Management Science

Management Science

Decision Making Through Systems Thinking

2nd Edition

HANS DAELLENBACH
Emeritus Professor of Management Science, University of Canterbury, Christchurch, New Zealand.
DONALD McNICKLE
Associate Professor in Management Science, University of Canterbury, Christchurch, New Zealand.
SHANE DYE
Senior Lecturer in Management Science, University of Canterbury, Christchurch, New Zealand.

B L O O M S B U R Y
NEW DELHI • LONDON • OXFORD • NEW YORK • SYDNEY

BLOOMSBURY INDIA
Bloomsbury Publishing India Pvt. Ltd
Second Floor, LSC Building No. 4, DDA Complex, Pocket C–6&7,
Vasant Kunj, New Delhi 110070

BLOOMSBURY, BLOOMSBURY ACADEMIC INDIA and the Diana logo are
trademarks of Bloomsbury Publishing Plc

First published in India 2023
First edition 2005
This edition 2012 published by PALGRAVE MACMILLAN
Now published by Bloomsbury Academic

ISBN: 978-93-56403-36-9
10 9 8 7 6 5 4 3 2 1

Printed and bound in India
For sale in the Indian subcontinent only

To find out more about our authors and books
visit www.bloomsbury.com and sign up for our newsletters

Contents

Preface

The subtitle '*Decision making through systems thinking*' indicates the focus of this text, namely to explore management science/operations research (MS/OR) within a broad systems thinking framework. It is this aspect that sets it apart from most other introductory MS/OR texts. Their emphasis is on mathematical tools and techniques of what has become known as **hard operations research**, and they offer little more than a few platitudes on the system context in which MS/OR work occurs.

The use of MS/OR is to provide insights for informed decision making. The vast majority of that decision making occurs within organizations or, in other words, within systems. Therefore, MS/OR can be viewed as a way of thinking with a system focus. This necessitates a good understanding of systems, system concepts, and system control. What is included in the system defined to analyse a particular problem and what is left out — the critical system boundary choices — may have important consequences for the people actively involved, as well as those passively affected.

Rather than assume that the usual starting point for an MS/OR project is a relatively well-structured problem, with clearly defined objectives and known alternative courses of action, the text steps back to the inception phase of most projects; namely, the presentation of a problematic situation, where the issues are still vague, fuzzy, and not yet seen in their proper systemic context. It demonstrates several aids to capture the problem situation in its full richness. This will facilitate gaining a more comprehensive understanding of the various issues involved, which in turn increases the likelihood that the problem formulation addresses the 'right' issues at an appropriate level of detail to provide insights and answers relevant for decision making.

Such an approach will also help the reader appreciate that for many decision situations there is no unique 'right' answer, but that the answer is affected by the world view accepted as relevant by the people involved, and by the boundary choices made for the system chosen. Much of Western Education encourages students to think in terms of a single right answer to problem solving. The MS/OR instructor thus faces a challenge to help students gain confidence in working within a mode of thinking which departs from such a narrow focus and which offers benefits that often go beyond the immediate concern. (See the special issue of *INFORMS Transactions on Education*, 12(1), September 2011, devoted to the challenge of teaching soft OR.)

These are the topics of Part I, together with graphical aids for depicting systems or views of important aspects of a particular system. Their aim is to make system modelling more accessible to the beginner.

Most hard operations research texts woefully neglect this essential foundation for effective MS/OR work. Their emphasis is on techniques and their mathematical development. However, applying techniques to 'problems', no matter how elegant the mathematics, without the underpinning of systems thinking needed to gain a sufficient grasp of the problem situations, will result in what Russel Ackoff [(1960) 'Case histories five years after,' *Operations Research*, March-April] coined as 'the surgery was successful, but the patient died.' He also adds that 'The surgeon (the operations researcher) cannot survive many such deaths.' Does not some of the disillusionment about operations research experienced in business and industry since the 1980s have its roots exactly in this emphasis on techniques, at the expense of systems thinking? A solid understanding of system concepts is as essential for hard OR that uses sophisticated mathematical modelling as it is for soft OR methodologies that seek culturally, politically, and socially acceptable compromises or accommodations in conflict situations.

Part II gives an overview of, and contrasts the two major strands of management science, i.e., hard OR and soft OR, and their overall methodologies. While most analysts who use hard OR agree on the general form of the hard OR paradigm, soft OR covers such a wide range of approaches that no single methodological framework can capture them all. Not only do they differ in terms of their specific aims — problem structuring, learning, conflict resolution, contingency planning, as well as problem solving — but also in terms of their suitability for specific problem situations. Of necessity, the chapter devoted to soft OR can only scratch the surface of this vast area. It is restricted to an introductory survey, exploring and contrasting the same case under three of the best known approaches.

Part III looks at two topics that unfortunately are again neglected by most MS/OR texts, but that any successful modeller needs to be thoroughly familiar with. First, most projects involve costs and benefits. These may be of a monetary or intangible nature. Which cost and benefits are relevant for a particular problem? Some of these costs and benefits occur in future periods. How do we deal with that?

Second, much decision making involves planning over time in response to future events. The sequencing of decisions becomes an integral aspect of the problem. How can this be captured by the models?

Part IV is largely devoted to hard OR. A number of MS/OR techniques borrow a leaf or two from managerial economics, in particular the principle of marginal analysis.

A variety of restrictions may be imposed on the decision process, relating to limited resources or qualitative properties the solution has to satisfy. What effects does this have on the solution and the process of obtaining it? What kind of insights can we derive from analysing these effects? The concept of shadow prices is introduced here in general terms and then in the context of linear programming.

Most decisions are made under various degrees of uncertainty about the outcomes. What is uncertainty? How do we react when faced with uncertainty? How can we model uncertainty? We make an excursion into waiting lines, simulation, and decision and risk analysis.

We return to the topic of decision making over time by exploring, albeit all too briefly, how to capture the dynamics of system behaviour through simulation.

Finally, there is a brief discussion on how the decision process needs to be adapted if we explicitly acknowledge the fact that the decision maker may be faced with conflicting goals.

Part IV thus gives an introduction into several well-known OR techniques. However, the emphasis is not on the tools themselves, but on how these tools should be used within a systems thinking framework, and what insights we can get from their use. The text is not an elementary introduction to MS/OR techniques. At an introductory level, although interesting and fun, these techniques are often reduced to the triviality of cranking a computational handle for a drastically simplified toy problem, devoid of most real-life semblance. Why not let software crank that handle?

Furthermore, the astronomical computational speed of even the modest laptop and the easy availability of MS/OR software have practically eliminated the need to know the inner workings of advanced hard OR algorithms, such as the simplex method, the various integer and non-linear programming techniques, and the intricacies of the plethora of search algorithms. Such details are needed for software developers, but not for the practising MS/OR analyst.

Rather than discuss concepts in the abstract, they are demonstrated using practical case studies derived from projects that the authors have been involved in or that have been reported in the literature. Some of them had to be trimmed to reduce their complexity and render them amenable for inclusion in the limited space of a textbook, but they have retained the essentials of their original flavour. Most chapters also have one or more case scenarios for the reader to test his or her understanding of the material. Although much simplified, they are again derived from actual projects, some of them undertaken by our honours students.

In Parts III and IV, whenever possible, the quantitative analysis is demonstrated using the power and flexibility of spreadsheets. The text uses Microsoft Excel©, but this choice is more one of convenience, rather than preference. Any other spreadsheet software with optimizer or solver capability and the facility for generating random variates will do.

The use of spreadsheets implies that the level of mathematics involved remains at a fairly elementary level and does not go beyond high school mathematics and statistics. In Parts III and IV, the emphasis is not on the mathematics, but on the concepts and the process of quantitative decision making. The book lives on the principle of 'never let the mathematics get in the way of common sense!' Any instructor who deplores the apparent lack of mathematical rigour may do well to weigh the points raised in Chapter 20 before dismissing this text.

By the time the reader has digested the wealth of learning opportunities offered by this text, he or she will approach all types of problem solving — not just those suitable for quantitative modelling — from a more comprehensive, more enlightened, and insightful perspective. Hopefully, the reader will also have been encouraged to reflect on and become more critical of his or her own way of looking at the world.

The main audience of the text is at an introductory undergraduate or MBA level for a 50- to 80-hour course on analytical decision making, where the emphasis is on methodology and concepts, rather than mathematical techniques. This is the use we have put it to at the University of Canterbury. It is sufficiently challenging for the MBA level, where the focus should be on insights rather than techniques. The real-life case studies used in many chapters make the text particularly relevant and attractive to mature MBA students. However, it is also suitable for self-study and as recommended background reading to set the stage for an introductory course in MS/OR, systems thinking, and computer science.

The text puts the techniques into their proper perspective in the decision making process. Rather than see them as the central and most important part of the analysis, it recognizes that they are powerful analytical and computational aids, but that they usually constitute only a small portion of the total effort that goes into any project. It is not the tools that 'solve a problem', but the process in which they are used.

Thanks go to several people who have contributed in various ways to this text and its precursors, but in particular to Ross James and Nicola Petty who have used its precursors and made numerous valuable suggestions for improvements. And then there are the thousands of students who read the text and whose questions and queries for explanations have led to saying some things more simply and clearly.

The scholar and teacher who has undoubtedly shaped the whole approach to systems thinking and MS/OR more than anybody else is the late C. West Churchman. This text is dedicated to him.

1

Management science/ operations research and systems thinking

Learning objectives

- Appreciate/recognize that most human activity occurs within systems.
- Appreciate that decision situations within systems are often complex and need a new way of thinking.

Introduction

This chapter aims to whet your appetite to learn more about the complexity and challenge of effective problem solving. We will briefly describe five real-life situations that each involved making recommendations as to the best course of action to take. Three look at commercial situations, while the other two deal with issues of public decision making and policy. They are intended to give you a feel for the great variety of decision making problems, in terms of the areas of application, the types of organizations involved, the degree of complexity, the types of costs and benefits, as well as their importance. In each instance a systems approach, based on systems thinking, will lead to more insightful decision making.

1.1 Real-life complex decision situations

Call centres

Since the early 1990s, call centres have become an ever more predominant interface between all types of organizations and individuals wanting information, service or assistance, such as requests for emergency services, reporting of crimes to the police, requests for information from the Inland Revenue Service, help from software providers, inquiries about policies and filing of claims to insurance companies, inquiries about products and services to retailers, and not to forget the oldest of such services, telephone directory assistance.

Callers to a call centre, who are more likely than not put on hold, would obviously like to speak to a real person as quickly as possible. Some callers may become impatient and renege if they deem that the time on hold is too long. On the other hand, the call centre does not want to have staff sitting around idle, waiting for calls. Idle operators are costly. Effective operation of a call centre requires a judicious balancing of these opposing aims. Determining 'best' staffing levels is one of the main concerns for call centre management.

The problem is made more difficult by the fact that some aspects, such as salaries and equipment, can be expressed in monetary terms, while others, particularly for emergency service call centres, largely defy any attempt to express them in this way. How do you evaluate a 10% increase in the waiting time which may result in a 40% increase in the likelihood of a loss of life or of serious injury?

Example 1-1: Financial services call centre

The financial services industry is a major user of call centres for generating new business where the products offered may be insurance, loans, savings, credit card and other banking services. The case in question concerns a call centre of a regional company specializing in personal loans of up to £15,000 for periods between 1 and 5 years. This market is particularly competitive with several nationally known companies offering similar borrowing terms. The company stimulates new business by advertising on television, in newspapers, and by direct mail.

Calls received by the centre fall into three categories: enquiries from new customers, enquiries from existing customers, and trivial calls. The call lengths vary, from more than 10 minutes for the first category to less than half a minute for the third.

It is the first category of calls that generates new business and hence profits. If any of these callers renege because too long on hold, potential business is lost, something the firm tries to avoid. So the firm wants to find staffing levels that balance two costs which vary in opposite directions: the cost of staff and the 'cost' of lost business.

Reliable forecasts of call rates over time for each category are the most crucial input into planning best staffing levels. Determining such forecasts is subject to a number of complicating factors. For all categories, there are pronounced intra-day, intra-week, and seasonal variations. The call rates are also affected by bank holidays, seasonal festivities, and 'national' events, such as important football matches. Furthermore, promotional drives cause spikes in new customer calls, followed by a gradual decline. Different advertising media have different response rates. And there is the vexing problem that it is impossible to know to which category abandoned calls belong. Generating reliable call rate forecasts is thus far from simple.

This is a type of problem faced by many organizations, private or public, called a **waiting line** problem. Here are other examples:

- the number of tellers or cashiers a bank, an insurance office, a post office, a supermarket, etc., should have during various times of the business day;
- the number of crews needed by a repair or service outfit, like an appliance service firm or a photocopying machine service firm;
- the number of nurses and/or doctors on duty at an emergency clinic during various hours of the week;
- the degree of redundancy built into equipment to prevent breakdowns.

Vehicle scheduling

Pick-up and delivery firms, like courier services, collect and drop off goods at a number of places. The locations of these pick-ups and drop-offs may differ daily. New pick-up requests may be generated during the day, the mix of requests and their number varying by the hour. Certain of the customers may specify a given time period or 'time window' during which the visit must occur. The vehicles used may have different carrying capacities. The length of time drivers can be on the road in one shift may be subject to legal restrictions. Add to this the fact that traffic densities on various city roads, and hence the travel times between locations, fluctuate during the day. It is also clear that, even for a small problem, the number of possible distinct sequences for visiting all locations is very large. For example, for 10 locations, there are $10! = 3{,}628{,}800$ different itineraries, while for 20 the number grows to $2{,}432{,}902 \times 10^{12}$. Although a majority can be ruled out as bad, it is still no trivial task to select the best combination or sequence of pick-ups and deliveries from those that remain, such that all complicating factors and constraints are taken into account. It may even be difficult to decide which criterion should be chosen for 'best'. Is it minimum distance, or minimum time, or minimum total cost, or a compromise between these considerations?

Example 1-2: Bulk beer deliveries by tankers

The brewery in this case supplies tap beer in tankers to pubs, bars, and hotels scattered over a large rural area. A few large customers receive deliveries twice a month, while most others only receive on average one delivery a month. A beer tanker has several compartments of differing sizes where the liquid is kept under pressure. Delivery is always made in full compartment quantities. The beer slopping around in partially filled compartments would lose its fizz and endanger the stability of the truck. A trip usually makes deliveries to more than one customer. The person in charge of scheduling deliveries has to take several factors into account:

- customers must not run out of tap beer; there are latest delivery deadlines;
- the size of storage tanks may differ from customer to customer;
- tanker trucks in the fleet have different compartment configurations with different capacities;
- some of the larger customers insist that delivery may not made outside specific time windows;

- parts of the road network from the brewery to customers and between customers include hilly countryside; there are maximum weight restrictions on some road sections, particularly bridges;
- average travel times for fully loaded, partially loaded, and empty tankers, as well as corresponding fuel costs, are known for each road section of the network;
- a trip may exceed eight hours only under exceptional circumstances.

The task of the scheduler is to develop a delivery schedule that takes all these factors into account, while trying to minimize total delivery costs. These consist of fuel costs, tanker driver wages, and other variable vehicle costs that vary depending on the schedules chosen.

Similar types of combinatorial sequencing problems are faced by airlines for the scheduling of aircraft and air crews, public bus or railroad companies for the scheduling of buses or engines and drivers, or the city rubbish collectors for determining their collection rounds.

Environmental and economic considerations

Commercial and industrial activities are often in direct conflict with protecting and safeguarding the natural environment from being adversely affected. While economic activities can easily be measured in monetary terms, the loss or degradation of the natural environment, such as water and air pollution, the loss of native flora and fauna, the loss of wilderness areas, scenic beauty, and so on defy being captured in dollars, pounds, euros, or yuan. How should national and local governmental agencies deals with such issues? What are the responsibilities of private enterprise in this respect?

Furthermore, such situations often involve entrenched political aspects, as the next example shows.

Example 1-3: The Deep Cove project

The waters discharged into Deep Cove from the Manapouri Power Station in Fiordland National Park at the bottom of New Zealand's South Island is so pure that it does not need any chemicals to neutralize harmful bacteria or other contaminants. Several years ago, a US firm applied for the rights to capture this water and transport it with large ocean-going tankers to the US West Coast and the Middle East. It would have entailed the building of a floating dock close to the tail race of the power station, where up to two tankers could berth simultaneously. The project would provide employment for about 30 people in an economically depressed area of New Zealand, and the New Zealand government would collect a water royalty. It would thus make a substantial contribution to both the local and national economy.

The firm showed considerable responsibility in planning the whole operation to keep the environmental impact in the fiord as low as economically feasible. For instance, all staff would be flown into Deep Cove daily, allowing no permanent residence. All rubbish would be removed. No permanent structures would be erected. Tanker speed in the fiord would be reduced to keep swells low. There would be extensive safety measures to avoid oil spills, etc. Not surprisingly, environmental groups were opposed to this project. Here are some of their reasons: first, it would have introduced non-tourist commercial activities in the waters of a national park, which is against the charter of national parks. They feared that the removal of up to 60% of the tail race water for extended periods would alter the balance between fresh water and salt water, and affect the sound's unique flora and fauna, which has evolved over millions of years. The big tankers would speed up the mixing of the fresh water layer on top of the salt water base, affecting the ecological balance even further. Due to the severe weather conditions in that part of the country, accidents resulting in oil spills would be difficult to prevent, even with the best of intentions, with potentially disastrous consequences. It could introduce rats, thereby endangering rare birds. It would make poaching of rare birds and lizards easier.

The New Zealand government had the final say. What should it do? Given the potential environmental impact, a decision could not be made on economic grounds alone. It required a careful balancing of important economic, political, and environmental factors. There were conflicting objectives, i.e., maximizing the economic welfare of New Zealand, versus minimizing irreversible environmental impacts to preserve a unique wilderness area for the enjoyment of future generations, as well as limiting the intrusion of commercial activities into a national park.

Problems of multiple and conflicting objectives occur frequently, particularly in the public sector. **Multicriteria decision making** approaches may help in dealing with such conflicts. They explore trade-offs between monetary and intangible objectives. Similarly, problem structuring methods can be used for clarifying different viewpoints and helping to find accommodations between conflicting aims.

Disease control and eradication

Towards the end of the twentieth century, national health services stepped up efforts to combat various types of cancer through early diagnosis — breast cancer, cervical cancer, bowel cancer. New vaccines for various diseases have been and are being developed, such as for the several types of hepatitis, the ever-modifying flu strains, and so on. Both these developments give rise to nationwide campaigns to reach the population affected. Some involve considerable investments in equipment, recruitment, and training of staff. Their full roll-out may take months, even years.

Example 1-4: Cancer screening policies

Breast cancer is currently the biggest single cause of mortality for women in developed countries. Recent statistics show that in the UK about 1 in 11 women will develop breast cancer during her life and of those afflicted a substantial number will die as a result of the disease.

Breast cancer incidence and aggressiveness varies with the age of the patient. It starts usually with a small growth or lump in the breast tissue. In its early stages, such a growth is usually benign. If left untreated, it will enlarge and often become malignant, invading adjacent tissue, and ultimately spread to other parts of the body — known as 'metastasis'. The rate of progression varies from person to person and with age. The age specific incidence of breast cancer rises steadily from the mid-twenties through the reproductive years. At menopause there is a temporary drop, after which the rate climbs again.

About 95% of all potentially cancerous growths discovered at a pre-invasive stage can be cured. It is thus crucial that it can be detected as early as possible. In the 1970s, screening trials were made in Sweden, England, and the US in an effort to reduce breast cancer mortality. It is now generally accepted that mammography is the most effective method for detecting abnormal tissue growth. Research shows that for women aged 50 and over mammography can detect about 85% of all abnormal tissue growths that could develop into breast cancer within the subsequent 12 months after a screening. This is significantly higher than for other methods of screening. The percentage of potentially cancerous growths detected at an early stage drops substantially as the time interval between screenings becomes longer. Note, that there is, however, a small risk that repeated screening itself may cause a cancer to develop — another factor to be considered.

As the need for the introduction of an effective screening policy finally became recognized by both health professionals and governments, there was still some controversy as to the 'best' screening policy to use. A screening policy is defined by the age range of women to be screened and the frequency of screening, e.g., all women between the ages of 50 and 65 at yearly intervals.

In addition to the medical factors and partially avoidable loss of human lives involved, there were economic aspects to be considered. In 2000, the cost of a screening was between £50 and £100, while the equipment cost was in the range of £200,000 to £300,000. Each machine used full-time can perform around 6400 screenings per year. As the age range and frequency of screening is increased, the number of machines and trained personnel needed also increases. Acquiring these machines and training the personnel required thus involved an enormous capital outlay and could not be done 'overnight'. So, the problem faced by health providers was (and still is for new programmes): what policy offers the best compromise between economic considerations and human-suffering, and what strategy should be adopted for introducing the policy chosen to the whole country, given budget considerations that affect the rate of equipment procurement and staff training. The National Health Service Screening Programme in the UK began in 1988, inviting women aged 50 to 64 for screening every three years. By 2005, the programme was extended to age 70. The mortality rate from breast cancer for women screened regularly is estimated to be about 35% lower than for those who opt out of screening.

As for the Deep Cove project, decisions by publicly funded health providers cannot be made on costs alone. Social, cultural, and equity issues have to be addressed, and inevitably there are also political considerations to take into account.

Differing perceptions of issues and conflicting aims

There are many decision situations where the specific events or issues that raise concerns and trigger an intervention are not well-understood. The various people involved or affected may not only have different perceptions of what the issues or concerns are in the first place, but also disagree about appropriate aims. Furthermore, the decision making powers of those involved may differ. Hidden agendas and internal politics may come into play, adding more complexity. For such situations, accommodations can only be found with the help of analytical methods or methodologies that specifically cater for these aspects. The next example, reported by M. Winter [(2006) 'Problem structuring in project management,' *J. of the Operational Research Society*, 57(1): 802-12], demonstrates this within the context of branch retail merchandising.

Example 1-5: Branch specific ranging

In the mid-1990s, Tesco, the UK's leading food retailer, explored means for tailoring the various products and services offered in its retail stores much more specifically to the local social, cultural, and economic conditions of the store location. The project team set up to look into this concept called it 'branch specific ranging' (BSR). It also discovered early on that BSR was not simply a matter of developing relevant data files on the local conditions in which each store operated and then using this information as a basis for product selection. It was more than just an information technology project.

In fact, the team quickly discovered serious disagreements within the organization about a number of aspects: What was the essence of BSR? What did the firm want to achieve by BSR? What were the likely problems in operating BSR? And last, but not least, if Tesco went ahead with introducing BSR nationwide, what problems might arise and how should they be managed? Should the concept first be trialed at one store to gain greater insight?

The situation the team faced exhibited all the nasty attributes that define complexity: differing views on the meaning of BSR, conflicts on its wider aims, conflict between different product branches about the nature of local conditions, disagreement on how to go about analysing the situation, and, if it ever came to it, on how to implement BSR.

Unless Tesco top management dictated a 'solution' to be implemented, possibly against the preferences and wishes of lower levels of management, progress could only be made by a meeting of minds, which first developed a strategy of how to go about investigating the issues associated with BSR and then applied that strategy to come to an agreement on actions which all 'players' involved could live by.

This is usually achieved by a lengthy process, starting out with canvassing the views of all people intimately involved in BSR, followed by one or more workshops under the guidance of a skilled facilitator. In the Tesco case, the soft systems methodology, one of the **soft operations research** approaches or **problem structuring methods** surveyed in Chapter 7, was applied to find an acceptable strategy.

1.2 Common features

What have all these problem situations in common? A number of things! First, there is somebody who is dissatisfied with the current situation or mode of operation and sees scope for doing something better or more effectively, or sees new opportunities or new options. In other words, this somebody would like to achieve one or several goals, or maintain currently threatened levels of achievement.

Second, the answer to the problem, or the solution, is not obvious. The problem situation is complex. The interested parties may disagree on what the relevant problem is. There may be conflict on objectives. They may not have enough information about the situation to know or discover all the consequences of decision choices. Elements of this are present in the Deep Cove, the breast cancer and the BSR projects.

Third, the interactions between various elements or aspects may exhibit high computational complexity that the human mind cannot evaluate in the detail desirable to make an informed decision. All, except the BSR project, have aspects of this nature.

Finally, the settings within which these problems exist are systems.

What is a system?

Chapters 2 and 3 explore various system concepts in detail. So, for now, we define a system as a collection of things, physical or abstract, entities, or people that relate to each other in specific ways, i.e., that are organized and follow specific rules of interaction. Collectively, they have a given purpose, i.e., they aim to achieve or produce outcomes that none of its parts can do in isolation. However, we should also quickly add that in the real world systems do not exist or create themselves spontaneously, ready-made for us to discover. No!

- **Systems are human inventions.**
- **We conceive or view something as a system for our own purposes.**

This is an important insight to which we will return in subsequent chapters.

Systems thinking

If we are to deal effectively with the complexity of systems and decision making within systems, we need a new way of thinking. This new way of thinking has evolved since about 1940 and could be labelled 'systems thinking'. **Management science/operations research (MS/OR)**, **systems engineering** and **systems analysis** are strands of this mode of thinking that are particularly suitable if most of the interactions between the various parts of a system can be expressed in quantitative terms, such as mathematical expressions.

Since the early 1970s, MS/OR analysts and systems thinkers, mainly in the UK, have complemented the mathematics based MS/OR toolbox — renamed **hard OR/hard systems approaches** — with a number of analytic, but non-quantitative methods and methodologies that go under the label of **soft OR/soft systems approaches**. Some are based on formal systems ideas, whereas others use ad hoc processes that have proved successful for certain types of structures or problems, while still being rooted in systems thinking. All are decision processes which help decision makers to explore problems in much of their complexity with a view to developing an acceptable and sometimes even best compromise solution. They frequently give answers to important 'what if' questions, such as for example 'How is the best solution affected by significant changes in various cost factors?' or 'What is the effect of uncertainty in a critical aspect?' They provide the decision maker(s) with valuable information and insights on which to base an informed decision, rather than their being mainly guided by intuitive, emotional, or political considerations alone.

Although political considerations may be unavoidable and may, in the end, sway the decision one way or another, the use of such decision processes increases the degree of rationality in decision making, be it in the private or public sector. Note, however, that they are not intended to replace the decision maker, with whom must rest the final decision.

1.3 Overview of what follows

As we have seen, most decision making in today's world deals with complex problem situations. They are often ill-defined, subject to conflicting forces and goals. One of the major reasons for this complexity is that these problem situations occur within a system context. The systems we are interested in are created and controlled by humans. The human element can therefore not be excluded from the decision process.

Although we, as humans, are endowed with amazing faculties of reasoning and insight, most of us are unable to cope with more than a few factors at the same time. Without computers, our computational abilities are slow and limited. We have difficulties processing and digesting large quantities of information and tracing complex interrelationships and interactions. Professor Herbert Simon, the 1978 Nobel Prize Laureate in Economics, coined in his acceptance speech the concept that human decision making is limited by **bounded rationality**. It is therefore all the more important that decision making is guided by systematic and comprehensive methodologies that helps us make effective use of our extensive but still limited powers of reasoning.

This text is an introduction to MS/OR methodologies. MS/OR approaches are not a panacea, capable of developing solutions or improvements for all problematic decision situations. However, they have proved successful for problem situations that involve management problems which lend themselves to rational analysis. Usually, they deal with questions of the effectiveness and/or efficiency of various activities or operations. The discussion looks at how systems thinking forms the basis for MS/OR approaches and what is good and bad practice. The methodologies are not intended to deal with dilemmas of a psychological or ethical nature.

Part I covers systems thinking and system models, regardless of which specific problem solving approach is applied. This implies an understanding of essential system concepts. Problems do not occur in a vacuum, but are embedded in **problem situations** — their context. In order to identify the problem correctly, we need to understand this context in much of its richness and complexity. The analyst who takes short-cuts in this crucial phase of any MS/OR project, risks solving the wrong problem.

Part II gives an overview over the two prominent strands of MS approaches: hard OR, where problems lend themselves to quantification, and soft OR, where the problem situation has high human complexity with conflicting values, and where the stakeholders involved may have different perceptions about the problem situation.

Much decision making involves costs and benefits. Which costs and benefits are relevant for a particular decision? Some costs and benefits occur over time. How should their timing be correctly included in the analysis? And many decision making problems involve not simply a single decision point, but a sequence of decisions over time, where later decisions are dependent on earlier ones. These aspects are the topics of Part III.

Finally, Part IV explores how constraints on the decision choices affect decision making, how to deal with uncertainty and incorporate it into the decision making process, and how to balance conflicting multiple objectives. Several of the best known hard OR techniques — marginal analysis, linear programming, queueing, simulation and system dynamics, decision and risk analysis, and multicriteria decision making methods — are used to demonstrate these aspects. In order to gain greater insight for informed, rational decision making, the emphasis is not primarily on the intricacies of the mathematical models and their solution methods, but rather on conceptual aspects of the approach.

Further reading

Ackoff, R.L. (1978) *The Art of Problem Solving*, New York: Wiley. Part 1 deals with problem solving. Part 2 presents six cases. Includes Ackoff's fables. Enjoyable. Many valuable lessons. A clear must and reminder for analysts with some practical experience. The emphasis is on 'Art' — something largely learned from experience, and consequently somewhat lost on the beginner.

Pidd, M. (2009) *Tools for Thinking: Modelling in Management Science*, 3rd edn, Chichester: Wiley. Chapter 1 discuss the need for a new mode of thinking to deal with complex situations.

PART I

Systems and systems thinking: Introduction

Except for the most trivial daily actions, most decision making happens within the context of systems — all sorts of organizations, from family units to major corporations, from local government to international institutions, and all sorts of activities and operations. You may wonder: 'Since science has been one of the major driving forces of modern civilization, why don't we simply use the scientific method for decision making within systems? Hasn't it proved itself highly successful in the biological and physical sciences and, by extension, in all branches of engineering?' There are a number of reasons! First, experts in science and the philosophy of science do not agree on what the scientific method really is. There is much anecdotal evidence that what sets scientists and researchers on the path of successful breakthroughs are often ingenious hunches, and that the scientific method is only used after the fact to test and confirm the results. But even disregarding these controversies, most real-life decision making does not neatly fall into a pattern of observation, followed by generating hypotheses to be confirmed or refuted through experimentation. Each decision situation may be unique in terms of the context and people involved. Experimentation under the same conditions in a world of constant change is impossible. The decision may deal with future planned activities or operations that do not yet exist.

Most importantly though, while scientific research attempts to understand the various aspects of the world we live in, decision making attempts to change aspects of this world. Furthermore, decision making does not occur under idealized conditions in a laboratory, but out in the real and often messy and turbulent world. So, the methodology has to be able to cope with the complexity of the real world, and has to be comprehensive and flexible, while still delivering the results in the often short time frame within which most decision making has to occur. Neither is it so important that the methodology used satisfies strict scientific principles of inquiry. It is more important that it is transparent and leads to good decision making.

Part I sets the platform of concepts and ideas needed for applying one of these MS methodologies. Chapter 2 gives a few examples of the complexity in today's decision making, discusses effectiveness and efficiency — concepts often misunderstood, and shows that systems may exhibit unexpected counterintuitive behaviours. It then contrasts the traditional reductionist and cause-and-effect thinking, underlying the scientific method, with systems thinking.

Chapter 3 studies system concepts and types of systems in detail and highlights them with examples. Since viewing something as a system is a human conceptualization, it is by definition subjective. We explore the meaning of this. The behaviour of systems is the prime concern of systems thinking, and we study various modes of controlling system behaviour.

In order to identify the right problem, we need to understand the context or problem situation in which it occurs and its stakeholders — the roles various people play. This and how to describe and summarize the problem situation are the topics of Chapter 4. We will use mind maps, rich pictures, and cognitive maps — diagrammatic aids — to capture essential aspects of the problem situation. Chapter 5 studies system models, effective approaches to the process of modelling, and good properties of models. It explores how to represent aspects of special interest in the form of system diagrams.

References

Checkland, P. and Scholes, J. (1999) *Soft Systems Methodology in Action, includes a 30-year retrospective*, Chichester: Wiley. A seminal work. Chapters 1 to 5 of the 1983 reprint present a most authoritative discussion and history of systems thinking.

Churchman, C.W. (1971) *The Design of Inquiring Systems*, New York: Basic Books. An early scholarly text, raising important questions.

Churchman, C.W. (1968) *The Systems Approach*, New York: Dell Publishing Co. Provocative. Dialectic view of different ways of systems thinking.

Habermas, J. (1971) *Knowledge and Human Interests*, Boston: Beacon Press. Advanced material covering the philosophical basis relevant for systems thinking.

Jackson, M.C. (2000) *Systems Approaches to Management*, New York: Kluwer/Plenum. A comprehensive and critical review of all systems methodologies based on systems thinking. A must for any serious student in systems thinking.

Klirr, G.J. (1991) *Facets of Systems Science,* New York: Plenum Press. Part 1 gives a guided tour on systems science at a mathematical level. Part 2 is a collection of papers on general systems theory. Neither are for the faint-hearted. (There is an extensive literature on **general systems theory**, dealing with concepts, principles, properties of systems, and systems behaviour, not specific to a given field of application. At its inception in the 1940s and 1950s, great hopes were placed on this theory to enhance and unify our understanding of systems and their use for the betterment of the human race. Unfortunately, it has not lived up to these expectations. Much of the theory is of such a general nature that it is of little practical use.)

Maani, K., and Cavana, R. (2007) *Systems Thinking, System Dynamics: Managing Change and Complexity*, Auckland: Pearson. Also contains detailed discussion on five real-life cases.

Pidd, M. (2009) *Tools for Thinking: Modelling in Management Science*, 3rd edn, Chichester: Wiley.

Pidd, M. (ed.) (2004), *Systems Modelling: Theory and Practice*: Chichester: Wiley.

Schön, D. (1987) *Educating the Reflective Practitioner: Toward a New Design for Teaching and Learning in the Professions*, San Francisco: Jossey-Bass. Covers basic responsibilities of any person claiming to be a professional.

2
Systems thinking

Learning objectives

- Be able to recognize reductionist thinking, cause-and-effect thinking, and systems thinking.
- Appreciate that, faced with complexity, systems thinking must complement reductionist and cause-and-effect thinking.
- Be able to identify whether an outcome of a decision is planned or unplanned, and/or counterintuitive.
- Be able to distinguish between efficiency and effectiveness, and determine whether an action is efficient and/or effective with respect to achieving a desired goal.

Introduction

Why is there a need for systems thinking in dealing with many of today's decision situations? Why are the traditional analytic methods used by engineers, economists, and accountants for the last 100 years no longer adequate to come up with the 'right' solutions? After reading this chapter, you will be able to give a tentative answer to these two questions.

2.1 Increased complexity of today's decision making

What is 'complexity'? W.R. Ashby, one of the fathers of modern systems thinking, defined complexity as the quantity of information required to describe something [(1973) 'Some peculiarities of complex systems', *Cybernetic Medicine*, 9/2: 1-6]. This includes the number of parts and their interrelations that make up that something, that 'whole'. Complexity is thus in the eye of the beholder. For example, the neurosurgeon views the brain as a highly complex system, while for the butcher the brain of a calf is only one of some 30 different cuts of meat. It seems that the more we know about something, the more complex we see it. The same is true for decision making.

The second half of the twentieth century has been marked by the unprecedented realization of the complexity of even everyday decision making, let alone decision making in government and business. Where before we saw few and only limited interdependencies, technological progress has raised our awareness of many complex interactions. Untold innovations in agriculture, industrial and chemical processes, engineering, and air travel have encroached on our natural environment on a huge scale, a scale so large and unforeseen that we are only now beginning to realize its potential impact on the future of humankind. Similarly, the global communication/information technology explosion since the introduction of the Internet and smart phones offers virtually instant access to local and global information collecting and sharing banks. It has revolutionized private and commercial communication, has given access to shopping and banking at the touch of a button in the privacy of your home, has globalized commercial dealings in the financial and raw material stock exchanges, opened new ways for higher education, and changed the world of entertainment. Its cultural impact on both developed and developing countries may well turn out to be the greatest leveller the human race has ever experienced.

Hand-in-hand with the accelerating rate of innovation in technology and communications has been the ever-increasing complexity of various large infrastructures that regulate our daily lives and supply services that we take for granted, such as water, sewerage, power, gas, transport, health, police, fire fighting, emergency and civil defence, education, a multitude of government regulations and laws, and so on. Few of them stand alone. They are heavily interdependent. A planned change, a hiccup or breakdown in one may have serious consequences for another, as exemplified by the disruption to private and commercial communications when a fault shuts down a mobile network.

The lowering of trade barriers and the easing up of the flow of investment funds over the last four decades has given untold power to a few huge multi-national corporations — the oil giants Exon Mobil, Royal Dutch Shell, and BP; the car manufacturers Toyota, Volkswagen, and Ford; the electrical and electronics producers General Electric and Samsung Electronics; the food giants Nestlé and Unilever; the pharmaceutical companies Johnson & Johnson, Pfizer, and Roche; or the beverage producers PepsiCo and Anheuser-Busch Inbev, just to name the largest in their group, not to forget the world bankers such as Royal Bank of Scotland and Barclays in the UK, Deutsche Bank, the French BNP Paris, HSBC of HongKong, Chase Manhattan and Citigroup of the USA, UBS of Switzerland, and Mitsubishi of Japan. These corporations command financial and human resources and technical know-how which give them means to influence world events that far exceed the power and control of all but a few national governments. Neither do we fully know the sinister penetration of crime syndicates, such as the Mafia, triads, Japanese yakuza, South American drug bosses, and Russian crime syndicates into legitimate business ventures, or the effects of this.

Along with these developments came the widening gap between the rich developed countries, with their ever-increasing demand for energy and raw materials, their consumption and waste mentality, and the poor underdeveloped and developing countries, where traditional subsistence farming has been replaced by large-scale planting of cash crops subject to widely fluctuating world prices, leading to unsustainable indebtedness towards the developed countries and hopeless impoverishment of their rural population and their ever-growing city slums.

Add to this the problems of overpopulation, the collapse of the communist power bloc, the resurgence of ethnic-based nationalism and religious fundamentalism, both erupting in bloody conflicts and insurgencies, the legitimate call for women's equality in this male-dominated world, the 1998 economic crises that started with the collapse of the banking systems in several of the Asian 'economic miracle' countries and soon threatened the world economy, the even more devastating partial melt-down in 2008/9 of some banking sectors in the US and the UK, the renewed 2011 banking crisis, coupled with the threat to the euro, triggered by the risk of insolvency of several members of the European Economic Community, the uncertainties and unanswered question of genetic engineering in both agriculture and medicine, and the looming environmental threats (deforestation, ozone depletion, greenhouse gases) of a planet that continues to be exploited and abused for the sake of short-term profit and greed, economic growth, and political and economic power. Today's world has thus increased in complexity and interdependence to a point where the traditional methods of problem solving based on the cause-and-effect model can no longer cope. Let us study briefly three very different examples.

Example 2-1: Construction of the Aswan High Dam in Egypt — 1960 to 1976

Many of the 'great' technical achievements have not just brought the increased well-being used for justifying them, but also unexpected undesirable consequences, some of which may far outweigh the benefits hailed. The construction of the Aswan High Dam in Egypt is cited as an example.

Heralded as the key to Egypt's entry into the world of plenty, it initially increased agricultural production in the Nile Delta. However, it also caused an unprecedented increase in schistosomiasis — a highly debilitating disease spread by water snails that thrive in the irrigation canals. In the 1970s, it was claimed that 60% of Egypt's *fellahin* or farm workers were affected.

Fertile silt, which prior to the building of the dam annually renewed the fertility of the land it inundated, is now trapped behind the dam. In its place a massive increase in the use of fertilizers is needed to maintain output. That, together with poor drainage, causes salinization, annually rendering large tracts of land unsuitable for agriculture. The loss of the silt previously carried past the Delta into the Mediterranean has caused the sea to encroach onto the land, leading to further loss of land. The loss of the nutrients previously fed into the Mediterranean destroyed the sardine fisheries which provided an essential part of the population's diet. Finally, uncontrollable growth of water hyacinth in Lake Nasser causes excessive loss of water through evaporation.

So, the erection of the Aswan High Dam had a number of unexpected and unplanned consequences, some of them disastrous. Few were predicted and taken into account when the decision to build the dam was made. That decision, in fact, was largely a political power play between the USA and the old USSR, both hoping to incorporate Egypt within their sphere of influence.

Example 2-2: Deterioration of urban transport

In response to the suburban population drift and increased car ownership after World War II, and encouraged by the automobile industry, most metropolitan areas were facing increasing traffic congestion. Massive improvement of the road network and provision of city centre parking facilities looked like a very responsible public policy to city planners. In many cities, particularly in the USA, public transport facilities were neglected and did not keep up with the population demographics. Encouraged by the large bus manufacturers, city fathers replaced environmentally friendly electric trolleys and trams with diesel buses. Fare hikes, low service frequency, and dilapidated facilities could not match the convenience of the private car. This accelerated the shift from public to private transport, and the story continued — the end result ever more serious traffic congestion in the access roads used by commuters.

Again, we see that seemingly good responsible decision making resulted in unexpected outcomes which only temporarily improved access to the city centres. It is interesting to speculate what would have happened if city mayors had opted to upgrade public transport to bring the people from the suburbs into the city, rather than upgrading

Example 2-3: Assessment of unit production costs

Many firms compute the unit production cost at each machine centre by adding up all material, energy, and labour costs incurred at that machine centre and then dividing the total by the number of parts produced. The efficiency of a machine centre is assessed on the level of its unit production costs: the lower the unit production costs at a machine centre, the higher its efficiency. This rule works well for simple, one-stage production processes, where the firm works at full capacity and has no difficulties in selling all its output.

However, this same rule runs into serious trouble when we are faced with complex multi-product production processes. Usually, each machine centre produces many different parts — often in small lots — which are used as input into later stages of the production process. If the centre supervisor is judged on the basis of unit production costs, then he or she will have a strong incentive to have all machines and operators producing parts all the time. If subsequent machine centres do not require the parts immediately, they will temporarily be stored in a warehouse or on the production floor. The costs of keeping these stocks are normally not attributed to the machine centre that produced them. So, the machine centre's efficiency looks good, but the firm ends up with excessive intermediate parts stocks that are costly to finance and maintain and, furthermore, run the risk of becoming obsolete before they are required.

Activity

For each of Examples 2-1, 2-2, and 2-3, list three aspects that contribute to the complexity of the situation.

2.2 Efficiency and effectiveness

Efficiency

Example 2-3 demonstrates how the concern with efficiency for a particular operation or division of a firm may lead to an overall deterioration of the performance, in this case profit generation, of the firm as a whole. The firm may be very efficient in the use of its resources, but this efficiency is not put to effective use in terms of the firm's overall objectives or goals.

So, what is efficiency and what is effectiveness? Everyday language often confuses these concepts.

Efficiency looks at how well resources are used in a given activity. The higher the level of output achieved for a given set of inputs or resources or, alternatively, the lower the inputs or resources needed for producing a given level of output, the higher the technical efficiency of the activity.

We distinguish between technical and economic efficiency. Driving a car so as to maximize the ratio of distance travelled to fuel consumption is technically efficient. This may mean that you travel at between 60 and 80 km per hour, always accelerate very gradually, and plan your speed such as to avoid any unnecessary use of the brakes. If the vehicle is used for commercial purposes, e.g., a bus service, such a mode of driving may be economically inefficient, since it ignores wage costs for the driver as well as the potential earning power of the vehicle. For economic efficiency, in terms of maximizing the difference between revenues and total costs, the vehicle may often have to be driven in a technically inefficient way. The gain in added revenue may well outweigh the increased costs of a technically inefficient operation.

Effectiveness

Effectiveness looks at how well the goals or objectives of the entity or activity are achieved.

Consider the following example: a bus service forms the backbone of a city's public transport system. Its objective is to provide convenient but cost-effective commuter transport, where 'convenient' may be defined as 'no residents having to walk for more than five minutes from their home or work place to catch public transport'. Economically efficient operation of each vehicle is now only one aspect of the system operation. The choice of bus routes, the frequency of service at various times of the day, the type of vehicle used and how they are maintained, as well as the fare structure all determine the effectiveness of the transport system in terms of its objectives and the resource constraints imposed on it.

Efficiency versus effectiveness

> **Operating various parts of a system in their most efficient manner does not necessarily mean the system as a whole is effective in terms of achieving its objectives.**

Consider the operation of a hospital. The fact that its testing laboratory, its physiotherapy service, its blood bank service, and so on, are all operated efficiently in a technical and economic sense is not sufficient for the hospital as a whole to operate effectively. For instance, the tests ordered from the laboratory may be of the wrong type or may be redundant in the sense of not adding any additional information for correct diagnoses. The fact that they are executed efficiently does not imply that their use was effective. Effectiveness implies that these services are used and coordinated properly to achieve the objectives of the system as a whole.

Why do managers of all sorts of organizations, profit-making as well as non-profit-making, private and public, seem to be so concerned with efficiency? Working with a fixed budget — a limited amount of funding to spend over a given period of time — any pound spent on a given activity means one pound less for another activity. Hence the overriding concern to make every pound go as far as possible. Now, most firms or organizations operate with some waste or not fully utilized resources. Most managers' natural reaction is to eliminate such waste or underutilized resources. As we have seen, the consequences for the firm as a whole may, however, not turn out to be as beneficial as expected.

Here is another example.

Example 2-4: Machine spare parts

Walk through any factory and you will see machine spare parts accumulating dust. They tie up the funds spent to purchase them. These funds are seemingly 'idle'. Hence, it looks like a good idea to reduce the stock of spare parts and free up the funds for productive use elsewhere in the firm. But wait a minute! The reason why the spare parts were purchased was to reduce the down-time resulting from a machine part breaking down. If the parts are in stock, no time is lost waiting to get them. If the supplier is overseas, procuring them could easily result in a few weeks' delay or expensive air freighting. So, lack of adequate stocks of spare parts may result in prolonged down-time during which the machine is 'idle'. The loss of profit from the loss of output may far outweigh the cost of funding adequate stocks of spares. Therefore, elimination of such seemingly 'idle' spares may not be cost effective.

The real problem in Example 2-4 is not one of being efficient in the sense of eliminating idle resources but, rather, one of being effective in terms of the operation of the firm as a whole. This translates itself into finding the proper balance between the cost of the investment in stocks of spares and the cost of machine down-time incurred if the firm is short of spares.

This same theme occurs with respect to productive capacity of all sorts — machine capacities, runway capacity at airports, staffing levels in service industries, to name just a few. The difficult question to answer is: at what point is there real excess capacity in terms of the overall costs for the organization as a whole, rather than in terms of seeming 'idleness' over long periods of time?

Complementarity of efficiency and effectiveness

This discussion may have given the impression that efficiency is the enemy of effectiveness. Far from it! It is only the narrow concern with efficiency at the exclusion of the overall goals of the organization which is detrimental. True efficiency looks at the overall goals. Hence, the effectiveness of decisions and policies taken by the decision makers is enhanced. The goals of the organization will be achieved at lower costs, with fewer resources, or with increased benefits — in other words, more efficiently. The two are thus complementary. Effectiveness deals with 'doing the right thing', efficiency with 'doing things right'.

Activity

- What actions on your part would make studying this text more efficient? (Example: agree with your flatmate(s) not to be disturbed while studying it.)
- How would you judge that your studying of the text was effective?

2.3 Unplanned and counterintuitive outcomes

In all these cases we see a common theme: seemingly rational decisions are made on the basis that 'Action A will cause the desired outcome B to be realized.' But in addition to B, the decision also causes C, D, and E.

Some outcomes are unintended, unpredicted, and may partially or wholly negate the sought for economic or social benefits of the intended outcome.

Responsible decision making clearly must consider the undesirable and/or additional beneficial effects of unplanned outcomes on the system as a whole. Consideration of such outcomes may well sway the decision. A comprehensive systems analysis is more likely to uncover most of the unplanned outcomes than a narrow cause-and-effect analysis (see Section 2.4 for cause-and-effect thinking).

Some of the outcomes actually realized, both planned and unplanned, may be 'counterintuitive' — what happens appears at first glance to contradict what common sense and intuition tells us should occur.

Examples 2-5 and 2-6 demonstrate this.

Example 2-5: High profit margin business principle

It is a generally accepted business principle that a firm should push those products which offer the highest profit margin. Consider the following simple example: a firm produces two products on the same assembly line as shown in the figure below. Both cost the same to produce, i.e., £90/unit, but product A has a profit margin of 50%, while B only achieves 40%. (The profit margin is [profit/selling price] x 100%.)

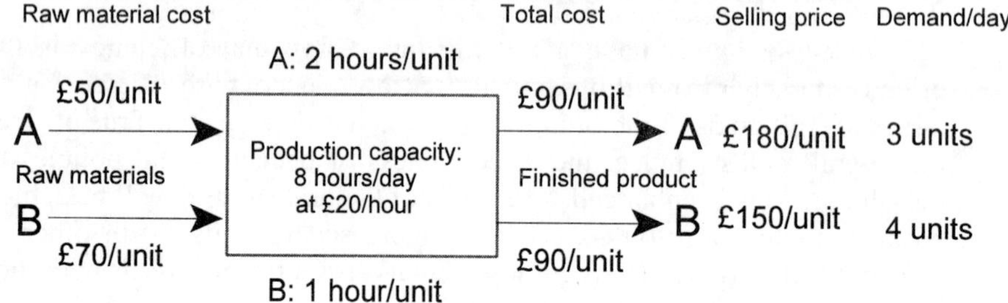

Given the limited demand for each product, it seems intuitively appealing that the firm should produce as many of A as it can sell, i.e., four, and then use up the remaining production capacity of 2 hours to produce two units of B. The daily profit is then 3 x £90 + 2 x £60 = £390.

Interestingly, in this example a reversal of the above business principle produces a better result. Namely, the firm should produce as many as possible of the product with the lower profit margin and only then use the remaining production capacity to produce the one with the higher profit margin. The resulting output of four units of B plus 2 units of A has a total profit of £420 — higher by £30.

This is a counterintuitive result. Why does it happen? The answer is simple. The business principle ignores vital system interactions: the different profit contribution per unit production capacity used of each product. Every hour of capacity used by product B produces a profit of £60, while an hour of work on product A only achieves £45.

Example 2-6: The Hawthorne experiments

A famous example is given by experiments conducted around 1930 among workers of the Hawthorne Works factory of the Western Electric Company in Illinois. A group of workers was subjected to a number of successive changes in their work environment to determine the effects on their performance. One of these experiments involved changing the lighting in their work space. As expected by the researchers, improved work space lighting increased the productivity of those workers affected, but contrary to expectations the control group who had not benefited from any change also showed improved productivity. When the lighting was restored to its original level as part of further experiments, rather than causing a decrease in productivity, it resulted in a further increase. Both results were completely counterintuitive. How could this be explained?

The explanation was found in the discovery by the researchers of what became known as the 'Hawthorne effect' — an increase in worker productivity produced by the psychological stimulus of being singled out and made to feel important. Somebody seemed to care, looking for how their work environment could be improved — factors initially overlooked. This was felt not only by the group subjected to the changes, but also by the control group.

In conclusion, outcomes that at first seem counterintuitive are usually not mysterious events. Most often, they can be explained by a comprehensive systems view.

Activity

For each of Examples 2-1, 2-2, and 2-3, list:

- the planned desirable and undesirable outcomes (sample answer for Example 1-1: low waiting time is planned, desirable; idle staff is unplanned, undesirable);
- the unplanned desirable and undesirable outcomes (Example 1-1 continued: low waiting times will lead to a low rate of complaints against the service, which is desirable and usually not planned and vice versa for high waiting times);
- Can you identify any counterintuitive outcomes? (Example 1-1 continued: long waiting times or slow response rate may increase the number of calls received, since some callers who give up may redial later several times, falsely raising the call rate.)

2.4 Reductionist and cause-and-effect thinking

How is it that, all too frequently, our decision making process seems to be so singularly linear? There is the desired outcome Y — here is action X which will cause Y to happen! Russell L. Ackoff—a philosopher, operations researcher, and systems thinker — gives us an answer in his paper 'Science in the Systems Age' (1973). He says that the intellectual foundations of the traditional scientific model of thought are based on two major ideas.

The first is **reductionism**: the belief that everything in the world and every experience of it can be reduced, decomposed, or disassembled into ultimately simple indivisible parts. Explaining the behaviour of these parts and then aggregating these partial explanations is assumed to be sufficient to allow us to understand and explain the behaviour of the system as a whole.

Applied to problem solving, this translates into breaking a problem down into a set of simpler subproblems, solving each individually and then assembling their solutions into an overall solution for the whole problem. 'Division of labour' and 'organizational structure along functional lines', such as finance, personnel, purchasing, manufacture, marketing, and R&D, are clear manifestations of this. However, we know that even if each is operated with the highest economic efficiency, the sum of the individual solutions does not necessarily produce an overall solution that is best for the system as a whole. The operation of a hospital (see p. 18) is an example of this.

The second basic idea is that all phenomena are explainable by **cause-and-effect relationships**. Aspect X is taken to be the cause of Y, if X is both necessary and sufficient for Y to happen. Hence, 'cause X' is all that is needed to explain 'effect Y'.

Viewing the world in this way, everything is explained by decomposing it into parts and looking for cause-and-effect relationships between the parts. But the examples above show that it may be inadequate to examine the causal relationships one by one. New relationships or properties may emerge through the interaction between the various parts or aspects of a situation — known as **emergent properties**. Some of these are usually planned, others may be unexpected and counterintuitive.

Furthermore, causal relationships may not be simply one-way. There could be **mutual causality** or **feedback** between two things, i.e., X affects Y, but is in turn affected by Y. X and Y are interdependent. Dealing with one alone, while ignoring the other, may not achieve the desired results. For example, poverty may result in poor health which in turn may increase poverty. Dealing with both simultaneously, rather than just with each individually, is likely to be much more effective in improving both. Chapter 3 will pick up mutual causality and feedback in more detail.

Case study 2-1: Power saving project

Our University Energy Committee held a meeting discussing ways to save power. The following argument between two committee members was overheard:

A: 'Clearly, every light turned off means some power saved. Hence, one of the major tasks of this committee is to educate all members of the university, and in particular all staff, to turn off lights whenever they are the last to leave a room, a lecture hall, or a corridor.'

B: 'Admittedly, a policy of turning off lights may generate some immediate power savings. But the greater frequency of turning lights on and off will burn out light bulbs more quickly and result in higher light bulb replacement costs. Furthermore, dark corridors and lecture halls may increase the incidence of accidents and the potential for crime, possibly imposing higher costs on the university community as a whole.'

A: 'The brief of this committee is to save power. Anything else is not our concern!'

B: 'Then we should point out to the Vice-Chancellor that the brief given to this committee is too narrow. The brief should be to find ways to save power that reduce costs to the University community as a whole, rather than consider exclusively how to lower the power bill.'

What are the desired planned outcomes and what could be the undesired, unplanned and/or unexpected or counterintuitive outcomes of the action proposed by A? Discuss the arguments put forth by A and B in terms of efficiency and effectiveness.

2.5 Systems thinking

From about 1940, a number of researchers from various scientific disciplines, biology, mathematics, communication theory, and philosophy, started to recognize that all things and events, and the experience of them, are parts of larger wholes. This does not deny the importance of the individual elementary parts or events. But the focus shifts from the parts to the wholes, namely to the **systems** to which the parts are seen to belong. This gave rise to a new way of thinking — **systems thinking**. Something to be explained is viewed as part of a larger whole, a system, and is explained in terms of its role in that system.

This new mode of thought has immediate consequences on decision making within a system context, namely that, for effective action in terms of the system as a whole, it may not be sufficient to use reductionist and cause-and-effect thinking by studying the individual parts or aspects in isolation. In order to get a true picture, it is essential to study their **systemic** role in the system.

However, this does not imply that systems thinking should replace reductionist and cause-and-effect thinking. The two approaches are in fact complementary. We cannot conceive of parts if there is no system to which they belong, neither can we talk of a whole unless there are constitutive elements that make up the whole. Cause-and-effect thinking gives attention to the details of each component, systems thinking to their systemic role in the system. Each may ignore or miss crucial aspects. More often than not, both modes of thinking are needed to gain a fuller understanding of a system. When we emphasis one, the other is implied. They are like the object and its shadow.

Chapter 3 defines systems and studies various aspects and properties of systems. Chapter 5 explores how to define a system and capture certain system aspects using diagrammatic methods.

Activity

Remember how you learned to drive a car and analyse the learning process you went through.

- List three tasks you mastered using:
  - reductionist thinking (e.g., starting the motor);
  - cause and effect thinking (e.g., pressing the brake pedal to slow down).
- Give two examples for why mastering each task of driving a car separately is insufficient for learning to drive safely.

2.6 Chapter highlights

- Today's world in a modern society is becoming increasingly more complex.
- Traditional rational thinking is still largely based on reductionist and cause-and-effect modes. These may not be able to cope with complexity and lead to narrowly focused, piecemeal decision making, which may result in unplanned outcomes and which, from an overall point of view, may be ineffective.
- Systems thinking takes a comprehensive view, focusing on the whole and explaining the role of the parts in terms of the whole, rather than the other way around.
- Systems thinking strives for effectiveness in terms of the system as a whole, rather than narrow efficiency of its parts.
- Systems exhibit not only the planned and desired outputs, but also unplanned and often undesirable outputs. Some outputs may seem counterintuitive.

Exercises

1. A few years ago, our city administration was looking for ways to reduce the city budget deficit. The parks and recreation department decided to reduce the cost of rubbish collection by eliminating rubbish bins in most public areas, except those catering especially for tourists and visitors to the city. 'We must encourage our citizens to carry their rubbish away rather than dumping it into the bins,' asserted the head of the department.
   (a) List the planned and unplanned outcomes of this decision.
   (b) Discuss the decision in terms of efficiency and effectiveness.

2. Consider the Deep Cove Water Export Project briefly described in Example 1-3.
   (a) Contrast the different views, in terms of efficiency and effectiveness, taken by the firm, the government, and environmental protection groups.
   (b) List the planned outcomes and the unplanned outcomes of the proposal.
3. Consider the Breast Cancer Screening Policy Project described in Example 1-4.
   (a) Contrast the different views, in terms of efficiency versus effectiveness taken by the government, health professionals, and the female population aged 50 to 70.
   (b) List the planned outcomes and the unplanned outcomes of the example policy stated.
4. For the following examples discuss the relevance of efficiency versus effectiveness:
   (a) the Aswan High Dam Project in Egypt (Example 2-1);
   (b) the deterioration of urban transport (Example 2-2);
   (c) the services call centre (Example 1-1).
5. For each of the following examples list one or more counterintuitive outcomes:
   (a) the Aswan High Dam Project in Egypt (Example 2-1);
   (b) the deterioration of urban transport (Example 2-2);
   (c) the assessment of unit production costs (Example 2-3).
6. Some systems experts stress the importance of the three Es, i.e., efficiency, effectiveness, and efficacy. What does 'efficacy' add to efficiency and effectiveness?
7. In your own words, discuss the difference between efficiency and effectiveness. Give two real-life practical examples for each. Give an example where a narrow view of efficiency interferes with effectiveness, and one where efficiency enhances effectiveness.
8. In Example 2-4, it was assumed that any delay in output of the machine causes a loss of sales. Assume now that there is no loss of sales for a (reasonably short) delay in output. How does this change the argument about stocking or not stocking spare parts? Answer the same question as though there were other machines available with sufficient capacity that could produce the same products, possibly at a somewhat higher cost.
9. Briefly discuss an instance of mutual causality present for the following:
   (a) the Aswan High Dam Project in Egypt (Example 2-1);
   (b) the deterioration of urban transport (Example 2-2);
   (c) poverty, the general health of certain segments of society, and educational achievement;
   (d) the inflationary spiral (relating prices to wage levels).

Further reading

Ackoff, R.L. (1974) 'The systems revolution', *Long-Range Planning*, 7(6): 2–20.

Ackoff, R.L (1973) 'Science in the systems age. Beyond IE, OR, and MS', *Operations Research*, 21(3): 661–71.

Checkland, P. (1985) 'From optimization to learning: a development of systems thinking for the 1990s', *Journal of the Operational Research Society*, 36(9): 757–67.

Hill, P.H. et al. (1986) *Making Decisions – A Multidisciplinary Introduction*, Lanham: University Press of America. Delightful book. Chapters 1 and 2 are relevant for systems thinking.

Pidd, M. (ed.) (2004) *Systems Modelling: Theory and Practice*, Chichester: Wiley. Chapters 1 and 2 talk about the need for MS/OR and systems thinking.

3
System concepts

Learning objectives

- When viewing something as a system, be able to tell if it is an out-there view or an inside-us view.
- Appreciate that a system definition is subjective and depends on the observer's worldview and prior knowledge about the situation.
- Be able to identify which aspects are system components, which ones form its environment, identify the controllable and the uncontrollable inputs, the system outputs, and the system behaviour, activity or transformation.
- Be able to distinguish between the narrow system of interest and the wider system of interest.
- Be able to recognize boundary judgements implied by a system definition for both the narrow and the wider system of interest.
- Be able to judge if an emergent property is planned or unplanned, desirable for achieving the goal(s) of the decision maker or detrimental.
- Be able to recognize feedback loops in system behaviour and determine whether they are positive or negative.
- Be able to determine whether a control is open-loop, feedback or feed-forward.

Introduction

In Chapter 2 you saw why it is useful to know about systems. This chapter studies the most important system concepts in more detail. We first explore how to define systems, what is so special about them, and what differentiates them from a mere collection of parts. Next, we study system behaviour and the importance of emergent properties of systems — the main reason for viewing something as a system. We then briefly look at various classifications of systems. Our main interest is the control of systems — control aimed at achieving certain desired goals. This is the topic of the last section.

3.1 Pervasiveness of systems

We are constantly surrounded by things we view as **systems** or that belong to systems. Planet Earth is viewed as a part of the **solar system**. Our whole life is spent in, and shaped and controlled by **social systems**, such as the family, the school, our work place, and interest groups we join, participate in, and drop out of. Some of us exploit **political systems** or are frustrated by them. Life without a **telephone system** would be difficult. The Internet has become our favourite **communication system**. In high school or university, we learn about **number systems**. Modern management would collapse without **information systems**. We expect our rights to be protected by the **legal system.** When our **digestive system** strikes, we suffer. What differentiates us from other animals, is our brain, part of our **central nervous system**. New systems are conceptualized or invented by the thousand every day.

At first sight, these things seem to have little in common. So, why are they all referred to as systems? They are all assemblies of things or entities that we view as interconnected or standing in clearly defined relationships with each other. They may have evolved into these relationships through natural physical processes, such as the solar system or a biological system. These are **natural systems**. Or they have been created by humans, such as **human activity systems**, such as most social systems, business and industrial entities or parts of them, or **abstract systems**, such as number systems or information systems. In this text, **we will be mainly interested in human activity systems, how to describe the relationships between their components, their behaviour, how to control them, and what aspects and considerations lead to effective decision making.**

Figure 3-1 is an excerpt from *Webster's 9th New Collegiate Dictionary.*

sys-tem n [**LL** systemat-, systema. fr Gk systemat-, systema. fr. synistanai to combine, fr. syn- + histanai to cause to stand – more at STAND] (1619) **1**: a regularly interacting or interdependent group of items forming a unified whole {a number ~}: as **a** (1): a group of interacting bodies under the influence of related forces {a gravitational ~} (2): an assemblage of substances that is in or tends to equilibrium {a thermodynamic ~} **b** (1): a group of body organs that together perform one or more vital functions {the digestive ~} (2): the body considered as a functional unit **c**: a group of related natural objects or forces {a river ~} **d**: a group of devices or artificial objects or an organization forming a network esp. for distributing something or serving a common purpose {a telephone ~} {a heating ~} {a highway ~} {a data processing ~} **e**: a major division of rocks usu. larger than a series and including all formed during a period or era **f**: a form of social, economic, or political organization or practice {the capitalist ~} **2**: an organized set of doctrines, ideas, or principles usu. intended to explain the arrangement or working of a systematic whole {the Newtonian ~ of mechanics} **3 a**: an organized or established procedure {the touch ~ of typing} **b**: a manner of classifying, symbolizing, or schematizing {a taxonomic ~} {the decimal ~} **4**: harmonious arrangement or pattern : ORDER {bring ~ out of confusion – Ellen Glasgow} **5**: an organized society or social situation regarded as stultifying: ESTABLISHMENT 2 – usu. used with the syn see METHOD – sys-tem-less.

Figure 3-1 Excerpt from *Webster's 9th New Collegiate Dictionary*

It lists more than a dozen different meanings of the word 'system', including the everyday language use as a procedure or scheme, or as a derogatory term for 'the ruling social order' or 'the establishment'. Have you recently 'beaten the system', implying you got around some rule you did not like?

Our view of a 'system' will be much more restrictive. The key terms are 'interacting', 'interdependent', and 'forming a unified whole'. Furthermore, it is not the notion of 'systematic', in the sense of carefully using a rational method or following a well laid-out plan or procedure, that primarily concerns us here, although we will go about any applications of system concepts in a systematic way. The key emphasis is on **systemic**, i.e., 'pertaining to systems', using systems ideas, or viewing things in terms of their role in a system. The term 'organized' captures much of the system notion.

3.2 Out-there and inside-us view of systems

One of the prime sources of confusion when calling an organized assembly of things a system is what could be termed the **out-there** view of systems in contrast to the **inside-us** view of systems. When we talk about our solar system, we have in mind the sun and its nine planets, of which Earth is one, and how the planets are linked to the sun and each other by gravitational forces. Similarly, an electric power system is viewed as the collection of power stations and their equipment, the power transmission grid, the local distribution network, with its transformers and power lines, and the various control stations that regulate the flow of power, as well as what the power system does, i.e., generate electric power and distribute it to its users where it is 'consumed'. A computer information system consists of the pieces of data collected, the rules used for collecting the data and their transformation into pieces of information, the storage of this information in electronic form, the programs for processing, storing, cross-referencing, manipulating, retrieving, and presenting this information on screens or in printed form, the computer equipment needed to perform all these activities, and finally the users.

In each of these examples,

the system is seen as the physical and abstract things that make up the whole assembly, their relationships, and what the system does. This is the out-there view of systems. It is seen as absolute; it exists or will exist sometimes out there; it is viewed as independent of the observer.

While most informed people today would agree on the same definition of the solar system, no such agreement can be expected for what things make up a particular electric power system or a computer information system. The reservoirs for power stations, the water catchment areas that feed them, and the annual water inflow patterns as part of the system were not listed. This is a seemingly arbitrary choice of what is viewed as belonging to that system. Another observer might have included these aspects as integral parts. One of our colleagues, who is an expert in the efficient operation of such systems, would have included the pricing structure for electricity as part of the system, something partially controllable by the power company. So, we see that different people may define the same 'system' in different ways, deliberately choosing what to include and what to exclude.

The choice of what to include or exclude will largely depend on what the person viewing something as a system intends to do with this definition, i.e., the purpose of defining something as a system. The system is no longer seen as existing independently of the observer; it is not out there; it has become a mental construct, personal to the observer! This is the inside-us view of systems.

The confusing thing is that in everyday language the word is usually used in an out-there meaning. This even happens if the assembly of components is a human construct or view, such as an industrial or business operation. It is described as if it existed independently of the observer. Unfortunately, even systems experts sometimes fall into this trap. So, when we say 'something is a system', what we really mean is that we '**view something as a system**' for a given purpose. Most often, it is simply a convenient means to express and organize our thoughts.

Systems as a human conceptualization

In this text, it is the inside-us view of systems that is important. Systems are seen as human conceptualizations. Although they may exist out there, it is only the human observer that views something as a system.

For instance, the grandfather taking his grandchild for a walk along an estuary may see it as a beautiful place to share the wonders of nature with his grandchild, while the jogger, crossing their path, may see the track along the estuary as part of a fitness course. The biology student studying the estuary will see it as an ecological system, where plants, insects, and all sorts of aquatic life forms interact with each other and are affected by the tides. The engineer working for the local catchment authority will also see it as a system, in fact, a subsystem of a larger water drainage system under her management. The grandfather or the jogger will hardly view the estuary as a system, while the biology student and the engineer each see different systems. But when the engineer takes her wind surfer onto the estuary, she too will not see it as a system, but simply as an enjoyable playground.

That systems are human conceptualizations is clearly driven home by the fact that the majority of systems we conceive in our role as analysts are not our personal view of some existing real assembly of things. They are visions (i.e., mental conceptualizations) of things that may not exist yet, things we plan to realize, such as a major planned change to an existing operation, still to be implemented. Sometimes, these visions are idealizations of what we would like to see, idealizations that we know will never come fully true, but which we strive to realize as closely as economically feasible.

3.3 Subjectivity of system description

The way something is viewed as a system depends on the personal interest of the observer. The purpose of studying an organized assembly of things as a system will determine the type of system seen. However, any two people viewing the same situation with the same purpose in mind may well form surprisingly different conceptualizations of that organized assembly of things. The reason for this is that the way an individual views a situation is affected by factors highly personal to that individual — aspects of which the person may not even be fully aware.

Worldview of observer

These personal factors include upbringing, cultural and social background, education, practical experience, and personal values or beliefs. For example, a firm may be viewed differently by each of its three co-owners: the first (the materialist) views it as a system to increase his wealth, the second (the idealistic artist) as a system to exercise her creative drive, and the third (the humanitarian) as a system to provide employment for the people in the town in which he lives. So, one of the skills all budding management scientists have to learn is to see a situation through other people's eyes. Hopefully, this will also make them more aware of their own way of looking at the world.

These personal factors are all captured in the concept of ***Weltanschauung***. This German word translates as **worldview.** It operates like coloured spectacles that taint things, distort a few, emphasize some, obscure others. It works as a filter that channels a person's view in a given personal way, which allows attributing meaning to what he or she observes that is congruent with his or her *Weltanschauung* or worldview.

Effect of previous knowledge

Reality is even more diverse and confusing. Partial knowledge, or an a priori obvious interpretation, or what we are told about something may affect what we observe or end up seeing. Consider the three shapes in Figure 3-2. We immediately recognize them as an isosceles triangle, a circle with a point at its centre, and a sector of a circle. In fact, each of these shapes is a different view of the same object. Can you guess what that object is? To verify your guess, look at Figure 3-3 over the page.

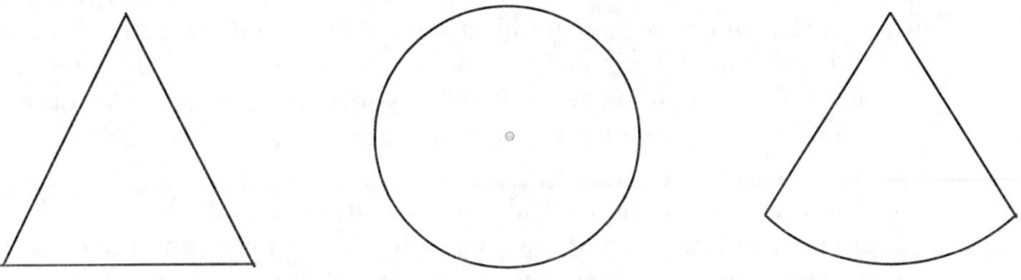

Figure 3-2 Geometrical shapes

The triangle is the silhouette of the cone seen level with its base. The circle is the view from above, while the sector is its silhouette as seen from a position opposite the cone at a height about half its size.

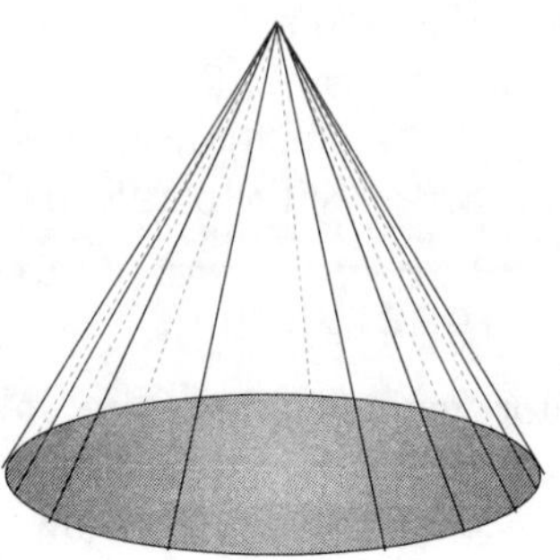

Figure 3-3 A cone

System definitions are subjective

For all these reasons, the way you view something as a system is to a large extent subjective. It is important for you to recognize that other people, viewing the same system, may not share your definition. Not only may they attribute a different purpose to the system, they may also include and exclude different aspects. But, and this is an important 'but', one definition cannot be labelled 'right' or 'valid' and another 'wrong' or 'invalid'. As long as each is logically consistent, each one is valid for its owner. The only conclusion that may be drawn is that one may be more effective, insightful, useful, or defensible in terms of the aim or purpose for viewing that entity as a system. This is an important aspect of systems thinking that may be difficult for a novice to accept. It is simpler, more comforting, less threatening to think in terms of a single unique answer or solution — the 'right' answer. However, systems thinking is not a matter of black-and-white, but of shades of grey. Often, there is not one single 'right' answer, but several possible and defensible ones.

Naturally, this discussion deals with the age-old controversy of **objective** versus **subjective**. Is there objectivity? From what you have read so far, you must conclude that we are firm believers that objectivity, at least in its traditional meaning of 'the expression or interpretation of facts or conditions as perceived without distortion by personal feelings or prejudices — in other words, independent of the observer's mind' — is an illusion. It is not an operational concept.

What is out-there in the real world can never be fully known. All we have are perceptions of an unknown reality, constructed and reconstructed as we learn more and gain more insights. Our mind can only capture our personal perceptions coherent with our worldview.

The only operational meaning that objectivity may have is what the systems thinker R.L. Ackoff (1974) calls 'the social product of the open interaction of a wide variety of individual subjectivities' — a sort of **consensual subjectivity**. So, wide consensus of interpretations on many things is thus not excluded. Modern scientific knowledge is based on such consensus. But, as the two examples below show, this is all that it is, a consensus. Or, to quote Albert Einstein: 'The only justification for our concepts is that they serve to represent the complex of our experiences; beyond this, they have no legitimacy.'

Consider the interpretation of 'what is insanity?' We look at past views of 'possessed by the devil' either with abhorrence or a benign smile. Future generations may think of the current view of 'deep-seated emotional disturbances due to maladjustment to the social environment, particularly during early childhood' as rather naive.

Probably the most famous example comes from Physics. Newton's laws of dynamics have been and still are some of the most successful scientific theories of profound theoretical and practical importance ever put forward. Not only were these laws corroborated by countless experiments and observations, but they also fully proved their practical value in mechanics — the building and working of all machinery on which modern life is based. Yet, at the beginning of the twentieth century Einstein showed that, when considering motions with velocities comparable to that of light, or when attempting to analyse the mechanics of atoms and subatomic elements, Newton's laws, seen as inviolate for over two centuries, break down and must be replaced by postulates of relativity and quantum theory. However, this in no way diminishes the continued importance of Newton's laws for operations with bodies of ordinary size, as dealt with in industry and much of space science.

Even Einstein's theory of relativity was challenged in late 2011 when an experiment by scientists at CERN seemed to indicate that neutrinos can travel faster than the speed of light.

So, if you hear somebody state with emphasis 'The facts prove it!' or 'Looking at it objectively ...' be suspicious. The person is either a fool, possibly a naive one, or a politician trying to pull the wool over your eyes.

3.4 Formal definition of the concept 'system'

We choose to define a system as follows:

1. **A system is an organized assembly of components. 'Organized' means that there exist special relationships between the components.**
2. **The system does something, i.e., it exhibits behaviours that are unique to the system. For human activity systems, this behaviour happens over time.**
3. **Each component contributes towards the behaviour of the system and its own behaviour is affected by being in the system. No component has an independent effect on the system. (A part that has an independent**

effect and is not affected by the system is an input. See point 5 below.) The behaviour of the system is changed if any component is removed or leaves.

4. **Groups of components within the system may by themselves have properties 1, 2, and 3, i.e., they may form subsystems.**
5. **The system has an outside — an environment — which provides inputs into the system and receives outputs from the system.**
6. **The system is viewed by someone to be of special interest for a given purpose.**

The relationships between components may be uni-directional and/or causal, i.e., part A affects part B, but is not in turn affected by B. They may be mutual, i.e., A and B both affect each other. Mutual influences or causality increase the complexity of system behaviour.

The crucial ingredients of a system are therefore its **components**, the **relationships** between the components, the **behaviour** or the **activities** of the system, its **relevant environment**, the **inputs** from the environment, the **outputs** to the environment, and the **special interest of the observer**. This is depicted diagrammatically in Figure 3-4, which shows two overlapping systems.

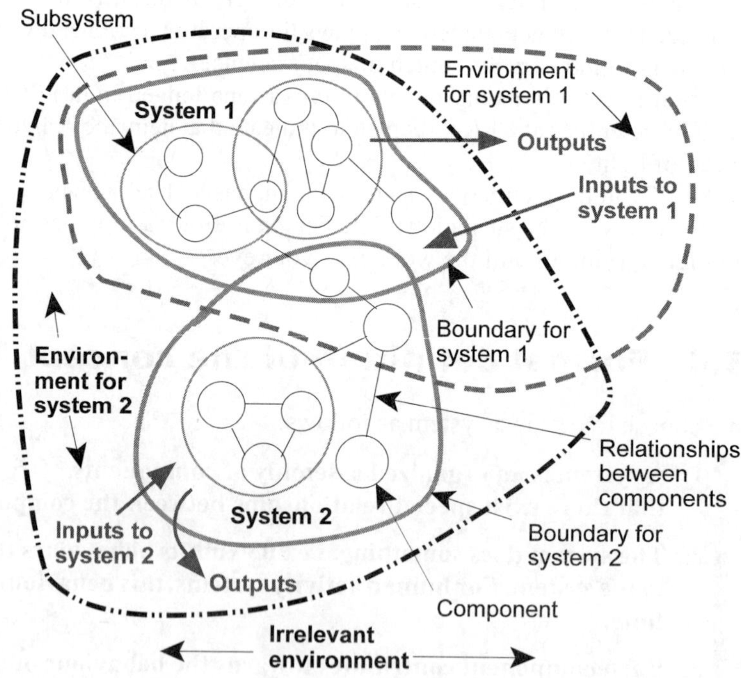

Figure 3-4 Environment, systems, subsystems, and components

A system is not a mere collection of parts that do not interact. It is not a **chaotic aggregate**, such as a pile of rocks. Adding a few parts to a chaotic aggregate or removing some does not change its nature. Doing so in a system will affect its behaviour. Similarly, a chaotic aggregate has no purposeful activity, while a system does, or at least is capable of, purposeful activity under specific conditions.

System components do not have to be physical. They can be abstract, such as information, variables that measure things, such as cumulative costs or levels of achievement, or relationships between physical or abstract things. In fact, most systems of interest in decision making often consist only of abstract things and their relationships.

An example of two overlapping systems is the operation of a fire service and an ambulance service, sharing the same facilities and communication subsystem.

What a system does — its activity — is of prime interest to the observer. The system behaviour consists of a **transformation process**, i.e., **inputs from the environment are transformed into outputs**. Living plants are an example of such a transformation process. When exposed to light, they transform water and carbon dioxide (inputs) into carbohydrates and oxygen (outputs). Another example is a factory, which transforms raw materials, funds, labour and expertise of people (inputs) into finished products for sale to customers, thereby producing profits (outputs).

The relevant environment of a system consists of all those aspects that affect system behaviour in any form, and those aspects that are affected by it but do not in turn affect it. (If they did, they should be included as part of the system.) They are viewed as being outside the system. They provide inputs to the system or receive outputs from the system. Inputs are things the system needs to function but does not produce for itself or, if so, only in insufficient quantities, such as resources or information. Inputs may also be in the form of constraints on the behaviour of the system, e.g., by setting quality standards or providing equipment and other facilities with given limited capacities.

Many of the inputs are **uncontrollable** or assumed to be so. They are given and cannot be affected by the decision maker. However, aspects over which the decision maker has control are **controllable inputs**. The control may be in the form of being able to select the value of a **decision variable**, choosing one of a range of actions to take, a decision about the amount of certain **resources**, such as funds, to be made available to the system, or a set of **decision rules** to follows whenever the behaviour of the system exhibits certain conditions or a specified event occurs.

Outputs are things the system 'releases' to the environment, such as goods and services, information, funds, and waste products. They also include **measures of performance**, i.e., indicators of prime interest of how the system responds to the controllable inputs, as well as other indicators of system behaviour. The purpose of studying a system determines which measures of performance an observer may wish to consider.

The relevant environment is in turn embedded in an even larger environment — 'the universe' — which is assumed not to affect the system; neither is it affected by the system, i.e., is irrelevant and can be ignored.

Finally, the person studying a system has a purpose for doing so. This could be to gain a better understanding of system behaviour, e.g., for a natural system. For human activity systems, the 'observer' is usually the decision maker, interested in how to control system behaviour, e.g., how to achieve maximum output.

3.5 System boundary and relevant environment

The separation between a system and its environment means that there is a **boundary**.

> **Boundary selection is the most critical aspect of systems thinking. Boundary choice determines not only the nature of the system transformation process and the form of the outputs, but also who will benefit from the desirable outputs and who will suffer undesirable consequences.**

For example, the productivity of a system operation may be enhanced at the detriment to another operation viewed as outside the system. Is this good and intended, or, on the contrary, bad and unintended, and why? Hence, we must question, in a critical sense, our **boundary judgements**, i.e., justify the boundary choices made in terms of their consequences and reassess them as we learn more about the system.

Similarly, what is considered the relevant environment also gives rise to critical boundary judgements, i.e., the choice of boundary for the relevant environment. For what defensible reason can an aspect of the environment be viewed as insignificant and hence be ignored, i.e., judged as irrelevant? Or which undesirable consequences of system outputs into the environment can be ignored as insignificant or irrelevant to the study, such as effects of pollutants discharged into waterways, or the social consequences resulting from closing a factory or splitting a community in two by putting a four-lane highway through it. Each of these choices involves value judgements that the analysts needs to evaluate critically.

For each boundary choice, the analyst must be on the lookout for implicit assumptions or boundary judgements. For instance, a system for the future operation of an entity or parts of an entity, such as a firm or government department, may use past data to estimate inputs. This implies that the future behaviour of the environment will be similar to its past behaviour (e.g., the demand for an entity's products or services will be the same, or the current trend will continue), that changes in the system outputs will have no effect on relevant inputs into the system (e.g., it will not stimulate or curtail demand for the entity's products or services), and that the system has no control over these aspects, when in fact such control is possible (e.g., demand for the entity's products or services can be affected through promotion).

3.6 Brief examples of system descriptions

A traffic system

A network of roads and their connections, i.e., road intersections, road forks, and motorway interchanges, and their physical characteristics and traffic controls, which affect their carrying capacity, as well as the vehicles using the roads at any given point in time, can be viewed as a traffic system. The relationships between the components consist of their geographic location relative to each other and how they are linked together.

Does a traffic system do anything? The road network connects places with each other and thus allows vehicle movement from each point in the road network to all other points. It transforms vehicles at given source locations (inputs) into vehicles at given destination locations (outputs). If a road section (such as a critical bridge over a river) is removed, some locations may become isolated from the rest of the system or more difficult to access. Traffic flows in different streets affect each other. As a consequence, the traffic behaviour changes.

What constitutes the environment of a traffic system? To answer this question, we need to look at the inputs and outputs of the system. The major physical input consists of the people who want to go from one place to another and the type of vehicles they use. They enter the system, become components, and then leave the system at their destinations. Traffic controls, such as green waves, and so on, are abstract inputs. Note that if the vehicles are removed, the road network ceases to be a traffic system. There is no transformation process present.

A regional traffic network can be viewed as containing several subsystems, one for each town or city, each of which has similar properties to the system as a whole.

The person viewing the network as a system could be a traffic engineer. His aim may be to observe certain system performance measures — the outputs of interest to him, such as the change in traffic flow along various crucial road sections between 7 am and 6 pm. The scheduler of a fleet of pick-up and delivery vehicles may be another person interested in the road network as a traffic system. His or her aim is determining the sequence of pick-ups and deliveries for a given vehicle, which has the shortest distance, or which takes the shortest time given the traffic densities likely to be encountered during the trip.

A motor vehicle

A car is often cited as a typical example of a system. It is a complex assembly of thousands of individual parts. Its major components — the engine, its steering mechanism, its suspension, the electric parts — are complex subsystems by themselves. Their relationships consist of how they are fitted together and how they interact. It is an easy trap to view an assembled car as a system — indeed, in its out-there meaning, existing independently of the observer. But a car by itself, say parked on the road, in a garage, or exhibited in a car museum, is not a system. It does not do anything on its own. More is needed for a system. To be a means for transporting people and goods, it also needs a driver and a destination, plus fuel, plus a road network for a road vehicle. The road network and all its properties form the environment of the car-driver system. Without them it remains an inert assembly of parts.

Cars could, though, form part of different systems. For example, for a car collector, cars become a hobby — part of a personal enjoyment system. For the car salesperson, the cars in the sales yard are part of a profit making system.

Note that most cars have many components — trim, interior comforts, a stereo, a central locking subsystem — that do not contribute to their intended role as a means of transport. It is still part of a transport system without these. However, remove the wheels, and the car ceases to be a system for a means of transport. If it has an external power pick-up link, as in some cross-country vehicles or tractors, it may be used as a system to provide motive power for the operation of machinery. Its purpose changes.

A water reservoir

A water reservoir can be viewed as a system. Its inputs are the inflows from its catchment area. Water released into a conduit — a canal or a pressure pipeline — or over its spillway are its major outputs. What does it do? It stores water temporarily over time. Its components are: water and the controls on the two water release gates for the conduit and the spillway. The dam and other physical aspects of the reservoir are part of its environment. So are the inflows. The person interested in viewing it as a system could be the controller of a power station or of an irrigation scheme. The water reservoir illustrates another point. It can be viewed as a subsystem of a larger system, such as a hydro-electric power system or an irrigation system.

A stock control system

An appliance wholesaler stocks Brand X television sets. Periodically the firm places a replenishment request for Brand X with its manufacturer. The sets arrive n days later and are added to those still in stock, if any. The firm receives orders from retailers for Brand X, which it ships m days later. The activities of replenishing the inventory, storing the sets, and removing sets for delivery to retailers can be viewed as a stock control system. The inventory of sets is one of its components. Replenishment requests placed with the manufacturer, but not yet received, and the orders received from retailers, but not yet shipped, are other components. The placements of replenishment requests are controllable inputs and the receipts of retailer orders are uncontrollable inputs. The environment consists of the storage capacity, the length of time it takes between placing a replenishment request and the receipt of the set, n, and the demand pattern for Brand X from the retailers. Depending on the purpose of viewing this as a system, the cost structure of the operation, for example, also forms part of the environment. The person interested in this system could be the MS/OR analyst who wishes to determine the replenishment policy that minimizes the overall costs of the system.

A sawmill

A sawmill cuts up logs into a variety of products — planks, beams, framing materials, posts, and trim. An industrial engineer may see a sawmill as a system for converting raw materials in the form of various types of logs into a wide range of different finished products, including by-products, such as off-cuts and sawdust. The aim is to determine a facility and equipment layout and processing rules that provide an efficient and safe operating environment. The owners of the sawmill may see it as a system for producing a financial return on their investment. An MS/OR analyst may see parts of it as a system for cutting logs into end products intended to satisfy a given composition of customer demands at the lowest possible cost. Table 3-1 lists the components, activities, relationships, inputs and outputs, and the transformation process for each of these three views.

Table 3-1 Three different systems views for a sawmill

Systems view	Industrial engineer	Owners	MS/OR analyst
Purpose of viewing entity as a system	• study physical layout of equipment, product handling, and operating rules	• assess financial return on investment	• study effect on costs of different cutting patterns to meet customer demand
System components	• buildings, yards • equipment, vehicles • operators • logs in yards • intermediate and finished products	• subsystems, such as log procurement, production, warehousing, marketing, distribution, finance • funds invested • work force • equipment	• processing subsystems • stock of logs • intermediate and finished product stocks
Activities of system	• various processing operations • moving of cuts • drying of cuts • storage • equipment maintenance	• purchasing of logs • conversion of logs • warehousing of products • marketing • distribution	• subsystem product conversions
Relationships between components	• process sequence • location of fixed equipment • feasible cutting patterns	• subsystem outputs become inputs to other subsystems • communications between subsystems	• subsystem outputs become inputs to other subsystems • feasible cutting combinations
Inputs from environment (C) = controllable	• types of logs • supplies (oil, fuel) • processing rates and capacities • operating rules (C) • maintenance policy (C) • task assignments to operators (C)	• log supply • market demand • commercial laws • funds (C) • equipment (C) • hiring and firing (C) • pricing policy (C)	• logs available • cost data • processing rates and capacities • product demand to be met • operating rules (C) • cutting pattern selection (C)
Outputs	• finished products • by-products • processing capacity use • bottlenecks • equipm. capacity use	• cash flow projections • return on investment • market share	• projections for total operating costs to meet given customer demands
Transformation process of system	• facilities use for converting logs into finished products	• wealth at time t into wealth at time t+1	• converting equipm. capacities, logs, and customer demands into operating costs
Time frame	• continuous over day	• monthly/quarterly over year	• specified number of periods (days/weeks)

The industrial engineer takes a highly detailed view of the physical characteristics of each piece of equipment, such as its dimensions, maintenance and safety requirements, its potential location, its processing rates, and the various ways different pieces of equipment may interact with each other. The inputs and outputs of the system are both physical (logs, products), as well as abstract (operating rules, operating statistics, such as output capacities, bottleneck locations, and so on).

In contrast, the owners have little interest in the details of the physical side of the operation. Seeing the firm as a profit generating system, they take an aggregate view. For them, the firm consists of several interdependent subsystems, each with its own mission. The outputs of one become the inputs of others. Their prime concern is the effective coordination of subsystems' interactions and the financial consequences in terms of profit and cash flows for the firm as a whole. These are the firm's major outputs and performance measures, not the products it produces. Inputs are mainly financial (funds) and abstract (policies on pricing, and so on).

An MS/OR study has some aspects of both of the preceding systems. It keeps much of the details on the physical product flow as in the engineering system, but possibly at a lower level of resolution. In fact, best operating rules and processing capacities derived in the engineering study become abstract inputs into its system definition. But it also retains the financial implications for all activities which are associated with the multi-stage process of converting logs into finished products, as in the profit generating system. Again, it is not the physical products that comprise the major outputs of the system, but the overall cost implications of the operations.

Level of resolution in system description

As these three views of a sawmill demonstrate, the purpose of studying the operations as a system strongly influences the level of detail or the degree of **resolution** used for representing the various components, the system inputs and outputs. The industrial engineer's system adopts a very high level of resolution, showing minute details of equipment operations. On the other hand, the owners' system has a much lower level of resolution, where complex details of the production subsystem are aggregated into a few relationships that measure the financial implications of converting logs into finished products. The MS/OR analyst may go for an intermediate degree of resolution. Its exact level will depend on the purpose of the study — a low level of resolution for aggregate monthly planning, a high level of resolution if the study is to come up with a detailed daily operating schedule.

Arbitrariness of system description

This discussion drives home the point that there is considerable arbitrariness in how a system is defined, where its boundaries are placed, and its level of detail or resolution. As a rule, the choice should be the smallest system needed for achieving the purpose for which the system is defined. Furthermore, the analyst may make simplifications and approximations to reduce the system complexity to a level he or she can handle with the resources available. Both are a matter of judgement.

Activity

The principal views her high school as a human activity system.

- List its major components, inputs, outputs, and its environment. (An example of the four items: teachers, government, minimum contact hours, number of students suspended, demographic location of school.)
- Do you see your description as an 'out-there' or 'inside-us' view?
- What is the underlying worldview of the school principal? (Example: maintaining discipline is essential.)
- What is the system transformation process? (Hint: which major input is transformed into the major output?)
- List three performance measures. (Example: number of students suspended.)
- List three (possibly arbitrary) choices you made as to where to draw the system boundary. (Example: limited computing facilities assumed unchangeable.)
- Redefine the boundary by including one of these aspects as an integral part of the system. How might this affect the major transformation process? (Example: changes in computing facilities opens up new ways of teaching.)

3.7 Systems as 'black boxes'

The complexity of real life may be such that we have no, or only incomplete, knowledge of the inner workings of a system, even if we are able to identify the physical components. Often, the major reason for this lack of knowledge is that the system behaviour is affected by random aspects. In other cases, the relationships between components is only partially understood. This is the case for human brain functions. So, there is no full understanding of how humans learn. Similarly, in spite of the enormous progress made in meteorology, weather systems are only partially understood. As a result, weather predictions are unreliable. Computers or other machinery fail for a myriad of reasons. It may be impractical to keep track of individual causes which often exhibit mutual causality. Hence, only aggregate records are compiled.

In each of these examples, the inside of the corresponding system is left largely empty. All we know are the inputs into, and the outputs from, the system. To the lay observer, it looks like one of those black control boxes, with many wires into and out of the box, but no way of knowing what is under the cover. If our aim is to predict the output of such a system in response to various inputs, we may indeed not have to know the details of its inner workings, even if this were possible. In such instances, all we need to discover is the form of the functional relationship between inputs and outputs, i.e., the mathematical form of the transformation process. Various statistical tools may help in this task. After proper testing, these relationships can then be used for predicting the corresponding phenomena, such as the most likely weather pattern resulting from certain meteorological (input) conditions, or the long-run daily breakdown patterns for, say, 24 looms in operation at a carpet or cloth factory — information needed for planning a repair service.

In other situations, the transformation process is known exactly. However, rather than represent it in full detail, it may be adequate to view the inner working as a black box and simply express the various activities of the transformation process with a single functional relationship. Instances of this are intricate multistage chemical processes, as in an oil refinery, where a yield table is used for transforming, say, crude oil into a range of refined products. This approach is frequently used as a substitute for the transformation process of a subsystem which receives inputs from and provides outputs to other components of the system. For example, the subsystem for the conversion of logs into finished products in the sawmill profit maximizing system is most likely to be included in the form of a black box.

3.8 Boundary choice and hierarchy of systems

The purpose of viewing something as a system affects what aspects should be included as part of the system and what aspects are more appropriately placed into the relevant environment, in other words, where to place the **boundary of the system**. The two systems for the sawmill — a cost minimization system (1) and a profit making system (2) — clearly demonstrate this. System (1) takes the equipment and its properties as given. There is a given assortment of logs available. Similarly, the assortment of various finished products to be produced is set. These are some of its uncontrollable inputs from the environment. It selects a combination of cutting patterns to transform all or some of the logs into the required finished products so as to minimize costs. For system (2), the boundaries are set much wider. It is not a set of logs that are its input, but the prevailing capacity of the logging industry to supply various types of logs. The volume of logs acquired for processing are a controllable input. By investing additional funds, the output capacities of its facilities can be increased. The facilities are not part of the environment. While the general market conditions are a vital aspect of the firm's environment, its own customer demand can to some extent be affected through promotional activity.

The sawmill demonstrates another point. System (1) is completely contained in system (2). Some decisions of system (2), such as the volume of each type of log purchased and composition of finished products to be produced, become the inputs of system (1). They form part of its environment. So, we have a system within a system. It is unimportant that the degree of detail shown for the two systems may be different.

In fact, these are only two of a whole sequence of nested systems related to the sawmill. The firm itself is embedded in a system of regional sawmills, all sharing the same forest resources. The system of regional sawmills is embedded in the system covering the national wood processing industry. The latter in turn is included in the system for the whole national economy. This nesting of systems within systems within systems is referred to as a **hierarchy of systems**. It is depicted in Figure 3-5. The containing system becomes the environment of the contained system.

In most instances, the containing system exercises some control over the contained system. The controlling system may set the objectives of the contained system, monitor how well it achieves these objectives, and have control over crucial resources needed by the contained system. The controlling system is then referred to as the **wider system of interest**, while the contained system becomes the **narrow system of interest**. The wider system (including its own relevant environment) thus becomes the relevant environment of the narrow system. For the sawmill, if cost minimizing system (1) is the narrow system of interest, then sawmill profit maximizing system (2) and its environment is its wider system of interest.

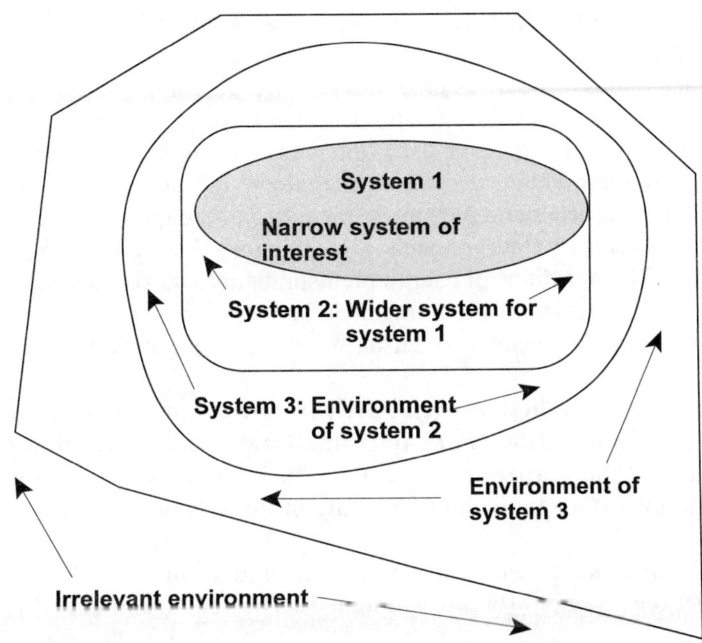

Figure 3-5 Hierarchy of systems

The advantage of viewing two systems in a hierarchy of a narrow and a wider system is that their relationships are shown in their proper context. It may show how the performance of the narrow system is hampered or constrained by aspects of the wider system. Changes in the wider system may become prerequisites to performance improvement in the narrow system of interest.

Similarly, the relationships between various inputs into the narrow system are clarified. For example, two inputs first seen as independent of one another may turn out to be highly affected by the same factors when seen in their proper relationship within the wider system. This could be the case for the cost of labour in the sawmill cost minimization system for the various subsystem operations. All labour costs may depend on the same union contract.

Activity

High school as a system (continuation of Activity, p. 39):

- Describe two subsystems and their major components.
- Describe briefly the wider system of interest.
- Define a hierarchy of three systems, with the high school as the smallest one.

3.9 Behaviour of human activity systems

System state

As pointed out earlier, the behaviour of a system is of prime interest to the person studying it. How do we describe the behaviour of a system? We show how various characteristics, properties or attributes of each component change as inputs change and/or as it is affected by changes in other system components. Consider the stock control system. Its dynamic behaviour can be traced in detail if, at any moment in time, we know the number of units in inventory, the number and size of replenishment requests in process and the status of each, and the number and size of retailer orders in process and the status of each. The inventory is a system component. Its attribute is its size. The attributes of each replenishment are its size and its status. That status is normally expressed as the number of days remaining until the replenishment arrives and is added to the stock. We usually refer to these attributes as **state variables**.

At any point in time each state variable assumes a given value, numerical or nominal. The set of values of all state variables at that point in time is called the 'state of the system'. The behaviour of a system is completely known if we know how the state of the system changes over time.

When we start observing a system, the initial values of all state variables are inputs (either observed or arbitrarily assigned). They change in one of two ways:

1. The change in a state variable is the result of an input into the system — the placement of a replenishment request or the receipt of a customer order in the stock control system. The first is a controllable input, the second is not.
2. The change in a state variable of a component is a consequence of the activity of the component itself or of its relationship with other components. Each day, the state variable counting the number of days until arrival in stock decreases by one. Once it arrives, the component disappears, but the state variable for the level of inventory increases by the size of the replenishment.

Variety of system behaviour

System behaviour can be almost infinitely varied and complex, even for very simple systems. To demonstrate this we borrow the fascinating example from the (British) Open University text (Beishon and Peters, 1981).

Example 3-1: A moving text strip

Consider one of those old-fashioned newscaster strips, where advertising and news headlines march across the front of a building, each letter formed by a specific pattern of on and off light bulbs. Assume that the display panel is 7 light bulbs high and 100 light bulbs long, allowing for only 20 letters to be shown at one time. The behaviour of this system is given by the changing patterns of light bulbs on and off. Each possible pattern is one state of this system.How many different states does this system have?

> Since each light bulb can either be on or off, the state variable for each light bulb has two values. If there are only two light bulbs, then for each of the two states of the first bulb there are two states for the second bulb, i.e., there are 2 times 2 or 2^2 possible states. For three light bulbs it is 2 times 2 times 2, or 2^3. You now see the pattern. For 700 light bulbs it is 2^{700} different states. This is slightly larger than 10^{210}, i.e., a number consisting of a 1 followed by another 210 zeros. Most of us have great difficulties in grasping how big this number really is.
>
> To put it into perspective, consider the number of atomic particles contained in the entire universe. This has been estimated as being in the order of 10^{73}, an infinitesimally small number compared to the number of states for the 700 light bulb newscaster, which is a rather small one compared to the one that existed in the 1960s and 1970s on London's Leicester Square which had 30,000 bulbs! And this is dwarfed by the capacity of a high resolution computer monitor that can display up to 1024 × 768 (almost 800,000) individual dots or pixels. We will not even try to express the number of possible states.

The huge variety of system behaviour is another dimension that adds complexity to decision making.

In real-life systems studies, we are rarely interested in the minute details of the complex system behaviour. This would quickly outstrip our cognitive and computational capabilities. Our concern is, rather, with the aggregate or average system behaviour. For example, in the road network the traffic engineer is hardly interested in the movement of every vehicle but, rather, with 15-minute or half-hour averages of the capacity use or traffic flows along certain road sections over the course of a given weekday. This will indicate which road sections and intersections are prone to becoming traffic bottlenecks. Or the traffic engineer may want to collect information on the number of trips made from a given suburb of the city to various other parts of the city for planning future road needs. Summary measures for selected state variables will suffice for this purpose.

Even in the relatively simple stock control system, the MS/OR analyst studying it may summarize the inventory behaviour over time by its average.

Emergent properties

The behaviour of the road network as a traffic system highlights another important aspect. A traffic bottleneck at a given intersection as a result of high traffic flow cannot be associated with an individual vehicle travelling through that intersection. Similarly, the traffic density at a given point in the network is a product of many components acting together. It makes no sense to associate traffic density with a single car.

> **The system exhibits behaviours or properties that none if its components may exhibit individually. Such properties only emerge from the joint interaction or behaviour of the components that form the system, hence their label 'emergent properties'. This phenomenon is often summarized by 'the whole is greater than the sum of its parts'.**

Human activity systems are usually created or formed in order to produce desired emergent properties. Consider again the car/driver as a system of components (engine, wheels, and so on, plus driver, plus road network). This system is more than simply a complementary collection of components arranged in a given pattern; it was created specifically as a mode of transport. None of its parts has this property by itself.

Viewed individually, the various subsystems that make up a sawmill are not capable of producing a profit. Only by coordinating their activities properly does the potential for producing a profit emerge. Again, this is a planned emergent property.

Unfortunately, all too often some emergent properties are not desirable, or even planned. The examples in Chapter 2, such as the side effects of building the Aswan High Dam (Example 2-1), the deterioration of urban transport (Example 2-2), or the effects of the traditional method of assessing machine efficiencies (Example 2-3), clearly highlight this. One of the compelling reasons for using a systems approach to problem solving is exactly to predict better the planned desirable emergent properties and the unplanned undesirable emergent properties resulting from a given decision. It is then possible to take suitable countermeasures or alter the original design to alleviate or avoid undesirable emergent properties at the planning stage, before they occur.

Activity

High school as a system (continuation of Activities, pp. 39 and 41):

- list three state variables and their attributes (example: state variable — contact hours for a given student; attribute — number of hours);
- list two desirable planned and two undesirable unplanned emergent properties of the high school system (example: socialization of students — planned, desirable; vandalism — unplanned, undesirable).

3.10 Different kinds of systems

As in all scientific disciplines, systems are classified according to various distinguishing properties. Being aware of them helps in understanding system behaviour.

Discrete systems

In the newscaster light bulb display (Example 3-1), the state of the system is any one of a huge number of individual states, each characterized by a pattern of on-and-off bulbs. The pattern changes so rapidly that our eyes are deceived into seeing a continuously moving string of letters. However, that movement consists of a sequence of displays of individual patterns, each one held for a fraction of a second. So, the state of the system jumps through a sequence of discrete states. Such systems are called **discrete systems**. A discrete system changes its state at discrete points in time. Between these times, the state of the system remains unchanged. The state variables of the stock control system also change in discrete jumps, e.g., Q units added to the stock upon arrival of a replenishment.

Here are a few other examples of discrete systems:

- For the services call centre (Example 1-1), the number of telephone lines or the number of operators busy are two of the important state variables. Each can only be an integer.

- In a predator/prey system, the state is described by the number of predators and number of prey alive at any point in time. Both are discrete variables.
- In the loom repair system (p. 39), two state variables of prime interest are the number of machines operating and the number of machines broken down at any given point in time — again, discrete variables.

Continuous systems

A commercial airliner flying from Airport A to Airport B is a component of an air traffic control system. It changes its position continuously. Four of its state variables are: its two geographical coordinates, its elevation, and its ground-level speed. The position of every aircraft within the area monitored by the air traffic control system is defined by these four state variables, whether flying or on the ground. This is an example of a **continuous system**.

The water reservoir system is also a continuous system. The water level in the reservoir, as well as the inflows and outflows, are continuous variables. Many industrial processes, particularly in chemical and petrochemical plants, should be viewed as continuous systems. The value of certain state variables may be monitored constantly, e.g., to initiate action for keeping the temperature of a liquid within a given narrow level. Similarly, the process used by warm-blooded animals to maintain body temperature within a narrow range is also a continuous system.

Some state variables that may assume any real value may nevertheless change their values only at discrete points in time. For example, in the water reservoir system, the water outflow for irrigation changes at discrete points of time whenever the sluice gate is adjusted, opened or closed.

Although a continuous system may change continuously, in many cases its state is usually also observed and recorded only at regular discrete points in time, say, every 10 minutes. The closer consecutive recordings are taken in time, the more accurately the system actual behaviour is approximated.

Many systems have both discrete and continuous state variables. Furthermore, the 'observer' of the system may, for reasons of simplicity or convenience, approximate a continuous state variable as discrete or a discrete variable as continuous.

Deterministic and stochastic systems

If the behaviour of a system is predictable in every detail, the system is **deterministic**. For example, in most studies the solar system is viewed as a deterministic system. The trajectory of every planet can be predicted almost exactly. Animated neon advertising signs that go through a regular pattern can be viewed as deterministic systems. A sequence of traffic lights along a one-way street is set at a fixed pattern during certain hours of the day so as to produce a green wave. When operating in this mode, it is a deterministic system.

Given the same starting conditions, a deterministic system will always exhibit exactly the same behaviour, i.e., go through the same sequence of system state changes.

Some systems' behaviour may be affected by **uncertain**, **random** or **stochastic** inputs. Such systems are called **stochastic systems**. ('Stochastic' derives from the Greek *stochos*, meaning 'aiming at', or 'guess'.) Sections 15.2 and 15.8 (pp. 422 and 438) discuss possible causes of uncertainty and approaches used for modelling stochastic system inputs.

The traffic network and the stock control systems both are viewed as stochastic systems. The number of vehicles entering various boundary points of the traffic network or the demand pattern in terms of the number of TV sets ordered by all retailers in the stock control system vary randomly over time.

It is also the case that we may model uncontrollable inputs as random in order to keep the narrow system of interest to a manageable size, rather than because such inputs are inherently unpredictable. This is particularly the case when it may be too expensive in terms of time and funds to ascertain in sufficient detail and accuracy complex interactions in the environment that produce these inputs. The cost of such accuracy may exceed the potential additional benefits that could be gained.

If the variations in behaviour are minor, we may choose to approximate it with a deterministic system. In the stock control system, the random demand may be replaced by its average. The Swiss railroads, known for their almost pedantic punctuality, can for most purposes be adequately approximated as a deterministic system.

Closed and open systems

The father of General System theory, Ludwig von Bertalanffy, introduced the concepts of **closed and open systems**. A closed system has no interactions with any environment. No inputs, no output. In fact, it has no environment. In contrast, open systems interact with the environment, by receiving inputs from it and providing outputs to it.

Viewing systems in the out-there mode, none are closed systems. Any real-life system has an environment with which it interacts, even if only in a small way. So, the concept of a closed system is only of theoretical interest. With no interactions with an environment, its behaviour is regulated entirely by the interactions among the components of the system.

Scientists, particularly in the biological and physical sciences, may try to create artificially closed systems that are, as far as physically possible, insulated from their environment. Their only inputs are the initial starting conditions. By providing different initial conditions, the analyst observes how system behaviour responds. Note, however, that these conditions are imposed as inputs to the system from outside, hence these systems are not truly closed. Unfortunately, some social scientists give 'closed system' a different meaning — a rather unhelpful misuse of the term, leading to confusion.

Systems defined for decision making are always open systems, since by definition the decisions or the decision making rules are inputs into the system. Stochastic systems are always modelled as open systems since the specifications for the randomness in behaviour are imposed by the analyst. These specifications may be derived from actual observations of the real-life counterpart of the system modelled, or from theoretical considerations for planned systems or phenomena not fully understood.

The steady state of a stochastic system

A stochastic system may exhibit some remarkable and surprising characteristics in its behaviour. It may become trapped in the same final state, if one exists, even if it starts out from different initial conditions or initial states of the system. However, more commonly, stochastic systems in the long-run tend to approach a **state of equilibrium**, also called a **'steady state'**. This state of equilibrium is independent of the state the system starts out from.

The term 'steady state' is a misnomer. It is not a particular state that once reached is maintained in perpetuity. Rather, it refers to the system's **long-run behaviour**.

> **The state of equilibrium is characterized by the values which certain state variables that measure long-run averages tend to approach if the system 'functions' or operates for a sufficient length of time.**

In a services call centre, they are the long-run average number of operators busy and the long-run average length of time callers have to wait prior to receiving service. In a predator-prey system, they are the long-run average size of each population.

Few stochastic systems ever reach their state of equilibrium. Small or large random disturbances, e.g., a sudden random surge of emergency calls, or a severe storm in an ecological system, may disrupt system behaviour and push it away from these long-run averages. But, in each case, the system will gradually approach the same or a new state of equilibrium again.

Activity

Give two examples for each of the following:

- a discrete system;
- a continuous system;
- a deterministic system;
- a stochastic system;

and show why they are that type of system.

3.11 Feedback loops

As mentioned in Section 2.4, the behaviour of system components may exhibit mutual causality, i.e., component A affects component B, which in turn affects component A. This is known as a feedback loop. Such feedback may be indirect via other components, e.g., A affects B, which affects C, which in turn affects A. This is depicted in the top loop of Figure 3.6. The arrow inside the loop shows the direction of the influence relationships. Note that it is usually the state of a component that affects the state of another component, and so on. Feedbacks are a common feature in most human activity systems and natural systems. They often are the main cause of complexity.

Figure 3-6 represents the feedbacks present in a toilet cistern mechanism. Water flows into the cistern via an inflow pipe C and out via outlet F. The water level A in the cistern is one of the state variables of the system. If level A is at its maximum, valve B keeps inflow pipe C closed. If the flushing lever D (an external disturbance of the system) is activated, mechanism E opens outlet F, and lets the water in the cistern empty out via F. As level A in the cistern lowers, valve B opens, causing the inflow via C to become positive (for this to work, the inflow via C must be at a much lower rate than the outflow via F). Once level A falls below a trigger point, mechanism E blocks outlet F, cutting off the outflow. This now allows level A to rise. When full, valve B closes, cutting the inflow via C to zero. (Note the arrows do not depict flow of water, but cause-and-effects between system components.)

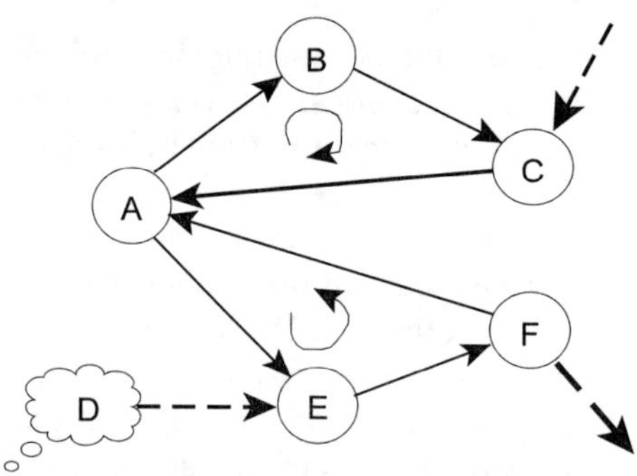

Figure 3-6 Feedback loops

Negative and positive feedback loops

Feedback can act positively or negatively.

> **Positive feedback increases the discrepancy between the future state of the system and some reference state, such as an equilibrium or a desired target state. In other words, the system state tends to deviate more and more from its reference state. In contrast, negative feedback decreases the discrepancy between the future state and the reference state.**

(Note that 'positive' and 'negative' do not imply 'good' and 'bad'.)

In the cistern example, a full cistern, i.e., its level at its maximum, is the desired target state. If a disturbance occurs (lever D is activated), level A is displaced from its target, but is brought back to it by the two feedback loops A–B–C–A and A–E–F–A. Both loops act negatively, restoring the level of A to its target.

Positive feedback tends to lead to instability. The system either explodes, for example, by having some of its state variables take on larger and larger values, or it kills itself. The meltdown of a nuclear reactor, without the presence of a counter-mechanism, is an example of a positive feedback.

Although a number of theoretical examples, particularly from mathematics and economics, exhibit positive feedback, most natural and human activity systems rely on negative feedback. They either try to reach a goal or strive to maintain or preserve existing relationships, properties, or equilibria. In all cases, the system has built-in mechanisms that steer the system back towards the goal, or the desired relationship or equilibrium if it is displaced from it through some external event.

Section 5.5 (p. 97) shows how diagrams help identify feedback loops and whether they are positive or negative. Feedback loops play a central role in system control.

Activity

Describe the feedback loop for:

- a thermostatically controlled heating system;
- the market system assumed to balance supply and demand for a product.

3.12 Control of systems

Our main reason for viewing something as a human activity system is to exercise effective control over its behaviour. Control is achieved by imposing something on the system in the form of inputs — a set of decisions, or decision rules, or simply an initial state for the system — that will affect some activities in the system, and therefore the behaviour of the system, in desired ways. We shall refer to them as **control inputs**. Note that if we impose decision rules on the system it may seem, at least superficially, as though the system exercises control by itself. The fact that its behaviour will change if the system is made to obey a different set of rules clearly shows that this apparent self-control is imposed from outside.

Three conditions are needed for exercising control over system behaviour:

1. a target or goal for the system to reach (for deterministic systems, this may be a particular system state; for stochastic systems, it may be a desirable steady state);
2. a system capable of reaching the target or goal (this is rather obvious; the difficulty is that for stochastic systems there may be no way of guaranteeing that this goal is ever reached or approached sufficiently closely); and
3. some means for influencing system behaviour (these are the control inputs — decisions, decision rules, or initial states; how these control inputs affect system behaviour is an important aspect of studying systems).

System theory distinguishes between three types of controls: **open loop controls**, **closed loop** or **feedback controls**, and **feed-forward controls**.

Open loop controls

Open loop controls are inputs imposed on the system based only on the prediction of how the system behaviour responds to them. No account is taken of how the system actually responds to the control inputs. Open loop controls are often in the form of a recipe or a set of rules to follow. For example, in the sawmill cost minimizing system the control inputs will be in the form of a schedule of detailed cutting patterns to apply to each log to be processed.

We will find that for many MS projects the recommendations derived for controlling the system are in the form of open loop controls. However, for many situations open loop controls are not adequate or effective. Assume you use the following five steps for starting the engine of your vintage British sports car:

1. insert ignition key into ignition lock;
2. depress clutch pedal and use gear lever to shift into neutral (assume you always leave the car in gear when the engine is off);
3. pull choke button half way out ('what is a choke?' some of you may ask; it is a vintage car because it has one!);
4. turn ignition key clockwise to red mark (this engages the starter motor), hold for two seconds, and then return key to black mark);
5. after the engine runs for ten seconds, push the choke back in fully.

It is clear that this does not guarantee that you can start the car's engine successfully. For example, the person who used the car before you may have left it in neutral. Touching the gear lever will immediately indicate this, so you will skip step 2. The engine may still be hot from a previous run, hence no choke is needed; or it may be very cold, and the choke has to be pulled out completely and the engine run for more than ten seconds. The engine may start already after one second, so you return the key to the black mark without waiting two seconds. The engine may not start within the two second interval, in which case you may continue holding the key to the red mark for much longer. In fact, what you are doing is adjusting the controls used for starting the engine to how the car responds to the controls. The behaviour of the system becomes a source of feedback to adjust your controls.

Closed loop or feedback controls

Under this type of control, information about the system behaviour, possibly in response to previous control inputs, is fed back to the controller for evaluation. This may lead the controller to adjust the control signals. The classic example for this is how most people adjust the temperature of a shower. Standing safely outside the shower, we turn the shower control valve to a setting somewhere midway between 'cold' and 'hot'. After a few seconds, we tentatively put in a hand to test the temperature of the water flowing from the shower head. This information is interpreted by our brain. If the temperature feels too cold, we respond by turning the control valve clockwise to increase the flow of hot water relative to the flow of cold water. If it is too hot, we turn the control counter-clockwise. We then wait again a second or two to check the result. This process continues until the water temperature feels right.

In systems terms, the controller supplies some initial control inputs to a **feedback control mechanism.** The latter is a component of the system, while the controller itself is outside. The initial control inputs are usually in the form of decision rules or a decision strategy (... if such and such is observed, do this and that ...). These decisions rules are used by the control mechanism to issue **control signals** that steer the system in a desired direction. Information about the resulting system behaviour or outputs is then fed back to the control mechanism for evaluation. The latter adjusts the control signals in accordance with the decision rules. So, the loop from the control mechanism to other parts of the system is closed by a feedback loop from these parts back to the control mechanism. For this reason, such types of controls are referred to as **closed-loop controls** or **feedback controls**. The top portion of Figure 3-7 depicts this.

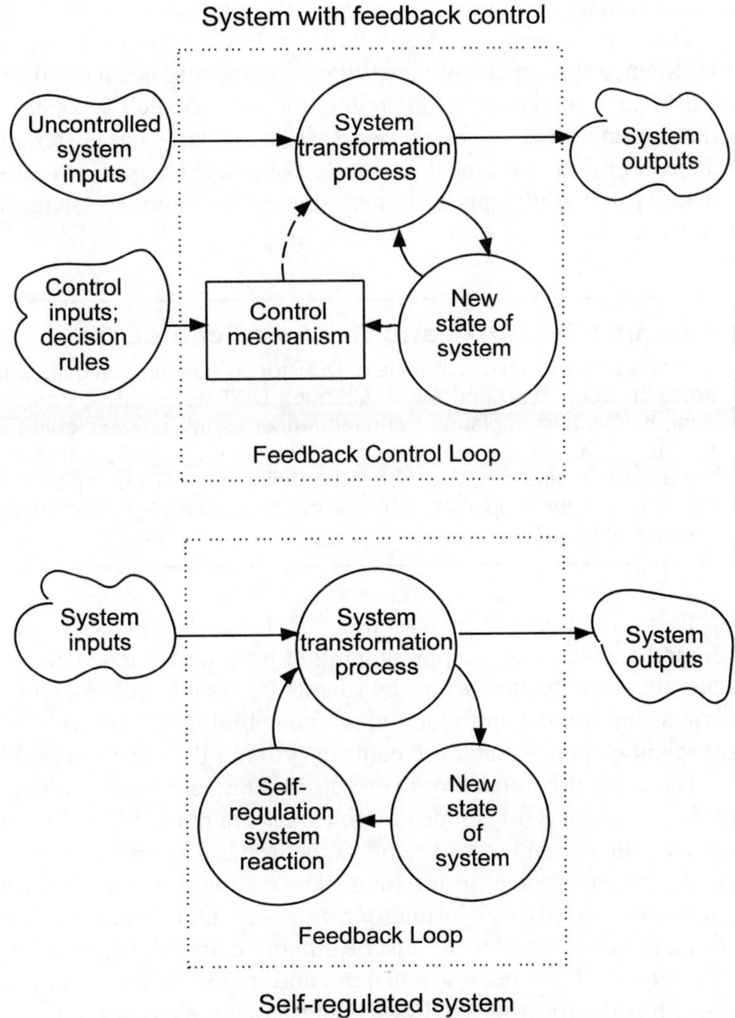

Figure 3-7 Feedback control and self-regulation

Self-regulation

Feedback loops also occur in many natural systems, particularly biological and ecological systems, where they help regulate the behaviour of such systems. Consider a predator-prey system. Assume that a large proportion of the predator population has been wiped out by a storm. This will lead to an explosion of the prey population. The smaller predator population thus finds very favourable conditions for multiplying and will grow beyond its original level. This added pressure will in turn reduce the prey population, with excess predators now also dying off due to lack of food, and so on. Through a series of oscillations of ever-decreasing magnitude, the previous natural equilibrium between the two species will re-establish itself after a while.

This type of feedback has nothing to do with control. There are no human inputs to influence system behaviour. What is happening is a natural self-regulation, which is different from control. Self-regulation returns such a system to its natural equilibrium. Human control of natural systems usually has different goals, such as the eradication of some aspect of nature considered a pest or a health menace. Unfortunately, many attempts at human control of natural systems have had disastrous results.

Example 3-2: DDT and the American eagle

The classical example is the use of DDT for combating mosquito and agricultural insect pests between 1950 and 1980. Although DDT admirably accomplished this desirable goal, it also had unplanned consequences, such as weakening the egg shells of a number of predatory birds. As a consequence, these bird populations crashed almost to the point of extinction. Only belated banning of DDT use and other rescue measures saved a number of species, such as the American eagle, the condor, and the pelican, from being wiped out.

There is obviously a lesson to be learned from such events, namely that a comprehensive systems approach might have prevented such near-disasters. In fact, state agencies dealing with environmental issues are now very cautious in giving permission for the introduction of new biological controls without having seen sufficient evidence that these controls will not develop into problems themselves.

The present controversy over genetic engineering of animal population or genetically modified (GM) foods is another case in point. Should we believe the claims of private industry and some scientists that the use of GM technologies is safe and will greatly benefit society in the long-run, or should we be more cautious and demand much more extensive and long-term testing, undertaken by agencies and scientists without any vested interest? Just bear in mind that it took over 20 years before the full effects of DDT use became apparent, and it took half a century before we discovered that chlorofluorocarbons (CFCs), hailed as a harmless gas, safe for all sorts of uses, are the prime cause of the ozone depletion that occurs each year over the Antarctic and to a lesser extent also over the Arctic region. Not to mention the billions of dollars of profit at stake for some of the giant and powerful multinationals at the forefront of GM seed production. The tobacco industry has taught us that we must be cautious when evaluating claims from powerful vested interests as to the safety of their products.

Feedback control and self-regulation

The lower portion of Figure 3-7 shows that feedback control and self-regulation differ in important ways. Feedback control receives an extra input of decision rules supplied by a human controller. The rules governing self-regulation are internal to the system. They are usually the result of natural evolution, such as the process for maintaining the body temperature of all warm-blooded animals.

Feed-forward control

A feedback control mechanism **reacts** to changes in some critical state variables or outputs. Rather than react to events after the fact, feed-forward control **predicts** how changes in inputs (uncontrollable or controllable) are likely to affect system behaviour and then sends control signals that will guide system behaviour to reach the desired targets as closely as possible, thereby counteracting the effects of input disturbances. This is the type of control used by an experienced driver of a car. It is also commonly used for the control of chemical processes. Similarly, most successful firms attempt to forecast future economic trends and technological change in order to take advantage of growth opportunities or avoid potential disasters due to an economic downturn or a change in technology. Again, these are applications of feed-forward control.

Feed-forward and feedback are often combined into a single control strategy.

Response lags in systems

Consider again the temperature adjustment of the shower water. You have observed that turning the shower valve does not instantaneously change the water temperature. In fact, the response is delayed for a short time and then occurs gradually, either increasing or decreasing to a new level. The time delay between the moment when the control signals are applied and their effects have been fully realized is called a **lag**.

If the flow into a canal bringing water to a hydro-electric power station is increased, it may take a few minutes or even hours before the increased flow reaches the pressure pipes leading to the turbines and allows additional turbines to be operated. Such a lag is a **transport lag** (also called a 'pipeline lag' in analogy to a pipeline operation). Such lags are common in industry and commerce. Placing a replenishment request for Brand X does not result in an immediate increase in the inventory level of Brand X. It takes several days for the goods to arrive from the supplier.

Most feedback loops are also subject to a transport lag. By the time the information on the state of the system has been processed by the control mechanism, that information may already be out-of-date, hence the need for feed-forward controls.

A second kind of lag of great importance is the **exponential lag**. Here, the control signal has an immediate, but gradual effect. An example of this type of lag is the temperature change in a gas oven. Although the temperature starts rising immediately if the temperature controls are raised, say from 175°C to 250°C, it will take several minutes for the oven air temperature to reach that new level, since some of the heat is lost to the oven walls, the oven dish and its contents.

Stochastic systems tend to approach their steady state asymptotically. This is an example of an exponential lag response.

The response of a system to control signals may exhibit both a transport lag, as well as an exponential lag, one following the other. Natural systems also exhibit response lags to changes in inputs.

Activity

High school as a system (continuation of Activities, pp. 39, 41, 44):

- Who provides control inputs to the system? Give at least two 'controllers'.
- What type of control inputs are they? Open loop, feedback, feed-forward? Are any feedback controls positive or negative? (Do not confound 'positive' and 'negative' with the type of criticism offered by teachers.)
- Are there any response lags and, if so, of what type?

Case study 3-1: Blood bank operation

A local hospital blood bank collects blood from volunteer donors. They donate one pint of blood each time. Text messages or postcards remind them that their last donation was three months ago and invite them to donate again. Some do so promptly, others delay, and some do not respond for various reasons, such as having moved away, being ill or under stress, and so on. The attrition of blood donors due to age, change of domicile, and so on, causes the pool of blood donors to decrease over time. To restore the pool of donors the blood bank periodically organizes a drive to recruit new donors — poster appeals, visits to factories, and appeals on local radio stations.

The amount of blood collected obviously depends on the number of active donors and on the frequency with which they call in to give blood. For the reasons listed earlier, the amount collected also fluctuates on a daily basis, and there is a weekly pattern, as well as spikes after each donor drive.

Each donation is stored in its own sealed bag and classified as to type, A, B, AB, and O. All blood collected is tested for various diseases. If it is disease free, it is added to its corresponding blood type stock, available for transfusions to patients. The demand for fresh blood originates either in the hospital's accident and emergency unit or from surgeons' requests for scheduled elective surgery. Hence, the requirements for blood also fluctuate on a daily basis.

Fresh blood has a shelf life from 26 to 49 days, depending on the preservative added. For this blood bank, the shelf life is 35 days. Hence, any blood not used within the shelf life is outdated, i.e., removed from stock and destroyed. This is highly undesirable. If the blood is collected from volunteer donors, it is morally wrong to discard it. If it is collected from paid donors it is costly. This blood bank does not pay its donors.

Some fresh blood is put aside for the generation of by-products, such as platelets, plasma, and so on, immediately after collection and testing. It is by such withdrawals of fresh blood that the director of the blood bank has limited control over the daily stock of fresh blood kept for transfusions.

There are other complications. Blood transfused to infants should by preference be fresh, at most a few days old. Each bag of blood requested for transfusion has to be type-matched to the blood of the patient. So, it is not just the total stock of blood that has to be monitored, but also the composition by type. There is also a tendency by some surgeons to request more blood than they expect to need, just to be cautious. Type-matched blood is temporarily stored in a refrigerator near the operating theatres. For various reasons, such as over-ordering of cautious surgeons, not all blood requested is used. Any type-matched blood not used within two days is returned to its corresponding stock.

Blood is used from stocks on a first-in, first-out basis, i.e., the oldest stock goes out first. (Some blood banks use a last-in, first-out policy, i.e., the freshest blood is used first.) If a surgeon requests blood for elective surgery and the right type of blood is not available, the elective surgery may have to be postponed.

However, postponement is not an option for emergency operations. If a shortage occurs, the blood bank calls in 'emergency donors', usually members of the police and fire service with the right type of blood. As a last resort, blood may be helicoptered from another blood bank that can spare blood of the required type, which is costly.

The director of a blood bank is thus faced with several partially or totally conflicting objectives: (I) avoid, as far as possible and reasonable, having to notify surgeons scheduled to perform an elective surgery that their requests for blood cannot be satisfied due to stock shortages; (ii) avoid having to make costly emergency requests; (iii) avoid having to outdate blood (which is morally wrong); and (iv) keep operating costs as low as possible. If the blood bank is operating efficiently, then better performance with respect to (I) and (ii) invariably means worse performance on (iii) and vice-versa.

Assume that you have been asked to study this 'problem'. As a first step, you must define a relevant system. You realize that this system may not capture all aspects of the problem situation. In fact, you may start with a simple system and study the boundary choices that implies. Next, you bring in additional aspects as dictated by questionable boundary choices of the simple system, and so on. A table, similar to Table 3-1 (p. 37), may help you to identify inputs (both controllable and uncontrollable), outputs, system components, and the environment by your definition.

3.13 Chapter highlights

- This text, in common with most social and natural sciences, thinks of systems as human conceptualizations — the inside-us view.
- System descriptions are therefore subjective to the person viewing something as a system. They are affected by the worldview assumed by the person(s) defining the system. Different people (or different worldviews) may define different systems for the same entity or phenomenon studied, and each one may be an effective or good view for its intended purpose. Definition details will also be dependent on the resources (time, funds, training, tools and equipment for analysis) available to the analyst.
- There may be no unique 'right' system definition, but several defensible ones which reflect different perceptions and worldviews.
- The choice of system boundaries is a critical aspect of a system definition. It assigns each aspect or thing to be a component of the system or to be part of its environment. The central concept of a system is that it transforms inputs from the environment into outputs to the environment.
- Two or more levels of nested systems form a hierarchy. The containing system is the wider system of interest to the contained or narrow system.
- Systems have emergent properties that none of its parts or subsets of parts have by themselves.

- The state of a human activity system at any point in time is completely defined by the values of all its state variables. Its behaviour can be described by how its state changes over time.
- Some subsets of system components may form feedback loops. Positive feedback loops cause the system to deviate from its reference state, while negative feedback loops take it closer to the reference state.
- Feedback loops may exhibit transport and/or exponential lags.
- Finding good ways of controlling a system to enhance desirable emergent properties or reduce the effects of undesirable emergent properties is often the reason for 'building' systems.
- The control inputs can take the form of open-loop, closed-loop or feedback, and feed-forward controls.

Exercises

1. Consider a university as a system. Identify a possible relevant worldview of an observer, the transformation process of the system, the mission or objective of the system and what system aspects are used for measuring the system performance, the inputs into the system, including control inputs, and the outputs from the system, and the major system components, including possible subsystems, from the following viewpoints:
   (a) a student attending the university to acquire theoretical and practical training for a professional career;
   (b) an academic staff member who sees the university as a system for pleasant gainful employment;
   (c) the chief executive officer of the university who sees the university's major role as one of advancing knowledge in view of enhancing its world recognition.
2. Consider the operation of a small urban fire department as a system. It is funded and operated by local government on behalf of its tax-paying residents. Identify a possible relevant worldview of an observer, the system transformation process, its mission or objectives, its measures of performance, its inputs, including control inputs, its outputs, and its major components, and the explicit and implicit boundary judgements made, from the point of view of:
   (a) the local taxpayers;
   (b) the chief of the fire department.
3. Give an example of a hierarchy of systems:
   (a) in a governmental setting;
   (b) in an educational setting;
   (c) in a sports setting;
   (d) in a law enforcement setting.
4. List some of the state variables used for defining the state of the system for:
   (a) the university as a professional training system (refer to Question 1(a));
   (b) the fire department (refer to Question 2(a)).

5. In fewer than 100 of your own words state what the main reasons are for using a systems approach for problem solving.
6. Give examples of emergent properties for the following types of systems:
   (a) a river system receiving untreated chemical or sewage discharges;
   (b) a computer information system;
   (c) an intersection traffic control system;
   (d) a firm;
   (e) the police department.
7. Give two examples (different from any listed in the text) for:
   (a) discrete systems;
   (b) continuous systems;
   (c) deterministic systems;
   (d) closed systems (as an approximation);
   (e) open systems;
   (f) stochastic systems.
8. For the following situations/systems, identify the type of control/regulation mechanism present:
   (a) assembly instructions for a kit-set;
   (b) inflating a car tyre at a service station air pump;
   (c) the car/driver system on a motorway or freeway, where constant speed can be maintained;
   (d) the car/driver system on a curvy, hilly two-lane road with traffic in both directions;
   (e) an automatic wage payment system, where wages are directly credited to the recipients' bank accounts;
   (f) a firm has the following system to replenish its raw material stocks: whenever the stock level falls below a critical level, called the 'reorder point', a quantity of X tonnes is ordered;
   (g) the fermentation process for converting the sugar in grapes into alcohol works as follows: after the yeast starter has been mixed with the grapes, the number of yeast cells multiply and convert the sugar in the grapes into alcohol; as sugar is depleted or the concentration of alcohol builds up, the growth in the number of yeast cells is inhibited until it stops, and most yeast cells die; at that point, fermentation stops;
   (h) a stockbroker constantly watches the price changes in various company shares and tries to predict future price movements; this information is then used for making buying or selling decisions on various shares;
   (I) an automatic thermal heating system controlling the water temperature in a swimming pool.
   (j) a solar water heating system which works on hot water rising.
9. Identify the types of lags found in the following systems (note that there may be several types of lags present):
   (a) the system for replenishing products from a supplier who will deliver the goods 10 days after receipt of the order;
   (b) the system for clearing cheques or interbank funds transfers used by banks, where all cheques or transactions presented before 4 pm on each day are processed overnight for credit or debit to the corresponding accounts;

(c) a system of reservoirs used for hydro-electric power generation;

(d) the temperature of a heated swimming pool, where heating starts when the water temperature differs from the target setting by two degrees.

10. Consider the blood bank operation (Case study 3-1, p. 54).

(a) Assume that the director of the blood bank uses the following rules to control the stock of blood for each blood type. At the end of each day, she determines the amount of fresh blood which is 32 days old. If that amount is larger than some critical number, she withdraws an amount of blood equal to the excess above the critical number, using the most recently collected blood. What type of control is she using? Why do you reach that conclusion?

(b) What emergent properties are generated by the system? Which are planned and which are unplanned? Which are desirable and which are detrimental?

(c) The control inputs available include: donor drives, withdrawal of blood for by-product generation, frequency of donation, calling up emergency donors, the length of time type-matched blood is kept in temporary storage (and hence not available for other uses). For each, determine what type of control it is, and whether the response to it involves a lag.

Further reading

Beishon, J. and Peters, G. (eds) (1981) *Systems Behaviour*, 3rd edn, London: Harper & Row. A collection of articles on systems and systems thinking.

Lane, A. (2000) *Systems Thinking and Practice: a Primer*, Milton Keynes: Open University Press. T205, T306, and T551 course material. Basic and informative.

Pidd, M. (2009) *Tools for Thinking: Modelling in Management Science*, 3rd edn, Chichester: Wiley. Excellent text. Systems concepts covered in chapters 1, 3, and introduction to part 2.

4

The problem situation

Learning objectives

- Be able to identify the six elements of a problem description.
- Be able to identify the stakeholders of a problem situation and their roles.
- Be able to create a mind map for a problem situation, based on a written description or personal observation.
- Be able to draw a rich picture, based on a written description or personal observation.
- Be able to create a cognitive map, based on a relatively simple narrative of a problem situation, and identify core constructs and emerging themes.

Introduction

Before we can apply the concepts studied in Chapters 2 and 3 to describe a relevant system for an issue of concern or problem we want to study, we need to come to grips with the context within which the issue or problem occurs, i.e., the problem situation. Seeing the problem in its proper full context will facilitate identifying its stakeholders — the people involved — and all other aspects of the problem situation, including those which the issues of concern triggered the need for an investigation. This is the subject of the first two sections. Next, we explore three effective ways to capture the problem situation. These are mind maps, rich pictures, and cognitive maps. The last is demonstrated in some detail with a practical application, which we will take up again when we explore soft systems approaches to decision making in Chapter 7.

A full grasp of the problem situation and its stakeholders is also a prerequisite in our critical search for setting appropriate boundaries to both the narrow system of interest and its relevant environment or the wider system of interest. The last section of the chapter broaches that topic. Chapter 5 studies several diagrammatic aids or approaches to capture or represent core aspects or relationships of systems.

4.1 What is a 'problem situation'?

The **problem situation** is the context within which the problem occurs. It is the aggregate of all aspects that can or may affect or shape the problem or issue of concern. Figure 4-1 attempts to capture this.

It is the complex of relationships and conflicts, stemming from the people involved, their worldviews, and their goals and aims, the physical relationships and constraints impacting on the situation, the structures and processes used or potentially available that govern the behaviour, the control and actions made possible by the resources, the uncertainties associated with any of them, and last, but not least, the consequences stemming from their interactions for all those involved, or directly and indirectly affected, where the latter may include not only people, but also other species and the environment.

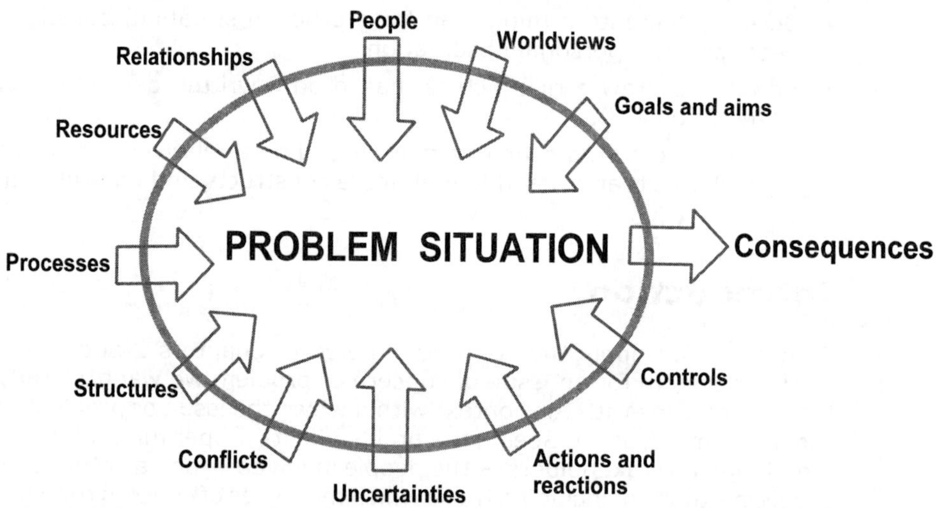

Figure 4-1 Issue context — the problem situation

But first, what is 'a problem'? How do problems manifest themselves? For a problem to exist there must be an individual (or a group of individuals), referred to as the **problem owner** — usually its decision maker — who:

- is dissatisfied with the current state of affairs within a real-life context — does not like what is happening, or has some unsatisfied present or future needs, i.e., has some goals or objectives to be achieved or targets to be met;
- is capable of judging to what degree these goals, objectives, or targets have been met and whether that degree is satisfactory; and
- has control over some aspects of the problem situation that affect the extent to which goals, objectives, or targets can be achieved.

The six elements of a problem are: (1) the decision maker(s), (2) the decision maker's objective(s), (3) the associated decision criteria, (4) the performance measures, (5) the control inputs or alternative courses of action, and (6) the environment or context in which the problem occurs.

To clarify these concepts, consider again the sawmill in Section 3.6 (p. 36). The owners of the firm have become concerned about the firm's decrease in profitability over recent times. They have instructed the sawmill's CEO to investigate that matter. He becomes the 'problem owner' or decision maker and adopts the objective of the firm's owners to achieve a satisfactory return on their investment. One possible decision criterion used for judging whether or not this objective has been achieved is 'the rate of return on the owner's investment reaches at least 18% before taxes', a rate considered satisfactory by the owners. Its associated measure of performance is the ratio of net profit over the owners' investment. Any alternative course of action — such as a combination of the type and quantities of logs to purchase, the type and quantities of finished products to produce, and the best rules for processing logs into finished products, and so on — that raises the return to 18% or above satisfies the criterion and is a solution. Note that no solution may exist that meets this criterion.

An alternative decision criterion could be to 'maximize annual profits', with the annual level of profits being the measure of performance. Once we find a course of action where no other action exists that has a higher profit, the criterion is satisfied.

The problem owner may have goals that impose a constraint on a given output rather than being a target for which to strive. For the sawmill, the CEO may want to make sure that the volume for a certain type of clear timber produced meets the demand of a particularly important customer, even if this implies a reduction in profits.

The context of the problem is given by all the aspects that directly or indirectly affect the measure of performance and over which the decision maker has no immediate control, or which are taken as 'givens' with respect to the issue(s) to be investigated.

Distinction between objective and decision criterion

Unfortunately, these two terms are often confused in the MS literature. *Webster's Collegiate Dictionary* defines an objective as 'the end towards which effort is directed, an aim, goal or end of action'. Examples are: achieving the highest profit, gaining a 40% share of the market, finding the shortest distance between two locations in a road network, a water purity that safeguards the survival of flora and fauna in a river or estuary, a high degree of equity between various interest groups, and so on.

The achievement towards an objective is captured by an appropriate performance measure. If it can be expressed quantitatively, it is referred to as the **objective function**.

A criterion (its plural is 'criteria'), however, is defined as 'the principle or standard on which a judgement or decision is based'. Both 'principle' and 'standard' imply a rule. So, a criterion is the rule for judging whether, or how well, the performance measure achieves the objective.

Another example may help. An ambulance service wants to find the 'best' location in a small city, where 'best' is interpreted as 'reaching any emergency as quickly as possible'. This is the objective. One possible measure of performance is 'the sum of all times to reach every road location in town'. The associated criterion is to minimize that sum. This would locate the ambulance service at the centre of gravity of the city with the largest part of locations reachable in a relatively short time, but some after only an extremely long time. An alternative performance measure could be 'the sum of the squared times', and its associated criterion 'minimizing that sum'. This would penalize long times more than short times, thus favouring a solution to keep the long times shorter. A third possible criterion is to minimize the performance measure 'the maximum time between the ambulance service location and all other locations in the city'. This would tend to reduce the longest time.

In many situations, there may only be one relevant performance measure and associated criterion to evaluate how well an objective has been achieved. For example, the objective 'achieve the highest profit' has the performance measure 'profits' and the criterion 'maximize profits'. Criterion and objective then coincide.

Complexities of problem definition

In real life, determining the six problem elements may not simply be a question of asking the decision maker. The dissatisfaction felt may just be a vague feeling that things could be better. The analyst's job is then to explore and clarify the problem situation in order to shed more light on the real issue(s) of concern.

A decision maker may also be vague or fuzzy about objectives and, consequently, about performance measures and decision criteria. The analyst will then have to help the decision maker to externalize objectives and preferences. The setting of realistic performance criteria may have to wait until the analysis is well-advanced, because only then will it become possible to explore the range of available solutions. If it turns out to be easy to improve performance, the decision maker may aspire to a higher level of achievement, and vice-versa if it is difficult.

Furthermore, the decision maker may not be aware of the full range of alternative courses of action available. Discovery of new decision choices is one of the exciting and rewarding aspects of MS/OR work.

Further complexities arise if there are multiple decision makers who may have different worldview, who may see the problem situation differently, and hence may have potentially conflicting objectives. Such conflicts can usually only be resolved by a compromise. One of the **problem structuring methods,** discussed in Chapter 7, may help to bring about at least a partial consensual understanding about the problem situation. This may allow agreement on a choice of action, even if no consensus can be reached on objectives.

Many projects may are also be initiated by parties other than the decision maker, but who have vested interests in the matter. They may have no direct or indirect control over the problem situation, the possible courses of action, and the resources needed. Often such projects aim to convince the 'real' decision maker to take action, if the results of the analysis show that this is in the interest of the wider community. While the project is undertaken, the real decision maker may not be involved. The objectives assumed are likely to be the ones of the interest group and may not necessarily coincide with those of the final decision maker.

In most real-life applications, problem definition will not be achieved in a single pass. The initial definition usually goes through a series of progressively more detailed reformulations and refinements as deeper insight into the problem is gained. To some extent, problem formulation continues until the project ends. It is, however, in these early stages where the ultimate success or failure of a project most often has its roots!

Activity

Referring to Section 1.1, define the six problem elements for:

- the service call centre (Example 1-1, p.2);
- the Deep Cove project (Example 1-3, p. 4).

4.2 Stakeholders or roles of people in systems

As we have seen in the previous section, any human activity, particularly problem solving within a system context, involves people. We mentioned the problem owner, the decision maker, other parties affected who have no control over the situation, and the analyst. They all assume various roles. We refer to these roles as **stakeholders**. Let us now formalize this.

- The **problem owners** are the persons exercising control over certain aspects of the problem situation, in particular over the choice of action available to affect change. Most often, they are also the decision makers. There may be several levels of problem owners: (a) those who have the ultimate power over all controllable aspects in the wider system of interest, and in particular the level of controllable resources made available, but who may have delegated part of that power to others, and (b) those who have been given limited powers to make decisions and initiate change within the narrow system of interest or some subsystem.
- The **problem users** are those who use the solution and/or execute the decisions approved by the problem owners or decision makers. They have no authority to change the decision or initiate new action. Any apparent decision making is simply an application of prescribed rules. If any discretionary powers are given, they are very limited in scope and, again, within specified rules.
- The **problem customers** are the beneficiaries or victims of the consequences of using the solution. In many instances, they may be given no voice or have no means to affect the analysis or its outcomes. They may also include future generations or even other species. Which ones should be included in the analysis gives rise to critical boundary judgements (see Sections 3.5 and 4.10).
- The **problem analysts or solvers** analyse the problem and develop a solution for approval by the problem owners or facilitate accommodations between them.

All roles are always defined with respect to the narrow system. Definite identification of who the various stakeholders of a problem situation are becomes fully clear only once the relevant system has been defined, although the analyst may have a fair idea about who most of them are very early in the analysis.

Some examples will clarify these roles. Recall the staffing level problem of the service call centre in Example 1-1 (p. 2). The call centre manager is the problem owner. He or she has the final say over any decision about staffing levels and hence assumes the role of decision maker. The manager may have delegated the implementation of the staffing levels to the technical supervisor, who then assumes the role of problem user. He/she has limited discretionary power over fixing the duty roster, i.e., which operator works when. The telephone operators and the people placing calls are the problem customers. They are the beneficiaries or victims of the service performance resulting from the staffing levels chosen. They may have no direct voice in the process, but be heard only through the use of a complaints process. Finally, the decision maker hired a specialist in waiting line problems to study the problem and make recommendations. That person assumes the role of problem analyst.

In this instance, each stakeholder role is assumed by a different person or group of persons. For many situations, the same individual may act in two or more roles. Assume you are considering the replacement of your current car. You have limited finance and borrowing capacity, a wish list of desirable and absolutely essential features that your new car should meet, and a choice of options: a range of new cars, as well as suitable pre-owned cars. In this case, you are the problem owner, the problem user, the problem customer, as well as the problem analyst — all roles coincide.

Note again that the terms 'problem owner', 'user', 'customer', and 'analyst' refer to roles people assume and not to the individuals themselves. As we have seen, one person may assume more than one role simultaneously or consecutively.

Importance of clear role definition

Why are we concerned about role definition? First, any one of these roles can in fact be the initiator of an MS/OR project. The role of the sponsor will colour the nature of the project, i.e., stamp it with a corresponding focus and worldview. If initiated by the decision maker, the project will usually be of a substantive nature, leading to real change, with a relevant system for the project clearly defined within the span of control of the decision maker. The relevant worldview is the one held by the decision maker. If it is initiated by any of the other roles, its nature is usually descriptive. Its initiator will tend to use it as a means for educating or persuading other stakeholders of the problem situation. It will only become substantive if its findings are adopted and acted upon by the real problem owner. The appropriate choice of the relevant system for such projects and an appropriate worldview may be more problematic and possibly controversial.

Unless the problem analyst is fairly clear about the roles of the various participants in the problem situation, the project may set off in the wrong direction from its inception. It goes without saying that the analyst must attempt to see the problem situation through the relevant worldview of the project sponsor, and not let his or her own view contaminate it.

The problem customers may be future generations. A project may affect them adversely, e.g., depriving them permanently of enjoying a wild river by damming it for power generation, or burdening them with stores of radioactive materials. Non-human species are all-to-often the victims of human activity, e.g., through the destruction of wildlife habitat by clear-felling forests or the killing of fish through pollution. It is essential that somebody takes up the defence of their interests — gives them a voice by proxy.

One of the difficulties sometimes encountered at this stage is that the existing assignment of 'stakeholders' is inappropriate. For example, the person having the control over the decision process may not have access to the information needed for effective decision making, while the person with the information may have no decision making authority. For effective decision making, it may first be necessary to change the organizational structure and reassign decision making roles. Only then will the structure and climate of the organization be conducive to embarking on an MS study proper. One of the problem structuring methods in Chapter 7 may be useful for bringing about the required organizational change.

Activity

Who are the stakeholders for the Deep Cove project in Example 1-3 (p. 4)?

Example 4-1: Breast cancer study (continuation of Example 1-4, p. 5)

If the study is initiated by the Director of Public Health, the highest level of decision maker for health issues in the governmental administrative structure, the prevailing worldview is likely to be 'the effective allocation of public funds'. This would ultimately lead to evaluating trade-offs between allocating funds to breast cancer screening and other uses within the health system. The entire health system becomes the wider system of interest. The output of the study would be a recommended screening policy, a schedule for its implementation, and a total cost. If that total cost exceeds the budget allocation, this may lead to cuts somewhere else, or it may call for changes in the breast cancer screening policy in order to bring its cost in line with budget expectations.

In contrast, if the study is initiated by a medical practitioners (a problem users' group) or by the 'Women for Health' (a problem customer group), the relevant worldview would be reducing/avoiding preventable deaths and reducing personal suffering and trauma by women and relatives affected, with the relevant system limited to the relationship between screening policies and breast cancer mortality. Wider issues of allocation of public funds may not be considered. The study would be used as evidence to persuade the Health Department to divert the necessary funds for a national screening policy.

4.3 Problem situation summary — mind maps

Acquiring a sufficiently complete and detailed understanding of the problem situation is a necessary condition for a successful system intervention. The analyst must get a thorough'feel' for anything that may impact on the outcome. Figure 4-1 (p. 60) gives a list of things to look out for. **Mind maps**, **rich picture diagrams** and **cognitive maps** are highly effective diagrammatic aids with which to capture these aspects.

What is a mind map? When you think about something, a phenomenon, an issue or a problem, a host of thoughts are evoked in your mind: things, aspects and concepts, including fears and aims, data and facts, possible actions and reactions by yourself, by other people or organizations involved and their consequences, both planned and unplanned, desirable and undesirable that may results from such actions, and the wider context or environment of it all. A mind map is all this, or a judiciously chosen subset, put down on paper in headings, slogans, or sentences.

The things are arranged in a meaningful way. Arrows from one entry to another indicate the direction of a causal relationship. Simple lines indicate other meaningful affinities or hierarchies. No formal conventions are used. You may introduce your own, such as using solid lines for strong relationships, broken lines for weak ones, or enclosing entries that form a subgroup inside a circle or 'cloud'. Figure 4-2 is a mind map of what gets evoked in the mind of one of the authors when he ponders on the mode of transport for going to work on some mornings.

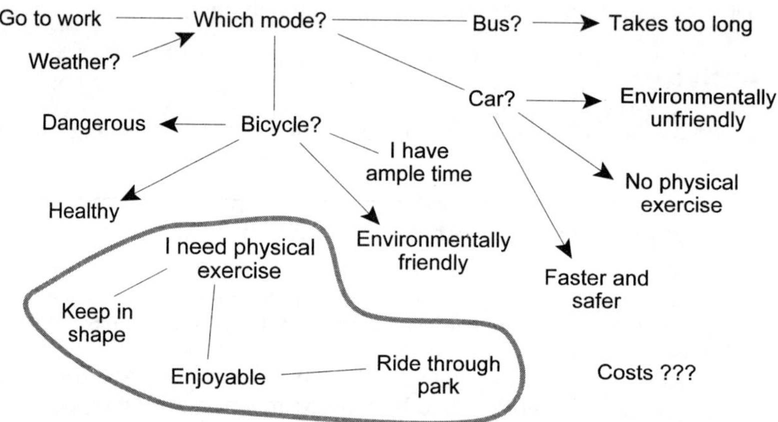

Figure 4-2 Mind map of dilemma of going to work by bicycle

Mind maps can easily be used for capturing and consolidating the thoughts and ideas of several people, borrowing rules of brainstorming. An effective way to go about it is to write down each item on a sticky note as it is evoked. These are initially stuck on a whiteboard or big flip chart. As more and more concepts and relationships are elicited from the participants, the sticky notes are rearranged and appropriately connected by lines or arrows. This is an effective way to help bring about a consensus among the participants on the problem situation. Differences of view or disagreements can also easily be depicted by showing alternative configurations side-by-side. Once complete, the final version can be digitally photographed or copied on paper.

In contrast to a formal written description, which by necessity has to be sequential, a mind map shows the situation in much of its complexity at a glance, so-to-speak. It can be 'read' in any direction with all aspects remaining 'present' for instant reference. The information contained in it can be processed in parallel, while a verbal description can only be processed linearly. It is thus a much more effective and potent vehicle to present a situation or to use as a basis for communication than a formal write-up.

Activity

Draw up a mind map for the Deep Cove Project in Example 1-3 (p. 4).

4.4 Rich picture diagrams

Rather than show the various aspects in words or short sentences, Checkland (1999) suggests drawing a cartoon-like pictorial summary of everything (or almost everything!) the observer knows about the situation studied.

As is true for mind maps, rich pictures can be taken in as a whole. Since all features are always in front of you, it encourages you to keep an open mind about the problem situation.

Note that term 'rich picture' does not, in the first place, mean a drawing. It is simply a more colourful term for situation summary. Representing it by a cartoon-like drawing is an effective way to capture its essential elements.

'But I'm no good at drawing!' you object. Neither are we. The representations used are very simple: stick-like figures, clouds, blobs, circles, and boxes of lists, some slogan-type writing, and arrows depicting connections and relationships or time sequences. Figure 4-3 is a rich picture for the dilemma of one of the authors of whether or not to go to work by bicycle.

Figure 4-4 on the next page shows some types of symbols commonly used. You will quickly discover that the talent needed is not an ability to draw well, but simply a bit of imagination. In fact, drawing rich pictures is fun.

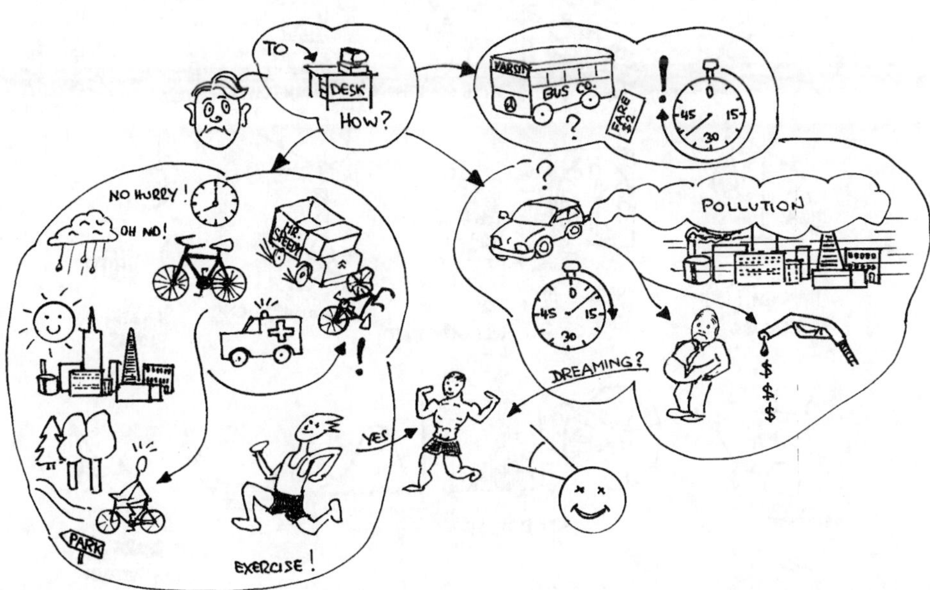

Figure 4-3 Rich picture of dilemma of going to work by bicycle

There are good reasons for sticking to hand-drawn pictures. They convey their tentative, provisional nature, capturing the situation at this point in the investigation, with some current features to be amended and other aspects to be added as more is learned about the situation. Note that the temptation to use computer clipart is great.

Don't! The result is usually stilted and contrived, giving it a 'finished' quality, rather than a work in progress.

Although your prime interest may only be a particular issue, it pays to assemble as wide a picture as is reasonably possible and not only include those aspects that seem

Figure 4-4 Sample symbols for rich pictures

directly related to the issue that triggered the study. Only then will you have some assurance of not missing interactions, relationships, and sources of data that could turn out to be essential. Even so, you will have to use judgement as to what details to include and what to leave out, or as to an appropriate level of resolution. You will have to strike a balance between the desires for completeness and parsimony. For instance, you may draw a book entitled 'Rules' as a reminder rather than list the detailed rules. Slogans, coming out of some person's head, are often highly effective summaries of details.

It is usually revealing to also sound out the problem users and problem customers and ask for feedback on your picture. You may discover new aspects or other angles of the situation. New aspects may be added, some entries redefined or deleted, relationships adjusted. In some sense, a rich picture is never finished. It is often redrawn. It will remain a central point of reference during the entire project and a useful reminder for all involved, even after moving on to other issues.

Naturally, you can only give your perception of the situation. Therefore, you will need to remind yourself as you proceed to keep an open mind, to avoid letting your own worldview or preconceived ideas taint the 'picture', to refrain from imposing an assumed structure on the situation or viewing it as 'the problem of such-and-such'. The latter may be particularly unhelpful, since other people may see different aspects of the situation as 'the real problem'. At this point, you do not want to commit the analysis unwittingly to a given direction before you have gained a full understanding of its complexity and crucial interrelationships.

All of this is easily said, but more difficult to stick to. We all have a natural tendency to classify problem situations and give them a name. It gives the illusion 'of having the situation under control'. Take truancy at primary school or at high school. 'Oh this is simply a lack of discipline in the home!' The 'problem' has been labelled and hence 'solved' — end of discussion. Taking such a view will narrow our focus of attention. It may lead us to overlook the social complexity of truancy and effective means with which to limit its adverse effects on the truant, the family, and society.

Most importantly, as is the case for a mind map, a rich picture is not a system description. The term 'system' implies that any interconnectedness is organized and not coincidental. By assuming such organized interconnections, you may impose a structure on the situation which may not be present or, if present, focuses your attention in a given direction, rather than encouraging you to keep an open mind. Only once you have reached agreement with the problem owner on which issue is to be analysed, will you be ready to define a system relevant for that issue.

In some instances, it may be instructive to supplement the rich picture with other types of diagrams, such as a chart depicting the flow or processing of material or information. For example, a manufacturing operation may best be captured by a process diagram depicting how material moves from work station to work station, the tasks performed at each station, the quality inspection points, the data collection points, and so on, including pointers for alternative ways to accomplish the same thing. It may be supplemented by notes about difficulties encountered at each work station and various options suggested for alleviating them. (More on such diagrams in Sections 5.5 and 5.7, pp. 97 and 105.)

4.5 Guidelines for mind maps and rich pictures

Three major components are represented in mind maps and rich pictures:

1. **Elements of structure:** These are those aspects of the situation that are relatively stable or change only very slowly in the time frame implied in the situation, such as the physical structures, buildings and equipment, the products involved, as well as logical, functional, or intellectual structural aspects and their properties, existing organizational divisions, information and data sources.
2. **Elements of process:** All dynamic aspects that undergo change or are in a state of flux, such as activities that go on within the structure, flow and processing of material or information, and any decision making that goes on.
3. **Relationship between structure and process and between processes:** How does the structure affect or condition process? What are the rules governing process? How does one process affect or condition other processes? What are the direct or indirect consequences of such relationships? For example, if a firm only collects information on sales executed, but fails to record customer orders received but not executed because of stock shortages, it is not in a position to estimate the actual demand for that product.
4. **The various stakeholders:** This category shows the problem owners, the problem users, the problem customers, and the problem analysts.

For human activity systems, a mind map or rich picture should include not only **'hard' facts**, but also **'soft' facts**. Hard facts are the physical structure and processes, data records and their statistical interpretation, information links, anything on which there is widespread agreement, or what might be labelled 'objective'. Soft facts cover the social and political aspects of the problem situation — or what could broadly be called 'the climate' of the situation. This includes opinions, gossip, hunches, inter-personal relationships (friendships, hostilities, power, egos) coming to the surface, perceived agendas and sacred cows, synergies, and symbiotic relationships. This climate is often an important determinant of the various worldviews held by the stakeholders. Unless the climate is sufficiently well-understood, essential aspects of these worldviews may escape the analyst.

All known areas of concern, actual or potential issues or problems should also be shown. In rich pictures, this can be done in a number of ways. One is to use the focus symbol of Figure 4-4 (p. 68) pointing at the area of concern. Another is to show a balloon, coming out from an area of concern or a person, containing a question or a short slogan with a question or an exclamation mark. If opposing values, or benefits versus costs have to be weighed, this can be depicted by scales with the baskets containing appropriate words, possibly with a question mark at the top of the scales. Opposing or conflicting views by various people involved can easily be shown by two crossed swords.

The rich picture should also be annotated to define symbols that are not self-explanatory or provide brief footnotes on why certain aspects are excluded or represented only in a cursory way, and so on. It may also be interesting and revealing to indicate where you enter into the picture, your interest or role.

Novices may believe that each item shown needs to be connected to one or more other items. They end up with a map or picture where every item is connected directly or indirectly to every other item. Some connections between items are useful to indicate relationships, such as cause-and-effect, symbioses, precedence, or processes. However, excessive use of connections may inadvertently impose a system structure. Remember again, a mind map or a rich picture is not a system description.

Your mind map or rich picture should not look like one of the system diagrams discussed in Sections 5.5 to 5.7. If it does, you imposed a system structure on the problem situation.

4.6 Uses and strengths of rich pictures and mind maps

The main use of rich pictures and mind maps is for communicating with other people about complex and problematic situations. They are rarely included in a formal report, since they need to be talked about rather than shown. The reaction of many analysts to rich pictures, in contrast to mind maps, is one of scepticism. 'Cartoons have no place in serious analysis!' Give the rich picture a chance! You will discover that precisely because they are unconventional, unexpected, and a fun tool, they are more likely to catch and retain your listeners' attention and interest — in fact, have them become active participants.

Interconnections, relationships, and direct and indirect consequences become more clearly visible; understanding is enhanced. Since the whole map or picture is constantly present, if you make a reference to aspects previously discussed, you do not have to rely on the listeners' memory; instead, you can point directly to the entry on the map or picture. Queries can also refer to the map or picture, and hence will be more focused and more precise. Misunderstandings are reduced. Missing aspects become more obvious.

It allows identification of the people who own the problematic situation, the people in positions of power, such as the decision makers, the people who will execute any decisions taken, and the people who will enjoy the benefits or suffer the consequences of the results. It pinpoints the sources and types of data. But most importantly, it will help identify existing or potential concerns, conflicts, and problems. It may point out that the particular issue is embedded in other areas of concern that may have to be resolved before the original issue can be tackled. Sometimes, particularly in a learning context, a mind map or rich picture is drawn simply to gain a better understanding of a complex situation as a whole. It will firm up the choice of the problem to be studied and show it within its complete context. This will help in selecting appropriate boundaries for the system and the scope of the analysis.

Activity

Draw a rich picture for what aspects and considerations have relevance for deciding whether or not to study at a tertiary educational institution or to complete your degree. Clearly show your worldview.

Case study 4-1: SkyWalker

Jess Sky and Jill Walker joined up by chance for the winter traverse of the Black Cuillin on the Isle of Skye — peaks of which dreams are made ... or nightmares, as the one of the advertisements claims — and are glad they did. Both in their early thirties and unattached, they hit it off well. Jill recently quit work as a travel agent and is looking for a new challenge. Jess is a software consultant.

While celebrating the successful traverse, they hatch the idea of offering a mountain climbing travel service, where clients can log on to a website, inquire about a given climb or walk, and get detailed advice and guidance as to transport access, accommodation, eating places, mountains guides, geographical and geological information, weather, and so on — in short, everything that a climber or walker would want or need to know, personally tailored to their degree of skill, age, and spending power. It would also offer to do all the necessary bookings. Full of enthusiasm, they agree that this idea deserves exploring, as well as a second bottle of Australian Shiraz.

They quickly come up with a fitting name: SkyWalker, but then disagree — amicably, mind you — about how to proceed. Jill wants to start small by initially providing advice only on climbs and walks in Scotland, and then gradually expand to include the Lake District and Wales. If the venture takes off well, expansion to include the Alps and other regions on continental Europe and ultimately the world should be explored. In contrast, Jess feels that such a strategy is risky, since it invites competition, possibly by an established outfit that offers similar personal services for visiting cultural sights. She thinks that their best strategy is to gather all required information for the whole of the British Isles and maybe even the Alps, with which she is very familiar, and only then launch their service. She also is adamant about developing most of the necessary software herself rather than farm some of it out, again eliminating the possibility that somebody else may get to know about their venture and possibly steal it, as has happened before, she points out strongly. Although Jill does not voice it, she thinks that Jess's fears are a bit exaggerated.

While Jess prefers to have their data base covering all areas complete when the website is launched, Jill is of the opinion a more flexible approach could work quite successfully, namely, cover initially only the most popular sites. Information about new sites would be gathered at the time of such inquiries. Their data base would then gradually expand and become more complete. Anyway, to offer top service, they would have to update their information continually, and be prepared that some inquiries may need special research that is not on the original data base.

However, this raises the question of how to charge for their service. Should it be a service offered only to subscribers who pay an annual fee, or should there be a charge for individual inquiries, or possibly a combination, with lower inquiry fees for subscribers, rather than one or the other? The latter choice might encourage repeat customers to take out a subscription. And what would be a reasonable level of fees? Obviously, the service would appeal mainly to people who are relatively well-off.

Both agree that SkyWalker should be launched as quickly as prudently possible, since other people might have similar ideas and could pre-empt them. Jill points out that her idea of concentrating initially only on Scotland would allow them to launch within three or four months, while going Jess's way would take eight to ten months.

The other difficulty is how to raise the necessary finance. Jill has some £50,000, enough to cover her living expenses for about a year and the cost of gathering detailed and intimate local information on the most important Scottish locations. She guesses that this should not take more than three months. Jess has been living hand to mouth. She needs financial support for developing the website, which she thinks will take at least three months if she does it all herself, less if parts are farmed out or bought in. It would take her another three to four months or so to organize the information she has accumulated over the last six years about climbs in the Alps, since she would need to follow some of it up with visits, for which she would also require financial support.

Jess does some quick calculations and figures that she would need at least £20,000 for developing the software and other incidental costs, more if some parts are bought in, and another £30,000 for firming up the information about the Alps. The launch itself would need promotion — another £10,000 at least. Furthermore, the revenue during the first few months of operation will be insufficient to cover their salaries and the cost of updating their data base. At a rough guess, they would need about £120,000 in addition to Jill's £50,000. This raises another problem, namely how to divide the stakes in the enterprise. Relevant to this issue is that, in contrast to Jess, Jill sees the whole venture as an exciting challenge rather than largely as an opportunity to become rich.

Jess and Jill approach you to help them capture this problem situation, so that both of them get the full picture of it. What would you do? (A mind map, maybe?)

4.7 Cognitive mapping

Cognitive mapping is a tool C.L. Eden developed in 1979 as an adaption from Kelly's (1955) theory. The latter explains how individuals make sense of their world, attribute meaning to events and experiences, and develop and understand connections between experiences. In contrast to mind maps and rich pictures, which are also suitable for representing a group's aggregate perception of the problem situation, a **cognitive map** only captures the subjective, personal perception of a single individual. These are captured as a network of succinct statements, called **constructs**, expressing concepts — ideas, goals, concerns, preferences, or actions. The constructs are linked together by arrows, which indicate the direction of connections, i.e., which concept leads logically to which other concept(s). Figure 4-5 gives a simple example.

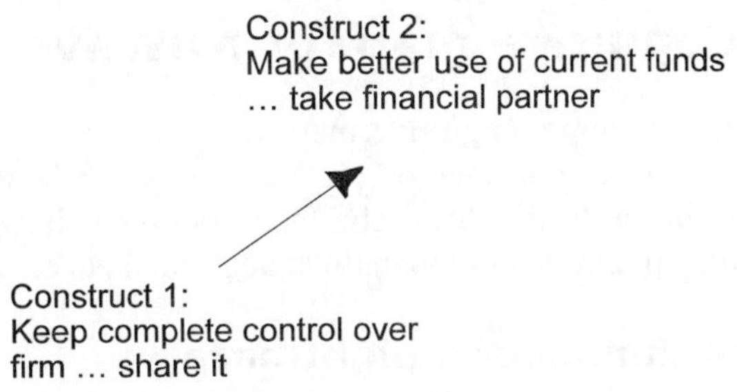

Construct 2:
Make better use of current funds
... take financial partner

Construct 1:
Keep complete control over
firm ... share it

Figure 4-5 Constructs and links

Constructs are usually composed of two **poles**. The first pole may often express a given desirable concept (idea, meaning, goal) or a potential action. The second pole denotes a contrast or opposite. The second pole is not necessarily a logical opposite, but an alternative idea, goal, concern or action that forms a contrast in the mind of the individual. For example, the first pole of construct 1 in Figure 4-5 is something the individual would like to happen: 'keep complete control over firm'. Its contrasting pole is something the individual would rather not do: 'share it' (with another person). There are other statements, which could be plausible contrasts, such as a rather vague 'give up total control', or 'sell firm and be an employee'.

The two poles are shown separated by an ellipsis (...) which is read as '*rather than*'. So, the construct becomes: 'keep complete control over firm *rather than* share it'. If the second pole is the logical opposite of the first pole, it is may not be shown explicitly after the ellipsis. A final goal, a constraint, or a piece of information may have no relevant opposite, and hence only one pole is stated.

Both poles should be expressed in the individual's own words, since the way something is said may have associated connotations that go beyond the words themselves, such as the strength of a preference, ambiguities, conflicts, or even contradictions that may need clarification when the map is analysed.

Eden stresses that the wording should be action oriented — a verb or noun implying an action. The map should reveal the consequences or implications of these actions, which in turn may be other actions, the logical sequence ultimately leading to the final outcomes. The latter may often be desired outcomes or goals.

In Figure 4-5, the first pole of construct 1 leads to the first pole of construct 2. If this is not the case, i.e., the first pole of a construct leads to the second pole of another construct, then a negative sign (–) is attached to the head of the arrow. Similarly, a negative sign on the tail of an arrow implies the second pole leads to the first pole of the following construct. Furthermore, it is not implied that the second pole of a construct logically always leads to the second pole of the next construct (as happens to be the case in Figure 4-5).

A word of caution. Although a cognitive map may on first glance look like a representation of system components, they are not system models. Its constructs are perceptions and views about a problem situation, and goals and potential actions available to the individual for whom the map is created. They are **not** system components.

4.8 Cognitive map for NuWave Shoes

Let us now develop a cognitive map for a personal problem, faced by Elly Schuhmacher, the owner-manager of NuWave Shoes. We will first give a short verbal description of the 'difficulties' she faces and then show how her perceptions can be mapped out. (Ignore the numbers in square brackets on your first reading.)

Elly Schuhmacher's nightmare

Just over a year ago, Elly jumped at the opportunity to go into business on her own, taking over a failing niche-market, high-fashion shoe factory from an old family friend and converting it into one offering funky shoes to the yuppie generation. With an overdraft of £90,000 from a sympathetic bank and her own savings of more than £40,000, plus a loan from her parents, her funky shoes were an instant success rather than a flop [1], as some sceptics predicted, with sales only restricted by limited production capacity rather than demand [2]. However, her cash position was tight and not as good as expected [3], due mainly to two reasons: a threefold rise in raw material stocks [4], locking up cash [5], and the slow rate of collections from the retailers, the latter taking an average of 50 days to pay, rather than the 30 days net asked for by NuWave [6].

Elly knows that she can easily double sales with little additional effort [7] if she gets new machinery more suitable for her style of goods [8]. But that will require £140,000 new capital. How to raise that is her immediate dilemma [9]. The bank turned down her loan application unless she injects more equity capital [10]. She has no other funds, and neither can she raise more from her parents [11]. A priori, her only option seems to be to take a financial partner [12]. But NuWave is her baby, and she wants to keep complete control rather than share it [14]. Last night she had a nightmare that somebody else was sitting at her desk and giving her orders. She looks again over her options:

1. Do nothing now, i.e., continue with the current mode of operation [7]. Another few years of deprivation on a measly £400 a week for slaving away 60 to 70 hours a week? It would take her three to four years to build up enough retained earnings to upgrade the machinery [8]. Can she wait that long? Competition may grab the opportunity and step in to fill her potential market [15].
2. Get a business partner to inject £70,000 [12]. Together with an equal-size bank loan this would cover the new equipment cost and provide the additional working capital needed, but would reduce her equity share to 50% — her nightmare come true [13]!

Could she perhaps make better use of her current funds [16]? For instance, offer a discount for prompt payment [17] to speed up collections from retailers. It will reduce her margin and, hence, profit [18], but if it frees half of the current £150,000 tied up in accounts receivable [19], she is already halfway home.

She again studies the latest balance sheet. Her gaze is caught by the investment in raw materials. 'Do we really need over £90,000 dollars of RM stocks? Could we not operate efficiently with less?,' she asks herself [20]. The current stocks cover four to five months' worth of usage! Admittedly, when they started out with only £30,000, a few deliveries had to be delayed [21]. In the long-run, that will give NuWave a reputation for unreliability — something she wants to avoid [22] since it will ultimately have a negative impact on sales and, hence, profits [23].

A cognitive map for Elly's dilemma

Rather than read this narrative several times, highlighting pertinent aspects, you will get a more truthful picture of how Elly perceives her problem by developing the map, sentence by sentence or thought by thought. We take the sequence of statements as a reflection of her thought processes. That in itself may reveal other crucial aspects, such as the strengths of preferences and dislikes for certain ideas. So, reread the first paragraph of the narrative again. It will lead to the first constructs in Figure 4-6 (p. 77).

Ignoring the historical reference, the first statement is 'her funky shoe sales were an instant success, rather than a flop, as some sceptics predicted' (labelled [1]). Its abbreviated form '[1] Funky shoes instant success … a flop' mirrors the essential of her actual wording. (Recall that the ellipsis reads as '*rather than*'.) The first construct is usually entered about 2/3 down a blank page (at least A4 format, but A3 is even better), or on a sticky note that we place on a big whiteboard. This placing will hopefully leave enough space to add other constructs below as well as above. In our case, no other constructs lead to it. Hence, it shows up at the bottom of Figure 4-6. The second part of the same sentence gives the next construct, i.e., '[2] Sales restricted by production capacity ... demand'. It is a natural successor or follow-on thought of construct [1], as indicated by the arrow from one to the other. The next two sentences contain four related constructs ([3] to [6]) which have no direct relationship with constructs [1] and [2], so we place them a bit to the side. Constructs [4] and [6] lead into [5], which in turn leads into [3]. No contrasts are explicitly stated for constructs [4] and [5]. We could have ended these constructs with the ellipsis, implying the logical opposite. Instead, we chose contrasts that seemed to reflect the situation better. It is though essential that these choices are checked out with the individual once the map is analysed.

The first sentence of the second paragraph provides the next two constructs. Construct [7] 'Potential sales easily doubled' shows no immediate contrast. Neither does [8]. Rather than invent suitable opposites now, which may not reflect Elly's thought process, it usually pays to wait and see if suitable opposites reveal themselves subsequently. This is the case here when Elly ponders on option 1 further on (... do nothing now ...). Can you spot them? Construct [7] is a logical successor to [2], while [8] follows [7].

The sentence following refers to her dilemma of how to raise the £140,000 (construct [9]) needed to finance the new equipment. Some reflection indicates that raising these funds sounds like a goal that she wants achieve. Ultimate goals usually have no opposite pole. Furthermore, it is a mapping convention to show such goals or final outcomes at the very top of the map, with sub-goals and actions that lead to these goals below. (Note that at this point we do not know whether there are even higher order goals, so it may be prudent to leave some free space above.)

Continuing in this fashion, we develop Figure 4-6. We hasten to say that this map is a sanitized version — the placement of constructs reorganized to have them spread out evenly and, if possible, to avoid intersections of arrows. Most first drafts will look cluttered, with new constructs squeezed in between other constructs, some constructs or arrows crossed out, and many arrows intersecting. Furthermore, it is the map as interpreted by one of the authors. Another person might have derived a slightly different map. Either may equally well serve for further analysis, if the wording and the connections in each can be logically defended. (The reader is encouraged to consult the practical advice in the article by Eden et al. (1995), which can be downloaded free from the www.banxia.com website.)

A problem owner can develop such a map on his or her own, expressing their personal train of thought. In practice, cognitive maps are usually drawn by an analyst trained in the method, either while interviewing the problem owner or on the basis of a taped interview. It goes without saying that a map drawn during an interview will need considerable tidying up. The analyst invariably will have to go back to the problem owner for clarification on exact wording of poles, particularly second poles, or eliciting missing second poles, and verifying the correct direction of arrows. This may result in substantive changes in wording, as well as the addition of new constructs and links. In fact, critical analysis and discussion of the map will generate considerable further insight into the problem situation and result in a better understanding for both the problem owner and the analyst.

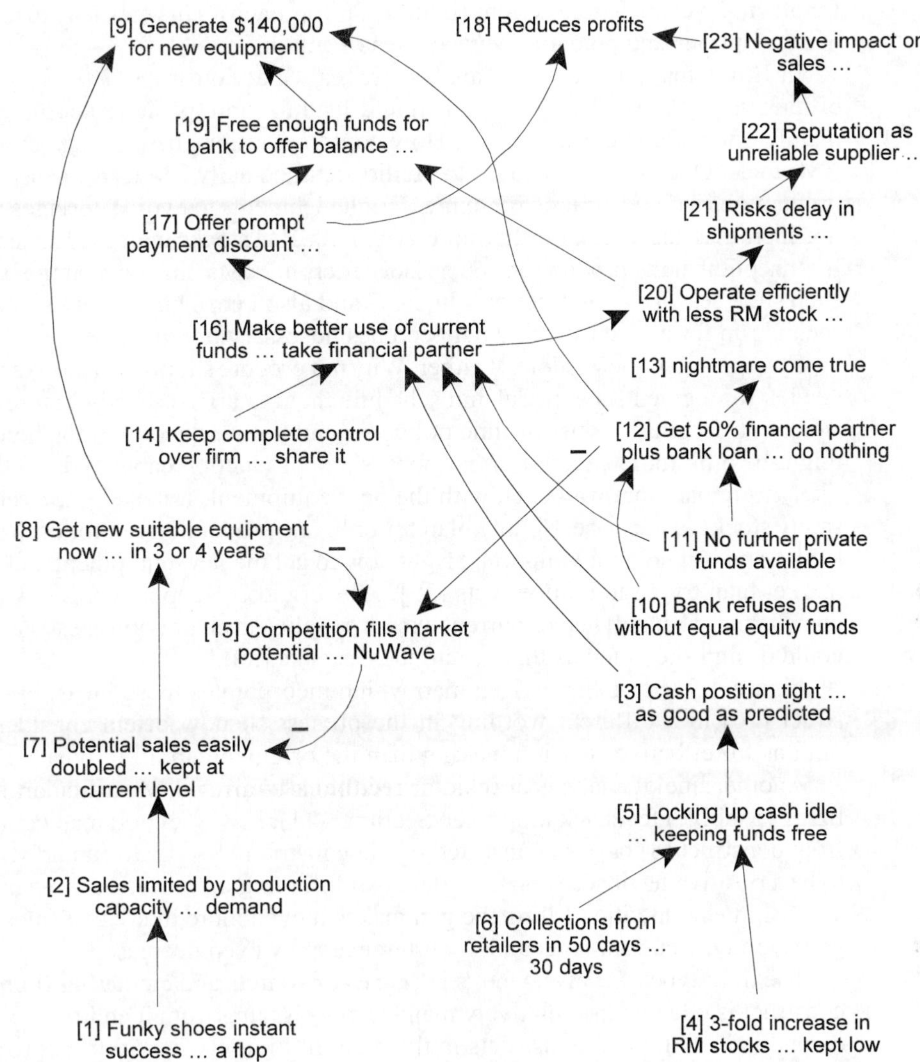

Figure 4-6 Cognitive map for NuWave's owner-manager

Analysing the map

Once the problem owner is satisfied that the map is a sufficiently valid representation of her or his thought process and vision of the problem situation, the map should be analysed along a number of lines. The aim is to make sure that the various paths from information, via actions, to goals are correct and complete. This is done either from top to bottom, or from bottom to top. In both approaches, it is important to question whether there are other, as yet uncharted possible actions that may also achieve the desired goals (top-down approach) or whether a given action opens up the possibility for other, as yet uncharted actions (bottom-up approach). This may lead to the discovery of new options and potential new courses of action.

In Elly's map, a bottom-up analysis reveals that construct [20] ('Run operations efficiently with less RM stock ...) should lead to more positive actions, rather than mainly undesirable consequences. How could operations be run efficiently with less RM stock? One obvious action is to predict detailed daily RM usage based on planned production [24] and arrange for express replenishments to avoid shortages [25] even if this increases costs [26]. Furthermore, why have RM stocks increased so dramatically? It turns out that the production supervisor orders all RMs only once at the beginning of each shoe season — summer or winter — and also keeps high safety stocks in case a second run for a given shoe model becomes necessary or attractive.

Elly questions the wisdom of either. Why not procure supplies in the exact quantities needed for a given shoe model and schedule them to arrive shortly before production is about to begin — a just-in-time policy — and not weeks or months before [27]? It might be a bit more costly. Furthermore, since production capacity is so tight, and is likely to remain that way even with the new equipment, it makes little sense to keep safety stocks just in case. Simply plan for only one production run for each shoe model [28]. 'And is it not more important right now to get the new equipment and capture the market than trying to reduce costs [29]?' she argues. 'Keeping costs low can always come later.' That still leaves current excess supplies from previous seasons' models. 'I could design shoe models that use up these stocks [30].'

Figure 4-7 shows the revised map which incorporates these ideas, changing construct [20] to a different wording in the process. It now offers considerably more options for effective decision making than the original map.

Another line of analysis checks for **feedback loops** and, in particular, for destabilizing (positive) feedback loops (see Section 3-11). Elly's revised map contains a loop from construct [8] back to construct [7] via construct [15]. Unfortunately, it turns out to be a positive feedback loop. Its effect is reinforcing, i.e., waiting three or four years and risking competition filling the gap makes it even more likely that sales may never go beyond the current level and, by inference, may even decrease.

The third type of analysis looks for **core constructs** and **emerging themes**. A core construct is one that has relatively many arrows issuing from it and/or leading to it, in comparison with other constructs in the map. In Figure 4-7, construct [16] sticks out with eight links — four arrows in and four out. Except for constructs [12] with five links, all the remaining ones have four or fewer links. Construct [16] is therefore a pivotal construct. Any attempt to find a solution to Elly's dilemma is likely to revolve around it, i.e., involving paths that lead through it to the final goal. Viewed together, [16] and [12] mirror Elly's key dilemma. Given her true nature as a determined woman, 'Doing nothing' (the opposite pole of [12]) does not seem an option she would really contemplate. If we eliminate it, the two constructs can be collapsed into one that reflects her true dilemma: 'Make better use of current funds ... get a 50% financial partner plus bank loan'. As a first strategy, she will therefore investigate the amount of funds she can free by the five actions of constructs [17], [28], [24], [27], and [30]. If it is enough, her final choice is a foregone conclusion. The bank may also be favourably inclined when presented with such detailed analysis.

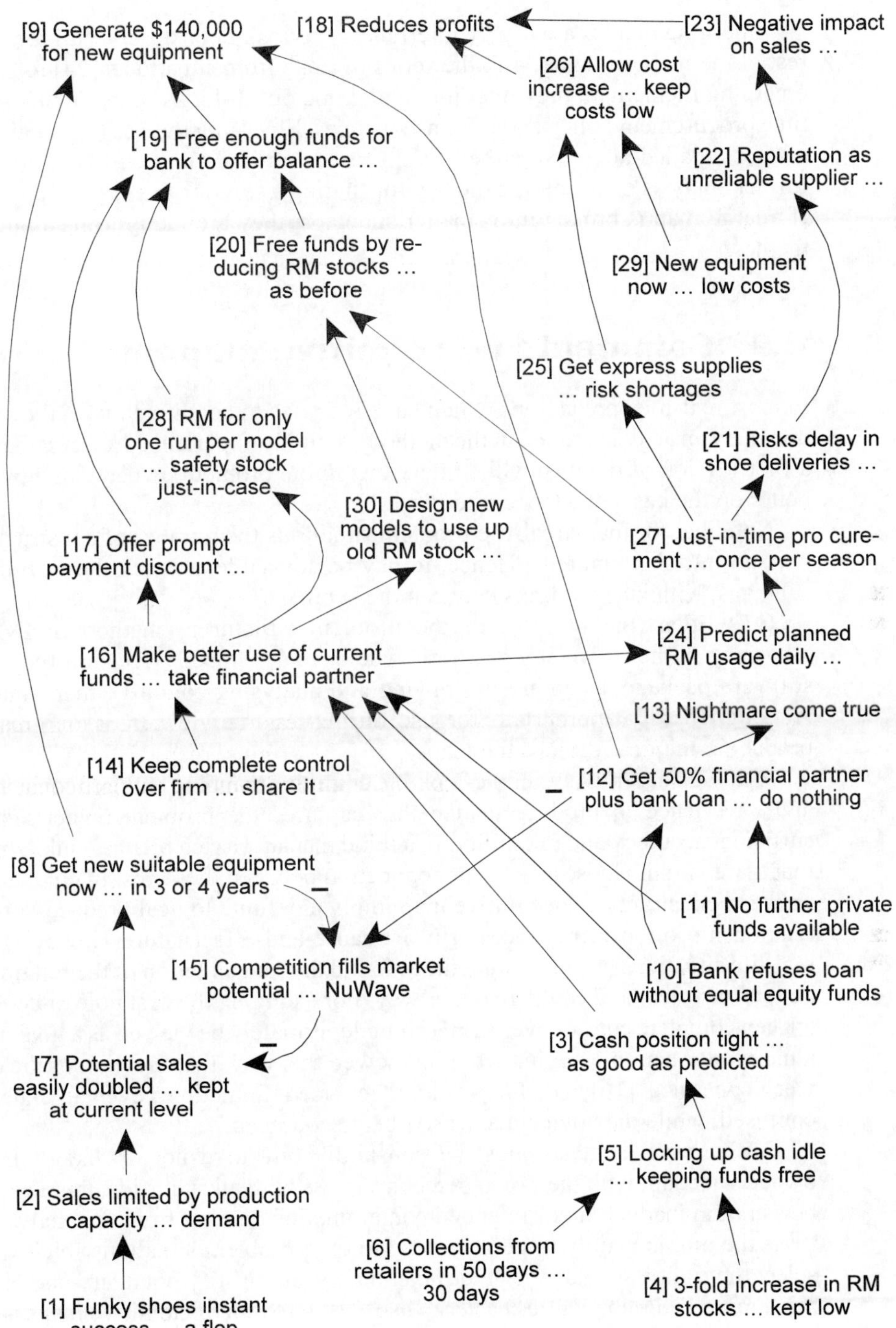

Figure 4-7 Amended cognitive map for NuWave's owner-manager

Emerging themes are highly interlinked groups of constructs with few links to the rest of the map. In Figure 4-7, the series of links from constructs [24] to [18] form an emerging theme with only one link in and one out. It looks at the option of a just-in-time procurement policy and its consequences. Emerging themes may again be singled out for detailed attention, either giving rise to an issue that will become a focus for further analysis or as holding the key for finding a solution to the problem in question. If a large map is broken into smaller submaps, they are likely to be along emerging themes.

4.9 Comments on cognitive mapping

In most real-life applications which have recourse to cognitive maps, they are usually drawn by an analyst trained in the method. A highly experienced analyst may construct a first version of the map while interviewing the problem owner. The novice will do better on the basis of a taped interview.

Note that for many real-life problem situations the number of constructs in a map may go into the hundreds. Hence, it may be advisable to break the map into several submaps, with labelled links between the submaps.

C.L. Eden (the inventor of the problem structuring method SODA) and his associates at the University of Strathclyde have developed 'Decision Explorer', a PC software package, as an aid in drawing and analysing cognitive maps interactively. Although hardly appropriate for use during an interview, it is of great help for producing the final draft of the map.

Although deceptively simple-looking, cognitive mapping requires considerable skill and experience to produce a map that captures the problem owner's views with sufficient accuracy and reliability. In a mind map and a rich picture, links simply mean that there is some loose affinity or connection between the items. In contrast, the links between constructs in a cognitive map imply a definite logical predecessor-successor relationship, often but not necessarily of a cause-and-effect nature. However, faced with real-life situations, we have sometimes found that the direction of the relationship may be far from clear and could go either way. For example, the first pole of construct [14] ('Keep complete control over firm') could legitimately be viewed as a goal, rather than a motive for action resulting from it. Viewed this way, the direction of the arrow between constructs [16] and [14] would be reversed. Sometimes even an expert may get confused, while the novice may easily be discouraged.

Furthermore, analysts must be constantly on guard not to distort the problem owner's account with their own perceptions. As with all such aids, there could always be a certain inadvertent or intended contamination coming from the analyst.

If the aim is mainly to get a good grip on a problem situation which will help to select the right issue, identify the stakeholders, and justify boundary choices, we find mind maps and rich pictures easier to use. The strength of cognitive maps is that often they are more than simply a summary of the problem situation. As we have seen when analysing and enhancing Elly's map, the map provided a clear strategy for further detailed investigation. In fact, cognitive mapping often goes beyond capturing the problem situation and already explores aspects of problem solving, as was the case here.

In Chapter 7, we will briefly explore how it forms the first phase for SODA — a conflict resolution technique for multiple decision makers.

Case study 4-2: SkyWalker (continuation of Case study 4-1, p. 72)
Draw individual cognitive maps for Jill and Jess, being careful not to contaminate the maps with statements made by the other person. Identify core constructs in each. Identify differences and common ground between the two maps.

4.10 Problem definition and boundary selection

Recall that the purpose of obtaining a sufficient understanding of a problem situation is to delineate the problem to be analysed. This does not simply mean identifying the correct issue of concern, but also its scope, form, and level of detail or depth. These should all be appropriate to generate useful insights and answers for decision making or problem solving. Part of this involves a critical evaluation of which aspects of the problem situation should be included in the analysis and which aspects can be ignored. Those included either become part of the narrow system of interest or its environment. In other words, we have to select the boundaries for both the narrow system of interest and its relevant environment. As pointed out in Section 3.5, boundary selection is the most critical facet of systems thinking.

Critical systems heuristics, developed in 1983 by Ulrich (see Further reading in Chapter 7), is currently the most comprehensive framework for subjecting boundary selection to thorough scrutiny. Several problem structuring methods (see references to Part 2: Rosenhead and Mingers, 2000) devote considerable effort to assess which aspects should be considered and which ones can be ignored during a particular phase in the analysis. We will limit our comments to some general points.

Boundary selection fixes the scope, direction and focus of all subsequent analysis. It not only determines which inputs are considered controllable, but also whose benefits and costs are included in the performance measure, and in particular which potential stakeholders are reduced to problem customers, possibly mere victims without any say or recourse.

It may also be highly instructive to contrast different worldviews and analyse their effect on the appropriate boundary choices. The added insights invariably gained will contribute towards a more comprehensive understanding of the problem situation and a revised definition of the problem.

Selecting the wrong boundaries may result in solving the wrong problem. It may make it difficult, or even impossible, to implement the solution, or may reduce the potential benefits that could have been derived.

Let us now use the summary portrayed in Figure 4-7 to define Elly's problem. Her initial concern was how to raise the £140,000 needed to finance the new equipment. Her statements indicate that she does not want to consider taking a financial partner — its her nightmare! That either leaves doing nothing, which is potentially crippling, or finding most of the funds internally, particularly via actions emanating from construct [16]. With this focus, the critical problem elements become:

- Decision maker: Elly Schuhmacher.
- Objective: Generate enough funds to purchase the new equipment.
- Performance measure: Amount of funds freed.
- Decision criterion: Funds generated are at least equal to £140,000.
- Alternative courses of action: combination of size of discount offered to customers; just-in-time procurement policy based on better prediction of RM usage; new model designs to absorb previous season's excess RM stock; emergency in-freighting to avoid shortages; one run per model, no safety stocks for second production runs.
- Boundaries for narrow system of interest (as indicated by major system inputs): old and new production output capacity and cost structure; potential demand and shoe wholesale prices; proportion of retailers taking up prompt-payment discount offer for various levels of discount. (She may want to investigate the effect on funds released for different proportions of retailers taking up the option.)
- Boundaries for wider system of interest: no countermove by competition within the near future; bank amenable to make up shortfall (e.g., in the form of a mortgage on equipment), if sufficiently small; no fashion shift away from funky shoes.

The stakeholders affected, but not involved in the decision making process, include the retail stores. They are not adversely affected, but are offered a new prompt-payment discount option. Only NuWave's competitors could be adversely affected by Elly's pre-emptive move to expand production capacity, but then that is in the nature of competition. (Any employees of hers will also be problem customers or users.)

4.11 Some conclusions

As we have seen, how problem owners and/or analysts perceive the problem situation involves a fair degree of arbitrariness. It is strongly affected by the purpose of the analysis, the worldviews of the analysts and/or problem owners, and the resources (time, funds, people) available for the job. You should therefore not be surprised if different people see the problem situation differently and may disagree on which issues need to be studied first. Such disparity of views is to be expected. No view can be ruled out as invalid, unless it lacks internal logic or is incompatible with the problem owner's own worldview. However, this does not imply that all problem situation summaries are equally useful, particularly if they are incomplete or their focus is biased.

Furthermore, a problem situation summary should not be in the form of a system description, since this may impose a given structure biasing the analysis. At this stage, it is crucial to keep an open mind. Nevertheless, sufficient mutual appreciation of the conflicting views is needed to reach a partial consensus on the problem situation. Only then may an agreement emerge as to which issue is to be studied and how.

4.12 Chapter highlights

- The problem situation is the context in which a problem is embedded. Most problem situations involve several interconnected issues. Each could become the focus for analysis. The full context is needed for correctly defining the problem situation.
- Identifying a problem means defining the decision maker, his or her objective(s), the performance measure for assessing the level of achievement towards the objective, the criterion for judging when the objective has been achieved, the alternative courses of action, and the relevant environment in which the problem is embedded.
- Stakeholders are the people or entities that are, in one way or another, connected to the problem, either as the person(s) owning or having the problem and controlling crucial aspects of the problem, the person(s) who will use the results of the analysis, the person(s) who will analyse the problem, and those that are affected by the results and may not have any direct or indirect influence over the actions taken. A person may assume more than one stakeholder role at the same time or at different times.
- Mind maps, rich pictures, and cognitive maps are useful tools for problem situation summaries. They are not system models. They serve as a basis for discussion with other stakeholders. They show the problem in its full context, help identify and define the issue or problem to be analysed, the stakeholders, the potential actions, and facilitate selecting appropriate boundaries of the analysis.

Exercises

1. Draw a mind map for the service call centre in Example 1-1 (p. 2).
2. Draw a mind map for the Deep Cove project situation in Example 1-3 (p. 4).
3. (a) Draw a mind map for the balance of your tertiary education in view of the kind of career you envisage for yourself and the possible obstacles to it.
   (b) Identify the various stakeholders and their roles.
4. (a) Draw a mind map for the breast cancer screening situation in Examples 1-4 (p. 5) and Example 4-1 (p. 65), as viewed from the point of view of the Director of Public Health.
   (b) Identify the various stakeholders and their roles.
   (c) Redo the exercise but from the point of view of a woman advocate for breast screening.
5. For the blood bank in Case study 3-1 (p. 54), draw a mind map and identify all stakeholder roles.
6. For the blood bank in Case study 3-1 (p. 54), draw a rich picture and identify all stakeholder roles.
7. Consult the Internet about the ozone hole that has developed over the Antarctic in the late southern hemisphere winter since the 1980s and draw a rich picture of its causes, its detrimental effects on the planet's flora and fauna, including us humans, and the measures already taken to combat it. (Note that the *Guardian* reported in October 2011 that there are now definite signs that a similar phenomenon seems to develop over the Arctic.)
8. Consider the interview below between a young graduate (Y) from the University of Mexico and the priest (P) his mother called in to settle the dispute with his father about what he should do over the next year or two. Draw a cognitive map for Y based on this.

P: Son, tell me about how you see your future.

Y: I'm torn between wanting to take a year off rather that go for a job now, you know, travelling around Europe, not stay home, spend some time in St. Tropez, you know, and enjoy the girls —

P: St. Tropez, where they bathe topless? Mm … Go on.

Y: — yes, rather than settle down, you know, no more playing around. Settling down would please dad.

P: You mean get a job and marry Iñez now?

Y: I guess … not wait a year or two. But it may already be a bit late to find a good job this year. The really good jobs always go first. Maybe one of father's friends might help.

P: You know what kind of job you would like?

Y: Yeah, a job with one of those big international consulting firms. Many of their projects involve travel all over the world. That would be awesome! No dull factory job for me.

P: Travelling seems really important to you. Why?

Y: I want to see the world, meet people, have excitement.

9. In late 2011, Bill Dodge, the supervisor of Customs at the Christchurch International Airport (or CIA), became alarmed about a number of aspects of the customs operation under his management. He received approval to call in an MS/OR consultant to study the operations. The interview reproduced below took place between Bill Dodge (B) and the consultant (C). Draw a cognitive map for (B) based on this interview.

C: So that I can put things into context, what is Customs' primary role at CIA?

B: Clearly, it must be border protection, i.e., prevention of importation of illegal goods (drugs, pornographic material, and so on), prevention of entry into New Zealand of prohibited aliens, and full assessment of import duties.

C: And I guess that you are not achieving these goals to your satisfaction, right?

B: Yes, for a number of reasons. First, most critically, there is insufficient staff capacity to deal properly with all the tasks loaded onto us. Our current staff ceiling is simply too low, although HQ considers it about right. Government processing standards require us to process all PAX of an incoming flight within a set maximum of 30 minutes — rather than taking as much time as needed to do our duties properly. Second, our present shift schedule was OK eight years ago, when most of flights arrived during day time, but it no longer fits the current pattern. Our flight arrivals and departures are spread over almost 24 hours each day. And, so far, the Customs Officer Union has insisted on continuing the present schedule, rather than allowing us to adapt it to the current needs.

C: Why is that?

B: The present shift schedule results in lots of overtime and many special call-outs. As a consequence, officers get their wage topped up with very high overtime pay, rather than just getting their normal salary. This is, in fact, one of the major reasons for choosing to work at CIA rather than other Customs jobs, such as sea freight import processing or investigations. It's ironic, but my reading of the situation tells me that, although most officers are keen on the extra pay for the first one or two years, they begin to resent it in the long run. They dislike the disruption of their family or social life. The extra money does not compensate enough for it. They particularly dislike the special call-outs.

C: What are special call-outs?

B: Calling in off-duty officers for a duration of two to four hours to process an incoming flight, either because no shift is on duty or the shift on duty is short-staffed and unable to handle the traffic.

C: Is it possible to eliminate most overtime and call-outs by changing shift schedules?

B: Not so much for overtime, since late arrivals of incoming flights might still require the staff beyond their scheduled quitting time, but it would reduce special call-outs needed to process scheduled flights outside the current shifts. There still would be special call-outs to meet non-scheduled flights and the irregular Deep Freeze traffic which occurs mainly between 02.00 and 06.00 hours. I bet if we come up with a shift schedule that still offers reasonable overtime, say about 50% of the current level, and eliminates all special call-outs for scheduled flights, leaving only the occasional unscheduled flight, a majority of officers would vote for it. So, one of the aims of this exercise is to demonstrate that it is possible to leave sufficient overtime opportunities for those who want it, rather than force it on everyone. With a hefty reduction in overtime costs we could live within our current budget, rather than having to apply for special funding every six months to cover the cost overrun. I hate getting the heat from HQ over that twice each year. It does not look good on my annual job evaluation. In fact, I think that if I can show a permanent and guaranteed reduction in overtime costs they might even be willing to give favourable consideration to increasing my staff ceiling. That would allow larger shift crews and hence enable us to meet the processing standard more regularly, rather than the 70% or less as at the present. Meeting these processing standards is a real problem. How can we meet them 100% all the time? It would require an excessively high staff level with a large portion of the staff being idle much of the time.

C: I am afraid that is correct. What is the current shift schedule?

B: We run two shifts each day: 06.30 to 15.30, and 15.00 to 23.00, with a 30-minute lunch break around the middle of the shift. The overlap is needed for a proper hand-over of processing a flight. With the second shift ending at 23.00, we have to schedule overtime or special call-outs every day to process several incoming flights between 22.00 and 01.00. There are five days a week when we have departing and incoming flights between 05.00 and 06.00, i.e., before the first shift is fully operational, since they get 15 minutes to change into uniforms and we need at least 15 minutes to brief the team.

C: I presume other work can be postponed and executed later when there are no flights.

B: Yes, administration and correspondence can wait for up to a week, rather than being done right away. Some other jobs can be delayed for a day or two. But two people are needed to staff the customs office for airport freight every weekday from 9.00 to 16.00.

C: I see, but it seems that two shifts would not cover the current flight schedule.

B: No. We would still need some overtime or special call-outs, but not every day. Also, on mornings where there are early departing flights, but no incoming flights, only two officers are needed. Maybe we should look into the possibility of having shifts of various sizes, rather than each shift with a full complement of 15 officers. It would also help if the Union agreed with flexible shift start times, as long as they only differ by up to four hours, rather than insisting that a given shift has the same start time every day. Flexible shift times would to allow having officers on duty when they are needed, rather than having a mismatch between staff needs and availability.

C: Is the union's position on shift schedules very entrenched or a bargaining strategy?

B: A bit of both, I guess. The current schedule gives high pay, and as a former union member I can understand that the union delegates wish to protect that and not be seen as being soft on anything that threatens current conditions. Also, the union contract will be up for negotiation later this year, and they want to start from a strong position, rather than compromise before then. Mind you, they are reasonable chaps, not bloody-minded, and if we can come up with an acceptable compromise that shows them as having firmly protected their members' interests, I am fairly confident that they will be willing to put it up for a vote. The important aspect is that it must satisfy both those officers who want to top up their salary though overtime and those who would rather not have these disruptions to their daily lives.

C: Are there any other aspects about the union contract that I should know about?

B: Let me see. Yes. All staff get four weeks' vacation plus seven statutory holidays. Also, officers may attend training courses and have sick leave provisions. These entitlements add up to about 18% of their regular working hours. We call this the X-factor.

Further reading

Eden, C.L., Ackermann, F. and Cropper, S. (1995) *Getting Started with Cognitive Mapping*, Glasgow: Banxia Software. Informative step-by-step guidelines for cognitive mapping; documentation for Decision Explorer® (see http://www.banxia.com).

Kelly, G.A. (1955) *The Psychology of Personal Constructs*, New York: Norton. Developed the original theory of personal constructs within a psychological context.

Lane, A. (2000) *Systems Thinking and Practice: a Primer*, Milton Keynes: Open University Press.

Lane, A. (1999) *Systems Thinking and Practice: Diagramming*, Milton Keynes: Open University Press.

Naughton, J. (1984) *Soft Systems Analysis: An Introductory Guide*, Technology Course T301: Block 4, Milton Keynes: Open University Press. Down-to-earth text. Together with its *Workbook,* this is one of the best accounts of the use of rich pictures and systems diagrams.

Open University, Milton Keynes: the systems modules in their technology series have a number of relevant CDs on systems thinking, systems concepts, and diagramming.

5
System models

Learning objectives

- Appreciate that system models and diagrams are approximations, subjective to the individual making them.
- Be able to specify/identify the elements/aspects that make up a system description or model.
- Be able to apply the system identification rules for identifying inputs, outputs, and system elements.
- Appreciate that systems modelling is a process of enrichment and reformulation.
- Be able to draw a causal loop diagram, and identify positive and negative feedback loops.
- Be able to draw an influence diagram.
- Be able to draw a material flow chart.
- Be able to draw a precedence chart for the tasks of a project, calculate its earliest completion time, and identify the critical tasks.
- Be able to draw a decision flow chart.

Introduction

We are now ready to define a relevant narrow system of interest for the issue identified as the problem. This is often referred to as **system modelling**. The first section discusses various types of system models, while the next describes two common approaches to system modelling. This is followed with pointers on what constitutes good modelling.

Diagrams are an effective approach to highlight salient aspects of systems — their structure, the internal system interactions between components, the cause-and-effect and precedence relationships, the inputs from and the outputs to the environment, the flow of material and information inside the system, and the logic of decision rules. These topics are taken up in the last three sections.

5.1 Types of system models

The word 'model' has many meanings. The one of interest to us is defined in *Webster's Collegiate Dictionary* as 'a description or analogy used for helping to visualize something (as an atom) that cannot be directly observed', although in some cases we may be able to observe certain aspects of it. This seems to be exactly what we do when we define a system. Therefore, **a system model is a representation of all or parts of a system**. As a system is an abstract mental construct — a personal conceptualization and hence not independent of that person (recall the concept of 'consensual subjectivity', pp. 30–1) — so a model is another abstraction at a different level. It is not the real thing.

A model may be **iconic**, **analogous**, or **symbolic**. Iconic models are reproductions of physical objects, usually to a different scale and with less detail. A car model, or the small-scale aircraft tested in a wind tunnel for the aerodynamics of the real thing, or an architectural mock-up of a building, are all iconic models.

Analogue models are representations which substitute the properties or features of what is modelled by alternative means such that the model is able to mimic whatever aspect of the real thing is of interest to the modeller. For instance, the constantly updated picture that an air traffic controller observes on a radar monitor is an analogue of the air traffic in a given sector of the air space. Similarly, the three-dimensional vision produced by computer software on the screen, allowing the observer to see an object from any desired direction or angle, or enabling the observer to walk through a building, is an analogue model.

Symbolic models

Symbolic models are representations of the relationships between various entities or concepts by means of symbols. By the time you reached tertiary education, you would have encountered and been bombarded with thousands of all sorts of symbolic models. Every newspaper, technical magazine or school book contains graphs, depicting how a given variable varies as a function of another variable, such as the stock exchange index over time, or statistical charts, e.g., pie charts of how funds are allocated or bar charts comparing the values of various variables of interest. Geographic maps, hierarchical charts of the command structure in an organization showing who reports to whom, flow diagrams depicting how material and information flow through an organization, or diagrams depicting the sequence of decisions that need to be made, are all examples of symbolic models. Such models are extensively used for communicating all sorts of data and information. In Sections 5.5 to 5.7, we will study several such graphical and diagrammatic models.

However, the most common symbolic models are the mental pictures we form in our minds or the descriptions that we make verbally or in writing about something, an object, an entity, an operation, a process, or an interconnected set of abstract concepts, such as a logical argumentation or a theory. Our daily life is literally a never-ending journey from model to model, although most of the time it remains outside our formal awareness. What we call 'experience' is a huge memory bank of mental models to which we add new ones daily. This is what allows us to recognize a car when we see one, and not mistake it for a rubbish container, although closer inspection of what people accumulate in cars shows that many are used as rubbish containers. But, as a colleague pointed out, this is preferable to dumping it out of the window.

Mathematical models

Another type of symbolic model extensively used in hard OR is a mathematical model. We use mathematical expressions, such as functions, equations, and inequalities, to represent the relationships between system components. You may have come across the mathematical expression for the distance s a free falling object travels in a vacuum in t seconds: $s = 0.5gt^2$, where g is the constant of gravity. This is a mathematical model, although your high school teachers may not have called it that.

This book focuses on symbolic models — mental, diagrammatic and mathematical, although even the last two invariably start with a verbal model. The methodology of hard OR is taken up in Chapter 6.

Models as approximations

As Webster's definition states, a model is only a partial representation of what it is supposed to capture. It will contain various approximations and simplifying assumptions, some of little significance, others of great consequence. However, it is essential that the analyst carefully records the form of the approximations and assumptions made. There are three major reasons for this: (1) to ensure that all stakeholders of the model are aware of the model's limitations; (2) to highlight the need to study changes in system behaviour by modifying these approximations and assumptions, if this is possible; and (3) to ensure that, if the model is revisited some time in the future in view of making modifications, the analyst is fully aware of any approximations and assumptions incorporated in it.

The type of approximation and assumptions made will reflect the training, experience, and personality of the analyst, the resources, particularly in terms of time and funds, available, as well as the purpose of the study. There is always a degree of arbitrariness present. Hence, there may be several good models for the same system.

Unfortunately, analysts may introduce assumptions into a model without being fully aware of doing so. For example, data used in the model, such as demand for a product or service, are often based on past experience. They may even have been collected while a different mode of operation was in use. If the model is used for predicting or controlling future behaviour of the system, the implicit strong assumption is that the nature, form, and pattern of past data are valid predictors for the future after the new system has been implemented. This may or may not be the case. Furthermore, what may be obvious to you may not be obvious to somebody else. So, it pays to record all assumptions carefully.

Activity

For each of the following, indicate the type of model and why: (a) the wiring diagram of a TV set; (b) a thermometer; (c) a weather chart; (d) a play station game; (e) a porcelain statue; (f) the normal distribution.

5.2 Approaches for deriving a system model

A system description or model consists of specifying:

- the **transformation process(es)** or activities of the system;
- the **boundary** of the system, i.e., what is inside the system — the narrow system of interest — and what makes up its environment, or the wider system of interest;
- the **components** and **subsystems** of the narrow system involved in the transformation process, and the **dynamic relationships**, and **stable relationships** or the **structure**;
- the **uncontrollable inputs** into the system from the environment, the **control inputs** or **decisions,** and **decision rules**; and
- the **outputs** of the system, desired and undesired, planned and unplanned, and which ones serve as the **performance measures** for the system.

How should we go about this task? There are two main approaches: (a) identifying and fitting a known basic structure; and (b) analysing the processes and defining a suitable structure from first principles.

A structural approach

The issue chosen for detailed study may strongly suggest a typical structure usually found for situations of that sort. For instance, the issue may be the excessive length of time that the customers requesting a service may have to wait before being served. This immediately suggests a 'waiting line' structure, as depicted in Figure 5-1, with customers arriving randomly at a service facility, joining the queue in front of the servers, advancing in the queue by one position each time a customer ahead of them has been served, until it is their turn to be served by the next server who becomes free. The system transforms customers in need of service into customers served.

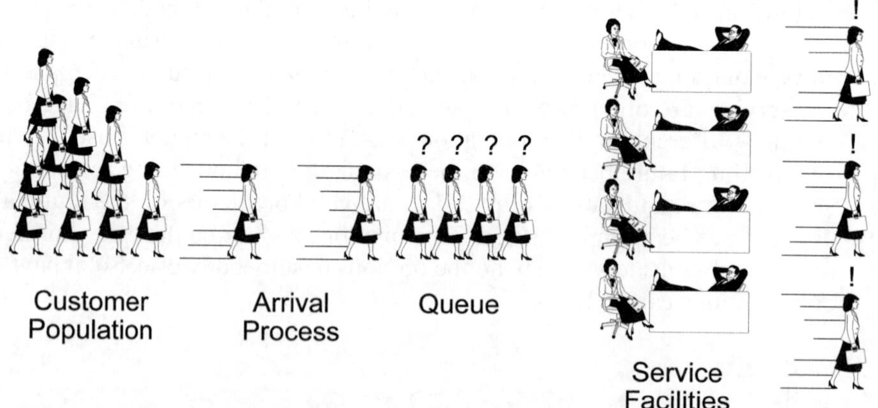

Figure 5-1 Waiting line structure

In a waiting line structure, the components of the system are customers, one or several queues, and the server(s). The stable structure of the system is given by how customers pass through the system. After arriving, they wait in the queue in front of the service facility, are served by the server(s) in a specified sequence or priority, e.g. first-come first-served, and then depart from the system. The dynamic aspects or processes are given by the random arrivals of customers from a given 'population' in the environment (the arrival process), how they progress to the front of a queue, and the service activity where both a customer and a server are engaged jointly — a transient relationship.

Customer arrival times and service times are the uncontrollable inputs. The control inputs are the number of servers on duty and the service priority rules imposed. The arrivals obey a given (assumed) known arrival pattern, such as being completely random. Once 'arrived', each customer becomes a temporary component of the system.

The novice will take customer departures as the output of the system. This, though, is of little use. Typically, the analyst is interested in several performance measures, such as the average waiting time of customers in the queue, the average total time a customer spends in the system, and the average time the servers are idle. Customer departures are only of interest in that they help determine how long each customer spends in the system.

Using a known basic structure allows fast progress towards defining a complete system model. Once the basic structure has been identified, the analyst will immediately know which aspects of the situation form the narrow system of interest and which are part of the environment, the type of components to look for, the usual relationships between them, the underlying processes, and the usual inputs and outputs of the system. He or she will know what input data are needed, and the form of suitable system performance measures, and also have a fair idea which quantitative tools, if any, are most appropriate for analysing the situation. He or she may have access to commercial software specifically developed for the model structure chosen.

A structural approach is clearly the preferred way to go, if the transformation process of the situation closely fits the assumption implied by the structure. However, if aspects are present that depart from that structure, there is a serious risk that the issue is 'forced' into an inappropriate model.

This approach also presupposes that the analyst is sufficiently familiar with the most common types of system models, not simply on a theoretical level, but also through practical experience. A novice may lack both. Using a process approach to build a system model from first principles may then be safer.

A process approach

Here, no a priori assumptions about the underlying system structure are made. An appropriate system structure is developed by tracing how inputs, controlled and uncontrolled, are transformed into outputs. This approach is more challenging, but also more difficult. Chapter 6 demonstrates its use for a real-life case.

What is the best way to go about it? The worldview of the problem owner dictates the objectives to be pursued and the form of the most appropriate evaluation criteria. Some objectives may give rise to constraints on particular aspects. One or more may be in the form of maximizing or minimizing a corresponding performance measure — the system output of prime interest to the problem owner. Next, we identify all aspects of the narrow system of interest over which the problem owner exercises some control and the extent of that control, and then those which the wider system imposes on the narrow system. Finally, we define the transformation of inputs into outputs, and how the system components interact with each other in that process.

The following four rules help in identifying the components, the inputs, both controllable and uncontrollable, and the outputs of the system:

1. any aspect, controllable or uncontrollable, that affects the system, but in turn is not affected by it, is a system input;
2. any aspect that is directly or indirectly affected by the transformation process, but in turn does not affect any other aspect of the system, is a system output;
3. any aspect that is part of the system's structure or is affected by an input or by other aspects of the system and in turn affects other aspects of the system, including outputs, is a component or a relationship;
4. any aspect that does not affect the system, or is not affected by it, or is not part of its structure is irrelevant and can be ignored.

Table 5-1 summarizes these rules. According to rules 1 and 2, there should be no feedback loops between the system and its environment. All aspects in such a feedback loop, except external control and data inputs, should be contained within the system. Any transactions across the system boundary are therefore either inputs or outputs.

Table 5-1 Systems identification rules

Question	**Is aspect affected from within the system or by an input?**		
Does aspect affect something inside the system?	Answer	YES	NO
	YES	**component or relationship**	**input**
	NO	**output**	**irrelevant**

In the real world, things may not be as clear-cut as assumed by these four rules. A given aspect may affect the system only marginally. The recurrent question is therefore: 'At what point does such an influence become a significant factor that should be taken into account?' If time and funds allow it, a prudent analyst will include rather more than less. If it turns out that its impact is negligible, it can always be discarded later on.

A simple, effective way of finding out whether an aspect is irrelevant or only marginally relevant is to look at its opposite or absence. If it does not change the relevant system definition or its relevant inputs, then that aspect can be ignored.

Novices get confused by the fact that the control over an input may only be partial since random aspects may alter its effect. This is best represented by separating it into two inputs, a target control input and a specific (but uncontrollable) stochastic disturbance of that control input. All random aspects that affect system behaviour are always specified as uncontrollable inputs, usually in the form of probability distributions.

Activity

- View a tertiary institution as a system for educating people. Look at it from the point of view of its chief executive (president or vice-chancellor). It transforms students who satisfy the entrance requirements into graduates (or dropouts) in a given field of study. The underlying worldview is that education is a worthwhile thing. Define the controllable inputs, the uncontrollable inputs, the outputs, including at least one performance measure, and the components of this system.
- Do the same, but now from the point of view of a student who sees education as a means for finding rewarding employment after graduation.

5.3 Essential properties of good models

Since models are not primarily for the analyst but, rather, for the problem owner or decision maker, they should satisfy some essential properties. In his article 'Models and Managers: Concepts of Decision Calculus', J.D.C. Little (1970) gives some useful hints for mathematical models. However, his comments apply to symbolic models as well. Models should be:

1. **Simple**. Simple models are more easily understood. A decision maker will more easily follow the logic of a spreadsheet than of a complicated set mathematical expression, which may do little more than the computations performed in a spreadsheet — admittedly more elegantly. To get simple models, the analyst may have to make suitable approximations and simplifications to the real situation. For example, although a given phenomenon (such as the demand for a product) is subject to small and possibly random fluctuations over time, it is approximated as occurring at a constant rate per period.

   To achieve a model that is transparent, i.e., where interactions and relationships are easily tractable, aspects of minor significance may even be deleted. For example, minor exceptions to the general rule are left out.

   However, sometimes an analyst may have no choice but to build a complicated mathematical model. The decision maker will gain confidence in such a model if he or she has the opportunity to experiment with it, e.g., by exploring whether changes in the input parameters produce intuitively reasonable changes in the best solution and, if not, whether counterintuitive results can be explained convincingly.

2. **Complete**. A model should include all significant aspects of a problem situation that affect the measure of performance. The problem here is to know, before the model is built, whether an aspect is likely to affect the 'best' solution in a significant way. Experience will obviously help. If a model is used repetitively many times and the cost of using it is significant, it may be necessary to build two models, a complex one with these aspects present, and a simpler one without them, compare their answers, and only then judge the significance of a particular aspect.

3. **Easy to manipulate and communicate with**. It should be easy for the analyst and/or the user to prepare, update, and change the inputs and get answers quickly and with a reasonable amount of effort and resources. In today's world of interactive user-friendly computer software, this property has become one of the standard selling points. (It reminds us of the situation faced by meteorological services in the 1970s, when meteorologists could produce accurate seven-day weather forecasts only by having very fast mainframe computers churn away for five days, ending up with an out-of-date two-day forecast! Clearly, the computation time needed then was excessive, robbing the answers of much of their value.)
4. **Adaptive**. Usually, reasonable changes in uncontrollable inputs and the structure of the problem situation should not completely invalidate the model. If they do, it should be possible to adapt it to the new situation with only relatively minor modifications. This is more likely if the model consists of a sequence of small modules that each perform a separable task or operation. Any structural changes in the problem situation may then require only modifications to one or a few modules. An adaptive model is often referred to as a **robust** model.

Some of these properties put conflicting demands on the modelling process. A simple model may not capture all significant aspects of the problem situation. A robust model may not be simple. A model that includes all significant aspects may not be easy to manipulate. Model builders have to balance these conflicting demands and come up with a suitable compromise. This compromise will, by necessity, reflect not only the training of the analyst, but also the available resources in terms of time and funds.

It should also reflect the likely benefits that can be achieved. It may be economically more advantageous to use simple quick-and-dirty rules that only capture 50% of the potential benefits, rather than develop a sophisticated and expensive mathematical model that may capture 90%. The costs of developing a mathematical model, collecting the required input data, computing the best solution, implementing the model, and finally operating and maintaining it, all increase much more than proportionately as the sophistication of the model increases, while the additional benefits go up less than proportionately — the economic principle of decreasing marginal return and increasing marginal cost (discussed in Chapter 12).

However, satisfying these properties to a high degree may not be enough to convince a problem owner or user to implement the answers of the model. That depends to a large extent on the **confidence** the latter has in the model's ability to produce useful information or, loosely speaking, in the model's **credibility**. It will, in the end, determine the model's fate. This adds a new dimension to the notion of desirable properties of models. In fact, it may be more useful to talk about **desirable properties of the modelling process**, since user credibility and confidence are more related to that process and the interactions between user and modeller than to the model itself.

There are two further desirable properties:

5. **A model must be appropriate for the situation studied.** By this is meant that the model produces the relevant outputs **at the lowest possible cost** and **in the time frame required for effective decision making**. For example, for the NuWave case

in Section 4.8 a simple spreadsheet for month-by-month cash flow projections may well be an appropriate choice of model if the objective is to provide a quick estimate of the firm's cash flow and its profits, whereas a simulation study which models the progress of every batch of shoes along the production line will not, unless it also produces suitable financial measures. And even then, its level of detail may be excessive, and therefore inappropriate, for the situation studied. On the other hand, if our objective is to estimate the maximum possible rate of production, or the size of buffer space needed between operations or machines, a detailed simulation model will be appropriate, whereas a financial spreadsheet will not.

6. **A model has to produce information that is relevant and appropriate for decision making.** Its output has to have direct bearing on the decision process, has to be useful for decision making, and has to be in a form that it can be used directly as input for decision making, without the need for further extensive translation or manipulation. This does not imply that the decision maker may not have to use judgement in interpreting the information produced. But the information should lead to insights that the decision maker could not easily obtain by other means.

If a model satisfies the last two properties, this will enhance the decision maker's confidence in the model and willingness to use its answers. Confidence in and credibility of the model are not necessarily the result of a logical analysis of the model, or even of an understanding of how the model works. It may be largely intuitive, based on a demonstration that the model gives usable, sensible, expected, and explainable answers in a timely fashion and with reasonable effort and expense. It will also be strongly influenced by the working relationship between modeller and problem owner/user and their involvement in the modelling process.

5.4 The art of modelling

One of the aims of this text is to render modelling less ad hoc, more scientific. However, there still remain aspects which are more akin to art than science. This means that some people will discover that they possess a natural talent for modelling, while others will find it hard going. So, how should one go about modelling?

Here are a few useful guidelines — some little more than common sense when approaching any new task, but, surprisingly, often ignored by the inexperienced.

Ockham's razor

William of Ockham, a fourteenth-century English philosopher stated a useful heuristic rule: 'Things should not be multiplied without good reason.' (Since Ockham was reputed to have a sharp and cutting wit, this heuristic has become known as Ockham's razor!) In terms of modelling, it means that the modeller has to be highly selective about which aspects to include in a model. All aspects that are not absolutely essential or that contribute little to its 'accuracy' or 'predictive power' should be excluded. A good model is as parsimonious as possible in terms of the variables or aspects included. In other words, it should be simple.

An experienced modeller is often capable of slicing through a messy situation and quickly selecting all aspects essential for a good model, and only those. But how should a novice go about applying Ockham's razor?

An iterative process of enrichment and reformulation

Successful analysts confirm that building a model is a process of successive rounds of **enrichment** and **reformulation**. We begin with a simple model — possibly quite removed from reality — and move in an evolutionary fashion towards a more elaborate model that more closely reflects the complexity of the perceived problem situation.

This advice seems harmless enough, yet it does require a certain amount of 'guts' to back off from the real problem situation in its full complexity, and knowingly commit the sins of omitting or distorting certain aspects. The aim is to discover how much of reality can be captured by a simple model. For example, our first model may ignore most aspects of uncertainty.

On the second round, we enrich the model without changing its basic form and structure by trying to incorporate additional aspects that may be important. In other words, we add bells and whistles and see how far we get. For example, we may allow some aspects to exhibit random behaviour and then trace the consequences of this on the rest of the system. This may indicate the need to introduce slack in the form of excess capacity or buffers to provide a reasonable level of protection against a sustained run of adverse effects.

If seemingly important aspects still remain excluded, we may need to abandon the original model and reformulate the problem. This may imply changing the structure and form, or even the nature of the model. For example, rather than use a normal feedback control (i.e., steer the system in reaction to system outputs and events actually observed), use feed-forward control (i.e., predict system outputs and future events to steer the system). Sometimes, it may be advisable or necessary to switch to a different problem solving methodology, such as switching from a quantitative approach, that by necessity largely ignores the human element, to a qualitative approach that can deal more effectively with interpersonal conflicts.

The new model may itself undergo another round of enrichment until including further aspects adds little to the accuracy or predictive power of the model, or when the additional complexity may jeopardize its successful implementation.

Use an incremental approach

Often the system for the problem of interest consists of a number of interacting subsystems with strong connections within each subsystem, but only one or a few relationships with other subsystems. Rather than model the system as a whole, it may pay to gain experience by initially concentrating on only one of the subsystems. Once mastered, a second subsystem is modelled, the outputs of which become inputs into the first subsystem, or the other way around. This may require some changes to the first subsystem. Proceeding in this incremental fashion, gaining experience at each step, the analysis is extended to cover the entire system. In many instances, it may even be possible to implement the intermediate results of the subsystems analysis at each step.

Working out a numerical example

For problems with strong quantitative content, a piece of advice which we often apply ourselves is to construct an example with representative numbers and play around with them. We carefully observe how variables of interest behave. Any recurrent regular patterns found may suggest a suitable mathematical structure. We may also find analogies with other problems we are familiar with either through experience or the literature. These may suggest reasonable approximations or assumptions which make it easier to translate the relationships or the average behaviour over time into mathematics. But even if we do not discover anything earth-shattering, working through a numeric example often provides valuable insights into the behaviour of the system.

Diagrams and graphs

If you are a visual person, like many of us, you will find it helpful to see things in the form of graphs or other drawings that express relationships or patterns. Typical patterns, such as nonlinear trends, regular fluctuations, or outliers in data plots, are more readily visible from a graph than from sequences of numbers.

The shape or pattern in the graph may suggest analogies with possible completely unrelated problem situations that you know. The same approach as used there may turn out to be suitable or can be adapted suitably.

Revisiting the rich picture, mind map, or cognitive map

System modelling invariably leads to the discovery of aspects, both soft and hard, that may be missing or different from the depiction in the rich picture, mind map or cognitive map that describes the original problem situation. It is good practice, for the analyst to revisit the map and fill in additional details, i.e., alter, add, enrich or expand relevant parts. Critical scrutiny of the changes within the full problem situation also adds an element of reality check: are they consistent with all other aspects present, or do the changes raise further questions? It may show the need to go back to various stakeholders, revisit the facilities and/or data sources for clarifications, more detailed analysis and additional data collection.

5.5 Causal loop diagrams

As a rich picture or mind map conveys the complexities of an unstructured situation more effectively than prose, so can various diagrammatic representations help in clarifying both the structure and process of a system. **Causal loop** and **influence diagrams** are particuiarly insightful for bringing out the transformation process of the system. It is often the first step for the process approach to modelling.

Causal loop diagrams and feedback loops

Causal loop diagrams depict cause-and-effect relationships between various aspects, entities, or variables. If item A affects item B, this causes one or more attributes of item

B to change, such as its numeric value or its status. This is depicted by connecting the two with a directed arrow. Changes in B may, in turn, become the cause of changes in C, and so on, resulting in a chain of cause and effects.

A positive sign (or the letter 's' for 'same direction') attached to the arrow head means that an increase in the value of item A causes an increase in the value of item B, while a negative sign (or the letter 'o' for 'opposite') indicates that the increase in A results in a decrease in B.

An arrow from an item further down in the cause-and-effect chain to an earlier item is a feedback loop, as discussed in Section 3.11 (p. 47). If the number of negative signs attached to the arrows on the entire loop is odd, the loop is negative, dampening the cumulative effect, while an even number of negative signs indicates positive feedback or a destabilizing cumulative effect.

Figure 5-2 is a causal loop diagram depicting a production/inventory system.

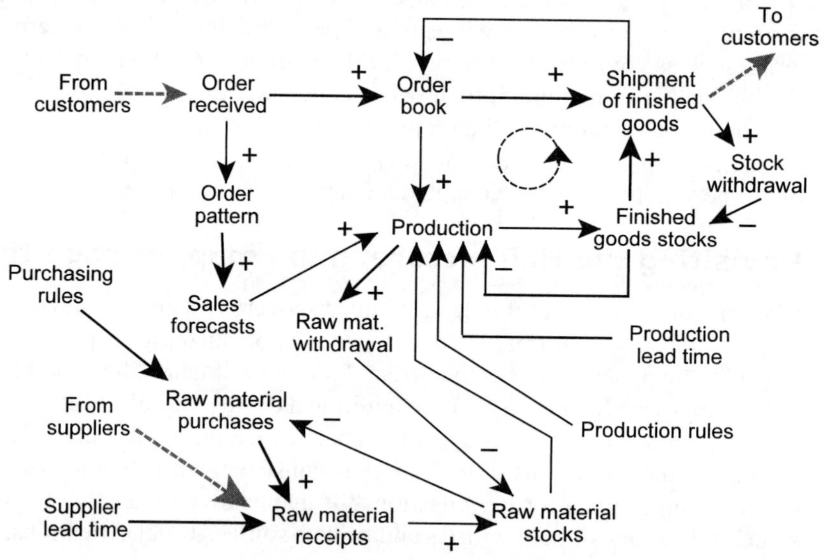

Figure 5-2 Causal loop diagram for production/inventory system

'Orders received' from customers are added to the 'order book' (the backlog of orders not yet shipped). 'Orders received' affects the 'order pattern observed', which in turn influences the 'sales forecast'. Increases in the 'order book' or the 'sales forecast' both cause an increase in 'production'. However, the response in 'production' will be delayed by the time it takes to initiate an increase and the time to produce the finished goods, labelled 'production lead time'. A rise in 'finished goods stocks' has a dampening effect on 'production'. Obviously, 'production' increases 'finished goods stocks'. Figure out the remaining relationships.

Some arrows have no signs attached. They are either constant inputs, such as the current production lead time, or they constrain an item or variable. For example, 'production' can only happen if 'raw material stocks' are sufficient.

The diagram contains two mutual cause and effects and three feedback loops (one shown by a circle), all negative, as desired. Find the other two and explain them.

A causal loop diagram similar to the one depicted in Example 5-1 on page 100 was used in the system dynamics study of the New Zealand Wine industry (Cavana et al., 1997).

Spray or fish-bone diagrams and **fault trees** are other versions of cause-and-effect diagrams. A spray diagram explores which primary factors may contribute individually or jointly to produce a given final outcome. Each primary factor may, in turn, be decomposed into more elementary factors, and so on. For example, customer dissatisfaction may be caused by product quality, salesperson error, or customer error. These primary factors in turn are broken down into more detailed factors. For product quality, this could be faulty product design, unsuitable raw materials, or manufacturing faults, the latter in turn broken into machine failure, incorrect machine adjustment, and so on.

A fault tree shows the sequence of two or more aspects or conditions that must be present at the same time to produce a final outcome. For instance, a collision at a railway crossing requires the simultaneous occurrence of a vehicle attempting a crossing and the train about to enter the crossing, each of which in turn requires the simultaneous presence of other factors, and so on.

Activity

Develop a causal loop diagram of all the aspects that may influence you (or should have influenced you) on whether or not to pursue graduate studies after completion of an undergraduate degree. Does it have any feedback loops?

5.6 Influence diagrams

Influence diagrams are more formal versions of causal loop diagrams. They are particularly useful when using a process approach. They depict diagrammatically the system transformation process. Figure 5-4 shows the diagrammatic conventions used. The notation identifies the nature of the various elements included: uncontrollable inputs, control inputs, outputs, **state variables** representing the status of attributes of system components, and the direction of the influence relationship. Each attribute of a system component has its own separate state variable.

For numeric attributes, the state variable measures its value. For instance, in the production/inventory system depicted in Figure 5-2, 'raw material withdrawal' is a system component. It has only one attribute, i.e., the quantity or the rate of raw materials withdrawn. This is its state variable. It reduces the value of 'raw material stocks', another state variable, by the same amount.

However, influence diagrams are equally effective for depicting non-quantitative relationships, such as the presence or absence of a given property, or a qualitative description captured by a gradation 'very strong' 'moderately strong', 'average', 'weak', and 'absent'. (Note that this gradation could also be expressed numerically by a five point scale of 5, 4, 3, 2, 1.)

Example 5-1: New Zealand wine industry

The New Zealand wine industry grew from a few hundred hectares in the early 1970s to over 10,000 hectares by the year 2000. The causal loop diagram in Figure 5-3 explains what factors affect wine production and the planting of new vineyards. The model makes the strong simplification that the wine industry is homogeneous, i.e., that all grapes and wines follow the same behavioural patterns.

One feedback loop is highlighted by the arrows with thick lines. There are four more, one of them positive. Identify them and find which one is the positive one. Fortunately, its destabilizing effect is counteracted by another loop with which it shares most of the causal links.

Since all aspects shown can be expressed quantitatively, the relationships can be captured in mathematical form. Using system dynamics software, such as *ithink* (see Section 17.6, p. 505), it is possible to trace out numerically the effect of various policies of grower support, of the government excise duty, or of the world price of wines.

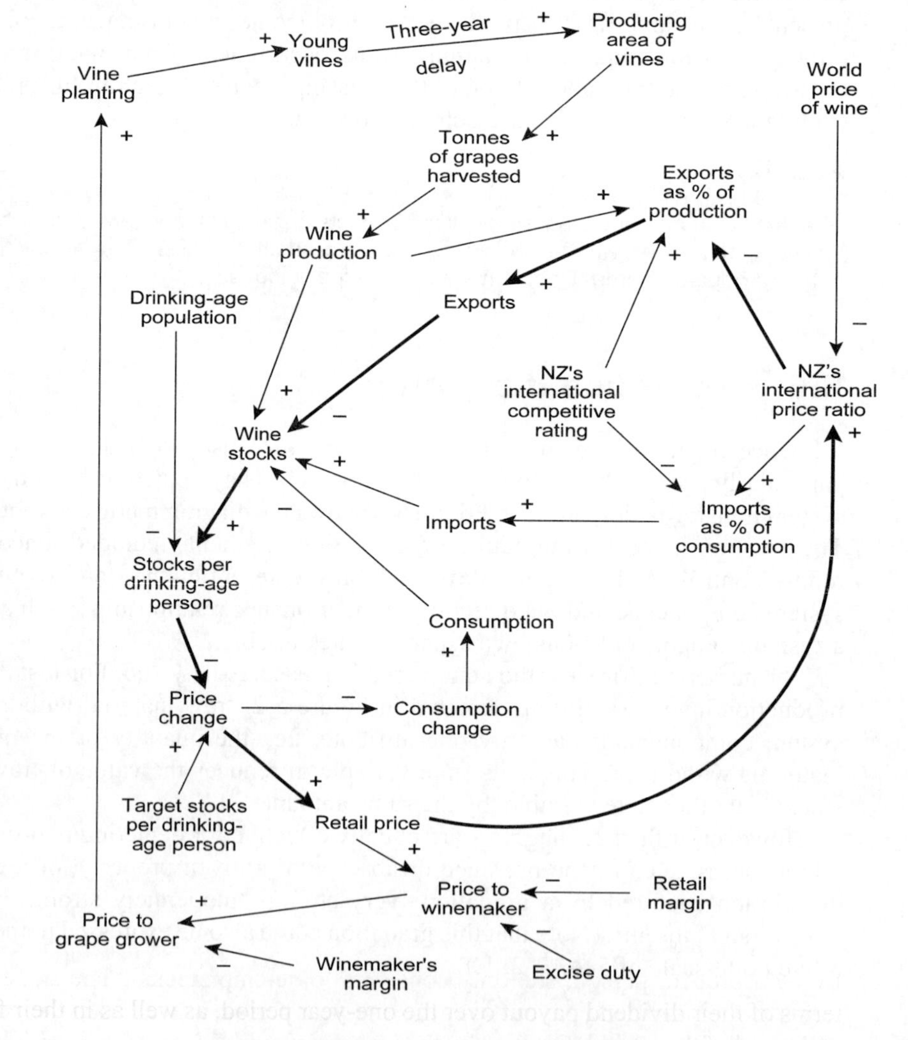

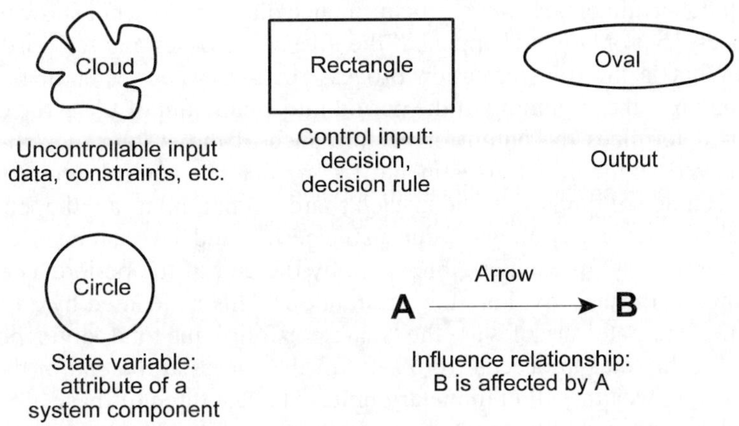

Figure 5-4 Diagrammatic conventions for influence diagrams

Using the symbols depicted in Figure 5-4, Figure 5-5 shows the influence diagram for an investment decision in shares.

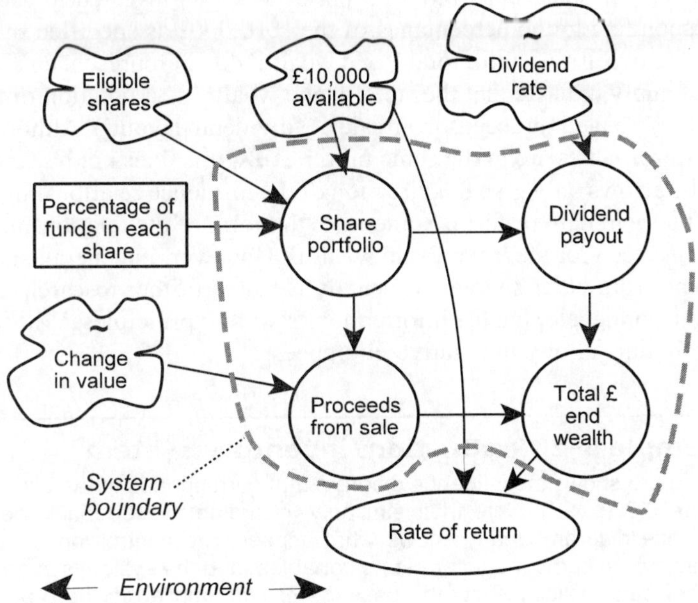

Figure 5-5 Influence diagram of investment system

Assume an investor considers putting £10,000 into company shares for one year. Being a prudent person, she only considers 'blue-chip stocks'. The shares differ in terms of their dividend payout over the one-year period, as well as in their final value at the end of the period. Obviously, the investor would like to determine a portfolio of shares (i.e., a combination from various firms) that yields the highest return on the £10,000 available. However, the influence diagram does not show that maximization process, but only what happens if the investor chooses a given portfolio of shares.

What is the transformation process of this system? It transforms the input of £10,000 at the beginning of the period into an amount of £X at the end of the period. This determines the output or performance of the system, i.e., the 'rate of return' achieved on the initial investment of £10,000. The control input (or decision) is the 'percentage of funds invested in each share'. Other inputs are the 'eligible shares', the likely 'dividend payout rates' during the period, and the 'change in value' (capital gain or capital loss) of each eligible share by the end of the period. The last two are not known with certainty, i.e., they are random. This is denoted by a tilde (~) over their name. The state variables are the 'share portfolio', the total 'dividend payout' over all shares, the total 'proceeds from sale' of the shares at the end of the period, and the 'total end wealth', all in monetary units. The last three of these are also uncertain or random, given that some of the inputs are random. The boundary of the system is delineated by the half-tone broken line which encloses the four state variables (done here only for demonstration).

This diagram does not show a physical flow of money or funds over the year. The arrows simply indicate an influence relationship of an input or a state variable on another state variable or an output, but not necessarily a physical flow of anything. For instance, the 'share portfolio' is a list of amounts invested in each 'eligible share', corresponding to the percentages of the '£10,000', as specified by the control input. Even the two arrows into 'total £ end wealth' do not represent an actual flow of funds. They simply indicate that the 'total £ end wealth' is a function of the other two state variables (in fact, 'proceeds from sale' + 'dividend payout'). Although in this example, all state variables are in the same unit, i.e., £s, this does not have to be so.

The arrows only give the direction of the influence relationships, but no indication as to their strength or form. Sometimes the form of the relationship is obvious, as we have just seen for the 'total £ end wealth'. However, in general, such information has to come from other sources. It usually requires further research, data gathering and analysis, or developing the information from first principles. Without it, the influence diagram only allows qualitative inferences.

Example 5-2: Production/inventory system

Figure 5-6 shows the influence diagram that corresponds to the causal loop diagram in Figure 5-2 (p. 98). Note their similarity, including the feedback loops. However, the influence diagram clearly shows what aspects are control inputs and uncontrollable inputs, which components are state variables, and the system's outputs. Unfortunately, neither can explicitly show the passage of time implied in the process. For instance, 'finished goods stocks' is affected by the 'production rate', by 'stock withdrawals', both occurring over time, and by the 'finished goods stocks' carried forward from before. This explains the arrows leading back from 'finished goods stocks' to itself.

Although at first glance it may seem that several of the arrows show a flow of material, this is not so. For instance, the arrow from 'raw material stocks' to 'production rate' relates information as to the availability of raw materials. Obviously, the production rate is restricted by the amount of raw materials on hand. It does not signify a flow of raw material to the production process. Similarly, the arrows from 'production rate' back to 'raw material stocks' convey information as to the amount of raw materials used in the production.

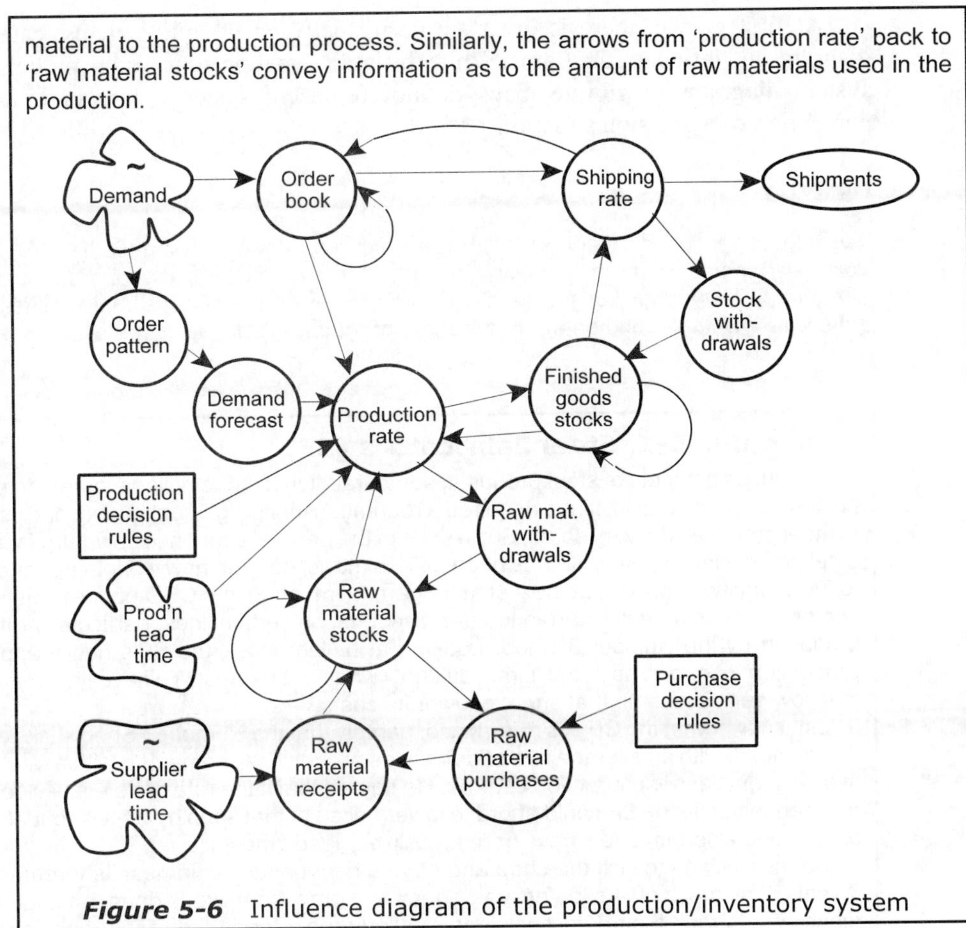

Figure 5-6 Influence diagram of the production/inventory system

Here are a few ground rules to remember: by the very definition of an input, arrows can only leave a cloud (an uncontrollable input) or a rectangle (a control input), but must never enter either of them. Again, by the definition of an output, arrows can only end at an oval (an output), never leave one. Circles (state variables) must have at least one arrow entering that originates either at a cloud, rectangle, or another circle, and at least one arrow leaving to another circle or an oval. They cannot be the head or the end of a chain of influences.

Influence diagrams and causal loop diagrams help explore complexity in a system. As mentioned earlier, an influence diagram is often an effective means with which to define a relevant system for the issue studied. In such instances, it becomes a substitute for a more formal system definition based on the four-rule scheme summarized in Table 5-1 (p. 92). As with rich pictures, both facilitate and clarify the communication process between analysts, and between analysts and clients. However, there are situations where an influence diagram may not be a suitable vehicle to bring out the structure of a decision problem unambiguously and clearly. One or the other of the diagrammatic aids in the next section may be able to shed more light on the problem and its structure.

(At first glance, there is great similarity between cognitive maps, causal loop diagram, and influence diagrams. While the latter two represent system models and are system diagrams, cognitive maps do not represent systems, but an individual's perception of a decision situation.)

Activity

Develop an influence diagram for the service call centre in Example 1-1 (p. 2). The diagram should show at least two outputs: the total cost of the operation and the frequency distribution for the length of time callers have to wait until their calls are answered. Both depend on the number of operators on duty.

Case study 5-1: Steel Fabricators (SF)

SF produces a variety of steel products, some traditional industry lines, others to special customer specifications. It had acquired a reputation for its high quality work and its ability to meet promised delivery dates. So, in spite of the general economic downturn facing the steel processing industry, SF has been able to attract enough new work to operate close to full capacity. However, at the last management meeting, the CEO pointed out that the competition has recently started to offer discounts on certain lines, particularly on those produced by the Number 3 Shop. Looking at E. Lim Nate, the SF's newly appointed production manager, he adds: 'Lim, you know what that means. We have little choice but to follow suit. Shake up that shop to lower its costs.'

Lim knows what the CEO is referring to, namely that the Number 3 Shop sticks out like a sore thumb with an average rate of defectives of over 12%, compared with a rate of less than 2% for all other production centres. He figures that if the rate of defectives could be reduced to that level, SF could afford to lower prices of that shop by 5% without affecting profits, and also trim a few days from its delivery lead times.

So, he decides to visit the shop and have a serious talk to James, its foreman. This reveals that most of the defectives seem to come from work done on four of the machines. In fact, their defective rates regularly reach one-third of the machines' total output, while the remaining machines are not out of line with the rest of the plant. Although James is well aware of the problem, he tells Lim bluntly: 'My guys are following the rules for maintenance and machine adjustments issued by the machine's manufacturer to the last bloody detail.'

Indeed, some months ago, after he was been promoted to foreman of the shop, he says that he looked into this matter. He discovered that these machines tended to get out of adjustment over time, with a resulting increase in the rate of defectives. Re-adjusting the machine brought the rate down again, although it was still considerably higher than for other machines. At that time, the machine operators adjusted the machines whenever they figured that the rate of defectives was getting excessive, somewhere between every 45 and 50 minutes, less than the one hour recommended in the manufacturer's operating manual. He thinks that machine age can be the only logical explanation. 'They should be replaced,' he adds. There is one bright spot. About half of the defectives can be reworked on another machine, although that takes one operator about 12 minutes per part. The other defectives unfortunately have to be scrapped.

Back in his office, Lim checks the files for their date of purchase. They are only five years old and should last for another eight to ten years. Checking the manufacturer's website, he discovers to his consternation that no changes have been made to their specifications. This essentially rules out advanced age as the reason for the problem. He feels thwarted. This morning he was all fired up to tackle the defectives problem of Number 3 Shop. And now the situation looks rather hopeless, particularly since the manufacturer seems to be of no help! But maybe lowering the run time between adjustments even further might produce positive results. He decides to investigate this.

Next morning, Lim calls James. He asks him to watch one operator for a whole hour and mark down the exact time when a defective part is produced. By ten o'clock, James brings him the result. Defective parts were produced after 12, 22, 32, 38, 42, 46, 50, 54, 56, 60 minutes. When questioned whether this is typical, James replies that things vary a bit from run to run, but that the general pattern is similar. He also says that the reason why all numbers are even is that it takes two minutes to produce one part. As an afterthought he mentions that a normal re-adjustment takes about 6 minutes.

Develop an influence diagram that shows how the difference between the revenue from selling good parts and all costs incurred for the parts produced for one machine over an eight-hour day is affected by the time between machine adjustments. This difference covers material costs for all parts and the wage cost for the operator of the machine, including the wage cost or reworking defective parts. Assume that the machine operating costs are negligible. Note that the time between adjustments does not have to result in an integer number of adjustments per hour.

5.7 Other system diagrams

Flow charts are another type of diagram, depicting logical and temporal relationships.

Material or information flow charts

The temporal flow of materials or goods through a process, or the logical sequence of processing, storing, and retrieving information can be depicted by a material or information flow chart. This is demonstrated by an example of a beer-making process.

Beer production

The process of making beer consists of converting grain starches to sugar and then fermenting it with yeast to produce an alcoholic, lightly carbonated beverage. It is a multistage process under strict hygienic and temperature-controlled conditions. Barley (or some other starchy grain) is steeped in water for 40 to 50 hours, raising the water content in the grains to about 45%, thereby activating germination. This increases their malt content. The 'green barley' is then dried in a kiln, screened to remove little roots that may have formed, and stored temporarily in a silo.

The actual beer production process starts with crushing the barley to 'grist'. It is mixed with two to three times the volume of water to produce a mash, where enzyme action releases the sugar. This liquid, called 'wort', is separated from the husks and spent grains, mixed with hops in a copper kettle, and boiled for up to 90 minutes to stop germination and infuse the bitter and aromatic qualities of the hops into the liquid. At the same time, undesirable aromas are allowed to evaporate. The spent hops and other insoluble proteins are removed in a whirlpool separator. The wort passes through a cooling stage where additional oxygen is added. The liquid is stored in huge stainless steel vats, yeast is added, which initiates fermentation of the sugar into alcohol, releasing CO_2 in the process.

Fermentation takes from two to ten days, depending on the type of beer. It is arrested by cooling the liquid, removing most of the yeast, and transferring the green beer into conditioning and maturing vessels for several weeks, where slow fermentation continues under pressure, raising the level of dissolved carbon dioxide to the desired level. The beer is once more filtered to remove any clouding. The bright beer is stored until it is bottled, pasteurized, labelled, and packed, ready for shipment to customers.

If you fully grasped this lengthy explanation, congratulations. If not, the material flow chars in Figure 5-7 might help.

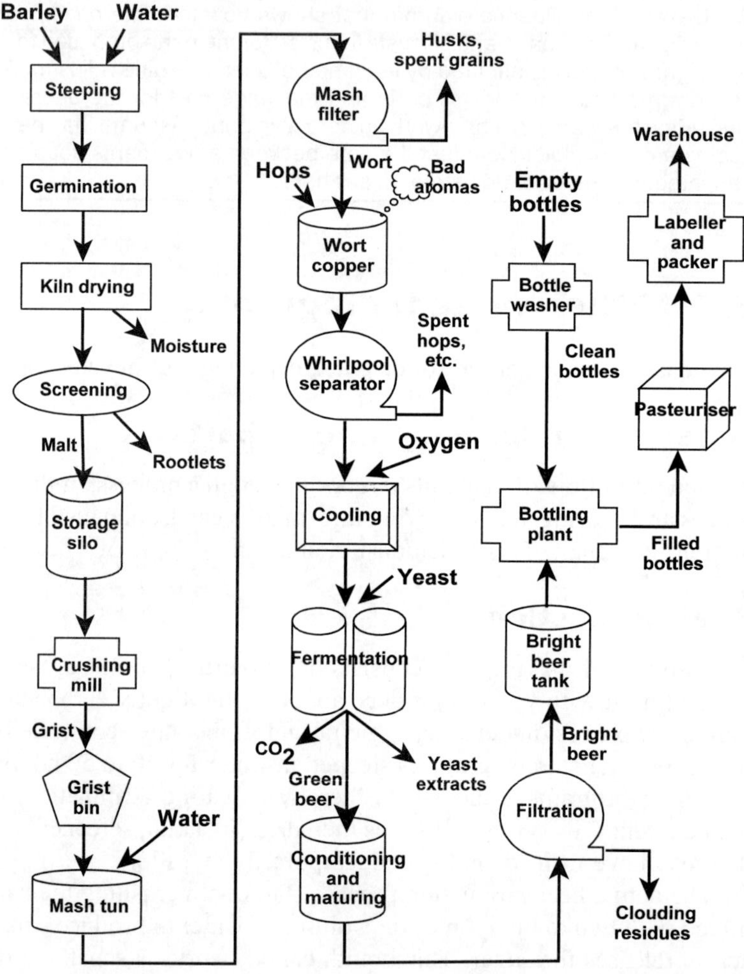

Figure 5-7 Material flow for beer-making process

It is obvious that such a diagram allows you to visualize the system quickly and without much explanation, except maybe for a table of keys to the symbols used. It is much more effective than the verbal descriptions that are often confusing and difficult to follow. If drawn entirely as a horizontal sequence, adding a time scale below the flow diagram also shows the temporal phasing of the process.

Most manufacturing firms use material flow charts to introduce new employees or visitors to their operations. Capture the flow of information and data, instead of goods, and you get an information flow chart. They are essential for making sense of the myriad links involved in the generation of data and information at various sources, where and in what form they are stored and updated, by whom and for what purpose the data and information may be further processed, analysed and combined, thereby producing new information, and who has access to it at what level of security.

Activity

Draw a material flow chart for the blood bank operation in Case study 3-1 (p. 54).

Precedence charts

Many projects consist of a large number of individual tasks that have to be performed in a specific sequence. While some may be done simultaneously, others can only be started after one or several other task(s) have been completed. The task(s) may also have to share scarce resources, such as equipment or specific job skills. Construction jobs, overhauls and maintenance of large installations, research and development projects, a major move into new facilities, even the production of a film or a show all require a coordinated plan for the execution of the all tasks that make up the project.

Figure 5-8 on page 108 shows the 26 tasks for building a house and their temporal sequence. The arrows indicate the precedence in which the tasks have to be performed. Preparing building plans is the first task. Once that has been completed, an application for obtaining the building permit can be filed, at the same time as making arrangements for financing the project, and so on.

Computing the minimum elapse time for completing a project — critical path scheduling

The times required for each task are indicated by the number next to the top left of each box in Figure 5-8. Task 1 'Prepare building plans' takes two weeks. That task is completed by the end of week 2. This is indicated by the bold number to the bottom right of the corresponding box. Task 2 'Obtain building permit' and task 6 'Arrange finance' can only be initiated after completion of task 1, i.e., at the beginning of week 3. Task 2 is completed four weeks later, namely by the end of week 6 (2 + 4), again shown by the bold number to the right of the box. Tasks 3, 4 and 5, 'Prepare building site', 'Pour foundations', and 'Build floor', take one week each and are completed by the end of week 9. Tasks 6, 7, 8 and 9 can be done in parallel with 2 to 5. Tasks 6 to 8 take five weeks and can be finished at the earliest by week 7. Since task 10 has to wait for both these subsequences to be completed, it only can be started at the earliest at the beginning of week 10, i.e., after task 5 has been completed. Note the subsequence of tasks 6 to 8 could be delayed by up to two weeks without delaying the start of task 10. But a delay in any of tasks 2 to 5 will delay completion of the project.

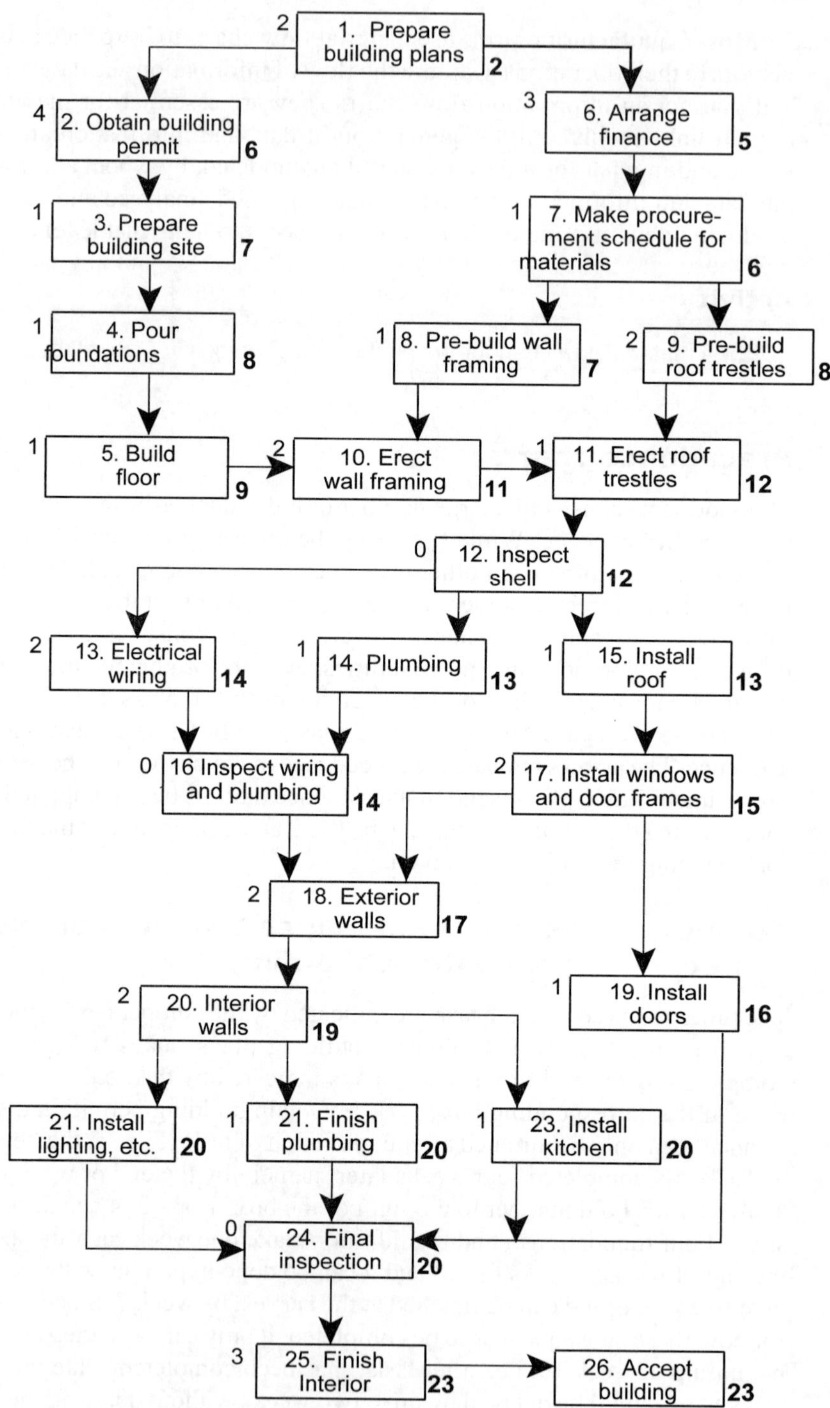

Figure 5-8 Precedence chart for building a house

Task 11 can be started when both tasks 10 and 9 are done. Since task 10 has a later completion date than 9, task 11 can only start at the earliest after week 11. Using this logic, verify that the earliest the house can be accepted is at the end of week 23.

There is at least one path of consecutive tasks from start to end where any delay will cause the project as a whole to be delayed. These are called **critical tasks**. Which are critical in Figure 5-8?

Precedence charts are used to determine which sequence of tasks is critical. These are those that need to be tightly controlled so as to avoid any delays. This type of analysis is called **critical path scheduling**. It is extensively used for initial planning and day-to-day control of all sorts of project work that involve multiple tasks, some of which can be done in parallel.

Activity

Construct a precedence chart for a market survey, where the letters in brackets list the predecessor tasks, and the number is the length of the task in days:

- A: design preliminary questionnaire [2]
- B: determine sampling design [3]
- C: test preliminary questionnaire [A; 4]
- D: prepare final version of questionnaire [C; 1]
- E: prepare list of people to be surveyed [B; 2]
- F: print required number of questionnaires [D, B; 5]
- G: recruit interviewers [B; 4]
- H: train interviewers [G, D; 2]
- I: conduct interviews [E, F, H; 10]
- J: process questionnaires [I; 3]
- K: analyse results [J; 5]
- L: write survey report for sponsor [K; 2]

Can you determine the number of days required to complete the survey? Which tasks are critical?

Decision flow charts

A decision flow chart shows the logical sequence of alternative choices available, conditions tested and resulting actions taken, and so on, for each possible path from the initial situation to a final outcome. You may have been introduced to decision trees in an introductory course in statistics. They are a type of decision flow chart.

The Lubrication Oil Division (analysed in more detail in Chapter 6) produces various types and grades of lubrication oils. Customer orders for these products vary in size quite considerably — small orders from local service stations, large orders from wholesalers and big national department store chains. A customer order received for a given product can be executed in two different ways. The first is to make a special production run for the exact amount ordered and ship it direct to the customer. The second is to withdraw the product requested from inventory and ship it. Since small production runs are uneconomical, small orders are met from inventory. Special production runs are only made for large orders. The customer order processing clerk uses the following criterion to decide if a customer order is small or large: if the order is equal to a cut-off point L or larger, the order is considered 'large', if smaller than L, it is 'small'.

Meeting small orders gradually reduces the inventory. Sooner or later not enough is left in stock to meet the last small order received. At this point, a new production run of size Q is scheduled to replenish the inventory. Once the product has been added to stock, the small customer order that triggered the replenishment is shipped.

Again, congratulations if you understood this fully at the first reading. Now study the corresponding decision flow chart of Figure 5-9, which is much easier to follow.

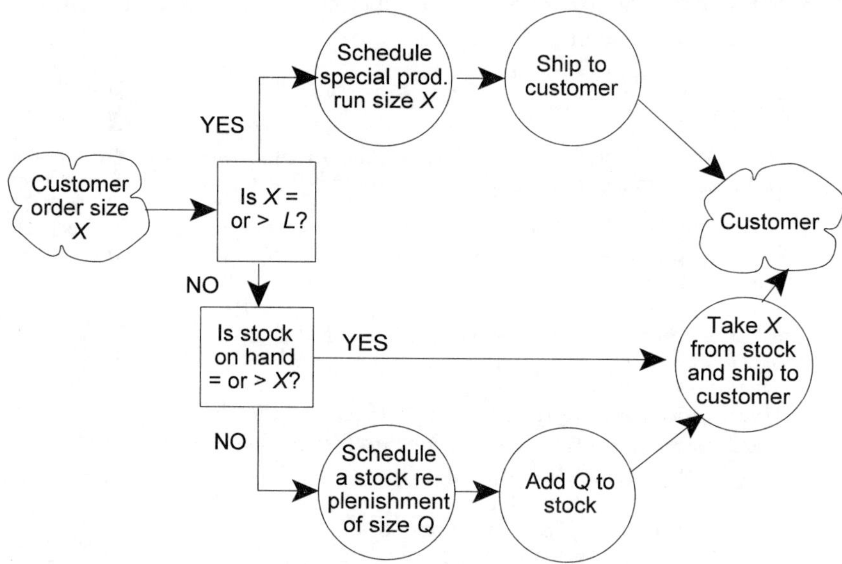

Figure 5-9 Decision flow chart for a production/stock control problem

Activity

> You are inviting a group of friends to a formal dinner party. Draw a decision flow chart for the various decisions you need to make. Include such aspects as: cleaning, who to invite, whether you do the cooking yourself, or cater out for parts of it, and so on.

5.8 Chapter highlights

- A system definition is a symbolic model. This model should clearly indicate the system boundary, the controllable and the uncontrollable inputs into the system, its activity, behaviour or transformation process, and the outputs of the system.
- A structural approach makes use of typical, known structures or configurations, while a process approach defines the system from first principles.

- Good models are simple, complete, easy to manipulate and communicate with, adaptive to changes in the problem situation, and appropriate and relevant for decision making for the problem studied. Some of these properties are in conflict.
- Modelling is an iterative process of enrichment and reformulation. Few models are 'final' after a single pass.
- Causal loop diagrams and influence diagrams show the influence relationships between system components, controllable and uncontrollable inputs, and system outputs, thereby delineating the system boundaries.
- Other diagrammatic models highlight the sequence of processes, the flow of material, precedence relationships between different activities, or the logic of the decision process.

Exercises

1. For the service call centre situation in Example 1-1 (p. 2), apply a process approach to define a suitable system for exploring how many telephone operators the centre should hire, so as to explore the trade-off between waiting time and centre operating costs. Use any diagrammatic aid you judge suitable to reveal its structure.
2. For the breast cancer situation in Example 1-4 (p. 5), seen from a governmental angle, apply a process approach to define a suitable system for exploring the consequences of different breast cancer screening policy choices on the various conflicting goals. Use any diagrammatic aid you judge suitable to reveal its structure.
3. Draw a causal loop diagram for the breast cancer screening situation in Example 1-4 (p. 5).
4. Develop a causal loop diagram for the NuWave Shoes problem in Section 4.8 (Elly Schuhmacher's nightmare, pp. 74–5). How does it differ from Elly's cognitive map?
5. Consider the relationships between unemployment, poverty, public health expenditures, family breakdown, and crime. Draw a causal loop diagram.
6. Draw an influence diagram for how the various aspects and decision choices affect the mortality rate in the breast cancer screening situation described in Example 1-4 (p. 5). What boundary judgements are implied by the system defined in the diagram?
7. Draw an influence diagram for the blood bank operation described in Case study 3-1 (p. 54). It should clearly show the direct or indirect effects of the controllable actions and decisions on the two performance measures of shortages and outdating. Note that the aspect of optimization is not shown, only the results of decision choices, and so on. What boundary judgements are implied in the system defined by the diagram?
8. The production process for an electric toothbrush consists of the following operations: PVC compounds are procured from a local supplier. PVC is used for: (a) moulding the tooth-brush case, which houses the motor and battery; (b) the housing of the recharging unit; and (c) the holder for the brushes (which slots into the recharging unit). Rechargeable batteries are purchased from a supplier, and are installed in the toothbrush case. The firm produces its own electric motors from parts purchased from suppliers. It also makes its own brushes, using purchased bristle material, which is moulded into PVC. Once the toothbrush and recharging unit are assembled, all parts plus one spare brush and an instruction booklet are packaged into a cardboard box. Draw a material flow chart for this process.
9. Draw a material flow chart for the bread-making operation in a commercial bakery.

10. The tasks for making kite kits are as follows: [predecessors; time in minutes]
    A: cut cloth to shape of kite [2]
    B: sew seams and sleeves on cloth, attach dowel slots [A; 8]
    C: cut plastic dowels [3]
    D: attach metal end pieces to dowels [C: 2]
    E: measure and cut string, spool on roll [4]
    F: pre-assemble parts of the frame [B, D; 1]
    G: roll up kite around remaining dowels [F; 1]
    H: package rolled-up kite, string, and assembly and flying instructions [E, G.; 2]
    (a) If one person does all the tasks, how long does it take for one kite? Which tasks are critical?
    (b) If two people can work at the same time, side by side, each doing different sets of tasks simultaneously, how does that change things?
11. Assume that you have at most £10,000 available to buy a 'pre-loved' car. Draw a decision flow chart for this purchase decision. You may not want to spend all the money. You may buy from a dealer or privately. You may want to have the car professionally inspected.

Further reading

Cavana, R.Y. et al. (1997) 'A policy making framework for the N.Z. wine industry', *System Dynamics*, IX(1):1–19. Figure 5-3 is an adaptation of the one in this paper.

Lane, A. (2000) *Systems Thinking and Practice: a Primer*, Milton Keynes: Open University Press. Course material for T205 and T306.

Lane, A. (1999), *Systems Thinking and Practice: Diagramming*, Milton Keynes: Open University Press. Course material for T205 and T306.

Little, J.D.C. (1970) 'Models and managers: concepts of decision calculus', *Management Science*, April.

Naughton, J. (1984) *Soft Systems Analysis: An Introductory Guide*, Technology Course T301: Block 4, Milton Keynes: Open University Press. Down-to-earth text. Together with its *Workbook*, this is one of the best accounts of the use of rich pictures and other systems diagrams.

Open University, Milton Keynes: the systems modules in the technology series have a number of relevant CDs for systems thinking, systems concepts, and diagramming.

PART II

MS/OR methodologies

Part II surveys how systems thinking is applied in the two major strands of MS/OR methodologies, i.e., the hard OR/hard systems and the soft OR/soft systems views. For a better understanding of their underlying paradigms, process and practice, it is helpful to consider first their scope and areas of application.

Jackson and Keys (1984) classify problem situations along two dimensions: **complexity** and **divergence of values and interests**. Complexity refers to the number of elements or aspects in a problem situation and their interactions. Few elements and well-defined, linear, stable interactions imply low complexity, while many elements, many interrelationships, dynamic and not well-understood relationships in a turbulent environment imply high complexity. Complexity is either **technical** — the physical and logical relationships and/or the mathematical and computational nature of the problem and its context, or is caused by a **degree of uncertainty** — the higher the degree of uncertainty present in a situation, the higher the level of complexity.

Divergence of views is divided into **unitary**, **pluralistic**, and **conflicting/coercive**. 'Unitary' implies stakeholders share a common worldview. 'Pluralist' implies multiple compatible worldviews that differ in emphasis, but allow trade-offs to reach mutually acceptable compromises. 'Conflicting/coercive' implies irreconcilable, competitive worldviews that render voluntary compromise difficult, and where differences in power relationships imply that one party is coerced into accepting a 'solution' imposed by another. This constitutes an extreme case. In practice, differences in power may range from the subtle effect of claims to expertise, seniority, or status to the dependent employee/ employer relationship and, ultimately, to the coercive force of the absolute dictator or law enforcer. Attempts at deception by one party are included here. A term, such as 'asymmetry or distortion in communications' would be a better description than 'coercive'. Few, if any, any real-life situations are ever entirely free of such distortions (Ulrich, 2003). Most real-life situations involve aspects of all three views.

Some examples may clarify these distinctions. A multinational firm has *m* manufacturing plants, each with limited production capacity. It operates *n* distribution centres. How much should each factory produce and ship to each distribution centre so as to meet the known demand at each centre. The objective is to minimize the sum of all production and shipping costs. This problem exhibits low technical complexity in terms of logical structure, as well as computational effort. It also has zero degrees of uncertainty.

Contrast this with the problem faced each morning by the scheduler of a pick-up and delivery service, who faces a large number of requests from clients all over the city. He or she has to develop itineraries for the *m* vans available, subject to vehicle capacities, fixed driver shifts, and time windows specified by clients. The objective is minimization of total costs. If all requests are known, this problem also has zero degrees of uncertainty. However, it exhibits high technical complexity, both in terms of its logical structure and the computational difficulties.

Since both problems involve cost minimization as the objective, they fall into the 'unitary' sphere. Neither involves uncertainty. If the demands for the distribution centres are uncertain — they may fall within a likely range — or only a portion of the customer requests in the van scheduling problem are known at the beginning of the day while the rest come in any time during the day, the degree of uncertainty is raised, while not necessarily affecting the degree of technical complexity.

The breast cancer situation of Example 1-4 (p. 5) falls into the pluralist sphere. There are multiple stakeholders with partially conflicting but reconcilable values and interests. However, its technical complexity is low. The physical structure is well-known. Since extensive data on statistical incidences of breast cancer and the success of treatment outcomes are available, its degree of uncertainty is also low.

On the other hand, the 'Greenhouse' debate is at the other extreme: highly conflicting worldviews and extreme differences in economic and political power between stakeholders (e.g., economically powerful oil companies versus weak citizen-based environmental groups, politically powerful countries versus small Pacific island states, political parties with radically different views), high technical complexity because of multiple physical, environmental, and economic interactions and processes, which are not fully understood, and a high degree of uncertainty as to future scientific, technological, and economic developments, as well as political uncertainties.

These three dimensions classify the three main streams of MS/OR approaches, as shown in Figure II-1. (The areas have fuzzy boundaries. They overlap. The volume of each area is not intended to reflect the number of problem situations contained.)

Functionalist systems approaches assume that systems catch or represent aspects of existing or future reality, largely independent of the observer. Different observers would basically agree on the same system and share the same goals or objectives — sometimes referred to as 'objective' (i.e., meaning a consensual subjectivity). Note that this does not imply that different observers and modellers may not draw their system boundaries differently, put main emphasis on different systems aspects, or select a different degree of resolution to model the system. The main concern of functionalist systems approaches is with 'How to do it' questions, assuming that the 'What to do' questions have already been resolved. Hard OR, systems engineering, systems analysis, and cybernetics are the prime methodologies. They have seen numerous successful applications in situations of high technical complexity and where uncertainty can be captured by probability distributions. However, they only cope with low human complexity and a low to medium divergence of interests (such as multiple objectives rather than differences in worldview).

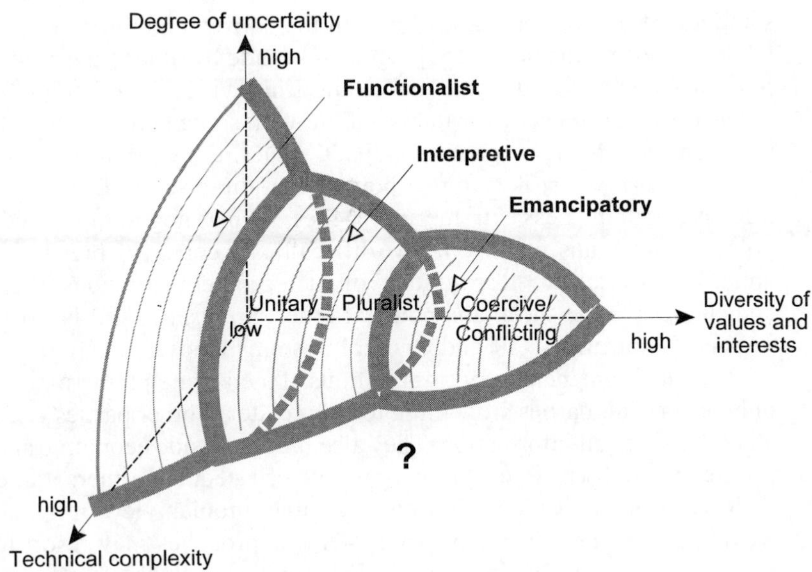

Figure II-1 Problem situation classification and systems approaches
(adapted from Jackson, 2000)

Few activities in today's world have not been touched by hard OR analysis, from private business and industry to public and environmental issues, from government policies to personal leisure activities. You flip a light switch and become a customer of a hard OR project controlling power generation. You use a cell phone and you profit from several different hard OR analyses. Even cricket, baseball, and yachting strategies have been successfully subjected to hard OR.

Interpretive systems approaches adopt a 'subjectivist' approach to systems thinking. The system defined reflects the observer's worldview and perceptions. It is not assumed to exist in this form in reality, but is seen as a personal conceptualization of what the observer sees as a useful and convenient representation of inter-relationships between the various aspects and stakeholders. Although interpretive approaches allow a certain divergence of interests and views, they assume there is a sufficient sharing of interests between stakeholders. Hence they consider it to their advantage to cooperate.

Interpretive systems approaches focus mainly on 'What?' rather than on 'How?' questions. Their main aim is to learn more about the behaviour of the system in view of bringing about, if not a shared set of values, at least a shared commitment to action. They can cope with a fair degree diversity of interests and values, but have greater difficulty in dealing with technical complexity and uncertainty, responding to the latter mainly on an intuitive or contingency level. These approaches are increasingly being applied for practical problem solving in both the private and public sectors.

Emancipatory systems approaches also take a 'subjectivist' view. However, the various stakeholders may have partially or radically different, conflicting or opposing worldviews that may be irreconcilable. They may disagree on which 'facts' are relevant, and on their interpretation. They see different relevant systems and choose substantively different boundaries for both the narrow and the wider system of interest, while contesting the boundary judgements made by other stakeholders. They may be in a conflicting or confrontational relationship with each other and possibly unequal in terms of their power over the situation, with some being in the role of victims.

Their main focus is again on 'What?' issues. For extreme cases of 'coercion', the 'coerced' may see strikes, direct political action, or civil disobedience as their only effective options. Less extreme approaches, such as negotiation, mediation, law suits, political campaigns, and so on, have difficulties to cope with high technical complexity and high uncertainty. 'Resolutions' of such problem situations may involve reforms and changes in the social and political order. So far, MS/OR has offered little in this respect. **Community OR** and **Critical Systems Heuristics** are the exception.

The label 'emancipatory' is ambitious. True emancipation of all stakeholders can only occur if all parties are willing to appreciate all other parties' views and interests, and fully share all information. They also must set aside economic and political power differences and seek a resolution of problems as equal partners, rather than imposing their will from a position of power — a rather utopian view of human nature.

Interpretive and emancipatory systems approaches may resort to a functionalist methodology when dealing with those 'How?' aspects that can be quantified.

Chapter 6 demonstrates our version of the hard OR methodology with a real life case. It cycles through a well-defined set of steps, from exploring the problem situation to implementation of the solution. By necessity, the treatment is succinct. Its aim is to give you an informed appreciation of the methodology, without going into details of MS/OR techniques and tools. These are the topic of Part IV of this text.

Chapter 7 discusses common aspects found in many soft OR approaches. Three are studied in some detail. However, the treatment never goes beyond an appreciation level. Unfortunately, competent use of these methods requires considerable experience and exposure. Most cannot be mastered by reading a textbook, even one devoted exclusively to a given method, but are learned by hands-on practice under the guidance of an experienced facilitator or by participating in specialized workshops.

Implementation of recommendations, the difficulties associated with it, and the professional and ethical responsibilities of the analyst conclude this overview.

References

Checkland, P. and Scholes, J. (1999) *Systems Thinking, Systems Practice, includes a 30-year retrospective*, Chichester: Wiley.

Jackson, M. (2003) *Systems Thinking: Creative Holism for Managers*, Chichester: Wiley.

Jackson, M.C. (2000) *Systems Approaches to Management*, New York: Kluwer/Plenum.

Jackson, M. and Keys, P. (1984) 'Towards a system of systems methodologies', *Journal of the Operational Research Society*, 35: 473–86.

Rosenhead, J. and Mingers, J.C. (eds) (2000) *Rational Analysis for a Problematic World Revisited*, Chichester: Wiley.

Ulrich, W. (2003) 'Beyond methodology choice: critical systems thinking as critically systemic discourse', *Journal of the Operational Research Society*, 54(4): 325–42.

6

Overview of hard OR methodology

Learning objectives

- Appreciate that the hard OR methodology is an iterative process with forward and backward linkages.
- Be able to judge when problem scoping, rather than a firm project proposal, may be more appropriate for a given problem situation.
- Be able to determine whether a project proposal contains all aspects the problem owner/decision maker should know in order to be able to make an informed decision as to whether to proceed or not.
- Be able, for a relatively simple problem situation, to apply a process approach to formulate a mathematical model via a suitable system diagram and enhance and/or reformulate it to incorporate additional aspects.
- Be able to apply the EOQ model to a stock control problem, and perform error and sensitivity analysis.
- Be able to judge whether the final project report contains all aspects the problem owner/decision maker and users need to know for implementing the solutions and for its continued use (if relevant).

Introduction

Operations researchers broadly agree on the basic steps of what is a good hard OR practice, although they may package some activities differently or place their emphasis on different aspects. This chapter gives our preferred version of the hard OR methodology — together with points of practical experience.

The first six sections cover a general overview of the hard OR methodology, while the remainder of the chapter demonstrates the various steps with a real-life application. The appendices give samples of report writing.

6.1 Hard OR paradigm overview

Hard OR approaches explicitly and implicitly are based on the following assumptions:

1. The problem has been clearly defined, i.e.,
   - the objectives of the decision maker are known and there exist criteria to ascertain when they have been achieved;
   - if there are conflicting objectives, trade-offs can be defined;
   - the alternative courses of action are known, either as a list of options or a set of decision variables;
   - the constraints on the decision choices are known; and
   - all input data needed are available or can be collected at reasonable cost.
2. The problem is relatively well structured, i.e.,
   - the relationships between the variables are tractable;
   - system behaviour can be captured in mathematical models; and
   - the computational effort for determining solutions is economically feasible.
3. The problem can be sufficiently well-insulated from its wider system.
4. Optimization of the objectives, whenever possible, is the ideal.
5. The problem is of a technical nature, devoid of politics; people are mainly seen as passive objects.
6. If there are multiple stakeholders, a consensus can be reached about all aspects that affect how well the objectives can be achieved.
7. The decision maker has the power and authority to implement the 'solution' or enforce implementation through the hierarchical chain of command.

(In Chapter 7 we shall contrast these assumptions with the ones for soft OR.)

Although in practice not all of these properties may be satisfied for a particular problem, a hard OR approach may still provide valuable insights to the decision maker(s), provided the nature of the approximations and assumptions made and their implications are clearly spelled out, understood, and extensive 'What-if' analysis is performed.

The particular hard OR version presented in this chapter relaxes some of these assumptions. In particular, it does not assume that the problem is presented in a fully defined form, ready for building a mathematical model, but that it must first be extracted and identified from the problem situation. Similarly, a high degree of implementation can only be achieved if human factors are not ignored.

With this proviso in view, any OR project with a happy ending goes through three major phases:

- problem formulation or problem scoping;
- problem modelling; and
- implementation of recommendations.

Each phase consists of several steps. This is depicted in Figure 6-1. As shown, it is not a linear process, starting with 'summarizing the problem situation' and ending in 'following up solution use'. In practice, it is an iterative process where we may have to go back to earlier phases or steps to overcome unexpected difficulties, fill in omissions uncovered at a later stage, and alleviate or eliminate undesirable consequences. There are also forward linkages. At each step, we keep future steps in mind and are on the lookout for difficulties we may encounter. It may lead us to alter our initial approach and look for countermeasures, whenever possible.

The process starts out in the real world — a concrete world. For the modelling phase, we move into the world of systems — an abstract world. As we proceed to implementation, we return to the real world. On the other hand, the nature of the analysis goes from the qualitative and possibly ill-structured world in the early stages of the problem formulation to the quantitative and more structured world in the modelling phase, and then back to the qualitative world for implementation.

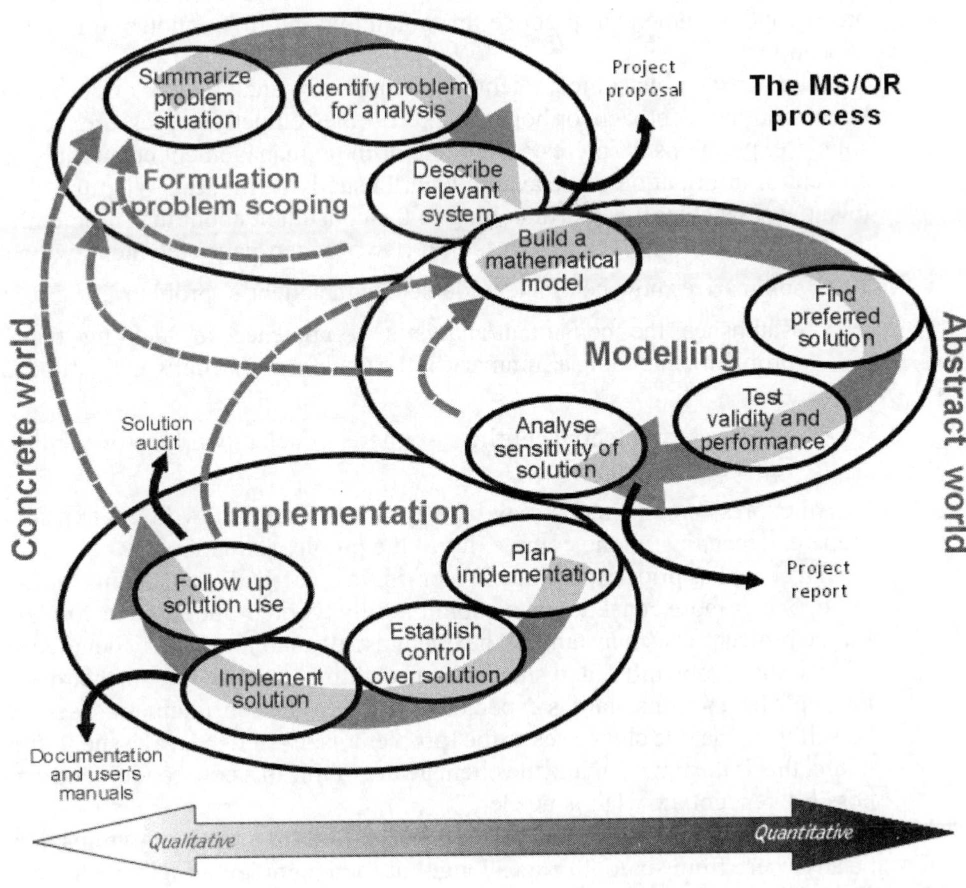

Figure 6-1 Hard OR methodology

6.2 Problem formulation and/or problem scoping

The first phase aims to identify the issue to be analysed and define a relevant system for it. The level of depth, the detail, and the level of resolution of this definition depends on a number of factors — prior knowledge about the problem, its complexity, and the relationship between problem owner or project client and problem analyst.

Use of external consultants

While in the early history of OR, some government agencies, such as the UK Coal Board, many banks, and large industrial and commercial outfits ran their own in-house OR groups, from the 1980s onwards, MS/OR work was increasingly farmed out to external consulting firms. Even the few remaining internal groups are now expected to compete for internal work and justify their existence by being profitable, just like any outside consultant (Fildes and Ranyard, 1997). Added to this is the widespread public and commercial practice of obtaining multiple quotes for any sizeable expenditure.

If an outfit — our project client — wishes some analytic work done, but does not know whom to approach, or hopes to exert some competitive pressure, he or she may solicit 'expressions of interest' from one or more management consulting firms. The amount of information made available will usually be modest. What the client wants to know is whether it is worth talking to the consultant about the 'problem'.

The consultant is expected to submit a two- to ten-page statement, which

- summarizes how he or she understands the client's 'problem';
- establishes the consultant/analyst's competence in tackling that type of 'problem', including a summary of the track record in delivering value to clients; and
- indicates any potential conflicts of interest, such as working on similar projects with a direct competitor.

An expression of interest may take anywhere from a few hours to a few days to prepare, depending on the complexity of the problem situation.

If a client has prior experience in working with MS/OR consultants, he or she may invite one or more consultants to submit a fully worked-out quote or formally tender for the project. In such instances, the client usually submits a fairly detailed statement of what the 'problem' is, and should also be willing to enter into further discussion to firm up what the consultant is expected to deliver. The consultant must satisfy him- or herself that what the client sees as the 'problem' is, in fact, the real issue. If there is any doubt, this is the time to make the client aware of this in a non-condescending way and possibly renegotiate what is needed.

A formal quote or detailed tender is in the form of a **project proposal**. This may be anywhere from six to 20 pages long, but for a complex project could be considerably more. It may take several days or weeks to prepare. Hence, its cost to the consultant can be substantial — easily running into thousands of pounds.

In some instances, the consultant may be unable to make a formal project proposal without substantial additional information about the problem situation. This in itself may be costly in terms of time. The consultant may then propose to be paid to undertake a **scoping study**. Its aim is to firm up any recommendations and to explore the risks involved, both in terms of potential benefits and likely costs.

Problem formulation or problem scoping?

If the potential benefits are certain and justify the cost of the analysis, the first phase takes the form of a complete problem formulation, producing a detailed definition of the relevant system. On the other hand, if not enough is known about the potential benefits and costs of a project, or the project is large and highly complex, it may be advisable to scope the problem first. Scoping means identifying the nature of the problem and assessing what an in-depth analysis could produce and the risks involved; in other words, whether the projected costs of undertaking the project will justify its likely benefits. In that case, the relevant system is only defined in broad terms by identifying the major subsystems and delineating its approximate boundaries. A complete system definition will wait to see if the project proceeds to the problem modelling phase. This is the reason why in Figure 6-1 'Describe relevant system' is shown overlapping into phase 2.

If the problem owner and analyst are one and the same, a scoping exercise may gradually turn into a full problem formulation, as the analyst/problem owner learns more about it. No formal project proposal may be written up. The analyst proceeds directly to the modelling phase.

When the problem owner/client engages an analyst/consultant, then problem scoping usually leads to a formal project proposal, submitted to the client for evaluation and approval.

Problem formulation and problem scoping follow largely the same steps. They only differ in the depth of the analysis. We will study both at the same time, although problem scoping will receive more emphasis.

You are already familiar with what is involved in the three steps of problem formulation or scoping from our discussion in Chapters 4 and 5. The first step — summarizing the problem situation — is preferably done by means of a rich picture or a mind map. It helps us to focus on the issue to be analysed within its full context and helps us in step 2 to identify the right problem. We suggest that at this point you briefly remind yourself again of the material in Sections 4.1 and 4.2 (pp. 60–5), i.e., the six elements that define a problem, the complexity of problem definition, and the stakeholder roles.

For the third step, defining a relevant system, we usually have recourse to diagrammatic aids. In particular, influence diagrams often are ideal for bringing out which aspects are inputs and outputs, and which system components form the transformation process of the narrow system of interest.

However, for problem scoping we will not necessarily define the system in all its intricacies. We are mainly interested in where to draw the boundaries of the narrow system and wider system of interest. At this point, we do not need a highly detailed understanding of all the interrelationships and interactions observed or assumed. We only need to understand enough for making a competent project proposal. There is little justification for investing considerable effort in analysis when we do not even know if the project will go ahead. Therefore, how far we proceed in defining a relevant system depends on many factors.

For problems that fit into a well-known structure for which commercial software is available, it may limit itself to assessing the suitability of that structure and identifying the boundaries of the system. The details will be fleshed out at the beginning of the modelling phase.

For simple situations that do not fit a known structure, the phase may end with an influence diagram that provides an adequate definition of the relevant system. For highly complex situations, the system definition may remain coarse and tentative, and at a low level of resolution. Rather than draw a detailed influence diagram, we make do with a simplified causal loop diagram or other diagrammatic representation.

In fact, sometimes not enough may yet be known about the problem situation and the nature of the problem to be in a position to make a definite proposal for a full-scale study. In such instances, the more prudent approach is to suggest a **preliminary study** with the aim of assessing whether a full-scale study is justified.

6.3 Project proposal and go-ahead decision

Once the analyst has obtained a sufficient understanding of the problem and has drawn the boundaries of the relevant system, he or she has to make a judgement about whether hard OR can be successfully applied to find a 'solution' to the problem. The analyst must weigh the following questions:

- Can the problem be expressed in quantitative terms?
- Are the required data available or can they be generated at a reasonable cost?
- Does the cost of the analysis justify the likely benefits to be derived from the implementation of the results? What are the risks?
- To what extent can the project sponsor's expectations be met?

To answer these questions, the analyst must give cursory considerations to the modelling and implementation phases. We see the forward linkages in action almost from the start. Obviously, previous OR experience will be of great help here — little comfort to the novice management scientist.

If the analyst is reasonably satisfied that the answer to all these questions is affirmative, the scoping phase may conclude with a formal project proposal recommending that it be undertaken. The problem owner will base his or her decision about the future of the project on this document.

Even if the project skips the project scoping phase, it will still be useful to take care when answering the three questions above. The insights gained at this stage may well change the assessment of the project's benefit and/or costs, and lead to a change of direction or its abandonment before any significant effort is wasted.

The formal project proposal is, no doubt, a most critical piece of work in any study. The quality of its presentation and soundness of the reasoning used often make the difference between its acceptance or rejection. In a certain sense, it is the analyst's sales pitch. However, in contrast to most sales transactions, where the relationship between seller and buyer is often terminated when the goods exchange hands, the acceptance of a project proposal by the problem owner signals the beginning of an even closer relationship. It is therefore important that the analyst gains the confidence of the problem owner by being scrupulously honest as to the likely benefits and costs.

The analyst should not promise more than he or she knows can reasonably be delivered with the resources likely to be available. It would be unethical to do otherwise. If he or she is an external consultant, the client may have the legal power to insist on promises being delivered without covering the cost of the additional work needed. Since OR modelling claims to have much in common with scientific investigations, it should also be guided by the ethics of scientific research.

Major potential difficulties that could derail or delay the project should be brought into the open and discussed, and responsibilities for action clearly assigned.

Estimation of project cost and likely benefits

The likelihood that a project is undertaken will largely depend on whether its predicted benefits will justify its costs and whether the problem owner's expectations can be reasonably met. If both benefits and costs can be expressed in monetary terms, a project is beneficial if the **present value** of the difference between all benefits and its cost over the useful life of the project is positive (Sections 10.1 and 10.2 explain present values and financial evaluation of projects).

Costs

How much will it cost to undertake the project? Almost certainly more than you will think initially. The costs cover:

- the time spent by the analyst(s) and by all other individuals external to the entity that commissions the project, such as sub-contractors;
- the time of senior staff supervising the analyst(s) and managing the project;
- the time spent by the people internal to the organization, including their supervisors/managers;
- software that has to be purchased or for which annual licences have to be bought;
- any other equipment and hardware needed for the analysis and the continued use of the 'solutions', including stationery;
- the time to be spent on implementation of the 'solution' and the initial monitoring of its use;
- any other incidental costs, such as travel, accommodation, communication, and so on; and
- contingencies to cover underestimation of the time projections, due to unforeseen delays, unexpected complications, including mis-communications; this is particularly essential if the project proposal involves a firm quote, rather than an estimate or a cost-plus arrangement.

How is the time of an analyst charged out? By the time he or she spends on the project? Hardly. First, the full cost of an analyst is not simply the salary, but also includes fringe benefits and other costs associated with his or her employment, such as personnel administration and other overheads. Second, the analyst does not spend 100% of the time working on a given project, but also attends staff meetings and training courses, reads technical journals, prepares proposals. And do not to forget that an occasional client may never pay for a project done or may dispute some charges. As a consequence of these factors, the likely utilization in terms of hours chargeable to clients runs to no more than 60% to 70%.

A reasonable contingency multiplier is about 2, equivalent to a doubling of the analyst's pay rate. So, if an MS/OR analyst receives a salary of, say, £60,000, equivalent to about £30 per hour, it is not excessive to charge out his or her time at twice that amount, and that of the project supervisor at four times or more.

Benefits

For projects dealing with environmental, health, or social issues, many of the benefits cannot be adequately captured in currency. Take the preservation of nature or scenic beauty, or the prevention of fatal accidents. How much is it worth to prevent the destruction of some ecologically important estuary or a wildlife habitat? Similarly, the monetary evaluation of the benefits of noise abatement or pollution control, or the social benefits of pre-school education can hardly be measured in dollars, pounds, or euros. A comparison of benefits and costs may therefore be far from simple.

But, even if we look only at monetary benefits, providing a reliable answer for what the likely benefits are going to be may not be straight forward. At this point in the life of a project, the analyst may have only scant information about the potential size of the benefits. As pointed out earlier, it may be advisable to propose a preliminary study for assessing the economic feasibility of the project. Such projects are similar in nature to research and development ventures. These have to be funded based on vague potential, rather than hard facts. Some will succeed and reap great benefits, others will fail. The expectation in undertaking such projects is that, on balance, long-term benefits will outweigh long-term costs.

However, the analyst should make a serious and honest attempt at predicting the likely benefits beyond mere guesses. It may require developing a simplified model of the proposed operation or system. This can then be used to compute approximate lower bounds to estimates of benefits. It will also give a better picture of the likely costs for undertaking the project.

Prior expectations

Frequently, the sponsor of the project may have certain prior expectations about what the project should achieve and the time frame within which it should be completed. Even if the project is beneficial from a cost/benefit point of view, it may not meet these expectations. The sponsor should be made aware of this. It could well be that the sponsor's expectations or the time frame available are unreasonable. The analyst may then try to alter these expectations through reasoned arguments, based on a preliminary study or experience from similar projects.

Also, analysts must also keep in mind that they may inadvertently encourage the formation of unreasonable expectations. Proper and diplomatic management of the sponsor's expectations is an important aspect of any project. Inappropriate expectation may easily derail a project.

Format of project proposal

A project proposal should be relatively short — six to 20 pages — and presented to a professional standard, with correct spelling, grammar and syntax, and consistent formatting. Its visual effect is as important as its content.

Your language should be concise, clear, and simple. Be wary of pompousness, fad words, or 'business speak'. Do not use OR jargon, unless you know for certain that the readers are fully conversant with it. Reasoning should be logically developed and complete, with one point leading to the next. Sounds obvious, but is often violated!

Writing a competent, well-presented report is an integral part of the professional image you wish to convey to the problem owner. One of the most common causes for complaints we hear from employers of novice MS/OR analysts is the often abysmal writing skills of many fresh graduates. It is difficult to come across as credible and professionally competent if your boss has to rewrite your reports before they can be presented to the sponsor of a project. In fact, it is the quickest way to lose your job.

The report should briefly summarize the problem situation, motivate the proposed approach in non-technical terms, list the steps of the analysis, and the data and the resource needed (time, funds, computational capabilities). It should indicate the nature and approximate size of the benefits, if this is possible at that stage, or justify why this may not be possible, showing a list of costs and a detailed timetable for completing the project. It should give a clear recommendation on whether the project should proceed or not. If relevant, it is also advisable to indicate briefly why other potential approaches were discarded.

If the analyst is an external consultant, then he or she must provide supporting evidence of competence and address questions of confidentiality (e.g., who is authorized to have access to confidential data and who may remove such data from the premises).

The proposal should start out with an executive summary.

We recommend that the analyst offers an oral presentation to the problem owner and the problem users. Do not hesitate to use the rich picture. It may be a catalyst for an animated discussion. Questions, doubts, and anxieties — which invariably crop up — can be dealt with, clarified, and alleviated on the spot.

Again, such an oral presentation must be professional, i.e., clear, to the point, logically developed, and not extending much beyond half-an-hour. If you use Powerpoint© or similar software, make sure that a projector and a screen are available, and test that the projector works. Most important though, rehearse your entire talk, using the software, and time yourself carefully. In fact, one rehearsal may not be enough!

If the problem owner or decision maker finds that the likely results justify the cost of the analysis, including the cost of eventual implementation, and has confidence in the analyst's competence to bring the project to a successful completion, he or she will usually give the go-ahead to proceed with the project.

6.4 Problem modelling phase

It is this phase that distinguishes the hard OR methodology from soft OR. Often, hard OR is viewed as synonymous with a collection of powerful mathematical tools and techniques, such as linear programming, computer simulation, and statistical methods. We shall see that this is a rather blinkered view, which we find unhelpful, even detrimental to achieving the full potential of hard OR modelling.

The problem formulation or scoping phase may not have come up with a detailed definition of the relevant system. Therefore, step 4, building a mathematical model, may start out with finalizing the definition of the relevant system in the detail and resolution needed for translating it into quantitative terms. If the analysis done for step 3 showed that the problem fits a well-known structure, this simply means fleshing out the details. However, for a complex problem that does not fit a known structure, step 3 may only have delineated the boundary of the system. Hence, considerable further work needs to go into defining a relevant system, usually using a process approach. This may be in the form of a detailed influence diagram. Sometimes, it may be useful to have two or more levels of diagrams: a high-level system structure diagram, showing categories of inputs, the interactions between subsystems, and the major outputs, supplemented with a detailed influence diagram for each subsystem.

However, even if step 3 ended in a complete definition of the relevant system, it is advisable to revisit it carefully. The passage of time may have changed your perception of the problem.

Once satisfied with the system definition, we build a mathematical model. Sometimes, a spreadsheet is all that is needed to capture the quantitative relationships between the inputs, the state variables for the various components, and the outputs. If the problem fits a well-known structure, such as a linear program or a network, readily available commercial software can be used for formulating a mathematical model and finding a solution. However, in many instances, we may have no choice but to build a special-purpose model that expresses the relationships between control inputs, state variables, and outputs. Such models may consist of numerous equations and inequalities. Notice that at this point we are well into the abstract world. The model is not the real thing.

As discussed in Section 5.4, building a mathematical model is in part an art. The final model version of the model may be the result of a process of enrichment and reformulation.

In step 5, finding the preferred solution, we manipulate this model in order to explore the response of the system performance to changes in controllable and uncontrollable inputs, i.e., we explore the set of feasible solutions or the **solution space**. The aim is to find the preferred solution in terms of the problem owner's objective(s). If the problem owner is interested in one major objective, say profits, this means finding the optimal solution — the one that maximizes profits.

Readily available optimization software may deliver the optimal solution without the analyst having to explore the solution space.

Testing and validation of model and solution

Step 6 establishes the model's credibility. Validation has two facets:

1. **Internal validity or verification**: Checking that the model is logically and mathematically correct and that the data used is correct. It means carefully verifying that all mathematical expressions correctly represent the assumed relationships. If they have been translated into a computer program, it is advisable to print not only the final solution, but detailed step-by-step intermediate results. If computationally feasible, these should be verified numerically with a hand calculator for a sufficiently wide range of inputs. This also involves verifying that each expression is dimensionally consistent. For example, if the right-hand side of an equation is in terms of kilograms per hour, so must the left-hand side. The correctness of all numerical constants should be verified. Rather than insert the numerical constants directly into the various formulas, all input data should be entered in data tables. These are then referenced by all formulas that use them. This ensures that any data changes will automatically be carried forward to all formulas.

   The prudent analyst does much of the checking for internal validity while developing the model. Thus, establishing internal validity cannot be divorced from the actual model building — a clear example of how various steps overlap or happen concurrently, at least in part.

   Complex models consisting of many separate submodels also have to be checked for logical consistency. Have the parts been fitted together correctly?

2. **External validity** (also simply referred to as **validation**): Is the model a sufficient representation of reality? Does it provide insight and answers useful and in the appropriate form for decision making? This is far more difficult to establish than internal validity. 'What is or is not a close enough approximation?' is largely a question of judgement. The answer should depend on the purpose of building the model and the intended use of its solution. A rough approximation may well be good enough for an exploratory planning model, while a model intended for detailed day-to-day operational decisions may need to be an accurate representation of reality. So, again, we see that validation overlaps with both the definition of the relevant system (step 3 of the methodology) and the model building (step 4) (see Landry et al. (1983) in Further reading of Chapter 8).

   Stakeholders should all recognize that it is not possible to prove that a model is externally valid. It is only possible to show it to be wrong. Hence, external validation is a question of establishing the **credibility** of the model. Satisfying the essential properties of good models, discussed in Section 5.3, will also enhance its credibility. If the model is credible, the user will have confidence in it.

External validity can often be assumed if the model mimics reality accurately. Hence, the analyst needs to analyse how the model responds to changes in inputs. Are they as expected and, if not, why are they different? Complex systems often exhibit counterintuitive behaviour. A model's validity is put into question unless such behaviour can be convincingly explained.

Model testing itself looks at how the model and its solution perform. What improvement in benefits or cost does it offer over the current mode of operations? If the project deals with a proposed future system, what is the range of the potential benefits that can be expected? The answers to these questions will determine whether the project is abandoned, re-oriented, or allowed to continue on its current course.

What-if or sensitivity analysis

Finally, in step 7 — sensitivity analysis — we ask 'what if' questions. How is the preferred or optimal solution affected by individual or simultaneous changes of uncontrollable inputs into the system? How costly are errors in inputs in terms of reduced benefits achieved if a solution based on incorrect inputs is implemented? Both are referred to as **sensitivity analysis**.

Sensitivity analysis is, without doubt, the most important step of hard OR. It must become second nature for any operations researcher. The insights gained from it may be more valuable than finding a good, or even the optimal, solution.

Extensive sensitivity analysis is also an integral part of checking external validity — another instance of the linkage between various steps.

Project report

For projects that need the owner's approval for implementation, the modelling phase ends with a detailed project report on the analysis done, its findings, and the analyst's recommendations about implementation. Further action will largely depend on this document. Its format is a more detailed and extended version of the project proposal — again preceded by an executive summary of the findings and recommendations. By this point, the analyst is ready to give firm estimates of the potential benefits and costs of implementation. The appendices should:

- give details on technical aspects of the quantitative model(s) used, such as a listing of the mathematical formulas and/or the computer programs written (the latter may be provided in digital form, a CD or data stick);
- justify the assumptions and simplifications made in the analysis and their likely effects on the findings;
- report on important findings of the sensitivity analysis performed; and
- list all input data and how it should be updated for continued use of the model.

The project report must be complete and stand alone. As pointed out for the project proposal, to be credible, the project report must be to a high professional standard in terms of content and presentation.

Both the strengths and weaknesses of the analysis and conclusions reached should be spelled out. This is also for the analyst's own protection. He or she cannot then be accused of negligence, or having misled the problem owner by hiding important aspects. It forms part of the analyst's professional ethics!

Should the project be abandoned?

As the analysis progresses, the analyst must periodically assess whether the project should continue or be abandoned. The viability of a project is put in question when the likely benefits to be derived from implementing its results do not justify the additional cost to be incurred for completing it. If this seems to be the case, professional ethics require that the analyst report this fact to the problem owner(s) or sponsor(s). The points raised on estimation of project costs and benefits are all relevant here.

Note that this assessment does not take into account the costs already spent up to this point, but only the additional costs for completing the project. Why do we ignore the costs already spent? The reason is that nothing can be done about them; they are a 'sunk cost' (see the detailed discussion on this in Chapter 9, pp. 244–5). However, if any further costs are justified by the likely benefits, it is still worthwhile proceeding.

We cannot undo costs already spent. It is therefore important that we discover as early as possible that further costs may not be recovered by the project's benefits. This will allow culling a project before large amounts of resources are wasted, hence the need for regularly assessing a project's continued viability.

6.5 Implementation phase

If the problem owner accepts the analyst's recommendation to proceed, the project enters the solution implementation phase. In step 8, planning implementation, the analyst, in consultation with the project sponsor, prepares a detailed plan of all implementation tasks, their assignment to individuals, and a schedule for their coordination.

Step 9 establishes procedures for maintaining and establishing controls over the solution. It specifies for what range of values of crucial uncontrollable inputs the current solution remains valid and the exact procedure for updating the solution when inputs stray outside these ranges, including who is responsible for enacting them.

Step 10, the actual implementation of the solution, executes the changes required to switch from the current to the proposed mode of operation. By that time, the analyst has prepared self-contained user's manuals. These should be written at a level compatible with the education level of the users. The analyst, preferably jointly with the project sponsor, may organize and conduct training sessions on any changes in work procedures for the various users.

Although implementing the solution comes almost at the end of a project, planning for it starts at the very outset of any project, when the first contacts are established with the problem owners and users, and continues through all other steps. It implies establishing good lines of communications, exploring and managing prior expectations, particularly unrealistic ones, keeping the problem owners and users informed about the progress of the project, and consulting with them. Experience shows that the more the problem owners and users are actively involved in the project, the more they own the results, and the keener they are to implement the results and make them work.

Finally, after the new solution has been in use for some period, the analyst returns and performs an audit (step 11). This consists of establishing the extent to which the solution fulfils its promises in terms of the benefits achieved and the costs incurred, as well as checking for continued proper use of the solution and recommending possible changes in the light of the practical experience gained. This may give rise to a final project audit report.

Chapter 8 discusses in more detail the implementation process, the obstacles to implementation, and how to overcome them.

6.6 Nature of the hard OR process

Forward and backward linkages

The various steps are usually initiated in the sequence shown, but each step may overlap with preceding and/or subsequent steps. When we start identifying the problem to be analysed, we may need to gather more specific and more detailed information about the problem situation. This may call for changes to the rich picture, i.e., we return from step 2 to step 1. By the time we get to the project proposal (end of step 3), we may already have explored, at least tentatively, a general form of the mathematical model (step 4). Not only may this allow us to determine rough estimates of potential benefits, but it may also affect the boundary choices and the level of resolution for the relevant system.

The choice of the most suitable mathematical model should be influenced by how costly both its detailed development and ultimate implementation are expected to be. For example, if its use presupposes a level of training and skills which goes far beyond the norm for the type of employee in that position, we may opt for a simpler model or for rules that only approximate the optimal solution. This is likely to capture less of the potential savings or benefits, but will have a better chance of successful implementation. The experienced analyst will constantly be on the look-out for such forward and backward linkages between phases, as well as between steps within a phase.

Iterative process

The methodology is iterative. This means that the analyst may go back to previous steps and redo or modify part of the analysis already done. For example, attempting to define a relevant system may point to contradictions or missing aspects in the problem situation. Before proceeding, this aspect should be resolved. It may, in turn, lead to changes in the relevant system. During the solution step, the analyst may discover that the software and computing facilities needed to perform the computations are very costly, negating some or all of the expected financial benefits. Implementation of the model could therefore not be justified. The analyst may have to iterate back to the model building step and formulate a computationally less demanding model. Unfortunately, it may even happen that during implementation, crippling oversights in the problem formulation are discovered which render part or most of the model irrelevant, or even change the nature of the issue. If the problem owner agrees, the analyst may have to start almost from scratch with a new problem formulation.

Few projects sail through all the various steps without iterating back to earlier steps in the analysis. You should therefore clearly keep in mind that, even if we discuss the steps separately in their natural sequence, they overlap.

Data collection

Many OR texts show a separate 'data collection' step. Figure 6-1 shows none. This is not an oversight! The reason is simple. Data collection does not occur at a given point in the analysis as a separate step, such as for testing a statistical hypothesis. We start collecting and assessing data and identifying data sources when we meet the problem situation for the first time. As we proceed, we continue collecting more data for describing the relevant system. Collecting and evaluating data occurs in parallel with any of the 11 steps, even the audit at step 11.

The specific properties and forms of various data will dictate the mathematical form of the relationships in the model. Hence, for most projects, a representative sample of data will have to be collected prior to building a mathematical model. We will ask such questions as 'Are the relationships linear or non-linear?', or 'What type of probability distribution best describes the random phenomena?'. But the bulk of data may not have to be available until the model is ready for implementation in step 10, although its collection may have to be initiated well before that.

Sufficiently accurate time estimates for performing certain activities and their cost may only be determined by actual observations, say, by taking time measures.

In many instances, the data may not be in the form required or may not even exist. It is important that the analyst ascertains before step 3 whether the required data sources exist and, if so, in what form. If the data are missing or not available in a useful form, action has to be initiated to start the collection of the data in the form required.

Furthermore, an assurance by various stakeholders that all the data are available and easily accessible should be treated with a healthy degree of suspicion. It pays to show a lively interest in ascertaining what data were actually collected and study their format. We have encountered situations where assurance was given that several years of data were readily available, only to discover that the collection format had recently been changed and that the latest computer facilities had no device to read data files on obsolete storage media.

Lack of sufficient data may seriously delay completion of the project.

Is the past representative of the future?

One further important word about data. Most data available reflect the current or past mode of operation. If the proposed project substantially changes that mode, such data may no longer be relevant for future operations. What we really want are data as they will be once the proposed system has been implemented. However, such data are not yet available, so we have to do with what we got, but we must make adjustment so that the data become relevant for the proposed system. For instance, if demand for products shows a trend, up or down, that trend needs to be extrapolated. If equipment is replaced, the labour cost for the new equipment has to be ascertained. Past sales records may not be an accurate estimate of the level of future demand since lost sales, due to shortages, may not have been recorded. The blind use of past data implies hidden, unintended system boundary judgements.

6.7 Lubricating Oil Division situation summary

We now demonstrate the methodology with a case where one of the authors was the principal analyst.

How was the project initiated?

The project dealt with the operations of the Lubricating Oil Division (LOD) of a major US oil company. The LOD produced and stored about 400 types of automotive and industrial lubricating oils and greases, for ultimate sale to over 1000 wholesale and retail customers. The impetus for the project was a report by the firm's internal auditors to the Vice-President of Finance that, in their judgement, the current average stock turnover achieved by the LOD of 12 times per year was well below the company target of 24. (Stock turnover measures how many times per year the entire stock is renewed.) As a result, the funds tied up in inventories were seen as excessive. This concern was passed on to the Vice-President of Manufacture who, in turn, informed the manager of the LOD, with a request to report to him in due course the measures he intended to take. In response, the manager of the LOD approached the in-house OR group at the company headquarters for help. That is where the analyst came in.

The initial request was somewhat vague — the manager wanted advice. Therefore, the first phase of the project was clearly in the nature of problem scoping. There was no guarantee that a project might ever eventuate.

Learning the stakeholders' technical jargon

The analyst's first action was to arrange a guided tour of the offices and facilities of the LOD. Remembering people's names was one of his weaknesses. So, whenever he met new people, he immediately noted down their name and function on a notepad. He made a conscientious effort to understand, learn, and use the largely unfamiliar technical terminology which he encountered. If he did not understand something, he was not ashamed to ask — even at the risk of looking a bit dumb.

It is important not to assume that somebody else's technical meaning of a term is the same as yours. So, he checked it out to avoid any confusion and misunderstanding.

Details of the operations

If he had been familiar with rich pictures at that time, he would have drawn up something like Figure 6-2. Starting in the top left-hand corner, it shows what triggered the study and the implied worldview, namely, a concern for economic efficiency of investments. The core of the picture describes the various operations of the LOD and its relationships with other parts of the refinery operation and its customers. Here are some additional comments.

Production of lube oils and greases was done in batches varying from 400 litres to 100,000 litres. Many products were sold in several container sizes — from large drums to small cans. The LOD carried 804 different product/container-size combinations. As shown in the rich picture, some customers placed such large orders for a single product that each was met by special production run and shipped directly to them.

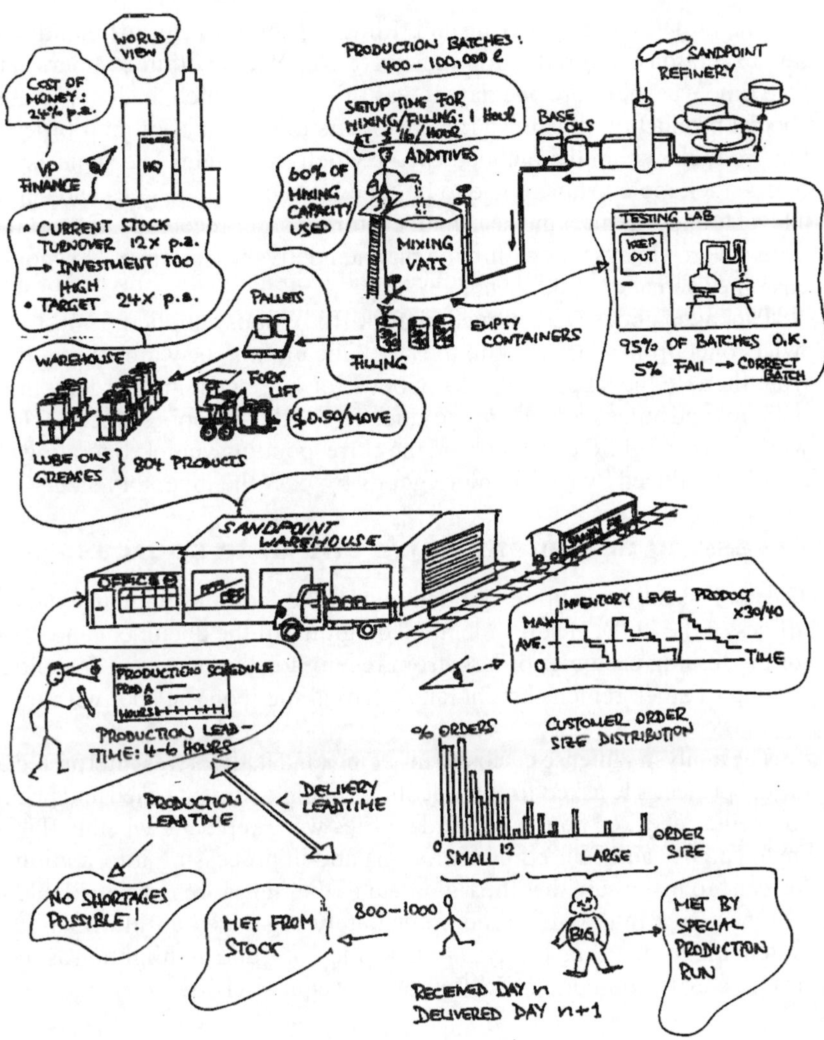

Figure 6-2 A rich picture for the Lubricating Oil Division

Other, usually smaller, customers placed orders that were met from warehouse stocks. As these stocks were sold off, they were replenished by an appropriately sized production run. The manager proudly pointed out the firm's policy of shipping any goods to the customer within two days after receipt of the order.

Various base oils and additives were mixed to specified recipes in mixing vats. The vat size chosen depended on the size of the batch. The base oils were drawn from storage tanks, fed from the refinery. After mixing, the finished product was tested to ensure that it met the desired specifications. Once a batch passed the tests, the finished lube oil was filled into containers, usually within 4–6 hours. Each mixing and filling run incurred a fixed set-up or change-over cost that varied from product to product and depended on the sequence of oils made. The pattern for grease production was similar.

The LOD's existing mixing and filling capacities were sufficiently large that, with rare exceptions, all production runs were completed within 24 hours. The production lead time was therefore one day. It was this aspect which made it possible to schedule special production runs for large customers after receipt of their orders and still ship the products within the planned two-day delivery cycle. The same aspect also meant that a stock replenishment had to be scheduled only once sales had depleted stocks to a level too low to meet the last small customer order received. As a result, all customer orders were always met within the planned delivery lead time. No shortages or unmet customer demands could occur.

Packaged goods were moved by forklifts. Goods supplied from stock were moved twice, once from production to the stock location in the warehouse and a second time from there to the shipping docks. Goods for large customer orders, in contrast, were only moved once, i.e., from production to the shipping docks. Hence, the total workload for forklift operators and the corresponding vehicle operating cost and wages could be reduced by having more goods by-pass the inventory stage.

Assessing document flows and data sources

The analyst followed up the guided tour of the facilities with an extended visit to the offices of the LOD. He drew detailed diagrams of the document and information flow for processing customer orders, from receipt to shipment, and for initiating and processing of stock replenishment, and verified them on the spot with the people doing each task.

The analyst's intense curiosity in seeing all data files was interpreted as enthusiasm for the project. He asked for photocopies of all documents used and print-outs of computer files, checked how far back data files were kept, and whether during that period any changes had occurred in operations and in processing information or in data file formats, to make sure that the right data in the right form was available when needed.

Once back in the office, he immediately organized all information gathered in a systematic form, filling in any gaps from memory, and highlighting aspects that needed further clarification or verification on subsequent visits.

6.8 Identifying the problem to be analysed

Identifying the issue to be analysed

The rich picture indicates a number of possible issues:

1. tighter coordination of the mixing and filling operations so as to reduce the cost of changing over from one product to another, particularly on the filling machines;
2. lengthening the production lead time from one to two days; this would allow for better sequencing and coordination of the mixing and filling workload, and might possibly reduce the number of operators needed to perform the same tasks;

3. lowering the minimum customer order size which triggers a special production run, thereby having fewer orders met from stock, or do the reverse, i.e., increasing the trigger point and have more orders filled from stock; and
4. increasing the average stock turnover — the aspect about which the Vice-President of Finance voiced strong concerns.

When questioned, the LOD manager ruled out issues 1 and 2. The mixing and filling equipment had been upgraded substantially only the previous year. He did not want another disruption of this sort. He was also adamant that lengthening the production lead time would lower customer service and be contrary to company policy.

He considered that the project should address the issue raised by the statement of the Vice-President of Finance about the inadequate average turnover of stocks and its implication that too much money was tied up in inventories.

What is the relationship between stock turnover and funds invested in stocks? As shown in the rich picture, the normal inventory behaviour over time for each product has a typical saw-tooth pattern. Each tooth corresponds to one stock replenishment and represents one complete stock turnover for that product. The fewer stock turnovers per year, the larger must be each stock replenishment.

For example, if the demand for a given product is 120,000 litres per year and the size of each stock replenishment is 5,000 litres, the stock turnover is 24 times per year. If the stock turnover is reduced to 12 times per year, then each stock replenishment must be equal to 10,000 litres. The stock turnover for each product is directly linked to the size of its stock replenishment, which was controllable by the LOD.

Discussions with the LOD manager showed that he shared the worldview revealed in the statement of the Vice-President of Finance; namely, to assure the most efficient use of funds. The Vice-President saw funds tied up in stocks as lying idle and saw a high stock turnover as a sign of efficiency. Given the current average stock turnover of 12 times per year, decreasing all replenishment sizes by half would allow meeting the Vice-President's target of a stock turnover of 24. However, from the rich picture we see that every mixing and filling run also involves a set-up — the time operators spends preparing a mixing and filling run and the lab technician needed to test the products. Increasing turnover for a given product means more stock replenishment and hence more production set-ups. As a consequence, the time spent by operators on set-ups will also increase. At an average of $16 per hour, this can well mean that any savings made by reducing investments may be lost by higher annual labour costs.

The size of stocks needed also depends on what customer order size is viewed as large. Lowering the cut-off point for large orders reduces the demand met from stock. Consequently, less stock is needed, which in turn translates into a reduction in investment. But lowering the cut-off point means more customer orders are met by special production runs, causing an increase in the annual production set-up costs.

Changing the size of stock replenishments and the cut-off point for large orders results in some costs decreasing and others increasing. A narrow efficiency approach focused only on investments may thus not be in the best interest of the firm (unless, for other reasons, the firm wishes to reduce its investments regardless of the effect on operating costs). All costs that change in total as a result of a change in policy become candidates for inclusion in the performance measure.

There is a further point. The Vice-President's target was an average stock turnover of 24. However, this does not imply that each product carried should meet this target. In fact, each product has its own optimal turnover rate, some considerably smaller than 24, others well above that. The average over all products may not be 24. Hence, the optimal policy may deviate from the Vice-President's target. The LOD manager should understand that meeting that target could result in higher overall costs. Hence, some management of prior expectation was required right from the start of the project.

The hierarchy of systems involved

The problem is embedded in a hierarchy of systems. The widest system of concern is the company as a whole, with the refinery as one of its subsystems. The LOD, in turn, is a subsystem of the latter. Within the LOD system, production/inventory control operations forms one of its major subsystems. It is the narrow system of interest. Since the LOD operation as a whole has control over the resources needed by the narrow system, it becomes the wider system of interest.

Stakeholders

With the narrow and wider systems of interest tentatively chosen, the analyst knew enough about the situation to identify the various stakeholders. These were defined with respect to the narrow system of interest.

The role of analyst was assumed by an in-house consultant of the company.

There were several levels of problem owners or decision makers. This is typical of problem situations with a hierarchy of systems. At the top was the Vice-President of Finance who coordinated the use of funds within the firm. She stated the criteria by which investments of funds were to be evaluated. The Vice-President of Manufacture (refinery system) operated within these criteria. He delegated making day-to-day operational decisions on production and stock control for packaged products to the manager of the LOD (LOD system). For projects that did not involve any major investments, the latter was the immediate decision maker. However, he had to refer any decision on large investments to the Vice-President of Manufacture.

A priori, the only new use of funds of the project was the cost of the project itself. Once that was completed, the analyst might recommend a change in the level of investment in inventories. Any such recommendations would then be evaluated in terms of the investment criteria specified by the Vice-President of Finance.

At this point in the analysis, the cost of undertaking the project — a transfer of funds between departments within the company — was the only use of funds which had to be evaluated. As it turned out, even that exceeded the manager's authority and hence had to be referred higher up. But, once approved, any changes to the day-to-day operation of the LOD were under his control as long as they did not require additional investments. It was his worldview that the problem solver had to use as a basis for determining the goal or aim of the project.

However, it is important to confirm that the worldviews of all levels of problem owners are compatible. If not, the stakeholders at the various levels should be made aware of the conflicts and the need to have them resolved prior to proceeding further.

Persistence of conflicting worldviews between various levels of decision makers is likely to result in serious suboptimization, i.e., the benefits gained may be wholly or partially negated by additional costs inflicted elsewhere in the organization, e.g., in another subsystem at the same or at a different level. (Recall the discussion on efficiency in Section 2.2, p. 17, and boundary choices in Section 3.5, p. 34.)

Resolution of conflicts in worldviews is usually beyond the scope of hard OR, since it deals with organizational issues. A soft systems approach may be more suitable.

For the LOD, the analyst already ascertained that there was basic agreement between the worldviews of the Vice-President of Finance and the LOD manager. Both saw return on investment as the ultimate company goal. This translated into maximizing profits or minimizing costs. However, conflict could arise if the optimal solution did not meet the stock turnover target set by the Vice-President of Finance. This aspect needed to be addressed in the project proposal.

To determine the problem users, we needed to identify who was in charge of initiating production runs for stock replenishment or large customer orders. These 'decisions', within the policy defined by the problem owner — the LOD manager — were made by the stock officer. Any changes to the rules of the inventory/production control policy had to be such that her level of education and training was sufficient to deal with them. Any training and other costs, such as upgraded computing facilities, had to be taken into account in the project recommendations.

The customers of the LOD were the problem customers. Recall that the LOD manager was adamant that any new policy had to maintain or improve the current level of service offered; hence, the two-day delivery lead time had to be maintained. The employees for the various operations and in the office were also problem customers, since their work would be affected by any changes in the mode of operations.

Problem elements

In summary, the six elements of the problem were:

- immediate decision maker: the LOD manager;
- objective: achieving low operating cost for the LOD's operation, subject to maintaining the same level of customer service;
- performance measure: the total operating and investment costs of the LOD;
- decision criterion: minimizing total costs;
- alternative courses of action: the size of stock replenishment batches and the cut-off point for classifying customer orders as large or small; and
- wider system of interest: the LOD operation and the refinery.

6.9 A system for stock replenishments

Having settled on the problem to be analysed, the analyst proceeded to define a relevant system. A cursory inspection showed the presence of all the usual inventory/production control aspects. An experienced analyst would be tempted to use a structural approach, selecting one of the standard production/inventory control models. This, together with an identification of the products to be controlled, would delineate the system boundary. However, for the LOD a more careful analysis revealed that there were aspects not normally found in a typical production/inventory structure. In particular, different rules applied to meet large and small customer orders. Hence, a process approach, starting from first principles, was more appropriate.

What is a suitable level of resolution for the system definition? At this point, little was known about the potential savings the project may produce. So, opting for problem scoping, rather than a full problem formulation, was more appropriate. Initially, only a high-level system structure diagram was needed, such as in Figure 6-3. It connects the various subsystems and indicates the system boundaries.

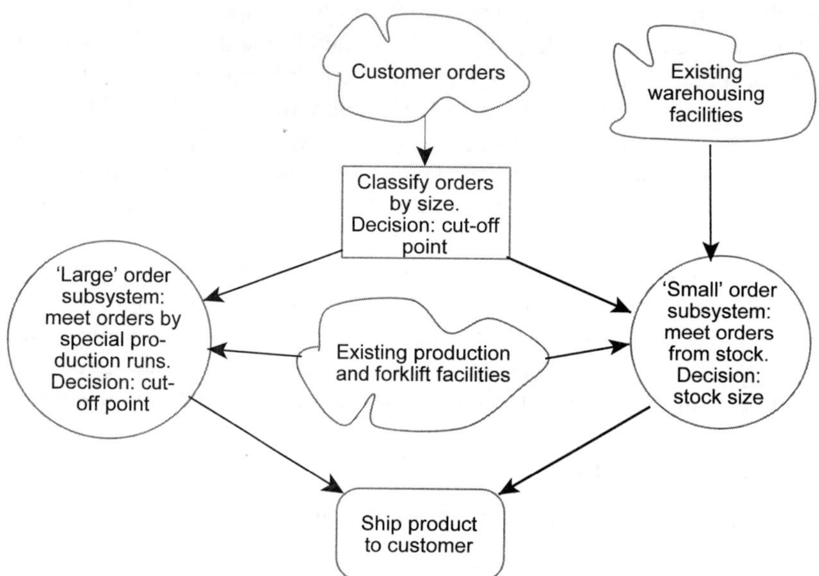

Figure 6-3 High-level system structure diagram for the LOD

The uncontrollable inputs were incoming customer orders, and the existing operations and warehouse facilities. Orders were classified as 'large' or 'small'. The processing of each class was a separate subsystem. One subsystem met large orders by scheduling a special production run, and the second processed small orders from inventories and replenished stocks periodically. Existing production facilities and capacities, including the forklift operation to move stock, were shared and taken as inputs. Similarly, existing warehousing capacity for the 'small order subsystem' was given. Specifying the inputs, both controllable and uncontrollable, delineated the boundaries of the narrow system of interest in sufficient detail for problem scoping.

It was also important to notice that the two input controls, i.e., the **cut-off point** classifying a customer order as large, and the **stock replenishment size**, had to be specified individually for each of the 804 products. What could be a good pair for one product, might be bad for another. The products were independent of each other. In some sense, there was not one big problem, but 804 small problems, one for each product. Their only interdependence was that they shared the same production and warehousing facilities. Their combined usage of these facilities could not exceed the existing capacities.

There was one more consequence of this. The measure of performance of the narrow system, i.e., the total operating cost of the LOD for meeting customer demands, was the sum of the 804 costs for the individual products.

Boundary judgements, explicit and implicit

Figure 6-3 shows customer orders and existing warehouse, production and forklift facilities as uncontrollable inputs, beyond the control of the LOD manager. They were, though, not outside the control of the wider (controlling) system, i.e., the firm as a whole. What was assumed here was that the firm deliberately chose not to use that control and to leave them unchanged. However, how they were used was assumed controllable and was bound to change as a result of the study.

The demand for the firm's products could also be affected by promotion and other actions. Since a large proportion of the 'customers' were company-owned wholesale distributors, even the pattern of demand could to some extent be controlled. The firm could have given each of these 'customers' a schedule when they had to place orders. That schedule would have been coordinated over all outfits so as to achieve desirable patterns, such as an even flow of orders or synchronizing ordering for certain products to allow them to be combined into a joint special production run. Again, the LOD deliberately decided that such controls were not part of this study.

There was also the assumption that the base oils and additives used for the blending of oils were always available when needed.

All such assumptions must be noted down and listed in the project proposal and final project report.

Activity

- Before you proceed to the next section, reread the four questions at the beginning of Section 6.3 (p. 122). Try to answer each from the information and discussion in Sections 6.8 and 6.9. If you cannot, indicate why or what additional information you would need to do so.
- List the additional boundary judgements made in the LOD case for costs, base oil availabilities, and operating capacities, and discuss their implications.

6.10 Project proposal for the LOD

At that point in the analysis, the analyst could answer the first two of the questions listed in Section 6.3, i.e., the problem could be expressed quantitatively and the required data seemed to be available, or could be determined at a reasonable cost. The LOD had a complete electronic data base on all customer orders processed for at least the previous two years. The customer order pattern for all products could be extracted from that base. Cost data on products and the production and warehousing operations could either be obtained directly from cost accounting data or computed without major expenses by observing operators' time and materials required for various tasks.

The third question about potential benefits and costs of the analysis was somewhat more difficult to answer without actually solving the problem, which begs the question. No mathematical model had yet been formulated, neither had any detailed product input data been collected. The analyst had only rough ranges for the product cost factors and a general idea of which aspects should go into the measure of performance.

The way to deal with this dilemma is to make simplifications. With the help of the stock officer, half a dozen representative products were identified, covering the range from small to large volume. She had access to approximate product values and information about the mixing, filling and testing operations from which a rough guess as to the total set-up cost could be derived. A call to the Finance Section of the firm confirmed that investments were supposed to achieve a return of at least 18% per year before taxes. This was the opportunity cost for the use of funds. At this stage, it seemed appropriate to have recourse to one of the most basic inventory control models that are part of the hard OR tool box. This model determines the best stock replenishment size under the assumption that all orders are met from stock. The model to be developed for the LOD was much more sophisticated and therefore likely to produce larger savings. Consequently, the cost estimates obtained from the simple model were a very conservative lower bound. This cost was then compared with the annual the cost of the current practice and the resulting cost savings were extrapolated for all 804 products.

In the LOD case, the cost savings for the six products used as a sample ranged from \$32 to \$253 per year, with an average of \$117 and a standard deviation of 30. Using standard statistical estimation principles, a 95% interval estimate for the predicted savings over all 804 products is approximately \$94,000 + or – 1,700.

A rough estimate as to the total time input by analysts, cost accounting and data processing, as well as LOD staff was about 120 days. At an internal charge-out rate of \$600 per day, the cost of the analysis would be recovered within about half a year — lower than the acceptance criterion of one year used by the company for 'research' projects of this type. So, this rough scoping exercise seemed promising.

However, a more prudent approach was, first, to undertake a preliminary study to find a more reliable savings estimate, based on a version of the proposed model, and using a stratified random sample of around 5% of all products. If the results confirmed the guesstimates, then a recommendation for a full-scale study could easily be supported. On the other hand, if a more detailed preliminary study showed that the potential savings were much smaller than initially estimated, then this fact would be discovered before a costly full-scale commitment had been made — a more sensible approach in this case. Such a study could be completed in about 16 working days.

In this project, much of the groundwork done in a preliminary study could also be carried forward to a full-scale study. As a consequence, the total expense of a preliminary study followed by an extension to all products would not be appreciably higher than undertaking a full-scale study from the start. This was because a substantially larger portion of the total cost of a full-scale study was incurred for data collection, computation of the optimal policies, and their implementation, while the cost of the modelling phase was relatively small.

A further reason for opting for a preliminary study was that we were dealing with a fairly large number of products. For only a few dozen products, much of the justification for a preliminary study would disappear. The cost of a full-scale study would then be only be minimally larger.

An important factor for whether to go for a preliminary or a full-scale study hinges on which phase of the analysis incurs the most substantial portion of the cost. If it is the modelling phase, the tendency is to opt directly for a full-scale study. If it is the implementation phase, as in the LOD case, a preliminary study is less risky.

Appendix 6.1 contains a project proposal for a preliminary study. If it were written by external consultants, it would also give a summary of the analyst's credentials, such as his or her educational background and a list of major projects completed, as well as comments about how confidentiality of data would be managed.

Study Appendix 6.1 before continuing!

6.11 Complete LOD system definition

For the LOD problem, the project proposal, reinforced by an oral presentation, completed phase 1 of the OR process. The analyst's recommendation for a full-scale study was approved. The project entered the modelling phase. Its first step was to define, in sufficient detail, a relevant system. It took the form of the influence diagram reproduced in Figure 6-4, which shows the transformation process of control inputs and uncontrollable inputs into outputs, via the state variables of system components. Recall that it does not show the optimization aspect. That is another system.

The analyst already identified the control inputs for each finished product; namely, the size of stock replenishments and the cut-off point for classifying customer orders as large or small. The system performance measure and main output of interest was the sum of operating costs over all products of the LOD. Just in case the new policy required more warehouse floor space, the latter became another output of interest.

'Total operating cost' is rather vague. Costs are incurred over time. But the LOD was not really interested in the total cost for a particular year, say, the most recent 12-month period. Instead, the aim was to devise decision rules for the future. Since that future was unknown, the analyst assumed that it remained similar to the past — a fair assumption for a stable system such as the LOD. So, the total long-run average cost over a given time interval, such as one year, became the measure of performance. This choice is arbitrary. An interval of one month would work equally well.

The total operating cost is made up of the sum of the costs that change if the control inputs changes and those that are not affected. There is little point in including the latter. They can always be added in at the end, if need be. So, the term 'total operating cost' only relates to those costs that, for the firm as a whole, change if the control inputs change. They are the **relevant costs**.

As we already saw, total cost is the sum of the individual costs incurred for each of 804 products. The cost structure has the same form for each. Only the data inputs differ. Hence, the influence diagram only has to cover one generic product. Once translated into a mathematical model, it can be applied to each product individually.

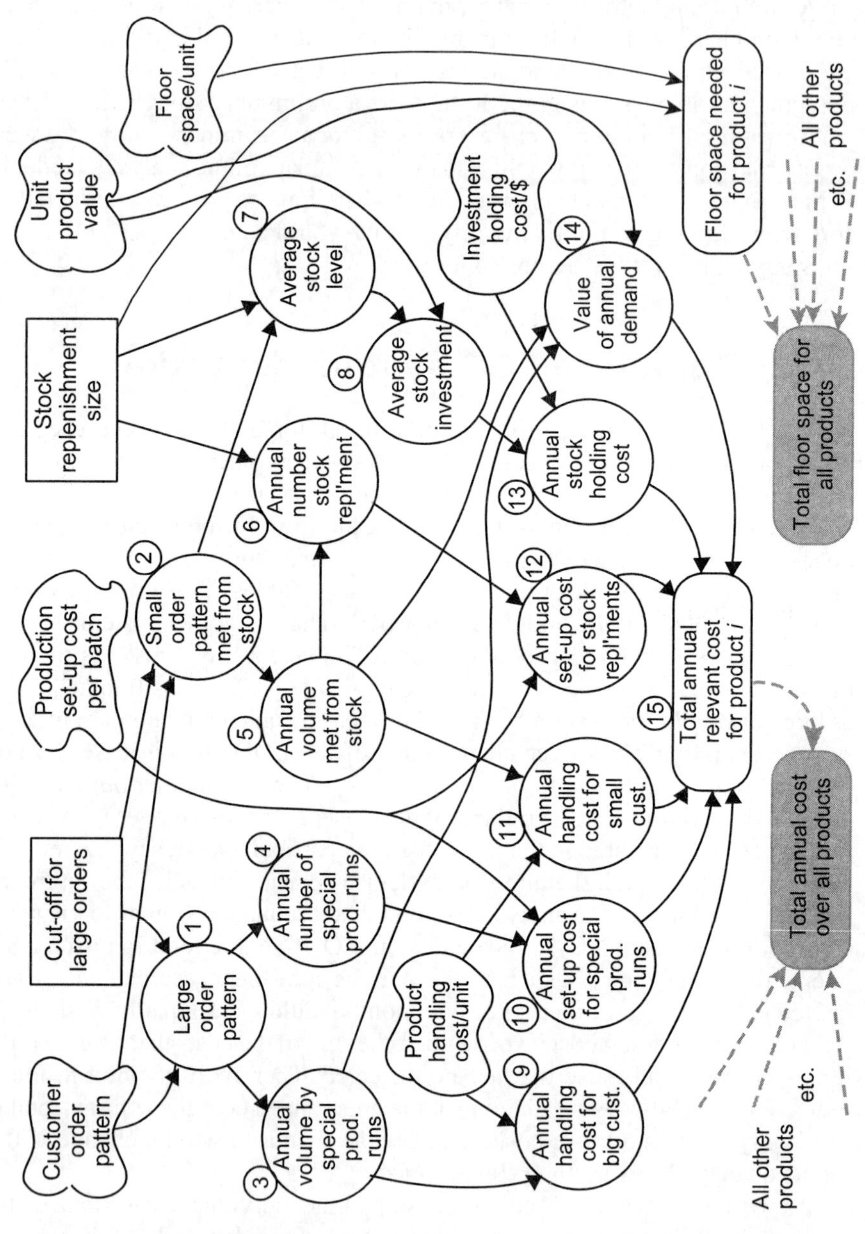

Figure 6-4 Influence diagram for the LOD system

The influence diagram in Figure 6-4 can be translated into a mathematical model for one generic product, *i*. The same pattern is repeated for all other 803 products. The overall performance measure (shown in grey tone at the bottom) is the sum of the 804 individual 'total annual relevant costs'. Similarly, the total warehouse space required (also shown in grey tone) is the sum over all products.

When drawing an influence diagram, start out with inserting the rectangle(s) for the control input(s) — in the LOD case 'cut-off for large orders' and 'stock replenishment size' — at the top of the diagram and the oval(s) for the output(s) at the bottom.

Next, map out the transformation process in a logical top-down sequence. For the LOD, the 'cut-off for large orders' splits the 'customer order pattern' — a data input — into two groups: large orders met by special production runs and small orders met from stock. Therefore, two sets of arrows issue from 'cut-off for large orders' and 'customer order pattern' to the two state variables 'Large order pattern' (circle 1) and to 'Small order pattern met from stock' (circle 2). The state variable 'Large order pattern' determines the 'Annual volume (met) by special production runs' (3) and the 'Annual number of special production runs' (4). Recall that products shipped directly from production are handled only once. So, the 'annual volume by special production runs' and the input data 'product handling cost/unit) together determine the 'annual handling cost for large customers' (9). Similarly, each special production run incurs a set-up cost. The 'annual number of special production runs' and the data input 'production set-up cost per batch' determine the 'annual set-up cost for special production runs' (10). The state variables 9 and 10 are contributors to the output 'total annual relevant cost' (oval 15). Explain all other relationships.

The influence diagram allows us to trace the effect of any choice of decisions on the two output measures. The choices over all 804 products only yield a feasible solution if the total floor space required is no more than the space available.

If a full-scale study indicated that this constraint was violated, either all stock replenishment would have to be made smaller so that the products would fit into the available warehouse space, or the LOD had to add more warehouse space.

A proposal to add more warehouse space would be a new project — an investment evaluation (as covered in Chapter 10). The difference in total costs between the restricted solution (that fit into the available warehouse) and the cost of the unrestricted optimal solutions would be the savings resulting from building a new warehouse of an appropriate size. If these savings, discounted over the life of the warehouse, exceeded the discounted sum of construction, maintenance, and operating costs, building a new warehouse would be financially attractive.

6.12 Mathematical models

A mathematical model expresses, in quantitative terms, the relationships between the various components, as they were defined in the relevant system developed in the formulation phase. Sometimes, it may be possible to represent these relationships in a relatively simple table using a spreadsheet. Often, it may be more convenient or necessary to formulate the relationships with a mathematical expression or a whole system of mathematical expressions, such as equations (e.g., $Q=ax+by$), inequalities (e.g., $ax+by \leq c$), or functions (e.g., $f(x) = ax+[b/x]$).

Before proceeding, it will be useful to define some terminology. The controllable aspects of a problem are referred to as the **decision variables** or the **alternative courses of action**, the latter term being mainly used if the choices available are discrete and usually few in number. For example, when you consider replacing your car with another one, the alternatives may be: do nothing (i.e., keep the current car), replace it with a car of type A, B, C, ..., or K. A decision variable, on the other hand, can be any integer or any real-valued variable in a given range. In the LOD problem, the 804 pairs of 'size of a replenishment' and 'cut-off level for classifying customer orders as large or small', one set for each product, are the decision variables. Both may assume any non-negative integer value (number of containers, e.g., drums, or cases of containers, e.g., cartons of one-litre cans).

Those aspects that measure how well the objectives of the decision maker are achieved form the **performance measure** or **measure of effectiveness**. If it can be expressed as a function of the decision variables, then we usually call it the **objective function**. For the LOD problem, the relevant measure of effectiveness was the sum of total annual costs over all 804 products carried.

Our aim may be to find values for the decision variables that maximize or minimize the objective function, respectively. For the LOD, the aim was to find the lowest total annual cost. Minimization of the objective function became the optimizing criterion.

The uncontrollable inputs are often referred to as **parameters**, **coefficients**, or **constants**. For example, the initial purchase price and the fuel consumption are input parameters into the car replacement decision, while the value of a product, or the production set-up cost were input parameters in the LOD problem. They were uncontrollable inputs from the wider system or the environment.

Mathematical expressions that limit the range of values that a decision variable can assume are called **constraints**. The limits are (uncontrollable) inputs. For instance, you may impose conditions on the minimum capacity of the engine or on the maximum average rate of fuel consumption that a car must satisfy to be a possible candidate. Similarly, the total amount of warehouse floor space available to store all products in the LOD problem was limited to 3600 square metres. Any solution, i.e., combination of decision variables, that required more than that was not viable, i.e., was **infeasible.**

Since the early 1950s, operations researchers have developed many **general-purpose models**. They are the ones commonly used in a structural modelling approach. Linear programming and its numerous extensions, network models, waiting line models, and inventory models are some of the best-known. They have a clearly defined mathematical structure and an associated solution method, usually in the form of an algorithm (Section 6.19 briefly discusses solution methods). They are commonly referred to as OR techniques and form the core of most OR teaching and textbooks.

For problems which do not fit a particular OR technique, the analyst uses a process approach to build a **special-purpose model**. Its structure is specifically tailored to the problem. It may also imply devising a suitable solution technique.

If all inputs and relationships are known with certainty, the model is **deterministic**. If certain inputs are uncertain or random, then the outputs of the model are also uncertain or random. If probability distributions can be specified for the random inputs, the resulting model is **probabilistic** or **stochastic**.

Why build mathematical models?

A pharmaceutical company which does research to develop a medical treatment will first test a large number of compounds or a combination of compounds on laboratory animals. The one or two that have shown exceptional promise may then be tested on humans. In contrast, when a management scientist wants to determine the best mode of operation for an existing process, there are no convenient guinea pigs available, neither is experimentation on the existing facilities a viable option. It would be far too disruptive, too risky, and usually too expensive.

Frequently, the problem deals with potential projects that are still on the drawing board. The entity may not yet exist. Hence, real-life tests are not even possible. But, even if real tests could be done, the time delay caused by testing one configuration, let alone several dozen different ones, means that real-life testing is out of question. In most cases, such tests may take several months or years to become conclusive. The final answer may only be available when the problem has long become irrelevant! Mathematical models are therefore the only practical way to obtain answers to such problems quickly and reasonably inexpensively.

With today's interactive mathematical modelling packages, such models can be developed fairly easily — often within a few hours or days of analysis. The exception may be models that attempt to represent the entire operation of a firm, such as an entire oil company, consisting of the extraction of crude oil, the transportation to the refineries, the detailed operation of the various processes at each refinery, and, finally, the distribution of the refined products. Such a project may take several person-years to complete. The major costs are the salaries of the analysts.

Mathematical models are usually easy to manipulate, particularly with the help of computers. They allow quick exploration of the effects on the objective function of changes in the inputs. In contrast to real-life experiments, a new or updated answer may often be found within a few seconds of computer time. It is these attributes which make mathematical models the workhorse of hard OR.

Important considerations when building mathematical models

When building a mathematical model, the analyst must keep the **essential properties of good models**, discussed in Section 5.3, firmly in mind. In particular, the model should be as simple as possible, while still capturing all essential aspects. It should be robust and, above all, appropriate for the situation, and provide the output relevant and in a useful form for decision making.

As we have seen in Section 3.5, any system definition implies **boundary judgements**. Analysts make some deliberately to keep the problem within manageable bounds or by necessity, because some aspects may be beyond their control. Good practice requires that these be critically justified and recorded. Similarly, when capturing the system's structural relationships, analysts may find it necessary to introduce further assumptions or boundary judgements. Some may be implied by the form of model used. Again, it is essential that these are critically evaluated. Are they appropriate or a sufficiently good approximation to reality? How may they affect the outputs from the model? Could they even invalidate the model's outputs?

Two types of boundary judgement may be made without deliberate consideration. The first, the validity of using past data to predict the future, has already been covered. The commonly implied second boundary judgement is more pernicious and difficult to deal with. As the discussion on efficiency in Section 2.2 and on the hierarchy of systems in Section 3.8 shows, most systems are, in reality, only subsystems of some bigger entity. They share resources with other subsystems, and receive inputs from and give outputs to other subsystems. The implicit assumption we make when 'optimizing' a particular subsystem is that all other subsystems are already operating at their optimum and that any changes made will not affect that — a rather big ask! There may be little we can do about how the operations of other subsystems affect the subsystem studied, except making those in control aware of it. However, it is crucial to ascertain how changes in the subsystem studied may affect the operation of other subsystems. Little is gained if the improvements in one subsystem cause a deterioration in another.

Activity

For each of the following descriptions, indicate whether it involves the use of a mathematical model. If yes, identify its components, i.e., decision variables, uncontrollable inputs, performance outputs (including the objective function), constraints, and so on, and discuss the boundary judgements made.

- The height of males of age 20 in a given city tends to follow a normal distribution with an average of 178 cm and a standard deviation of 4 cm. Current policy states that all recruits to the police force must be at least 174 cm tall. Hence, a certain proportion of persons interested in police work are excluded by this criterion.
- The distance you can throw a rock depends on the weight of the rock, the angle of your throw, and the initial velocity once the rock leaves your hand.
- The amount an addicted gambler is willing to bet in a casino.

6.13 Mathematical model for the LOD: first approximation

In the next two sections we will demonstrate the modelling process of enrichment and reformulation, discussed in Section 5.4.

We already discovered that the connection between products is given by the constraints on warehouse space available and the mixing and filling capacities. A first obvious simplification is to ignore these constraints. If the best unconstrained solutions for all products satisfy the constraints, then these are not restricting and ignoring them was a good guess. If any one of the constraints is violated, e.g., more space than available is needed, we enrich the model by appropriately amending the unconstrained solutions or by embarking on a new round of building a more comprehensive model.

We identified two decision variables: the cut-off point for when a customer order size is classified as large, and the stock replenishment size. As a first simplification, we would rather deal with only one decision variable per product. Note that the original issue raised by the manager of the LOD concerned the size of the investment in stocks. Our first simple model deals only with that.

Checking back with the influence diagram, we now consider only the consequences that follow from state variable (2). This is the stock replenishment subsystem in Figure 6-3. However, rather than simply ignore the decision variable for the cut-off point, we fix it at an arbitrary value, say $L = 12$. In other words, we do not use it as a decision variable, but treat it as another fixed input. This determines the order pattern for demand met from stock (circle 2) from which we can easily calculate the annual volume met from stock (circle 5). This becomes an uncontrollable input into the stock replenishment subsystem. Furthermore, the subsystem for dealing with large orders (circles 1, 3, 4, 9, and 10 in Fig. 6-4) is not affected by the stock replenishment policy and can be ignored at this point.

We are now ready to build the first approximation for a mathematical model. We use the relationships — the arrows — in the influence diagram to form mathematical expressions. Each state variable is expressed as a function of the inputs and/or other state variables which have arrows terminating at the variable in question. Proceeding stepwise down the diagram, we can ultimately assemble an expression for the 'Total annual relevant cost for product *i*' (oval 15).

We start arbitrarily with circle 6. The incoming arrows indicate that the 'Annual number of stock replenishments' is a function of the annual volume of demand met from stock (circle 5 — an input now), denoted by D_1, and the stock replenishment size, Q — the single decision variable of this first approximation. The larger the value of Q, the fewer replenishments needed to fill that demand. A little bit of thought (or trial and error) shows that

(circle 6) Annual number of stock replenishments = D_1 / Q

The annual set-up cost for stock replenishments (circle 12) is a function of the annual number of stock replenishments (circle 6) and the production set-up cost per batch, s. In fact, it is the product of the two:

(circle 12) Annual set-up cost for stock replenishments = $[\, D_1 / Q \,]\, s$

The rich picture (Figure 6-2, p. 133) shows that the inventory for each product follows a saw-tooth pattern over time — each time stocks are filled by a replenishment (the decision variable), they are gradually reduced by withdrawals to meet the pattern of small customer orders (circle 2). Approximating these stock withdrawals as a constant rate, it follows that each tooth is a right-angled triangle. Hence, the average stock level (circle 7) is half its height, or

(circle 7) Average stock level = $0.5Q$

If each unit in stock has a value of v (an uncontrollable input), the

(circle 8) Average stock investment = $0.5Qv$

Each dollar invested per year incurs a penalty of r, so

(circle 13) Annual stock holding cost = $0.5Qvr$

A bit of thought shows that circle 14 is a product of two inputs:

(circle 14) Value of annual demand = vD_1

Circle 11 is also the product of two inputs:

(circle 11) Annual handling cost for small customers = $h_1 D_1$

Summing up these intermediate results gives the total annual relevant cost for the first approximation, denoted by $T(Q)$:

$$T(Q) = 0.5Qvr + (sD_1 / Q) + h_1 D_1 + vD_1 \tag{6-1}$$

$T(Q)$ is a function of one decision variable, Q. Naturally, it is also a function of other inputs in the form of cost and demand parameters. It is customary not to show these explicitly as arguments in $T(Q)$. However, it would be useful to indicate that $T(Q)$ is, in fact, expressed for a given fixed cut-off point L.

Our decision criterion is to find a value for Q that minimizes expression (6-1). Note that for any given cut-off point L, the last two parts of (6-1) are constants that do not depend on the decision variable Q. Hence, the value of Q that minimizes (6-1) is the same that minimizes

$$T(Q) = 0.5Qvr + (sD_1 / Q) \tag{6-1A}$$

By differential calculus it can be shown that the optimal value of Q which minimizes (6-1A) if given by

$$Q^* = \sqrt{\frac{2\,s\,D_1}{v\,r}} \tag{6-2}$$

Expression (6-2) is known as the **economic order quantity formula (*EOQ*)**. It is the simplest, but also the most widely used inventory control mode. In fact, it is the model incorporated in most inventory management software commercially available.

Example 6-1: Economic order quantity

Consider the following example: a given product Y has a total demand in drums of D = 7132. For a cut-off point of L = 12, only D_1 = 4140 is met from stock, the rest is met by special production runs. The product value is v = \$320/drum, the production set-up cost s = \$18, and the holding cost penalty r = \$0.18/\$ invested/year. By expression (6-2), the optimal EOQ is

$$EOQ = \sqrt{2(4140)(18)/(320)(0.18)} = 50.87.$$

Since Q can only have integer values, we round the result to 51. By (6-1A) the relevant annual cost is

$$T(EOQ) = 0.5(51)320(0.18) + 18(4140/51) = \$2,930.$$

Activity

For the following input data: D_1 = 3600, s = \$20, v = \$15, r = 20%, h_1 = \$0.50, determine:

- the annual relevant total cost $T(Q)$ for Q = 300;
- the optimal Q^* = EOQ and its associated annual relevant total cost $T(Q^*)$.

6.14 Second approximation for the LOD model

For the first approximation, we fixed the cut-off point for classifying customer orders arbitrarily at $L = 12$. This allowed us to discover that the EOQ formula could be used for finding the optimal stock replenishment size Q. The annual volume of demand met from stock, D_1, is one of the input parameters of the EOQ formula. That formula is still applicable even if D_1 changes, for instance, as a result of a change in the cut-off point L. Is it then not possible to find the best joint values of Q and L by a simple process of enumeration? Right! For all possible values that L can assume, we determine the optimal value of Q and also compute the total cost associated with the corresponding combination of L and Q. The lowest of these total costs will allow us to identify the jointly optimal values of L and Q.

An interesting feature emerges. The first simple model developed for finding the optimal stock replenishment size becomes a submodel of the new model. Such **nesting** of one model inside another model occurs reasonably often.

The total cost now also has to include those costs associated with special production runs. Since it is a function of two decision variables, L and Q, we will denote it as $T(L,Q)$. The influence diagram in Figure 6-4 shows that there are two additional costs associated with L, the annual handling cost for large customer orders (circle 9), and the annual set-up cost for special production runs (circle 10):

(circle 9) Annual handling cost for large customers $= h_2 D_2$

where D_2 is the annual demand from large customers (circle 3), i.e., the sum of orders equal to or larger than L, and h_2 is the corresponding unit handling cost, and

(circle 10) Annual set-up cost for special production runs $= s\,N$

where N denotes the annual number of special production runs for large customer orders (circle 4). It is given by the number of orders equal to or larger than L. For any L, both D_2 and N can easily be determined from the large order pattern (circle 1).

Note that the annual handling cost for small customers (circle 11) changes proportionately to the demand met from stock, D_1. The latter increases if the cut-off point L increases and decreases if L decreases. So this cost becomes a function of a decision variable and cannot be ignored, as for the simple EOQ model. However, the total product cost $(D_1 + D_2)v$ remains constant, and can therefore be omitted.

The total relevant cost for $T(L,Q)$ is therefore as follows:

$$T(L,Q) = [sN] + [h_2 D_2] + [0.5Qvr + sD_1 / Q] + [h_1 D_1] \qquad (6\text{-}3)$$

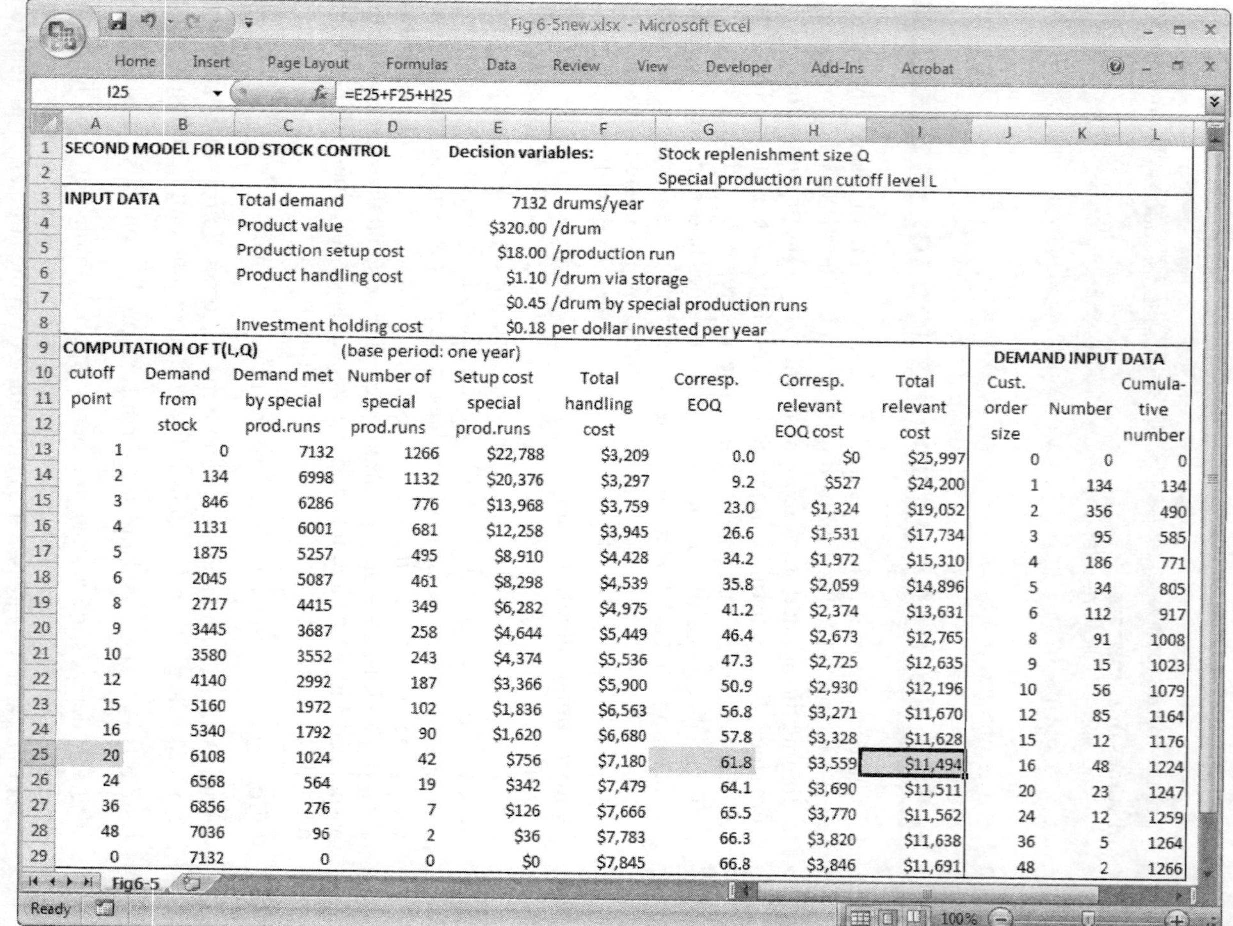

SECOND MODEL FOR LOD STOCK CONTROL — **Decision variables:** Stock replenishment size Q; Special production run cutoff level L

INPUT DATA

Total demand	7132	drums/year
Product value	$320.00	/drum
Production setup cost	$18.00	/production run
Product handling cost	$1.10	/drum via storage
	$0.45	/drum by special production runs
Investment holding cost	$0.18	per dollar invested per year

COMPUTATION OF T(L,Q) (base period: one year)

cutoff point	Demand from stock	Demand met by special prod.runs	Number of special prod.runs	Setup cost special prod.runs	Total handling cost	Corresp. EOQ	Corresp. relevant EOQ cost	Total relevant cost
1	0	7132	1266	$22,788	$3,209	0.0	$0	$25,997
2	134	6998	1132	$20,376	$3,297	9.2	$527	$24,200
3	846	6286	776	$13,968	$3,759	23.0	$1,324	$19,052
4	1131	6001	681	$12,258	$3,945	26.6	$1,531	$17,734
5	1875	5257	495	$8,910	$4,428	34.2	$1,972	$15,310
6	2045	5087	461	$8,298	$4,539	35.8	$2,059	$14,896
8	2717	4415	349	$6,282	$4,975	41.2	$2,374	$13,631
9	3445	3687	258	$4,644	$5,449	46.4	$2,673	$12,765
10	3580	3552	243	$4,374	$5,536	47.3	$2,725	$12,635
12	4140	2992	187	$3,366	$5,900	50.9	$2,930	$12,196
15	5160	1972	102	$1,836	$6,563	56.8	$3,271	$11,670
16	5340	1792	90	$1,620	$6,680	57.8	$3,328	$11,628
20	6108	1024	42	$756	$7,180	61.8	$3,559	$11,494
24	6568	564	19	$342	$7,479	64.1	$3,690	$11,511
36	6856	276	7	$126	$7,666	65.5	$3,770	$11,562
48	7036	96	2	$36	$7,783	66.3	$3,820	$11,638
0	7132	0	0	$0	$7,845	66.8	$3,846	$11,691

DEMAND INPUT DATA

Cust. order size	Number	Cumulative number
0	0	0
1	134	134
2	356	490
3	95	585
4	186	771
5	34	805
6	112	917
8	91	1008
9	15	1023
10	56	1079
12	85	1164
15	12	1176
16	48	1224
20	23	1247
24	12	1259
36	5	1264
48	2	1266

Figure 6-5 Spreadsheet computations for $T(L,Q)$ of the LOD two-decision variable model

6.15 Exploring the solution space for *T(L,Q)*

Figure 6-5 shows the output from a spreadsheet for product Y. It calculates, for a range of values of L, the associated optimal value of Q (using the EOQ formula), and all cost components adding up to the total relevant cost. The lowest cost of $11,494 is obtained for the combination of $L = 20$, and $Q = 61.8$. However, both L and Q have to be integers. Hence, Q is rounded to the nearest integer 62.

The optimal policy is to meet all customer orders of a size $L = 20$ and larger by scheduling a special production run, supply customer orders of less than 20 from stock, and replenish inventory by an amount $Q = 62$ whenever it does not cover the last small customer order received. This occurs about every third day. The volume of demand met from stock is 6108 drums. The balance of 1024 is supplied by special production runs.

It turns out that goods are stored on pallets of four drums each. Management may therefore prefer to use a Q that is a multiple of 4. Verify that $Q = 60$ has a lower cost than $Q = 64$. The lowest total annual relevant cost for multiples of 4 is now:

$$T(L = 20, Q = 60) = \$756 + \$7{,}280 + \$3{,}560 = \$11.495$$

or about one dollar larger than the minimum cost.

Figure 6-6 shows the total relevant cost as a function of L. Note that it is fairly flat. Hence, even moderate adjustments to the optimal values of L and Q will cause only negligible cost increases above the minimum total relevant cost.

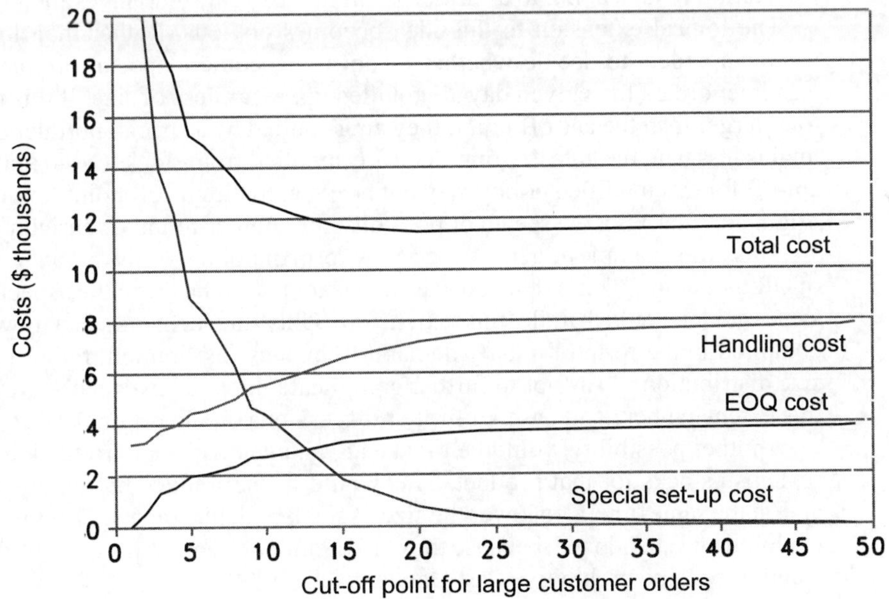

Figure 6-6 Total relevant cost *T(L,Q)* for product Y

How does the second model compare with regard to cost to the policy of $L = 12$ and $Q = 80$ currently used by the LOD? Using expression (6-3), the total annual relevant cost of the current policy is equal to

$$T(L = 12, Q = 80) = 18 \times 187 + 0.45 \times 2992 + 0.5 \times 80 \times 320 \times 0.18 + 18 \times 4140/80 + 1.10 \times 4140 = \$12{,}502$$

or about \$1,007 higher than the recommended policy for the second model — a rather substantial saving. Furthermore, the average investment in stock is reduced by \$3,200, a reduction of 25%. (Verify these numbers, using expression (6-3).)

Are there any aspects that the second model has not captured? Since it deals with each product separately, it still ignores the constraints on the productive capacity and the warehouse space. But as we have already outlined, those will only be considered once the optimal policy has been found for all products. At that point, the overall effect on capacities can then be assessed. Otherwise, the model seems to be a good representation of the real situation.

There are still some opportunities to streamline the model. Some of you may have wondered whether the LOD would make more than one special production run if several customer orders of size L or larger are received for the same product on the given day. Why not combine them into one larger run and split them only at the time of shipping, thereby saving on production set-up cost?

Combining orders leads to a new idea. If one or more small customer orders were also received on the same day as large customer orders, they could all be combined into a single large special production run. Hence, in such cases, even some small orders would be met without the goods going through the inventory stage. The effect of this would be that a slightly larger fraction of the total demand was supplied by special production runs, leading to a further small decrease in stock investments.

The logical extension to this idea becomes obvious. Rather than look at single customer orders to decide whether or not to schedule a special production run, all customer orders for a given day are totalled up, regardless of size. If this total is equal to or larger than the cut-off point, they are supplied by a special production run. If the total is less than the cut-off point, they are supplied from stock. (Note that the optimal cut-off for this modified policy may not be equal to the cut-off point found best for the original model.) So, we see an opportunity for another round of enrichment.

This is an example of generating a new form of policy — always an exciting aspect of OR modelling. This extension was in fact adopted. The fortunate aspect was that the same model could handle this extension. Only the demand data now had to be compiled in the form of a daily demand frequency distribution, rather than an order size distribution. So as not to further complicate the issue, we shall, however, ignore this extension here and base all further discussions on the original $T(L,Q)$-model.

Another possibility would be to take advantage of special production runs also to replenish stocks for that product. This would further reduce production set-up costs and, at the same time, also lower the size of stock replenishments. This third model was explored and abandoned, because the computational effort required to find the optimal solution became prohibitive (see Daellenbach, 1979).

Activity

Using expression 6-3 in Section 6.14, verify the results in Figure 6-5 on page 150 for a cut-off point of 8.

6.16 Testing the LOD model

The LOD model is based, at least in part, on well-tested production/inventory control theory. Hence, there is little doubt about its external validity. Internal validity is tested by verifying the spreadsheet calculations by hand for a typical product.

Testing of the solution of the second LOD model for its performance pretty much follows the steps outlined in the project proposal (Appendix 6.1). The 804 products were grouped into four classes: three classes for lubrication oils and one for all greases. The classification of oils was based on the distribution by annual sales-value volume — the method commonly used for grouping products for production/inventory control purposes. The high-volume A class products comprise the group of the biggest selling products that make up about 50% of the total annual sales value, the low-volume C class products comprise the slowest selling products that make up about 10% of the total sales value. All other products fall into the medium-volume B class. Usually, the breakdown in terms of number of products in each class is roughly 10% for A, 40% for B, and 50% for C.

A stratified random sample of about 5% of all products was seen as appropriate. Fixing the size of each subsample proportional to the annual sales-value volume recognized the fact that the larger the sales volume of a given product, the larger the potential savings were likely to be. The results are shown in Appendix 6.2. They show that the annual expected savings in costs amounted to over $90,000.

Since testing was done product by product, other aspects of importance, such as the variations in the daily workload for mixing and filling, and warehouse space usage, could not be observed. However, rough extrapolations of capacity usage on an annual basis indicated a workload similar to the current one. This was due to two opposing changes in the pattern of operations that as good as cancelled each other out. The proposed policies in general had higher cut-off points and, hence, used less capacity for special production runs. However, smaller stock replenishments resulted in more mixing and filling set-up capacity being taken up.

6.17 Sensitivity and error analysis of LOD solution

Once the optimal solution has been found, two further issues need to be addressed:

1. How does the optimal solution respond to changes in the values of the input parameters?
2. What is the error, in terms of loss of benefits or savings, incurred for using 'an optimal solution' derived on the basis of wrong values for input parameters?

Although both may be called **sensitivity analysis**, we reserve this term for the first, while the second is more appropriately referred to as **error analysis**.

Sensitivity analysis

Sensitivity analysis explores how the optimal solution responds to changes in a given input parameter, keeping all other inputs unchanged. We will demonstrate this, using the total cost expression (6-1A). If expression (6-2) is inserted in (6-1A), and simplified and rearranged, we get

$$T(EOQ) = \sqrt{2Dsvr} \qquad (6\text{-}4)$$

(Note, expression (6-4) is only valid for the optimal *EOQ*, not for other values.)

How do expressions (6-2) and (6-4) respond to changes in the input parameters D, s, v, and r? Assume that one of them changes by a factor k, i.e.,

$$[\text{new value}] = [\text{original value}] \times k$$

Then $T(Q)$ changes by a factor of $\sqrt{k}$, while the EOQ changes by a factor of $\sqrt{k}$ for D and s, but a factor $1/\sqrt{k}$ for v and r. So, a 50% ($k = 1.5$) increase in the demand or the set-up cost increases both the *EOQ* and its total cost by a factor of $\sqrt{1.5} = 1.225$ or by about 22.5%. But a 50% increase in the product value reduces the *EOQ* by a factor of $1/\sqrt{1.5} = 0.8165$ or 18.35% (100% – 81.65%), while $T(Q)$ still increases by 22.5%. For a more modest and more likely short-term increase in the demand of, say, 5%, the increase in the *EOQ* and its cost is only about 2.5%.

Sensitivity analysis has three main purposes:

1. If the optimal solution is relatively insensitive to reasonably large changes in input parameters, the solution and the model are said to be **robust**. It increases the credibility of the model. The decision maker and user can place more confidence in the validity and usefulness of the model. It is true for the EOQ model.
2. For scarce resources, sensitivity analysis finds information about the value of additional amounts of each resource. (This is a concept of high importance to both economics and OR and is taken up in more detail in Chapter 13.) So, if warehouse space turns out to be limiting, then sensitivity analysis with respect to warehouse space will tell us by how much total costs will change.
3. There may be considerable uncertainty about the value of some input data. Sensitivity analysis is used for exploring how the optimal solution changes as a function of such data. If the best solution remains unchanged or is only slightly affected for reasonably large departures of these data from their most likely range, then the decision maker can put much confidence into the solution. On the other hand, high sensitivity of the best solution to minor changes in these data would be a signal for caution. Either greater effort must be expended to obtain highly accurate estimates for the data, or a play-safe policy is implemented instead.

Activity

Current values are: $D = 4140$, $s = \$18$, $v = \$320$, $r = 0.18$. Find the percentage change in the optimal *EOQ* and the associated minimum cost *T(EOQ)* for:

- an annual change in demand *D* from 4140 to 2070;
- a decrease in the annual cost per dollar invested *r* from $0.18 to $0.09.

Can you explain why the change in *T(EOQ)* is the same in both cases, while the changes in the *EOQ* are in opposite directions?

Error analysis

Many of the input parameters are estimated from past data. They are then used for optimizing the operation in the future. There is no guarantee that the future will be similar to the past. For instance, demand for a product may increase or decrease appreciably. The holding cost may increase due to a worldwide rise in interest rates, and so on. So, incorrectly estimated input parameters may have been used in the model. The 'optimal' solution derived on that basis is only optimal on paper, but not in reality. How much does the use of incorrect input data cost in terms of the loss in potential benefits or potential savings? Error analysis explores this aspect.

Say the (incorrect) value p actually used is equal to k times the correct value P, or $p = kP$, where $k < 1$ means it is smaller, and $k > 1$ means it is larger than the correct value. A bit of mathematical manipulation shows that the percentage increase of the true cost over the minimum cost is given by

$$\{ [(k+1) / 2\sqrt{k}] - 1 \} \times 100\%$$

A rather surprising fact emerges. This percentage error is only a function of k and not the actual values of the parameters. The data below provide some examples:

Value of *k*	0.2	0.5	0.8	1.2	1.5	2	4
Implied % error in parameter	-80%	-50%	-20%	+20%	+50%	+100%	+300%
Cost increase over minimum	34%	6.1%	0.6%	0.4%	2.1%	6.1%	25%

For example, overestimating any of D, s, v, or r by 100% results in an increase of actual costs incurred over the minimum possible cost of only 6.1%. These numbers show that EOQ model is very insensitive to fairly large errors in the input parameters, confirming once more its robustness. There is little need for highly sophisticated, and hence very accurate, demand forecasts when using the EOQ model, neither is there a need to estimate the various cost parameters to a high degree of accuracy.

Error analysis is done for two main reasons:

1. To determine the accuracy needed for estimating input data; the more sensitive the solution is to input errors, the more accurate input parameters need to be.
2. To establish ranges for changes in input parameters over which the current policy remains near-optimal. As long as the input parameters stay within these limits, there is no need to recompute the optimal policy. The gain in benefits or savings is too small to warrant the cost of updating. This is an important input for step 9 of the hard OR methodology; namely, control and maintenance of the solution.

Activity

Using the data in the previous Activity on p. 154, determine the percentage error in true costs incurred if:

- the set-up costs are incorrectly assessed as $14.40 and $25.90, rather than $18; and
- the holding cost penalty is incorrectly set at 0.144 and 0.259, rather than 0.18.

6.18 Project report and implementation

The next step in the analysis was to prepare the project report. The projected savings were about $1000 below the crude estimate of the project proposal, but well within the interval estimate. Given this favourable result, the report recommended extending the preliminary study to all products. Study now the project report in Appendix 6.2. Again, note its format.

The project report also touched on implementation, in particular to the fact that the effects of the new policy would occur gradually over about six months, as more and more of the product stocks fell within the range of the new recommended *Q*s.

Human factors became important considerations that needed to enter planning for implementation and the transition itself. Chapter 8 discusses these aspects.

Case study 6-1: Steel Fabricators (continuation of Case study 5-2, p. 104)

Lim wishes to pursue the idea of experimenting with the run length to decrease the rate of defectives. Obviously, the ultimate goal is to get the highest possible net return from the four machines in question, which is not necessarily achieved by minimizing the rate of defectives. He figures that this seems like an ideal project for a student in the MS/OR programme at the local university, and it would allow him to grant a favour to his former lecturer who approached him last year about possible student projects.

Assume that you have been assigned to study this problem in the role of an external consultant. Prepare a written project proposal to study the problem of the high rate of defectives. (You will have to gather all required data, either by direct observation or from cost accounting data. A reasonable guess for data collection is about 16 hours of your time. You will have to estimate the times for all other analysis, and so on, yourself.)

6.19 Solution methods

The optimal solution for the EOQ model was derived by calculus, but we could have used trial-and-error. For many mathematical models, more powerful approaches are needed. We briefly review the common approaches used in hard OR.

Enumeration

If the number of alternative courses of action is relatively small, in the tens rather than thousands, and the computational effort to evaluate each alternative is relatively minor, such as finding the optimal *L* in the LOD case, then finding the optimal solution by evaluating the performance measure for each alternative or each discrete value of the decision variable may be simple and swift. The best solution is the one which achieves the best value of the performance measure — a minimum or a maximum value.

Enumeration is commonly used if the problem deals with a one-off situation. Rather than spend considerable resources in time and funds to develop a more elegant and efficient solution approach, enumeration may be the cheapest way to find the best alternative. It is also more readily understood by the decision maker.

Search methods

If the performance measure to be optimized is in the form of an objective function in one or several decision variables, various search methods may reduce the computational effort to find the optimal solution. Several successful search methods are based on the idea of eliminating successively more and more of the solution space which has been identified as not containing the optimal solution, until an arbitrarily small interval remains which will contain the optimal solution, hence their label **interval elimination methods**. Some of the more famous such methods developed by mathematicians over the years have been given colourful names, such as 'golden-section search'.

Interval elimination methods, however, only work if the objective function is well-behaved. If the objective function contains only one decision variable, this implies that the function is either U-shaped or unimodal, i.e., has only one single maximum (for a maximization problem) or one single minimum (for a minimization problem), as depicted in Figure 6-6 (p. 151).

Algorithmic solution methods

The most powerful solution methods are based on an **algorithm**. This is a set of logical and mathematical operations performed repeatedly in a specific sequence. Each repetition of the rules is called an **iteration**. To start off the algorithm, an initial solution has to be supplied. At the first iteration, the incoming solution is improved upon, using the rules of the algorithm. The new solution so generated becomes the incoming solution for the next iteration. This process is repeated until certain conditions — referred to as **stopping rules** — are satisfied. These stopping rules either indicate that the optimal solution has been found, or that no feasible solution can be identified (if the initial solution supplied was also not feasible), or that a certain maximum number of iterations has been reached or maximum amount of computer time has been exceeded. Most search methods are based on some algorithm. Figure 6-7 summarizes this approach as a flow diagram.

To be a practical solution method, an algorithm has to meet four properties:

1. each successive solution has to be an improvement over the preceding one;
2. successive solutions have to converge closer and closer to the optimal solution;
3. convergence arbitrarily close to the optimal solution should occur in a reasonable number of iterations; and
4. the computation effort at each iteration has to be sufficiently small to remain economically acceptable.

For practically all real-life problems, the computations invariably have to be performed by computer. Many of the general-purpose hard OR techniques, such as linear programming (discussed in Chapter 14), use algorithms for finding the optimal solution. Becoming thoroughly familiar with these algorithms is usually the major part of most intermediate and advanced MS/OR university courses.

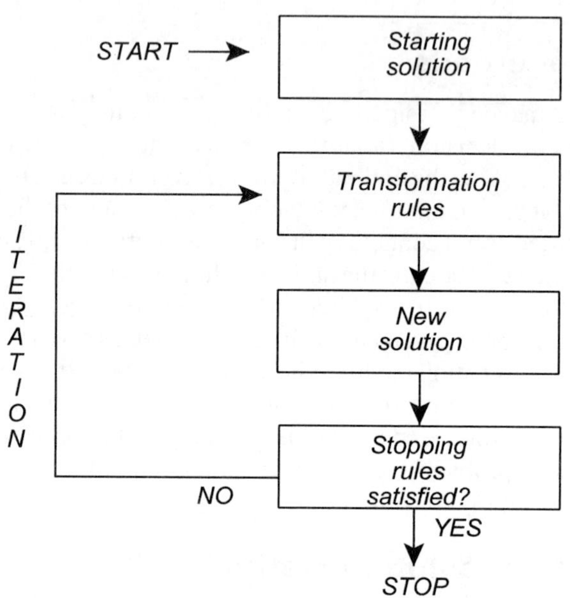

Figure 6-7 General flow diagram for an algorithm

Classical methods of calculus

In some instances, classical methods of differential calculus can be used to find the optimal solution. This is the case for problems involving an objective function with one or two decision variables that can assume any real-valued number, as is the case for the EOQ. The basic idea can easily be grasped graphically. Consider the U-shaped function $f(x)$ in the variable x of Figure 6-8. It first decreases as x increases from a to b and then increases as x increases further. Additional insight is gained by studying how the slope of the function changes as x increases. The slope of the function at any point $x = p$ is given by the tangent to the function at point p. Observe that to the left of b, the tangent is downward sloping, i.e., its slope is negative, while to the right b it is upward sloping, i.e., its slope is positive. As x increases from a, the slope becomes less and less negative, at b itself it is horizontal or 0, and as x moves away from b it becomes more and more positive. The minimum of $f(x)$ is assumed at b, where the slope is 0. (Note, however, that if $f(x)$ is badly behaved there may be other points where its slope is zero and where no minimum or maximum occurs!)

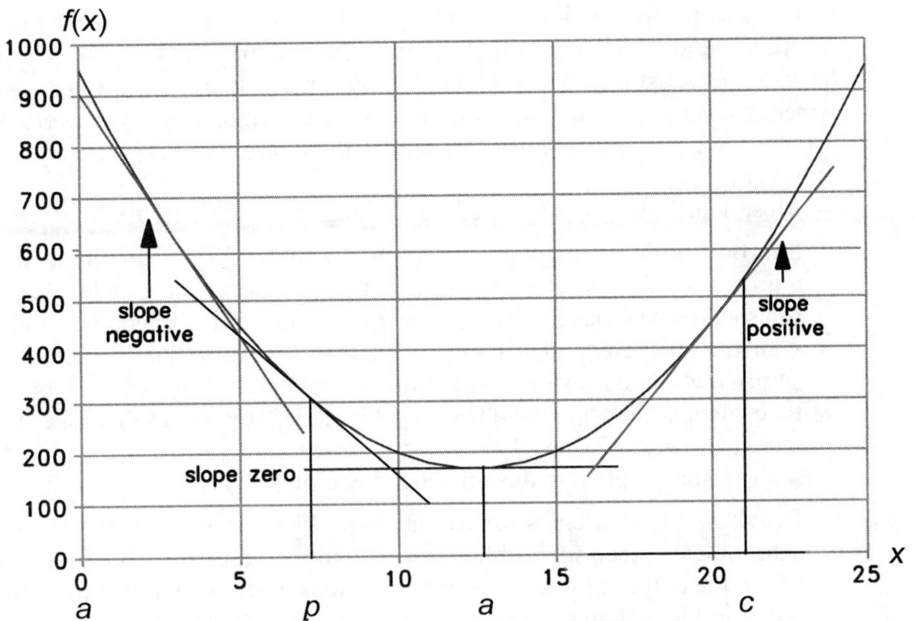

Figure 6-8 A function and its derivative

The **derivative** of $f(x)$ measures the slope. It is denoted by $df(x)/dx$ or simply by $f'(x)$. To determine the minimum, we find the derivative $f'(x)$ and determine the value of x_0 for which $f'(x) = 0$. (We also check that $f(x_0)$ is a minimum by verifying that for a value of x just less than x_0 the derivative is negative, while for a value of x just larger than x_0 it is positive.)

The analogous reasoning can be used for finding the maximum of a function that has the shape of a U upside down. We leave it up to you to work out the details.

Heuristic solution methods

Some models are of such a degree of complexity, or computationally so intractable that it is impossible to find the optimal solution with the computational means currently available. There are also instances where it is possible to find the optimal solution, but the potential benefits do not justify the computational effort needed. Heuristic solution methods may then be the only practical alternative.

Heuristic methods use the human mind's ingenuity, creativity, intuition, and experience to find good solutions or to improve on an existing solution. For example, repeatedly packing boxes of various sizes into a container will teach you the following simple heuristic rule: insert the biggest packages first or else you may not be able to fit them in later on.

It is a process of learning how the measure of effectiveness responds to various solution strategies and then of exploiting the insight gained to devise or discover promising solution rules. Sometimes, it may be possible to find explanations why the rules are successful. At other times, they may be adopted simply because trials show that they work. Although it may sometimes be possible to prove that a given heuristic solution method finds the optimal solution, this cannot be guaranteed. The analyst may have to be satisfied with finding a good, rather than the optimal solution. The American Nobel Laureate for Economics, Herbert Simon, coined the word '**satisficing**' for this. So, heuristic solution methods often result in satisficing, rather than in optimizing.

Most heuristic solution procedures belong to one or a mixture of four strategies:

- **Solution-building strategies:** A complete solution is constructed, one element at a time, according to a set of specific rules. Consider the problem for a travelling salesperson who has to visit each of *n* cities once. The objective is to find the tour with the shortest total distance travelled. A simple heuristic, that often gives surprisingly good results, is as follows: construct a tour by adding one city at a time, always choosing the one (not yet included) closest to the last city added. The bulk beer delivery problem in of Example 1-2 (p. 3) is a type of travelling salesperson problem with some added complications.
- **Break-make strategies:** A complex problem is broken into several smaller subproblems. Each subproblem is solved individually in an hierarchical sequence, where the output of lower-order subproblems become inputs into the next higher-order problem, thereby constructing a solution to the whole problem. This strategy was used for finding the optimal solution for the LOD problem. First, the overall problem of supplying the 804 products to the firm's customers was split into 804 individual subproblems. Each of those subproblems was broken into two lower-order subproblems, one of finding the optimal stock replenishment policy for each possible large orders cut-off point, and then using the results as input into finding the combined optimal large order cut-off point and stock replenishment size. The set of these individual subproblems became the solution to the overall problem. In this instance, it is the overall optimal solution.
- **Modification/improvement strategies:** Specifically designed heuristic rules are used to modify one decision choice of an 'initial' solution. If the modified solution improves the objective function, the change is retained and becomes the next 'initial' solution. If not, the heuristic is applied to another decision. The process stops when no further improvements can be found. For example, for the complete tour of the travelling salesperson problem, derived by a solution building strategy, the following heuristic may discover shorter tours: interchange pairs of consecutive cities; if it shortens the tour, retain it, otherwise not. Once done for all consecutive pairs, the process stops.
- **Search-learning strategies:** Applying a systematic tree-search, at each branch more is learned about the shape of the solution space. This allows the elimination of sequentially more and more of the solution space that is unlikely to contain the optimal solution. Once only a few branches are left, these may be explored exhaustively. The way most players play 'battle-ship' or 'mastermind' uses a search-learning strategy. The information gained by each trial is used to eliminate portions of the solution space and guides the next trial.

Sometimes, different heuristic strategies are applied in sequence (as for the travelling salesperson problem) or in combination.

Simulation

As we have seen in Chapter 3, the behaviour of a system can be accurately described by how the state of the system changes over time. Keeping a detailed record of these state changes and extracting statistics about the average value of critical variables can give useful information about the performance of the system in response to different operating policies. Collecting such data from the observation of the 'real' system may not be possible for a number of reasons — it may be too costly or too time consuming; it may even mean damaging or destroying the system; or the system may not exist yet. So, we imitate, step by step, how the system would behave over time. This can be done with paper and pencil, but is usually more efficient by computer. Such an imitation is called **simulation**. For complex dynamic systems, particularly if they also involve random aspects, simulation may be the only way to collect information about how the system performs under various policies. Again, as for heuristic problem solving, all the analyst can expect is to be able to identify good policies, rather than the optimal one.

Simulation is one of the more important tools for the MS/OR analyst. It is not only used for identifying good, if not optimal solutions, but it is the ideal vehicle for verifying how well the solution derived by other methods is likely to perform in the real world, as well as demonstrating to users how the solution works.

It is discussed in detail in Chapter 17 and Sections 18.6 and 18.7.

Case study 6-2: Steel Fabricators (continuation of Case studies 5-2 and 6-1, pp. 104, 156)

You obtained approval for undertaking the project and collected the following data:

- Raw material cost: £16.20 per part
- Cost of reworking defective parts £4.50
- Operator wage: £16.00 per hour
- Employee fringe benefits (vacation pay, pension fund contribution, insurance): 25%
- Net selling price: £26.40 per part
- Cumulative number of defectives produced for five one-hour test runs:

	Test run	1	2	3	4	5
	6 minutes	0	0	1	0	0
Machine	12 minutes	1	1	1	0	0
run	24 minutes	2	3	3	1	1
time	36 minutes	5	5	5	4	3
	48 minutes	8	7	9	7	7
	60 minutes	12	11	13	12	11

The machine run time does not include the time for making an adjustment.

- If you have not done so yet for Case study 5-2, develop an appropriate influence diagram that measures the gross profit for one machine for an eight-hour shift. (Gross profit is the difference between revenues and all costs, which are a function of the decision variable. It excludes all fixed costs.) Use it to formulate a mathematical model. Create a spreadsheet with a row for each state variable, the output variables (gross profit, number of good parts produced, average rate of defectives) and columns for a machine adjustments after every 12, 18, 24, 36, 48, and 60 minutes (which include the adjustment time).

- Using the results of the spreadsheet, plot the gross profit as a function of the time between adjustments. By trial and error or systematic search, find the number of minutes between adjustments that maximizes the gross profit contribution per eight-hour shift. Determine this time accurate to a full minute. Is this the number you would recommend? Why, or why not? What is your recommended solution and its corresponding gross profit contribution and rate of defectives?
- List all major approximations made for the model in (a). How reasonable are they?
- Perform separate sensitivity analysis for changes of plus and minus 10% and 20% of the rate of defectives, and plus and minus £1 and £2 to rework defectives. How sensitive is the solution?

6.20 Reflections on the hard OR methodology

We have seen that Phase 1 of the hard OR methodology ends with a definition of a relevant system for the problem of interest. Phase 2 takes that system and translates it into a mathematical model. It then applies mathematical methods to find a 'solution', usually one that optimizes some measure of performance.

It is revealing to view this process as a linked sequence of systems, where the output of one becomes the input into the next. This is depicted in Figure 6-9.

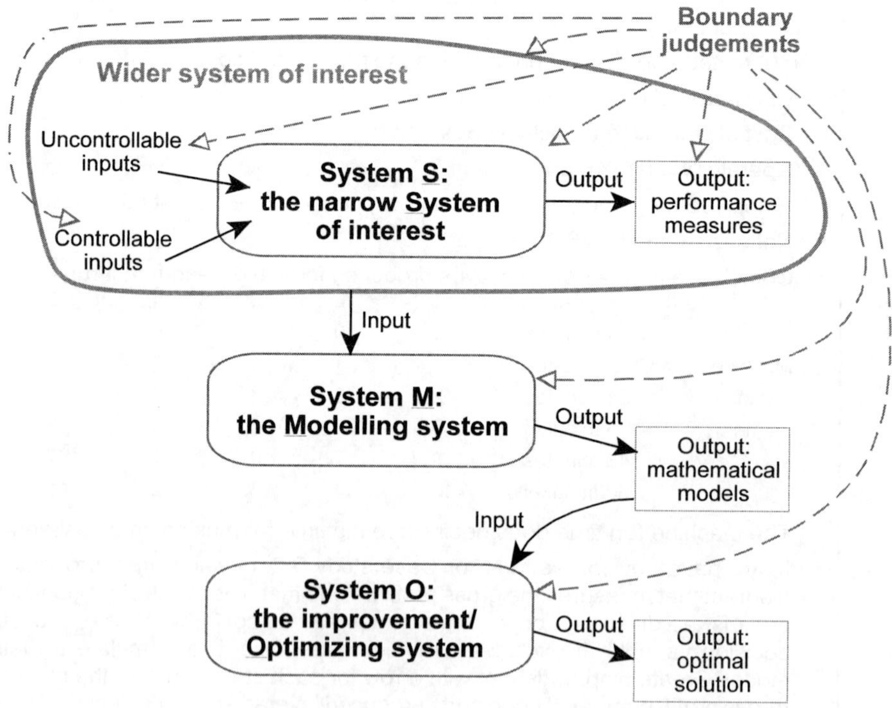

Figure 6-9 Structure diagram for hard OR

Phase 1 develops the narrow system of interest, **S**. The process of building a mathematical model can itself be viewed as a system — a **modelling system**, **M**. It uses as input system S, and then translates the transformation in S into mathematical expressions — a model. This is its output. That model, in turn, becomes the input into an **improvement/optimizing system**, **O**. System O manipulates the mathematical model by exploring its solution space, often with a view to finding improvements in the performance outputs of system S. This manipulation could involve the use of sophisticated mathematical techniques, particularly if the aim is to find the best control inputs to system S that optimize its performance. Boundary judgements affect all aspects.

6.21 Chapter highlights

- The hard OR methodology is an iterative process that covers three well-defined phases: problem formulation, mathematical modelling, and solution implementation, each consisting of several steps, with forward and backward linkages.
- Phase 1 is either a complete problem formulation or a problem scoping study.
- Problem scoping usually leads to a project proposal that makes recommendation as to whether to proceed, and if so, how.
- Phase 1 may produce a complete definition of the relevant system, e.g., using an influence diagram, the identification of a typical, known system structure to be fleshed out in the problem modelling phase, or only a low resolution description, delineating the boundaries of the relevant system using a high-level structure diagram. Boundary choices must be critically evaluated for their implications.
- A mathematical model expresses the system relationships in quantitative form. By manipulating the inputs (both controllable and uncontrollable) it is possible to explore the solution space of the system, possibly with a view to finding the solution that achieves the best value of the performance measure.
- By necessity, mathematical models are always approximations of the 'real thing', not the 'real thing' itself. This may imply further boundary judgements.
- The model's final version is not usually derived in a single pass, but is the result of an iterative process of reformulation and enrichment. This process terminates when the analyst is satisfied that the model approximates and captures most significant relationships of the real situation and that it will produce answers that are insightful, relevant, and appropriate for decision making. The analyst must find a balanced compromise between simplicity and completeness.
- For problems that involve finding an optimal solution, a number of often powerful techniques, methods, and approaches have been developed. Familiarity with them forms a core aspect of training in hard OR.
- Sensitivity analysis explores how the optimal value of the performance measure responds to changes in uncontrollable inputs, while error analysis establishes the loss in true benefits incurred if a solution based on erroneous uncontrollable inputs

is used (instead of the truly optimal solution). Both help establish how robust the model and its solution are.

- Verification of the model and its input data, and validation of both the model and the modelling approach are important features for establishing the credibility of a model and the sponsor's and user's confidence in its results.
- The project report is the document that allows the problem owner to decide if the findings should be implemented. It should disclose both the strengths and the weaknesses of the model and its solution.
- Concern for implementation is an ongoing process from the start of a project.
- The hard OR methodology can be viewed as a sequence of linked systems: a formulation system, a modelling system, and an improvement system.

Exercises

1. Read the Champignons Galore summary in Appendix 9.1 (pp. 265–70). That case is used for the purpose of identifying a suitable system, and so on.
   (a) Draw a high-level system structure diagram, similar to Figure 6-3, delineating the boundaries of the relevant system.
   (b) Discuss the boundary judgements implied by your boundary choices.
   (c) List stakeholders and the six problem elements.
   (d) Draw an influence diagram for computing the annual cost as a function of the number of flushes per growing/harvesting cycle.
   (e) Assume that you have been asked to do a scoping study and prepare a project proposal for finding the optimal policy for the number of flushes. Assume that, at the time you write the project proposal, no cost data, or yield, and picking rate data have been collected yet. Such collection is therefore part of undertaking the project. Also, based on the situation summary, no estimates of potential savings can be derived.
2. Consider the 'Sawmill as a cost minimizing system' in Section 3.6 (pp. 36–9).
   (a) Identify the stakeholders of the problem.
   (b) List the six problem elements.
   (c) Draw a high level diagram, similar to Figure 6-3, showing the boundary of the relevant system and its major subsystems.
   (d) Discuss the boundary judgements implied by your boundary choices.
3. ELMO, a manufacturer of electric motors, has just purchased a machine tool for winding coils of electric motors. Initial trials with the machine indicate that the number of rejects produced varies with the running speed of the machine. The results of the six trials for various speed settings are as follows:

Speed	30	40	50	60	70	80	90 coils/hr
Trial 1	1	2	3	5	6	8	11 rejects
2	0	1	4	6	7	9	10 rejects
3	1	3	4	4	5	7	9 rejects
4	2	3	2	4	5	7	11 rejects
5	2	1	2	4	7	10	10 rejects
6	1	2	3	5	6	7	10 rejects

Rejects have to be scrapped. The material cost of each coil is €2.60. The machine operator is paid at a rate of €22/hour. It costs €6 to operate the machine for one hour. 10,000 good coils have to be produced for a given type of motor. The total cost of producing this batch is used as the performance measure for setting the machine speed. Note that to end up with 10,000 good coils more than 10,000 coils will have to be wound. The size of the batch that needs to be scheduled is equal to 10,000/(1 – fraction of rejects). The fraction of rejects is a function of the machine speed.

(a) Develop an influence diagram showing the relationship between the running speed of the machine and the total cost of producing the batch of 10,000 coils.

(b) What boundary judgements are implied by the system defined in (a)?

(c) Use that influence diagram to derive mathematical expressions for each state variable and the performance measure of total costs. Combine these expressions into a single expression for total costs as a function of the machine speed setting. Does that model make additional boundary judgements? If so, what are they? (Note such further assumptions may be in the form of simplifications.)

(d) Develop a table or a spreadsheet containing one row for each variable and one for the total cost and columns for the running speeds listed above. Graph the results and identify the range where the lowest cost is likely to lie. Use the table to determine the best speed setting.

4. (a) Develop a spreadsheet to compute the total annual cost corresponding to expression (6-1) in the text for values of $Q = 24, 32, 40, 48, 56, 64, 72$, using the data listed in the Example box on p. 148. Find the optimal solution to the nearest integer value by trial and error.

(b) Reproduce the spreadsheet of Figure 6-5, including all calculations for the same data.

5. One of the products in the LOD is only sold in multiples of 4 drums. A total of 120 orders were received last year as follows:

Order size	4	8	12	16	20
Number of orders	70	32	11	5	2

They were evenly spread over the entire year with very few days having more than one order. The sales pattern for the coming year is expected to be fairly similar. The combined mixing and filling set-up cost is $15. The product handling cost is $1/drum for orders supplied from stock, and $0.40/drum for orders met by a special production run. Each drum has a value of $400. The stock holding cost is $0.18/$1/year. (It is suggested that you develop a spreadsheet similar to Figure 6-5.)

(a) Assume that all orders of more than 8 drums are met by a special production run. What is the optimal inventory replenishment size, its total annual cost, and the overall total annual cost for meeting the entire demand?

(b) Find the combined optimal policy for meeting customer demand, i.e., an optimal cut-off point for special production runs and an optimal stock replenishment policy. What is the minimum cost associated with the optimal policy?

6. Consider the following data for another LOD product: product value $180/drum, production set-up cost $12/set-up, product handling cost $1.50/drum via storage, $0.30/drum via special production run, investment holding cost 25% on the value invested per year; and the demand distribution as follows over a period of one year covering 250 working days:

demand	0	2	4	6	8	12	16	20	24	32
days	82	65	32	23	17	10	8	5	4	4

(a) Using the EOQ model, find the optimal stock replenishment size if the cut-off point for direct replenishments is set at 12 drums. Note that the demand is not given as a frequency distribution by customer order size, but by total demand for each day. The implication is that special production runs are made to cover all customer orders for a given day, rather than individual customer orders. (This is the extension briefly mentioned in Section 6.8.)

(b) Develop a spreadsheet similar to Figure 6-5 for finding the joint optimal values for the stock replenishment size and the special production run cut-off point.

7. A liquid is mixed in a mixing vessel and then packed into one-litre cans on an automatic filling machine. It takes the mixing technician two hours to mix the liquid, regardless of the amount to be mixed. The cost of the ingredients used is £1.60/litre. Two machine operators take 30 minutes to prepare the machine for a filling run. Cans are filled at a rate of 60/minute. Both machine operators have to be present while the machine is filling cans. The cost of a can, including its label, is £0.15. The labour costs for the technician and the machine operators, including the cost of fringe benefits earned, amount to £18 per hour worked. The firm aims for a rate of return on its investments of 24% per year.

(a) Determine the cost of preparing a batch of 3600 cans for the product in question.

(b) The annual demand for that particular product is 180,000 cans. Use the EOQ formula to find the optimal batch size and its relevant total annual cost.

(c) The cans are packed into cartons of 48 cans each. Cartons are stored on pallets. Each pallet holds 24 cartons. The practice is to always produce a batch which results in a multiple of full pallets, i.e., a multiple of 24 times 48 cans. If this practice is to be continued, what batch size would you recommend as best in terms of total costs?

8. Last year, Q-Imports sold 750 sets of stainless steel cutlery, imported from Germany at a cost of £60 per set, including airfreight. The firm sells the sets to retailers at £96. Sales occur at a fairly steady even rate throughout the year. The sets were imported in two shipments, the first of 250, the second of 500. For each shipment, the firm incurs clerical costs, bank charges, and custom agent clearing charges, totalling £200. Q-imports usually finances most of its purchases by bank overdrafts. The current overdraft rate is 18% per year. There are also insurance costs for storing goods in inventory amounting to 2% of the value of the goods. The manager of Q-Imports expects that sales this coming year will be about ⅓ higher than last year's. He therefore plans to place two orders of 500 sets each.

(a) What would be the total annual cost of the proposed ordering policy?

(b) Could he do better? Why and how?

9. A-Electronics sells about 2000 of its new sim chips per month at a price of $35/chip. The production cost are $25/chip. The current policy is to replace any chips that fail within the first six months of installation. The dealer doing the replacement also gets $10 to cover the labour cost for the replacement. The competition has recently increased its guarantee period from 6 to 9 months. A-Electronics is now under pressure to follow suit, or even go to a 12-months guarantee period. The engineering department has collected extensive data on replacements of chips, both under guarantee and after the guarantee period. They show the following picture, where time refers to the number of months after the initial installation of the chip:

Time	3	4	5	6	7	8	9	10	11	
Replacements	0	1	2	2	5	5	6	6	9	
Time	12	13	14	15	16	17	18			
Replacements	9	13	14	18	22	23	27			per 1000 chips

(a) Management would like to know the increase in annual costs of extending the guarantee period from 6 months to 9, 12, 15, or 18 months. You need to find a functional relationship between the time and the number of replacements. What approximations, assumptions or boundary judgements do you make?

(b) By how much would monthly sales have to increase to recover the increase in guarantee costs?

Answer both questions by building an appropriate spreadsheet.

10. A manufacturer assembles pumps from parts purchased from subcontractors. For a particular type of pump, it takes a technician 8 hours to set up the assembly line. His pay, including all fringe benefits, is £24/hour. Other production set-up costs, such as picking up the required number of parts from subcontractors, amount to £80. Once the technician has set up the assembly line, four people perform the actual assembly of the pumps. They can assemble 24 pumps per day. The value of the assembled pump, including all parts and labour costs, is £216. The firm estimates that its stock holding cost is 25% per year on the average stock investment. The annual demand for that pump is about 1250. The replenishment policy used is to start a new assembly run of Q pumps whenever the stock for that pump has been depleted. Hence, the technician will prepare a new assembly run one or two days prior to the time the inventory for that pump has been sold. Once assembly has been started, each day's production of 24 pumps are available for sale. In other words, during production, some of the pumps are sold, and once a batch has been completed, fewer than Q pumps remain in stock. (Note that this situation is slightly different from the EOQ model developed in this chapter, where the entire batch Q is added to stock as a single lot.)

(a) Adapt the influence diagram of Figure 6-4 for this situation. Note that there is no special production run option. That whole section is deleted, but the section dealing with the average inventory investment is now more complex and needs more detail.

(b) Using this influence diagram, develop a set of expressions that will ultimately culminate in a total relevant annual replenishment and inventory cost.

(c) List the approximations that you made to develop the total cost expression.

(d) Using enumeration by spreadsheet, find the optimal replenishment size and its cost.

The following computational exercises on sensitivity and error analysis are most conveniently done using the spreadsheets developed for the original exercises above.

11. For the example used in Figure 6-5, explore the effect on the optimal EOQ and its cost for the following changes in input parameters:

(a) changes in the replenishment set-up cost from \$18 to \$12, \$24, and \$36;

(b) changes in the investment holding cost from 18% to 12%, 24%, and 30%.

12. For the optimal solution to the ELMO coil production problem in exercise 3, do the following sensitivity analysis:

(a) changes in the size of the order from 10,000 to 5,000, 20,000, and 40,000;

(b) changes in the rate of defectives per hour, which currently runs at 0.0125 × (running speed of the machine)^2, to 0.0015, and 0.001 × (running speed)^2.

13. For the example in Figure 6-5, perform error analysis for the following cases:

(a) A true replenishment set-up cost of \$12 and \$24, rather than the \$18 used.

(b) A true investment holding cost of 12% and 24%, rather than the 18% used.

(c) The list of percentage errors for the EOQ error analysis on page 155 is not only valid for errors in the annual demand, but also for errors in the replenishment set-up costs or the ratio of replenishment set-up costs and investment holding cost; use this result to estimate the approximate effect of the following errors:

- an error of –80%, –20%, +50%, and +100% in the set-up cost; and
- true set-up costs and holding cost penalties of \$12 and 12%, \$15 and 25%, and \$24 and 15%.

14. For the ELMO coil production problem of Exercise 3, perform the following type of error analysis (note that the results of Exercise 4(e) will be useful):
    (a) a true size of the order of 20,000 rather than 10,000.
    (b) a true coefficient for the rate of defectives of 0.001 rather than 0.00125.
15. Discuss the following apparent contradiction: if at the start of an MS/OR project all costs and potential benefits were known accurately, the project would not get off the ground. However, if the total costs and potential benefits can only be ascertained with some confidence after the model has been tested for performance, but prior to its implementation, the correct decision may be to proceed with implementation. What implications does this have for evaluating costs and benefits of MS/OR projects?
16. Based on your analysis of the ELMO case in Exercises 3, 12, and 14, as well as additional analysis as to the potential savings of the best solution over the current policy, write a short project report, following the format in Appendix 6.2.
17. What information/insights is the (a) manager or decision maker; and (b) the problem analyst looking for in sensitivity and error analysis? Use your own words.
18. Why is establishing internal and external validity important for (a) the decision maker/user of the solution; and (b) the analyst of the problem?

Further reading

Ackoff, R.L. and Sasieni, M.W. (1968) *Fundamental of Operations Research*, New York: Wiley. An update of Churchman et al.; excellent coverage of modelling principles in Chapters 1 to 4.

Checkland, P. and Holwell, S., 'Classic OR and 'Soft' OR — An Asymmetric Complementarity', in Pidd, M. (2009) *Tools for Thinking: Modelling in Management Science*, 3rd edn, Chichester: Wiley, 45–60.

Churchman, C.W., Ackoff, R.L. and Arnoff, E.L. (1957) *Introduction to Operations Research*, New York: Wiley . The first complete OR text published. In contrast to most US published MS/OR textbooks (Ackoff and Sasieni excepted), it gives full coverage to modelling principles in Chapters 1 to 7. Chapter 2 has a complete case history of an OR project. (Out of print.)

Daellenbach, H. (1979) 'A family of inventory models with demand met either from stock or by special production runs', *Engineering and Process Economics*, June 1979: 141–6.

Fildes, R. and Ranyard J.C. (1997) 'The success and survival of or groups: a review', *Journal of the Operational Research Society*, 48: 336–60.

Landry M., Malawian, J.-L. and Oral, M. (1983) 'Model validation in operations research', *European Journal of Operational Research*, 14/3, November: 207–20.

Landry, M. and Oral, M. (1993) Special Issue: Model Validation, *European Journal of Operational Research*, 66/2, April. A series of articles on model validation. The editors' conclusions show that the validation issue cannot be divorced from the questions of 'What is science?' and 'Is OR/MS science?' Extensive bibliographies on validation and the process of science.

Pidd, M. (ed.) (2004) *Systems Modelling: Theory and Practice*: Chichester: Wiley. Chapter 4 discusses principles of modelling.

Williams, T. (2009) *Management Science in Practice*, Chichester: Wiley. Focus on practical skills needed by practitioners; Part III has discussion of the stages of a project similar to this chapter.

Also check out the Internet for guidelines on report writing and covering letters.

Appendix 6.1

PROJECT PROPOSAL
PRODUCTION/INVENTORY CONTROL STUDY
LUBRICATION OIL DIVISION, SANDPOINT REFINERY

Table of Contents

1. INTRODUCTORY STATEMENT

On 17 March 20XX, Mr Black, Manager of the LOD, approached the Management Science Group at the Company's Headquarters with a request to study the LOD production/inventory operations of packaged goods and make recommendations concerning appropriate stock levels. It is my understanding that this request is a follow-up on remarks in the Company's internal auditors' report about the current level of investment in stocks at the LOD. In particular, the auditors pointed out that the LOD's average stock turnover of packaged goods was well below the Company's target of 24 times per year, resulting in a level of funds tied up in packaged goods judged as excessive.

I arranged for a visit to the LOD's production and warehousing facilities at Sandpoint on March 27 and 28, during which I had extensive discussions with Mr Black, Mary Clarke, the stock control clerk, Bill Quick, the data processing supervisor, and all four operations supervisors. I also consulted with the Cost Control Department at Headquarters. The following report outlines my recommendations for a preliminary study, briefly motivates and describes the proposed analysis, and lists the resources required and a timetable for undertaking the study.

2. EXECUTIVE SUMMARY OF RECOMMENDATIONS

It is recommended that the Company's Management Science Group undertakes a preliminary study of the production/inventory operations. The study would develop a model for finding optimal stock replenishment sizes as well as the minimum size when it becomes more economical to meet individual customer orders by a separate mixing and filling run. Based on this model, reliable estimates as to the potential savings in operating costs can be computed with the aim of establishing whether a full-scale investigation can be justified. The results of the study would be available within 4 weeks and the internal charge to the LOD would amount to $7,200.

3. STATEMENT OF THE PROBLEM SITUATION

The auditors' report states that the LOD's stock turnover rate over the last two years averaged 12 times per year and, hence, is well below the company's target rate of 24. As a result, they conclude that the amount of funds tied up in stocks is about twice as high as it should be.

2

What are the cost implications of a given stock turnover rate? For the current customer delivery policy and production lead time, the average amount of funds tied up in stocks, and hence the cost of carrying this investment for any given product, is proportional to the size of its stock replenishment batches. On the other hand, the annual production set-up cost is inversely proportional to the size of replenishment batches. Any reduction in average stock levels and the annual cost of carrying the corresponding investment can therefore only be achieved by increasing the annual production set-up cost. It can easily be shown that there is a best size for each replenishment batch for which the sum of these two costs is at its lowest possible value. This also implies a best turnover rate for each product. It is likely to be different from product to product. Only by coincidence will the average turnover rate over all products be equal to the target rate of 24. A target turnover rate of 24 may thus not achieve the lowest total cost for the LOD operations.

If the objective is to reduce total investment in inventories, it is preferable to set an upper limit of the total amount, rather than a target turnover rate. The models can then be used for finding the least expensive policy to stay within this limit. This recognizes the fact that the best turnover rate is different from product to product.

The current customer delivery policy offers the opportunity to schedule special production runs for direct delivery to customers. The goods then by-pass the inventory stage. Furthermore, they will then only be handled once, rather than twice, reducing handling costs. This is currently done for those products where large customer orders occur frequently. A decrease in the cut-off point for which customer orders are met by special production runs reduces the fraction of the total demand satisfied from inventories. This, in turn, will reduce the best replenishment size, and hence the average investment in stocks. It will decrease product handling costs, but increase the annual number of set-ups incurred for special production runs and, hence, the annual set-up cost. It will also affect the best stock turnover ratio for the portion of the total demand met from stock.

The best policy is the one which sets a cut-off point for special production runs and a stock replenishment batch size that minimizes the sum of all relevant costs.

Annual cost reduction in operating costs for a sample of six products range from $32 to $253, with an average of $114 and a standard deviation of 30. A 95% interval estimate of predicted saving for all 804 products is $90,000 to $94,000. The cost of a full-scale study is estimated as 80 chargeable days or $48,000 at the internal charge-out rate of $600/day.

However, rather than embark on a full-scale study right away, it is advisable first to undertake a preliminary analysis. Its aim is to establish beyond doubt whether the potential savings of a full-scale study are justified by the cost of such a study. The reasons for such a recommendation are that: (1) at this stage it is difficult to give any reliable estimates of the potential savings that could be achieved without substantial additional effort and data collection; and (2) the cost of a preliminary study is about one tenth of the cost of a full-scale study, and the model developed can be carried forward to the full-scale study, reducing that cost accordingly.

If the findings confirm that all further costs for a full-scale study can be recovered within the first year of changing over to the new policy, i.e., within the one-year payback period required for such projects by the Company, a recommendation and timetable for such a study will be submitted for approval.

4. BRIEF DESCRIPTION OF PROPOSED ANALYSIS

The preliminary analysis will be done for a random sample of products. Its results will be extrapolated to all products carried by the LOD. The following major steps are involved:

(a) Development of model: After further on-site study, a model for the total annual relevant

3

cost, suitable for use on all products carried by the LOD, will be developed. It will be used for determining the best combination of stock replenishments and cut-off point for special production runs for each product. The objective is to minimize the total annual operating costs. The model will be in the form of a computer spreadsheet.

(b) Sample selection and data collection: In view of increasing the accuracy of potential savings estimates for the new policy, products will be grouped according to annual sales and a representative sample selected from each, making up about 5% of all products. Demand and cost data will be estimated for all products in the sample using readily available data from the LOD data base of customer orders and costing data from the Cost Control Department.

(c) Estimation of total saving: The total annual operating cost for the best policy will be determined individually for each product in the sample. These costs will be extrapolated for each product group, and finally to the entire product line. This extrapolation is an estimate of the total annual cost of using the best policy for all products. This estimate will be compared with the annual costs incurred for the current policy. The difference represents the potential annual savings. No change in the expected office costs of running the new policy is expected.

(d) Estimation of further expenses for a full-scale study: The expense in terms of internal employee charge-out rates, materials, and computer running costs for undertaking a full-scale study will be estimated.

(e) Forming of recommendations and preparation of project report: The recommendation will state whether a full-scale study should be undertaken, based on the normal company criterion that all expenses for such a study must be recovered by the savings generated within one year after implementation of the recommendations. If appropriate, the project report will also present a detailed budget of resources needed and a timetable for undertaking the full-scale study.

5. ASSUMPTIONS UNDERLYING THE ANALYSIS

The analysis makes the following assumptions about the operations of the LOD:

1. the future customer order pattern for all products remain unchanged;
2. the current capacities of the mixing and filling operations remain unchanged; and
3. the available storage space in the warehouse remains unchanged and is sufficient to carry any possible increase in total inventories; if this turns out to be not the case, the total annual costs for the adjusted policy would be slightly higher.

6. RESOURCES REQUIRED AND TIMETABLE

Task	Staff time (days): Analyst	Cost control	LOD	Elapse time
Model development	1		1	2
Sampling design	2		2	4
Data collection	4	3	3	8
Savings estimates	1			4
Writing recommendations	1			3
Totals	9	3	6	21 days
Chargeable costs:	9 days +	3 days	at $600/day	$7,200

Date: 11 April 20XX

Project analyst: I.M. Right, Management Science Group

Appendix 6.2

PROJECT REPORT
PRODUCTION/INVENTORY CONTROL FOR PACKAGED GOODS AT THE LUBRICATION OIL DIVISION, SANDPOINT REFINERY

Table of Contents

1. INTRODUCTORY STATEMENT

This report contains the findings of a preliminary study covering the production/inventory control operations for packaged goods in the LOD warehouse at Sandpoint Refinery. Mr Black, Manager of the LOD, approved this study on April 18, on the basis of the project proposal submitted to him by the Management Science Group on 11 April. We undertook the preliminary study during the period from May 27 to July 5.

The aim of the study was: (1) to develop a mathematical model for finding the best production and stock replenishment policy which minimizes the sum of all costs affected by the choice of policy; and (2) to estimate the potential savings in operating costs that can be achieved by using such a policy for all products.

2. EXECUTIVE SUMMARY OF FINDINGS AND RECOMMENDATIONS

The following major findings were made:

(a) Implementation of the policy proposed in this report for the entire product line of the LOD is estimated to result in annual savings of operating and investment costs of over $90,000. It will increase the average stock turn over to about 32 times per year.

(b) Total staff time needed for developing the necessary software, data collection, and policy implementation is projected at 100 days, of which 70 are chargeable to the LOD. That charge amounts to $42,000.

(c) The new policy could be fully implemented within 14 weeks.

In view of this highly favourable ratio of savings to costs, it is recommended that the LOD immediately proceeds with implementing the proposed model.

3. STATEMENT OF THE PROBLEM

The current production and stock replenishment policy for packaged goods followed by the LOD distinguishes between two groups of products: group 1 includes only high-volume products with frequent large customer orders, and group 2 includes all other products. Group 1 covers currently 78 products (all packaged in drums of 200 litres),while group 2 covers the remaining 726 products. Each group accounts for about 50% of the total dollar throughput. The production and stock replenishment policy is characterized as follows:

2

1. Group 1: any customer order equal to or larger than a given cut-off point is supplied by scheduling a special production run, while any customer orders below the cut-off point are met from stock. Stock is replenished periodically. Currently, the cut-off point for all products is 12 drums, while the stock replenishment size varies from product to product and covers between 2 and 6 weeks of customer orders supplied from stock.
2. Group 2: all customers orders are supplied from stock. Stock replenishments vary in size with the sales volume and cover between 3 and 12 weeks of sales.

Our analysis indicates that, in principle, the policy followed for group 1 products can be applied to all products, drums as well as products packaged in other containers. Furthermore, the choice of the best cut-off point depends not only on the customer order pattern, but also on the various production and warehousing costs.

Rather than classify products arbitrarily into these two groups, we decided, after discussions with Mr Black and other LOD staff, to build a model that allows all products to follow the group 1 policy, but with individually determined cut-off points and stock replenishment sizes. If the cut-off point for a product is set at a level larger than the largest customer order likely to be received, the policy for that product corresponds to the entire demand being supplied from stock.

Although some products exhibit a mild seasonal pattern, the model is based on the premise that the average demand remains constant over the year. The effect of this simplification is negligible. To adjust for trend, the optimal policy should be updated annually.

As a result of opting for a uniform policy for all products, the problem becomes one of developing a model which finds for each product a cut-off point and stock replenishment size so as to minimize the sum of all operating costs affected by the values chosen for these two variables. The relevant costs are: (a) the product raw material and production cost; (b) the mixing and filling operation set-up costs; (c) the product handling costs; and (d) the cost of holding products in stock, which consists mainly of the cost of funds invested in stocks.

The second aim of the study, namely the estimation of the potential savings that would accrue if the model is applied to all packaged goods, was achieved by extrapolating the results obtained from a sample to all products.

4. MAJOR STEPS OF ANALYSIS

These followed the steps outlined in the project proposal.

(a) Developing a suitable model: My initial visits to the LOD on 27 March were followed up by further visits on 26 and 27 May. After extensive discussions with Mr Black and his staff, we concluded that a model based on the group 1 policy should be used, in principle, for all products. A computer spreadsheet program was developed for finding the best policy. The details of the model and a sample output from the spreadsheet are shown in the Appendices to this report.

(b) Data collection for the sample of products to be analysed: In view of the large number of products, the model was applied to a sample of 5%, with the results to be extrapolated to all products. In order to achieve higher accuracy of the estimate, the products were grouped into relatively homogeneous classes. The usual distribution by annual dollar sales volume was applied, with three classes: high, medium, and low annual dollar volume. Since the production set-up costs of greases are considerably higher than for oils, a fourth class for all greases was created. The composition of the classes and the subsample sizes is summarized in the top portion of Table 1 below. Products to be analysed were selected by random sampling methods. The customer order pattern for each sample product was extracted from the 20XX customer order file, the most recent complete year of customer data available. Figures for all relevant cost factors were supplied by the Cost Control Department (CCD) or were computed based on rough time trials.

(c) Estimation of total savings: For each product in the sample, the best policy, consisting of the cut-off point for large customer orders and the stock replenishment size, was computed using the spreadsheet developed.

A simple simulation program was written to simulate the performance of the proposed and of the current policies for a given product. This program was used for estimating the total cost difference between the two policies for each product in the sample. This, in turn, provided all the input required for extrapolating the results obtained to the entirety of all products. The findings are summarized in Table 1.

Table 1 Estimation of potential annual savings

Class	High volume oils	Medium volume oils	Low volume oils	Greases
Overall:				
Percentage of total volume	45	35	12	8
Number of products	64	205	411	124
Subsample size	20	15	5	4
Ratio (# in class/subsample)	3.2	13.67	82.5	31
Per product:				
Average cost difference	$431	$147	$74	$39
Standard deviation	$125	$26	$21	$19
Extrapolation to class:				
Cost difference	$27,584	$30,135	$30,414	$4,836
Standard error	$1,000	$372	$425	$212
Estimate of total cost difference:		$92,969		
Standard error (of total estimate):		$1,168		

5. MAJOR FINDINGS

Table 1 summarizes the results of extrapolating the savings to the entire packaged goods product line carried by the LOD. It shows that implementation of the best policy for each product would generate savings over the current operating costs of over $90,000 per year.

A detailed comparison of the current and proposed best policy indicates the following:

(a) As expected, the best cut-off point differs from product to product. As a rule, it tends to be between 3200 and 4400 litres per order — somewhat higher than the current 2400 (which is equivalent to 12 drums). Hence, a larger proportion of all sales are supplied from stock than is currently the case.

(b) For most products, the best stock replenishment size is also smaller than the current policy, and this in spite of the higher cut-off point.

(c) A consequence of (b) is a substantial reduction in total investments, as well as warehouse space needed. This could well ease the current shortage of easily accessible warehouse space suffered by the LOD.

(d) The average stock turnover associated with the best policy seems to be substantially higher than the company target of 24 times/year. A rough estimate is around 32 times/year.

(e) The proposed best policy is relatively insensitive to reasonable shifts in the total annual demand and in most cost factors, i.e., changes in any of these items of up to 25% that

4

may occur after implementation of the best policy for a given product will only result in a small reduction in the potential savings. As a consequence, it will in most instances be adequate to update the best policy once each year, unless a given product is subject to major changes.

6. RECOMMENDATIONS FOR IMPLEMENTATION

Implementation of the model to all products will require computationally efficient programs to be developed for finding the best joint values of the cut-off point and stock replenishment. Furthermore, the format currently used for recording customer order data requires substantial data manipulation. Hence, considerable time savings can be gained in the future when the control variables are updated, if Information Systems Services (ISS) makes several small additions to the existing programs for recording customer orders and storing them in their data base. Implementation involves therefore mainly staff time, with the time of the analyst, CCD, and ISS chargeable to the LOD. No new equipment or stationery is needed. Table 2 shows the staff time for the various tasks. According to this schedule, the new policies could be in full use by the end of October.

Table 2 Staff resources required for full implementation

Task	Staff time (days): Analyst	Other staff	LOD	Completion
(a) Programs for use of model	12		1	week 4
(b) Alterations to data files	3	24 (ISS)		week 9
(c) Data collection	5	6 (CCD)	20	week 8
(d) Computation of policies	5			week 12
(e) Preparation of implementation plan	2		2	week 12
(f) Instruction of users	3		5	week 13
(g) Change-over to new policy	2		2	week 14
(h) Follow-up monitoring	8			week 26
Totals	40	30	30	
Chargeable cost:	40 days + 30 days		at $600/day	$42,000

The estimate of potential annual savings indicates that the cost of full implementation would be recovered by the new policies within less than half a year. However, it should be noted that the savings will only rise to their full potential level after a transition period. During this period, excess stock levels of those products with lower recommended replenishment sizes will be gradually reduced to their new lower levels, while products with higher recommended replenishment sizes will reach their new levels very quickly. Therefore, the savings in investment costs will only become fully realized once the new average levels have been achieved for all products. This may take up to 6 months.

Based on this analysis, I recommend that the model developed is implemented.

Date: 10 July 20XX

Project analyst: I.M. Right, Management Science Group

5

APPENDIX: SPREADSHEET COMPUTATIONS FOR FINDING OPTIMAL POLICY

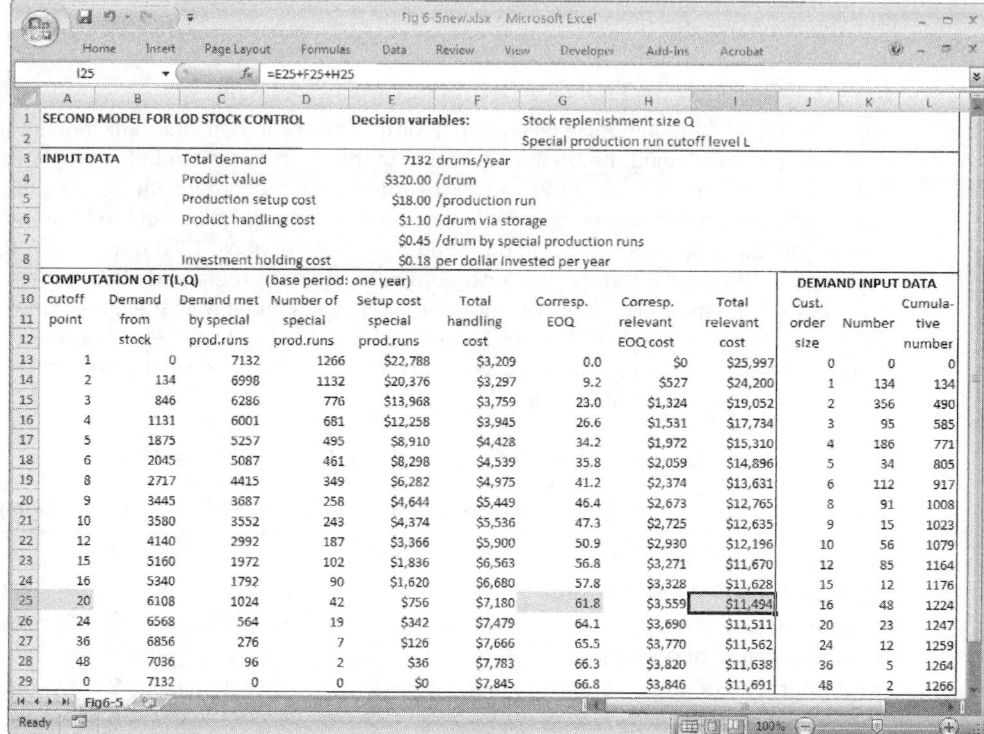

SECOND MODEL FOR LOD STOCK CONTROL — Decision variables: Stock replenishment size Q; Special production run cutoff level L

INPUT DATA

Total demand	7132	drums/year
Product value	$320.00	/drum
Production setup cost	$18.00	/production run
Product handling cost	$1.10	/drum via storage
	$0.45	/drum by special production runs
Investment holding cost	$0.18	per dollar invested per year

COMPUTATION OF T(L,Q) (base period: one year)

cutoff point	Demand from stock	Demand met by special prod.runs	Number of special prod.runs	Setup cost special prod.runs	Total handling cost	Corresp. EOQ	Corresp. relevant EOQ cost	Total relevant cost
1	0	7132	1266	$22,788	$3,209	0.0	$0	$25,997
2	134	6998	1132	$20,376	$3,297	9.2	$527	$24,200
3	846	6286	776	$13,968	$3,759	23.0	$1,324	$19,052
4	1131	6001	681	$12,258	$3,945	26.6	$1,531	$17,734
5	1875	5257	495	$8,910	$4,428	34.2	$1,972	$15,310
6	2045	5087	461	$8,298	$4,539	35.8	$2,059	$14,896
8	2717	4415	349	$6,282	$4,975	41.2	$2,374	$13,631
9	3445	3687	258	$4,644	$5,449	46.4	$2,673	$12,765
10	3580	3552	243	$4,374	$5,536	47.3	$2,725	$12,635
12	4140	2992	187	$3,366	$5,900	50.9	$2,930	$12,196
15	5160	1972	102	$1,836	$6,563	56.8	$3,271	$11,670
16	5340	1792	90	$1,620	$6,680	57.8	$3,328	$11,628
20	6108	1024	42	$756	$7,180	61.8	$3,559	$11,494
24	6568	564	19	$342	$7,479	64.1	$3,690	$11,511
36	6856	276	7	$126	$7,666	65.5	$3,770	$11,562
48	7036	96	2	$36	$7,783	66.3	$3,820	$11,638
0	7132	0	0	$0	$7,845	66.8	$3,846	$11,691

DEMAND INPUT DATA

Cust. order size	Number	Cumulative number
0	0	0
1	134	134
2	356	490
3	95	585
4	186	771
5	34	805
6	112	917
8	91	1008
9	15	1023
10	56	1079
12	85	1164
15	12	1176
16	48	1224
20	23	1247
24	12	1259
36	5	1264
48	2	1266

APPENDIX ON COMPUTATIONS PERFORMED

(Not shown here in detail.) This appendix gives, for each product, full details on input parameters used for finding optimal policies and the resulting solution in a table form. It also shows the results of the simulation runs and the cost incurred for the current policy. These form the basis for estimating the potential savings in Table 1. Details on sensitivity analysis performed are included also.

APPENDIX: DETAILED DESCRIPTION OF MODEL

(Not shown here in detail.) This appendix shows an annotated formulation of the total cost function for the *T*(*Q*,*L*)-model. It also lists all important assumptions, in particular that there are no warehouse or production facility capacity restrictions. If such a constraint turns out to be binding, once the optimal policies for all products have been computed, suitable adjustments would need to be made. It also refers to the opportunity to generate additional savings if the stock level is reviewed whenever a special production run is scheduled for a given product, and topped up at the same time. Extending the model to cater for this aspect would have increased its complexity substantially, adding several thousand dollars in model and software development, while only producing a small further saving. However, no tests were made to confirm this conclusion.

7

Soft systems thinking

'If we investigate our ideas, we have to be willing to give them up.'

Gordon Hewitt, PhD, Wellington, New Zealand

Learning objectives

- Appreciate what aspects distinguish PSMs from hard OR.
- Be able to distinguish between issues of 'What?' and 'How?' in a problem situation.
- Be able to draw a rich picture summarizing salient features of a problem situation (see Chapter 4).
- For Checkland's soft systems methodology, be able to:
  - perform Analyses One, Two, and Three for a relatively simple problem situation;
  - identify the six elements of CATWOE for an issue or vision of a problem situation chosen for more detailed study;
  - compose a suitable root definition expressing necessary CATWOE elements for a relatively simple issue chosen for analysis, and translate it into a conceptual model;
  - identify similarities and differences between the conceptual model and the 'real' world situation, and propose ensuing topics for discussion.
- Using a SCA mode of analysis, be able to identify potential decision areas and draw a decision areas graph (shaping), identify sets of mutually exclusive feasible action options and create an option tree (designing), identify the presence of any of the three types of uncertainties and their relative importance, draw a pair-wise comparison graph with respect to the objectives relevant (comparing), and suggest a plausible commitment package (choosing), for a relatively simple problem situation.
- For a simple problem situation involving two conflicting interest groups, each with a set of assumptions about objectives, boundary choices, and courses of action, create an assumption rating chart.
- Appreciate that, for many problem situations, facts and values are not separable, but that what we see as facts and their interpretation depends on our worldviews and values.

Introduction

In 1960, C.W. Churchman, a pioneer of MS/OR, voiced his serious misgivings about the ever-increasing mathematical bias and narrow focus on optimization of MS/OR. Rather than dealing with important executive-type decision problems, these trends condemned MS/OR to become tools for low-level operational problems. He challenged our MBA class at the University of California to step beyond the shackles of mathematics and address our efforts to the really important problems humanity was facing. His call for a change of heart remained a lonely voice for almost another decade. Stafford Beer, the originator of the **viable system model**, was the only exception — in fact, a precursor.

In the late 1960s and the 1970s, other voices took up the call: Russel Ackoff (University of Pennsylvania), Peter Checkland (University of Lancaster), John Friend and A. Hickling (Tavistock Institute of Human Relations), and Colin Eden (University of Bath) being some of the most prominent.

Rather than accept the narrow rationality of economic thought, they recognized that human decision making is far more complex and varied, and that it is also governed by other than economic values. Imposing a 'solution' that ignores these aspects simply shifts the problem to a new dimension. They also recognized that the process of decision making itself greatly affects whether or not a 'solution' is accepted. They expanded the narrow quantitative optimization focus to include ideas from other disciplines, primarily critical philosophy, sociology, behavioural psychology, and organizational behaviour, in order to tackle those important executive-type decision problems.

This blurring of boundaries between disciplines can be seen as part of the growing awareness that problems do not respect discipline boundaries, that a narrow economic efficiency focus alone is insufficient, and that human striving for quality of life, happiness, aesthetics, equality, and justice are equally valid and legitimate aims. The 2011 global movement against financial greed that started on Wall Street in New York and found echoes all over the world is a popular manifestation of this.

This chapter introduces the philosophy and processes of these alternative approaches to decision making. They go under the label of **soft OR**, and a subset of them is referred to as **problem structuring methods (PSMs)**. Their basic properties and working modes are presented first. The next five sections demonstrate three prominent and radically different problem structuring approaches: Checkland's **soft system methodolog**y, Eden's **strategic option development and analysis (SODA)**, and Friend and Hickling's **strategic choice approach**. The final two sections give a brief summary of further philosophical and methodological issues in soft systems thinking.

Finally, let us quote J. Mingers and J. Rosenhead (2011):

> Researchers and practitioners in soft OR/PSMs do not consider them as a challenge to or substitute for the established mathematical methods of MS/OR. Soft MS/OR could no more schedule an oil refinery than dynamic programming could help a group of disparate stakeholders with variable or nonexistent quantitative skills to agree on what subset of their shared problematic situation they should attempt to make progress with. The approaches are complementary.

7.1 Soft systems paradigm and working modes

Ackoff (1979) points out that 'Managers are not confronted with problems that are independent of each other, but with *dynamic* situations that consist of *complex problems that interact with each other* (author's italics)'. This quote, Ackermann (2011) says, brings up two other pertinent issues: 'that of being willing and able to manage the complexity rather than reducing it, and feeling comfortable with group members continually shifting and changing their understanding of the situation'. It is thus not surprising that the protagonists of soft OR/soft systems approaches correctly claim that the majority of real-life problem situations in business, industry, and government violate many, if not most, of the basic assumptions underlying the hard OR view of the world that we studied in Chapter 6.

We will now contrast the hard OR properties of Section 6.1, with the properties that fit the majority of soft systems approaches. (Review the beginning of Section 6.1 to refresh your memory.)

Properties of PSMs and soft systems approaches

Soft systems approaches were designed to deal with complex problem situations, which are messy, ill-structured, ill-defined, not independent of people — in other words, where different stakeholders have different, possibly conflicting perceptions about the problem situation and its major issues, often with conflicting worldviews, and where there may not even be agreement about the appropriate objectives. PSMs and other soft systems approaches cater for this diversity. They are characterized as follows:

1. Structuring the issues in a problem situation, rather than narrow-focused problem solving.
2. Facilitating dialogue between the various stakeholders with the aim of achieving a greater degree of shared perceptions of the problem situation, rather than providing an analytic decision aid to decision makers.
3. Addressing 'What?' questions first, and only then 'How?'questions, i.e.,
   - What is the nature of the various issues and how are they connected?
   - Who are the respective stakeholders for each issue?
   - Which issue should be addressed first/next?
   - What are appropriate objectives for that issue, given the various worldviews and the implied value systems of the stakeholders?
   - What are appropriate definitions of the system for each of the various issues to be considered, with particular emphasis on boundary choices for both the narrow and the wider system of interest?
   - Which changes are **systemically desirable** and **culturally feasible**?
   - How are these changes best brought about?
4. Requiring the stakeholders to work together to elicit from within their group a resolution to the 'problem' and accommodation for future action, rather than having it presented by an external expert/analyst consultant.

5. Changing the role of the problem solver/analyst to one of becoming a facilitator and resource person who relies on the technical subject expertise of the stakeholders.
6. Appreciating that the problem situation is dynamic, rather than static, and is evolving both in terms of its environmental context and the shifting perceptions of its stakeholders as the intervention progresses.
7. Appreciating that the human aspects inherent in a problem situation and the intervention process itself cannot be treated as separate unrelated issues since the intervention process changes the human dynamics in the problem situation.

'How?'questions, i.e., which means are the best for achieving the desired goals, must ultimately also be addressed by soft systems approaches. But they are often an anti-climax, almost obvious, rather than being centre-stage as in hard OR projects.

Chronological list of PSMs and soft systems approaches

Here is a list of PSMs and soft systems approaches. Some are fully-fledged methodologies, others have more the flavour of techniques, while still others provide a philosophical basis for sound professional practice. (Developers in parentheses)

1950s	**Gaming** (RAND Corporation)
1959	**Viable system model** (Beer)
1960s	**Metagame analysis** (US Arms Control and Disarmament Agency)
1969	**Strategic choice approach** (Friend and Hickling)
1969/81	**Strategic assumption surfacing and testing** (Mason and Mitroff)
1971	**Social systems design** (Churchman)
1974	**Interactive Planning**, or **Social systems sciences** (Ackoff)
1975	**Soft systems methodology** (Checkland)
1979	**Strategic option development and analysis** (Eden)
1980	**Hypergame analysis** (Bennett)
1980	**Robustness analysis** (Rosenhead)
1980–90	**Theory of constraints** (Goldratt)
1983	**Critical systems heuristics** (Ulrich)
1990–3	**Drama theory** (Bennett, Bradley, Bryant, and Howard)
1991	**Total systems intervention** (Flood and Jackson)
1995	**Multimethodology** (Brocklesby and Mingers)

Essential characteristics

In contrast to hard OR, it is difficult (possibly even questionable) to capture the characteristics and working mode of all PSMs and soft systems approaches in a single diagram, as in Figure 6-1 (p. 119). The majority use quite different, often ad hoc processes that have evolved through practical use and have proven themselves successful for specific types of problem situations. However, they all take a highly **subjectivistic view** of systems, i.e., systems reflect the worldviews of the stakeholders.

Several approaches were developed through **action research**, often within a practical consulting context. Some, such as Checkland's soft systems methodology, Churchman's social system design, and Ulrich's critical systems heuristics, are firmly based on philosophical foundations and systems theory. Gaming, metagame and hypergame analysis, and drama theory originate from the ideas of **game theory**, but abandon its rigorous axiomatic foundations and only retain its outer form, i.e., two or more players with opposing views. Other approaches, such as aspects of strategic option and development analysis and drama theory have psychological roots. Total systems intervention and multimethodology are meta-methodologies that help analysts determine which paradigm and method or combination of methods is most suitable for a given problem situation.

They have a number of properties in common. While hard OR deals mainly with the 'content' of the problem, giving only limited concern to 'process', soft approaches put equal emphasis on both content and process. At the very start of an intervention, process is used for extracting content and the underlying value systems. The methods seek to attain a reasonably comprehensive view of the issues within their wider context, although they recognize that true comprehensiveness is impossible, and it may not be necessary to obtain agreement on a workable course of action. The main aim at that stage is to gain a shared understanding and mutual appreciation about values, interests, objectives, choices for action, and the environment, and identify clusters of highly connected aspects. System and environment boundary choices are subjected to critical assessment and evaluation. They also recognize that a resolution of a problem does not necessarily require a full convergence of views, and that a mutual appreciation of views short of seeking consensus may be sufficient for an acceptable compromise and a commitment for action.

Iteration through, or flexible switching between, various modes of working is a prime feature. Several use software to aid in the structuring process and the exploration of choices. Most require a facilitator with thorough training and experience in the method and, most importantly, good interpersonal and negotiation skills.

Figure 7-1 is a compromise to capture general aspects of the working mode of the majority of methods. In parallel to hard OR, there are three major phases: formulation of the problem, system and action modelling, and implementation.

As mentioned earlier, most approaches are iterative, both between different steps within a phase and between phases, with strong forward and backward linkages. Different steps may be dealt with at the same time (shown by sets of black arrows in both directions). Change of perceptions, revelation of new aspects and their implications, or reaching of impasses may call for a return to an earlier step (as shown by the grey arrows). For several methods, the first two phases have considerable overlap. As more is learned about the problem situation and the issue selected, the working mode may need to switch from modelling back to formulation several times (as indicated by the solid grey arrow).

Activity

From your reading in Chapters 2, 3, 4 and 6, discuss why concern with the intervention process itself is essential when dealing with complex problem situations with multiple stakeholders.

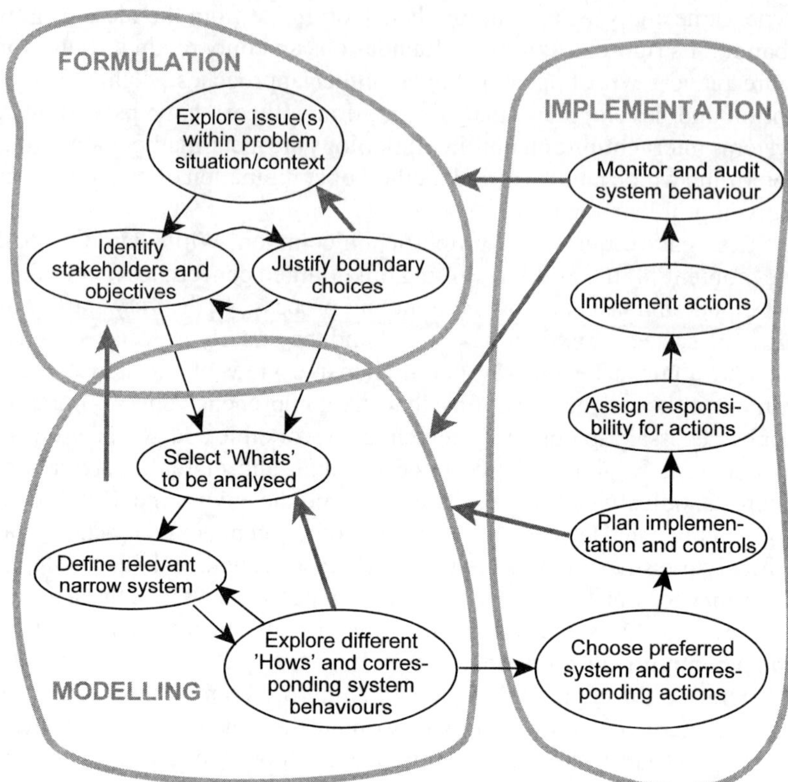

Figure 7-1 General working mode of PSMs

7.2 Checkland's soft systems methodology

Peter Checkland's soft systems methodology (SSM) is, without doubt, one of the most researched and rigorously based PSMs in terms of its theoretical systems premises and underlying philosophical reasoning. Although difficult to judge, it also seems to be the most widely applied, with numerous known applications, many of them documented in the literature.

Based on a programme of action research at the University of Lancaster in the late 1960s, the methodology evolved, using itself as a learning system. Each case investigated by the Lancaster research group in the early stages involved not an 'obvious' problem to be solved, but a situation which some people saw as problematical. Furthermore, different people saw different aspects as problematical, and multiple interpretations existed for many aspects. The group quickly realized that deeper and more insightful learning could be gained by exploring in parallel a meaningful subset of such interpretations, rather than just a single concern, as in a hard OR approach.

This culminated in the development of a 'seven-stage' methodology, presented in Checkland's ground-breaking 1981 book '*Systems Thinking, Systems Practice*'. As more experience was gained using the methodology over the following ten years,

Checkland and his co-researchers applied the methodology to undertake research itself — a process that is still ongoing. The '*SSM in Action*' text (Checkland and Scholes, 1990/1999) discusses a number of applications that demonstrate how the methodology evolved into a flexible and more fluid 'four-activity' process.

By necessity, the following brief treatment cannot pretend to give you practical know-how for applying the methodology. Its aim is more modest, i.e., to convey a flavour of its process and some of the underlying ideas.

The 'seven-stage' SSM process

The original seven-stage process remains the more easily understood version and is still more universally taught. Figure 7-2 shows a flow diagram of its iterative working. Black arrows show the logical sequence of the stages, while dashed grey arrows depict backward links.

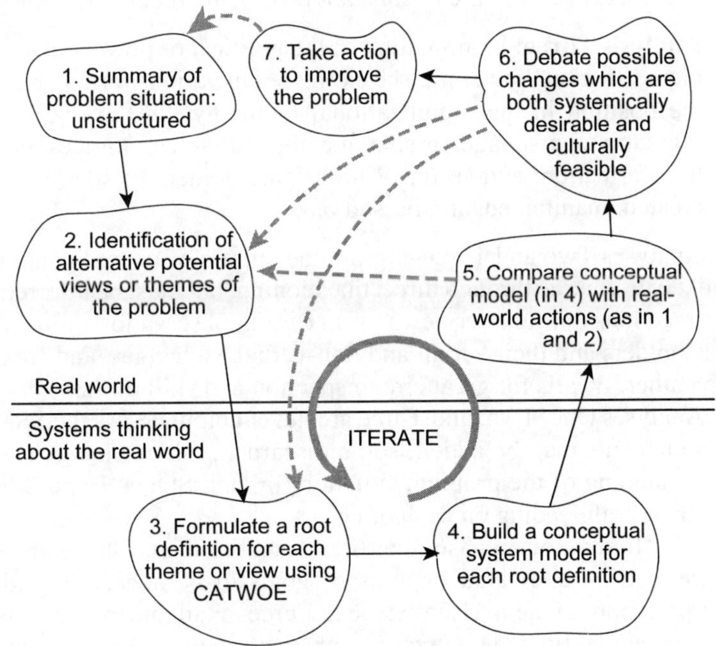

Figure 7-2 A flow diagram of the seven-stage SSM process (adapted from Checkland, 1983)

Stages 1 and 2: They form the 'finding out' phase of SSM. Stage 1 assembles a **situation summary** or a **rich picture** of the problem situation 'as is'. It should be a holistic view that contains elements of structure and process, as well as aspects of 'climate'. (You are encouraged to refresh your memory on rich pictures by reviewing Sections 4.4 and 4.5, pp. 67–71.)

Stage 2 enriches the picture by performing three types of analyses:

1. **Analysis One:** Examination of the intervention in terms of three roles. The 'client' role is assigned to the person or group of persons that caused the enquiry to take

place. The 'problem solver' role is taken by the person or group of persons that undertakes the investigation. The 'problem owner' role is a stakeholder or stakeholder group from whose point of view the problem situation may plausibly be viewed. For most problem situations, there are several different candidates or groups for this role. It is the problem solver who chooses who takes the role of problem owner(s). Note that the same stakeholder(s) may fill two or all three roles.

Analysis One also explores the reason why the problem owner sees various aspects as problematical, the problem owner's assumed worldview, and the resources (funds, time, people, data and facilities) available for the investigation.

2. **Analysis Two:** Examination of the social characteristics of the problem situation. What are the expected role behaviours or norms of the stakeholders? What are the values by which they are judged? Who controls role behaviour and norms? Who sets the values? Note that roles, norms, and values are interdependent. Each defines the other two. They are in constant flux, being redefined through their interactions.

3. **Analysis Three:** Examination of the political or power-related aspects of the problem situation. Power may be expressed in various forms: the authority implied by the position in the organizational hierarchy, the level of education, expertise, reputation, personal charisma, membership to committees, control over or access to information, and so on. Who are the holders of such powers? How is power created, maintained, and passed on?

Analyses Two and Three explore the culture of the entity studied. That culture is unlikely to emerge through direct questioning, but must be inferred from the behaviour and reactions during interviews, from careful observation of the interactions between stakeholders and their verbal and non-verbal exchanges, and from how they defer to each other. It calls for great circumspection and skill of those doing the analysis.

Analyses One, Two, and Three are never complete. As the SSM process proceeds, new elements may be added, some discarded, others changed. All three enrich the understanding of the problem situation. In fact, Stages 1 and 2 happen more or less together, both feeding on each other.

The 'finding out' phase identifies potential themes to explore, such as issues of concern to be alleviated or aims or goals to be achieved, and differing possible interpretations of them. Usually, the resources available for the investigation imply that only a meaningful and contrasting subset of up to a dozen can be studied in detail.

The initial emphasis should be on 'Whats' before addressing 'Hows'. What specific goals or aims should be pursued that are consistent with the worldviews of the problem owners? What aspect, such as organizational climate and organizational structure, may need to change to remove obstacles for achieving the goals? What are the information needs? Most 'Whats' ultimately also lead to 'Hows', i.e., how to bring about the desired change, where alternative means are explored.

Stage 3: The methodology now leaves the real world and enters the abstract world of systems thinking. Each interpretation of a theme is expressed as a **root definition** — a concise unambiguous statement, specifying the nature of the human activity system relevant to accomplishing the aim of the theme. A full root definition takes the form:

Let A, authorized by O, do T by doing X, benefiting or affecting C, to achieve Z justified by W, subject to E.

where

T stands for the 'transformation' of the system from a given state to another. X is the set of activities achieving this transformation. So, T stands for 'what to do' and X for 'how to do it'. The set of activities X should not simply map the existing structures of the problem situation. Checkland recommends that each T be judged on five E-criteria: Efficacy (does it work?); Efficiency (are resources required kept as low as possible?); Effectiveness (how well does it do it?); Ethicality (is it ethical to do it?) Elegance (is it aesthetically pleasing?).

O is the 'owner' or group of owners of the system with the power to abolish the system, i.e., to stop T.

A are the 'actors' who carry out the activities of T under the authority of O.

C are the beneficiaries or victims of T.

W is the worldview or set of values that make T meaningful. It is usually that of O.

E are the environmental resources and constraints that the system takes as given.

Any stakeholder or stakeholder group may assume one or more of roles O, A, and C. (The beginning of Section 4.2, p. 63, defines these roles.) In the guise of a memory aid, Checkland captures these six elements by the mnemonic letter sequence CATWOE. Few root definitions will explicitly list all components, particularly if some, such as A, C, and E are implicit in the wording or can be inferred from the context.

The novice is advised to start out with a clear definition of T, the transformation process. However, it is not a good idea to list in detail all relevant activities involved, as this leads to excessively long statements which may obscure the nature of the transformation, rather than focus on its prime aim.

Root definitions can either be **issue** based, placing emphasis on the core issue(s) the system is supposed to deal with, such as 'resolve conflicts in resource allocations to different users,' or **primary-task** based, specifying the primary tasks that need to be executed, such as 'allocate resources to different uses and apply them efficiently,' or a mixture of both. The set of root definitions explored should include both types. This will broaden perception and understanding of the problem situation, which may lead to clarifications and changes of elements, formulation of new root definitions, and/or discarding of others.

The first three stages correspond to the formulation phase of Figure 7-1.

Stage 4: The method now proceeds to system modelling. For each of the root definitions chosen to be pursued, we construct a **conceptual model**. The activities needed to achieve the system transformation T are expressed by appropriate verbs or action words. Arrows indicate the logical influence relationships and the precedence sequence between them. We shall refer to this model as the 'operating subsystem'. Subsets of activities may be subsystems themselves, which in turn could be decomposed further into submodels of activities at an even higher level of resolution.

It is important to keep in mind that Checkland sees conceptual models as intellectual constructs. There is no implication that in the real world the components and relationships contained in an operating system do exist or should exist. The models are idealizations of the minimum number of activities needed for the system transformation T to happen. They should only be developed from the corresponding root definition and nothing else. The novice will find task-based conceptual models easier to develop.

Following principles of formal system theory, the operating subsystem should be complemented by two additional subsystems, one for monitoring and controlling its performance, and the other for updating the performance criteria, and assessing and evaluating critical inputs, particularly those of a dynamic nature.

Note that insights gained at this stage may lead us to recycle back to Stages 1, 2, or 3 for updating or reinterpreting aspects or elements that the conceptual models show up as incomplete or questionable.

Stage 5: The process now returns to the real world. It compares the conceptual models with the problem situation, i.e., with what is perceived to exist in the real world. The aim is to develop an **agenda of discussion topics** with the stakeholders for Stage 6. So, we look for similarities and differences between the conceptual models and the real world. The emphasis should again be on 'Whats', e.g., 'What activities are missing or problematic?' rather than in terms of 'Hows', such as 'How is this activity done in the real world?' There may be several 'Hows' to achieve a given 'What'.

Stage 6: The **debate** at this stage should, whenever possible, involve representatives of all three types of stakeholders. Its purpose is to subject the implications of possibly conflicting worldviews to the collective judgement of the group in an open and non-defensive manner. The aim is to develop new ideas for change in the real world. These will often be in the form compromises or accommodations between the stakeholders, rather than a genuine consensus. To be considered for possible implementation, such changes must be:

- **systemically desirable**, i.e., they are more beneficial, and more effective and efficient to achieve the result aimed for than the current mode of operations; and
- **culturally feasible**, i.e., they are acceptable to all stakeholders.

Echoing Churchman's and Ackoff's call, Checkland also stresses that any action taken must be ethically defendable and aesthetically pleasing.

Each root definition is processed through Stages 4 to 6, some in full detail, others only in a cursory manner, depending on whether or not a particular vision promises new insights and new learning. The grey arrows in Figure 7-2 originating at Stages 5 and 6 indicate that the process may iterate right back to Stage 2 for a new round.

Stages 3 to 6 correspond to the modelling phase in Figure 7-1. Note that Stage 3 overlaps both formulation and modelling.

Stage 7: Plans are developed to **implement** some or all ideas for change that are deemed systemically desirable and culturally feasible. This may throw up aspects that have been neglected or misinterpreted, calling again for a return to an earlier stage.

Regardless of whether any changes are implemented, each completed cycle of this process will transform the original problem situation into a new one. The new situation should find the stakeholders with a shift in perception and at a higher level of understanding. It may then become the starting point for another learning cycle, i.e., the methodology returns to Stage 1. By involving all types of stakeholders in the process, it is hoped that change or implementation (Stage 7) is facilitated.

Note that nowhere in this short description of the process was the analyst mentioned. In fact, ideally, there is not one analyst, but the various stakeholders or a subgroup of them do the analysis themselves. If there is an analyst, her or his role is largely one of facilitation and advice about important 'do's' and 'don'ts' at various stages. As the stakeholders become more confident with the SSM process, the facilitating analyst becomes superfluous.

Activity

SSM explores changes which are 'systemically desirable and culturally feasible'. How does that differ from hard OR approaches?

The 'four-activity' SSM process

Checkland refers to this second version of SSM as sense-making. As depicted in Figure 7-3, it is an iterative process of four interconnected phases, (unfortunately) referred to by Checkland as 'activities' (not to be confused with the activities forming the transformation process). Each phase consists of a critical debate that encourages learning.

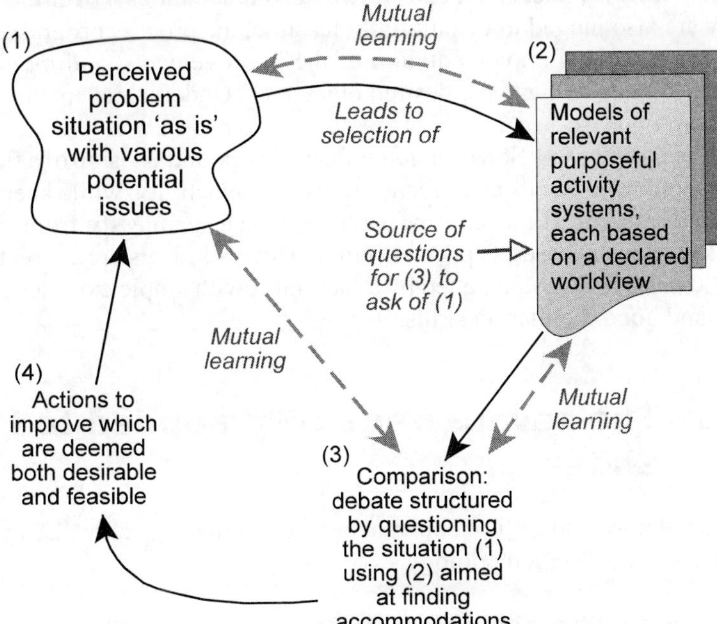

Figure 7-3 A sense-making model for SSM practice
(adapted from Checkland and Winter, 2006)

Phase 1 is a flexible amalgam of Stages 1, 2, and 3 of the seven-stage version. The problem solvers explore and experience the problem situation as fully as possible, including its underlying organizational, social, and political culture. While doing this, various themes of concern will emerge, each involving its own mixture of stakeholders O, A, and C, a specific worldview W of its problem owner(s) O, and a given environment E. For those themes or different interpretations of themes that are judged promising, appropriate root definitions are formulated. These are subjected to a critical debate, which enrich the perceptions of the problem situation, from which new or altered themes may emerge.

Phase 2 builds 'ideal' (conceptual) models for the transformation activities captured in each root definition carried forward from phase 1. They are subjected to a critical debate in terms of two perspectives: 'Do the ideal models achieve the transformations expressed in the root definitions?' and, considered from the perspective of the ideal models, 'Do the root definitions appear to be complete?' (as indicated in Figure 7-3 by the grey double-ended arrows). Negative responses may lead to reformulation of the ideal model or the root definitions, respectively. The second case implies a return to phase 1. The prime aim of phase 2 is to produce questions for the debate in phase 3.

Phase 3 is a structured debate comparing the ideal models with the actual problem situation, as perceived in phase 1. The comparison may indicate that important aspects in the problem situation do not feature in the ideal model. The process then returns to phase 2 for a redefinition of the ideal model, or phase 1 for a revision of the corresponding root definition.

The comparison may indicate that the ideal model offers systemically desirable improvements (Checkland calls them 'accommodations') over the actual situation. If they are also judged to be culturally feasible, the process progresses to phase 4.

Phase 4 plans implementation of the improvements, and monitors how well the improvements achieve the desired objectives. Underachievement may, again, lead to a return to phase 1 or 2.

The four-activity SSM version reflects Checkland's vision of a flexible process that, at any moment, has its main focus on one phase/activity, while keeping the other three actively present. It makes it possible to switch seamlessly from one to another and back. He views this as its prime strength. However, it also puts greater demands on the participants and should be led by a facilitator with ample experience in the methodology and good facilitation skills.

7.3 The seven-stage SSM applied to NuWave Shoes

We shall now study Elly Schuhmacher's dilemma in Section 4.8 (pp. 74–5) using the seven-stage SSM methodology.

Stage 1: The situation summary

In Section 4.8, Elly Schumacher's 'nightmare' was seen only from her own perspective. We studied it with the help of personal cognitive maps. In SSM, the situation summary is expanded to encompass all potential stakeholders. This is reflected in the rich picture of Figure 7-4, where the points of view of the production manager, the retailers, and the bank loan officer are also explicitly included. Find those aspects in the drawing!

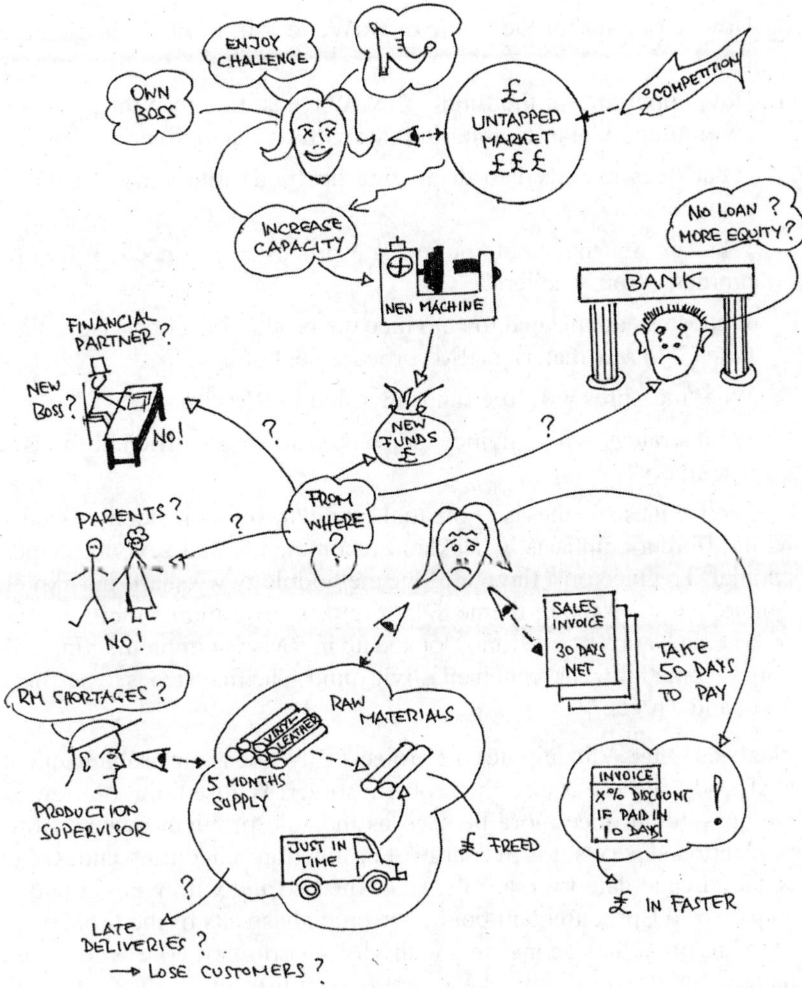

Figure 7-4 Rich picture for NuWave Shoes dilemma

Stage 2: Identification of potential themes

From the rich picture, we can glean potential themes or issues of concern for Elly. In practice, the details and full meaning of such themes are derived from talking to the people involved, rather than the rich picture. Several 'What?' issues, as well as a number of 'How?' themes, immediately spring to mind:

1. What should be Elly's long-term plans for NuWave? In particular, should she pursue her dream to capture the potentially untapped market or do something else, such as remain small and concentrate on high-price fashion shoes instead?
2. What sources of funds or combination should she pursue to finance any capacity expansion?
3. How important for the future of NuWave is it for her to keep full control over the firm?
4. How important for the future of NuWave is it to keep the goodwill of retailers by continuing to be a reliable supplier with no late deliveries?
5. What does she need to do to free up funds internally via more efficient asset management?
6. What prompt payments option and processes are needed to collect funds more promptly from retailers?
7. What steps are needed to convince the production supervisor to agree to a just-in-time (JIT) raw material (RM) procurement policy?
8. What measures will free funds invested in RMs?
9. What strategy will convince the bank to advance sufficient funds to purchase new machinery?

Each of these themes is a potential candidate for more detailed study. Some overlap, with different emphasis. Checkland recommends that several themes are studied in parallel. To give you a flavour of the methodology we shall first explore the relatively simple 'How?' issue of theme 8, before tackling a more ambitious 'What?' issue.

Theme 8 aims to free funds locked up in RMs via implementing a JIT procurement policy, something very much on Elly's mind. The first step is to perform Analyses One, Two, and Three.

Analysis One: Who initiates the project? Elly: she is the problem client. Who does the analysis? Elly: she is also the problem solver. Whose point of view is taken? Elly as the boss could once more be seen as the sole problem owner. However, since the production supervisor is in charge of production scheduling and RM procurement, he is a joint candidate for that role. His expertise and willingness to take active 'ownership' of a JIT procurement policy are crucial aspects of the problem situation.

Aims or 'Whats', consistent with Elly's worldviews (i.e., capture more of potential market, run firm profitably, keep control over firm, enjoy the challenge of running own successful business, be a trend setter in for funky shoe fashion) as the problem owner are: efficient use of funds invested in the firm. The productions supervisor's goals are running an efficient manufacturing operation, meeting delivery terms promised to retailers, and avoiding RM shortages.

Environment assumed as given for theme 1: current and future production set-up; RM procurement lead times; production lead times; time frame within which decisions for next season must be made; willingness of suppliers to adhere to JIT deliveries.

Resources available for the investigation: only Elly's intellectual abilities and her spare time, the production supervisor's expertise, sources on JIT procurement principles.

Problem content: the assets of prime interest are the RMs, both existing and future stocks. What actions can the firm take to reduce the funds invested in RMs?

All of these aspects are subjected to critical review in the light of all other aspects. Does the aspect reflect reality? For instance, should the production lead times be taken as given, or is there some leeway? Can they be shortened? Can suppliers' willingness to participate in JIT deliveries be taken for granted, or should steps to taken to secure their agreement?

Is the aspect needed and why? For example, knowledge of production lead times for each model produced is required because funds invested in RM are locked in during this time.

Are alternative interpretations more useful? For example, should RM shortages be avoided at all costs or only be kept sufficiently low?

Can an aspect be ignored? Should other aspects be added and, if so, why? For example, should specific emergency measures to avert shortages be included?

In the light of Analysis One, should the theme be restated differently, or would other themes be more insightful?

Analysis Two: Elly's roles are many: being the driving force of the business as the planner, manager, financial analyst, employer, and product designer — roles she has assigned to herself. Although there are expected business norms associated with each role, she largely sets her own expectations and values, and uses her personal, demanding standard for judging her performance. Her values are implicit in her worldviews. However, she might possibly want to explore whether she can fill all those roles successfully in the long run. For instance, would it be advantageous to use an external financial adviser occasionally? This may be a new theme to be explored.

The production supervisor occupied that position before Elly took over the firm, and she allowed the previous scope of that role, its norms, and expectations to continue.

Analysis Three: The power aspect is rather simple. Elly is the holder of power with respect to all her roles. She assigned the extent of her power to herself. It is doubtful that she set well-defined limits to her power, but largely plays it by ear, probably still learning and firming up the extent of her power; neither is she likely to consider any radical changes to any of that.

However, she relies heavily on the expertise of the production supervisor. This confers considerable power to him. In fact, it gives him control over the core aspect of the firm's operation. He determines the production schedule for the various models produced, calculates the amounts of RMs required, and sets the procurement schedule. Generating funds internally may well require that Elly, as the boss, revisits that aspect. If she wants to switch from the current mode of procuring all RMs to be in stock at the beginning of the production season to a more flexible JIT policy, she may have to renegotiate his job description.

Stage 3: Root definition

Theme 8 must now be captured by a root definition. The usual wording in these definitions appears almost archaic and convoluted. A task-based root definition is most appropriate for a 'How?' theme:

> **Root definition 1:** A system owned by Elly and jointly operated by Elly and the production supervisor to achieve a more efficient use of funds by reducing RM investments via JIT RM procurement and the use of RM remnants.

The four CATWOE elements explicitly listed are:

O: Elly
A: Elly and the production supervisor
W: achieve more efficient use of funds
T: reduce RM investment via JIT RM procurement and use of RM remnants

Missing are **E** and **C**. They can, however, easily be inferred. **E** consists of the existing and future production set-up, the ability and willingness of suppliers to deliver on a JIT basis, and the current stock of RM remnants. Elly is the primary beneficiary (**C**) of the system. The RM suppliers could be seen as victims (**C**) since they are marginally affected by the proposed policy.

The root definition should again be subjected to a critical review. Is it complete, or are essential aspects missing? A case in point may be that a change in the procurement policy requires a renegotiation of the production supervisor's job description. Root definition 1 contains nothing about that. This is, though, done deliberately. Changing the job description is another issue of concern to be added to the potential themes.

Stage 4: Conceptual model

How do we go about building a conceptual model? Or, more appropriately, how does a beginner learn about it? Practice with systems diagrams, particularly influence diagrams (see Chapter 5) helps. A conceptual model is not 'what is', if that exists, but shows the 'ideal' set of activities needed for the transformation of the root definition to be realized, and only those. The activities are linked together by arrows that indicate the logical and temporal sequence in which they have to occur. The 'ideal' should be that of the owner(s) of the root definition — Elly, in the NuWave case.

The idea of JIT procurement is that all RMs arrive shortly before the production run for a particular shoe model starts and not well in advance, thereby reducing the length of time funds are locked up in RMs and delaying payment for them. For this to happen, the suppliers have to be told at the time of placing RM orders the date on which goods should be delivered. So, the production supervisor must already have worked out a detailed production schedule in consultation with Elly, based on her choice of next season's range of shoe models. Working backwards like this, we can begin to build a logical and temporal sequence of activities. 'Decide on next season's range of shoe models (1)' is the first activity, shown in the oval near the bottom of Figure 7-5. It allows 'plan the production schedule (2)' to proceed. That plan enables the production supervisor to calculate all RM requirements (3), model by model. Armed with that plan and the list of RMs required, he can develop a detailed schedule of quantities and latest delivery dates for RM purchases (5). Since RM remnants from previous seasons are to be used whenever possible (4), the RM quantities to be purchased (5) are adjusted accordingly, as shown by the arrow from (4) into (5). Explain the sequencing of the remaining activities in Figure 7-5.

Activity (6) needs some explanation. Unless the suppliers adhere to the delivery schedules, the whole scheme will fail. If they do not, the materials may arrive too late, causing shortages, or arrive too early, resulting in RMs sitting around idle, locking up funds. Elly will have to negotiate JIT terms with suppliers and solicit their agreement.

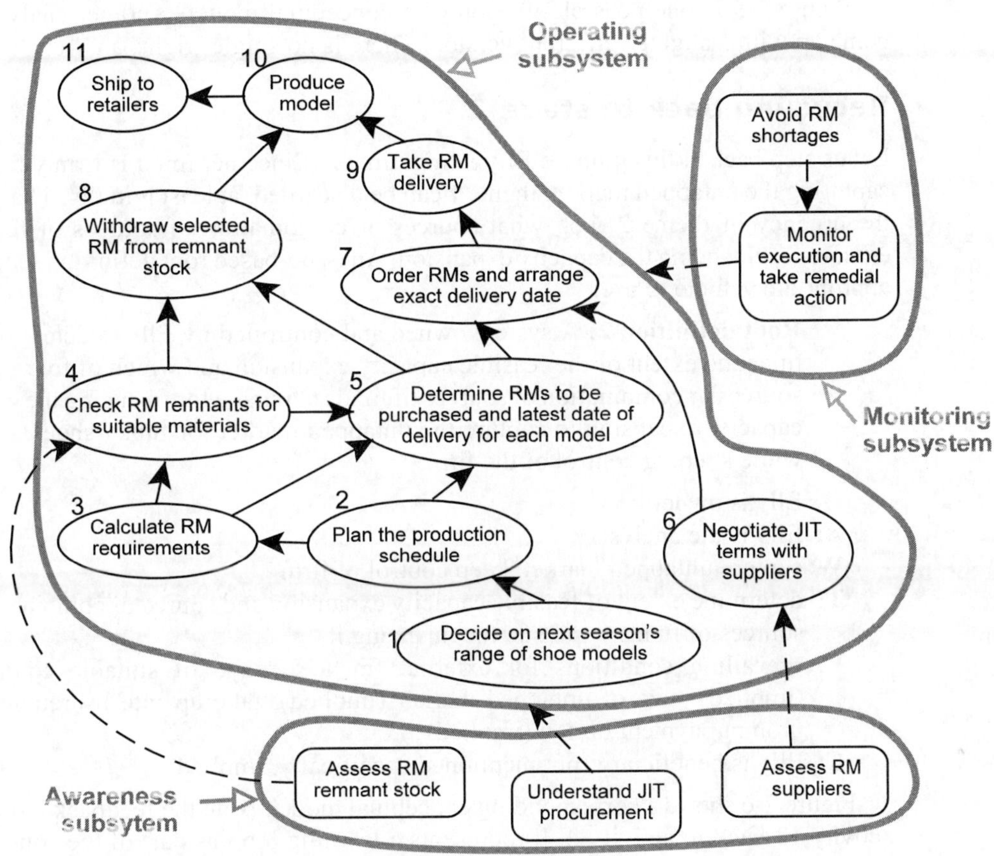

Figure 7-5 Conceptual model 1 for root definition 1

A scheme where timing is crucial needs constant monitoring, so that remedial action can be initiated to prevent any damaging deviations from the various schedules. This forms the monitoring subsystem. The awareness subsystem ensures that the activities of the operating subsystem are based on the correct information and know-how.

This model is, in turn, subjected to critical review. Does it contain all activities and links required for T and only those? There is, in fact, either a link or an activity missing in Figure 7-5. One way Elly plans to reduce RM remnants from previous seasons is to design models that use these remnants. To do this, she may even have to inspect the remnants prior to planning next season's range. So, activity (1) assumes that she is fully aware of the RM remnants available. An arrow from 'Assess RM remnant stock' to (1) or a new activity 'inspect RM remnants' as a predecessor to (1) would do.

Does it contain necessary activities which are missing or not implicitly implied by the root definition? If the latter is the case, the root definition may have to be revisited and possibly amended. The root definition does not explicitly mention 'ship (goods) to retailers'. The investment in RM will only be released when this happens. But it is such an obvious aspect that we shall not clutter up the root definition with it.

Figure 7-5 is one possible version of a conceptual model. Another analyst may come up with a slightly different version. There is no single 'right' answer.

Recycling back to stage 2

Let us step back at this point to Elly's 'nightmare'. Since her mind is firmly fixed on capturing the untapped market, theme 1 can be discarded, at least initially. That raises the urgency of theme 2, i.e., what sources or combination of sources of funds to explore for financing the capacity expansion. An issue-based root definition seems the appropriate vehicle to use:

> **Root definition 2:** A system owned and controlled by Elly to determine the extent of the feasible capacity expansion and which of four sources or combination of sources of funds to pursue for financing the capacity expansion to capture the untapped market for funky shoes, while keeping control of the firm.

O: Elly is owner
A: Elly is the analyst
W: capture untapped market, keep control of firm
T: determine extent of feasible capacity expansion and source or combination of sources of funds to pursue for financing it
E: prevailing conditions for external finance, range of suitable equipment (implied), size of untapped market (implied), take-up rate by retailers for prompt payment option (implied)
C: Elly is beneficiary (not mentioned specifically, implied)

Figure 7-6 shows a corresponding conceptual model. Note the feedback loop from activity 13 back to activity 2. It represents a learning loop as part of the conceptual model.

Stage 5: Comparing conceptual models with the real world

The Stage 5 comparison between what is present in the real world and each conceptual model highlights the following points for the debate at Stage 6:

- Both Elly and the production supervisor aim to run an efficient business. What does this mean in practical terms? Does it mainly consider cost minimization? And is this the prime objective? Hardly so for Elly, who has further goals.
- Existing RM stocking policies claim to be based on cost minimization, but ignore the ensuing cash flow effects, whereas both conceptual models focus mainly on the latter. Which is more relevant at this point in time for Elly? Is she willing to accept a reduction in profits to achieve her aim of capturing a portion of the untapped market for funky shoes?

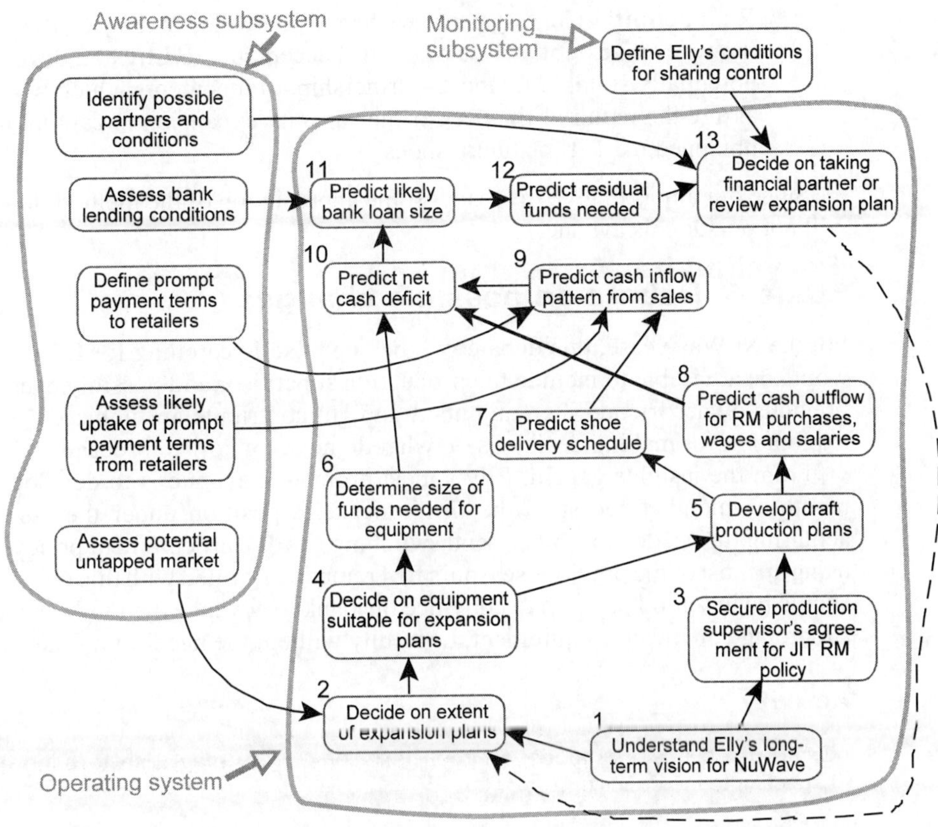

Figure 7-6 Conceptual model 2 for root definition 2

- What is the production manager's view of adopting a JIT procurement policy? Is he willing to implement it and, if so, does he need additional training? Both aspects need exploring and clarification.
- The conceptual model for root definition 1 focuses on the activities needed for operating a JIT procurement policy. In contrast, root definition 2 focuses on what sources of funds to pursue. Can conceptual model 1 not be seen as a subsystem for model 2? It expands activities (5) and (8) of Figure 7-6. Does that imply that model 1 should be explored fully as preparation for exploring model 2?
- Neither conceptual model directly addresses the important issue of financial control of the firm. In fact, both make a boundary judgement that sharing such control is not on the cards. Hence, only ways to capture the potential market with Elly remaining in full control are considered 'systemically feasible and culturally acceptable'. Is this an immutable constraint? Maybe further insights could be gained by iterating back to Stage 3 and exploring a suitable root definition for theme 3, such as:

Root definition 3: A system owned and controlled by Elly to identify the type and extent of loss of control acceptable to Elly and develop potentially suitable financial partnership arrangements which would assure the required finance for the capacity expansion to capture the untapped market for funky shoes.

Since our aim is to give the reader some appreciation of the methodology only, we will not pursue this avenue.

Stage 6: Debate on possible changes

For the NuWave case, this debate will be one of self-searching for Elly. However, it would be advisable to include the production supervisor and possibly even the firm's previous owner/friend. Such an outsider might contribute an 'unbiased' view to the exploration for making decisions on what do next, on how to proceed.

From the insights gained, Elly's most promising avenue is to develop a detailed month-by-month forecast of the firm's net cash position under the assumption of acquiring the needed machinery and switching to a JIT procurement policy, as well as using up most of the previous season's RM remnants. Armed with this information, she should be in a good position to convince the bank to advance the funds needed against a mortgage on the new equipment, hopefully without the need for a financial partner.

Activity

Develop a conceptual model for root definition 3. You may wish to bring additional aspects into the definition.

7.4 Concluding remarks on SSM

The seven-stage SSM version presented follows a well-defined iterative process. It tackles both the intellectual problems of interpretation, analysis, and synthesis involved in conceiving ideas for change, and the practical problems of facilitating the change process itself. It can be used by a group of people facing dilemmas or decision issues without the need for a professional facilitator. All it needs is an individual versed in the method, and able to guide and monitor the process without becoming dominant.

For the beginner, one of the more difficult aspect of the process is formulating meaningful alternative root definitions and developing corresponding conceptual models. Both must introduce sufficient variety and contrasting viewpoints, and thereby offer new insights into the problem that encourage learning.

The methodology offers little help and no guidelines on how to deal with disagreements and conflicts in views and values between stakeholders beyond stating that the debate at Stage 6 should be open and non-defensive, where all stakeholders feel safe to contribute freely. Few organizations offer all members equal freedom in terms of actions available and equal voice, power, and credibility, regardless of their position in the organizational hierarchy, their seniority, technical expertise, education, and access to information. Such differences tend to stifle free and open discussion. Yet, free and open debate is essential for gaining appreciation of the varied points of view of different stakeholders and encouraging learning. Similarly, if there are fundamental conflicts between firmly entrenched worldviews and stakeholders refuse to shift, no meeting of minds on accommodation may be possible. These are serious drawbacks of the methodology that even a highly skilled facilitator might not be able to overcome.

SSM therefore lends itself best to situations where the stakeholders share similar interests, where views differ mainly in emphasis and detail, rather than substance, and where power differences are minor. This will allow accommodation between stakeholders without the need to accept or impose compromises that satisfy no one.

In principle, a single individual can use SSM to investigate a decision problem that is largely of concern only to her- or himself, or for a problem situation concerning multiple stakeholders, but without explicitly involving them. In the second case, all that is needed is the ability to place oneself into the different stakeholder roles with an open mind and debate with oneself — in Churchman's terminology (1968), being able to play the devil's advocate to one's own ideas and views.

However, as Checkland points out, SSM is more than a problem structuring method. It is a mode of thinking that can be internalized and become second nature, the same as the process of the hard OR methodology can become second nature. It will then be applied on a more informal, heuristic basis, possibly only in parts. The debate remains largely internal to the person doing it.

Checkland (Checkland and Winter, 2006) also advocates that SSM, particularly its four-activity version, cannot only be used to deal with the content of a problem situation, but also with the process of carrying out such a content intervention. In other words, the content problem situation that triggers an intervention is embedded in a process intervention that explores how to undertake the content investigation.

Numerous accounts of interventions using SSM have been published in books and technical journals, many dealing with public sector situations. SSM has also become one of the major tools for exploring and planning information systems.

Case study 7-1: SkyWalker (continuation of Case study 4-1, p. 72)

Jess recalls that one of the lecturers in her MBA programme gave a short introduction to Checkland's SSM, and would like to apply it to the SkyWalker 'birthing' problem. All she remembers is that one starts with Analyses One, Two, and Three. Can you help her? As a start you might want to explore the following two issues:

1. How to launch the SkyWalker service and survive the first six months of operations (primary-task based). Write a root definition, identifying the CATWOE elements listed and reasons for those not specified, and develop the corresponding conceptional model. What questions for further investigation does the model raise and what aspects need to be resolved before taking any decisions?
2. Consider the alternative issue: to decide on whether to opt for a partial data base launch within 3 to 4 months, or a complete data base launch within 8 to 10 months (issue-based). Write a root definition, identifying the CATWOE elements listed and reasons for those not listed, and develop the corresponding conceptional model. What questions does the model raise and what aspects need to be resolved before taking any decisions? (Note: This root definition does not deal with the activities needed to launch the service.)

What insights can Jess and Jill gain from exploring these two root definitions?

7.5 Strategic option development and analysis

Strategic option development and analysis (SODA) (Eden, 1983) or 'Journey Making', as it evolved into in the late 1990s, is a method used by an analyst/consultant to facilitate group decision making in complex conflict situations that involve several **stakeholders**. These may have different perceptions of the problem situation, different values and goals, and possibly different vested interests.

SODA is based on four interacting perspectives:

- **Personal construct theory:** Cognitive psychology is the theoretical basis of the method. Individuals use language to express ideas. These are subjective and the language used is rich in meaning. An individual's perceptions of a problem situation can be captured by a **cognitive map**.
- **Nature of the organization:** Organizational decision making involves politics, forming of coalitions, and negotiation between stakeholders. Change in organizations often occurs through management of conflict.
- **Nature of consulting practice:** The role of the consultant is to help problem solving and securing commitment to action through facilitation and negotiation.
- **Technology and technique:** Recourse to computer software (*Decision Explorer*, available through www.Banxia.com) for cognitive mapping and quantitative analysis, and holding of SODA workshops, all designed to explore and manage complexity.

SODA is run by a consultant, skilled in the method, with a group of between two and ten people, who are all actively and substantively involved in the problem situation. The method is based on the premise that a sufficient degree of appreciation of the different views and interests among the stakeholders will allow the group to commit itself to an agreed set of actions without necessarily sharing compatible worldviews and values. It consists of four main steps:

Step 1: The consultant constructs a cognitive map for each stakeholder involved, based on one or two extended individual interviews with each (most likely with the help of the interactive *Decision Explorer* software).

Step 2: The consultant discusses each map with its owner, clarifies ambiguities and contradictions, and works with them through the map, checking for consistency and completeness. They explore it for possible uncharted actions and goals. Through this process, each member should gain a good understanding of his or her own views and perception of the situation.

You are already familiar with these two steps from Section 4.7, where the principles of cognitive maps are discussed in some detail, and Section 4.8, which demonstrates the process for NuWave Shoes.

Step 3: The consultant merges the maps into a **strategic map**, by combining identical or similar constructs, retaining the richer construct wording. Substantive conflicts between maps may be highlighted by alternative paths. The aim of the strategic map is to develop **emerging themes** and **core constructs**.

Emerging themes are in the form of clusters of constructs with many links between them and few links with clusters outside the group. Core constructs are those that have either many arrows leading into it or many leading away. Again, the *Decision Explorer* software facilitates the merging of maps and the identifying and analysing of clusters.

Step 4: All participants are now brought together in a **SODA workshop** with a consultant as an active facilitator for the process. The strategic map becomes the vehicle for discussion and negotiation. The consultant starts by taking the group through the merged map, its emerging themes and core concepts, and any still unresolved conflicts. The idea is to enable all group members to recognize their views as part of the greater picture. Then one or more related clusters are chosen for deeper analysis with the aim of getting a shared view, if not on goals then at least on actions. The consultant will attempt to bridge major differences in views and goals between stakeholders through negotiation. The workshop ends in success if the consultant can get the stakeholders to commit themselves to a set of clearly defined and spelled-out actions.

The perspective of 'personal construct theory' underpins Steps 1 and 2. Principles of organizational behaviour are recognized in Step 4. Technology, in particular the *Decision Explorer* software, is used in Steps 1 and 3, while consulting practice guides the process through all four steps.

Unlike SSM, where conflict resolution hinges on open and free debate, SODA provides specific mechanisms for that. Merging the individual maps into a strategic map depersonalizes the issues and places its ownership with the group as a whole, while at the same time allowing each member to see her or his own map reflected in it. It allows conflict to be managed, first by exposing it in the strategic map and then through negotiation in the SODA workshop.

In terms of Figure 7-1, problem formulation and modelling occur hand-in-hand in the first three steps, with the emphasis shifting more and more to modelling as the process moves towards and into Step 4. There is no proper implementation phase, unless the commitment for action includes the planning for its execution and the assignment of responsibility for who does what.

In contrast to SSM, SODA relies heavily on the competence of the consultant. Not only does this person need to have good interpersonal and facilitation skills, but also has to be a skilful interviewer (for developing the cognitive maps) and a skilful negotiator. The consultant holds a critical role throughout the entire process. He or she interprets each stakeholder's views through individual cognitive maps and works on each map with its owner, makes choices and interpretations while merging the maps, and finally guides and controls the facilitation and negotiations in the SODA workshop. It is also clear that the consultant does not remain an 'objective' or neutral outsider, but becomes an active participant and, thereby, an interested stakeholder in the process and, by extension, in the problem situation. Therefore, he or she shoulders a heavy responsibility.

A more recent version of SODA, known as the **oval mapping technique** operates in a four- to eight-hour workshop covering all phases, under the guidance of a facilitator. The only effective teacher for SODA is participating in a real-life application.

As is the case for SSM, SODA has been particularly successful in investigations addressing decision support and strategy, and policy analysis in the public sector, the police, corrections, the health sector, and public transport, among others — a majority with Colin Eden and Fran Ackermann, its primary developers, as the consultants.

NuWave Shoes continued

You may wonder how the process we started in Section 4.8 with the creation and analysis of Elly's cognitive map (Figures 4-6 and 4-7, pp. 77 and 79) would proceed further with the SODA method. So far, we only have Elly's contribution. Who could be additional stakeholders? The production supervisor, in charge of RM procurement, immediately comes to mind. He sees efficient management of RM procurement and shoe production, in terms of costs and maintaining the current reputation for reliability in meeting promised delivery dates, as his main aim. This is in partial conflict with Elly's view that, in the current crisis, cost efficiency can be sacrificed and reliability may not be seriously compromised if the occasional delivery is delayed by a few days.

Another, possibly more interesting stakeholder is the bank's loan manager. A satisfactory solution to Elly's problem requires that the bank comes to the party. Including the loan manager in the process directly, rather than simply as an external stakeholder whose views Elly can only second-guess, could well enhance the chances of a successful conclusion. (If the bank is more than simply a conditional provider of funds, but takes a more supportive interest in the venture, such an inclusion could be on the cards, although rather exceptional.)

In Section 4.8, Elly developed and analysed her own cognitive map. For the SODA process, we now need a consultant who does this for the other two stakeholders and then merges the three maps into a strategic map. The most likely emerging theme would remain around concept 16 ('Make better use of current funds ...') and its logical successors 17, 24, 27, and 19, dealing with freeing up funds. If the cash flow projections confirm that the bank loan can be properly serviced and partially repaid within in a two-year period, the bank may well commit itself to a further loan. A SODA (mini-)workshop would be mainly concerned with the terms for such a loan, i.e., security offered, its size, its duration, and the monitoring conditions the bank may want to impose, i.e., a close watch on how RM stocks and balances owed by retailers behave over time, and the steps to be taken if they go against the expected pattern.

Case study 7-2: SkyWalker (refers to Case studies 4-1 and 4-2, pp. 72 and 81)
Merge the individual maps for Jill and Jess into a strategic map and identify emerging themes.

7.6 Strategic choice approach

In the words of one of its developers, John Friend, the origins of the strategic choice approach (SCA) (Rosenhead and Mingers, 2000):

> are to be found in the experience of two pioneering research projects, in which operational researchers and social scientists worked together in observing strategic decision makers in action... The insights obtained... were to provide the foundations for the development of a set of relatively open, participative methods for representing the structure of interrelated decision problems and the various sources of uncertainty — technical, political, structural — which made them difficult to resolve.

During the 1970s, the approach was further developed and refined in a programme of action research in the Tavistock Institute of Human Relations. SCA attempts to formalize the way a group of people learns to cope with complexity and uncertainty in decision making. It has proved to be particularly appropriate and useful for contingency planning where the group participants represent stakeholder interests of several possibly only loosely connected organizations, such as local or national governmental agencies, educational institutions, or departments within a private organization, and where there is strong pressure for early decisions and early commitment to action.

In contrast to SSM and SODA, SCA has no formal theoretical foundation, but instead consists of a set of four ad hoc, complementary modes of working flexibly with a group of six to eight participants in intensive workshop sessions that are managed closely by a skilled consultant/facilitator.

Fundamental to SCA are the stakeholders' perceptions of the importance of three types of uncertainties, which also include such aspects as lack of knowledge, lack of externalization, ambiguities, and fuzziness:

UE — Uncertainties about the working environment: They are mainly of a technical nature and can usually be overcome fully or partially by forecasting, surveys, in-depth technical or costing studies of insufficiently known aspects, using statistical and other quantitative and qualitative techniques.

UV — Uncertainties about values, objectives, priorities, vested interests: These reflect the personal worldviews of the stakeholders or how the latter perceive the worldviews of the entity they represent. They are the most difficult uncertainties to get a grip on. Often, stakeholders are not fully aware of their values and preferences, while they try to hide or disguise vested interests. All three need to be brought into the open in a nondefensive manner. Only that will encourage shared understanding and appreciation of each other's positions.

UR — Uncertainties about the relationships/interconnectedness/interactions between decision areas or issues: How do decision choices for a given issue affect decision choices in other issues? What aspects are unknown, unclear, or fuzzy, or open to different interpretations?

Answers to these uncertainties often involve boundary judgements for both the narrow and the wider system of interest. In some sense, SCA can be viewed as facilitating learning about the complexity of the problem situation, which should lead to managing these three types of uncertainties more effectively. The process of SCA consists of working in four modes, as shown in Figure 7-7.

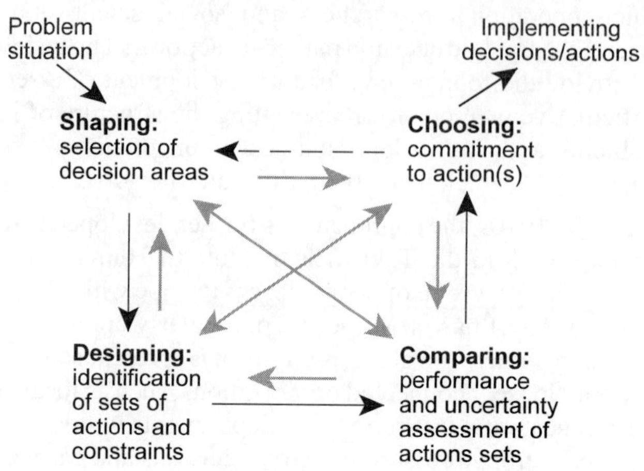

Figure 7-7 Four working modes of SCA
(adapted from Friend and Hickling, 1987)

They are:

Shaping involves identifying issues, also knows as **decision areas,** and deciding which to include or exclude. It is in the form of a decision graph — a network that shows which decision areas are linked with each other, the strength of the connections, and the importance, urgency, or priority of the decision areas. The output of this mode is an agreement on which subset of highly interconnected decision areas should be the (first tentative) **problem focus** for further study. This basically comes down to making boundary choices and boundary judgements about the narrow and wider system of interest.

Designing (analysis of interconnected decision areas) consists of defining mutually exclusive **action options** or alternative decision choices for each decision area. For situations that involve decision making over time, action options will include a timing element, such as 'now' or '12 months from now'. Action options in different decision areas are superimposed on each other, and tentative answers are given as to whether action options in different decision areas are compatible, incompatible, or whether compatibility is uncertain/questionable/unknown. Each set of compatible (or feasible) action combinations is referred to as a feasible **decision scheme**.

Comparing consists of defining a set of quantitative or qualitative objectives or performance measures and associated decision criteria (see Section 4.1, p. 61, for a discussion of the difference between objectives and criteria) for evaluating or assessing the strength and desirability of the various decision schemes. Some assessments may give rise to the use of hard OR techniques. For example, an action option may involve allocating a scarce resource to several activities, where the optimal allocation may be found by linear programming (see Chapter 14).

This comparison is done for each pair of decision schemes, resulting in a balance sheet or **comparative advantage graph** that may involve objective numerical outcomes or qualitative (arbitrary) point scales.

Choosing is a two-stage process: (1) evaluating decision schemes in terms of how they are affected by uncertainties and what remedial actions or **exploratory options** will help reduce critical uncertainties and clarify ambiguities; and (2) developing a final **action scheme** or commitment package, detailing the chosen action options and exploratory option and their timing, as well as what contingencies to keep in reserve for managing future uncertainties.

Although these four modes of working may be initiated in the order shown, the effectiveness of the method is considerably enhanced if the facilitator allows a flexible switching between modes in any direction, as depicted in Figure 7-7. Whenever working in a given mode tends to become bogged down, a switch to another mode may unblock progress. Insights gained from working in a given mode may lead naturally to reconsider a previous mode, such as a redefinition of the problem focus, changes in the action options, or the reassessment of action compatibilities and of uncertainties. It is also essential that areas of uncertainty and ambiguity are noted down as they are discovered during all stages of the process, rather than just at the choosing stage.

In terms of Figure 7-1, shaping and the identification of action options for designing are the formulation phase, while the rest of designing, comparing, and the first step of choosing form the modelling phase. Only the second step of choosing can be viewed as implementation planning.

Activity

For the Deep Cove Project of Example 1-3 (p. 4), identify aspects of uncertainty, ambiguity and/or fuzziness, and classify them by their nature.

7.7 SCA applied to NuWave Shoes

The developers of SCA provide the STRAD (for 'strategic adviser') interactive software to streamline the process. For small informal groups working around a desktop computer, STRAD facilitates making quick progress. However, we will now demonstrate the four modes of SCA using only the low-tech diagrammatic aids and tables, as suggested by Friend and Hickling (1987). As for SODA, active participation in a real-life exercise is the only effective teacher in mastering SCA.

The NuWave Shoes problem has only three potential stakeholders, Elly, the production supervisor, and the bank loan manager. The latter is an outsider to NuWave and only involved by proxy, i.e., via Elly's interpretation of his position. Even the production supervisor is only marginally involved. The human interactions between the stakeholders, which form a vital part of SCA, is missing (an aspect difficult to put into print anyway).

Shaping

Figure 7-8 lists seven major potential decision areas and arranges them as a network. Note how different representations are used to indicate the 'importance' and 'urgency' for decision areas, and to highlight the 'strength' of the links between them.

The three decision areas inside the grey bordered shape are the aspects of immediate prime interest for Elly. They form the initial problem focus. They include two urgent decision areas — timing of equipment purchase and how to free internal funds — as well as the important area of external funding.

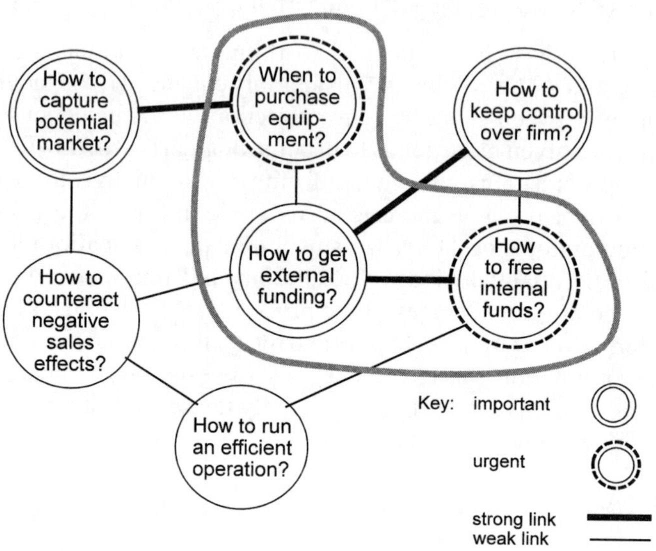

Figure 7-8 Decision areas graph

Designing

The set of mutually exclusive action options, which is deliberately kept small, is:

- When to purchase equipment:
  - — now
  - — later
- Freeing up of internal funds:
  - — offer cash discounts to retailers
  - — tighter credit for slow payers
  - — reduce RM stocks
  - — all three
- Procuring external funds:
  - — get additional bank loan
  - — take a financial partner
  - — both

These options are now checked against each other for compatibility. All combinations are arranged in a logical option tree that allows identification of feasible decision schemes, as shown in Figure 7-9. The decision areas are arranged along two dimensions: (1) urgency: purchase equipment, freeing internal funds, getting external funding; and (2) timing or logical sequence: all three to occur more or less at the same time in this case. The sequence in Figure 7-9 reflects the fact that the requirement for and size of external funding depends on freeing up internal funds.

Elly also arbitrarily decides that she will not consider decision schemes for a later equipment purchase that rely on taking on a financial partner.

Infeasible action option combinations are marked with an X and doubtful ones with a question mark. The feasible (and questionable) decision schemes are labelled A to L.

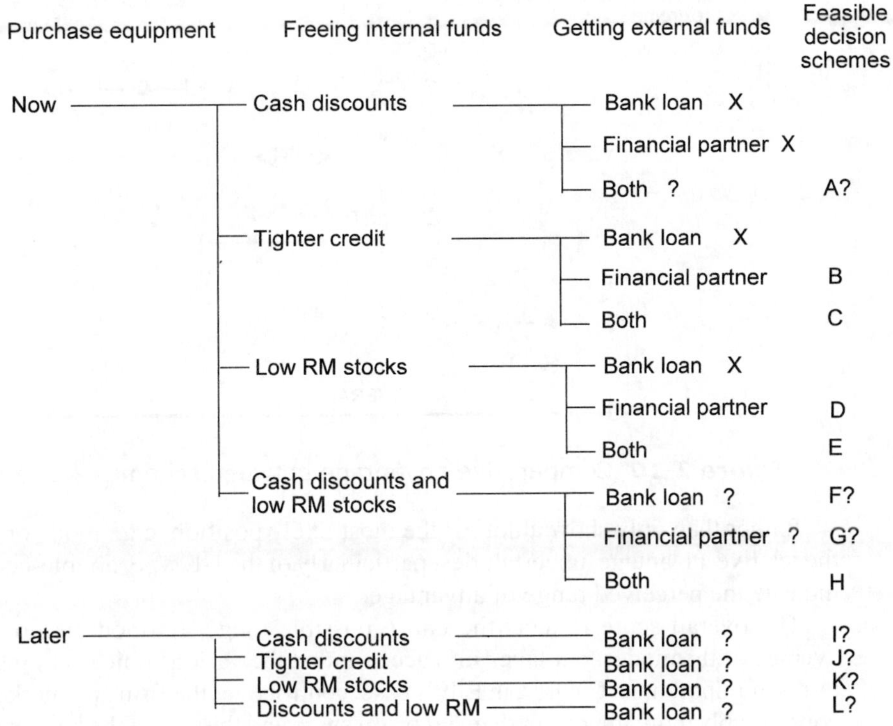

Figure 7-9 Option tree showing feasible decision schemes

Comparing

A subset of feasible decision schemes is chosen for further evaluation in terms of their performance. Elly considers the following objectives or performance measures:

- her degree of control of firm,
- the firm's share of potential market,
- her share of profits, and
- low need for external funding.

Each scheme is ranked, either on an arbitrary point scale or and by an objective measure. Armed with such assessments, the decision schemes are compared pair-wise on a gradation going from the extreme relative advantage for one scheme to the extreme relative advantage for the other scheme. Figure 7-10 depicts one way of displaying the comparison between scheme {C} and {F?}.

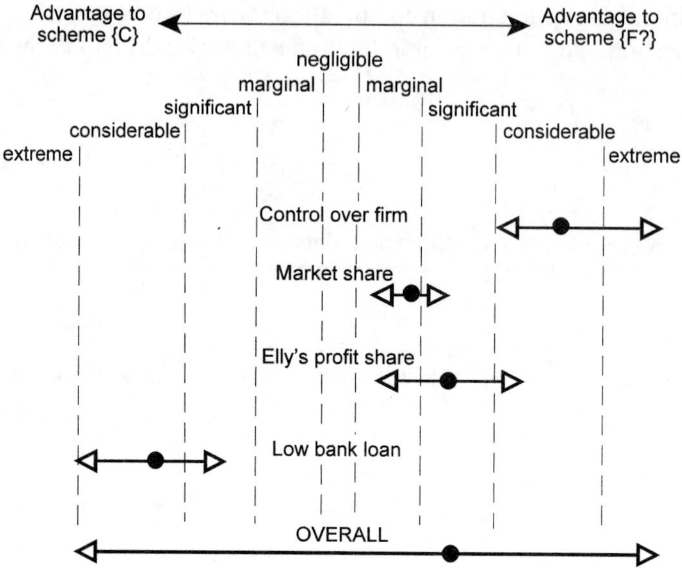

Figure 7-10 Comparative advantage between schemes {C} and {F?}

Rather than only show a dot for the most likely position, e.g., mode or average of the relative advantage, uncertainties, particularly of the UE type, double-ended arrows indicate the perceived range of advantage.

The overall score reflects the entire possible range. Its mode is not simply an average of the modes, but takes into account that the various objectives may differ in terms of importance. Clearly, in Elly's case, control over the firm and market share are considerably more important than her profit share and the size of the bank loan needed.

Such pair-wise comparisons are made for all combinations. This shows whether some schemes clearly dominate other schemes. The dominated schemes can then be eliminated. In this manner, the schemes are whittled down to a few preferred ones which become the input into the choosing mode.

Choosing

As pointed out at the end of the previous section, as the analysis progresses, areas of uncertainty and ambiguity will be discovered and recorded. It is not uncommon, that aspects that have been chosen as decision areas or objectives will also turn out to be areas of uncertainty. They now have to be classified as to type (UE, UV, UR). Some may straddle more than one type. For NuWave Shoes, the list shows:

Area of uncertainty	Uncertainty type
Share of the market that can be captured	UE + UR
Potential response of retailers to discounts and tighter credit	UE
Credit limit of the bank	UR
Effects of actions on Elly's profit share	UR
Effect of loss of control over firm due to an external partner	UV

Recall that UR means that the uncertainty is caused by the interaction between decision areas. So, the share of the market is affected by whether or not tight credit controls are instituted. This is why scheme {C}, with tight control, is disadvantaged against scheme {F?} without tight control, as shown in Figure 7-10. In contrast, the effect of how loss of control affects Elly is largely an issue of values, hence it is a UV-type.

Next, the areas of uncertainty are assessed as to their relative importance or **salience.** This may lead to proposing possible remedial steps or exploratory options that could reduce highly salient uncertainties. Such steps may render action schemes affected by these uncertainties more attractive. This is particularly crucial for action schemes which have been labelled questionable or doubtful, such as scheme {F?}. For example, Elly might want to sound out the bank loan manager as to his assessment of a loan for various amounts of internal funds freed (with the balance of funds needed to be covered by the bank). Similarly, if it is perceived that scheme {C} has a fair degree of uncertainty in term of how retailers will respond to tighter credit controls, this may lead Elly to undertake a survey of retailers.

She might also do some soul searching about why she feels that she wants to retain absolute control over the firm (recognizing that the simple act of getting a loan from the bank already means a certain loss of control). It may affect the importance she assigned to this area of uncertainty/ambiguity. In turn, this may lead to changes in the comparative advantage of various pairs of schemes, causing the process to recycle back to the comparing mode.

The outcome of this process is a commitment package or action scheme, most effectively shown in table form. Table 7-1 is its summary for NuWave Shoes.

Table 7-1 Commitment package for Elly in NuWave Shoes project

Decisions now		Future decisions	
Explorations	Actions	Deferred actions	Contingency plans
Purchase equipment:			
Make cash flow forecast based on exploratory option below	Place equipment order if bank offers loan		
Freeing internal funds:			
Find best discount level	Offer discounts	Explore feasibility of tighter credit controls	
Develop tighter RM forecasts and JIT scheduling	Reduce RM stock levels	Find ways to use RM remainders from previous seasons	
External funding:			
Prepare funding case	Negotiate with bank		Find silent financial partner if bank declines loan

The timing of actions and options becomes important, hence the action scheme may differ from the preferred decision scheme in detail and composition. Before Elly can commit herself to the purchase of the equipment, she needs to explore how the cash flow over time is affected by offering discounts to retailers for prompt payment and by the proposed JIT procurement policy for RMs. The larger output will mean more RM purchases, as well as other increases in working capital.

This presupposes that she has a detailed production schedule and traces its effects on the time pattern of RM usage, on shoe deliveries to retailers, and on the resulting cash collection pattern from retailers. Armed with these projections, she can enter into negotiations with the bank for securing the needed finance for her equipment. (Note that using SSM yielded the same conclusions.) The major contingency provision in the event that the bank declines the loan is to reconsider finding a 'silent' financial partner — silent in the sense that he or she only takes a financial but not operational interest.

In the usual multi-stakeholder case, each step involves extensive discussions, interchange of ideas, and negotiations between the workshop participants, carefully facilitated by the consultant, who would manage the process by judicious switching of working modes to encourage progress towards reaching a commitment package.

Case study 7-3: SkyWalker (refers to Case study 4-1, p. 72)
Apply SCA to choose a strategy for getting the service up and running successfully. Consider financial success, personal satisfaction, speed of getting service operating, and ability to secure external funding as goals or performance measures. Identify the nature of uncertainties and classify them as to type. Perform the steps of shaping, designing (option tree), and comparing (comparative advantage graph).

7.8 Survey of other PSMs

Strategic assumption surfacing and testing

Strategic assumption surfacing and testing (SAST) evolved in the 1970s (Mason and Mitroff, 1981) and owes much to Churchman's (1968) dialectic approach of playing devil's advocate, i.e., the deliberate contrasting of opposing perspectives. Its main area of use is for strategic planning and controversial policy decisions in complex situations involving several interconnected issues, where the situation challenges the status quo in the presence of polarization between groups of entrenched protagonists. The core aspect of SAST is the adversarial testing and questioning of assumptions, beliefs, values and worldviews that underlie strategies, as well as questioning the strategies themselves. The method consists of four stages:

Group formation: The participants, usually involved stakeholders or their representatives, are grouped into two or more small, homogeneous teams, such that the members within each team share similar views and values, and may have similar vested interest, while the views and values between groups are highly diverse. Consider a proposal to create a marine reserve along an ecologically vulnerable stretch of coast. One team may be made up of recreational anglers for whom this area is a favourite fishing spot and who put a high value on their right to enjoy this leisure activity. A second is a team of ecologically-minded individuals and government representatives from the Department of Conservation who wish to protect a unique ecological asset, and a third is made up of local commercial fishermen whose livelihood may be seriously affected by the proposal.

Assumption surfacing: Each team identifies the stakeholders, both those involved and those affected by their preferred strategy, and the assumptions and value judgements they have made about them. These often boil down to making boundary choices and judgements, which may or may not be seen as valid by other teams. Each team then positions their assumptions on an **assumption rating chart**, as shown in Figure 7-11. The horizontal axis measures how important an assumption is and the vertical axis how certain or confident the team is that the assumption is correct.

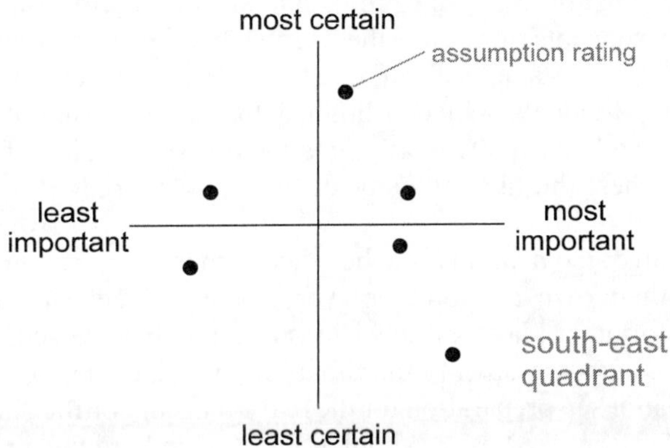

Figure 7-11 Assumption rating chart

The assumptions in the south-east quadrant (important but uncertain) represent a weakness that other teams will certainly challenge. They are candidates for further research in an attempt to increase their degree of certainty.

Dialectic debate: An external consultant facilitates an adversarial debate between pairs of opposing teams where each team critically evaluates the assumption-rating chart of the other. The aim is to identify weaknesses in the other team's assumptions, thus causing them to rethink their approach. Prime candidates for being challenged are: (a) questionable boundary judgements, such as the omission of potential stakeholder groups, including future generations or flora and fauna; (b) a failure to recognize assumptions made about them; and (c) logical flaws in assumptions.

Synthesis: Each team revisits their preferred strategy in the light of the learning gained during the dialectic debate. They meet again with the other team with the aim of forging a new approach to which both sides can commit themselves.

The consultant becomes an active participant in the process, both to manage the dialectic debate and to help in the strategy synthesis. SAST seems to be most suitable for issues that involve groups of professionals of equal rank and status.

Activity

For NuWave Shoes, give and justify your perception of the degree of importance and uncertainty for the following aspects:

- the share of the market that may be captured;
- the potential response of retailers to discounts; for tighter credit policy;
- the bank's credit limit;
- the potential loss of control due to taking an external financial partner.

Problem structuring methods based on a game metaphor

Operational gaming, **hypergame analysis**, **metagame analysis**, and **drama theory** all borrow concepts from game theory, but abandon its rigorous axiomatic foundations. They only retain its outer form, i.e., two or more players, opponents, competitors, or groups of individuals, with conflicting perceptions, different vested interests, motives and views, and different opportunities and decision choices, facing a complex decision situation where the final outcome depends on the joint effect of the actions taken by all parties.

The aim of the methods is to help decision makers gain insights into the situations, such as their own and other players' potential decision dilemmas, the potential reactions of other players to decisions or strategies chosen, and the resulting consequences or outcomes, *before* the situation is played out in real life. In some sense, they are simulations in preparation for the real events or conflict situation expected to arise. They differ from the type of simulations done in hard OR in that they occur with real individuals who interact or role-play with each other in real time under the firm control of a consultant. The latter plays an active and central role.

Operational gaming grew out of war games developed by the Rand Corporation in the 1950s. It has found uses in education (e.g., business games), job training, disaster planning, marketing, and war games. It follows a strict format with rules clearly spelled out to the participants. The game controller prepares a detailed game plan, sets the game rules and the starting conditions. The participants then play the game, usually through several rounds, where at each round they have to make certain decisions or take actions. The game controller determines the outcomes for each party and feeds that information back to them. At the end, the game play is analysed through all its moves and conclusions are drawn about the effectiveness of the strategies used. If used for learning or as a training device, this is done jointly with the participants.

Metagame and hypergame analysis are both 'played out' under the control of a consultant. Usually, only one side or party involved in the conflict situation is physically present. It 'simulates' their own and their opponents' possible play. Metagame analysis explores possible scenarios that could eventuate under the assumptions that all parties can predict each others' choices and their reactions to such knowledge, including their emotional responses to threats and promises, and their credibility. As a result of the insights gained, the party will be much better prepared to behave rationally in the real situation. Metagame analysis has been used for exploring international conflict situations, and policy and management conflicts in business organizations.

In hypergame analysis, each player is assumed to construe the game in possibly quite different terms. This is captured by the client defining for each player a perceptual game — her or his own strategies and the perceptions of the possible strategies and preferences for each of the other players, including emotional aspects, such as their willingness to honour an agreement, their sincerity and fears. Again, all feasible combinations of strategies by all players are explored. This reveals the strengths and weaknesses of the client's strategies, promoting better insight and, hence, better decision making.

In the late 1990s, the learning from these two methods led to the development of drama theory (also known as confrontation analysis), where the conflict situation is actually played out, so-to-speak, on the stage as dramatic episodes, with all their psychological emotions and irrationality. The method assumes that strong emotions, expressed in the confrontation, are often a precursor to changes in preferences. This, in turn, may bring about a redefinition of the game for which a common position can be achieved that the players all trust will be implemented.

Robustness analysis

One of the serious problems in strategic planning is how to cope with high degrees of uncertainties about the future, and in particular, how to develop strategies that do not foreclose potential future options, but leave the door open to cope with a large number of likely scenarios about what the future may look like. Conventional strategic planning approaches try to reduce or tame future uncertainties and identify the most likely future. In contrast, robustness analysis is a low-tech planning approach to cope with such uncertainties, mainly of the UE and UR type (in SCA's terminology).

It is often true that several future strategies all imply the same initial action or commitment. Each set of strategies that shares the same initial commitment is tested for success or acceptability over a reasonably wide range of possible future scenarios. The larger the fraction of all future scenarios for which a given initial commitment is acceptable, the higher the robustness of this commitment. Robust commitments offer flexibility and are desirable candidates for implementation.

Unlike most other PSMs, robustness analysis, developed in 1980 by Rosenhead (2000) needs no facilitator. It can also be used informally as a mode of thinking. In fact, it is good MS/OR practice to look for strategies that keep future options open.

There are other methods or approaches that can be viewed as PSMs, such as **decision conferencing** (a type of brainstorming and system designing, using interactive computer software that allows a group of people to network and interact with each other from different locations), **scenario analysis** (developing of representative futures or scenarios for a given problem situation, usually as inputs into further analysis), **stakeholder analysis** (a systematic procedure to identify all stakeholders of a project, their 'stakes' or interests and values, and so on, and then analyse the relationships between them), and the **theory of constraints** (a mode of thinking about technical and/or organizational change and how to deal with all sort of constraints, physical, intellectual, and relational, often in the form of bottlenecks).

7.9 Critical systems approaches, meta-methodologies

This last section looks at more recent developments in systems thinking and briefly considers some of their philosophical motivation.

Critical systems heuristics

One of the recurrent themes in this text is the vital importance of choosing appropriate boundaries for the system of interest and its relevant environment. The effectiveness and legitimacy of any system intervention depends on this. So far, we have been somewhat vague about how to select appropriate boundaries. Ulrich's **critical systems heuristics** (CSH) (1983/94) is the first and still the only systematic procedure for critically examining boundary choices and their underlying boundary judgements. It is derived from rigorous theoretical and philosophical reasoning.

Space does not allow us to develop the philosophical origins of CSH. We limit ourselves to a motivational overview, as we understand Ulrich's extensive writings. As seen in Chapter 3, we, as humans, interpret the 'real world' through our perceptions. These are affected by our interests, values, and our worldview. Which 'facts' we view as relevant for a given purpose and our interpretation of them depend on our interests, values and worldview. Hence, **facts and values are not separable**. This is well captured by the simple folk wisdom of 'we only see what we want to see'. Similarly, human activity systems are conceptualizations for a given purpose, usually to improve the effectiveness of an existing or planned entity, operation, activity, or organization. Different people may define the corresponding relevant system and its environment differently. In other words, the associated boundary choices involve a fair degree of subjectivity. But boundary choices determine which 'facts' and values are considered relevant and which ones are ignored. Values and worldviews, in turn, may shift as a result of a system analysis. Ulrich refers to these relationships as the 'eternal triangle of reference system, facts, and values'.

Boundary choices also limit the nature of improvements derived from the implementation of the system and how these improvements are distributed among the potential stakeholders. As the discussion on efficiency and effectiveness in Chapter 2 shows, improvements in the narrow system of interest may be at the cost of a worse performance in the wider system. Both aspects raise serious ethical questions.

Churchman, the first systems thinker to raise these questions in the 1960s, argued that, ideally, the answer lies in considering the totality of all relevant aspects, i.e., effectively pushing the boundaries for both the system of interest and its relevant environment farther and farther out. Only then can we judge whether an improvement is real and not to the detriment of somebody or something else. Leaving aside the difficulty of judging what is 'relevant', such a quest is both impossible and impractical in the light of uncertainties about effects, conflicts of interest, cognitive difficulties, the often limited time frames within which decisions have to be made, and the difference in power between stakeholders.

We cannot avoid making boundary choices. It may be impossible, even counterproductive, to include in a system all relationships of interest, nor may we understand all their effects on the various stakeholders. To quote Ulrich (1994)

> '... the implication of the systems idea is not that we must understand the whole system but rather that we need to deal critically with the fact that we never do.'

('Critically' in the sense of exercising careful judgements without bias and guarding oneself against error; making transparent the value judgements underlying them.)

The crucial words are: **we need to deal critically with the fact that we never will**. CSH is Ulrich's approach to do this. Its core consists of critically assessing a set of three boundary question about 'who and what is' and contrast the answers with 'who and what ought to be' for each of four types of stakeholders involved in or affected by the system. Ulrich does not claim that answering these question will produce the 'correct' boundaries. In fact, he stresses that there exists usually not one unique right answer, but that this process will lead to reflection, appreciation, and debate about legitimate alternative views and values. This, in turn, will hopefully result in more informed and appropriate boundary choices. The twelve questions are (note that Ulrich's classification of stakeholders differs from the one listed in Section 4.2, p. 63.):

- About the **client** or **beneficiary** (i.e., those for whom the system is designed):
  1. Who is (ought to be) the client of the system?
  2. What is (ought to be) the objective, goal, or improvement of the system?
  3. How is (ought to be) the improvement in the system measured?
- About the **decision maker** (i.e., those who yield control over the system):
  4. Who is (ought to be) the decision maker?
  5. What aspects are (ought to be) controlled by the decision maker, such as resources (in a broad sense)?
  6. What aspects are not (ought not to be) controlled by the decision maker, i.e. the system environment?
- About the **planner** (i.e., the professionals or analysts who develop the system):
  7. Who is (ought to be) involved in planning the system?
  8. What is (ought to be) the knowledge and expertise of the planner?
  9. Who guarantees (ought to guarantee) that the system developed achieves its planned purpose effectively?
- About those **affected by the system, but not involved in it** (i.e., the voiceless victims or beneficiaries, including future generations, as well as flora and fauna, who have no say in the control or development of the system, but may be affected negatively, as well as positively, by its consequences):
  10. Who of those involved in the system represent/argue (ought to represent/argue) the interests of those affected but not involved?
  11. What opportunities are (ought to be) offered to the voiceless affected to represent themselves?
  12. What worldviews of those affected but not involved are (ought to be) underlying the system design?

As a rule, the 'ought' mode implies shifts in boundaries to cover concerns, usually of the voiceless group of stakeholders, that are ignored or violated by the original boundary choices.

In Ulrich's words (Daellenbach and Flood, 2002, pp. 72–3) the checklist points 'can be used: first, to identify boundary judgements systematically; second, to analyse alternative reference systems for defining a problem or assessing a solution proposal; and third, to challenge in a compelling way any claim to knowledge, rationality or "improvement" that relies on hidden boundary judgements or takes them for granted.'

The last can be particularly helpful when confronting experts who, knowingly or unknowingly, hide value judgements behind references to facts or claims of expertise (such as 'you don't understand that because you lack subject expertise'). The interpretation of facts is not value-free, and values cannot be justified through a claim of expertise or using the 'correct' methodology.

Boundary critique along the lines of CSH should be standard practice for any system study, hard or soft. Its use is essential for public policy issues and public projects.

In fact, Ulrich says that CSH enables individuals to become competent citizens in public debates. However, as we shall see in the next subsection, CSH is more than a checklist for systematically uncovering boundary judgements.

Activity

Give answers to the 12 questions of CSH and justify them for

- the Deep Cove Project;
- the NuWave Shoes case.

Critical systems thinking

The name 'critical systems thinking' (CST) was coined in the late 1980s as a common label for two distinct research strands that called for a more comprehensive and critical approach to systems thinking (Ulrich, 2003). The first of these is Ulrich's work on CSH in the late 1970s and early 1980s. His major driving force was to develop a philosophical foundation for sound professional practice in the applied disciplines and, in particular, for those claiming to use systems thinking. His second aim was to propose a practical framework for such professional practice. His work is based on the philosophical and social theories of Kant (1781), Peirce (1878), Churchman (1968, 1971), and Habermas (1971). The core concept is boundary critique as exemplified by CSH.

The second is the work done at Hull University in the second half of the 1980s by M. Jackson, P. Keys, and others, aimed at developing a framework for critical professional practice through critical awareness and understanding of the strengths and weaknesses of methodologies, and the nature of the problem situation in question. Particular emphasis was placed on the implications of differences in power relationships between stakeholders. One of its criticisms is that the kind of open, unfettered, and participative debate between stakeholders, presupposed by many soft OR approaches, is unattainable, and that mechanisms for emancipating all stakeholders have to be provided to produce results that address their aspirations in the presence of coercive power. Flood and Jackson (1991) developed a meta-methodology, based on methodological pluralism, to guide professional practice in the use of management science approaches. It is briefly covered in the next subsection.

The Hull School's aim for emancipation of all stakeholders has yet to produce an effective mechanism beyond the call for direct political action. (In fact, Ulrich's polemical employment of boundary critique via CSH is, so far, the only approach for concerned citizens to make their voices heard, challenge the stated or implied boundary judgements made by planners, and pursue such endeavours in various forums of the public sphere. Although this is no guarantee for complete emancipative success, there are numerous instances where the concerns of citizens, repeatedly and insistently raised in the public sphere, have finally prevailed (Ulrich, 2003).

Ironically, the Hull School's strongly proclaimed commitment to 'emancipation as an act of faith' precludes critical questioning of one's own boundary judgements. Gordon Hewitt's short quote at the beginning of this chapter ('If we investigate our ideas, we have to be willing to give them up'.) is highly pertinent.

Total systems intervention

Total systems intervention (TSI) is an ambitious meta-methodology (Flood and Jackson, 1991) for critical guidance of the practice of systems intervention.

Flood and Jackson use the following metaphors or systems analogies for viewing an organization:

- **a machine** with coordinated division of labour, a clear chain of command and fixed (open-loop control) rules or procedures for doing things, all controlled from above, such as a bureaucracy (e.g., a military unit, local government administration, the manufacturing operation of most firms);
- **an organism**, consisting of systemically interrelated parts, with feedback loops and controls, where each part has its own needs to be met, with long-term survival of the organization as a primary goal (e.g., a firm promoting flexible responsiveness to its economic and technological environment);
- **a brain**, with high information gathering and information processing ability, which emphasizes learning, self-enquiry, creativity, dynamic goal seeking (e.g., a consulting firm, an R & D department, a highly decentralized firm with quasi autonomous operating units);
- **a culture**, consisting of individuals with shared interests, values, and beliefs, and interacting with a cooperative community-like spirit (e.g., a sports club, a professional association, lower, middle, and upper management levels in firms with highly shared goals, views and values, and high loyalty);
- **a political system**, consisting of groups or coalitions of individuals with different vested interests and values, and who use power to achieve their goals (e.g., parliament, a coalition government, the upper management level of a firm

made up of various factions who compete strongly for power and scarce resources); and

- **a coercive system**, held together through sanctions and/or authority enforced consensus (e.g., a prison, a single-party cabinet of government ministers who must support all majority decisions, the sole, ruthless employer in an economically depressed area).

For a given problem situation, an organization may exhibit features of several metaphors. Different analysts may therefore ultimately select different metaphors as the most appropriate one.

TSI consists of three phases:

Creativity: Use the organizational metaphors to think creatively about the problem situation faced and choose the most appropriate one for the next phase.

Choice: Select a system-based methodology or a set of complementary methodologies and techniques that is judged as most suitable and effective for both the metaphor and the problem situation. If a set of methodologies is chosen, then one is used in a dominant role and the others in supporting roles as needed and appropriate within the framework of the dominant one.

Implementation: The chosen methodology (or set of methodologies) is applied to bring about a coordinated change to the problem situation — a solution, resolution or dissolution — that enhances the organization's efficient, effective, and ethical functioning. (The term 'implementation' departs from the traditional meaning of putting the final results of the analysis to work.)

The 'creativity' and 'choice' phases correspond to the problem formulation stage in Figure 7-1, while 'implementation' primarily covers the modelling stage. Again, as for other hard and soft systems approaches, TSI is used iteratively, possibly for more than one metaphor, with continual backward and forward linkages, and possible switching of dominant and supportive methodologies as more is learned about the problem situation and the suitability of the metaphor used.

A thorough theoretical and practical knowledge on a wide range of methodologies, both hard and soft, is an essential prerequisite for the competent use of TSI. Only then will the analyst/consultant be able to identify the most fitting organizational metaphor and the most suitable methodologies. Currently, few analysts/consultants, except some academics, have such a background. This is clearly one of the major weaknesses of TSI, limiting its use. Having heterogeneous teams of analysts may partially overcome this weakness, but at increased costs of analysis. Furthermore, although not explicitly included in TSI by Flood and Jackson, both the creativity and choice phases will be remiss unless complemented by a rigorous boundary critique along the lines of Ulrich's CSH. It is also questionable whether the 'correct' choice and 'correct' use of methods provides sufficient validation for TSI's claim to bring about critical professional practice. TSI practice is still evolving. Flood and Jackson have separated ways.

Multimethodology

Multimethodology (Mingers and Brocklesby, 1997) shares some of the same aims as TSI, i.e., plurality of methodologies and methods. Rather than use a single best hard or soft OR approach, it combines approaches so as to better match the richness, complexity, and peculiarities of a particular problem and its organizational context. Different methods or parts of methods are applied at different stages of the analysis, or part of a method is combined with another at the same stage. For example, in Chapter 6, the hard OR methodology was supplemented by rich pictures (Stage 1 of SSM) as the most effective way for capturing the problem situation. Similarly, to overcome constraints to, or difficulties of, implementation of a hard OR solution, the various stakeholders may be brought together in a SODA or SSM workshop to find the best implementation strategy. During a PSM exercise, hard OR techniques may be used for evaluating or comparing the performance of alternative systems studied. The comparing phase of SCA, Stage 6 of SSM, or the preparation to Step 4 of SODA may profit of such 'trespassing' into hard OR. Similarly, the SAST assumption rating chart may be a useful device for assessing the relative salience of uncertainties in SCA.

Multimethodology recognizes a practice that inventive analysts have informally used almost from the inception of MS/OR.

As is true for TSI, effective practice of multimethodology requires good theoretical and practical competence in a wide variety of systems approaches.

7.10 Concluding remarks

It is fair to say that so far the major use of soft systems approaches, except for multimethodology, comes from the developers themselves, often within a consulting practice, and from a small group of acolytes, predominantly academics. Few users are sufficiently familiar with more than one approach, although this is changing with several universities, as well as some of the developers, offering courses and intensive workshops. However, such exposure alone is not sufficient for expertise. As has been pointed out earlier, the consultant also needs to have good skills in interpersonal relations, in facilitation and negotiation. These skills come naturally to a few, while others struggle to acquire them through long years of working with people.

None of the soft systems approaches seem explicitly to address the various issues of practical implementation. It is true that the active participation of many stakeholders in the project intervention process will hopefully pave the way for the implementation of the commitment package or recommendations made, since the stakeholders are more likely to own the solution. However, owning the solution is only a beginning — it removes some of the human constraints to implementation. Planning for the actual process of change, assigning responsibilities for who does what when, and monitoring implementation and the performance of the new system are other essential aspects that need to be dealt with. The 'monitoring subsystem' of SSM provides for the latter, provided it gets translated into action.

Finally, it is interesting to view the practice of PSMs within a system context, similar to the structure diagram for hard OR in Figure 6-9 (p. 162). This is done in

Figure 7-12. In contrast to hard OR, it is not a sequence of systems whose outputs become the input into the next system. System S is 'created' or defined within system M. Note again how boundary judgements affect all aspects.

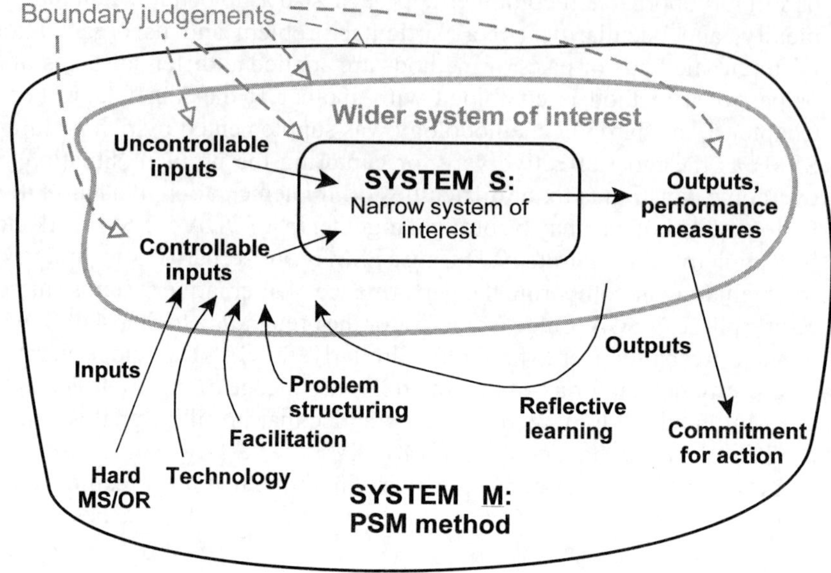

Figure 7-12 Structure diagram for PSMs

7.11 Chapter highlights

- While hard OR approaches stress mainly 'content', most PSMs put equal emphasis on process. They use participative debate to enhance understanding of differences of interests and views. They address primarily 'What' questions. All profess to be 'learning systems', used iteratively and flexibly. Most PSMs are the result of practical consultancy and/or action research, and rely on a consultant/facilitator to guide the process through its phases.
- While some PSMs are firmly based on system theory, others are also based on critical philosophy and/or borrow ideas from psychology, sociology, and organization theory.
- The seven-steps of SSM are a learning process that iterates through several alternative potential views or root definitions of the issues selected, develops a conceptual system model for each, and compares what 'is' in the real world with what 'ought to be'. This process encourages greater insights into the problem situation.
- SODA merges individual stakeholders' cognitive maps into a joint strategic map that helps to discover emerging themes and core ideas which become the focus for a decision analysis workshop, culminating in a commitment for action.

- SCA is a four-phase approach to explore and deal effectively with various types of uncertainties that may impede decision making. Its outcome is a commitment package for immediate and exploratory actions and for future contingencies.
- CSH is a practical approach to evaluate system and environment boundary choices and to reveal boundary judgements, particularly with respect to those stakeholders that are affected, but have no voice in the project. It should be the front-end of any system analysis, both hard and soft.
- CST attempts to address principles of critical professional systems practice and the difficulties any systems methodology faces in the presence of differences in economic, political, and authority-based power between the stakeholders.
- TSI views problem situations through one or more of six organizational metaphors and then matches it with an appropriate MS/OR methodology or combinations of methodologies.
- Multimethodology advocates the judicious combining of methods or the borrowing of parts of methods for various phases or aspects of an MS/OR intervention as a means to enhance its effectiveness and success.

Exercises

1. Consider the staffing problem situation faced by Bill Dodge in exercise 9 of Chapter 4 (p. 84). Formulate two alternative root definitions, seen from his point of view, the first task-based reflecting his objectives for border control, the second issue-based reflecting his desire for efficient and effective staff management. Identify the CATWOE elements.
2. Consider the blood bank situation (Case study 3-1, p. 54), and its rich picture or mind map. Draw a conceptual model for the following issue-based root definition:

   A system which allows the director of the blood bank to reconcile the conflict of potential blood product shortages versus outdating of fresh blood so as to derive a medically defensible policy for managing limited shelf-life blood stocks, collected from voluntary donors and needed for transfusions to patients in emergency and scheduled elective surgery, and for conversion into blood components administered to patients with blood deficiencies.
3. Consider again the Customs staffing problem situation in Exercise 9 of Chapter 4 (p. 84). Take the point of view of the consultant.
   (a) Formulate a task-based root definition for providing the client, i.e., Bill Dodge, with an effective tool for identifying technically feasible and culturally acceptable staff shift schedules that are flexible and offer some overtime. One of the requirements for the tool is that Bill Dodge can use it himself. Identify the stated and implied CATWOE elements.
   (b) Build a conceptual model for the root definition of (a).
4. Consider the cancer screening problem in Example 1-4 (p. 5). For the following root definition, construct a conceptual model: 'A system owned by the National Health Service and operated by local health boards for setting up a voluntary national screening service, equipped with the latest technology and staffed by fully-trained technicians, where all

women between the age of 48 and 70 are encouraged to be screened every second year. The objective is to have as high a participation rate as possible.' Note that acquiring the equipment and training additional technicians to operate the equipment, as well as the process of rolling out the service, are implied in that root definition.

5. Consider exercise 8 in Chapter 4. Combine your map for Y with the one shown below for his father (F) into a strategic map. Identify any emerging themes and/or core concepts.

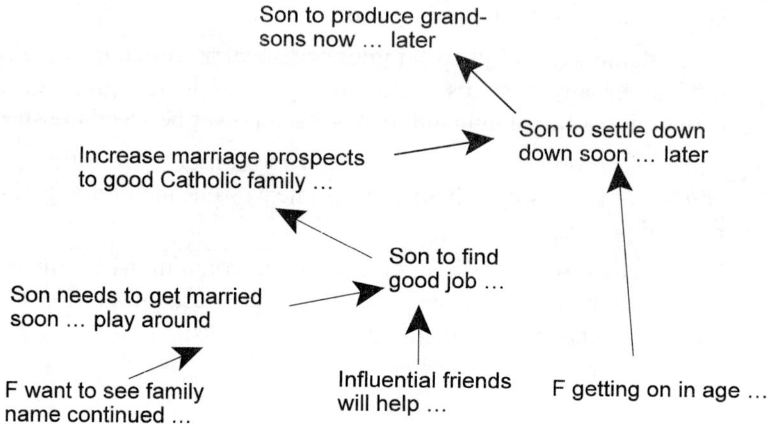

6. For the Customs staffing problem situation in exercise 9 of Chapter 4 (p. 84):
   (a) identify which aspects belong to each type of uncertainty UE, UV, and UR;
   (b) list the various decision areas;
   (c) draw a decision (areas) diagram, similar to Figure 7-8, showing both the importance and urgency of the decisions and their links;
   (d) select a subset that you judge is most important for Bill Dodge to investigate first; develop an option tree, showing all feasible decision schemes, similar to Figure 7-9.
7. For the blood bank in Case study 3-1 (p. 54):
   (a) identify which aspects belong to each type of uncertainty UE, UV, and UR;
   (b) list the various decision areas;
   (c) draw a decision (areas) diagram, similar to Figure 7-8, showing both the importance and urgency of the decisions and their links.
8. From the interview answers given by Bill Dodge for the Customs staffing problem situation in exercise 9 of Chapter 4 (p. 84), draw an assumption rating chart, similar to Figure 7-11, for the following aspects: (A) prevention of entry into the country of prohibited aliens; (B) prevention of importation of illegal drugs; (C) meeting Government guidelines for processing commercial flight PAX; (D) processing correspondence within three days; (E) meeting custom officers union demand for no flexible shifts, no short shifts, and no part-timers; (F) eliminating (most) overtime hours that are extensions of regular shift hours; (G) eliminating (most) special call-outs; (H) the reliability of PAX numbers supplied by the airlines prior to arrivals of aircraft; (I) arrival times of scheduled flights.
9. Discuss the distinction between 'What' and 'How' questions. Referring back to Figure II-1 (p. 115) and the basic properties of hard OR and soft OR approaches, why are the latter more suitable to tackle 'What' issues than hard OR approaches, while hard OR is more successful in situation with high technical complexity?
10. It seems obvious, why a proposal for introducing a change in a system or organization must be 'systemically desirable'. Explore why it also needs to be 'culturally feasible' to be

successful and accepted by the various stakeholders, particularly the users.

11. Ackoff, Churchman, and Checkland suggest that model builders should also consider the aesthetics of their models and the ethical implications of their boundary choices and recommendations. Discuss.

Further reading

Ackermann, F. (2012) 'Problem structuring methods 'in the dock': Arguing the case for soft OR,' *European Journal of Operational Research forthcoming.*

Ackermann, F. (2011) 'Getting 'Messy' with Problems: The Challenge of Teaching 'Soft' OR,' *INFORMS Transactions on Education*, 12(1): 55–64.

Ackermann, F. and Eden, C. (2011) *Making Strategy: Mapping Out Strategic Success*, London: Sage.

Ackoff, R.L. (1979) 'The Future of OR is Past', *Journal of the Operational Research Society*, February: 93–104.

Beer, S. (1985) *Diagnosing the System for Organizations*, Wiley, Chichester. Stafford Beer is the creator (1959) of the 'viable system model', a cybernetic model of organizations, which Beer started to implement for restructuring of Chile's economy under Allende. (Not covered here.)

Checkland, P. (1985) 'From optimization to learning: a development of systems thinking for the 1990s', *Journal of the Operational Research Society*, 36(9): 757–67.

Checkland, P. and Holwell, S. (2004) Chapter 3: 'Classic OR' and 'Soft' OR—an asymmetric complementary, in Pidd, M. (ed.), *Systems Modelling: Theory and Practice*, Chichester: Wiley, 44–60.

Checkland, P. and Poulter, J. (2006) *Learning for Action: a short definitive account of Soft Systems Methodology and its use for practitioners, teachers, and students*, Chichester: Wiley. Written at a very basic level specifically for inexperienced students and instructors.

Checkland, P. and Scholes, J. (1999) *Soft Systems Methodology in Action, includes a 30-year retrospective*, Chichester: Wiley. Accounts of several real-life applications.

Checkland, P. and Winter, M. (2006) 'Process and content: two ways of using SSM', *Journal of the Operation Research Society*, 57(12): 1435–41. Shows how SSM itself can be used as an overarching methodology for an SSM intervention.

Churchman, C.W. (1971) *The Design of Inquiring Systems*, New York: Basic Books. A scholarly text.

Churchman, C.W. (1968) *The Systems Approach*, New York: Dell Publishing. Provocative.

Daellenbach, H.G. and Flood R.L. (2002) *The Informed Student Guide to Management Science*, London: Thomson. Short, introductory descriptions of all major OR/MS concepts and tools.

Eden, C. and Ackermann, F. (2004) Chapter 9: Use of 'soft-OR' models by clients — what do they want from them? In Pidd, M. (ed.), *Systems Modelling: Theory and Practice*, Chichester: Wiley, 146–163.

Eden, C. and Ackermann, F. (1998) *Making Strategy—The Journey of Strategic Management.* London: Sage. Cognitive mapping, SODA, and Journey Making by the developers.

Flood, R.L. and Jackson M.C. (1991) *Creative Problem Solving, Total Systems Intervention*, Chichester: Wiley. TSI discussed by its developers.

Franco, L.A. and Montibeller, G. (2010) 'Facilitating modelling in Operations Research,' *European Journal of Operational Research*, 205(3): 489–500.

Friend, J.K. and Hickling, A. (2005) *Planning under Pressure: the Strategic Choice Approach,* 3rd edn Oxford: Butterworth-Heineman,. SCA by its developers, including several real-life applications.

Habermas, J. (1971) *Knowledge and Human Interests*, Boston: Beacon Press. Advanced.

Keys, P. (2006) 'On becoming expert in the use of PSMs', *Journal of the Operational Research Society*, 57(7): 822–9.

Mason, R.O. and Mitroff, I.I. (1981) *Challenging Strategic Planning Assumptions*, Wiley, New York. Original coverage of SAST by its developers.

Mingers, J.C. and Brocklesby, J. (1997) 'Multimethodology: towards a framework for mixing methodologies', *Omega, 25*: 489–509

Mingers, J.C. and Gill, A. (1997) *Multimethodology — The Theory and Practice of Combining Management Science Methodologies*, Chichester: Wiley. Combining different methods or parts of methods for analysis of different aspects of the same problem.

Mingers, J. and Rosehead, J. (2011) 'Introduction to Special Issue: Teaching Soft OR, PSMs, and Multimethodology,' *INFORMS Transactions on Education*, 12(1): 1–3.

Pidd, M. (2009) *Tools for Thinking: Modelling in Management Science*, 3rd edn, Chichester: Wiley. Introductory treatment of SSM in chapter 5, SODA and Journey Making in Chapter 6.

Rosenhead, J. (2006) 'Past, present and future of PSMs', *Journal of the Operational Research Society*, 57(7): 759–65.

Rosenhead, J. and Mingers, J.C. (eds) (2000) *Rational Analysis for a Problematic World Revisited*, Chichester: Wiley. An overview of the important properties of soft systems approaches, followed by a detailed account with case studies of several methodologies, written by various contributors. Good starting point for the 'basics' of and a 'feel' (1989 edition by Rosenhead.)

Ulrich, W. (2012) 'Operational research and critical systems thinking—an integrated perspective, Part 1: OR as argumentative practice,' *Journal of the Operational Research Society*, 63(7): 1228–47. Excellent exposition of CSH and TSI, their common aims and differences in interpretations.

Ulrich, W. (2012) 'Operational research and critical systems thinking—an integrated perspective, Part 2: OR as applied systems thinking,' *Journal of the Operational Research Society*, 63(7): 1307–22.

Ulrich, W. (2003) 'Beyond methodology choice: critical systems thinking as critically systemic discourse,' *Journal of the Operational Research Society*, 54(4): 325–42.

Ulrich, W. (1996) *A Primer to Critical Systems Heuristics for Action Researchers*, Centre for Systems Studies, University of Hull. Useful, practical guide for applying CSH.

Ulrich, W. (1994) 'Can we design future-responsive management through systems thinking and design?' *Interfaces*, Vol. 24, No. 4, July-Aug: 26-37. Ulrich's tribute to Churchman.

Viewpoint, *Journal of the Operational Research Society*, (2006), 57: 766–775. Thought-provoking dialogue about PSMs and their future by C. Eden, P. Checkland, and J. Friend.

INFORMS Transactions on Education, Sept. Issue 2011, Vol 12, No. 1, contains several articles on PSMs, PSM case reports, and the teaching of PSM, written by practitioners and academics. Instructive.

8

Implementation and code of ethics

Learning objectives

- Be able to identify difficulties and obstacles to implementation: those relating to the physical task of implementing the solution or recommendations, those relating to the problem owners and problem users, and those stemming from the wider system of interest.
- Be able to judge whether an implementation plan addresses all aspects that enhance its likely success.
- Appreciate the analyst's ethical responsibilities in any system intervention, including towards those affected without a voice.

Introduction

The majority of MS/OR projects are aimed at improving the operation of an existing system, or finding the best mode of operations for a new proposed system. The potential benefits of such a project can, however, only be secured if the solution to the problem is implemented. Contrary to the belief of most novice MS/OR analysts, implementation is not something tacked on to the end of the modelling phase. Rather, it must be a prime concern underlying all earlier steps in the analysis. Planning for implementation starts right from the outset of any project. This is the topic of the first two sections of this chapter.

Once a solution has been implemented, procedures and rules have to be put in place for the continued control, updating, and maintenance of the solution. These aspects are explored in Sections 8.3 and 8.4.

The chapter concludes with a discussion of aspects of personal and professional ethics for the analyst, particularly for projects that involve and affect stakeholders other than the analyst him- or herself.

8.1 Implementation and its difficulties

As shown in Figures 6-1 (p. 119) and 7-1 (p. 182), implementation of an MS/OR project is putting the results of the modelling phase to work, i.e.,

- specifying who does what, when; in other words, assign to each problem user the tasks he or she is to perform, when and how;
- training them in the proper use of the new rules; and
- making the changeover from the existing to the new mode of operation.

At first sight, the steps for accomplishing this seem straightforward. They are easily handled by a systematic approach, good organization, and coordination. Unfortunately, implementation is fraught with difficulties that are largely of a human nature. This is particularly pronounced for projects that deal with improving an existing operation.

To get a better 'feel' for one of these human aspects, just put yourself in the position of the stock clerk in the LOD in charge of the day-to-day replenishments of stocks (see Section 6.7), or the position of the personnel scheduler of a 24-hour service operation in charge of rostering individual employees to tasks and shifts. You have done these tasks for a number of years and considered that you did a competent job. Along comes this MS/OR analyst, called in by your boss or sent in by somebody higher up in the hierarchy. Most people will see this as a sign of lack of confidence in their ability to do the job properly, and hence will perceive it as a threat. What may make it even worse is that this whizz kid is probably fairly young, university trained, but with seemingly little practical understanding of the intricacies of your job. It would be rather surprising if you did not view any 'solution' proposed by this analyst with a fair degree of suspicion, unless you yourself were intimately involved in the analysis.

Problems of implementation can stem from three causes:

1. Those relating to the physical task of implementation:
   - the complexity of the solution;
   - the sensitivity of the benefits or costs (both tangible and intangible) to deviations from the formally prescribed rules; and
   - the extent to which the proposed solution deviates from current practice.

   The greater any of these, the greater the problems which have to be overcome.
2. Those relating to the problem users and other individuals affected by the solution:
   - their personalities, their motivation and pride in the job (e.g., does the proposed solution restrict their freedom of action, take away their responsibility, reduce their relative status, transform a challenging job that required years of experience into one of merely feeding data into a computer which then spits back what action to take?);
   - their ages (change is more difficult, routine becomes more entrenched with age);
   - their background and level of education (are the intellectual demands put on them too great?);
   - the importance of the tasks associated with the proper use of the solution in

relation to their other job activities (the less important they perceive these tasks to be, the less attention these tasks will receive); and

- the degree to which they perceive the solution to be a threat to their job security.

3. Those relating to the environment of the project:
   - the support given to the project and its solution by the problem owners (the less visible and explicit the support given to the project, the less cooperation it will receive from the problem users);
   - the organizational implications of the solution, such as the need for greater cooperation between departments (e.g., the user department becoming more dependent on information from other departments, or other departments perceiving the solution as interfering with their operations, either of which threatens compliance); and
   - the incentive systems for pay and promotions used by the organization (if the solution reduces pay or threatens promotional prospects, individuals may sabotage implementation).

Generally, hard MS/OR analysts pay full attention to the first factor, the question of technology. The tendency is to neglect or overlook the human factors of (2) and (3). They are qualitative in nature and evade the formal treatment that can be given to technology, but can nevertheless act as serious constraints on implementation. It should come as no surprise that neglecting these human constraints in a system can easily lead to a 'solution' that is one on paper only and is not workable in practice. From this point of view, implementation can be viewed as a problem of relaxing the human constraints versus adjusting the technical solution. On the other hand, the nature of a soft MS/OR approach is to give more attention to the factors of (2) and (3), sometimes to the detriment of (1). Some of the points stressed in this chapter are therefore specifically directed at hard MS/OR practice.

The human constraints may be relaxed in a number of ways. More involvement of problem users from the outset and more training may increase their understanding of the solution. It may be possible to identify individuals who could become obstacles to proper implementation and transfer them to other jobs of equal importance or status. The technical solution can be adjusted by simplifying the policy or decision rules, e.g., by going to quick-and-dirty rules that may capture only a substantial part of the benefits, but may be much easier to use and implement.

The literature on implementation is unanimous on one point — implementation and continued use of a solution are almost guaranteed if the problem owners and problem users 'own' the results of the analysis. Again, soft MS/OR approaches are geared to produce ownership as an integral part of the methodology, while for hard MS/OR projects, the analyst may pro-actively have to develop a process climate for this to happen. Users will develop a feeling of ownership if they can contribute to the project in meaningful ways with their experience and in-depth knowledge of the operations. A wise analyst will therefore keep them appropriately informed, submit all ideas of a non-mathematical nature to their scrutiny, and solicit their advice. If they feel that they have contributed in significant ways to the project and that their inputs have been valued, they will have an invested interest in seeing the solution put into practice and will take an active role in the implementation process.

In the LOD project, the stock clerk was the most important user stakeholder. She was pulled in as an active project team member from the outset and given the responsibility of liaising with all other potential problem users and problem customers. Similarly, the LOD manager was kept fully informed and regularly consulted during the project. Rather than have the analyst present the proposed solution to the staff of the LOD and interested refinery personnel, he fully briefed the LOD manager and coached him to give that presentation. Except for the EOQ formula, it contained no mathematics. The whole project conveyed a strong impression of active LOD participation and management support.

8.2 Planning for implementation

As pointed out before, planning for implementation must start at the outset of any project, when the first contacts are established with the sponsor(s).

Laying the groundwork for implementation

The groundwork for implementation is laid throughout the project as it progresses through its phases. This truth cannot be overemphasized. Except for purely technical projects, largely devoid of any human aspects, it is not sufficient to start planning for implementation once the solution to the model has been tested and the project report submitted to the sponsor. Not only could this result in serious delays in implementation because crucial input data may not be available, but the human aspect discussed in the previous section will most certainly have been neglected.

Laying this groundwork consists of the following aspects:

1. **Correctly identifying the problem owners and all problem users:** The first, because they will ultimately have to give approval for implementation; the second, because their full cooperation is needed for continued use of the solution.
2. **Establishing effective lines of communication** with the problem owners and problem users: Which channels, formal or informal, does the analyst use to communicate with various people in the sponsor organization? Who are the liaison people? To be effective, the lines of communication must be open, and there must be mutual respect and trust between the analyst and the problem owners and users.

   If the project is the first contact that the analyst has with them, trust and respect must be explicitly established and nurtured, because there is always the risk that the problem owners and problem users feel threatened by the project. Any signs revealing condescension or superiority by the analyst will only reinforce their mistrust, but particularly that of the problem users. The analyst has to be aware that such messages are more often than not conveyed by non-verbal body language, such as signals of impatience or 'knowing smiles'. Also, beware of offhand remarks to other parties, particularly in e-mails. They are bound to reach the wrong ears.

   As a rule, the analyst should start from the premise that the problem users have done their best, based on their training, education, and resources available. The analyst may know more about MS/OR modelling, but the problem users know much more about the problem, not only those aspects that are easily visible, but also those that may require extensive experience and exposure. It is easy to withhold such information, which will then become an obstacle to proper implementation. So, initially, it is the analyst who has to rely on them and learn from them, before he or she can start contributing to the problem.

3. **Exploring and managing prior expectations for the project:** As discussed in Section 6.3, a problem owner and/or problem user may have formed prior expectations about what the project will deliver in terms of benefits or the time frame for its execution. If these expectations cannot be met, these stakeholders may withdraw their support from the project, either actively or passively. This may jeopardize implementation. For this reason, the prudent analyst will explore and evaluate all prior expectations. If they are unrealistic or difficult to meet within the time frame and resources available, they should be confronted in a diplomatic manner. The analyst must also be aware, that he or she could unwittingly contribute to the formation of unrealistic expectations by promising more than can be delivered.
4. **Keeping the problem owners and problem users regularly informed** about the progress of the project and soliciting feedback and new ideas from them.
5. **Checking out availability and sources of all input data needed:** Are sufficient data available to draw valid inferences? It may take months to accumulate sufficient data, such as product demand, and so on. Unless missing data collection is initiated right from the start, undesirable delays in implementation will be unavoidable. If available, have any changes in their form or timing occurred during the collection period? If yes, you may be comparing apples with pears.
6. **Clearing access to data:** Who liaises over access to data? Who of the analyst team has access, when and where? May data be removed from the premises?
7. **Ordering of special equipment and commercial computer software** may have to be done well in advance of implementation.
8. **Developing all software** needed for implementation and continued use of the new solution. Such software has to be fully tested on real-life data, as well as for extreme data values. It should flag errors in data input or data that are questionable, e.g., falling outside their operational range. Nothing undermines the users' confidence more quickly than software that breaks down or produces answers that look suspect.
9. **Preparing detailed documentation for all computer software:** Lack of detailed documentation may render it difficult, if not impossible, to correct programming mistakes or make changes to the software in response to changes in the mode of operation. Best practice calls for detailed comments inserted in the software programs explaining the function of non-obvious statements.
10. **Planning and executing the change-over to the new mode of operation:** With the groundwork laid, the actual change-over from the current to the new mode of operation involves the following steps:

- Writing detailed users' manuals that translate the mathematical solution and/or the new systems structure and processes into a set of easily understood operating procedures and decision rules, appropriate to the level of education of the intended users. This includes tasks related to updating of the data bases needed for the continued use of the solution. The importance of complete users' manuals cannot be stressed enough. Incomplete, inaccurate, and badly written users' manuals are a prime cause for implementation failure or a rapid deterioration in the proper use of the implemented solution.
- Assign responsibility for the various tasks to each problem user. Tasks should be assigned to organizational positions as part of their job description, rather than to named individuals. This will ensure continuity if personnel changes occur.
- Preparation of special stationery or forms needed for using the solution.
- Prepare training sessions for all users, including printing of a sufficient number of users' manuals, and any other material needed for the training sessions.
- Plan the actual change-over to the new mode of operation. For large projects, it may be advisable to schedule implementation in stages rather than in one go in order to avoid straining the resources and facilities. In the LOD case, the solution reduced the stock replenishment sizes for low-volume products. It projected that their existing high stocks would take up to three months to reduce to the new maximum levels. On the other hand, the stocks of high-volume products would rise almost immediately. Simultaneous implementation of the policy for all products would thus risk creating serious warehouse space shortages. Hence, the policies for low-volume products were scheduled to be implemented immediately, while implementation for the high-volume products only proceeded at the rate at which warehouse space became freed up by reducing the stocks of low-volume products.

  For the NuWave Shoes project, take-up by retailers of prompt payment discounts was more likely to be successful if they were explicitly informed about the change in policy when they received the new season's catalogues or samples, rather than by a small print statement at the bottom of the invoice accompanying the shipment months later.
- Conduct the training sessions and inform all users of the change-over schedule.
- Execute the change-over.
- Schedule regular follow-up sessions with problem users during the early stages of the new mode of operation. It is hoped that this will reveal problems that could threaten the proper use of the solution, such as errors in the users' manuals or misinterpretations of rules, early enough before they may cause a loss of confidence in the solution.

Planning for implementation may call for the use of the **critical path method** (CPM), which is a topic in most texts on MS/OR techniques and production management. Figure 5-8 (p.108) demonstrates its application for a construction project.

In particularly complex and sensitive cases, the implementation planning and execution for the results of a hard MS/OR projects may be facilitated via recourse to a soft MS/OR approach, such as SSM.

8.3 Controlling and maintaining the solution

The environment in which most organizations operate is constantly undergoing change. This means that inputs into the system modelled and its environment are also changing. Such change may be quantitative or structural. Quantitative changes are those that only affect the magnitude of inputs into the model, e.g., a change in the volume of the annual demand for the LOD, or a new travel time from point A to B in a delivery problem due to road alterations. In most cases, the model remains a valid representation of the system. However, if the changes in the inputs are sufficiently large, then the current solution may need to be adjusted. Sensitivity and error analysis will provide guidelines as to when such an adjustment may be desirable. This reinforces the importance of performing such analysis with respect to all important inputs into the model.

A change in the form or nature of an input or in the systems environment is structural if it affects the influence relationships with one or more system components or state variables in the model. The original model may cease to be a valid representation, requiring affected functional or systemic relationships in the model to be reformulated. For the LOD problem, installation of new mixing and filling equipment might allow seamless change-over on the filling machine between container sizes for the same oil. Hence, all container sizes for each oil could be filled with a single mixing batch, reducing set-up costs considerably. The current model deals with each oil/container size combination individually. Such a structural change would require a new model that finds a joint optimal policy for several related products — technically a much more complex problem. Similarly, for the NuWave Shoes, if a major foreign RM supplier introduces substantial quantity discounts for large purchases, the potential cost impact of that could lead to a rethink of the just-in-time procurement policy.

Procedures have to be set up to monitor such quantitative and structural changes in the environment. This will allow timely corrective action to be triggered when the changes become significant. Spelling out these procedures and trigger points forms an important part of the users' manuals. A change is judged significant if the estimated improvement in benefits gained by adjusting the solution exceeds the cost of making the adjustment. Note that if the solution is regularly updated, say once every six months, the estimate only covers the period remaining until the next regular adjustment.

Establishing controls over the solution consists of:

1. Listing for each input (parameters, constraints) — both those that are explicitly included in the model and those that have been excluded as insignificant — the quantitative change in values for which the present solution remains optimal or near-optimal. Rather than indicate such permissible changes in absolute terms, it is more useful to give percentage changes. The latter often remain valid even after successive updates of the solution, while absolute changes could become out of date after one or two updates. For example, for the LOD project, any change in the rate of demand for a given product in excess of 50% became a signal for an update

of the control parameters, unless an annual update was less than three months away.

2. Listing of the structural form of the assumed influence relationships between inputs and state variables, and state variables and outputs, both for those explicitly included in the model and those excluded. Any MS/OR analyst will then be able to judge whether a given subsequent structural change in relationships invalidates the current version of the model. For the LOD project, any changes in equipment and processing procedures for customer orders could imply structural changes.
3. Specifying in detail how each input should be measured to assess if a change is significant, how frequently such measurements should be made, and specific events that may call for such measurements to be taken. For the LOD project, each product demand distribution was updated monthly by a forecasting method called **exponential smoothing**. Its updated monthly average was plotted on a statistical control chart. An out-of-control signal triggered a review of that product. The introduction of possible substitute products also triggered a review.
4. Assigning responsibility for the control of each item and who is to be notified if significant changes have been detected. Again, such responsibilities should be part of a job description for a given position. For the LOD project, the stock clerk was responsible for the majority of the control tasks, except those of a purely financial nature, such as changes in the cost of capital or changes in labour costs. Control of these was assigned to a position in the Cost Control Department. In the NuWave Shoe case, Elly would be in charge of monitoring the payment habits of retailers, while the production supervisor would be in charge of monitoring RM levels.
5. Specifying in detail how the solution has to be adjusted in response to quantitative changes in inputs and by whom, and what action has to be initiated to deal with possible structural changes detected. For the LOD project, the stock clerk was put in charge of updating the solution for quantitative changes in the input parameters, using the software developed by the Management Science Group. She was also in charge of updating all control parameters once a year and notifying the head of the Management Science Group if events occurred that could imply structural changes.

8.4 Following up implementation and performance

Monitoring implementation

The job of the MS/OR analyst is not finished once the solution has been implemented. There is always the danger that, over time, enforcement of the rules for using the solution becomes lax. Users may take shortcuts that do not seem to cause an immediate visible deterioration of the performance, but have a cumulative effect. Certain rules, or the reasons for them, may have been misunderstood or misinterpreted. Furthermore, even with the most comprehensive planning and greatest care, events unforeseen by the analyst will occur and remedial action may be taken by individuals who do not have the right information or training to make the proper changes. For all these reasons, it is essential that the analyst keep monitoring the performance of the model for some time after implementation.

Misapplication or misinterpretation of the solution usually requires corrective action. This may consist simply of once again going over the rules with the individuals in question. It could call for organizing follow-up training sessions, or even adjusting the solution rules to circumvent a recurrence of errors. Errors or unclear instructions may need revisions of the users' manuals.

It is crucial that the analyst does not underestimate the importance of such follow-ups. Neglecting this aspect could well result in the actual operation reverting back to the previous mode within a few weeks or months and the new solution being 'shelved'. Resurrecting it at that time may be quite difficult due to the negative attitude that most users will have developed towards it. It is quite natural that they will blame the solution or the analyst for the failure, rather than the improper use of the solution.

For example, follow-up monitoring revealed that the supervisor of the LOD grease operation continued using the old rules. He had worked in that plant for over 40 years and was not going to 'take orders from anybody who did not know the first thing about how to make greases', as he put it to the LOD manager. In the end, implementation of the solution for the grease plant could only be obtained by shifting him to another job. Sadly, he could not adjust to the new job either and was offered early retirement at full pension, which he accepted.

Performance audit

One of the final duties of the analyst is to make a performance audit on the solution. This means checking the extent to which the projected new benefit or reduced costs (both pecuniary and intangible) have been realized. **The benefits generated by the use of the new solution are estimated based on the solution's actual performance and not on theoretical formulas**, such as expression (6-3) for the LOD project (p.149). These benefits are then compared with the performance the old solution would have achieved.

To be valid, the comparison must be made using the same basis. For quantitative problems, this means the same input data. For instance in the LOD project, comparing the actual total costs for the last year of using the old solution with the cost of the first year of using the new solution is not a valid comparison, since it uses data from different years.

Any serious discrepancy between the projected and the actual benefits should be fully examined and properly explained.

This audit is not only important for the sponsor of the project, but also for the analyst. **Only then does the analyst get valid quantitative and qualitative feedback on her or his own performance**.

The final audit for the LOD project was done one year after implementation. The costs savings were estimated at $72,000 for that year. Given that the new policy was implemented in stages and only became fully effective after a four-month transition, this confirmed fairly well the original savings estimates. However, the costs of implementation were slightly more than $40,000. This was largely because of significant additions to the software produced, in particular, a demand forecasting system.

Full versus partial implementation

Full implementation of all recommendations is rare. It is more useful to talk about the degree of implementation achieved. The aim of the analyst should be to achieve a sufficiently high degree of implementation to capture the major portion of the potential benefits. As for mathematical modelling, to capture the last bit of benefits may not be justified by the additional cost incurred.

8.5 Ethical considerations

Ethics is the code of moral principles and values that govern the behaviour of a person or a group of people with respect to what is judged right or wrong by the society they live in. Sounds pretty straightforward! Unfortunately, it is far from that. There are a number of difficulties and grey areas. There are genuine conflicting views among people and societies about what constitutes ethical behaviour and what is not. Different societies and subgroups of society will tend to abide by different ethical standards. What is acceptable behaviour for one group, may be very objectionable for another. Neither do such standards remain static over time. Certain generally accepted industrial practices in the nineteenth century are now viewed as morally detestable. Many aspects of the new free market society that has sprung up in Russia with the demise of communism would be highly frowned upon even by the bastion of the free market, the USA. The sequence of financial crises — the stock exchange debacles of 2008 and 2011, and the partial melt-down of the banking sectors of 2009, repeated in 2011 — have raised fundamental ethical questions about traditionally tolerated or accepted behaviour of financial market operators and bankers.

Furthermore, we are also highly selective and inconsistent in choosing which ethical principles to apply or ignore in various situations. Many of us follow one code of ethics in our interactions with relatives and friends, another when interacting with people at large, and a third in our dealings with the tax authorities or the traffic police.

Ethics has occupied philosophers and religious leaders for as long as humanity has existed in the form of organized societal structures. The discussion that follows will therefore hardly scratch the surface of this fascinating subject.

Ethics as a basis for decision making

Ethics is relevant for decision making in at least two ways. First, it goes without saying that ethical principles should form the basis for all decision making. Without following ethical principles, decision making degenerates and becomes opportunistic, self-centred, inconsistent, and destructive to all stakeholders. What forms a minimal set of ethical norms has puzzled philosophers, from Pythagoras (6th century BC, better-known for his mathematical discoveries) to Bertrand Russell (1872–1970). Its discussion goes beyond the scope of this text. However, what is relevant is that in recent years decision making methodologies have been proposed that are largely based on ethical considerations. They consist of check lists for evaluating the decision process, the decisions, and the outcomes, and their effects on all stakeholders, with particular considerations to the problem customers. The process of boundary critique in CSH (Section 7.8, pp. 212–14) is an effective approach to uncover questionable ethical and value judgements.

Personal ethical considerations for analysts

But even within the MS/OR methodology, ethics and ethical considerations must concern analysts at a personal and professional level. Analysts must assume moral responsibility for the effects that their own involvement in a project and the recommendations derived from it have on the various the problem users and the problem customers — the third parties that benefit from or are the victims of the results of the project, but have no direct say in it. In Ulrich's classification (1983, 1996), they are those affected by the system but not involved in its planning, including other species, fauna, and flora. For example, the project may involve increasing the efficiency of personnel use, such as the nurses and doctors in a public hospital. Depending on the decisions taken, this could result in a considerable number of nurses losing their jobs, subjecting the others to increased work stress, while patients face potential increases in waiting times for elective surgery, and reduced quality and safety of care. It may even increase the risks of medical misadventure. While the nurses and doctors may be consulted to some extent, the patients have usually no say in the matter, unless there is a consumer advocate on the hospital board. The reason why plans for public projects invite interested parties to make submissions is exactly to give a voice to those affected but not involved in the planning.

How should analysts deal with such situations? If an analyst has personal, moral, or environmental objections to the possible outcomes of the project, then clearly he or she should decline participation. At the very least, the analyst should make a full disclosure of his or her moral objections and other possible conflicts of interest (such as personal gain or loss), and leave it up the problem owner(s) to make a judgement about whether any involvement in the project should continue. If yes, then the analyst must confront the issue of how these moral objections could influence the analysis and the results, and attempt to keep the analysis free of such personal biases as far as humanly possible.

The analyst must also be aware that in public advocacy processes he or she cannot assume the role of modeller and also be an advocate of vested interest without having the role of unbiased modeller put into question. For example, as a member of the official publicly-funded project team modelling an environmentally controversial project, you are supposed to take a neutral view. Both the model and your own credibility are jeopardized when you also become an advocate for vested interests, such as an environmental lobby group or the mining company who would benefit from the project.

This does not imply that analysts should not draw the problem owners' attention to any adverse consequences of both the project process and its final recommendations. In fact, this is one of their responsibilities, regardless of their own personal views for or against the project.

If a project involves rare undesirable or dangerous outcomes, such as contamination of an environment or the accidental exposure of people or animals to dangerous substances, care must be taken when making statements about their likelihood. Such outcomes are often the consequence of the simultaneous or conditional occurrence of a large number of separate events, which are only remotely connected. Their interdependence may be difficult to assess. Experts all too frequently claim that such events are independent. Unfortunately, true independence is rarely present, particularly if some are subject to human failure or error. History is replete with such instances. One form of Murphy's law says that if something goes wrong, all hell breaks loose.

But even if the analyst is personally neutral or favours the outcomes, the ethical responsibility remains not only to point out the positive aspects, but also to disclose fully the negative consequences, including ethical ones, without belittling them. The analyst must point out the ethical dilemma involved in trading off cost savings against the potential of loss of life, permanent injuries, and irreversible detrimental environmental changes, regardless how negligible they consider their probabilities. It is part of critical boundary judgements. Furthermore, is it ethical to trade off potential injuries, loss of life, or environmental destruction for economic gains?

It is not the analyst's place to judge these consequences as to their desirability or otherwise, but to provide the decision maker with a relevant basis and complete information for making a fully-informed decision.

Professional ethics of the MS/OR analyst

The analyst must make sure that the analysis performed is not flawed from a professional point of view. This implies:

- Disclosing any vested interest in the project or its outcomes.
- Approaching the problem situation from the worldview of the problem owner(s) as far as this is possible and being aware of one's own biases.
- Keeping the problem owner(s) regularly informed about the project progress and immediately reporting the discovery of new aspects or a higher severity of undesirable consequences that may call for a re-assessment of the project.
- Fully documenting the model, such that any other analyst of similar training can understand and verify it. This implies recording of any assumptions, simplifications, and known omissions made, data ignored or discarded, as well as the proper justification of these aspects.
- For any data used as input, recording their sources, keeping data specifically collected for that purpose in raw form, or save operational data that, in the normal course of events, would be destroyed after some limited time period. Without such data it is impossible for a third person to verify the analysis.
- Verifying and validating the model; performing sensitivity analysis to evaluate the robustness of the model and its recommendation; and establishing ranges of critical input parameters for which the recommendations remain valid.
- Supplying the problem owner(s) with a report on the project, the analysis done, and its recommendations, at a level appropriate and agreed upon beforehand. It should cover what was accomplished by the study, as well as, even more importantly, what was not accomplished, and any possible weaknesses and limitations of the analysis done. Projects involving quantitative analysis should give technical details,

intended for persons trained in MS/OR, that describe in sufficient detail the model and solution method used.

- Scrupulously observing any ground rules about confidentiality for the disclosure of data and any reports produced, as laid out at the inception of the project. This should also cover what material may be removed from the premises of the sponsor and by whom. (That does not rule out whistle-blowing if written, well-founded and documented reports on adverse effects are repeatedly ignored by those in charge.)

These points just cover the most important ethical considerations. There are other obvious rules of moral conduct not unique the MS/OR projects, such as:

- Do not undertake a project that requires you to rubber stamp a conclusion or decision already reached, or do it only with the clear (written) understanding that you are in no way bound by such prior decisions or conclusions.
- Do not omit disclosure of aspects (such as roughly estimated data, ignored potential alternatives, lacking sensitivity analysis, critical assumptions, possible limitations) that you know will weaken your case. The temptation to do that may be strong. Mistakes and their consequences on the validity of the findings that are discovered after the report has been submitted should be disclosed immediately. Your own loss of credibility by admitting to mistakes may be of minor importance in comparison with the possible risks for other stakeholders if you fail to come clean.
- The report and its analysis should be written in such a manner that neither can be easily misrepresented or used for implying more than it should.

8.6 Chapter highlights

- The aim of most MS/OR projects (at least for those of a substantive nature) is to improve the performance of some existing or proposed entity or operation. The benefits of the project can only be achieved if the recommendations are implemented to a high decree.
- Problems of implementation relate to the physical task of change and to the human aspects involving the problem stakeholders. Neglecting the human aspects is often the prime cause for implementation failure.
- Helping the problem owners and users to get a feeling of ownership over the solution is seen as the key to successful implementation. Enhancing feelings of ownership is an integral part of many soft MS/OR approaches, but has to be explicitly fostered in hard MS/OR projects.
- Planning for implementation starts at the outset of a project.
- Only by following up on the implementation and assessing the proper use and performance of the implemented solution will the analyst discover what works well and learn from her or his own mistakes.
- Following an accepted code of personal and professional ethics is a moral obligation and enhances the credibility of the analyst.

Exercises

1. Professor Churchman, after reviewing the introduction to another MS/OR text by one of the authors, casually observed : 'Don't you know that implementation is the first phase of any MS/OR project?' This remark initially startled the author, particularly since Churchman's own 1957 text shows implementation as the final step of the analysis. However, as the author pondered this, he came to agree. In the light of the coverage you have seen of the 11-step hard MS/OR methodology of Chapter 5 or the 11-step soft MS/OR working mode of Chapter 7, critically discuss Churchman's statement. It may be helpful to distinguish clearly between the physical process of implementing the results and the substantive issues involved in implementation.
2. Discuss the parallels between the major MS/OR implementation principle of 'get the problem owners and problem users to own the project' and your own personal experiences of getting family members, friends, or colleagues to go along with some new activity or way of dealing with recurrent daily problems, or being at the receiving end of such pressures coming from them?
3. Assume that your project report for the ELMO case (Exercise 3 of Chapter 6) convinced management to implement the solution. Prepare a detailed plan for implementing, maintaining, and auditing the solution. Note that the machine operators (i.e., the users) are trained mechanics, but have no education beyond high school. Some may not even have graduated.
4. Sections 5.3 and 5.4 discuss desirable properties of models and model validation. The concept of model 'credibility' is raised. It also pointed out that it may be more useful to talk about 'desirable properties of the modelling process', rather than of the model itself. Integrating this with the material in Chapter 8, develop a list of such desirable properties that enhance the likelihood of full implementation and facilitate implementation.

Further reading

Churchman, C.W. and Schainblatt, A.H. (1965) 'The researcher and the manager: A dialectic of implementation', *Management Science*, February, 11. Philosophical analysis of the activities and attitudes by analysts and problem owners which are most appropriate for a climate conducive to proper implementation. See also the October 1965 issue of *Management Science* for a follow-up on this very provocative paper, particularly the comments by W. Alderson.

Cooke, S. and Slack, N. (1991) *Making Management Decisions*, 2nd edn, Englewood Cliffs, NJ: Prentice-Hall. Broad coverage, including behavioural aspects of management, at the expense of systems modelling. Relevant chapters: 1 to 5, 8 to 10.

Interfaces (1987) Special Issue: Implementation, May–June. The entire issue is devoted to implementation with particular emphasis on management information systems.

Schultz, R.L. and Slevin, D.P. (eds) (1975) *Implementing of Operation Research/Management Science*, New York: American Elsevier. A collection of papers on implementation. Read the one by A. Reisman and C.A. de Kluyver 'Strategies for implementing systems studies' for a pragmatic view of how to improve the chances for successful implementation.

PART III
Assessing costs and benefits, and dealing with time

The focus in Parts I and II was on systems thinking and systems methodologies in general, both hard and soft. The emphasis in Parts III and IV now shifts more towards hard OR, although even soft OR practitioners should be capable of correctly assessing the relevance and treatment of the cost concepts and have at least a rudimentary knowledge of the most basic hard OR methods presented in Part IV.

Most MS/OR analyses involve costs and benefits, expressed in monetary terms. A thorough understanding of the nature of costs and benefits is therefore essential. Only then will the analyst be able to identify those costs and benefits which are relevant for a given decision problem and those which can be ignored.

Unfortunately, these aspects, crucial for correct MS/OR practice, are generally neglected in MS/OR textbooks and barely touched on in university courses under the assumption that an introductory accounting and/or economics course provides sufficient background. As we shall see, accounting interprets and treats costs differently from what is needed for MS/OR analysis, while most economics courses restrict themselves to general definitions, lacking practical detail. The following three chapters intend to fill that gap.

If the word 'system' is used in various different ways, the word 'cost' has even more varied uses in our language, and each may imply different value judgements. Business people speak of the cost of goods and materials purchased for production or resale, the cost of equipment, the cost of operating the equipment, and the cost of workers and employees — referring to wages and salaries paid. It is relatively easy to put an exact monetary figure to each of these. But business people also talk of the cost of delivering goods late to customers, the cost of lost sales, the cost of a strike, either within their own organization or that of a supplier or a big customer, or the cost of rescheduling production to meet a rush job to a major customer. It is usually not possible to assess the exact 'cost' to such events.

In everyday language, the use of the word 'cost' becomes even more fuzzy: the social cost of unemployment in terms of despair, low self-esteem, increased suicide rate, increased crime, increased family break-ups; or the environmental cost of pollution; or the hidden cost of government actions and policies; or simply the cost of a missed opportunity!

Briefly expressed, the relevant costs and benefits are those which, for the system as a whole, change for different decision choices. A proper understanding of how costs and benefits arise and how they vary helps the analyst to incorporate them correctly in the analysis. Chapter 9 explores the nature and types of costs.

Often costs and benefits occur over time. How can we aggregate costs and benefits that occur at different points in time? This leads us to study discounting and expressing future cash flows in terms of their present value — the topic of Chapter 10. We shall also venture into when equipment, the efficiency of which deteriorates with time, should be replaced — an important hard OR application.

Time enters into the analysis also in a different way. A project may involve making decisions at various points in time in an environment that does not remain stable, but changes in predictable ways in the future. Chapter 11 studies how this affects the decision process and what implications this has on the length of the planning horizon needed for making correct decisions.

Each chapter applies the concepts discussed to a practical case study — a real-life MS/OR decision problem.

References

Collis, J. and Hussey, R. (2006) *Business Accounting: An Introduction to Financial and Management Accounting*, New York: Palgrave Macmillan.

Eldenburg, L.G. and Wolcott, S. (2004) *Cost Management: Measuring, Monitoring, and Motivating Performance*, New York: Wiley.

Moles, P., Parrino, R. and Kidwell, D.S. (2011) *Corporate Finance: European Edition*, Chichester: Wiley.

9

Relevant costs and benefits

Learning objectives

- Be able to recognize/determine whether a cost item is explicit or implicit, expressible in monetary terms or intangible, fixed or variable, and identify opportunity costs and sunk costs.
- Be able to correctly attribute costs and benefits to various aspects of an activity or operation.
- Be able to determine whether a given cost or benefit item is relevant for decision making, i.e., whether it affects the measure of performance in response to changes in the decision choices.

Introduction

As if the correct assessment of the variety of 'costs' were not difficult enough, accountants and economists — the two professional bodies dealing with costs and monetary benefits — apply partially different classifications, thereby compounding the ambiguity of their correct interpretation and use.

The first two sections look at how these two disciplines define various types of costs and benefits. Section 9.3 studies which types of costs are usually relevant for decision making.

In MS/OR modelling, we are usually concerned with how total costs and benefits change in response to a change in controllable inputs, decisions, or the mode of operation. Some costs and benefits remain the same, regardless of the changes. If we are only interested in finding the best decision, they can be ignored. The following sections considers a real-life case of decision making, where the main difficulty was ascertaining which costs were affected by the decision choices available, and how to take them correctly into account.

9.1 Explicit, implicit, and intangible costs

Part of the ambiguity when dealing with cost concepts arises from the fact that some costs involve an 'out-of-pocket' transfer of funds from one party to another, while others do not. The first are called **explicit costs**; the second, **implicit costs**. The payment for goods or equipment purchased from a supplier is an explicit cost. The annual reduction in the recorded 'book value' of a piece of equipment, called 'depreciation', is an example of an implicit cost. No funds change hands. It is simply a convention used by accountants to reflect the fact that, through use and ageing, a piece of equipment has lost some of its original value. By the time the firm disposes of this item, its book value is expected to have been reduced from the original purchase price to its current disposal value as scrap or second-hand equipment.

Several of the examples of costs mentioned in the introduction to Part III, such as the cost of late delivery, the cost of reduced productivity and disruption caused by rescheduling production in response to some emergency, the social cost of unemployment, and so on, are also examples of implicit costs.

The difference between these examples and depreciation is that it is relatively easy to put an exact figure on the amount of depreciation, while it is usually difficult to assess the 'cost' of a late delivery. If a late delivery is a very exceptional occurrence, happening for reasons beyond the control of the firm, and if the customer has been notified prior to the delivery due date, there may be no cost. However, if late deliveries occur repeatedly for the same customer, the firm runs a high risk of ultimately losing that customer. The 'cost' to the firm is the possible loss of profits that future sales to that customer could have generated. The potential for future profits through sales is also called **goodwill**. So, the firm may suffer a loss in goodwill with its ensuing financial implications. Such costs are also referred to as **intangible costs**. Their assessment is often based on guesswork, and therefore highly subjective to the assessor.

The amount of depreciation assessed on a piece of equipment will usually have no effect on decision making, except in so far as it affects the timing of taxes paid (given that depreciation reduces the taxable income). On the other hand, intangible costs clearly may seriously affect which decisions are preferred or best.

Accountants also classify some cost and benefit items as intangible. The two main ones are goodwill and reserves for doubtful accounts receivables (credit customers who are seriously in arrears in their payments). The balance sheet item 'goodwill' usually arises from the acquisition of a going concern where the purchase price exceeds the net value of the assets acquired. This excess is seen as representing the growth in potential earnings of the firm. It is recorded as an asset. It is depreciated in the same way as most fixed assets. Similarly, the reserve for doubtful accounts receivable is recorded as a form of asset value reduction shown on the liability side in the balance sheet.

Although accountants refer to these items as intangible assets or intangible costs, their interpretation of the term 'intangible' differs from its use in MS/OR. They refer to actual entries in the accounts of the firm. In MS/OR, we refer to potential future costs or loss of benefits that should be recognized as relevant for the correct evaluation of decision alternatives. However, no cash transaction or entry in the accounts of the firm is implied or will occur if a decision is implemented.

9.2 Different views of cost concepts

Accountants' view of costs

Accountants are basically historians. They record costs as the amount paid to buy goods, such as raw materials and supplies needed for manufacturing operations, goods for resale, equipment and facilities, and to acquire services, employees' time, insurance coverage, access to information, and the use of funds. This allows them to determine the financial position of a firm as at a given point in time, i.e., what the firm owns in the form of various assets, and what the firm owes to its creditors and has set up as reserves for potential losses. The difference between these two represents the equity position of its owners. These three aspects are summarized in the **balance sheet**. Furthermore, accountants record in detail how this equity position changes over time, usually over quarterly and 12-monthly periods. This gives rise to the **profit-and-loss statement**.

The balance sheet and the profit-and-loss statement allow current and potential investors in the firm to assess how well the current investments in the firm are doing. Producing these two documents is also a legal requirement for all firms, for assessment of taxes as well as for the protection of creditors of the firm. These are the main purposes for financial accounting.

For facilitating pricing decisions, and monitoring and control of costs, accountants have extended the cost concept to the notion of **standard costs** — a measure indicating what it should cost **on average** to produce a given item or service under normal operating conditions. Actual historical costs vary from standard cost in the short run due to unexpected events, such as price fluctuations of raw materials or varying productivity of the work force. Significant deviations (or what cost accountants call 'variances') from standard costs are flagged and brought to the attention of management. In the absence of inflation or deflation, actual average historical cost will approximate standard costs in the long run, since the latter are, in fact, derived from the former.

Accountants' classification of costs

Accountants classify costs into two main categories: **prime** or **direct costs** and **overhead** or **indirect costs**. Prime costs are those directly identifiable with a specific end product or service. This includes the purchase costs of goods or materials used in the production process and the costs of all labour directly attributable to the production of that product or service. Prime costs tend to increase or decrease (often proportionately, but not necessarily so) with the volume of output. It is fairly obvious that if the level of output doubles, the amount of materials needed to produce the goods also doubles. Similarly, a doubling of the level of service offered will in most cases also double the labour input and its cost.

Overheads cover the cost of all support activities that are not directly attributable to a particular product or service, or that are shared by all or a group of products or services. Examples are salaries and fringe benefits of executives, managers, supervisors; various support staff, such as maintenance, personnel, and other administrative services, including vacation and holiday pay for these employees. The cost of borrowed funds, such as loans or mortgages, are also overheads.

Most overheads, but not all, remain fixed over a wide range of output levels. For example, the same administrative support staff may be needed even if the output of the firm decreases or increases within a fairly wide range around the current level. Only a change in output level beyond that range may result in a change in overheads, e.g., by requiring more staff or additional shared production facilities. Similarly, the interest cost of loans taken up to finance the purchase of plant and equipment will have to be paid regardless of the level of output of the plant.

For product or services costing purposes, all overheads will ultimately be allocated on some suitable basis to the individual products or services. This allocation by necessity involves a varying degree of arbitrariness. The most commonly used basis for allocating overheads is in proportion to the amount or the cost of direct labour involved in producing each product or service.

The distinction between prime costs and overheads is often not clear-cut, particularly if the costs do not vary proportionately with output. Furthermore, some costs may be classified as overheads because the efforts or 'cost' of identifying which portion is directly attributable to each product or service may be excessive, while increasing the accuracy of their unit costs in only a minor way.

Economists' view of costs

Economists measure the cost of a resource in terms of the earning power or the opportunities foregone by not applying the resource in question to some other potentially available use — in fact, the best alternative use of the resource. Economists thus argue that the implicit cost of a resource is equal to what it could earn if it were used for its best available alternative activity now or at some future point in time. This cost is called the **opportunity cost** of the resource. Being an implicit cost, no funds change hands. For resources owned by the firm, it is not the original cost of acquiring them that is relevant any longer, but the return on its best alternative use.

Economic theory shows that, if all individuals and firms follow this principle consistently, this will lead to the most efficient use and the optimal allocation of resources for the economy as a whole. In practice, this is a somewhat naive view. The world is not quite that simple. People and firms do not consistently act according to such strict rational principles. Individuals and firms often do not pay the true cost of the use of many resources. They pay nothing for so-called 'free goods', such as the environment, and even cause damage by air and water pollution. They may not pay the true cost for 'public goods', such as the use of the road network. The tax collection on heavy vehicle road use does not cover the cost of the damage trucks cause to road surfaces. Firms do not pay for the damage to public health, both physical and mental, caused by their activities or their products (effects of pollution, smoking, alcohol, fatty unhealthy foods, effects of gambling on other family members, and so on). Economists claim that 'user-pay' policies can handle this — theoretically true, but highly problematic to achieve in practice; just look at the complexity and misuse of carbon tax credits that are likely to be exploited by crime syndicates, while greenhouse gases continue to grow.

The most common application of the opportunity cost concept concerns situations in which a resource enjoys several potential uses at the same point in time, since using the resource for one purpose precludes its use for any other purpose.

Economists' classification of costs

The main classifications used by economists are **fixed costs** and **variable costs**, on the one hand, and **short-run costs** and **long-run costs**, on the other. Fixed costs are those that are not affected by changes in output levels, in contrast to variable costs. There is thus some analogy between the accountants' distinction of direct costs and overheads and the economists' distinction of variable and fixed costs. However, the analogy is far from perfect. For example, a given machine may be exclusively dedicated to the production of a single product, or an office may solely be used for providing a given service. Some costs associated with their use, such as depreciation of the machine or actual or imputed rental of the office, may not change with output level but remain constant per period (say, one year). They are classified as direct costs by accountants, even if they are in the nature of fixed overheads, but as fixed costs by economists.

In the short-run, investments in capital goods, such as equipment, buildings, land, and so on, are taken as given. They are not easily changed without often substantial new investments of funds. They restrict the firm's output to a given range. Hence, the cost of using these resources is fixed. On the other hand, other aspects of a firm's operations, such as the amount of raw materials and labour used, usually vary in proportion to the output level. Hence, they are variable costs.

In the long-run, however, the composition of all inputs into a firm's operation can be altered. The number and type of machines, the number and size of facilities, and so on, can be changed. Hence, in the long-run all costs become variable.

In general, economists use costs to derive normative statements about how a firm should operate under market conditions. Their view of costs is thus more akin to the prescriptive focus of the management scientist. Hence, we will find the economists' classification of costs more useful for decision making than those of the accountants.

The problem management scientists face is that for most projects the source of cost information comes from the cost accountants. It is thus crucial to be aware of the different interpretations of cost. It may mean that the cost factors supplied by the cost accountants have to be dissected into their individual components and then reassembled differently.

9.3 Relevant costs and benefits

Which costs and benefits should a decision maker take into account when evaluating the monetary effects of alternative decision choices? The short answer is:

> **All costs and benefits that, for the system as a whole, change as a consequence of any of the decision choices! Any costs or benefits now or in the future that in total terms remain the same, regardless of the decision choice, are irrelevant.**

As is true for most short answers, this only tells part of the story. In many instances, it may be difficult to determine which costs and benefits change until the analysis has been completed. Fortunately, any costs included in the analysis that are not affected by the decision choice will not influence which decision is best, **provided such costs are included in the correct manner**. It is obvious that if the same constant is added or subtracted from the monetary outcome of each decision choice, their ranking is not affected. (We already used this principle when we ignored the annual value of product costs for the LOD case in Chapter 6, expression (6-1A), p. 148.) It is therefore more important to include costs in the correct manner, rather than worrying about whether a cost item should be included or not.

Having said this, we will nevertheless review which costs and benefits are relevant. This discussion will clarify grey areas and improve your understanding. For each cost and benefit, we attempt to answer the following question: Does this cost item (in terms of its current or future impact for system as a whole) increase or decrease if any of the decision choices is implemented or does it remain the same, regardless of which decision is taken? If it changes, it is a relevant cost item; if it remains the same, it can be ignored. Let us consider a few examples!

Explicit costs

It is quite obvious that explicit costs that would be incurred if a given decision choice were implemented, but not if another choice were made, whether fixed capital investments or variable with the output level, are relevant costs. However, this does not tell us the correct way of including explicit costs, particularly if they are of a fixed nature — more about that later. And what about costs incurred in the past and clearly associated with the project or activity in question?

Sunk costs

To answer this question, let us assess on whether or not the results of an MS/OR project should be implemented. Consider the LOD case study in Chapter 6. The LOD manager has received the final project report. For discussion's sake, assume that this report states that the potential cost savings amount to $36,000 per year (considerably smaller than the correct figure quoted in the Appendix 2 to Chapter 6) and that a further $32,000 will have to be spent for implementation of the new policy. This is in addition to the $7,200 already charged to the LOD for the preliminary study. Recall that the firm's criterion for accepting any investment of this nature requires that the estimated first-year benefits must exceed the cost of the project. Should the LOD manager give the go-ahead for implementation or not?

One line of reasoning is to state that the results of the project should not be implemented, since the total cost of the project (consisting of the initial $7,200 for the preliminary study plus the additional $32,000 for implementation of the results) exceeds the estimated first-year savings of $36,000 by $3,200. The firm would be worse off by $3,200 if it proceeded.

What is wrong with this reasoning? It is true that the total cost for the project, including the additional work needed for implementation, is $3,200 larger than the estimated first-year savings. On the other hand, the expenditure of a further $32,000 will provide estimated first-year savings of $36,000, a gain of $4,000. Hence, within one year of implementation the firm would be better off by this amount compared with abandoning the project now. So, if the LOD manager uses 'the recovery of all **further** costs within one year' as the criterion for accepting new projects, then he should go ahead with implementing the recommendations.

The fallacy in the first line of reasoning is that the $7,200 has already been spent. Nothing can be done about it. None of the decision choices available to the LOD manager will recover the funds already spent. They are a **sunk cost**. Sunk costs are irrelevant for decision making.

Had the LOD manager known, prior to engaging in the preliminary study, that the total cost for the project would be $39,200, while the estimated first-year's savings would only come to $36,000, the project would never have got off the ground. The $7,200 cost of the preliminary study would not have been spent. However, the manager did not know this at that time. He made the best choice on the basis of the information available then. Hindsight shows that this was the wrong choice. Taking the funds already spent into account again now would only lead to making another error in choice — one that can be avoided!

Sunk costs may sometimes be hidden in cost data derived from accounting records. Depreciation charges on a machine included in the unit production costs for a given item may be a case in point. If the annual depreciation charge is only an accounting entry made to reduce the initial purchase cost to zero over a specific minimum number of years, as dictated by tax regulations, aimed at reducing the incidence of tax on profits, then it is not a relevant cost item. The initial purchase price of the machine is a sunk cost and, hence, is irrelevant. Only that part of the depreciation that reflects the reduction in the machine's resale value due to wear and tear is a relevant cost item.

(Note that the loss in resale value of the machine due to aging may be relevant for a different decision, such as whether or not to keep the machine for a further time given its earning potential, or to dispose of it right now and replace it with a more efficient machine, as we shall see in Chapter 10.)

This is not to deny that, in the long-run, the survival of the firm depends on whether or not it can generate enough funds to replace all existing equipment and buildings at the end of their productive life. Hence, even the loss in value due to aging becomes a cost that has to be recovered from the sale of the products or services produced. But this becomes a product pricing matter — a different decision.

As is often the case in MS/OR, answers are not clear-cut, but depend on the circumstances and purpose of the analysis. This reminds us of that firm that advertised for a 'one-armed' operations researcher. When the CEO was questioned why the firm wanted a 'one-armed' applicant, he replied that he was sick and tired of their responses that 'on the one hand, you should do this; on the other hand, it may be advantageous to do that!'

Opportunity costs

Firms own, or are in control of, many resources, such as raw materials, machinery, buildings, and funds. Some of these resources were purchases, others were created by the firm's own operations. They are currently used for some purpose, but many could be put to alternative uses. How should such resources be valued? What is the 'cost' of their use? These are important questions. Their correct answer will determine whether these resources are put to their best use or not.

Consider again the LOD problem and, in particular, the investment of funds in finished goods. What is the cost of these funds? You may say that this depends on the source of these funds. You could reason that if they are raised through loans from a bank, the cost of these funds is the interest charged by the bank. On the other hand, if they come from retained earnings (profits accumulated and not paid out as dividends to the shareholders), there is no cost. What is wrong with this reasoning?

It ignores the return the firm could earn on these funds from alternative uses. Assume the firm has alternative investment opportunities, such as the acquisition of shares of another company that earn a high return or the purchase of a machine that can produce a highly marketable and profitable product, thus raising the firm's profits. Using the funds for investment in finished goods means that these same funds cannot be used for the best of these alternative investments. Therefore, the firm foregoes the return on this lost opportunity. The return foregone becomes the real cost of using these funds for investment in finished goods.

Since the assessment of this cost is based on the best alternative opportunity foregone, it is called an **opportunity cost.** All resources available to the firm or, for that matter, to any organization should always be valued at their opportunity cost. This will assure that these resources are used efficiently. (However, it would be unethical to divert resources from essential social services to other uses offering a higher return.)

Example 9-1: Cost of warehouse space — LOD case

What is the cost of the current warehouse space available to the LOD? As was the case for the use of funds, this item is relevant for assessing the cost of holding goods in stock for future sale. The cost accountant would claim that the cost of warehouse space is equal to the total maintenance costs incurred for the warehouse, the operating costs, such as electricity, cleaning, heating, and depreciation on the warehouse over a given period. The opportunity cost, on the other hand, depends on the return that could be earned for the best alternative use of the warehouse. This cost is not recorded in the accounting records, which only show historical costs. The latter may be larger or smaller than the opportunity cost.

Assessing opportunity costs requires that the analyst goes beyond accounting records. It may need some research into potential alternative uses. In the LOD case, some analysis may show that, because of its location, there is no alternative use for the warehouse as such, only for its land. The best alternative use for this land is as parking space for refinery employees, which currently has to be rented from the city at \$528 per parking space per year. This cost, expressed on an equivalent square metre basis (say 12 m^2 per parking space) would then correspond to an opportunity cost for warehouse space at the LOD of \$44 per square metre per year. Alternatively, if another division of the firm currently has to rent warehouse space adjacent to the refinery at \$56 per square metre per year, and the LOD warehouse would be a suitable alternative, the opportunity cost would amount to \$56 per square metre (minus extra transport costs).

Should maintenance and operating costs be added? The answer is 'yes', if these costs vary as a function of the warehouse space used by the LOD, and 'no', if they are incurred regardless of the level of usage. In general, interest charges on the funds invested in the warehouse land and building are irrelevant since they do not depend on the level of usage of the warehouse. They are a consequence of a sunk cost. If no alternative use exists for the warehouse, including its possible disposal, and maintenance and operating costs do not depend on the level of usage, the opportunity cost of warehouse space could well be zero.

Replacement costs

The historical cost paid for a resource or for goods is not a relevant measure for their value. Rather, it is the replacement cost which is relevant. For example, a cable manufacturer purchased a large quantity of copper wire at £1.63 per kilogram. A few weeks later, the price of copper wire increased to £1.84. It would then be incorrect to value the copper wire still in inventory at its original purchase price of £1.63. Any copper wire used up would have to be replaced at the higher cost of £1.84. Furthermore, copper being a world commodity, any stock on hand presumably could be sold also at the higher price of £1.84/kg. Replacement costs are a type of opportunity costs.

Future costs and benefits

Opportunity costs could well be in the form of the value of the resource for use at some future point in time. Future costs may, however, often happen in the form of explicit costs. For example, at the end of the productive life of a piece of equipment, a plot of land used for mining, or a facility built on some rented land, a substantial removal, disposal, or restoration cost may have to be incurred. This cost is a direct consequence of the decision choice and, hence, is a relevant cost. The huge decommissioning costs of nuclear power stations are a case in point.

The converse could also be true, i.e., the resource has some residual value at the end of the planning horizon. This is particularly true for land and buildings, but also for equipment, if they have a positive disposal or **salvage value.**

Intangible costs

Intangible costs may significantly reduce the worth or effectiveness of a decision alternative. For example, in terms of explicit costs (wages, and so on) alone, it is clearly much cheaper for a store to have few cashiers to serve customers. But excessive waiting times for customers may ultimately cause some customers to switch to another store. This potential loss of future business may be far more costly in the long run than the cost of additional cashiers. A decision on the best number of cashiers to have on duty should take into account the possible incidence of such intangible costs.

Given the difficulty and ambiguity in assessing intangible costs, the analyst may be tempted to ignore them. This is not advisable. Every effort should be made to determine a valid monetary equivalent for these costs. **If this is not possible, the analyst should perform extensive sensitivity analysis to ascertain how the best decision changes as the (assumed) value of intangible costs varies.** If intangible costs have been ignored, this fact should be clearly stated in any report on the project. This will forewarn the decision maker that her or his final conclusion should take the possible presence of intangible factors into account in qualitative ways. Armed with extensive sensitivity analysis, the decision maker will find that this task is greatly facilitated.

Activity

Find an example for each type of costs discussed in this section for: (a) owning and operating a car; and (b) your cost of living.

9.4 Champignons Galore — problem formulation

We now look at an account of an MS/OR project, where the major effort of the analysis was the correct assessment and use of various costs, and their presentation in a convincing form. You should now carefully study the situation summary in Appendix 9.1 in this chapter. You will not obtain the full benefit of the analysis that follows, unless you have a clear understanding of the Champignons Galore (CG) problem situation. You may have to read it more than once. (If you have not done so yet as part of exercise 5 in Chapter 5, it will be helpful to represent the situation as a rich picture diagram and identify the various issues to be analysed.)

Problem definition

The discussion is confined to only one of the options considered by Gérard Mousse; namely, the reduction of the number of flushes in each production cycle from the current five to four, three, two, or one. The aim is to learn if this will increase the annual output of mushrooms and to explore its effect on the firm's profits. In accordance with this option, Gérard Mousse would like to know the best number of flushes to use. We shall assume that he interprets 'best' as that policy that maximizes the annual profit for the current production facilities available.

The annual profit is the difference between the annual revenue and the total annual costs. If prices remain constant, annual revenue is equal to the sum of the products of the total annual output of mushrooms and other products, and their net unit selling price. Determining total annual costs is more involved. We need to study in detail the nature of the various costs. This allows us to identify those that are affected by changing the operating policy — therefore relevant — and determine the form of the relationships between the number of flushes per production cycle and annual revenue and costs.

Influence diagrams are an ideal tool for establishing these relationships. So, we will now formally define the problem, summarize the relevant system, and then construct the associated influence diagram.

Referring to Section 4.1 (p. 60-1), the essence of the problem is defined by identifying the decision maker, her or his objectives, the performance measure(s), the decision criterion, and the alternative courses of action. The decision maker is Gérard Mousse. His objective is to achieve a high annual profit. The performance measure is the annual profit, the decision criterion is maximizing this measure. Finally, the alternative courses of action are the number of flushes in each cycle. To keep things simple, we will assume that none of the potential constraints, such as the size of the market and the availability of raw materials, particularly straw, will become effective.

System definition

The firm's annual profit is mainly affected by how the various costs of inputs into the process (raw materials, labour, and so on) and revenues from the outputs produced change as a function of the number of flushes. The system description thus only needs to focus on these relationships. Little additional insight will be gained by expanding the system definition to include the biological details of mushroom growing. We will simply treat those aspects as black boxes. As a consequence, the system can easily be divided into five subsystems. Each deals with a given task or operation and its associated costs and revenues. Our choice is:

Subsystem 1: the operations of phase 1 (composting and tray preparation). Its major inputs are raw materials and supplies for compost making, power, and labour, and the unit costs of all external inputs. The empty trays, after they have been removed from the sheds and cleaned (an output of subsystem 2), are also an input. Its outputs are trays ready for the growing phase, and tray preparation costs. Peak heating is included as part of that subsystem. Trays are the major system component relevant to this subsystem.

Subsystem 2: the operations associated with loading and emptying sheds. Its major inputs are the trays prepared by subsystem 1 (output of subsystem 1), sheds having completed the harvesting phase (output of subsystem 3), which includes the trays of spent compost, supplies, packing material, labour, and the unit costs of all external inputs. Its outputs are sheds ready for the next harvesting phase, empty trays, the costs of its operations, and the sales revenue of packaged spent compost. The system components of prime concern to us are trays and sheds.

Subsystem 3: the harvesting operation. Its major inputs are sheds ready for harvesting (output of subsystem 2), labour picking rates for each successive flush, and labour pay rates. Its outputs are mushrooms (measured in kilograms), ready for sorting, the cost of picking mushrooms, and sheds having completed a full cycle. Sheds and kilograms of mushrooms are its major system components of interest.

Subsystem 4: the sorting and packing operations. Its inputs are mushrooms (output of subsystem 3), packing material and supplies, and labour, and the unit cost of all external inputs. Its outputs are mushrooms delivered to customers and the canning factory, the cost of its operations, and the revenue of mushrooms sold. Its major system components are mushrooms.

Subsystem 5: the biological and climate control subsystem. Its inputs are some supplies, power, and labour. Its outputs are sheds climatically controlled for best growth and harvesting, and the cost of this control. The latter is the only part of interest to us. Sheds are its major system component.

Each subsystem receives external inputs and provides some outputs, some of which become inputs to other subsystems. These form the links between the subsystems. They are also linked together by the decision variable; namely, the number of flushes in each harvesting cycle, which affects the system as a whole. Furthermore, various subsystems are subject to biological factors, such as the length of time needed to produce compost, the duration of the growing phase, and the duration of each flush.

A suitable influence diagram

You need to keep clearly in mind that the influence diagram only shows the significant influence relationships between inputs, state variables, and outputs. So, it is a limited view of the system. It does not include aspects and relationships that reflect the tasks a given subsystem performs, neither does it include the decision criterion used for optimization.

For the CG problem, the inputs consist of the decision variable, the various process and biological relationships of mushroom production, and the cost and revenue factors. The output of prime interest is the annual profit, which is the measure of performance. All other aspects of the system definition are not reflected in the influence diagram.

Activity

Before you study our version of a suitable influence diagram for the CG problem, we strongly recommend that you draw your own. Not only will this be a valuable exercise in becoming more proficient in this useful tool, but it will also force you to think carefully through the problem. Only then should you compare your diagram Figure 9-1.

In Figure 9-1 (p. 252) we chose to show each of the first four subsystems as a separate sequence of relationships, each receiving external and internal inputs, and having costs and/or revenues as the output to the system as a whole. While the cost relationships of each subsystem are fairly straightforward, the relationship between the decision variable, i.e., the number of flushes in each cycle, and other state variables, such as the length of each cycle, the number of cycles per year, and the output per cycle, may need some explanation.

Recall that the duration of the growing phase is 28 days, while each flush takes on average seven days. Together, these two determine the state variable for the length of a complete cycle (circle 1). The shorter each cycle, the more cycles can be scheduled per year for each shed. With the 65 sheds constantly in use, each carrying 400 trays per cycle, the number of cycles per year (circle 2) determines the annual number of trays needed per year (circle 3). The latter is one of the internal inputs into subsystems 1 and 2. Similarly, the length of each cycle (circle 1), together with the yield of mushrooms of each successive cycle, determines the cumulative yield per cycle per tray (circle 4). This, in turn, with the annual number of trays (circle 3), fixes the annual output of mushrooms (circle 5), the output of subsystem 3.

Activity

Explain how the number of flushes/cycle (decision variable) and the number of trays/year (circle 3) affect the annual picking cost (circle 10).

9.5 CG — analysis of costs

The next task is to examine all cost and revenue items listed in Appendix 9.1 and associate them with the inputs to the subsystems in the influence diagram. To determine which cost factors are relevant, we answer for each the question: Does the annual cost for the firm as a whole change if the decision changes from its current number of five flushes per cycle? If the answer is 'yes', that particular cost factor is relevant; if 'no', it can be ignored. Note that we may still wish to add it in as a cost that remains constant for all decision choices. We then get a complete picture of the net profit. However, including or excluding such fixed costs in the measure of performance will not affect which decision choice is optimal.

As is clear from the influence diagram, the effect of the number of flushes on the total annual cost may not be direct, but indirect via other system variables.

Table 9-1 states the relevance of each cost factor listed in Appendix 9.1, its nature, and the corresponding input parameter that captures its effect.

There is no question that some costs, such as raw materials and wages, are proportional to either the number of trays prepared per year or the mushroom output in kilograms per year. Fringe benefits, such as vacation and sick pay, pension fund and other employer contributions on wages vary in proportion with the wage payment. As the wage bill changes, so will such items. Hence, they are a variable cost. Note that accountants may include some of these costs for reasons of convenience and tradition, particularly fringe benefits, as part of various overheads. (The prudent analyst will analyse the composition of overheads for such items and, if necessary, re-allocate them appropriately.)

Table 9-1 Analysis of CG cost factors

Section	Relevance	Nature of effect	Input parameter
Compost/tray preparation:			
raw materials	yes	proportional./tray	preparation cost/tray (1)
electricity	yes	variable/tray	preparation cost/tray (2)
diesel fuel	yes	proportional/tray	preparation cost/tray (3)
maintenance on vehicles	yes	variable/tray	preparation cost/tray (4)
vehicle depreciation	no	constant	fixed cost
yard/build. maintenance	no	constant	fixed cost
yard workers' wages	yes	proportional/tray	preparation cost/tray (5)
salary J. Brownsey	no	constant	fixed cost
Shed loading and maintenance:			
supplies and diesel fuel	yes	proportional/tray	shed cost/tray
compost packing material	yes	proportional/tray	shed cost/tray
tray repair and maint'nce	yes	proportional/tray	shed cost/tray
vehicle maintenance	yes	variable/tray	shed cost/tray
vehicle depreciation	no	constant	fixed cost
shed workers' wages	yes	proportional/tray	shed cost/tray
Climate control:			
electricity	no	approx. constant	fixed cost
materials	no	approx. constant	fixed cost
lab. maintenance	no	constant	fixed cost
equipment depreciation	no	constant	fixed cost
new equipment	no	sunk cost	excluded
Picking, sorting, packaging:			
packing materials	yes	proportional/kg	sorting/packing cost/kg
supplies and electricity	yes	variable/kg	sorting/packing cost/kg
new equipment	no	sunk cost	excluded
maintenance equipment	yes	variable/kg	sorting/packing cost/kg
equipment depreciation	no	constant	fixed cost
diesel fuel trucks	yes	proportional/kg	sorting/packing cost/kg
maintenance trucks	yes	variable/kg	sorting/packing cost/kg
depreciation trucks	no	constant	fixed cost
wages for sort./pack.	yes	proportional/kg	sorting/packing cost/kg

continued (p. 253)

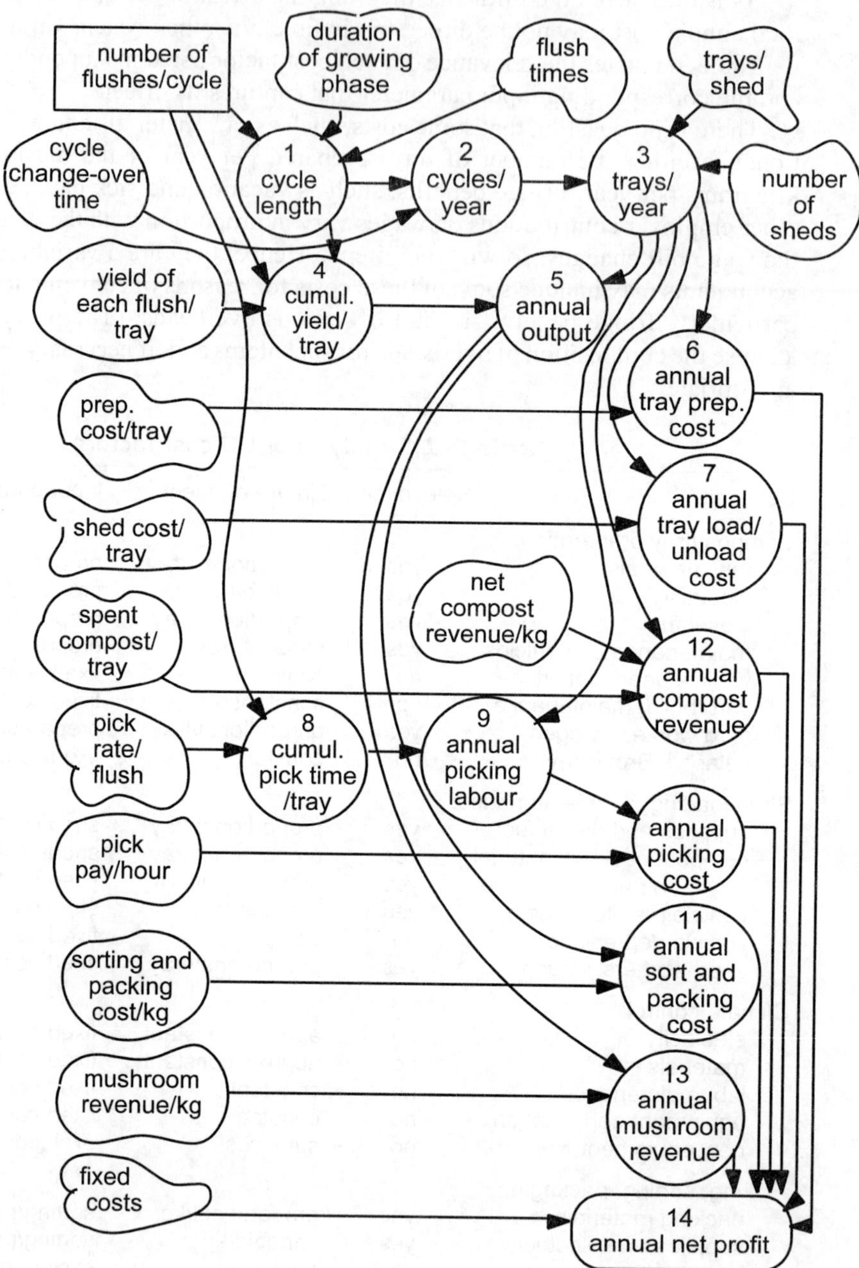

Figure 9-1 Influence diagram for CG problem

Table 9-1 Analysis of CG cost factors (continued)

Section	Relevance	Nature of effect	Input parameter
wages for drivers	yes	variable/kg	sorting/packing cost/kg
salary J.Fleurette	no	constant	fixed cost
wages picking	yes	variable/hour	picking pay/hr
vacation/sick pay	yes	variable/hour	picking pay/hr
Local marketing:			
salary J. Marchand	no	constant	fixed cost
travel J. Marchand	no	approx. constant	fixed cost
Other costs:			
office supplies	no	approx. constant	fixed cost
new equipment	no	sunk cost	excluded
company cars running cost	no	approx. constant	fixed cost
depreciation company cars	no	constant	fixed cost
office salaries	no	approx. constant	fixed cost
gardener	no	constant	fixed cost
maintenance office	no	constant	fixed cost
depreciation office bldg	no	constant	fixed cost
insurance, mortgage interest	no	constant	fixed cost
salaried employees accident insurance, pension fund	no	constant	fixed cost
worker accident insurance and pension fund	yes	proportional/€ paid	added to preparation and shed cost/tray, sorting/packing cost/kg, and picking cost/hour
salary C. Mousse	no	constant	fixed cost
travel C. Mousse	no	approx. constant	fixed cost

Some costs are fixed and, hence, can be excluded, such as insurance and mortgage interests on buildings. Salaries of administrative employees and managers and the associated fringe benefits are unlikely to change for an increase in output of up to 20% and, hence, are fixed. Depreciation on equipment and vehicles depends on whether it is mainly affected by usage or by age. In the first case, it is a variable cost; in the second, it is fixed. Given the relatively small amounts involved, we shall arbitrarily assume that such depreciation is a fixed cost.

Most supplies and electricity usage are affected by the level of activity, but not necessarily proportionally. Again, to keep things simple, we assume that these costs are approximately proportional to the level of activity, i.e., either the number of sheds prepared or the output of mushrooms. The exception is the section dealing with climate control. The sheds are in constant use for either the growing or harvesting phases, except for the two days of change-over from one cycle to the next. But even during those two days, the cooling of the sheds continues, hence the annual power cost is constant. Similarly, since the firm cultivates its own mycelium, the annual cost of supplies, and so on, is not affected by fairly large variations in the output level. All costs of the climate control section can thus be treated as constant. Even if some of these sheds remained unused during certain times, say as a result of reduced market demand, the climate control cost remains a fixed cost at a lower level, not affected by the decision variable.

Maintenance of yard equipment and vehicles, and of the sorting and packing equipment is likely to be affected by the level of activity. Hence, it is viewed as a variable cost, for simplicity approximated as proportional to the output level.

The travel costs of both the marketing manager and Gérard Mousse are partially affected by the mushroom output. The more mushrooms available, the larger must be the selling effort, which requires more travel. However, it would be difficult to determine a suitable mathematical relationship between output and travel cost. Given the small amounts of funds involved, we simply take them as fixed.

The tray maintenance, repair, and replacement costs are proportional to the level of activity. Most damage to the trays occurs during handling. The more handling, the higher this damage, so it is assumed to be proportional to the number of trays prepared.

The mushroom picking costs clearly are affected by the output level of mushrooms. But the relationship is somewhat complex, since the picking rate decreases with each additional flush. We shall analyse this aspect in more detail when we look at the mathematical model of total costs.

The two revenue sources are sales of mushrooms and sale of spent compost, both proportional to the volume of output of each.

Activity

Consider the costs listed in Table 9-1.

- Under what conditions is it correct to treat yard and building costs as fixed?
- The picking, sorting, and packaging section currently employs two drivers. Jennifer Fleurette guesses that a third driver is only required if the mushroom output goes up by more than 20% (resulting in considerable idle time), while an increase in output of more than 8% but less than 20% can be handled by overtime in the short run. Does this change the nature and relevance of that cost? Why or why not? (Note that such cost behaviour is quite common when 'work' capacity increases in discrete steps. Explain why an assumption of proportionality is a reasonable approximation, once the number of 'work' units gets large or workers can be used for other tasks.)
- Some costs, such as electricity or maintenance have the following form: cost = [fixed portion] + [variable portion], where the latter is a function of output. How would you deal with that?
- The section supervisors receive an annual bonus, based on productivity increases in their section. How would you treat this?

9.6 Mathematical model for annual CG profit

We now list the mathematical form of the relationships represented in the influence diagram of Figure 9-1. Rather than using mathematical notation, we explain them in plain English. Most of the expressions are simple enough to be self-explanatory. If you have doubts about any of them, we suggest that you check them by working out a few examples using assumed numbers. That usually helps.

All expressions are defined for a decision choice of n consecutive flushes in each cycle, where n can be 5, 4, 3, 2, or 1. The expressions are labelled by the numbers shown in each circle or output.

1. Length of each cycle:
[cycle length] = [growing phase duration] + [average flush length] × n = 28 + 7n

2. Number of cycles per year:
[cycles/year] = [days in year]/([cycle length] + [cycle change-over time])
= 365/([cycle length] + 2)

3. Number of trays prepared per year:
[trays/year] = [number of sheds] × [trays/shed] × [cycles/year]
= 65 × 400 × [cycles/year]

4. Mushroom output per cycle per tray. The data collected by Jennifer Fleurette for sheds 5 and 6 allow us to compute the average yield for each consecutive flush. In practice, it would be advisable to collect data on about a dozen cycles, rather than just two. Verify from the data listed that a new flush seems to start at regular intervals of about seven days. (A graph highlights this pattern clearly.) So, we add up the amount picked for each consecutive seven-day interval for both sheds and divide this sum by two. This gives the average yield for each flush per shed. Dividing these numbers by 400 gives the following average yields and cumulative average yields per tray for each consecutive flush:

flush n =	1	2	3	4	5
average yield kg/shed	9189	6432	2841	1711	1044
or kg/tray	22.97	16.08	7.10	4.28	2.61
cumulative yield kg/tray	22.97	39.05	46.15	50.43	53.04

5. Annual output of mushrooms:
[annual output] = [trays/year] × [cumulative yield/tray for n flushes]

6. Annual tray preparation cost:
[annual tray preparation cost] = [preparation cost/tray] × [trays/year]

7. Annual shed loading and unloading cost:
[annual shed cost] = [shed cost/tray] × [trays/year]

8. Mushroom picking time per tray. The picking time per kg increases with each consecutive flush. As for the yield, Jennifer's figures allow us to compute an average picking rate for each consecutive flush. To test your understanding, compare the answers you compute with the ones shown below:

flush	1	2	3	4	5
kg picked/hour	10.804	9.629	6.938	5.085	4.176
hours per tray	2.126	1.670	1.024	0.841	0.625
cumulative hours/tray	2.126	3.796	4.820	5.661	6.286

9. Annual number of hours required for picking mushroom output:
[annual picking labour] = [trays/year] × [cumulative hours/tray]

10. Annual cost of picking labour:
[annual picking cost] = [annual picking labour] × [picking pay/hour]

11. Annual sorting and packing cost:
[annual sorting and packing cost] = [annual output] × [sort. and pack. cost/kg]

12. Annual compost revenue:
[annual compost revenue] = [spent compost/tray] × [trays/year]
× [net compost selling price/kg]

13. Annual mushroom revenue:
[annual mushroom revenue] = [annual output] × [mushroom revenue/kg]

14. Annual net profit is given by total revenue less total costs:
[annual net profit] = [annual mushroom revenue]
\+ [annual compost revenue]
− [annual tray preparation cost]
− [annual shed cost]
− [annual picking cost]
− [annual sorting and packing cost]
− [annual fixed cost]

To apply this model, we now have to compute the various cost factors used in expressions 6, 7, 10, and 11.

9.7 Computation of cost factors for subsystems

We will demonstrate how some of the cost coefficients are computed for use in the mathematical model. It is important to remember that all costs compiled by the accountant and reported in Appendix 9.1 refer to the preceding financial year. During that year, the policy used was to let each harvesting cycle go through five flushes, i.e., $n = 5$. We shall also assume that there is no inflation. This implies that the cost factors derived will remain the same and, hence, valid for the future.

Preparation costs per tray: This covers all costs of the compost making and phase 1 tray preparation that vary proportionally with the number of trays prepared per year. They are thus best expressed in the form of an average preparation cost per tray.

For $n = 5$ flushes per harvesting cycle, the cycle length is $28 + 7 \times 5 = 63$ days. The average number of cycles per year is then $365/(63 + 2) = 5.6154$ cycles. With 65 sheds in constant use and each shed carrying 400 trays, the annual number of trays required is $65 \times 400 \times 5.6154) = 146{,}000$ trays.

Applying the classification of Table 9-1 to the data for tray preparation in Appendix 9.1, the costs that vary proportionally to the number of trays prepared amount to €6,243,310 (items numbered 1 to 5 in the table), including €428,211 for wages. The total cost of waged labour also has to include the cost of any fringe benefits and other wage-related contributions paid by the employer. We can assume that the figure on the total wage payments compiled by the accountant includes vacation and sick pay. So, no adjustment for this is needed. However, the accountant also lists under other costs for the preceding year accident insurance and pension fund contributions. These contributions are incurred on the totality of all wages paid. The percentage contribution rates for each are 2.5% for accident insurance and 4% for employer's pension fund contributions, or a total of 6.5%. This amounts to €27,834 on the €428,211 wages paid for this section. The total variable cost for this section is thus

Materials, power, fuel, and so on	€5,815,099
Waged labour	€428,211
Fringe benefits 6.5%	€27,834
Total waged labour cost	€456,045
Total variable cost for 146,000 trays	€6,271,144

This gives an average tray preparation cost of €42.96.

Shed cost per tray: Using the classification of costs in Table 9-1, verify that the analogous reasoning as for the tray preparation leads to a shed cost per tray of €5.40.

Mushroom pickers gross pay per hour: The accountant lists the hourly pay rate for mushroom pickers at €9.20. This is exclusive of all fringe benefits supported by the employer. The accountant also quotes that the vacation and sickness pay is limited to the equivalent of 8% of the total annual pay of a picker. Adding to this the accident insurance and pension fund contribution, total fringe benefits of 6.5% + 8% = 14.5% have to be added to the hourly pay rate. The hourly cost to the firm is thus €10.53.

Sorting and packing costs per kilogram of mushrooms produced: The total variable cost for materials, and so on, and labour, including the 6.5% cost of fringe benefits amount to €6,353,911. The annual output is equal to the cumulative yield per tray multiplied by the number of trays per year, i.e., 53.043 × 146000 = 7,744,205 kg. This gives a sorting and packing cost of €0.8205 per kilogram of mushrooms produced. (It is here important to show sufficient decimal places, since it will be multiplied by millions. Therefore, any small rounding error will be magnified.)

9.8 Analysis of CG problem by spreadsheet

The input data for the mathematical model in Section 9.6 is reproduced in Figure 9-2, while Figure 9-3 shows the spreadsheet computations. It first computes the various intermediate variables as a function of the number of flushes per cycle. These are then used in the cost and revenue computations. The last line shows the difference in annual profits in comparison with the current policy of five flushes per harvesting cycle.

The annual profit is higher for two, three, and four flushes than for the current policy. The highest profit increase is obtained for three flushes per harvesting cycle (shown shaded). The increase is almost €1 million per year. It also results in an increase in mushroom output of 844,245 kg, or slightly more than 10%. This is a highly interesting aspect of the policy of three flushes per cycle, since it also achieves another of Gérard Mousse's objectives. Based on this analysis, he would be advised to reduce the number of flushes from five to three per harvesting cycle. This would achieve his objectives of both increasing output and profits at the same time. The increase in output is the equivalent of seven additional sheds under the current policy of five flushes. Any decision on adding more sheds can therefore be postponed by another few years.

CHAMPIGNONS GALORE LTD			
INPUT DATA:			
Picking cost:	**€**	**€**	
Labour/hour		9.2	
Fringe benefit 14.5%		1.33	(incl. 8% vacation pay, 2.5%
Total/hour		10.53	accident ins., 4% pension funds)
Tray preparation:			
Materials		5,815,099	
Labour	428,211		
Fringe benefit 6.5%	27,834	456,045	(incl. 2.5% accident ins.,
Total for 146,000 trays		6,271,144	4% pension fund)
per tray		42.9560	
Shed cost:			
Materials, and so on		588,343	
Labour	188,231		
Fringe benefit 6.5%	12,235	200,466	(as above)
Total for 146,000 trays		788,809	
per tray		5.4032	
Processing cost:			
Materials, and so on		4,121,198	
Labour	2,096,444		
Fringe benefit 6.5%	136,269	2,232,713	(as above)
Total for 7,744,205 kg		6,353,911	
per kg		0.8205	

SUMMARY OF INPUT DATA:				
Number of trays/shed	400	Flush	Yield (kg)	Picking hrs
Number of sheds	65	1	9189	850.5
Revenue/kg	€3.60	2	6432	668.0
Sorting and packing cost/kg	€0.82047	3	2841	409.5
Picking cost/kg	€10.53	4	1711	336.5
Preparation cost/tray	€42.96	5	1044	250.0
Shed cost/tray	€5.40			
Fixed cost/year	€2,914,294			
Compost revenue/tray	€8.40			

Figure 9-2 Spreadsheet input data for CG problem

EVALUATION					
Flushes per cycle	1	2	3	4	5
Tray and volume computations					
Cycle length in days	37	44	51	58	65
Number of cycles/year	9.865	8.295	7.157	6.293	5.615
Yield/tray in kg	22.973	16.080	7.103	4.278	2.610
Cumul. yield/tray in kg	22.973	39.053	46.155	50.433	53.043
Picking hours/tray	2.126	1.670	1.024	0.841	0.625
Cumul. picking hr/tray	2.126	3.796	4.820	5.661	6.286
Number of trays/year	256,486	215,682	186,078	163,621	146,000
Total output/year in kg	5,892,136	8,422,914	8,588,450	8,251,800	7,744,205
Revenue and cost computations in €					
Mushroom revenue	21,211,689	30,322,491	30,918,420	29,706,482	27,879,138
Compost revenue	2,154,486	1,811,727	1,563,059	1,374,414	1,226,400
Tray preparation cost	11,017,629	9,264,824	7,993,182	7,028,487	6,271,573
Shed cost	1,385,840	1,165,366	1,005,414	884,071	788,863
Picking cost	5,744,763	8,625,051	9,447,924	9,757,619	9,668,026
Sorting and packing cost	4,834,338	6,910,773	7,046,591	6,770,379	6,353,911
Fixed cost	2,914,294	2,914,294	2,914,294	2,914,294	2,914,294
Net profit	−2,530,689	3,253,910	4,074,075	3,726,045	3,108,871
Difference	−5,639,560	145,040	965,204	617,174	0

Figure 9-3 Cost and revenue computations for CG

Postscript: When this solution was submitted to the management for consideration, CG's CEO responded with disbelief. In the case write-up in Appendix 9.1, his response is the one attributed to the father of Gérard Mousse. However, three years later, management changed its mind and reduced the number of flushes per harvesting cycle to three, a delay that may have cost them up to €3 million!

Case study 9-1: Vinyl Products Ltd

Vinyl Products Ltd produces various types of adhesive tapes, such as flesh coloured vinyl for bandages, electrical insulating tape, and so on. Depending on the type of tape, it is either produced on the older and more expensive Classic line or the newer and more efficient Modern line. Both lines are currently used for about one and a half shifts per day. In an effort to reduce production costs, Jan van Glug, the production engineer, experiments with various different production options. He comes up with a proposal which, he claims, will reduce production costs by well over €300,000 per year. The proposal implies that the equivalent of about half a shift of work is moved from the Classic line to the Modern line. This would increase the workload of the Modern line by about a quarter of a shift and leave it still well below the current maximum two-shift policy, but would reduce the Classic line to a one-shift operation.

At the weekly planning meeting, he presents a sample of the potential savings that could be obtained for switching bandage vinyl from the Classic to the Modern line. That particular product accounts for a bit more than one tenth of the Classic line current one-shift capacity. Here is the window on his laptop that he projects to the wall screen in the conference room:

	Classic line	Modern line	Savings
Speed of production (m^2/hr) 600	1200		
Adhesive applied (kg/m^2)	0.275	0.25	
Adhesive cost/year at €15/kg for 140,000 m^2	€577,500	€525,000	€52,500
Variable machine hours for production	233.33	116.67	
Size of batches in m^2	5,000	10,000	
Annual set-up time in hours	56	28	
Total machine hours for 140,000 m^2	289.33	144.67	
Labour cost €20/hr + 25% fringe ben.	€ 7,233	€3,617	€3,616
Overhead* allocation/machine hour	€102	€78	
Total overhead allocation	€29,512	€11,284	€18,228
Total net savings			€74,344

* Overhead includes recovery of the initial machine cost, i.e., machine depreciation.

Upon seeing this statement, Pieter Klever, the firm's long-standing accountant, reports that switching production from the Classic line to the Modern line would result in a significant change in overheads allocation. Reducing the work load on the Classic line by half a shift would increase its overhead rate by roughly a third from the current €102 to above €130 per hour, whereas the Modern line overhead rate would decrease by only about 15%, given its greater efficiency. As a consequence, the standard production costs of all the remaining products made on the Classic line would increase substantially. This would either reduce their profitability or force corresponding price increases, which could affect sales. Some previously profitable products may even become unprofitable. Also, the increased profitability of products made on the Modern line would probably not justify any price reductions or, if prices were reduced marginally, this was unlikely to increase sales noticeably. He therefore recommended against such a switch.

When asked if the overhead allocation rate on the Classic line could not be left at its present level, Pieter was adamant this would violate company policy that the products produced on each machine have to recover all costs, including the proper overhead allocation. If this were done in this instance, then pressure would build to use this kind of ploy in other instances. It would invalidate proper costing of all products.

- Analyse Jan's cost projections and discuss their relevance for the decision of whether or not to switch production lines. Are there any relevant costs that he missed?
- Discuss the accountant's arguments. What is your recommendation?

9.9 Chapter highlights

- Traditional accounting practices record the historical financial performance of an organization. Accounting cost control focuses on allocating all costs, variable and fixed, to individual products or services. The aim is to determine average costs or 'standard costs'. These may be suitable for pricing decisions and to assess current performance under the assumption of no changes in the level of activity or operation.
- Opportunity costs reflect the loss in benefit forgone for not using a resource for its best alternative use.

- Intangible costs reflect the detrimental effect on benefits and costs that do not lend themselves easily to being expressed in monetary terms.
- In MS/OR analysis, only those costs and benefits are relevant that change for the organization as a whole as a function of the different decision choices or different values of the decision variables. This includes opportunity costs and intangible costs, but excludes all fixed costs that are not affected by a change in decision choices.
- Accounting data of standard costs may therefore not be inappropriate, because they may include irrelevant fixed costs but exclude relevant variable costs. Furthermore, accounting records do not show opportunity costs, but show sunk costs that are irrelevant for decision making.

Exercises

1. Compare opportunity costs and intangible costs and discuss their differences and similarities, if any.
2. Discuss why opportunity costs are a form of implicit costs.
3. Why are opportunity costs relevant for decision making?
4. Give an example of explicit costs, implicit costs, fixed costs, variable costs, opportunity costs, sunk costs, and intangible costs for each of the following types of entities:
   (a) an industrial firm, such as a manufacturer of household appliances;
   (b) a merchandising firm, such as a department store;
   (c) a service industry firm, such as a restaurant;
   (d) a public service organization, such as a hospital;
   (e) a local government agency, such as the water supply authority.
5. Consider the LOD operation described in Chapter 6 (p. 132 ff).
   (a) Classify the following cost factors as to their nature for the LOD in general (explicit, implicit, fixed, variable, opportunity, sunk, or intangible cost, and under what assumptions): v, s, r, h_1, h_2, cost of warehouse space, cost of warehouse maintenance, cost of office staff involved in operating the new system, fringe benefits of office staff, salary of LOD supervisor, original building cost of warehouse, cost of operating filling equipment.
   (b) Redo (a), but classifying all cost factors in relation only to the LOD project, not the firm as a whole.
6. The following four questions refer to Table 9-1 of the Champignons Galore case:
   (a) The depreciation for yard vehicles is currently classified as a fixed cost. Assume now that CG adopts the optimal cycle length of three flushes. The number of trays to be prepared increases from 146,000 to 186,078, a 27% increase. When Charles Brun hears this, he casually mentions to Roger Munny that this implies that due to the much higher usage the yard vehicles may have to be replaced earlier than under the previous scheme. What implications, if any, has this on the relevance of depreciation?
   (b) Charles Brun also points out that, while the compost stacking machine can easily cope with the increased workload, this is not the case for the current assortment of forklift tractors. In fact, he reckons that at least one additional forklift tractor will have to be purchased. Its operating and maintenance costs, as well as its depreciation, would be

identical to the ones for the current tractors. What is the effect of purchasing another tractor on the annual costs under the new system?

(c) The amount of work for climate control is considerably more intensive during the 26–28 day growing phase than during the harvesting phases. Under the new system, the number of cycles per year also increases by 27%. Karl Scharf worries that he and Tina Paille will not be able to handle the increased workload without getting a part-time assistant. How does this affect the relevance of costs for climate control?

(d) The increase in the level of operations due to the higher volume of mushrooms requires additional working capital (funds invested in inventories of all sorts, an increase in the level of outstanding customer bills, increased bank account balances required for daily operations, and so on). Gérard Mousse proposes to raise the additional funds by getting a bank loan of €300,000 at an interest rate of 15%. The loan will be paid off through retained earnings. How does this affect the imputation of costs?

7. A firm sells a range of chemical products in a variety of containers: plastic bottles of 0.3 and 1 litre, cans of 1 and 5 litres, and so on. Each product goes through the following production process. The first stage is mixing the basic ingredients. This is done in vats of 100, 500, 1,000, 4,000, and 10,000 litres. An operator measures out the ingredients and adds them to the vat chosen for mixing in a prescribed sequence, with the mixing blades activated at various times. The ingredients are stored in the nearby chemicals warehouse. For safety reasons, each ingredient has to be handled individually, i.e., removing the desired quantity from the stock of ingredients if it comes in containers of the correct size, or else bringing a drum or bag from the storage area to the scales and measuring out the required amount, and then returning the balance to the warehouse. Most products require between 5 and 20 ingredients, but some are made up of up to 50. Once mixed, some of the products have to go through a homogenization process, i.e., the mixing vat is covered and the mixing blades rotated at extremely high speed. The entire mixing operation can take anywhere from 1 to 6 hours.

When mixing is completed, a 0.5 litre sample undergoes a series of tests in the lab. About 5% of all batches mixed fail one or several of these tests. If this happens, the lab technician returns an upgrading report to the mixing operator. That report spells out what additional quantities of ingredients have to be added to bring the batch up to specifications. The time taken for this is on average about 60% of the original mixing set-up time. It occasionally means also that the size of the batch becomes larger than originally ordered. Naturally, the upgraded batch has to be re-tested. Over the last five-year period, no batch has failed a test twice. Test results are usually available within 30 minutes.

Once a batch has been cleared, it is put into containers. Plastic or rubber lines are hooked up to connect mixers filling machines: one for each size container. To eliminate any contamination which could potentially be hazardous to the operators and the users of the products, these lines have to be thoroughly cleaned after each use. Furthermore, the lines deteriorate with use and have to be discarded after 80 uses. A new line has a cost of €60.

Prior to filling a new batch, the containers have to be made ready, the labels inserted into the machine, the filling machine adjusted for the viscosity of the product to be filled (this controls the quantity filled), and the lines from the mixer hooked up to the filling machine. Two operators are engaged in these preparations for a total of 15 minutes each. A trial batch of 12 containers is then filled and inspected. The last three containers are tested for weight. One of the containers is also returned to the testing lab for confirmation of its content. This container is then labelled with the batch number and date, and kept for at least eight months. The time taken for these final tests is 15 minutes, during which the filling machine is stopped. Although the two machine operators keep busy, such as making final re-adjustments to the machine, the production engineer views this time as essentially unproductive. Once the sample can has been cleared by the lab, filling takes place at full machine speed. The containers are packed into cardboard boxes by hand by up to four labourers. The boxes are sealed, labelled, and then placed on pallets, which are stored in the finished goods warehouse. During the machine set-up and testing, these labourers are kept busy with other productive work. Their wages during set-up are therefore not chargeable to the product being filled. Filling time depends on the batch size. The 1-litre machines can fill up to 300 cans or 180 bottles per minute.

Consider product X. Its ingredients cost €5.50 per litre of finished product. Preparation for mixing takes 2 hours. This includes the cleaning of the vat. The actual mixing operation is proportional to the size of the batch and takes 20 minutes for every 1000 litres of mix. The two laboratory technicians test 20 to 40 products each day. They also spend some 2 hours per day testing raw materials shipped by suppliers. Hooking up the mixers to the filling machine takes 5 minutes. This is done by the mixing operator. The actual filling occurs at a rate of 200 cans per minute. Four packers are needed for packing the cans into boxes, and so on. Cleaning the filling machine and the hook-up lines after a run takes another 10 minutes for two people. Cleaning is done using cleaning solvents and neutralizers. For this particular product, it takes 12 litres of fresh cleaning solvents to clean the vat, filling machine, and hook-up lines at a cost of €1.50 per litre. Furthermore, the first two cans filled cannot be used, since even after thorough cleaning, there may still be some small amounts of residue left in the filling mechanism, which is washed out by the flow of chemicals to fill the first two cans. Consumption of power during all these operations is about €0.16 per 1000 litres of product. Can labels cost 2 cents/can, while a carton for 24 cans has a cost of 60 cents, including the label.

The wage rate for the mixing operator and the two filling machine operators is €16 per hour, while the packing labourers at the filling machine are paid €12 per hour. The weekly salary of lab technicians is €800 for a 40-hour week. Any increase in the lab workload of more than 10% requires overtime or the addition of a part- or full-time technician.

Other costs involved in inventory control include clerical costs at the accounting department. Currently about three persons are fully occupied in maintaining computerized inventory records, including the processing of customer orders, preparation of customer delivery documents, preparation and processing of stock replenishments. It is estimated that each stock replenishment takes about 20 minutes of clerical time for all processing involved. Only about 20% of their time is taken up by processing stock replenishments. Clerks are on monthly salaries of €2,400 and work a 40-hour week.

There are two types of overheads. Plant overheads are charged at 50% of direct labour cost. General overheads are assessed at a rate of 64% on direct labour cost. General overheads also includes fringe benefits of 30%, such as vacation pay, pension fund contributions, health and accident insurance, cafeteria subsidies, and so on. The company wishes to earn a return on its investment of 15% after taxes. The current marginal tax rate is 33%.

The company rents its premises. The cost accountant has figured out that each square metre of floor space has an annual cost of €40. One pallet stored in the warehouse requires 1.44 square metres of floor space. Pallets are stored three high. For each pallet area, 0.56 square metres of floor space is needed for access aisles. The filling machine requires a floor space of 10 by 15 metres, while a vat needs about 9 square metres of floor space. The premises consist of a separate building. It is not subdividable and has to be rented as a whole unit. Currently, there is ample floor space available for expansion. Maintenance of the plant area has an annual cost of €12 per square metre.

The current inventory replenishment policy used by the firm is based on the economic order quantity model. Identify all costs relevant for determining the EOQ for the product in question. Develop a table similar to Table 9-1 for classifying all costs mentioned. You may wish to review some of the material in Chapter 6 dealing with the EOQ model. Recall that there are two types of relevant costs for the EOQ model, those that are fixed for each replenishment, regardless of its size, and those that are associated with the cost of holding goods in stock, usually assessed on the average inventory level.

8. For the cost factors developed in exercise 7, find the optimal replenishment size and its annual cost, using the EOQ model of Chapter 6, for an annual demand of 160,000 litres.

Further reading

Collis, J. and Hussey, R. (2006) *Business Accounting: An Introduction to Financial and Management Accounting*, New York: Palgrave Macmillan. Part Three discusses costing.

Eldenburg, L.G. and Wolcott, S. (2004) *Cost Management: Measuring, Monitoring, and Motivating Performance*, New York: Wiley. Parts One and Two discuss costing issues.

Samuelson, W.F. and Marks, S.G. (2012) *Managerial Economics,* 7th edn, International Student Version, New York: Wiley. Chapter 6 discusses costs relevant for decision making.

Appendix 9.1

Champignons Galore — Situation summary

Champignons Galore (CG) is a French commercial grower of mushrooms. Cultivated mushrooms grow under carefully controlled climatic and hygienic conditions, usually in complete darkness in caves, cellars, or specially constructed sheds. CG uses sheds.

The production process

Mushrooms are grown on a base of specially prepared compost. CG makes its own compost. It buys straw from the surrounding farms and wheat growers. In fact, CG buys well over 50% of all straw locally available. This straw is mixed with animal manure and other organic materials. The mixture is stacked into long snakes or rows of about 2 × 2 metres dimension. This operation is done with a special-purpose stacking machine. Once stacked, the mixture naturally undergoes a fermentation from inside out which transforms it slowly into compost. This creates a substantial amount of heat which further contributes to the process. Outside temperatures and the amount of natural rain can affect the speed of fermentation. Sprinkler systems are used for controlling the humidity level of the mixture.

After 1 to 2 weeks when the insides of the stacks have become compost, the stacking machine turns the stacks inside out. This speeds up complete fermentation of all material.

The whole process takes anywhere from 2 to 4 weeks, depending on the time of the year and the outside temperature. New stacks of compost are started at regular intervals to guarantee a constant supply of fresh compost for the production process.

The mushroom production itself consists of three phases. In phase 1, the compost is put into 30-centimetre deep wooden trays. These are topped with peat. The trays and their contents are then sterilized to kill any diseases or unwanted seeds, and so on. Once sterilized, the trays are injected with laboratory grown mycelium (mushroom spawn), covered with casing soil, and treated in a process called 'peak heating'.

Phase 2 is the mycelium growing stage. The trays are stored on shelves in growing sheds. The inside of the sheds is almost completely dark and kept within carefully controlled temperature and humidity ranges. The growing phase lasts about 26 to 28 days. During this time, the mycelium propagates throughout the entire bed in each tray.

The third phase is the cropping stage. The mushrooms, which are the fruiting bodies of the plant, appear in a sequence of 'flushes' at intervals of 6 to 8 days. Within 1 to 2 days of breaking through the casing soil, the mushrooms are harvested.

The yield of the first two flushes is substantially higher than for the subsequent flushes. Also, the size of the mushrooms becomes smaller in the later flushes. As a result, the amount of labour needed to pick the mushrooms appearing in the later flushes increases markedly after flush two. The reason for both these phenomena is that each flush reduces the nutrient content of the compost until, after about 5 to 6 flushes, it is almost exhausted. At that point, the trays are removed from the sheds.

The 'spent' compost is packed into bags for resale as mulch to home gardeners or commercial vegetable growers. The trays are cleaned and returned to the compost filling station, ready for use in a new production cycle. Emptying a shed, preparing it for the next cycle, and loading it with a fresh batch of trays takes about 2 days.

Like composting, phase 1 of the production process is done on a continuous basis. New trays are prepared daily for phase 2. With the number of sheds currently in operation, one or two sheds start on phase 2 every day. As a consequence the sheds are on a continuous rotation, with each shed at a different stage in the process. This provides a fairly constant output level for the operation as a whole.

Picking of mushrooms is done by hand. For this reason, the width of the trays and their spacing on the shelves in the sheds is such that a picker can easily reach to the middle of each tray, working either from the floor for the lowest shelf or from a ladder that rolls along the shelves for the upper two shelf levels. In order to maintain strict hygiene, any person entering a growing shed has to pass through a lock where shoes and clothing are automatically sterilized.

The freshly picked mushrooms are sorted by size and quality. The very small ones are used by a canning factory, operated by CG at a different site. Most of the high-quality product is exported to England and Scandinavia, while the second grade mushrooms are sold on the local French market or used in the canning operation.

The firm currently operates 66 sheds, each capable of storing 400 trays. There are 65 sheds in continuous in use for the growing and harvesting phases, except for the 2 days needed to clean a shed and prepare it for the next cycle. At all times, one shed is not in use on a rotational basis and undergoes major maintenance/repair work which takes 5 to 6 days per shed. Trays also need regular repairs and replacement. On average, a tray last four years.

The people

Gérard Mousse is the principal owner of the firm, having taken over from his father as managing director two years ago. Before that, he was the firm's marketing manager. He has six people in supervisory positions reporting to him. Roger Munny is the chief accountant and also serves as office manager. The compost and tray preparation sections are managed by Charles Brun. It is said of him that with his super-sensitive nose — a most striking feature in his face — and by sticking his right index finger into the fermenting stacks, he is able to judge the correct temperature and humidity level of the stacks as well as, and with less effort than, the scientific tests Gérard Mousse tried to convince him to use. His portion of the operation is highly mechanized, using the rather expensive compost stacking machine, forklift tractors, the automatic sprinkler system, the tray filling machine, the sterilization and peak heating ovens.

Michel Boîte is in charge of the gangs filling and emptying the sheds, shed maintenance and cleaning, repair and maintenance of trays, as well as disposing of the spent compost.

Karl Scharf and his laboratory assistant, Tina Paille, are responsible for the climatic control of the sheds. They are by far the most scientifically trained employees of the firm.

Picking and sorting of the mushrooms and the dispatch to the customers, all highly labour intensive operations, are managed by Jennifer Fleurette.

Jean Marchand has recently been hired as the marketing manager in charge of domestic sales as the sole member of that department. Gérard Mousse retained control over international marketing contracts and promotion.

The problem

When Gérard Mousse took over control of the firm after his father's retirement, his initial efforts went mainly into developing the export markets in England and Scandinavia. This led to increasing requirements for a top-quality product. To meet the additional demand, ten new sheds were added to the original 56 in operation at the time Gérard assumed the top position. Otherwise, Gérard did not make any major changes to the operation or its management. The exception was hiring the German scientist Karl Scharf to improve quality control.

It may also be worth mentioning that, as one of his first actions after taking over the management of the firm, he upgraded the staff cafeteria and the staff changing facilities — a deed that earned him the respect and loyalty of his waged and salaried staff, and contributed strongly to staff morale and productivity.

Given the potential for increased export sales, Gérard now sees upgrading the production capacity for top-grade product as one of his priorities. The firm's current facilities do not really allow the construction of more sheds, unless the firm adopts the rather expensive two-level sheds. A plot of land, two kilometres to the south of the existing plant and suitable for a maximum of 32 sheds, had recently been offered for sale. This opens up the option of going to a two-site growing operation, with the composting and phase 1 done on the current premises for both sites. Gérard doubts that the firm will need more than about 10 to 16 additional sheds within the next five years. Hence, only a small portion of the site would be used productively. However, this option would provide the firm with sufficient breathing space for further expansion for a long time. The increase in transportation cost for trays and mushrooms is an added disadvantage of the two-site option.

Gérard wonders whether it would be possible to increase the output of top-grade mushrooms at the current site without the need to construct new sheds. He has always wondered about the reasons why his father had used a five-flush harvesting cycle, although he is aware that practically all commercial mushroom growers, using the same system as CG, seem to follow this policy. In fact, he recently discussed this issue with his father when he visited him with his young family at a weekend. His father was very sceptical that any gains could be made by adopting a policy with a smaller number of cycles. His main argument was that if this were advantageous, the mushroom industry would have adopted it long ago. Gérard is not convinced by this argument, since the mushroom industry is hardly known for its initiative in researching anything else but how to grow the perfect mushroom.

Being a cautious businessman, he decides to cost out the three options. He remembers bumping into an old university friend, John Smart, at a recent function in London, where he discovered, with some envy, that John Smart had continued his university study, getting a PhD in MS/OR at a British university. He had recently accepted a teaching position at his old Alma Mater and mentioned that he was looking for potential student projects. Would this problem not be an ideal project? He contacts John who asks him to gather some data on various aspects of the operation, such as the costs of various tasks and the yield for each consecutive flush.

Data collected

Gérard asks Roger Munny to compile a preliminary list of various cost items incurred in the production of mushrooms. Jennifer willingly agrees to keep an exact tally of the quantity of mushrooms harvested each day over the entire harvesting cycle for sheds 5 and 6 which were just coming on-stream for producing mushrooms. It turns out that Jennifer goes a step further by also recording for each day the number of hours worked by the pickers harvesting mushrooms in these two sheds.

Below is a list of the various cost and revenue items compiled or collected by Roger Munny, based on the preceding financial year:

1. **C. Brun's section** (composting and tray preparation):
   - €5,493,557 for raw materials (straw, manure, peat, casing sand, sterilization agents, and so on; most raw materials were purchased regularly, some such as straw almost daily; hence raw material stocks were small and remained fairly constant over the entire year)
   - €267,844 for electricity for peak heating, operation of tray filling equipment, and so on
   - €27,911 for diesel fuel for yard vehicles
   - €25,787 for maintenance and repair costs on yard vehicles
   - €123,000 for depreciation on yard vehicles and equipment

- €86,520 for yard ground and building maintenance and repair costs
- €428,211 for yard workers' wages, including vacation pay
- €36,400 for salary of C. Brun

2. **Michel Boîte's section** (shed loading and unloading):
    - €51,333 for supplies (sterilization and cleaning chemicals for sheds)
    - €219,102 for packing material for spent compost
    - €24,451 for diesel fuel
    - €12,211 for vehicle maintenance and repairs; €35,600 depreciation on vehicles
    - €44,898 for repair and maintenance of sheds
    - €281,346 for replacement, repair, and maintenance of trays
    - €188,231 for wages, including vacation pay
    - €31,200 salary of M. Boîte

3. **Karl Scharf's section** (climate control):
    - €37,866 for electricity for climate control
    - €34,613 for materials (mycelium, laboratory supplies, and so on)
    - €12,452 for laboratory maintenance, cleaning, and so on
    - €33,200 for depreciation on climate control and lab equipment
    - €55,800 for new climate control and lab equipment
    - €68,400 for salaries of K. Scharf and Tina Paille

4. **Jennifer Fleurette's section** (picking, sorting, and packaging):
    - €4,071,758 for packing materials
    - €14,881 for supplies
    - €6,554 for electricity
    - €24,600 for new sorting machine
    - €4,212 for sorting and packing equipment maintenance
    - €14,600 for depreciation on sorting and packing equipment
    - €5,602 for maintenance and repair of sorting and packing shed
    - €18,006 for diesel fuel for trucks
    - €5,787 for truck maintenance and repairs; €37,800 depreciation on trucks
    - €2,044,324 for wages for sorting and packing staff only, including vacation pay
    - €52,120 for wages for drivers
    - €36,000 for salary of J. Fleurette
    - Pickers hourly wage: €9.20; vacation and sick pay allowance: 8% on wages

5. **Local marketing:**
    - €34,800 for salary of J. Marchand
    - €26,922 for travel and daily allowances

6. **Other costs:**
   - €48,766 for office supplies
   - €32,688 for new office equipment and computers
   - €3,435 for office building electricity
   - €12,111 for fuel and maintenance costs for two company cars
   - €6,600 for depreciation on company cars
   - €288,420 for salaries of office staff; €22,600 gardener
   - €8,688 for office building maintenance
   - €190,000 for depreciation on all buildings and sheds
   - €1,360,000 for mortgage interest; €124,005 fire and property insurance
   - €301,887 for accident insurance on waged workers (2.5%)
   - €8,517 for accident insurance on salaried employees (1.5%)
   - €483,019 for pension fund contribution on waged workers (4%)
   - €34,069 for pension fund contribution on salaried employees (6%)
   - €72,000 for salary of G. Mousse
   - €35,210 for travel costs for G. Mousse

Current revenue, net of sales commissions:

- Mushrooms €3.60/kg
- Spent compost €8.40/tray

Yield and picking data collected by Jennifer Fleurette:

day		kilograms picked in		hours pickers spent in	
		shed 5	shed 6	shed 5	shed 6
February	2	452	576	45	66
	3	912	797	78	83
	4	1463	1620	124	140
	5	2043	1304	191	119
	6	2495	2710	220	241
	7	1302	2003	129	176
	8	496	205	55	34
	9	0	298	0	48
	10	983	1160	94	103
	11	1224	1567	131	172
	12	1498	1364	161	129
	13	1373	1112	141	120
	14	1057	761	118	71
	15	467	0	48	0

16	0	421	0	65
17	232	365	36	64
18	786	613	109	81
19	848	907	123	112
20	595	426	81	61
21	264	225	46	41
22	0	0	0	0
23	0	289	0	43
24	323	180	69	35
25	368	423	71	81
26	404	407	80	82
27	301	198	61	42
March 01	242	0	50	0
02	0	0	0	0
03	175	204	39	44
04	238	153	49	36
05	98	311	24	54
06	307	144	56	34
07	118	121	26	27
08	94	87	23	21
09	56	69	15	17

10
Discounted cash flows

Learning objectives

- Be able to determine the present value of a stream of cash flows over time and find its equivalent annuity.
- Be able to determine whether a proposed investment project should be accepted or rejected.
- Be able to suggest a discount rate appropriate for a given project.
- Be able to recommend which of two or more mutually exclusive investment projects with possibly different initial outlays and differing productive lives is preferred.
- Determine when a piece of equipment should be replaced, based on economic considerations alone.

Introduction

Many MS/OR projects involve costs and benefits, occurring not at a single point in time, but spread over several periods. For example, a project may involve big initial investments in plant and equipment, followed one or two years later by a cash inflows over many years, as that plant and equipment produces goods or services to meet customer demands. Should this project be undertaken?

You have already come across a similar example. The project report in Appendix 6.2 recommended a full-scale study to find the optimal replenishment policies for all finished products carried by the Lubricating Oil Division. That recommendation entailed spending some \$42,000 now, with the expectation of generating annual total savings in costs of about \$93,000 for several years. The decision for going ahead with this study hinged on whether the flow of promised savings over several years justified spending the additional development costs. In that instance a (somewhat arbitrary) criterion was used; namely, that the estimated savings had to recover these costs in less than a year. For the majority of MS/OR projects, a similar type of analysis will have to be done as part of the recommendations for implementation.

To determine the net monetary outcome of projects with costs and benefits spread over several years, we have to aggregate the costs and benefits into a summary measure. Is the net monetary outcome of a project simply equal to the difference of total benefits and total costs, regardless of when the individual cost and benefit items occur in time? The answer to this question depends on whether the current value in terms of the purchasing power of £1 received, say, one year from now is exactly the same as the value of £1 received now. If this is so, then the answer is yes; otherwise, adding costs or benefits occurring at different points in time would be like adding apples and oranges.

This chapter demonstrates how costs and benefits that are spread over several time periods can be aggregated into a single meaningful measure which allows valid comparisons of projects with different streams of monetary flows. We will study decision criteria for deciding whether such projects are advantageous from a purely financial point of view.

The first three sections demonstrate several important concepts of financial mathematics, which have become integral tools of all spreadsheet programs, and have removed the tedium of having to consult financial tables, as was the case prior to that. However, in order to understand fully the principles involved, we cannot avoid delving briefly into the mathematics of discounting future cash flows.

Section 10.4 explores various considerations for setting an appropriate discount rate — an important topic extensively discussed in text on corporate finance, but usually neglected in most MS/OR texts.

We apply these concepts to a typical MS/OR problem of when equipment whose effectiveness deteriorates with age should be replaced — the 'replacement problem'.

10.1 The time value of money

Compounding

For an interest rate of $r = 8\% = 0.08$ per year, a sum of £100 left in a savings account for a year accrues to £100(1 + 0.08) = £108. Left for a second year, it will grow to £100(1 + 0.08)(1 + 0.08) = £116.64. This growth process is called **compounding**. An investment of C_0 at time 0, compounded at a rate r per period, will grow by the end of n periods to a future value F_n of

$$F_n = C_0(1+r)^n \tag{10-1}$$

If the period is a fraction $1/k$ a year, the compounding rate is adjusted to r/k. (This approximation slightly overstates the correct value. It gets worse the shorter the compounding period. For instance, for $r = 0.08$, £100 compounded half-yearly grows to £108.16; for monthly compounding it grows to £108.30. In some circumstances it is advisable to use continuous compounding or discounting.)

Discounting

The process of converting a future value into its **present value** (PV) is called **discounting**. Its formula is

$$PV = C_n / (1+r)^n = C_n\, \alpha^n \tag{10-2}$$

where the ratio $\alpha^n = 1/(1+r)$ is called the **discount factor**, while r is referred to as the **discount rate.**

Net present value of a cash flow over time

Consider a cash flow over time, consisting of an initial cash amount C_0 at time 0, followed by a series of cash outlays and cash receipts, $C_1, C_2, \ldots C_{N-1}, C_N$, occurring at the end of each period. The **net present value** (NPV) of this cash flow is given by the formula:

$$NPV = \sum_{n=0}^{n=N} C_n \alpha^n \tag{10-3}$$

(Recall that $\alpha^0 = 1$.)

Consider again the Champignons Galore case in Chapter 9. We explored whether CG should reduce the number of flushes per growing cycle from the current five to fewer than five. We discovered that by going to three flushes per cycle, the annual profit would increase by about €965,000. Some additional analysis indicates that the increased output can only be disposed of by decreasing the selling price, while at the same time increasing sales promotion. This lowers the annual net savings in the first five years to yield the following profit increases:

Year	1	2	3	4	5
Profit increase	€320,000	€360,000	€450,000	€600,000	€800,000

Furthermore, the increased output requires investment in additional yard equipment and trays totalling €1,200,000. This equipment and the trays have a productive life of five years and then need to be replaced. The owner of CG, Gérard Mousse, wants any new investments in the firm to earn an annual return of at least 18%, otherwise he does not view it as being financially attractive.

Champignons Galore expansion project: detailed *NPV* computation						
Year	Change in cash flow €	Discount factor for 18%	Present value for 18%	Present value for 12%	Present value for 24%	Present value for 30%
0	-1,200,000	1.000000	-1,200,000	-1,200,000	-1,200,000	-1,200,000
1	320,000	0.847458	271,186	285,714	258,065	246,154
2	360,000	0.718184	258,546	286,990	234,131	213,018
3	450,000	0.608631	273,884	320,301	236,019	204,825
4	600,000	0.515789	309,473	381,311	253,784	210,077
5	800,000	0.437109	349,687	453,941	272,886	215,463
Net present value			262,777	528,258	54,885	-110,464

Figure 10-1 Spreadsheet *NPV* calculations for different discount rates

Figure 10-1 explores how the *NPV* responds as the discount rate varies. For r = 0.18, the *NPV* = €262,777. The initial investment is therefore financially attractive. As expected, as r increases from 0.12 to 0.30, the *NPV* decreases and ultimately becomes negative. This relationship is depicted graphically in Figure 10-2.

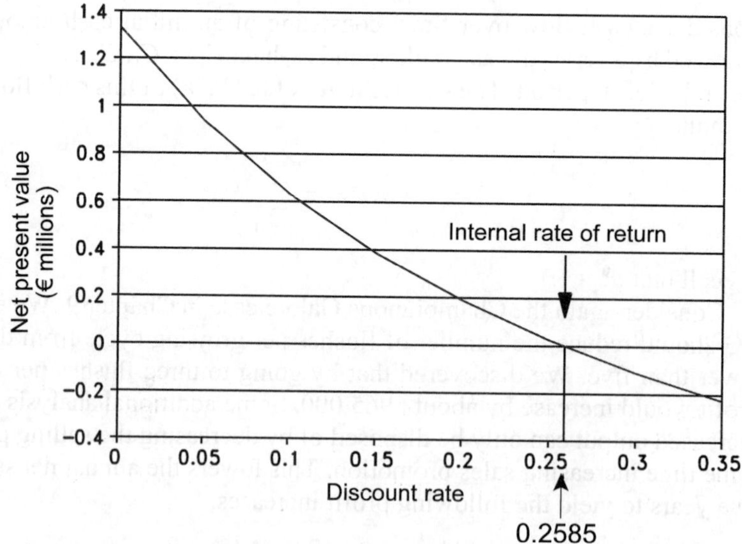

Figure 10-2 Relationship between discount rate and *NPV*

The internal rate of return

Figure 10-2 shows that for a discount rate of 0.2585 the *NPV* is exactly equal to zero. The discount rate for which the *NPV* is equal to zero is called **the internal rate of return** (IRR) or **the marginal efficiency of capital**.

Activity

- What is the *NPV* of a cash flow of –£1,400, +£1,000, +£1,000 occurring at the beginning of years 1, 2, and 3, respectively, at a discount rate of 25%?
- What is its *IRR*?
- If the *NPV* of a cash flow at the discount rate of 10% is positive, is the *IRR* larger or smaller than 10%? Why?

10.2 Accept/reject criteria for financial projects

The previous discussion provides us with two alternative criteria for deciding whether to accept or reject a project from a purely financial point of view:

> **Given a target rate of return of r^*,**
> **if $NPV_{r^*} \geq 0$ (net present value criterion)**
> **or if $IRR \geq r^*$ (internal rate of return criterion)**
> **accept the project,**
> **otherwise reject the project.**

These two criteria give the same answer if a project's cash flow consists of an initial cash outlay, followed by a string of cash inflows. The CG project has this pattern. So, if the target rate of return is $r^* = 18\%$, then the project is accepted under both criteria, since $NPV = €262,777 \geq 0$ and $IRR = 25.84755\% \geq 18\%$.

Unfortunately, if the cash flow has more than one reversal from negative to positive amounts and vice-versa, there may be two or more distinct *IRR* values for which the $NPV = 0$. For example, the cash flow pattern of –£720, £1,700, –£1,000, has two *IRR*-values of 11.11% and 25%. If the target rate of return is 20%, the $NPV = £2.22$. Under the *NPV* criterion, we get an unambiguous answer of 'accept this project'. Under the *IRR* criterion, we do not know which *IRR* value the target rate of return should be compared with, if any. For this reasons, financial analysts recommend the use of the *NPV* criterion in preference to the *IRR* criterion. We will follow this advice.

Activity

- The *NPV* of the cash flow of –£1,400, +£1,000, +£1,000 occurring at the beginning of successive years is 40 at a discount rate of 25% (example from previous Activity). If the target rate of return is 20%, should this project be accepted? Why?
- Can you tell if its *IRR* is less than 25% or greater than 25%, without computing it? Can you tell if it is less than 20% without computing it?

10.3 Annuities and perpetuities

A cash flow consisting of equal amounts C in each year is called an **annuity**. However, by extension, any equal-amount cash flow at regular intervals, regardless of the length of each period, is also referred to as an annuity. If it occurs at the beginning of each period, it is a **prepaid** annuity, if at the end, it is a **post-paid** annuity. Its NPV is equal to the sum of the discount factors multiplied by amount per period:

$$NPV = C \sum_{n=0}^{n=N} \alpha^n \tag{10-3}$$

For example, assume that at the end of each of the coming five years, you receive a payment of C=€84,030.40, i.e., a post-paid annuity for five years. The computations for its NPV are as follows:

Period	1	2	3	4	5
Amount €	84,030.40	84,030.40	84,030.40	84,030. 40	84,030.40
α^n	0.847458	0.718184	0.608631	0.515789	0.437109

Sum of discount factors 3.127171

NPV (84,030.40) 3.127171 = €262,777

If the constant cash flow C occurs for ever — a **perpetuity** — then the NPV (for the post-paid case) is given by this simple formula:

$$NPV_r = C/r \tag{10-4}$$

Equivalent annuity

The above example demonstrates an interesting point. The original cash flow for the CG project has an NPV of €262,777. The annuity of €84,030.40 received at the end of each of five consecutive years also has an NPV of €262,777. The two different cash flows over five years have the same NPV. This property allows us to express any sequence of unequal cash flows as a equivalent sequence of equal cash amounts, or as an **equivalent annuity**, covering the same number of periods. The annuity of €84,030.40 for five years is thus the equivalent (post-paid) annuity for the original stream of cash flows of the CG project. It leads to the following important finding:

For an uneven cash flow over N periods, its equivalent annuity can be interpreted as the weighted average amount per period, with the discount factors serving as weights.

Expressing uneven cash flows in terms of equivalent annuities turns out to be very useful when comparing projects that have different productive lives.

10.4 Choice of target rate of return

What is the appropriate discount rate to use in evaluating the worth of a project? This is a rather complex problem — it is a topic extensively discussed in the financial theory literature. We shall only summarize its main options.

Opportunity cost basis

Since the basis for discounting is the opportunity cost associated with the use of funds, the most obvious choice for the correct discount rate is the rate of return foregone on the best alternative use of the funds. Unfortunately, the range of alternative uses of the funds available may change within a short time span and, hence, so will the best alternative use. Using a discount rate based on the opportunity cost concept would therefore result in rather inconsistent choices from one project to the next. Furthermore, the decision maker may not really be aware of all possible uses of funds.

In real life, this concept is not a practicable approach for setting a suitable discount rate. Furthermore, it also ignores the difference in degree of risk between various projects. Any rational decision maker should be willing to trade return against risk.

Desired rate of return – a policy choice

A logical alternative is to ask management or the decision makers to formulate a policy as to the minimum acceptable rate of return for investments of a given level of risk. This minimum acceptable rate is then used as the target discount rate for that level of risk. It will reflect the general economic climate and will therefore be less subject to short-term fluctuations. From an MS/OR point of view, this is the preferred approach. It puts the onus of choosing where it belongs, namely, on the decision makers.

A firm's average cost of capital

Any organization has recourse to a variety of sources of funds to finance its assets — the things it owns. For example, a limited liability company in the manufacturing sector will have somewhere between 40% and 60% of its funds financed by the owners — its shareholders. These 'equity funds' are in the form of share capital and retained earnings (i.e., profits re-invested in the firm, rather than paid out as dividends to the shareholders). The balance will be financed by liabilities, such as mortgages, debentures, short-term bank loans, and trade credit from suppliers. The latter is regularly renewed through new purchases.

If a firm runs into financial trouble, i.e., the value of its assets is less than the amount investors put into the firm, and the firm goes into liquidation, then the holders of secured liabilities, such as mortgages, will be repaid first. Funds owed to unsecured creditors are paid next from what is left over, with the owners paid last. The unsecured creditors and the owners may lose part or all of their investment. Hence, each source of funds is exposed to a different degree of risk of losing its investment. The higher the degree of risk, the more they will 'charge' for advancing funds. So, the cost of each type of funding increases with the degree of risk involved, with secured creditors being the cheapest and equity funds being the costliest.

Furthermore, a firm wants to be viewed as a good investment prospect for existing and new owners and creditors. Therefore, it will try to maintain a composition of funds or a capital structure considered appropriate for the type of business it is in with its associated inherent business risk. Any significant departure from these norms will cause the firm to be perceived as a more risky investment, increasing the cost of all its potential sources of funds.

It follows that the compositions of funds used for financing a firm's operations and the cost of each source dictate what it needs to earn to be viewed as a good investment. If its earnings do not cover the total annual cost of all funds — interest due plus dividends and capital gains expected by the owners — the return the owners receive on their equity is below the level the market expects. It may even result in their equity being gradually eroded and the firm ultimately defaulting on its creditors. Expressed differently, the firm's average return on its own investments must be at least equal to its **cost of capital**. The cost of capital is computed as the weighted average cost of all its funds — liabilities and equity — with the weights given by the proportion each source contributes towards the total capital of the firm.

Rather than base the cost of capital on the past, we take an opportunity cost approach. For each source of funding, we determine the cost to the firm of raising additional capital. This cost is easy to define for liabilities, such as a bank loan. It is equal to the interest rate charged. Finding the cost of equity funds is more difficult and controversial, and its study goes beyond the scope of this text. If the firm is financially sound and generates adequate profits, a simplified approach is based on the ratio of profits before taxes and the total equity.

The cost of capital is used as the minimum required rate of return and, hence, the target discount rate for any project proposal. Any project that has a positive *NPV* at that discount rate increases the net worth of the firm, since it recovers more than what is required on average for remunerating the firm's combined sources of additional funds. Projects that do not meet this criterion lower the net worth of the firm.

Note that it would be incorrect simply to use the cost of the funds actually raised for the project as the target discount rate. This would lead to inconsistent decisions, since this cost would change from project to project, as the firm endeavours to re-balance its capital structure to meet investors' expectations.

If the risk associated with a project is different from the average business risk of the firm, the target discount rate may need to be adjusted — up if the risk is higher, down if it is lower. Again something that should clearly be left to the decision maker(s) to decide upon and not the analyst.

Effect of choice of target discount rate

The choice of a target discount rate has a significant impact on the type of project an organization accepts. The higher the target discount rate, the lower the *NPV*. But more importantly, this gives also less weight to future cash flows, both positive and negative. It will thus favour projects with a low initial cost and/or quick recovery of the funds invested. It will favour the purchase of cheap equipment and plant, rather than more expensive equipment and plant with low running costs, thus sacrificing quality for cost. You go for the low-cost, second-hand car, rather than the Mercedes or Lexus.

When dealing with environmental projects, a high r^* will favour quick resource exploitation and environmental degradation rather than conservation. Similarly, abandonment costs that are incurred far in the future tend to contribute very little to the *NPV*. This explains why construction of nuclear power stations may be seen as more attractive by generators than other power sources, such as solar power, in spite of the fact that the cost of decommissioning a nuclear power plant 40 or 50 years in the future and the cost of the storage of nuclear waste material for hundreds of years afterwards may run into the billions. However, discounting reduces these costs to insignificance. Just consider that the present value of a £1 billion cost 40 years from now at a discount rate of 10% amounts is a mere £22 million — a small sum compared to the initial investment for a nuclear power plant. These are some of the reasons why environmentally concerned people argue that the discount rate appropriate for projects with high environmental impacts has to be very low or even zero.

Discounting of costs for public projects often raises serious ethical questions of equity between generations. Bluntly put, discounting implies that future generations do not count. The interested reader should consult the relevant discussion in Mishan (1981).

Activity

Why is it advisable/essential that normal commercial ventures be evaluated on the basis of their discounted cash flows, while discounting of costs and benefits of projects that involve safety, health, or environmental issues raises serious moral and ethical questions?

10.5 Spreadsheet financial functions

Spreadsheets have built-in financial functions that perform most discounting computations with a few easy key strokes. They allow the user to specify the timing of each cash flow — end of period or beginning of period — with end-of-period timing usually being the default.

The four financial functions which you will need most often are the following (the forms shown in Figure 10-3 is for Excel; they are similar for other spreadsheet packages; the major difference may be the sequence of the function arguments):

Net present value of a stream of cash flows: NPV(r, Xi:Yj), where [Xi:Yj] indicates the first and last in a row or column of cells containing the sequence of cash flows, occurring at the end of consecutive periods. The initial cash flow at the beginning of the first period (period 0) may have to be added as a separate undiscounted entry.

Present value of an annuity: PV(r, number of periods, annuity, fv, type), where the annuity is the constant payment per period, 'fv' and 'type' are optional arguments with a default value of zero. If type = 0, then the annuity is assumed to occur at the end of each period, i.e., post-paid, if type = 1, then the annuity is assumed to occur at the beginning of each period, i.e., prepaid. (For Excel, this function assumes that the annuity is a cash outflow, hence it returns a negative value if the annuity is listed as positive.)

Internal rate of return: IRR(Xi:Yj, initial guess for *r*), where [Xi:Yj] again denotes the first and last cells in a row or column of cells containing the sequence of cash flows, including the initial cash flow at the beginning of the first period. At least one value must be positive (a cash inflow) and one value negative (a cash outflow). This function finds the answer by an algorithm of successive approximations. If no convergence occurs by the end of 20 iterations, a corresponding message is shown. A better initial guess must then be supplied.

Equivalent annuity: PMT(*r*, number of periods, NPV, fv, type), where NPV is the net present value of the original sequence of irregular cash flows, including the cash flow at the beginning of the first period, with fv = 0 and type = 0 as defaults. For type = 0 the equivalent annuity is post-paid, while for type = 1 it is prepaid.

Figure 10-3 demonstrates the use of these functions for the CG project. The Excel formulas used are shown at the bottom and refer to the column and row identifiers listed at the margins. The equivalent annuity is computed as occurring at the end of each period.

	A	B	C	D	F	G
1	Champignons Galore Expansion Project Evaluation					
2						
3	Year	Cash flow				
4	0	-1,200,000				
5	1	320,000				
6	2	360,000				
7	3	450,000				
8	4	600,000				
9	5	800,000				
10						
11		Discount rate	0.12	0.18	0.24	0.3
12		NPV	528,258	262,777	54,885	-110,464
13		Equiv. annuity	146,544	84,040	19,991	-45,354
14		IRR	0.258476			
15						
16	Spreadsheet formulas in column C for discount rate of 0.12:					
17	C12	= NPV(C11,$B5:$B9)+$B4				
18	C13	= PMT(C11,$A9,-C12,0,0)				
19	C14	= IRR(B4:B9,0.5)				

Figure 10-3 The use of spreadsheet financial functions

10.6 Dependent and mutually exclusive projects

So far, we have assumed that the cash flow of a given project is not affected by whether any other projects are also implemented. If this is the case, the project in question is economically independent. An accept-or-reject decision can be made on its own.

In many instances, the cash flow for a given project is affected by the concurrent or subsequent acceptance of other projects, i.e., several projects together form an interdependent system. For example, one year prior to undertaking the stock control project (see Chapter 6), the LOD was considering the replacement of its main can filling machine with a substantially faster machine. In order to take full advantage of the increased filling speed offered, the carton packing equipment also needed upgrading. The savings in operating costs for the new filling machine therefore depended on whether or not the carton packing equipment was also upgraded and, if so, when. The two projects 'purchase of a new filling machine' and 'upgrading of carton packing equipment' are thus interdependent. It could well be that the purchase of the new filling machine is financially unattractive without upgrading the packing equipment, while undertaking both projects is highly attractive.

The interdependence may even be stronger. Project A may be a prerequisite for project B. For example, a power generating company may evaluate the construction of a hydro-electric power scheme that involves damming a river to create a reservoir. It may also explore the possibility of extending the scheme by adding an agricultural irrigation system. The irrigation scheme assumes the existence of the dam which is part of the hydro-electric project. It can therefore only be evaluated in conjunction with that project, while the hydro-electric project itself can be evaluated independently.

At the other extreme, two or several projects are mutually exclusive — only one of them can be accepted. For instance, there may be several filling machines that would have the required hourly filling capacity and would be suitable for the LOD. Each machine may have slightly different characteristics and hence different operating costs. Only one of them will be purchased, if any at all.

It may be helpful to think of these cases as points along a continuum of relationships, as depicted in Figure 10-4. At one extreme, there is the complete dependency — one project being the prerequisite of another. At the other extreme, the projects are mutually exclusive. To the right of 'prerequisite' we have decreasing degrees of complementarity. To the left of 'mutually exclusive' we have decreasing degrees of substitutability. At the centre, we have independence.

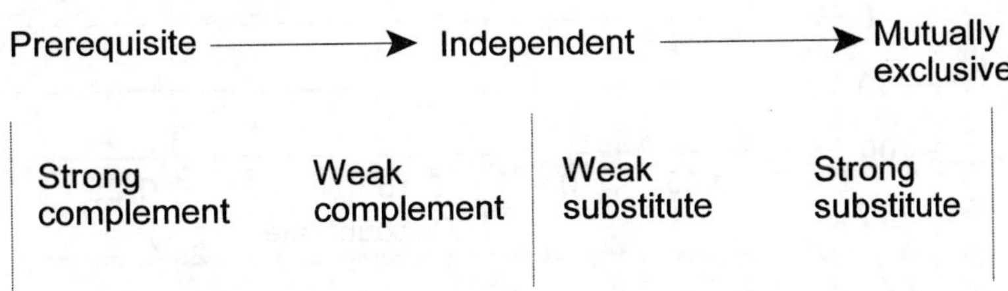

Figure 10-4 Range of interdependence of projects

Mutually exclusive projects may not only differ in terms of the initial investment, but also in terms of their productive lives. To make the right decision, the evaluation has to take these differences correctly into account.

Differing initial investments

Which one of the following two projects should be accepted, if any?

Project	Cash flow year 0	Cash flow year 1	Cash flow year 2	*NPV* for $r = 0.2$
A	£–2,000	£1,440	£1,512	£250
B	£–3,000	£1,500	£2,952	£300

Both projects have a positive *NPV* and are therefore acceptable. Project B has the higher *NPV*, hence it should be selected. By finding the present value of the difference between inflows and outflows, the *NPV* already takes into account that the two projects have a different initial investment. Both projects recover the initial investment plus more.

Figure 10-5 shows how the *NPV* of projects A and B vary as a function of the discount rate. For discount rates of less than 23.1%, project B has a higher *NPV* than project A. For discount rates of more than 23.1%, this positions is reversed. Therefore, for discount rates of less than 23.1%, project B is preferred, while for discount rates of more than 23.1%, project A is preferred.

However, if a fixed initial sum is available to undertake either project, the return that can be earned on the unused portion of funds must also be included in the analysis.

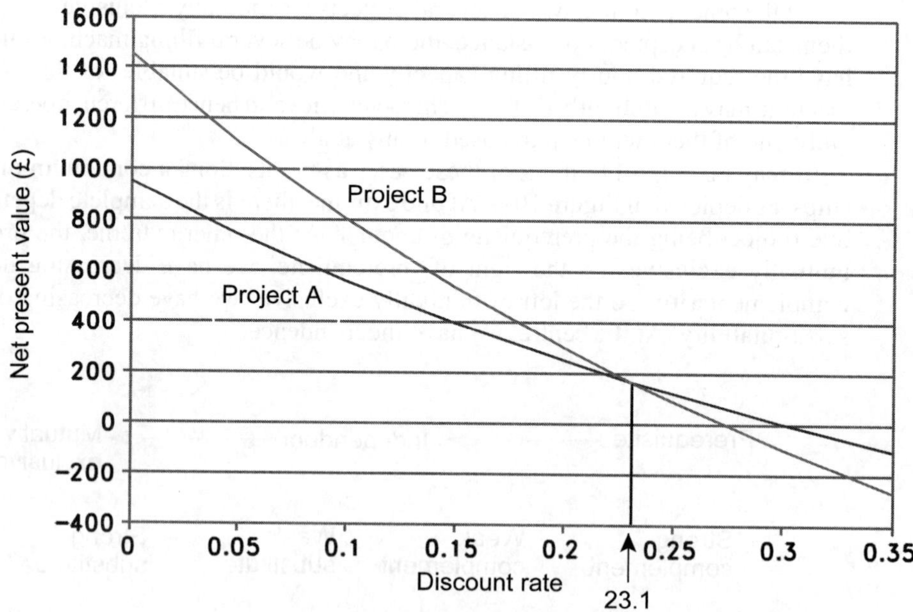

Figure 10-5 Comparing two projects as a function of the discount rate

Assume that £3,000 is available for use. Project A leaves £1,000 for investment elsewhere, such as another project or simply in bonds or a bank savings account. Say, the £1,000 is put into Project C, which offers £1,548 at the end of two years. The additional cash flow is then –£1,000, 0, £1,548. Discounted at the same r of 0.2, its NPV is £75. Hence, the combination of projects A and C yields a combined NPV of £325, or £25 more than project B.

Differing productive lives

Often mutually exclusive projects have different productive lives. For example, a building contractor has the choice between purchasing a utility vehicle or leasing it on a fixed-term contract. The purchased vehicle has a productive life of five years for his kind of usage, while the fixed-term lease runs for four years. The cash flow for each choice is shown in the top portion of Figure 10-6. The buy-option has an initial purchase cost of £44,000 at the beginning of year 1 (= end of year 0), followed by annual operating costs. These increase as the vehicle gets older. At the end of year 5, the vehicle is expected to fetch £14,000. Subtracting the operating cost of £7,700, this results in a net cash inflow of £6,300. Both options involve minor alterations to the vehicle at the beginning of year 1 at a cost of £1,000. The rental cost for years 1 to 4 is £14,000 per year. The operating costs are identical under both options. We also make the strong assumptions that all cash flows occur at the end of each year, except for the initial outlays. Management would like to know which option has the lower cost.

	A	B	C	D	E	F	G
1	**NPV FOR 'BUY' & 'SELL' OPTIONS**						
2	**INPUT:**						
3	Discount rate	0.2					
4	Year	0	1	2	3	4	5
5	Purchase	£44,000					(£14,000)
6	Operating	£1,000	£5,600	£5,800	£6,400	£6,900	£7,700
7	Leasing cost		£14,000	£14,000	£14,000	£14,000	
8	Cash flow for options:						
9	Buy	£45,000	£5,600	£5,800	£6,400	£6,900	(£6,300)
10	Lease	£1,000	£19,600	£19,800	£20,400	£20,900	
11	**EVALUATIONS:**						
12		NPV	Annuity	Equivalent			
13	Project	per cycle	factor	annuity			
14	Buy	£58,194	0.278650	**£16,216**	preferred option		
15	Lease	£52,968	0.321908	£17,051			
16	**Excel formulas for row**						
17		B14 @NPV($B$3,C9:G9)+B9					
18		C14 @PMT($B$3,G4,-1,,1))					
19		D14 @PMT($B$3,G4,-B14,,1)					

Figure 10-6 Mutually exclusive projects with different productive lives

This is a cost minimization problem rather than one of maximizing profit or wealth. How should 'costs' be evaluated? Can we simply compute the *NPV* for each proposal as it stands and then select the one with the lowest *NPV* cost? The *NPV* for each option is listed in the 'Evaluations' portion under '*NPV* per cycle'.

The 'lease' option has a far lower *NPV* over its productive life. However, the 'lease' option terminates after four years, while the 'buy' option goes to the end of year 5. What happens under the 'lease' option in year 5? We cannot ignore that.

Two mutually exclusive options with different productive lives cannot be compared unless adjusted for that difference. There are two main approaches to make them comparable. The first is to assume that each option is renewed several times until both reach the end of the productive life in the same period. The one with the better *NPV* is selected. There is no implication that such repetitions will actually be done in real life. It is only used as a trick to render the two options comparable.

The second approach finds the equivalent annuity for each option and selects the one with the best value — the buy option in this case. This approach is intuitively more appealing, computationally simpler, and extends to several alternative projects.

Activity

- Comparing the 'buy' and 'lease' options, we used an equivalent prepaid annuity. Would the 'buy' option also be the preferred one if we used an equivalent post-paid annuity for comparison? Why?
- 'Lease' payments have to be made monthly. Similarly, fuel costs have to be paid monthly. For the 'buy' option, service and maintenance costs occur at least twice a year. Given the difference in the timing of costs for the two options, a comparison based on an equivalent monthly annuity is more accurate. How do the inputs into the analysis have to be adjusted to accommodate this?

10.7 Replacement decisions

This section considers an application of discounting concepts to an important optimization problem; namely, the optimal time to replace a piece of equipment.

The performance of most machines or vehicles deteriorates with age. Ageing equipment becomes increasingly prone to breakdowns, repairs become more frequent and more substantial, and the quality and volume of its output decreases. As a result, operating and maintenance costs increase, while its potential for profit contributions decreases. Furthermore, its resale or salvage value also decreases, requiring a larger net outlay when it is replaced. Given these trends, it becomes more cost effective or more profitable to replace it with the latest model, even if the old equipment can still do its intended tasks and meet all capacity requirements adequately. This process is constantly going on — just look at the 'pre-loved' car market.

Situation summary of a replacement problem

Quiktrans is a small, regional goods carrier. It currently operates three articulated AZ tractor-trailer units. Two are starting their third year of operation, while one is three years old. Carey Bumps, the owner-manager, has just studied advertising leaflets on the latest AZ model. He is impressed by the reduced operating costs. At first glance, these figures look very favourable compared to the operating costs of his oldest unit. Should he upgrade his fleet now or wait another two years?

Following the recommendations of the long-haul carrier association, Carey has kept careful records of operating and maintenance costs on his units. The mileage run by each unit is very similar. The averages for each type of cost per truck are:

Operating year	1	2	3	approximate timing
Insurance, licence	€8,840	€8,640	€8,440	beginning of year
Maintenance	€11,952	€12,526	€13,048	end of year
Mech. overhauls	0	0	€3,041	beginning of year
Tires	0	€7,962	€8,008	beginning of year
Paint and bodywork	0	0	€11,951	beginning of year
Repairs	0	€2,044	€2,953	end of year
Variable running cost	€1.62	€1.64	€1.67	per kilometre

The initial purchase cost of the existing units was €255,000. He has some information about the expected costs of operations for the three units. In particular, according to his mechanic, each unit will need a new motor every three years. So if the oldest unit is kept on, its motor will have to be replaced right away. This will push up the mechanical overhaul costs for year 4 to €22,000. Similarly, he expects that major body and paint work needs to be done every second year. Naturally, if a unit is sold at the end of a given year, it is put on the market as is, without these jobs being done. He has compiled the table below, outlining these costs, as well as the variable running costs/km. The latter decrease slightly in the year the motor is replaced, but in general accelerate steeply with age.

Predicted costs in	4th	5th	6th	7th	year of operation
Variable running cost (€)	1.64	1.75	1.98	1.85	per kilometre
Repairs	4,000	4,000	8,000	15,000	[all at
Mech. overhauls	22,000	6,000	9,000	28,000	beginning
Paint and bodywork	0	15,000	0	15,000	of year]

The annual pattern for tyre replacement and regular maintenance is expected to continue as during the first three years.

Advertisements in the association's trade journal for second-hand units of a similar type, initial purchase cost of €255,000, and typical annual mileage of between 90,000 and 110,000 kilometres give the following maximum and minimum asking price in thousands of euros:

Age (years)	1	2	3	4	5	6	7
Maximum	210	160	118	94	62	29	20
Minimum	190	140	102	76	38	11	6

The advertised characteristics for the new model AZ unit list the following variable running costs per kilometre:

Operating year	1	2	3	4	5	6	7
Running cost/km (€)	1.40	1.42	1.45	1.43	1.54	1.73	1.65

First-year maintenance costs are predicted at about €10,000. Again, replacement of the motor is expected after about 260,000 to 300,000 kilometres. A replacement motor is tentatively priced at €24,000. This is €6,000 more than for the current models. The new unit is priced at €295,000 ready to roll. The insurance premium is expected to be €6,960, decreasing by €220 each year, while the licence cost remains constant at €2,200, rounded to the nearest €10. Carey's accountant suggests that an appropriate opportunity cost of capital is around 15%. What should Carey Bumps do?

Approach for analysing replacement problems

The old equipment should be replaced as soon as the total relevant cost for operating it for another period, say, one year, is higher than the minimum average cost per period for the new equipment. This leads to a two-step procedure:

- **Step 1:** Find the optimal age at which the new equipment should be replaced, if it is acquired. Associated with this optimal replacement age is a corresponding average cost per period, given by the equivalent annuity.
- **Step 2:** Compare this average cost with the total incremental cost incurred for keeping the current equipment for another period. If that cost is lower than the average cost for the new equipment, retain the old equipment for another period, otherwise replace it.

If the equipment is kept for another period, step 2 is repeated at that time by answering the question: 'Is the incremental cost for operating the old equipment for a further period lower than the minimum average cost for the new equipment?' This process continues until the incremental cost for operating the old equipment for another year becomes greater. At that point, the old equipment is replaced with the new.

The only complicating factor is that the cash flows occur at different points in time. They all have to be converted to a relevant common reference point in time.

Step 1: Finding the optimal replacement policy for the new unit

The manufacturer's advertisement contains estimates of the variable running costs per kilometre, but most other cost information has to be inferred from either the costs incurred or predicted for the current units. It is a fair assumption that many of these costs will be identical or follow a similar pattern. We shall assume that the costs for repairs, tyres, paint and bodywork, and mechanical overhauls for the new unit are the same as for the current units, except that the motor replacement costs at the beginning of years 4 and 7 are €6,000 higher. We shall assume that, starting from a base of €10,000, the annual maintenance costs increase also by about €500 per year. The resale value of the new unit is assumed to follow the pattern of the current model, but adjusted for the higher initial purchase price. For example, the resale value of a one-year-old AZ model truck is set equal to 295/255 times the average of the corresponding maximum and minimum asking price for the old unit, i.e., 0.5 × (€210,000 + €190,000) × 295/255, rounded to the nearest €100, or €231,400.

Finding the optimal replacement policy for the new unit boils down to a comparison of several mutually exclusive options; namely, replacing the AZ unit after every N years, where $N = 1, 2, 3, \ldots$. In fact, we shall assume that Carey Bumps will never contemplate keeping a truck for more than six years, so $N = 6$ is the highest option. These options all cover different productive lives. Using the equivalent annuity approach, the optimal replacement policy is the one with the lowest equivalent annuity.

Figure 10-7 shows the computations for this analysis. As usual, the top portion of the spreadsheet lists all input data. Each cash flow item is assumed to occur at a given point in time, either at the end (end/yr) or at the beginning (beg/yr) of a given year. This is indicated under the column 'timing'. In reality, many cash flow items, in particular the variable running costs, are spread throughout each year. However, accounting for this more accurately would complicate matters somewhat. (We would have to go to continuous discounting — a topic not covered in this text.) We will stick to this simplification, which will only result in small errors. The row for the variable running cost is simply equal to the running cost/km times the annual assumed mileage of 90,000 kilometres.

QUICKTRANS TRUCK REPLACEMENT PROBLEM							
DATA:	New truck cost		€285,000	Kilometres/year			90,000
	Discount rate		0.15	Discount factor			0.869565
				Year of operation			
Cost item	Timing	1	2	3	4	5	6
Running cost/km		€1.40	€1.42	€1.45	€1.43	€1.54	€1.73
Running cost/yr	end/yr	126,000	127,800	130,500	128,700	138,600	155,700
Maintenance	end/yr	10,000	10,500	11,000	11,500	12,000	12,500
Repairs	end/yr		2,000	3,000	4,000	8,000	15,000
Tyres	beg/yr		8,000	8,000	8,000	8,000	8,000
Mech. overhaul	beg/yr			3,000	28,000	6,000	9,000
Paint/body work	beg/yr			12,000		15,000	
Annual licence	beg/yr	2,200	2,200	2,200	2,200	2,200	2,200
Insurance	beg/yr	6,960	6,740	6,520	6,300	6,080	5,860
Cost summary by timing							
Total cost as of	beg/yr	9,160	16,940	31,720	44,500	37,280	25,060
Total cost as of	end/yr	136,000	140,300	144,500	144,200	158,600	183,200
Resale value	end/yr	231,400	173,500	127,300	98,300	57,800	23,100
EVALUATION							
Replace after year		1	2	3	4	5	6
PV cumulative costs		127,421	248,238	367,234	478,941	579,108	670,769
PV resale value		201,217	131,191	83,702	56,203	28,737	9,987
NPV of policy		221,203	412,047	578,532	717,737	845,371	955,783
Equiv. annuity	prepaid	221,203	220,397	220,334	218,607	219,293	219,611

Figure 10-7 Analysis for finding optimal replacement period

The beginning-of-year and end-of-year costs are summed separately. These two rows together with the row of resale values form the input into the *NPV* calculations. Each column in these computations refers to one of the six replacement options considered. The *NPV* for replacing the truck every *N* years is obtained as follows:

NPV(N) = (Initial purchase price for new unit) +
(Cumulative present value of all costs over *N* years) –
(Present value of resale value for a unit *N* years old)

For example, for $N = 2$, the computations are:

NPV(2) =	295,000 +	⟵	Initial purchase price
	127,421 +	⟵	*PV* of year 1 costs
	$16{,}940 \times 0.869565$ +	⟵	*PV* of year 2 beg/yr cost
	$140{,}300 \times 0.869565^2$ –	⟵	*PV* of year 2 end/yr cost
	$173{,}500 \times 0.869565^2$	⟵	*PV* of resale value end year 2

The cumulative present value of all costs over *N* years is recursively computed adding the year *N* present value costs to the *N*–1 cumulative present value costs.

The equivalent annuity is expressed as prepaid. For this particular application, this approach seems to be more natural.

The lowest cost is obtained for $N = 4$. Hence, the optimal policy is to keep the new AZ unit for four years and then replace it with a new one. Naturally, only one decision, namely, the first purchase, would ever be implemented based on this analysis. Any subsequent replacement decisions would be based on a new analysis, using up-to-date relevant information about new models and costs. (More on this in Chapter 11.)

It is somewhat surprising that the equivalent annuity costs for the various options differ by less than €3,000 per year. The cost function is thus fairly flat. This is a valuable insight. The final decision made by Carey may well also reflect other factors not explicitly included in the financial analysis, such as the level of goodwill created by having relatively new trucks and replacing them more frequently than implied by the optimal policy.

The second surprising factor is that the high cost of replacing the motor just one year prior to disposing of the unit does not turn out to be a deterrent for keeping the unit for a fourth year — a counterintuitive result.

Step 2: When to replace the old units

We are now ready for the second step of the analysis; namely, the decision about the timing of replacing the current units. These calculations are shown in the spreadsheet in Figure 10-8. It again lists all inputs in the top portion. The analysis is done for each current unit, one period at a time. For example, for the three-year-old unit, we want to establish if it is financially more attractive to operate it for a fourth year or replace it straight away. If it is replaced, then next year's annual cost is equal to €218,607 — the minimum equivalent annuity for the new truck found in the previous analysis. If the incremental cost of keeping the three-year-old unit for a fourth year is less than that, then it should be kept, otherwise it should be replaced.

Recall that the equivalent annuities shown in Figure 10-7 are expressed as prepaid annuities, rather than post-paid annuities. The incremental cost of keeping the old unit should therefore also refer to the beginning of the year. This cost consists of two elements:

Incremental cost = (Operating cost for another year) +
(Loss of resale value foregone by not selling now)

Since some of these costs are approximated as occurring at the beginning of the year, while others at the end of the year, all cash flows need to be expressed as of the same point in time — in this case as of the beginning of the year. The operating costs are given by the column labelled year '4' in Figure 10-8. A total of €38,240 of these costs occurs at the beginning of the year, while the balance of €165,100 occurs at the end of the year. Discounting the latter by one year and adding the two costs together equals €181,805 — the shaded entry in the intersection of row 'Total cost/year' and column year '4'.

QUICKTRANS REPLACEMENT OF CURRENT TRUCKS						
DATA		Year of operation				
Item	Timing	2	3	4	5	6
Running cost/km			€1.67	€1.64	€1.75	€1.98
Running cost/yr	end/yr		150,300	147,600	157,500	178,200
Maintenance	end/yr		13,000	13,500	14,000	14,500
Repairs	end/yr		3,000	4,000	8,000	15,000
Tyres	beg/yr		8,000	8,000	8,000	8,000
Mech. overhaul	beg/yr		3,000	22,000	6,000	9,000
Paint/bodywork	beg/yr		12,000		15,000	
Annual licence	beg/yr		2,200	2,200	2,200	2,200
Insurance	beg/yr		6,240	6,040	5,840	5,640
Cash flow summary by timing						
Total cost as of	beg/yr		31,440	38,240	37,040	24,840
Total cost as of	end/yr		166,300	165,100	179,500	207,700
Total cost/year	beg/yr		176,049	181,805	193,127	205,449
Resale value	end/yr	150000	110,000	85,000	50,000	20,000
Incremental cost of running truck			230,397	217,892	234,649	238,057

Figure 10-8 When to replace current trucks?

If the unit were sold right away, it would net €110,000 (the resale value at the end of year 3). Sold one year later at the age of 4 years, it will only bring in €85,000. The difference in resale value foregone, expressed in euros as of the beginning of the year, is equal to

Loss in resale value = (Resale value now) – (*PV* of resale value 1 period later)
= €110,000 – €85,000 × 0.869565 = €36,087.

The total incremental cost of keeping the three-year-old unit for a fourth year is €181,805 + €36,087 = €217,892. This is less than the minimum equivalent annuity of €218,607. Hence, the three-year-old truck should be kept for a fourth year.

At the end of its fourth year of operation, this analysis is repeated. Verify that now the total incremental cost for keeping the (then 4-year-old) unit for a fifth year is €234,649. This is more than the minimum equivalent annuity. It follows that the unit should be sold at the end of its fourth year of operations.

Although these calculations should normally be done at the appropriate time with the latest up-to-date cost information, they are here shown for trucks aged 2 to 5. Note the counterintuitive conclusion that the two-year-old units should be sold right away, while the three-year-old unit should be kept running for a fourth year. This seems to be the result of two factors: (1) the higher running costs in year 3 compared with year 4, and (2) the considerably greater loss in resale value suffered by a two-year old truck compared with a three-year old one.

In conclusion, we stress again that this analysis only considers the financial side of things. The decision maker may need to take other factors into account, such as company image, safety, or quality, before reaching a final decision. This may lead to a choice different from the one recommended by financial analysis alone. However, the decision maker will know exactly what the financial implications of this choice are.

Case study 10-1: Kiwi Wines

Kiwi Wines (KW) produces top-class wines. In contrast to most New Zealand wines, some of KW's wines are best aged for several years to bring out their full flavour and rich bouquet. Sue Keller, KW's owner-manager, wonders whether the firm should do the ageing of its wines itself or let its customers take responsibility for that aspect.

In the past, most wines were sold within one year of harvesting the grapes. This is between three and four months after bottling. Such wine is referred to as 'new wine'. However, Sue realizes that a substantial portion of those wines is drunk by the customers without being aged. Ageing the wines properly is bound to enhance the reputation of KW's wines considerably. This can only be guaranteed if KW does the ageing itself. However, this means that KW would have to build an addition to its bottle warehouse — a fairly expensive proposition, since the warehouse has to be climate controlled to provide the right storing environment. The cost of building the warehouse extension on land owned by KW is estimated at $300,000. It would be able to hold up to 360,000 bottles.

The cost of producing new wine is roughly proportional to the volume produced, since most of the costs incurred are in the value of the grapes used and the labour of picking and processing them. Although all grapes are produced on KW's own vineyards, Sue is of the opinion that any grapes used for wine making by the firm should be valued at the going wine grape market price, although she is not sure whether this argument is in fact correct, since no money changes hands.

Sue figures that once the wine has been bottled, the remaining cost of ageing the wines consists mainly of the interest paid to the bank for the funds invested in the wine, the cost of maintaining the warehouse and running the climate control installation.

The current bottle warehouse is owned by KW. There is no mortgage outstanding on it. The addition to the warehouse would need to be financed by a mortgage. Sue questions whether the warehousing cost should now also include the repayment of the loan and the interest incurred on it.

As the wine ages, its selling price goes up considerably. Therefore, at least some, possibly even all, additional costs might be recovered from the increased revenue generated through ageing. However, from a purely financial point of view, the best age to offer wine for sale is not necessarily the age when its flavour and bouquet are judged to be at their peak — four to five years on. So, before a decision can be made on whether the warehouse should be built, the question of the best age to sell the wines also needs to be settled.

The amount of grapes available each year allows producing more wine than can be stored, except possibly for a one-year ageing interval. (Note that, since wine making is an annual operation, if the wine is stored for two years, only 180,000 bottles of wine can be added to storage each year, given the warehouse capacity of 360,000 bottles. Similarly, storage for three years reduces the quantity that can be added to storage to 120,000, and so on.) Naturally, the whole harvest would be processed. But the plan is to store as many bottles as either the harvest or the warehouse capacity permits. Any excess bottles that cannot be stored would be sold as new wine.

Bottles stored for ageing are kept on racks. Proper ageing requires that they are turned several times per year. Just prior to selling, all wine, fresh or aged, is put into cartons of 12 bottles.

In the past, Sue has not accepted any new project that did not have a rate of return before taxes of at least 18% per year. The following additional data have been collected:

Warehouse addition: Extension to be built on vacant land owned by KW

Total construction cost: $300,000; completion date: three months after start
Expected useful life: 20 years, after which the extension needs major upgrading work and the climate control equipment has to be replaced, its total cost similar to the initial construction cost.
Financed by a 10-year mortgage of $250,000, the balance from internal funds
Interest rate of 12%, paid annually
Annual repayment on principal: $25,000
Additional storage capacity: 360,000 bottles
Climate control running cost: $32,000/year (independent of amount stored)
Fixed maintenance cost: $10,000/year
Building insurance: $3,600/year

Wine operation:

Current market price for grapes: $1,800/tonne
Average size of harvest available: 240 tonnes
Each tonne produces 920 litres of wine
Picking cost for grapes: $250/tonne
Cost of processing grapes, incl. fermentation and initial storage: $850/tonne
Bottling cost, incl. bottle and label: $0.36/bottle
Each bottle contains 0.7 litre
Ageing cost per year: $0.21/bottle
Cost of packing, incl. case: $1.18/12 bottles

Wine wholesale selling price:

Year sold	Fresh	1	2	3	4	5	6
Price/case ($)	72	86	110	136	148	156	160

Can you help Sue determine her best course of action; i.e., should the warehouse be built? Given that the fresh wine selling price depends on what the competition charges, she is also interested in knowing what the maximum fresh wine selling price can be before the no-ageing option is more attractive than the best ageing option.

Note that, as for the Quicktrans problem, the analysis consists of two phases. The first is to find the best number of years to age the wine if at all. The second is to use the information obtained to assess whether the investment in the warehouse extension is financially attractive.

For this case study, some of its difficulties are to identify which costs are relevant and which can be ignored as neither affecting the optimal time to age the wines nor whether the warehouse addition should be built (see Section 9.3). It also involves making some crucial boundary choices as to which aspects can be excluded as insignificant and which are taken as givens (see Chapter 3).

Furthermore, for the ageing process, practicable assumptions have to be made about what happens at the beginning and at the end of the 20-year period. Say, the optimal age to sell the wines is two years (not necessarily the correct answer!). Then 180,000 bottles of the wine pressed from the zero-year harvest are put into storage at the beginning of the first year, and 180,000 bottles from the first-year harvest are added at the beginning of the second year to fill the warehouse. From then on, at the beginning of each year 180,000 bottles of aged wine are removed for sale and replaced with the same quantity of fresh wine for ageing. At the end of the productive life of the warehouse addition, the ageing process stops. What are suitable assumptions about that?

10.8 Chapter highlights

- For normal commercial ventures with cash flows spread over time, a valid comparison between alternative projects requires that all cash flows be expressed as net present values, i.e., discounted at the target discount rate. The latter reflects the organizations weighted average cost of funds or the desired rate of return on its investments, as well as the degree of risk involved in the project.
- If the *NPV* of a project is positive at that rate of discount, then it is an attractive project from a purely financial point of view. (Naturally, the financial return of a project is not the only financial aspect in the decision of whether or not to undertake it. Other important considerations are the possible adverse effects on the organization's overall cash flow or the ability to raise the necessary funds.)
- Converting an uneven cash flow into an equivalent annuity provides additional insight into the project. The equivalent annuity can be viewed as an average cash flow in each period. It facilitates comparisons between projects, particularly those with different productive lives, such as finding the optimal replacement age.
- Financial evaluation of projects has been made simple by the various built-in financial functions of spreadsheets. (To avoid mistakes, it pays to check the conventions used. They differ between software packages.)
- For public projects, the appropriate choice of discount rate is far from clear, particularly for projects that involve questions of public health or safety, or irreversible environmental consequences. We have to ask ourselves whether there is any ethical or moral justification for discounting in such cases.

Exercises

All computational exercises should be done with the help of a computer spreadsheet.

1. The local town clerk of a seaside resort is considering two possible options for preventing or alleviating further encroachment of the sea on a newly developed housing estate for

holiday houses. The first option is to build a rock wall, reinforced by concrete. It would have an initial cost of €700,000 and would require little maintenance for about 20 years. The property owners would be charged an annual levy, which would bring in €30,000 each year. The second option is to raise the protective sand dunes, plant them with grasses for stabilization, and build wooden crossings for beach access. This would have an initial cost of €100,000. It would require annual maintenance of €20,000. No levy could be raised in this case. The town can borrow funds from the local banks at 10% per year. Use a planning horizon of 20 years for each option.

(a) Find the present value of each option. Which is the preferred option from a purely financial point of view?

(b) Since the annual levy would be paid by each property owner in two equal instalments and the maintenance costs would be occurred in early spring and early autumn in roughly equal amounts, the clerk thinks that annual discounting is not accurate enough. He asks you to compute the present value based on half-yearly discounting.

(c) Find the equivalent annual annuity for each option evaluated under (a).

(d) Assume now that both options essentially have an infinite lifetime. Find their present value under annual discounting. Which one is the better option now?

2. Consider the following two projects (£):

Year	0	1	2	3	4	5
Cash flow project A	–1000	–200	400	500	600	300
Cash flow project B	–500	–700	0	800	200	600

(a) Find the net present value for each for a discount rate of 15%. Which one would you accept, if they are mutually exclusive?

(b) Find the discount rate for which both projects have the same net present value. Discuss the meaning of this rate.

(c) Find the internal rate of return for each project. Using the internal rate of return criterion, which would you accept if the firm wishes to earn at least 15% on its investments?

3. You consider buying a car that has a cash price of £18,000. The dealer also offers you a monthly payment plan which requires an initial down-payment of £3,000 followed by 36 monthly instalments of £525. As it happens, the dealer has offered you £3,000 trade-in for your current car. This would just cover the down-payment. You could also take out a loan from your local savings bank. The bank's current interest rate is 15% per year on a declining balance basis. They would also insist that you repay the loan completely within 3 years. The minimum payment each month would be £400, covering both principal and interest. This would give you considerably more freedom in terms of choosing your payment schedule, as long as you repay the loan within three years. Which is the cheaper option?

4. A Canadian forest owner has just clear-felled 200 hectares of hillside trees and is evaluating which of two reforestation options is the more profitable. Option A calls for planting at a rate of 1600 seedlings per hectare at a cost of $2,000/ha. Thinning is scheduled at age 6 to a density of 800 trees per hectare at a cost of $400/ha. The remaining trees will be pruned at an additional cost of $600/ha. A second pruning is scheduled for age 10 at a cost of $800/ha. All trees will be clear-felled at age 35 at a cost of $3,000/ha. Their quality will make them suitable for saw milling. Hence, the estimated revenue is $64,000/ha. Option B calls for planting at a rate of about 1100 seedlings per hectare at a cost of $1,500/ha. A thinning is scheduled for age 14 at a cost of $2,000/ha. The thinned logs are then suitable for use as round wood and are estimated to fetch $3,600/ha. All remaining trees will be

clear felled at age 27 for use as pulpwood. The clear felling cost is \$2,200/ha. The revenue from the logs is estimated to be \$28,000/ha. Note that all prices are in terms of current dollars (i.e., either there is assumed to be no inflation, or future dollars have been adjusted to remove inflation effects). Which option is best if the forest owner wishes to earn a return of 5% on any investment?

(a) Build a spreadsheet for finding the *NPV* of all cash flows associated with each option over its productive life. Which spreadsheet functions do you need to use?

(b) Why can you not determine which option is best on the basis of these two present values? What is the recommended approach for comparing the two options? Do it. Which spreadsheet functions will you use?

5. A firm wants to determine which one of two different machine tools to purchase. The two machines differ in terms of purchase price, annual fixed and variable costs, as well as maximum output capacity. However, the quality of their output is identical. The following data have been prepared:

Model	1	2	
Initial purchase price	£30,000	£60,000	
Variable operating cost/unit	£1.50	£1.45	
Fixed annual operating cost	£18,000	£8,000	
Maximum annual output capacity	100,000	120,000	units
Expected resale value end of year 3	£7,000	£19,000	

Expected sales	year 1	year 2	year 3
amount	£60,000	£90,000	£120,000

Each unit is sold at a price of £2.00. Note that if model 1 is purchased, not all of the demand of year 3 can be met. It is also expected that at the end of year 3, this particular product will become obsolete. It will then be replaced by another product, requiring different machinery. The firm's policy is to accept projects only if they reach a 20% rate of return. Which machine should the firm purchase, if it wants to maximize the net present value of all cash flows?

6. A firm considers buying a new piece of equipment. Its purchase price is £30,000. Its profile for the predicted annual output, predicted operating and maintenance costs, and resale value is as follows:

Year of operation	1	2	3	4	5	6
Annual output	12,000	12,000	11,500	10,800	10,000	9,000
Operating costs	£3,400	£3,600	£3,900	£4,500	£5,400	£6,800
Resale value	£27,000	£24,000	£20,000	£15,000	£9,000	£2,000

Each unit produced brings in a net contribution of £2.50 (= sales price less material and labour costs). The firm works with a rate of return of 20% on its investments.

(a) Assume that all cash flows occur at the end of the year. Develop a spreadsheet for finding the optimal replacement interval. Does it satisfy the firm's criterion of earning at least 20% per year?

(b) For greater accuracy, approximate all continuous cash flows, i.e., the net contribution and the operating costs, by four equal amounts spaced at three-monthly intervals. Adapt your spreadsheet for this change. Does it affect the optimal replacement interval?

7. Management of ABC Printing is considering replacement of its current four-year-old guillotine. It has seen very heavy use. The production supervisor has looked into various possible options for upgrading the firm's cutting capacity. The two options which look the most promising are:

A Overhaul the current machine at a cost of €11,000. The machine would then gain at most another four to five years of productive use before it has to be sold for scrap. The manufacturer of the machine has provided some information on the expected operating cost and resale value of the overhauled machine:

Age of machine	5	6	7	8	9
Operating cost	€6,500	€7,200	€8,500	€10,100	€12,500
Resale value	€22,000	€18,000	€12,000	€6,000	€1,200

B Buy a new machine which has a current price of €35,000. The manufacturer is willing to take the old machine as a trade-in for €13,000 now. The operating cost and predicted resale value for the new machine are as follows:

Year of operation	1	2	3	4	5
Operating cost	€3,500	€3,600	€4,000	€6,000	€8,000
Resale value	€31,000	€26,000	€20,000	€12,000	€3,000

Naturally, if it is decided to overhaul the current machine, it still can be traded in at the resale values listed under option A for a new machine at a later date. The firm's policy is to require a rate of return of 18% on all new investments.

(a) Determine the optimal replacement interval for the new machine of option B.

(b) Should the firm overhaul the current machine and only purchase the new machine at a later date, and if so how much longer should the current machine be kept?

8. It is early 2012. Silicone Plastics Ltd is considering the replacement of one of its current injection moulding machines, purchased at the beginning of 2006 for $164,000. The operating log of that machine shows the following picture:

Year	2006	2007	2008	2009	2010	2011
Down-time hours	192	192	192	212	233	260
Reject rate	1%	1%	1%	1%	1.2%	1.6%
Repair costs	0	0	$146	$290	$590	$1,180
Overhaul costs	0	0	0	$2,867	0	0

Part of the down-time includes the weekly cleaning of the machine, which takes about four hours. It is expected that a major overhaul will be required every four years from the fourth year on, at a cost of around $3,000. The production supervisor also thinks that all other operating characteristics of the machine will continue at the same trend as up to now. Whenever possible, the machine is in use, producing at a rate of 78 kg per hour. The firm works one 40-hour shift per week, 48 weeks per year. The output of good parts (exclusive of rejects) required by the machine is 140,000 kg per year. This is expected to continue for the next few years. Overtime is scheduled as needed to meet this target. The amount of raw materials required is equal to the output produced. The current cost of the raw materials is $3,640/1000 kg. Three people are needed during the operations: a machine operator and two labourers. The latter are in charge of loading the machine and packing the output produced. The operator is paid at $16/hour, while the labourers receive $12/hour. All three are needed for the weekly cleaning of the machine. They also have to be paid during any down-time of the machine due to breakdowns.

The accountant has provided the following breakdown of overheads, all assessed on the direct labour cost: employee fringe benefits 20%, other factory overheads 28% (building maintenance, building depreciation, general lighting and power, salaried production staff), general company overheads 52% (general administrative staff salaries, building maintenance and depreciation, salaries for research and development and marketing, insurance, interest on loan capital). The firm's current average return on capital is 18%. In the past, new investment projects have usually been accepted if their rate of return exceeded this target.

The latest version of this type of machine has an initial cost of $246,000. According to the manufacturer, its reliability should be substantially better than that of older models. In particular, the reject rate should only be about 80% of the current model. Similarly, down-time other than regular weekly cleaning should also be about 50% less. The machine should be overhauled regularly every thee years at a cost of about $4000. No information on other repair costs is available, except that most spare parts seem to be about 30% less expensive for the new machine. Information obtained from a second-hand machine dealer indicates the following pattern of prices, as a function of the age of the machine which has had regular overhauls (in $1000):

Age	1	2	3	4	5	6	7	8
Resale value	$144	$132	$122	$112	$88	$64	$40	$14

(a) Construct a spreadsheet to determine the optimal replacement period for the new machine and find the optimal replacement period. This spreadsheet should show sufficient details of how all costs are computed and manipulated.

(b) Add a section to the spreadsheet for determining when the current machine should be replaced. It is now the beginning of 2012. At the beginning of what year should the current machine be replaced?

9. Discounting is pretty much the norm for commercial decisions. It is also extensively used for many public projects that have mainly pecuniary effects or effects that lend themselves to being easily expressed in monetary terms, such as flood control projects and similar public works. However, for projects that involve environmental, health, or social aspects there is considerable debate whether discounting is appropriate for evaluating their merit. Examples of this sort are: pre-school education, vaccination and other health promoting programmes, projects that involve prevention of loss of life, road-safety campaigns, conservation and environmental projects, recreational facilities for which charging may be difficult or discriminatory, and so on. What are the pros and cons of using discounting in such instances? What alternative criteria may be more suitable for evaluating their merit(s)? It may be interesting to do a limited literature search on this issue. Mishan (1981) may be a good starting point.

Further reading

Mishan, E.J. (1981) *Introduction to Normative Economics*, New York: Oxford University Press. Has a critical discussion on the implications of discounting, particularly with respect to environmental and intergenerational issues.

The mechanics of discounting and financial project evaluation are standard topics of managerial economics texts, such as W.F. Samuelson and S.G. Marks (2012) *Managerial Economics,* 7th edn, International Student Version, New York: Wiley, or any financial analysis or corporate finance text. The latter will also devote extensive coverage into the various theories for setting an appropriate discount rate.

11
Decision making over time

Learning objectives

- Appreciate that for dynamic situations, where decisions have to be made at various future points in time, controllable and uncontrollable inputs will affect the future state of the system.
- Appreciate that initial decisions may affect the range of choices available for future decisions.
- Appreciate that the length of planning horizon chosen for the analysis may affect what is the best set of initial decisions.
- Be able to select an appropriate length of the planning horizon for a cyclic or seasonal phenomenon.
- Be able to use a rolling planning horizon for a recurrent decision problem.
- Find the best procurement policy for time-varying requirements using the Silver-Meal heuristic and know when the planning horizon can be truncated.

Introduction

The type of decision processes we have studied so far were concerned with making a single decision at a given point in time, usually the present. For instance, the Champignons Galore case in Chapter 9 explored whether the cycle length should be shortened. In Chapter 10, we considered which one of several mutually exclusive investments should be undertaken. The future, if it is explicitly considered, only enters in so far as it affects the costs and benefits flowing from the decision.

The inventory control problem of the Lubricating Oil Division in Chapter 6 considered a string of decisions; namely, the periodic stock replenishment whenever the inventory for a given product has been depleted. At each decision point, the future in terms of the demand for the product and the incidence of costs, however, remained unchanged. In technical terms, the future is said to be **stationary**. As a consequence, each decision is identical to the first one.

In this chapter, the time element is explicitly incorporated into the decision process in several ways. All problems studied involve making decisions at several points in the future. Furthermore, the state of the system changes over time. Each future decision point may face a different state of the system — the latter being affected by changing inputs from the environment, as well as by prior future decisions. The future is not stationary, but **dynamic**. Hence, consecutive decisions are not identical and independent of each other, but tailored to the state of the system at the decision point.

When the time element enters into the decision process, the first question that must be addressed is 'How long into the future should we look?' The length of time that the model covers is called the **planning horizon**. We already used the concept of a planning horizon in some of the examples and case studies of previous chapters. For example, for investment and replacement problems we included all costs and benefits over the productive life of the investment in the analysis. Hence, the productive life of an investment became the planning horizon. For the stationary situation of the LOD stock control problem, we looked at annual costs. Hence, the planning horizon covered one year. However, the latter choice was arbitrary. The optimal replenishment policy would have been identical, even if the model had used a planning horizon of one month.

For dynamic situations, the choice of the planning horizon becomes more critical. The best sequence of decisions or the **decision policy** derived from the model may be affected by the length of the planning horizon chosen. The analyst is now faced with a new consideration. What is its most appropriate length? Section 11.1 gives some tentative answers to this question. The same theme is taken up again in Sections 11.2 and 11.5. Sections 11.2 and 11.4 study two production planning situations. Each one exhibits distinct features and calls for a different approach for choosing the planning horizon and finding the best sequence of decisions.

11.1 The planning horizon

The planning horizon is the length of time — number of weeks, months, or years — covered by the model. What is its most appropriate length for dynamic models? Before trying to answer this question, it is useful to clarify carefully our aim for modelling dynamic situations.

Aim of modelling dynamic situations

One of the rules of good MS/OR practice is to avoid taking any decision or action that will unnecessarily reduce the scope of future decision choices, as far as this is desirable and practical. In line with this, only those decisions are physically implemented which cannot be postponed any further without affecting costs and benefits unfavourably. No commitment is made on any decisions that only have to be implemented at later points in time. If the future is uncertain, the wisdom of this rule is obvious. The future may turn out to be different than we expected and the decisions not yet implemented may then be far from optimal. By keeping our options open, we will be in a better position to respond effectively to unexpected situations. But even if we pretend that the future is known, following this rule is equally advisable since, in real life, modelling the assumption of a certain future is only a simplifying approximation.

But why may it be necessary to consider future actions if we do not intend to implement them? Because the best initial decision may depend not only on future events, but also on future decision choices available. Only by including these future events and choices in our analysis can we be sure that the initial decision is best.

We are now ready to give a general answer about the most appropriate length of the planning horizon. It goes without saying that the longer the planning horizon, the costlier is the data collection and the more complex are the computations of the optimal policy. Furthermore, the further into the future we look, the higher the degree of uncertainty and the less reliable the information about distant events. For all these reasons, the analyst will want to keep the planning horizon as short as possible. Its minimum length should cover a time interval that includes all those aspects, activities, events, and decision choices in the future which would lead to one initial set of firm decisions being optimal when included and another when ignored.

Putting this into practice is far from simple. As the length of the planning horizon is extended, events and decisions towards the end of the planning horizon will, in general, influence initial decisions less and less. This is particularly true for costs and benefits. Even at a moderate discount rate of 10%, £1 received in 10 years is now worth only 38 pence, while after 20 years its present value now is less than 15 pence.

In a few special instances, the mathematical structure of the model helps the analyst to find a precise minimum interval or specify conditions which, once satisfied, allow the future to be ignored. In most cases, however, the actual choice of the length of the planning horizon is a partially arbitrary compromise between all the factors mentioned and the cost of data collection and computations.

Systematic sensitivity analysis with respect to the time interval covered may help in assessing the effects of future events on the initial set of decisions. This may lead to a better choice for the most suitable length of planning horizon needed for a particular problem situation. But it will also increase the cost and the time incurred for completing the project.

Such additional effort is justified if the project offers substantial benefits because of its size and importance. It is also justified if the model developed is intended for repeated and continued use on a regular basis. In either case, the cost incurred in getting the length of the planning horizon right will be recouped through lower costs or higher benefits in using the model. In most other situations, it pays to be conservative and select a planning horizon on the long rather than short side.

Planning horizons for seasonal processes

For some situations, the nature of the problem may strongly suggest a suitable length for the planning horizon. This is particularly the case for decision problems subject to a seasonal pattern for some of their crucial inputs. For example, a reservoir feeding a power generating plant may go through a natural annual cycle. Spring snow melt and rainfall may tend to fill the reservoir to its full capacity. The water stored is then used for generating electricity either over the following summer period, if the power is used mainly for air conditioning, or over the following winter period, if power is mainly used for heating. In either case, at the end of the 'season' the reservoir is expected to be empty. There is no planned carry-over from one year to the next. A new cycle starts each year. There is a natural break between consecutive annual seasons. A planning horizon of one year, starting with the beginning of the snow melt, is the natural and appropriate choice used by many hydro-electric power companies.

However, there are some very large reservoirs, particularly in Ontario (Canada) and in Sweden, that take several years to fill or empty under normal inflow and usage conditions. Substantial volumes of stored water are carried from one year to the next. Although the water inflow into the reservoir and the water usage may be highly seasonal, the planning horizon needs to be substantially longer, covering several years of operations.

We may still choose to use an annual planning horizon, even if there is a significant carry-over from one cycle to the next. The trick used is to create an artificial break between consecutive cycles. For example, the consumption of soft drinks and beers also has a seasonal pattern, superimposed on a more or less steady base rate. The lowest point of the seasonal cycle is chosen as the starting point of the annual planning horizon. The break between consecutive cycles is created artificially by specifying ending conditions for the state of the system. These then become the beginning conditions for the next planning horizon. Specifying such ending/ beginning conditions reduces or even eliminates the influence of later events on the current set of decisions. The size of finished product inventories, stocks of raw materials, or the work force are excellent choices for the ending and starting conditions between consecutive cycles. Again, good levels for these conditions may be determined through sensitivity analysis.

Rolling planning horizon

For ongoing processes with no natural breaks or end points, **a rolling planning horizon** approach is used. The process used is depicted in Figure 11-1. A planning horizon of T periods, e.g., weeks, months, or years, is used for determining the initial set of optimal decisions. These decisions are then implemented and their effects on the state of the system recorded. One period later, the problem is again analysed based on the updated state of the system. The planning horizon used remains constant at T periods by dropping the period just passed and adding a new period at the end of the previous planning horizon. This process continues indefinitely. After each period, the planning horizon is, so-to-speak, rolled forward by one period, hence the label 'rolling planning horizon'. Sensitivity analysis helps setting a suitable length for T.

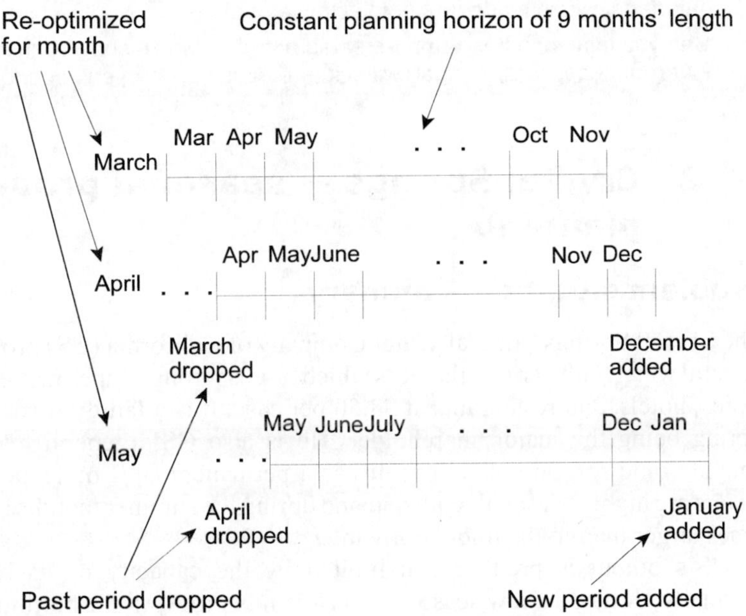

Figure 11-1 Rolling planning horizon of constant length

Effective planning horizon, active planning horizon

Implementation of decisions may not be instantaneous, but may consist of a sequence of activities which take several days, weeks, months, or even years to plan in detail and to execute. Decisions of this sort, scheduled for implementation early on in the planning horizon, may need to be planned prior to the start of the actual planning horizon. Therefore, such a **lead-up time** becomes part of the **effective planning horizon**. Similarly, developing the overall plan may take considerable time. During this interval, no decisions that are part of the plan can normally be implemented. Hence, this development time is also part of the lead-up time.

The effective planning horizon thus consists of two parts. The first part covers the lead-up time. During the lead-up time, firm commitments based on previous decisions will still be implemented as planned, since in most cases they can only be altered with heavy penalties. The second part is the **active planning horizon**, for which decisions can still be made. It is the focus of the planning exercise. The role of the lead-up time is to update the state of the system to the position it will be in at the beginning of the active planning horizon.

Activity

- If the set of future choices is different from the initial set, it seems reasonable that they need to be included in the analysis. But why is it necessary to consider them even if they are the same?
- Discuss the similarities and differences between the concept of a 'sunk cost' and 'future decisions made, but not yet implemented'.
- Can you think of other human-created activities which show regular cyclic behaviour (not necessarily annual) with clear breaks between each period?

11.2 Crystal Springs — seasonal production planning

Problem situation summary

The Crystal Springs Mineral Water Company of California (CS) produces carbonized mineral water with various flavours which it sells through supermarkets, corner grocery stores, hotels, and restaurants at $3.50 per case. It is a family-owned firm, with Sam Spring being the major shareholder. He is also CS's general manager, while his daughter and son do the selling. It has a permanent staff of 18 people. Sales of its waters are highly seasonal, with demand during the summer months being three to four times larger than in the middle of winter.

CS's output is pretty much limited by the capacity of its bottling machine. Normally, during the low season from November to April the bottling operation is run with one shift, staffed by a core of 12 employees, most of whom have been with the company for many years. During the hot season, when sales soar, a second shift is operated by hiring temporary staff who work alongside the permanent staff. Since temporary staff have to undergo training, they have to be hired about two weeks prior to the time the second shift starts producing, with planning, hiring notices, and actual hiring adding another two weeks. Sam Spring estimates that the cost of hiring staff for a second shift, including advertising and interviewing, amounts to about $18,000. Similarly, once the second shift is abandoned, CS again incurs a cost of about $15,000 for laying off all temporary staff.

The bottles are sold in cases of 12. Hence, all accounting and planning is in terms of cases, rather than bottles or volume. The production process is rather simple. Water is captured from a pristine natural spring on the firm's premises. Various minerals and flavourings are dissolved in the water. The water is piped to the carbonising machine and immediately filled into bottles which are sealed and labelled, all in one sequence of operations. The bottles are then put into cases. The cost of all ingredients, packing materials and labels, including power to operate the machines, but excluding any labour costs, comes to $3.10 per case.

There is some temporary storage space for about one week's production right next to the bottling machine. The normal mode of operation is to ship cases to the various stores directly off the production floor without storing them first. This temporary storage is sufficient to absorb the normal daily fluctuations in selling and shipping. However, any excess has to be moved into the cool store warehouse, some 50 metres away. Moving and storing cases incurs a handling and holding cost of about $0.15 per case stored per month. Any cases stored are carefully rotated to avoid storage in excess of two months. Sam Spring reckons that if CS is unable to meet all potential sales, unsatisfied potential customers simply buy another brand. As a consequence, any unmet demand is lost. Sam attempts to meet demand whenever physically possible, since he is afraid that lost sales could mean more than simply $0.40 of profits foregone per case. It could imply losing some customers to the competition for good.

Although total annual sales have increased by about 5% in each of the past four years, the percentages of annual sales falling into each month have shown a remarkably stable seasonal pattern. Their averages are:

Month	1	2	3	4	5	6	7	8	9	10	11	12
Sales percentage	3.5	3.1	4.7	8.0	7.4	10.3	13.8	14.4	14.0	9.9	4.7	6.2

The regular time (RT) shift cost is the same regardless of whether the shift works at full capacity or below. A shift can work up to 25% overtime (OT). OT is paid at a 50% premium above the RT pay. The capacities for a one- and two-shift operation, for RT and for OT, and the associated costs are as follows:

Operating mode	Capacity	Cost
1 shift on RT only	288,000 cases	$24,000/month
OT capacity for one shift	72,000 cases	$125 per 1000 cases
2 shifts on RT only	540,000 cases	$48,000/month
OT capacity for two shifts	125,000 cases	$144 per 1000 cases

OT capacity for a two-shift operation is less than twice the OT capacity for one shift due to reduced work efficiency. All other costs incurred are fixed overheads. They are not affected by the production schedule, and hence may be ignored.

It is now early December. Reviewing sales this year, Sam Spring expects that they will reach about 4,900,000 cases. He wants to develop a tentative aggregate production schedule for the coming year. The intention is not to implement it blindly, but to use it as a guide for the planning of temporary staffing needs, purchasing of various ingredients, scheduling of bottle and case deliveries to the plant, and for developing the vacation roster for the permanent staff. Nevertheless, Sam would like an aggregate production schedule that maximizes profits for the year. In the past, he usually planned for an end-of-December inventory of 50,000 cases of bottled water. He wishes to continue this practice.

(As an exercise, we suggest you draw a rich picture for this problem situation. The issue to be analysed is the development of a production plan that maximizes profits. Next, you should define a relevant system, following the suggestions in Chapters 4 and 5. Armed with these preliminaries, you will be ready to formulate a mathematical model which we can explore using a spreadsheet approach.)

Choice of planning horizon

This is a typical seasonal planning situation. Each calendar year forms a natural planning horizon. For Sam's intended use as an aggregate annual plan, it is sufficient to divide the planning horizon into monthly intervals. This implies that any changes in shift levels or the production rate are assumed to occur at the beginning of each month. When it comes to the implementation of production decisions, Sam will break the planned monthly aggregates into detailed weekly production schedules which he will adjust in the light of the demand and shipment pattern actually observed at that time.

Do we need to include a lead-up time? Changing the number of shifts needs to be initiated at least one month ahead, while changes in the production rate can be implemented with only one or two days' notice. Similarly, it takes only a few hours to develop a new annual production schedule. Therefore, shift changes require the longest lead-up time, adding the month of December to the planning horizon.

However, Sam also knows that, so far, there has never been a need to introduce a second shift prior to April. As a consequence, no lead-up time has to be included for a possible shift change at the beginning of January. With monthly periods, the one or two days needed to institute a change in the production level can be ignored. Also, if Sam is able to predict how many cases will be shipped out prior to the end of December, he can adjust the December output such that he ends up with an inventory of bottled water of approximately 50,000 cases. Hence, we can proceed without a lead-up time in the planning horizon, at least for the December planning exercise.

Influence diagram for production planning problem

Drawing an influence diagram for relationships between inputs, system variables, and outputs will facilitate the formulation of a mathematical model from first principles. Figure 11-2 shows our version of such a diagram.

The inputs into the system are demand predictions, production capacities for the four shift configurations, and revenue and cost factors. The major output of interest is the difference between total revenue and total relevant cost for the entire planning horizon. (This difference is not the net profit since no fixed costs are included!)

For each month, there are two decision variables: the number of shifts operated and the production level. The latter is only feasible if its value is within the production capacity for the shift level chosen, hence the broken lines from the shift level variable and the production capacities. Given the RT production capacity, the two decision variables also indirectly fix the OT output.

Each month is usefully viewed as a subsystem. The subsystems are linked by three state variables; namely, the ending inventory of bottled water and the number of shifts operated in month $t-1$, and the cumulative profit from month 1 to $t-1$. In some sense they are pseudo-outputs of the subsystem for month $t-1$ and become pseudo-inputs into the subsystem for month t. This feature calls for inventiveness in drawing the influence diagram. Rather than duplicate the subsystem relationships for each of the 12 months and connecting the subsystems through these pseudo-output/input linkages, we only show the relationships for one typical month t. The subsystem linkages are indicated symbolically by thick grey lines.

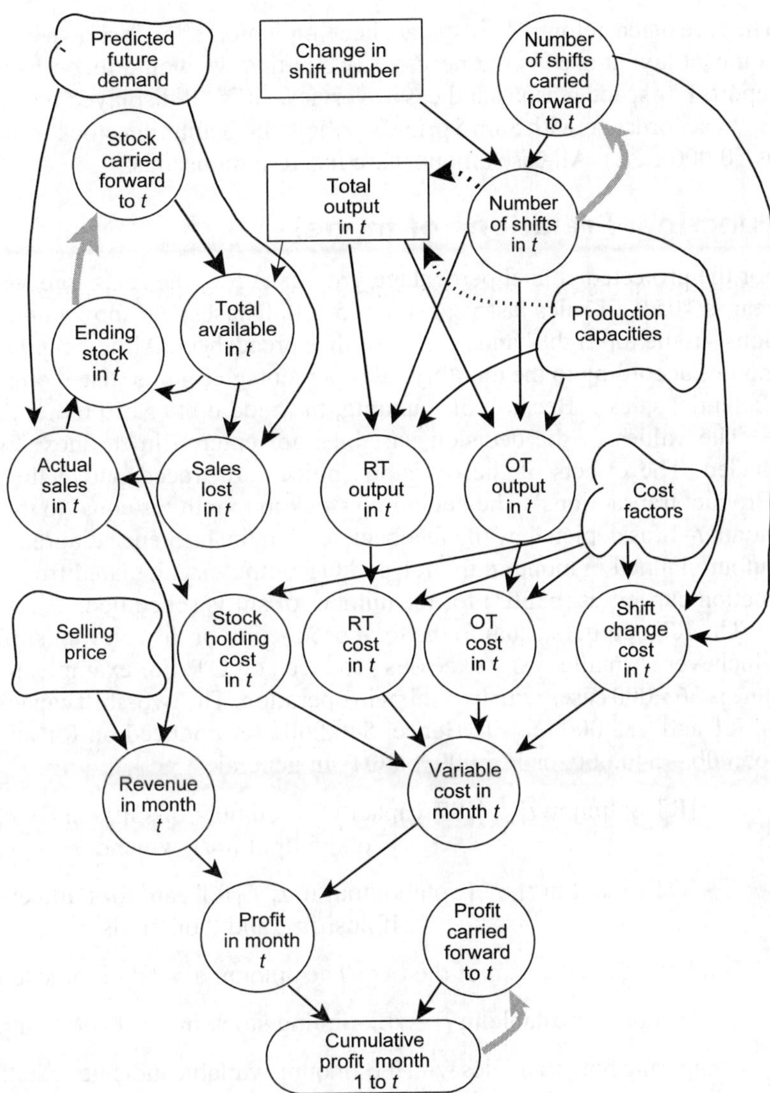

Figure 11-2 Influence diagram for multi-period production planning

11.3 Spreadsheet model for Crystal Springs

Two different general purpose optimizing techniques could be applied to find the optimal production plan for this problem. One is dynamic programming, the other integer programming, covered briefly in Chapter 14. While computer software exists for integer programming, no general purpose code exists for dynamic programming. For the CS case, either would be like using a sledgehammer to crack a nut.

The mathematical relationships for this production planning model are relatively simple. Some have the form of accounting equations. Others require a table look-up.

They are listed below. Their spreadsheet implementation is shown in Figure 11-3. (The compact layout used is not necessarily one that we would recommend for a business report. For space reasons and easy overview, it is all displayed on a single page.)

In accordance with Sam Spring's policy, the beginning stock in January is entered as 50,000 cases. All case amounts are listed in thousands.

Functional relations of model

For the projected annual percentage growth of 5%, the sales forecast for the coming year is 105% of sales last year or 5145 (1000 cases), as shown under 'Sales projections' in the top right-hand section of the spreadsheet. Allocating these sales over 12 months according to the monthly sales percentage figures (listed on p. 303), gives the 'Potential sales'. (Because of rounding, they add up to 5150 rather than 5145.)

The values of the decision variables are entered in the next two rows, shown shaded. The effects of the decision choices are traced out in the section entitled 'Product transactions'. The beginning stock in month t is equal to the ending stock in month t–1 (as depicted by the feedback loop in the influence diagram). Given the total output planned in month t, the RT and OT output is calculated from the table of production capacities (p. 303) for the number of shifts scheduled.

The RT output is equal to the total production or the relevant shift level capacity, whichever is smaller. Any excess is produced on OT. For example, the total output in June is 665,000 cases with two shifts in operation. The two-shift capacities are 540,000 on RT and 125,000 on OT. Hence, 540,000 are produced on RT and the balance of 665,000 – 540,000, or 125,000, on OT. In general

[RT output in t] = {[RT capacity for number of shifts in t], or
[Total output in t], whichever is smaller}

[OT output in t] = {[Total output in t] – [RT cap. for number of shifts in t]
if positive, and 0 otherwise}

Total output is the sum of the two. The amount available for sale in month t is:

[Amount available in t] = [Beginning stock in t] + [Total output in t]

Comparing potential sales with the amount available indicates whether there are any lost sales or any stocks carried forward. Lost sales are subtracted from potential sales to give actual sales. This gives the following expressions:

[Lost sales in t] = {0 if [Potential sales in t] ≤ [Amount available in t], or
[Potential sales in t] – [Amount available in t] otherwise}

[Actual sales in t] = [Potential sales in t] – [Lost sales in t]

[Ending inventory in t] = [Amount available in t] – [Actual sales in t]

We now have all the entries needed for calculating costs, as shown in the bottom portion of the spreadsheet. The material cost is the product of the unit material cost per 1000 cases and the total output. The ending stock is penalized in month t by a stock handling and holding cost:

DATA:	Capacity	Cost/month	Other revenues and costs in $1000:		Sales projections	
On operations:	1000 cases	in $1000	Raw materials/1000 cases	$3.1	Sales last year in 1000 cases	4900
1 shift	288	$24	Holding cost/1000 cases	$0.15	Annual percentage growth	5%
1 shift o/time	72	$9	Shift change cost/up	$18	Sales forecast coming year	5145
2 shifts	540	$48	Shift change cost/down	$15		
2 shifts o/time	125	$18	Revenue/1000 cases	$3.5	Desired ending stock	50

Month:	JAN	FEB	MAR	APR	MAY	JUNE	JULY	AUG	SEP	OCT	NOV	DEC	TOTAL
Sales percent	3.5%	3.1%	4.7%	8.0%	7.4%	10.3%	13.8%	14.4%	14.0%	9.9%	4.7%	6.2%	100%
Potential sales	181	160	242	412	381	530	711	741	721	510	242	319	5150
Total production	131	160	242	412	424	665	665	665	665	510	251	360	5150
Shift level	1	1	1	2	2	2	2	2	2	2	1	1	
Product transactions:													
Beginning stock	50	0	0	0	0	43	178	132	56	0	0	9	
R/T output	131	160	242	412	424	540	540	540	540	510	251	288	4578
O/T output	0	0	0	0	0	125	125	125	125	0	0	72	572
Amt available	181	160	242	412	424	708	843	797	721	510	251	369	
Actual sales	181	160	242	412	381	530	711	741	721	510	242	319	
Ending stock	0	0	0	0	43	178	132	56	0	0	9	50	
Lost sales	0	0	0	0	0	0	0	0	0	0	0	0	
Variable costs/month:													
Materials	$406.1	$496	$750.2	$1277.2	$1314.4	$2061.5	$2061.5	$2061.5	$2061.5	$1581	$778.1	$1116	$15965
R/T shift cost	$24	$24	$24	$48	$48	$48	$48	$48	$48	$48	$24	$24	$456
O/T shift cost	$0	$0	$0	$0	$0	$18	$18	$18	$18	$0	$0	$9	$81
Shift change	$0	$0	$0	$18	$0	$0	$0	$0	$0	$0	$15	$0	$33
Holding cost	$0	$0	$0	$0	$6.45	$26.7	$19.8	$8.4	$0	$0	$1.35	$7.5	$70.2
Total cost	$430.1	$520	$774.2	$1343.2	$1368.9	$2154.2	$2147.3	$2135.9	$2127.5	$1629	$818.45	$1156.5	$16605
Revenue	$633.5	$560	$847	$1442	$1333.5	$1855	$2488.5	$2593.5	$2523.5	$1785	$847	$1116.5	$18025
Total revenue minus total variable cost													$1419.8

Figure 11-3 Crystal Springs production plan — schedule meets demand without shortages

[Holding cost in t] = [Unit stock holding cost][Ending stock in t]

The RT shift cost for one or two shifts is obtained from the production cost table (p. 303). The OT shift cost is proportional to the OT output. For example, for June, the RT output of 540,000 has a production cost of $48,000. The OT production cost for one shift is $144/1000 cases or $18,000 for 125,000 cases. In general

[RT shift cost in t] = [RT shift cost for number of shifts in t]

[OT shift cost in t] = [OT output in t][OT cost/unit for shift level]

The shift change cost is only incurred if the number of shifts in month t is different from month t–1. It is allocated to the month in which the change takes effect. For example, an increase in the shift capacity effective for May means that the additional staff are hired and trained in the second half of April, but all costs are allocated to May. This approximation does not affect the total cost incurred over the entire planning horizon, while simplifying the spreadsheet computations. It is computed as follows:

[Shift change cost in t] = {[shift increase cost] if
[number of shifts used in t] ≥ [number of shifts used in t–1],
or [shift decrease cost] if
[number of shifts used in t] ≤ [number of shifts used in t–1],
and 0 otherwise}

The sum of all these costs is the total variable cost in month t:

[Total cost in t] = [Material cost in t]+ [Holding cost in t] + [RT shift cost in t]
+ [OT shift cost in t] + [Shift change cost in t]

The revenue in month t is equal to actual sales in t times the unit selling price:

[Revenue in t] = [Actual sales in t][Unit selling price]

The profit in month t (without accounting for any fixed costs) is the difference between revenue and the total variable cost in month t:

[Profit in t] = [Revenue in t] – [Variable cost in t]

Finally, the cumulative profit from month 1 to month t is (another feedback loop in the influence diagram):

[Cumulative. profit to t] = [Profit in t] + [Cumulative. profit to t–1]

It took about an hour to develop this spreadsheet.

Finding the best production plan

Having set up a spreadsheet, an obvious approach is to try out various schedules and let the spreadsheet compute the corresponding annual profit. Sam Spring will fully understand and can verify the logic used. In contrast, he would have to accept the output of a sophisticated mathematical optimization technique on faith. He is more likely to trust the results of a spreadsheet that he can play around with himself.

He will try a heuristic modification/improvement strategy (see Chapter 6, p. 160). The initial trial scheduled, shown in Figure 11-3, uses a 'chase strategy'. Production follows sales as closely as possible by setting production equal to sales and adjusting the number of shifts as needed. Since the two-shift capacity with overtime does not cover the high sales from July to September, we backtrack and increase production to its maximum capacity in the months prior to July, until all sales are met. June production increases to 665,000, with 43,000 cases added to the May production. The same sort of adjustment is made for December, including the provision of an ending stock of 50,000 cases. This policy has a total annual profit of $1,419,800.

This schedule does not use the RT production capacity efficiently. For instance, the March output is 242,000. This is 46,000 less than the one-shift RT capacity. Similarly, the two-shift RT capacity for May is underutilized by 116,000. By fully using the RT shift capacity in March and also producing 6,000 cases on overtime, it is possible to delay the start of the second shift by one month. This modification produces a small increase in profits of $6,450. The resulting schedule is shown in Figure 11-4.

Neither of these two schedules allows any lost sales. As a consequence, the amount of stock carried during the months of May to August is quite substantial. That stock is carried to cover sales in the three peak season months of July, August and September, where the maximum production capacity is less than potential sales.

The next modification reduces the amount of stock carried. Hence, some of the demand will not be met, resulting in lost sales. For instance, if production in May is restricted to 381,000 cases — 43,000 fewer than in the second schedule — then no stocks are carried forward from May to June, and the stocks at the end of June, July, and August are also reduced by the same amount. However, potential sales for September cannot be met completely, resulting in lost sales of 43,000. The monthly savings in stock holding costs is $150 for every 1000 cases, or $150(43)(4) = $25,800. The loss in gross profit per 1000 cases is the difference between the sales price and the total material cost, i.e., $3,500 – $3,100 or $400 per 1000 cases. For 43,000 cases this amounts to $17,200, or $8,600 less than the cost savings. Clearly, from a purely profit maximizing point of view this trade-off is advantageous. A similar (somewhat smaller) trade-off can be achieved by carrying no stocks from June to September.

The savings potential does not stop here. The new output for May still requires two shifts and is only 21,000 cases more than the maximum capacity of one shift with overtime. Delaying the introduction of the second shift until June, at the cost of additional lost sales in May, further profits by $21,066 over schedule 2, as shown in Figure 11-5.

Notice the ease with which we can explore such 'what-if?' questions in a spreadsheet. We simply reduce the production levels by successive small amounts first in May, then in June, and finally in July. If total profits increase, we keep these changes. We reverse them if profits decrease. The same heuristic modification strategy by trial-and-error is used to explore possible changes for April and May, and so on.

It may be that Sam Spring is not willing to lose almost 3% of the potential sales (i.e., [5150 – 4997] / 5150 × 100%) for an increase in profits of only $21,066. He may prefer the schedule in Figure 11-4 (however, note that it may be possible to improve upon that schedule without incurring shortages!), or one that lies between the second and the best schedule, allowing some lost sales in September, but none in August.

DATA:	Capacity	Cost/month	Other revenues and costs in $1000:		Sales projections	
On operations:	1000 cases	in $1000	Raw materials/1000 cases	$3.1	Sales last year in 1000 cases	4900
1 shift	288	$24	Holding cost/1000 cases	$0.15	Annual percentage growth	5%
1 shift o/time	72	$9	Shift change cost/up	$18	Sales forecast coming year	5145
2 shifts	540	$48	Shift change cost/down	$15		
2 shifts o/time	125	$18	Revenue/1000 cases	$3.5	Desired ending stock	50

Month:	JAN	FEB	MAR	APR	MAY	JUNE	JULY	AUG	SEP	OCT	NOV	DEC	TOTAL
Sales percent	3.5%	3.1%	4.7%	8.0%	7.4%	10.3%	13.8%	14.4%	14.0%	9.9%	4.7%	6.2%	100%
Potential sales	181	160	242	412	381	530	711	741	721	510	242	319	5150
Total production	131	160	294	360	424	665	665	665	665	510	251	360	5150
Shift level	1	1	1	1	2	2	2	2	2	2	1	1	
Product transactions:													
Beginning stock	50	0	0	52	0	43	178	132	56	0	0	9	
R/T output	131	160	288	288	424	540	540	540	540	510	251	288	4500
O/T output	0	0	6	72	0	125	125	125	125	0	0	72	650
Amt available	181	160	294	412	424	708	843	797	721	510	251	369	
Actual sales	181	160	242	412	381	530	711	741	721	510	242	319	
Ending stock	0	0	52	0	43	178	132	56	0	0	9	50	
Lost sales	0	0	0	0	0	0	0	0	0	0	0	0	
Variable costs/month:													
Materials	$406.1	$496	$911.4	$1116	$1314.4	$2061.5	$2061.5	$2061.5	$2061.5	$1581	$778.1	$1116	$15965
R/T shift cost	$24	$24	$24	$24	$48	$48	$48	$48	$48	$48	$24	$24	$432
O/T shift cost	$0	$0	$0.75	$9	$0	$18	$18	$18	$18	$0	$0	$9	$90.75
Shift change	$0	$0	$0	$0	$18	$0	$0	$0	$0	$0	$15	$0	$33
Holding cost	$0	$0	$7.8	$0	$6.45	$26.7	$19.8	$8.4	$0	$0	$1.35	$7.5	$78
Total cost	$430.1	$520	$943.95	$1149	$1386.9	$2154.2	$2147.3	$2135.9	$2127.5	$1629	$818.45	$1156.5	$16599
Revenue	$633.5	$560	$847	$1442	$1333.5	$1855	$2488.5	$2593.5	$2523.5	$1785	$847	$1116.5	$18025
									Total revenue minus total variable cost				$1426.3

Figure 11-4 Crystal Springs production plan — second shift delayed by one months, no shortages

DATA:	Capacity	Cost/month	Other revenues and costs in $1000:		Sales projections	
On operations:	1000 cases	in $1000	Raw materials/1000 cases	$3.1	Sales last year in 1000 cases	4900
1 shift	288	$24	Holding cost/1000 cases	$0.15	Annual percentage growth	5%
1 shift o/time	72	$9	Shift change cost/up	$18	Sales forecast coming year	5145
2 shifts	540	$48	Shift change cost/down	$15		
2 shifts o/time	125	$18	Revenue/1000 cases	$3.5	Desired ending stock	50

Month:	JAN	FEB	MAR	APR	MAY	JUNE	JULY	AUG	SEP	OCT	NOV	DEC	TOTAL
Sales percent	3.5%	3.1%	4.7%	8.0%	7.4%	10.3%	13.8%	14.4%	14.0%	9.9%	4.7%	6.2%	100%
Potential sales	181	160	242	412	381	530	711	741	721	510	242	319	5150
Total production	131	160	294	360	360	576	665	665	665	510	251	360	4997
Shift level	1	1	1	1	1	2	2	2	2	2	1	1	
Product transactions:													
Beginning stock	50	0	0	52	0	0	46	0	0	0	0	9	
R/T output	131	160	288	288	288	540	540	540	540	510	251	288	4364
O/T output	0	0	6	72	72	36	125	125	125	0	0	72	633
Amt available	181	160	294	412	360	576	711	665	665	510	251	369	
Actual sales	181	160	242	412	381	530	711	741	721	510	242	319	
Ending stock	0	0	52	0	0	46	0	0	0	0	9	50	
Lost sales	0	0	0	0	21	0	0	76	56	0	0	0	153
Variable costs/month:													
Materials	$406.1	$496	$911.4	$1116	$1116	$1785.6	$2061.5	$2061.5	$2061.5	$1581	$778.1	$1116	$15491
R/T shift cost	$24	$24	$24	$24	$24	$48	$48	$48	$48	$48	$24	$24	$408
O/T shift cost	$0	$0	$0.75	$9	$9	$5.18	$18	$18	$18	$0	$0	$9	$86.93
Shift change	$0	$0	$0	$0	$0	$18	$0	$0	$0	$0	$15	$0	$33
Holding cost	$0	$0	$7.8	$0	$0	$6.9	$0	$0	$0	$0	$1.35	$7.5	$23.55
Total cost	$430.1	$520	$943.95	$1149	$1149	$1863.7	$2127.5	$2127.5	$2127.5	$1629	$818.45	$1156.5	$16042
Revenue	$633.5	$560	$847	$1442	$1260	$1855	$2488.5	$2327.5	$2327.5	$1785	$847	$1116.5	$17490
									Total revenue minus total variable cost				$1447.3

Figure 11-5 CS production plan — best schedule, allowing some shortages

Considerations for practical implementation

Seasonal planning horizons have well-defined calendar start and end points. In the case of Crystal Springs, 1 January is the start and 31 December the end of the active annual planning horizon. The initial planning is done using these dates. As time progresses, more recent information about potential sales and stock levels becomes available and Sam will want to have a new look at the production schedule to see if any adjustments to the plan are advisable.

For example, assume that it is early April. Sales have been higher than expected, largely due to unseasonably warm weather. Long-term weather predictions indicate that this is likely to continue well into June. Should the second shift now be introduced in May rather than only in June? Should more stocks for future sales be built up?

To answer these questions, Sam will go back to the spreadsheet, update the sales forecasts from April on, and insert the current stock position at the beginning of April. The starting point of the planning horizon is now 1 April, since it must also include a lead-up time of one month. Should the end point also be extended by another three months? Given the rather definite break in the annual cycle at the end of December, we keep this date as the end point. Hence, for subsequent updates of the production schedule, the planning horizon becomes shorter and shorter. So, rather than talk about an annual planning horizon, it is more accurate the refer to it as a fixed date or fixed end point planning horizon.

Only towards the end of the current cycle, e.g., towards the end of the third quarter, may Sam wish to extend the planning horizon by a full annual season, in preparation for a preliminary mapping out of next year's schedule.

Activity

- Test your understanding by verifying each relationship in the spreadsheet numerically for several consecutive periods. March, April, May, and June cover most situations.
- If no shortages are allowed, can material costs be ignored? Why or why not? Are there other aspects that could be ignored?
- Since Sam uses the schedule to plan shift changes and build-up of stocks, would it be useful to go to shorter periods, say, of one or two weeks' duration? What difficulties does this bring up in terms of forecasting and computations?

11.4 Example of a rolling planning horizon

A rolling planning horizon is suitable when activities are not subject to a pronounced seasonality, but simply fluctuate in a predictable pattern. The following example of production planning in a manufacturing setting is a typical application where a rolling planning horizon approach is highly suitable.

For a particular household appliance, a manufacturer uses an electric motor type AC230/4. These motors are produced in batches of several hundred. Each new production run requires that the motor subassembly line is switched from one type of motor to another. That change-over has a cost of £960. No more than one run is made for any motor during any given week. However, a batch may well produce enough to cover the requirements for several consecutive weeks. Any motors not used in the week in which they are produced are stored for later use. The storage cost for the AC230/4 motor is 26% per year on its unit production cost of £80. This amounts to £0.40 per unit per week. All other costs are not affected by the size and timing of production runs. They are either fixed costs or variable costs that only depend on the total amount produced per year, but not on individual run sizes.

Based on the assembly production plan, the manufacturer can predict the number of motors needed each week, although unforeseen events may result in changes. The production manager would like to determine a production schedule for the AC230/4 motor so as to minimize the total long-run relevant cost.

What would be a suitable length for the active planning horizon? A tentative answer can be obtained from a stationary type analysis. If the requirements for the motor were the same in each week, then we could use the EOQ model (see Section 6.13). The average weekly sales over the next four months are 460. Using the EOQ formula in expression 6-2 (p. 148) for a weekly (rather than annual) model, we express all time-dependent inputs in terms of weekly figures. Hence, $D = 460$, $s = 960$, $r = 0.26/52 = 0.005$, and $v = 80$. The resulting EOQ is 1486, covering 3.23 weeks of average requirements. (Verify that the answer would be identical if all time-dependent inputs had been expressed in annual figures!)

However, in view of the highly fluctuating weekly requirements — 820, 1200, and 750 in weeks 1, 4, and 9, respectively, while only 50 to 100 in weeks 6 to 8, as shown below — the planning horizon should be considerably longer than three to four weeks. We will arbitrarily settle for an active planning horizon of eight weeks.

It takes about one week to prepare a change-over on the motor assembly line. Hence, the lead-up time is one week. This gives a total planning horizon of 9 weeks. Since the first week is the lead-up time where no decision can be made, we will label it week -1. The first rolling planning horizon will cover weeks -1, 1, 2, ... to 8. Its active part covers weeks 1 to 8.

Remember that the intention of this planning exercise is to implement only the first decision in the active part of the 9-week planning horizon. Subsequent decisions can wait. In fact, prior to implementing decisions for later periods, they will be re-evaluated in the light of the updated requirements and costs. The reason why they are included in the first place is simply to make sure that any possible effects they might have on the first decision are properly taken into account. Once the initial decision for week 1 has been implemented, the planning horizon is rolled forward by one week, the active portion covering weeks 2 to 9, and so on.

The following requirements are predicted over a 13-week period:

Week	-1	1	2	3	4	5	6	7	8	9	10	11	12	13
Number	460	820	220	450	1200	360	80	50	100	750	200	0	550	630

The Silver–Meal heuristic for dynamic replenishments

Rather than use an optimizing model, we will use a heuristic solution building strategy (see Chapter 6, p. 160) — the Silver–Meal heuristic [Silver et al., 1998]. Extensive tests have shown that it tends to give close-to-optimal, if not optimal, solutions.

Each replenishment covers the complete requirements for one or several consecutive periods. The Silver–Meal heuristic tries to minimize the average cost per period. The algorithm compares the average cost for successively longer and longer trial intervals. We continue adding additional periods as long as this average decreases. We stop when the average starts to increase. The only costs included are the change-over cost incurred for each replenishment and the holding cost on goods carried forward from the period in which they are produced to later periods.

First replenishment

Table 11-1 shows the calculations for weeks -1 to 8. No decision can be made for week -1. Hence, no cost calculations need to be made. (Its entries are shown in *italics*.) The week -1 requirement of 460 units is met from the stock of 480 carried into the planning horizon, leaving 20 to be carried in to week 1. These are used to meet partially the requirement in week 1. This leaves a net requirement of another 800 units still to be met. Hence, a replenishment has to be scheduled which covers at least this amount.

Table 11-1 Replenishment schedule for weeks -1 to 8

Week	Require-ment	Trial reple-nishment	Increm'l cost	Total cost	Average cost	Best run size	Stock at end of week
-2					*stock carried forward*		*480*
-1	*460*	*no decision to be made*					*20*
1	820	800	£960	£960	£960	1470	670
2	220	1020	£88	£1048	£524		450
3	450	**1470**	£360	£1408	**£469**	**lowest**	0
4	1200	2670	£1440	£2848	£712		
4	1200	1200	£960	£960	£960	1790	590
5	360	1560	£144	£1104	£552		230
6	80	1640	£64	£1168	£389		150
7	50	1690	£60	£1228	£307		100
8	100	**1790**	£160	£1388	**£278**	**lowest**	0

We now work through the algorithm. The first iteration covers a trial replenishment of 800 for week 1 only. Since all units produced are used up in week 1, the only cost incurred is the change-over cost of £960. This is also the total cost as well as the average cost for this first trial replenishment. (Ignore the last two columns in Table 11-1 for the moment.)

For the second iteration, the trial interval covers two weeks, i.e., the trial replenishment in week 1 is extended to include also the week 2 requirements of 220. The size of the trial replenishment is now 800 + 220 = 1020. The costs incurred consist of the change-over cost of £960 plus the incremental cost of carrying 220 units from week 1 to week 2. At £0.40 per unit per week, the holding cost is 220 × £0.40 or £88. The total cost for the two weeks is £960 + 88 = £1048, which averages to £524 per week, as shown in the column 'Average cost'. This is lower than the average cost for the first trial replenishment covering one week only. So, the process continues.

The third iteration covers three weeks. Adding the week 3 requirement of 450, the trial replenishment goes to 1020 + 450 = 1470. The total cost consists of the change-over cost, and the holding cost to cover the requirements for week 2 and 3. But the first two items are simply the total cost for the two-week trial replenishment. The 3-week total cost is found by adding the incremental cost to cover week 3, amounting to 450(£0.40)2, to the already computed 2-week total, i.e., £1048 + £360 = £1408. The average reduces to £469. We continue.

At iteration 4 the trial replenishment increases by 1200 to cover also the week 4 requirement. The incremental cost for week 4 is the cost of holding these 1200 units for 3 weeks from week 1 to week 4, or £1440. The total for a 4-week trial replenishment is £2848, or a weekly average £712. This turns out to be higher than that for the 3-week replenishment trial, so we have found the best week 1 batch size for the first replenishment. It is 1470, covering weeks 1, 2, and 3, as shown by the bold numbers. The last column in Table 11-1 shows the resulting inventory position at the end of each week.

Second replenishment

The process now restarts with finding the best run size for the replenishment to be scheduled in week 4. Verify that the average cost continues to decrease for the remainder of the planning horizon. We now have found the best replenishment schedule over the initial 9-week planning horizon. It consists of a replenishment of 1470 in week 1 to cover the requirements for weeks 1 to 3, and a replenishment of 1790 in week 4 to cover the requirements for weeks 4 to 8. Again, the last column records the resulting end-of-week inventory position.

Planning horizon roll-forward

Assume it is one week later. Week – 1 occurred as planned and a replenishment of 1470 units for week 1 was initiated. Of this first replenishment, 800 motors are still needed for the planned final assembly in week 1. This will leave a stock of 670 to be carried into week 2. The planning horizon is rolled forward by one week. We drop week – 1 and add week 9. The active interval covers weeks 2 to 9.

Due to a rush order, 100 units originally scheduled for week 3 are now already needed in week 2. The new schedule for weeks 2 and 3 is 320 and 350, respectively. No changes in requirements for weeks 4 to 9 are predicted.

Table 11-2 finds the new production schedule covering weeks 2 to 9. As shown in the last column, the planned stock of units carried into week 2 still covers the revised requirements for weeks 2 and 3. It simply confirms the original plan that no replenishment is needed in these two weeks. Although the actual holding costs are different from the original plan, there is no point in computing them, since they are already committed by the original decision.

The calculations for finding the best run size for week 4 are identical to those in Table 11-1. Adding week 9 confirms that the previously found best replenishment size for week 4 remains the same, with a new replenishment scheduled for week 9.

Table 11-2 Replenishment schedule for weeks 1 to 9

Week	Require-ment	Trial reple-nishment	Increm. cost	Total cost	Average cost	Best run size	Stock at end of week
-1					*stock carried forward*		*20*
1	*820*		*amount produced*			*1470*	*670*
2	320	previous decision confirmed					350
3	350	previous decision confirmed					0
4	1200	1200	£960	£960	£960	1790	590
5	360	1560	£144	£1104	£552		230
6	80	1640	£64	£1168	£389		150
7	50	1690	£60	£1228	£307		100
8	100	**1790**	£160	£1388	**£278**	**lowest**	0
9	750	2540	£1500	£2888	£481		
9	750	750	£960	£960	£960	750	0

The point of redoing these calculations was to find out whether the revised requirements caused a change in the planned decision to cover the week 2 requirements from the stock to be carried forward from week 1. Table 11-2 confirms that there is no change. In fact, regardless of any changes in requirements, as long as the planned stock carried forward into week 2 covers its requirement, the same conclusion will hold. Hence, there was actually no need to perform the calculations in Table 11-2. However, if the stock carried forward had been less than the requirement for week 2, a completely new schedule would then have to be developed.

Time now advances to the beginning of week 2. The week 1 activities happen as per the revised plan. The planning horizon is again rolled forward by one week, covering weeks 2 to 10, with week 3 being the first one where a new decision can be made. Some further changes in the final assembly schedule result in the following revised forecasts for the AC230/4 motor requirements:

Week	2	3	4	5	6	7	8	9	10	11	12	13	14
Number	320	210	1200	360	80	50	100	750	200	0	550	630	1050

The planned requirement for week 2 results in a planned stock of 350 to be carried forward to week 3. Does the smaller requirement in week 3 make it necessary to redo the calculations? The answer is 'No' for the following reasons. The smaller week 3 requirement results in a stock of 140 units carried into week 4. As a consequence the replenishment planned for week 4 will change. However, the decision to have no replenishment in week 3 still stands.

Time advances to the beginning of week 3. The planning horizon is again rolled forward by one week, with the first possible decision affecting week 4. Assume that the planned requirements for weeks 3 to 11 remain unchanged. Hence, the planned stock to be carried forward to week 4 is 140. The net requirement for week 4 is reduced from 1200 to 1060. The original schedule provided for a replenishment in week 4. This is still the case, but its size may be different due to the change in net requirements.

A new production schedule has to be developed. This is done in Table 11-3. The new schedule has a run of size 1600 in week 4 and a run of 1100 in week 8. Note that the small change in the week 8 requirement results in the week 4 production no longer covering week 8.

Table 11-3 Replenishment schedule for weeks 3 to 11

Week	Require-ment	Trial reple-nishment	Increm. cost	Total cost	Average cost	Best run size	Stock at end of week
2					*stock carried forward*		*350*
3	*210*	*no decision to be made*					*140*
4	1200	1060	£960	£960	£960	1600	540
5	360	1420	£144	£1104	£552		180
6	80	1500	£64	£1168	£389		100
7	100	**1600**	£120	£1288	**£322**	**lowest**	0
8	630	2330	£1008	£1388	£459		
8	630	630	£960	£960	£960	1100	470
9	220	850	£88	£1048	£524		250
10	200	1050	£160	£1208	£403		50
11	50	**1100**	£60	£1268	**£317**	**lowest**	0

This process of rolling the planning horizon forward one week at a time continues. No action is scheduled until the planned stock carried forward does not cover the requirements in the first period of the new active planning horizon. At that point, a new schedule is developed.

11.5 Minimum length of planning horizon

As briefly mentioned in Section 11.1, in a few special instances, the mathematical structure of the model or the solution method used for solving it may allow the identification a minimum length for the planning horizon or specifying conditions which, when satisfied, allow the planning horizon to be truncated. The astute reader may have already guessed that this is the case for the solution approach to the replenishment scheduling problem of the previous section.

Recall that we are only interested in the 'best' initial decision, i.e., whether or not to schedule a replenishment in the first week of the active planning horizon and, if so, what its best run size should be. For the situation in Table 11-1, the 'best' run size for week 1 is established once the trial replenishment covering the requirements for weeks 1 to 4 has been costed out and found to have a higher average than the trial replenishment covering only weeks 1 to 3. The rest of the analysis for finding the best run size for week 4 did not affect the best run size for week 1. There was, indeed, little point in continuing these computations. Similarly, the computations in Table 11-3 did not need to go beyond week 8. At that point, the best run size for week 4 had been identified as covering the requirements for weeks 4 to 7. Whatever happens after that will not affect this decision.

We see that for this particular production scheduling problem, in those weeks where a replenishment is needed, the solution method used allows us to truncate the active planning horizon as soon as we have found that the average cost per week goes up, while in all other weeks, where the incoming stock is sufficient to cover the requirements of the first active week, the active planning horizon is only one week beyond the lead-up time.

Activity

- Assume that there are no production capacity constraints and that only one batch can be scheduled for a product in any given period. Why is a plan to carry any stock forward into a period in which you also plan to make a new batch always more expensive than increasing the new batch by the same amount, while at the same time decreasing the size of the previous batch?
- If there is a maximum batch size limit, but more than one batch can be made in any given period, is it still more expensive to carry goods into a period in which a batch has to be scheduled? In fact, does the Silver-Meal heuristic still work? Try it out for the AC230/4 motor case and a maximum batch size of 1350.

11.6 Chapter highlights

- The behaviour of many systems is dynamic in the sense that uncontrollable inputs and events do not remain stationary but change over time. Uncontrollable events and decisions choices available in the future may affect what is the best decision now.
- The effect of future decisions and events on present decisions tends to become weaker the further in the future these events and decisions occur. One of the important problems faced by planners is how much of the future to include — how long the planning horizon should be?
- The effective planning horizon is made up of the lead-up time and the active planning horizon. New decisions can only be planned for the latter.
- The minimum length of the planning horizon should be such that any decisions and events occurring beyond the planning horizon will have no significant effect on what are the best decisions for which a firm commitment has to be made at the beginning of the planning horizon. Subsequent decisions will be reviewed later on.
- Regular seasonal cycles may provide a natural break for planning purposes. The planning horizon only needs to cover one cycle.
- For other scheduling problems over time, a rolling planning horizon may be a suitable approach. After each decision point, the planning horizon is shifted forward by one period — the first period (then completed) is dropped and a new period is added at the end, thereby keeping the length fixed.
- The Silver–Meal heuristic finds the 'best' production schedule to meet time-varying demand by minimizing the average cost per period. It allows all periods beyond the point for which that minimum has been achieved to be truncated.

Exercises

1. Consider the Crystal Springs example. Develop a spreadsheet to reproduce the results in Figure 11-3. If you find more elegant ways to handle some aspects, do so. (Note that to get everything on one page, the format is rather cramped. This is not necessarily a model to imitate.)
2. Still with CS, assume now that, as indicated in Section 11.7, it is early April. Sales have been somewhat higher than expected. Actual sales and production for the first three months were as follows:

Month	Jan	Feb	March
Actual sales	179	194	289
% increase over predicted	-1%	+21%	+19%
Actual production	129	206	320

Given the long-range weather forecast for another summer of heat in California, Sam Spring expects that sales are likely to remain at higher levels well into September and only then revert back to the previous level. There is also a problem with the union organizers who have been talking to his regular work force. His workers seem to be unhappy about the way overtime was scheduled in the past. If any overtime is scheduled, they want it to be for a minimum of at least 1 hour per day (the current maximum is 2 hours per day). In other words, overtime for producing between 36,000 and 72,000 cases for a one-shift operation and between 62,500 and 125,000 cases for a two-shift operation should be scheduled. He also expects that, due to having to offer higher moving allowances, the cost of adding a second shift would increase to $24,000. Similarly, due to increases in interest rates, the implied cost of holding stock has increased to $180 per 1000 cases per month. Sam has also been experimenting with the processing speed of his filling machine. He is pretty certain that he can increase the filling speed by 5% without affecting the safety or accuracy of the machine operation. He plans to implement this starting April. Finally, Sam has been advised by his raw material suppliers that, due to inflation, prices will increase in July, adding another 14 cents to the cost of producing a case. As a consequence of all these potential cost increases, he plans to raise the selling price per case to $4, effective from June. Given all these changes, Sam wants to develop a new production/shift schedule for the rest of the year. Use the spreadsheet of Exercise 1, making the necessary changes in input data to explore various possible schedules, trying to identify the highest profit solution.

3. A highway construction company rents specialized earth-moving equipment from a leasing company as needed during the various phases of a job. Such equipment has to be rented for one or more full weeks, even if it might only be required for part of the week. For a particular piece of equipment, the rental cost per week is £2000. Each time a unit is rented, there is a preparation and transport charge of £1200 by the leasing company. Each time a unit is returned, there is a service, cleaning, and transport cost of £1500. As an alternative to renting, the company can farm out some or all work during any given week to a local contractor at a cost of £1000 per unit short per working day. The weekly workload, shown in unit-days, i.e., the number of days' work that needs to be done during each week with this equipment, is as follows:

Week	1	2	3	4	5	6	7	8	9	10
Unit-days	6	10	8	14	7	15	0	4	5	7

Assume that each week has 5 workdays. Hence, a requirement of 8, for example, implies there is a need for one full unit and another unit for 3 days. But recall that rental charges cover full weeks only. At the beginning of the planning horizon, the company has one rental unit on hand. It can return it or keep it. There is no need for any units after week 10. Hence, all units rented at that time are returned. Develop a spreadsheet and try to find the optimal renting schedule by trial and error.

4. (Lengthy) Study exercise 9 of Chapter 4 carefully. If you have not done a cognitive map for Bill Dodge yet, it may be advisable to do so now. The brief for the consultant is to propose several good shift patterns and suitable rosters for the staff which differ in terms of amount of overtime, total staff size, and total weekly cost. Consider following additional data:

   - Summer schedule of commercial flights: (PAX = estimate of passenger number)

Arrival	Day	Time	PAX	Departure	Day	Time	PAX
1	Mon	00:30	180	1	Mon	07:10	380
2	Mon	16:20	370	2	Mon	09:20	160
3	Mon	18:30	280	3	Mon	18:40	360
4	Mon	23:10	250	4	Mon	20:40	260
5	Tue	09:50	400	5	Tue	07:50	300
6	Tue	14:30	180	6	Tue	11:20	360
7	Tue	19:50	360	7	Tue	21:10	180
8	Tue	20:50	180	8	Tue	22:10	360
9	Wed	00:30	380	9	Wed	07:50	180
10	Wed	15:40	360	10	Wed	09:00	380
11	Wed	23:10	250	11	Wed	18:50	320
12	Thu	01:20	180	12	Thu	07:30	180
13	Thu	15:40	360	13	Thu	09:00	180
14	Thu	20:50	400	14	Thu	19:00	400
15	Fri	00.30	190	15	Fri	06:00	360
16	Fri	16:10	380	16	Fri	07:30	180
17	Fri	17:10	280	17	Fri	18:30	360
18	Fri	22:30	180	18	Fri	20:20	250
19	Fri	23:50	370	19	Sat	06:50	180
20	Sat	00:30	330	20	Sat	07:00	350
21	Sat	05:50	200	21	Sat	07:30	320
22	Sat	14:50	180	22	Sat	08:00	180
23	Sat	16:30	190	23	Sat	18:10	180
24	Sat	20:50	360	24	Sat	18:30	200
25	Sun	00:40	190	25	Sun	06:20	360
26	Sun	15:20	200	26	Sun	07:30	180
27	Sun	18:40	400	27	Sun	17:10	180
28	Sun	23:50	360	28	Sun	19:30	400

   - Processing arriving passengers: It takes one minute to clear a passenger through immigration or passport control (primary processing). The maximum number of booths available is 10. For secondary processing, there is usually one officer for every 60 passengers arriving. In addition to this, one supervisor and one other customs officer staff the observation room which has a bank of TV monitors, one for each remote control camera in the arrival hall. Two others are roaming around in the arrival hall with sniffer dogs, one to check for drugs, the other for fruit (all fruit and vegetables are prohibited goods). Recall also that the officers form a team which assembles 30 minutes prior to the scheduled flight arrival for a briefing and the preparation of the arrival hall.
   - Processing of departing passengers: Regardless of the number of passengers on a departing plane, processing starts 30 minutes prior to the scheduled departure and involves always just two custom officers. If several flights depart less than 30 minutes

apart, no additional staff are scheduled. There is no extra time for briefing and preparation needed for departures.

- Deep Freeze mail arrival time schedule and staffing:

Day	Mon	Tue	Wed	Thu	Fri	Fri	Sat	Sun
Time	09:00	09:00	09:00	15:00	09:00	15:00	15:00	9:00
Staffing	4	2	2	2	2	1	4	2

  Assume that it always takes 60 minutes to process the mail.
- CIA freight office schedule: daily 10:00 to 16:00, two staff required.
- Clerical tasks: 64 hours each day Monday to Friday, 32 hours on both Saturday and Sunday. Note that up to 16 hours of a day's load can be shifted to the following day if need be, offering some flexibility for scheduling staff to cover these duties.

The hourly wage, including all fringe benefits, is $40 for customs officers. There are four permanent shift supervisors on the staff that should be able to cover all supervision duties, as well as do additional clerical work that cannot be assigned to customs officers. They are on annual salaries, with overtime compensated by extra leave.

(a) Use the following approach for developing a schedule of shifts: on one-millimetre graph paper block off rectangles corresponding to the number of people required for processing flights. Elapse time is measured along the x-axis, e.g. each one millimetre covering ten minutes, while the number of staff required is shown along the y-axis. Place the staff requirements for all other duties, except for clerical work, on top of the flight staffing requirements. (Clerical work will be added later.) Use different colours for each duty. For each flight arrival, the number of people required has to be computed from the expected number of passengers on that flight, given the government processing standards, up to a maximum of ten for the immigration booths. If several duties occur at the same time, the duties are juxtaposed on top of each other. The resulting graph will look like the skyline of a city.

You superimpose on to this pattern a set of shifts. Draw the shifts in easy-erase pencil. The shifts do not have to start at the same time each day, but it would be highly desirable that each weekday has the same total number of shifts. For instance, you may schedule two types of shifts each day: (1) three shifts of 12 officers, and (2) two shifts of two officers. The 2-officer shifts are used for processing departures. Assigning people to shifts will also be considerably simplified if each type of shift always has the same number of members. A shift should be nine hours long, which includes the paid meal break towards the middle of the shift, as flight processing duties allow. If a shift is relieved during a time when they are processing a flight, there must be a 30-minute overlap between the two shifts involved to allow for a smooth change-over. If two shifts overlap, then for the duration of the overlap, one shift is shown above the other. Arrange the start times of the shifts in such a way that you can meet most of the flights, as well as the other scheduled tasks. Any flights not covered, or only partially covered, by a shift will require the scheduling of overtime.

Once you have a tentative schedule, schedule the clerical duties during the times when there are no scheduled duties, but idle officers. It is a management policy that no overtime should be scheduled to undertake clerical tasks. So, you may have to increase shift sizes, if scheduled duties do not leave enough time free.

The aim is to minimize the amount of overtime scheduled, while at the same time keeping the total number of staff needed to a minimum. Obviously, there is a trade-off between the size of each shift and the amount of overtime. Total weekly overtime should not exceed 20%. Note that overtime has a 50% higher cost than regular time. Develop two or three different shift schedules, differing in their timing and size of the shifts. Compute the total weekly wage cost, including overtime pay for each.

(For the actual project, this approach was programmed in Visual Basic, which allowed the analyst to enter all data directly on the screen, move execution of clerical tasks around on the screen, and then superimpose trial shifts.)

(b) Develop a staff roster that assigns staff to shifts. Contractual arrangements require that, on average, each staff member works four out of six days. The kinds of rostering patterns that work well are cycles such as 'four days on/two days off', or 'five days on/two days off/five days on/three days off'. Such patterns have the effect that each staff member has the same number of weekends off. Indicate how many weeks it will take before a given person or whole shift team starts its cyclic pattern anew on the same day of the week.

5. An appliance manufacturer faces the following weekly requirements (in thousands of units) for a given subassembly, produced by the firm itself:

Week	1	2	3	4	5	6	7	8	9	10
Requirement	17	8	12	4	10	20	15	3	6	9

The cost of setting up a production run for this subassembly amounts to £500, while it costs £2 to store 1000 units from one week to the next, assessed on the ending stock on hand. Using the Silver–Meal heuristic, find the resulting schedule of production runs and stock holdings for the entire ten weeks. (Note that once you find the size of the production run in period 1, you simply start the heuristic anew from the first period not covered by that run.) What is the minimum length of the planning horizon required?

6. Referring back to Exercise 5, assume now that a production run of 25,000 subassemblies was scheduled for week 1. It is now the beginning of week 3. It turns out that, because of a power failure, only 22,000 subassemblies were actually produced. Furthermore, the actual total usage in weeks 1 and 2 amounted to 20,000 subassemblies only. The revised predicted requirements are now as follows (in thousands of units):

Week	3	4	5	6	7	8	9	10	11	12
Requirement	15	10	20	4	15	3	6	9	2	20

Determine a revised production schedule for this subassembly to the end of week 12, using the Silver–Meal heuristic.

Further reading

Silver, E.A., Pyke, D.F. and Peterson, R. (1998) *Inventory Management and Production Planning and Scheduling,* 3rd edn, New York: Wiley. For the Silver–Meal heuristic, see the chapter 'Lot sizing for individual items with time-varying demand'.

PART IV
Hard OR methods

Chapter 6 explored in some detail an 11-step paradigm for hard OR. As depicted in Figure 6-9 (p. 162), the hard OR approach deals with three systems:

- **System S:** the narrow system of interest which defines the interrelationships of the problem and how to judge system performance;
- **System M:** the modelling system that translates the interrelationships of system S and its performance measure(s) into a mathematical model; and
- **System O:** the improvement or optimization system that finds the preferred course of action or the most preferred values for the decision variables in the light of the performance measure(s) of system S.

While Parts I and II dealt mainly with system S, and Part III extended this to include system M and a rudiment of system O, Part IV deals exclusively with Systems M and O. This pursuit will lead us to study a number of MS/OR models and their associated solution and optimization techniques. However, the emphasis is not on the models, tools or techniques themselves. They are simply used as the vehicles to gain new insights into system behaviour and decision making when:

- the decision choices or decision variables are subject to constraints;
- there is uncertainty about the inputs into the system, causing the outcomes of decision choices to become uncertain themselves; and/or
- the performance is not measured by a single objective or goal, but by several, usually conflicting objectives.

So, Part IV is not a traditional introduction to MS/OR techniques and their solution methods. Although interesting and fun at an introductory level, they are often reduced to triviality, devoid of any practical application. Rather than study the intricacies of the techniques and solution methods with toy examples, we demonstrate the concepts and new insights derived from them using real-life practical case studies that we have been involved in or that have been reported in the literature. By necessity, some of them have been trimmed in order to reduce their complexity and render them amenable for inclusion in the limited space of an introductory text book, we hope without robbing them of their original flavour.

In the course of this journey, you will be exposed in Chapter 12 to the ideas of marginal analysis from economics — ideas that, in one form or another, appear in a number of tools and techniques, while Chapters 13 and 14 show how to deal with constraints, including modelling using linear programming, the transportation problem, integer programming, and networks. Chapter 15 deals with the various meanings of uncertainty and the difficulties of capturing uncertainty in general. Chapters 16 to 18 demonstrate a number of modelling approaches incorporating uncertainty, such as queueing and waiting lines, simulation, and decision analysis. Finally, Chapter 19 touches on the difficulties when faced with multiple objectives or goals, and covers one of the simplest methods, i.e., the aggregate value function approach.

Whenever possible, we shall use the power and flexibility of spreadsheets to do the computations. The text uses Excel and its solver capability, but this choice is one of convenience, rather than preference.

The use of spreadsheets implies that the level of mathematics involved remains at a fairly elementary level and does not go beyond high school mathematics and statistics. The emphasis of the exposure is not on the mathematics, but on the concepts and the process of quantitative decision making. The discussion lives on the principle of 'never let the mathematics get in the way of common sense!'

(As has already been the case in previous chapters, the format used for the spreadsheets is not necessarily one that we recommend you should use. While good practice usually has separate sheets for the inputs and the actual computations and the outputs, for reasons of space and easy overview we show all three on the same compact sheet.)

References

General texts

Albright, S. and Winston, W.L. (2012) *Management Science Modeling*, International edn, 4th edn, Cengage Learning EMEA. Contains add-ins for Excel 2010.

Anderson D., Sweeney, D.J., Williams, T.A. and Wisniewski, M. (2013) *Quantitative Approaches to Decision Making,* 12th edn, Cengage Learning EMEA. Introductory level, with CD.

Daellenbach, H.G., George, J. and McNickle, D.C. (1983) *Introduction to O.R. Techniques*, 2nd edn, Boston: Allyn & Bacon. Partially outdated, but contains aspects not covered in other OR texts.

Hillier, F.S., and Lieberman J. (2010) *Introduction to Operations Research*, 9th edn, New York: McGraw-Hill. A classic text, very comprehensive.

Jensen, P.A. and Bard, J.F. (2002) *Operations Research Models and Methods*, Chichester: Wiley.

Encyclopaedias

Cochran, J.J. et al. (2011) *Wiley Encyclopedia of Operations Research and Management Science*, 8 Volume Set (6408 pages), New York: Wiley. (A small fortune)

Daellenbach, H.G. and Flood R.L. (2002) *The Informed Student Guide to Management Science*, London: Thomson. Short, basic descriptions of all major concepts and tools. (Inexpensive)

Gass, S.I. and Harris, C.M. (2000) *Encyclopedia of OR and MS*, Hingham, MA: Kluwer Academic. Authoritative, mathematical treatment of concepts and techniques. (Expensive)

12
Marginal and incremental analysis

Learning objectives

- Appreciate the basic principles of marginal analysis.
- Compute the break-even point for an activity with total variable costs and total revenues that are proportional to the level of activity, and a fixed set-up cost.
- Find the break-even point graphically for an activity with nonlinear total costs and nonlinear total revenue.
- Be able to determine the marqinal cost and/or marqinal revenue for a given level of activity.
- Be able to use the principle of marginal analysis to find the optimal level of activity for well-behaved cost and revenue functions.
- Be able to apply the principle of incremental analysis for discrete variables or decision choices to find the optimal solution for well-behaved cost and revenue functions.

Introduction

Marginal analysis is one of the fundamental tools in economics. It forms the theoretical basis for deriving normative rules for a firm's optimal allocation of scarce resources to the production of goods and services, for selecting the optimal output and activity levels, as well as for product and service pricing decisions.

MS/OR problems often deal with decisions about resource allocation. Furthermore, several MS/OR tools, both simple and sophisticated ones, have borrowed the mode of thinking underlying marginal analysis. In fact, you already have encountered this type of reasoning in the truck replacement problem in Chapter 10. A clear understanding of marginal analysis is essential for MS/OR analysts.

The first two sections study the principle of decreasing marginal returns — one of the universal laws of economic theory — and its implications on the typical shape of total cost, total revenue, and profit functions. Section 12.3 makes a short detour into break-even analysis — a tool commonly used in business and industry. Next, we explore the typically observed relationships between marginal costs and marginal revenues and profits, and derive the basic principle of marginal analysis, which we demonstrate with a simple production example.

The starred (optional) Section 12.6 generalizes the concepts of marginal analysis to the case of continuous variables. It assumes a rudimentary understanding of differential calculus.

The last three sections extend the findings of marginal analysis to incremental analysis, where the decision variables assume integers or discrete values. Its usefulness is demonstrated with a transportation problem for a leading US manufacturer of ketchup which was reported in *Interfaces*, one of the MS/OR journals, readable even by novice MS/OR students.

12.1 The law of decreasing marginal returns

The term 'marginal' has a number of meanings. In everyday language, it usually implies 'just barely acceptable'. In economics, it relates to how a given function f(x) varies in response to an infinitesimally small change in the value of x — a rather different meaning. For example, a wheat farmer applies $x = 100$ kg of fertilizer to a plot of land. This results in an output of f($x = 100$) = 2000 kg of wheat for that plot. If the farmer increases the amount of fertilizer applied by a very small amount, say 0.1 kg, i.e., $x = 100.1$, the wheat output goes up to f($x = 100.1$) = 2000.8 kg, or an increase of 0.8 kg. However, that increase in output may only be valid for a small increase in fertilizer use beyond 100 kg. Increasing the use of fertilizers by another 0.1 to 100.2 kg may only result in an additional 0.78 kg of wheat, and so on. We are thus measuring the change in output for very small changes in inputs. If the change in input is infinitesimally small, the change in output becomes a **rate of change**. In economic theory language, that rate of change is referred to as the **marginal output** at a given level of input.

That rate of change is traditionally expressed in terms of a unit change in input (even if it may only be valid for an infinitesimally small change). In the above example, at an input of 100 kg, we can approximate the marginal output as 8 kg (= 0.8/0.1) per 1 kg of additional input. It reduces to approximately 7.8 kg (= 0.78/0.1) at an input level of 100.1 kg. Note that measuring the change in output for even small increases in inputs may yield more accurate approximations.

'Incremental change', on the other hand, relates to the actual numeric change in an output associated with a given increase of an input from its current level. In our example, an increase in fertilizer use from 100 kg to 101 kg will increase the wheat output from 2000 kg to 2007 kg, or an incremental output of 7 kg. For this example, it is less than the approximation found earlier for the marginal output of 8 kg at an input level of 100 kg.

In this example, the inputs and outputs are continuous variables. They can assume any real value, integer or fractional. If the input can only assume discrete values, integers, such as the number of tellers used by a bank during a given time period, or different models of equipment arranged in increasing output capacity, the marginal output for going to the next discrete value is always an incremental change. (However, for reasons of convenience, we shall use the label 'marginal' when the input x can assume a large number of values, such as all integers from 0 to N, where N is large. The label 'incremental' will be reserved when the input only ranges over very few values.)

Figure 12-1 shows how output changes as a function of input for the wheat production example. The incremental output is measured by the actually achieved increase in output in response to an increase in input from a specified level, e.g., 50 kg for a 10 kg fertilizer increase from 100 to 110 kg. The marginal output, on the other hand, is given by the slope of the total output curve at that level of input. This slope corresponds to the tangent to the curve. For instance, at an input of 100 kg of fertilizer, the slope of the output curve is 8 kg.

Although for many activities the output may vary proportionately to changes in an input over a wide range of operations, for other activities the increase in output may fall

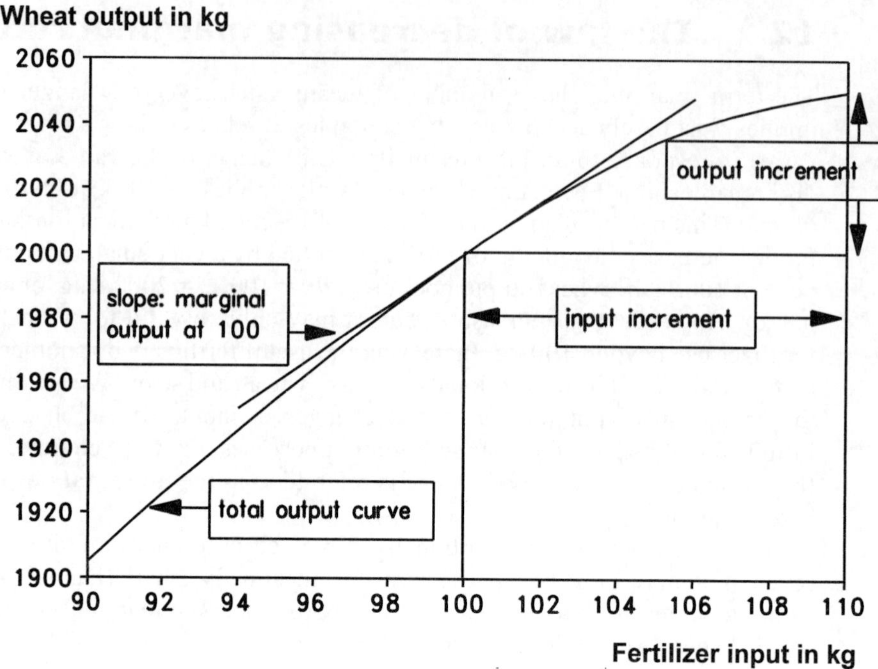

Figure 12-1 Marginal and incremental outputs

off from the very start. In the first case, the graph of the output as a function of the input is a straight line. The marginal output remains constant, or the operation shows **constant returns to scale**. In the second case, it is a curve whose slope becomes less and less steep, as in Figure 12-1, i.e., the operation shows **decreasing returns to scale.**

The law of decreasing marginal returns states that any activity will ultimately become subject to decreasing returns to scale, as a given input is increased while all other inputs remain unchanged.

The reasons for this are manifold. In the wheat production example, the stimulating effect of fertilizers on plant growth falls off. In manufacturing, increase in output may require overtime; it will ultimately cause congestion on the factory floor, create scheduling problems and a rise in errors, all interfering with smooth operations. As a consequence, marginal output falls and marginal costs increase. Similar effects occur in service operations. You will have observed that this is even true in the personal sphere, such as for leisure activities and the consumption of foods. Their appeal drops off.

It is also true for the revenue generated by increased output. After a certain point, increased output can only be sold by price reductions, such as sales promotions and one-off specials to dispose of excess output or stocks. Therefore, even revenue is ultimately subject to the law of decreasing returns.

12.2 Total costs, total revenue, profit

Polycompound — a production example

Polycompound produces silicone rubber for specific customer orders. At Polycompound, silicone rubber production is a two-step process. In step 1, the various ingredients, mostly silicon resins, plasticizer, fillers, stabilizers, pigment, and various other additives, are removed from storage, and mixed in a mixer in batches of 80 kg. During mixing, the blend is heated to temperatures of up to 140° C. The mixed blend is cooled and dumped into the hopper of a compounding extruder that forms silicon rubber granules. These are aircooled and then packed into 40 kg bags, shrink-wrapped and labelled for delivery to customers. Customer orders are always in integer multiples of batches, most in the range of 320 to 640 kg, or the equivalent of 4 to 8 batches. A few large customers place orders of up to 960 kg or 12 batches.

In Table 12-1, columns 2 to 4 list the various costs as a function of the number of batches *Q* in a production run. The set-up cost *F* covers the cost of preparing a new run and the cleaning of both the mixer and the extrusion section after completion of a run. This avoids contamination between runs and prevents any residues left hardening in the machines. The latter would require expensive scraping off and possible damage to the machines. This cost remains the same, regardless of the number of batches in a run.

Table 12-1 Production costs and revenues in £ per run

1 Run size Q	2 Set-up cost *F*	3 Material cost	4 Labour cost	5 Total cost TC(Q)	0 Total revenue TR(Q)	7 Profit	8 Marginal cost MC(Q)	0 Marginal revenue MR(Q)	10 Average cost AC(Q)
1	80	16	54	150	80	–70	150	80	150
2	80	26	94	200	160	–40	50	80	100
3	80	36	114	230	240	10	30	80	76.67
4	80	46	134	260	310	50	30	70	65
5	80	56	154	290	380	90	30	70	58
6	80	66	174	320	450	130	30	70	53.33
7	80	76	194	350	510	160	30	60	50
8	80	86	214	380	570	190	30	60	47.5
9	80	96	254	430	630	**200**	50	60	47.78
10	80	106	334	520	680	160	90	50	52
11	80	116	414	610	730	120	90	50	55.45
12	80	126	494	700	780	80	90	50	58.33

The amount of ingredients used for the first batch is slightly larger than for subsequent batches due to testing and adjusting of machines. All operations need constant supervision by one operator. Preparation of ingredients, testing, and adjustment of the extruder all involve additional labour. This reflects itself in higher costs for the first two batches, as shown in column 4. Up to 8 batches can be processed in a regular 8-hour shift. If a run exceeds 8 batches, it has to be completed on overtime, since stopping extrusion for more than 10 minutes requires a complete clean-down — the same as for a new set-up. Overtime incurs a penalty. If it exceeds an hour, it also requires the presence of a supervisor. This explains the increases in labour cost from the ninth batch on. Column 5 lists the total costs TC(Q).

The firm is only a small industry player and follows the prevailing price structure of the larger manufacturers, competing on quality rather than price. Total revenue TR(Q) is listed in column 6. The additional revenue, as the order size increases, decreases stepwise from £80 for an order of one batch to £50 for the twelfth batch. Finally, column 7 lists profits. Its maximum (marked in bold) is a $Q = 9$. (Ignore columns 8 to 10 for the time being.)

The shape of total costs, total revenue and profit, as a function of Q are depicted in Figure 12-2. Although these numbers are only defined for multiples of full batches, for greater generality we depict the relationships as continuous kinked lines.

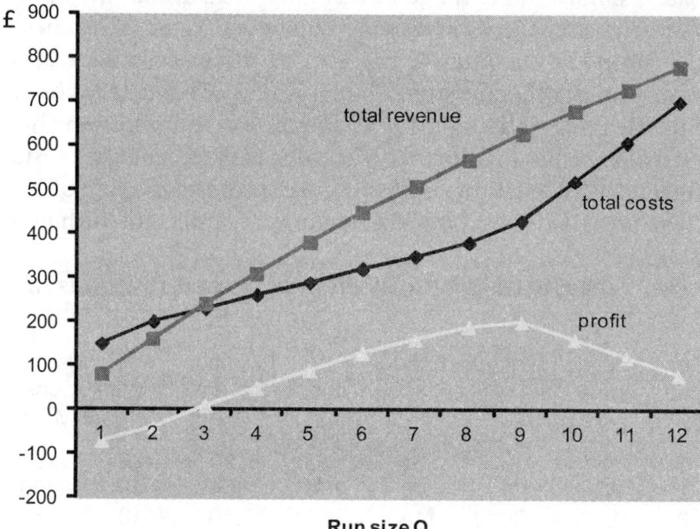

Figure 12-2 Total costs, total revenue, and profits

The shape of these curves is highly typical for most commercial, industrial, and agricultural activities. Total costs exhibit an initial phase of increasing returns to scale — the process becomes more efficient — and then ultimately fall prey to decreasing returns to scale. The result is an elongated S-curve. Total revenue is initial proportional to output, but then reflects decreasing returns to scale.

12.3 Break-even analysis

Observe what happens to profits as the run size increases. For run sizes of one and two batches, the total cost exceeds the total revenue. The firm is in a loss position. Since its pricing policy is dictated by the market, the firm cannot do much about that. At a run size of three batches the firm starts making a profit on the order. If the firm could refuse any orders of less than three without affecting its long-run sales prospects, it should do so.

Managers are often keen to know for what level of output the revenue generated covers the total cost incurred up to that point.

The level of activity or output of an operation at which total revenue recovers all costs is called the break-even point.

At the break-even point, profit is zero or has just become positive. Any output below the break-even point produces a loss, while above that point it generates a profit.

This in an important piece of information for deciding whether or not a venture should be undertaken, particularly when dealing in situations where there is considerable uncertainty about potential future demand for the product or service. If the activity breaks even at a relatively low level compared with potential demand, the manager can be confident that, even if sales fall considerably below expectations, the venture will not suffer a loss. On the other hand, a high break-even point when future sales are highly uncertain calls for caution. The risk involved may be too great.

For an activity measured on a continuous scale, there exists an exact point Q_0 where the activity breaks even. If both the variable cost and the total revenue vary in proportion to the level of activity, the break-even point can easily be determined mathematically. In this case, the total costs are given by

$$TC(Q) = F + VQ$$

where F is the fixed cost, independent of the level of activity, and V is the variable unit production cost. The total revenue function is given by

$$TR(Q) = PQ$$

At the break-even point, the total costs are equal to the total revenue:

$$PQ = F + VQ \qquad (12\text{-}1)$$

Solving expression (12-1) for Q we obtain

$$\text{Break-even point} = Q_0 = \frac{F}{P - V} \qquad (12\text{-}2)$$

Obviously, expression (12-2) only makes sense if the unit revenue exceeds the unit variable cost, i.e., $P > V$, otherwise that product should not be produced at all.

If the output is in discrete units, then there may be no value of Q for which total revenue is exactly equal to total cost. In such instances, the break-even point Q_0 is the first integer value of Q just larger than the ratio $F/(P–V)$.

There is another way of looking at break-even analysis. The denominator of expression (12-2), $(P–V)$, is the difference between the unit revenue and the unit variable cost. This difference is the **contribution** each unit (sold) makes towards covering fixed costs and profits. The larger the contribution that each unit makes towards the recovery of fixed costs, the lower will be the break-even point.

Example: Quiktrans

Remember Quiktrans in Section 10.7 of Chapter 10? Carey Bumps would like to know what the break-even point is for the new AZ truck if he sells the three-year-old unit at the end of its fourth year of operation.

In the first year, the fixed costs for the new AZ unit consist of the annual licence and insurance cost of €9,160, interest cost of 12% on the net investment €210,000 (i.e., cost of AZ truck less resale value of a four-year-old truck of €85,000) equal to €25,200, and that portion of the depreciation of the truck that is attributable to age, rather than mileage, which he estimates as 60% of the loss of €63,600 in resale value (i.e., €295,000 – €231,400) in the first year, or €38,160. These costs total €75,520.

The output of the truck consists of volume-kilometres carried. If we assume an average load for each trip, the output can be measured in terms of kilometres travelled only. The variable cost refers to the cost of the truck travelling for one kilometre (with an average load). This consists of the 'running cost' of €1.40, as specified by the manufacturer, the maintenance and tyre costs, and the mileage dependent depreciation. Using the estimates listed in Figure 10-7 (p. 287), and based on an estimated annual mileage of 90,000 km, the latter two amount to €0.156/km for maintenance and mileage (i.e., €10,000 for maintenance plus half of €8,000 for tyres, the sum divided by 90,000), and €0.283/km for depreciation (i.e., 40% of €63,600 divided by 90,000). All three costs add up to €1.839/km. It is reasonable to assume that this variable cost remains constant over a fairly large mileage range. Hence, the total cost function can be approximated as linear over this range.

Carey's accountant tells him that the revenue per kilometre for an average load amounts to €2.78. Again, this unit revenue can safely be assumed to remain constant over a wide mileage range, resulting in a linear revenue function.

From the assumptions about linearity of both costs and revenues, the contribution per 'unit output' towards fixed costs and profits is also constant and equal to €2.78 minus €1.839, or €1.171/km. Note also that the number of kilometres travelled is a continuous variable. Hence, expression (12-6) can be used:

Break-even point = €75,520 / (€2.78 – 1.839) = 64,492 km

This break-even point would change with the age of the truck as additional fixed costs are incurred and as the variable cost increases with the age and mileage.

A word of caution

The break-even point of expression (12-2) was derived on the assumption that both the revenues and variable costs are proportional to output. This made the mathematics simple, but is also its Achilles' heel. Although revenues are quite often proportional to sales, variable costs may frequently initially exhibit increasing returns to scale, followed by decreasing returns to scale. Expression (12-2) is then no longer valid. This is the case for the Polycompound example.

If sales stretch over a relatively long time period, it may be more insightful to measure the break-even point in terms of the point in time when total revenue recovers all costs incurred up to then, rather than in terms of output. In such instances, a firm may also often use a price skimming policy, i.e., charge high prices when the products or services are offered for the first time and then reduce the price in steps to capture those segments of the market not willing to pay the higher prices. This also violates the proportionality assumption underlying expression (12-2). A graphical approach, i.e., plotting how total costs and total revenue behave over time, will usually find an approximate value for the break-even point.

Nevertheless, break-even analysis remains a useful concept for evaluating the attractiveness and the risk of output decisions for both products and services.

Activity

- The average unit production cost for a run of 6000 units is £5. The variable production cost consists of the cost of raw materials (£2.50/unit) and wages (£1.50/unit). The item sells for £6.50. Was the run of 6000 units fewer than or larger than the break-even point?
- Sales of an item are slower than expected. Lowering the selling price is likely to increase sales and, hence, output. The manager refuses to do this since output has not yet reached the break-even point. Under what conditions may his reasoning be faulty? (Hint: Section 9.2 of Chapter 9 on costs may help.)

12.4 Marginal cost, marginal revenue, and profit

We shall now briefly explore the concepts of marginal cost and marginal revenue, and their relationship to profit.

Marginal costs, average costs

For a discrete activity, the **marginal cost**, denoted by $MC(Q)$, is equal to the difference in total costs $TC(Q)$ for an activity increase from Q–1 to Q:

$$MC(Q) = TC(Q) - TC(Q-1) \tag{12-3}$$

For the Polycompound example, the marginal costs are listed in column 8 of Table 12-1 (p. 329). Note that they decrease initially, become constant for the middle range and then rise again, corresponding to an initial phase of increasing returns to scale, followed by constant returns to scale, and ending with decreasing returns to scale. Its graph is U-shaped or concave.

Column 10 of Table 12-1 lists average costs, $AV(Q)$ = total costs/Q. They too produce a U-shaped graph. Observe the relationship between marginal costs and average costs. As long as the marginal cost for another unit of output is less than the average cost up to the previous output level, the average cost continues to decrease. This is the case up to a run size of $Q = 8$. As soon as the marginal cost becomes larger than the average cost, the latter starts to increase. This happens for a run size of $Q = 9$. Average cost is lowest just prior to that, i.e., for a run size of 8.

You already encountered this process with the Silver–Meal heuristic in Chapter 11. Study how we found the first replenishment in Table 11-1 (p. 314). Increasing the replenishment to cover period 2 demand also, the incremental cost (= marginal cost for adding period 2 demand) was less than the average cost for period 1. Similarly, the marginal cost for adding period 3 demand is less than the average cost for a replenishment covering the first two periods. However, the marginal cost for adding also period 4 demand exceeds the average cost over periods 1 to 3. Hence, we have found the lowest average cost replenishment.

Marginal revenue

The rate of change of total revenue is called the **marginal revenue**, denoted by MR(Q). For a discrete variable, it is given by the difference in total revenue between an output level Q and Q–1:

$$\text{MR}(Q) = \text{TR}(Q) - \text{TR}(Q-1) \tag{12-4}$$

For the Polycompound example, it decreases in several steps from £80 to £50.

Relationship between profit and marginal revenue and marginal cost

In Table 12-1 (p. 329) observe the relationship between these three concepts for the Polycompound example as the run size increases. The second batch incurs a marginal cost of £50, but generates a marginal revenue of £80. As a result the negative profit (= loss) decreases from –£70 by £30 to –£40. The third batch incurs a marginal cost of £30 and generates a marginal revenue of £80. The negative profit becomes a positive profit of £10. The increase in profit is again equal to the difference between marginal revenue and marginal cost at that level. Profits increase as long as the marginal revenue on the next batch added is larger than its marginal cost. Profits decline once marginal revenues becomes smaller than marginal costs.

These observations yield the following principle:

Maximum profit occurs at an output level Q^* where the following condition holds:

$$MR(Q^*) \geq MC(Q^*) \text{ and } MR(Q^*+1) < MC(Q^*+1) \tag{12-5}$$

In the Polycompound example, this happens for $Q^* = 9$.

Marginal analysis: a heuristic algorithm for finding the optimal activity level

We now have to convert this principle into a practical approach — an algorithm for finding the optimal level of activity. In terms of Figure 6-9, it is an optimization system O. We start out with a relatively small trial level of activity Q, such as the break-even point. Next, we increase the level of activity by a small amount, say one unit. The level of activity increases to Q+1. If $MR(Q+1)$ is larger than $MC(Q+1)$, then this increase is worthwhile. We continue this process of increasing the level of activity by 1 as long as the marginal revenue is larger than the marginal cost. We stop when the reverse becomes true, since this would cause the total profit to decrease.

The procedure follows a heuristic modification/improvement strategy (see Chapter 6, p. 160). The algorithm finds the optimal solution that maximizes profits, provided that total cost and total revenue are well-behaved functions, as depicted in Figure 12-2, and the starting point for the algorithm is a level Q for which the marginal cost is less than the marginal revenue, which is the case if a break-even point exists.

Activity

- Try this algorithm out for an alternative *TC*(Q) = 130, 170, 200, 300, 320, 340, 440, 460, 480, 500, 600, 620 for the Polycompound example. What happens?
- What conclusions can you draw from this with respect to the required shape of the total cost function?
- Does this algorithm work when total costs and total revenue are of the form used in expression (12-5) to derive the break-even point? Why or why not?

12.5 Finding the EOQ by marginal analysis

The discussion so far has developed marginal analysis within a production setting. The aim was to find the optimal level of a given activity by comparing marginal revenues with marginal costs. However, the principles of marginal analysis have a much wider scope of application.

For many MS/OR projects, the focus may be only on minimizing costs. No revenues are involved. Altering the level of some activity may increase certain costs, while offering savings in other costs. The savings achieved assume the role of 'revenues'. Marginal analysis then involves trading marginal costs for marginal savings. The following application is of that nature.

The EOQ model (see Section 6.13, p. 148, in particular expression 6-1A) consists of two relevant costs: the annual set-up cost sD/Q and the annual inventory holding cost $0.5Qvr$, where Q is the replenishment size, s the fixed set-up cost per replenishment, D the annual demand, r the holding cost per dollar invested per year, and v the unit product value in stock. We derived the square root formula for the EOQ by calculus. We shall now find the EOQ by marginal analysis. The product used as an example is packed into drums. The replenishment size is therefore a discrete variable; namely, the number of drums produced per run.

As Q increases from its minimum of 1 unit, the average inventory increases, causing additional holding costs. But at the same time, the number of replenishments decreases and saves some set-up costs. Therefore, the change in holding costs becomes the 'marginal cost', and the savings in set-up costs take the role of the 'marginal revenue'. The idea of marginal analysis is to continue increasing Q by small amounts as long as the marginal cost is less than the marginal savings gained. Once this condition reverses, we stop. The value of Q where this occurs is the EOQ.

Table 12-2 summarizes the iterations of the algorithm for an arbitrary starting level of $Q = 20$. Increasing Q from 20 to 21 decreases set-up costs by \$18(4140)/20 – \$18(4140)/21 = \$177.43, while holding costs increase by 0.5(21)(\$320)(0.18) – 0.5(20)(\$320)(0.18) = \$28.80. The 'marginal revenue' is substantially larger than the 'marginal cost'. So we continue increasing Q. Rather than increasing Q to 22, we make initially bigger jumps and backtrack if the last jump turned out to be too large. This will reduce the number of iterations needed and speed up convergence to the optimal solution. Condition (12-5) is next tested for $Q = 30$ and 31. Again, marginal savings exceed marginal cost. We continue in this vein. At $Q = 60$ and 61 marginal savings have become smaller than marginal cost. We now backtrack. The test for $Q = 51$ and

52 shows that, even for that level, marginal savings are smaller than marginal cost. We now have found the two values for Q which satisfy condition (12-5). The optimal Q is therefore 51.

Table 12-2 Marginal analysis for the EOQ model

Data: Product value v = \$320/unit; Annual demand D = 4140; Holding cost penalty r = 0.18/\$/year; Set-up cost s = \$18/set-up

Q	Set-up cost: sD/Q	Holding cost: $½Qrv$	$MR(Q)$	$MC(Q)$	Continue?
20	\$3,726.00	\$576.00			
21	\$3,548.57	\$604.80	\$177.43	\$28.80	yes
30	\$2,484.00	\$864.00			
31	\$2,403.87	\$892.80	\$80.13	\$28.80	yes
40	\$1,863.00	\$1,152.00			
41	\$1,817.56	\$1,180.80	\$45.44	\$28.80	yes
50	\$1,490.40	\$1,440.00			
51	\$1,461.18	\$1,468.80	\$29.22	\$28.80	yes
60	\$1,242.00	\$1,728.00			
61	\$1,221.64	\$1,756.80	\$20.36	\$28.80	no
51	\$1,461.18	\$1,468.80			
52	\$1,433.08	\$1,497.60	\$28.10	\$28.80	no

12.6* Marginal analysis and differential calculus

*This section assumes a rudimentary knowledge of derivatives.

The graph in Figure 12-3 shows typical total revenue $TR(Q)$ and total cost curves $TC(Q)$ in the same quadrant. The vertical difference between the two curves for any level of output Q is the profit $TP(Q) = TR(Q) - TC(Q)$.

Remember that the marginal revenue and marginal cost are given by the slope of the total revenue and total cost curves. In the general case, the slope of a function for any given value of its argument, Q in our case, is given by the tangent of the corresponding curve at Q. But the tangent to a curve is equal to the first derivative of the corresponding function. Putting these two things together, we see that the marginal revenue at any given output level Q' is equal to the first derivative of the total revenue function, evaluated at Q':

$$MR(Q) = dTR(Q)/dQ \text{ evaluated at } Q = Q'$$

By the analogous reasoning, the marginal cost at the output level Q' is equal to the first derivative of the total cost curve evaluated at Q':

$$MC(Q) = dTC(Q)/dQ \text{ evaluated at } Q = Q'$$

For what level of output is the profit maximized? From the graph, we see that the difference between the total revenue curve and the total cost curve is largest at the output level Q^*. At that point, the tangents to the two curves have exactly the same slope, i.e., $dTR(Q)/dQ = dTC(Q)/dQ$, both evaluated at Q^* (expression 12-6):

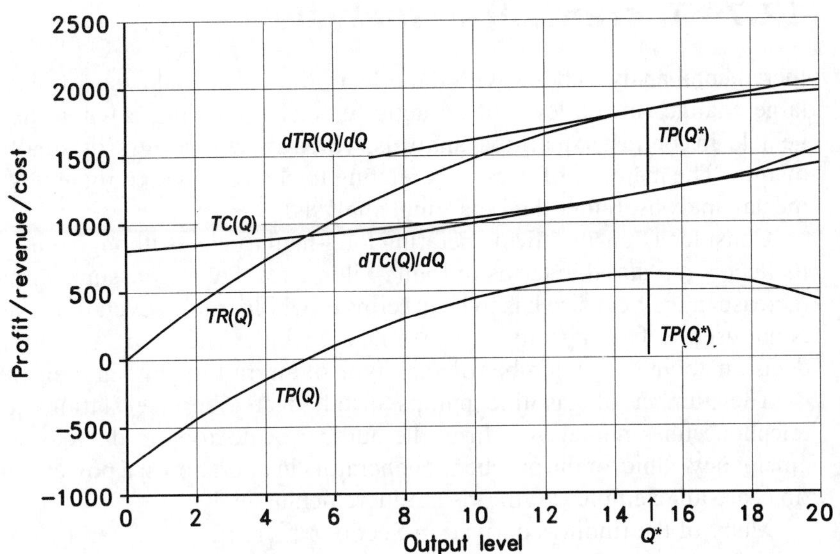

Figure 12-3 Marginal costs and marginal revenues

$$MR(Q^*) = MC(Q^*) \tag{12-6}$$

This is analogous to condition (12-5), except expressed for a continuous variable:

The optimal output level occurs where 'marginal revenue equals marginal cost'.

The stock replenishment example in Table 12-2 will be used to demonstrate this result. Recall again that the 'total revenue' is represented by the savings in annual set-up costs. Hence, $TR(Q)$ is the negative of annual set-up costs, i.e., $-sD/Q$, while the 'total cost' $TC(Q)$ corresponds to the holding cost, i.e., $0.5Qvr$. Taking derivatives of both expressions with respect to Q and setting them equal, we obtain:

$$sD/Q^2 = 0.5vr$$

Solving this expression for Q we obtain, to no surprise, the EOQ formula, expression (6-2).

There is an alternative way to derive condition (12-6), using the total profit function. As we have pointed out in Section 6.13 (p. 148), the value of x where the function $f(x)$ assumes its maximum can be found by setting the first derivative of $f(x)$ equal to zero and solving for x. Let us apply this to the profit function $TP(Q) = TR(Q)–TC(Q)$:

$$dTP(Q)/dQ = d(TR(Q) - TC(Q))/dQ = dTR(Q)/dQ - dTC(Q)/dQ = 0$$

Rearranging this last expression, we arrive again at condition (12-8).

Classical methods of differential calculus offer a simple and convenient optimization system O for determining the maximum or minimum value of a differentiable function.

12.7 Incremental analysis

Incremental analysis deals with the effect on revenue and costs of discrete and often large changes in the level of an activity, such as adding a whole new machine or vehicle, in contrast to marginal analysis, which assumes arbitrarily small changes at the margin. The majority of decisions relating to changes in activity levels call for incremental analysis, rather than marginal analysis.

Consider a transport firm operating long-haul trucks. Although the activity level of its fleet is measured in terms of tonne-kilometres that may assume any real value, an increase in the fleet size has to be in terms of whole trucks, even if the last truck added is not used to full capacity. Airlines face a similar situation, which will affect their decision about of the number of each type of aircraft to have in their fleet.

The number of gasoline pumps installed at a service station, the number of telephone lines rented by a firm, the number of doctors on duty in an accident and emergency clinic, or the number of generators in operation at a power station at a given time, are all examples giving rise to incremental analysis.

Many of the findings derived in Sections 12.1, 12.2, 12.4, and 12.5 were demonstrated based on exploring the effect of small, discrete incremental changes. This avoided having recourse to differential calculus. But the fundamental condition (12-5) also applies without modifications to incremental analysis.

The next example is a somewhat simplified account of a logistic problem faced by Heinz USA, the leading US manufacturer of ketchup. It is adapted from the paper by Kerke et al. (1990), published in *Interfaces*, one of the more readable MS/OR journals.

12.8 Heinz USA — a logistics analysis

Logistics deals with the transportation and distribution of goods. Many successful hard OR applications worldwide involve such issues.

Situation summary

Over 80% of the US tomato crop is grown in California and harvested from early July to mid-October. Part of this crop is immediately processed into various finished tomato products. A large portion, however, is made into tomato paste in factories located close to the growing areas. This paste is later converted into various other finished products at a number of plants throughout the US, with ketchup taking the greatest portion. Sales of finished products are also seasonal, but with a sizable steady demand throughout the year. The production pattern for finished products at the conversion plants tends to follow this seasonal demand, with as little as 600 tons in January and as much as 3700 tons in September.

Assume that this is January 1987. Heinz faces a vast logistics problem of how to transport large quantities of tomato paste from the factories in California to these conversion plants. This transport is by a specialized fleet of railway tankers. These are due to come off lease in early 1988. A team of analysts from finance and all major functional operating areas of Heinz, as well as three academics from Carnegie Mellon

University, is set up to identify and analyse various transport strategy options. Three options stand out:

1. Use a fleet of specialized railway tankers only. This involves a substantial initial investment, but low maintenance costs during the long life of the tankers. On the other hand, Heinz has to pay for the return trip of the empty tankers. Hence, round-trip haulage costs for the tankers are considerably higher than the one-way transport cost for the same volume of goods in regular railway box cars. If the tanker option is chosen, how many are needed?
2. Use giant pouches, similar in concept to the single-portion packets of ketchup available in fast food restaurants, except that these pouches contain 300 gallons of paste (i.e., more than 1 cubic metre). They are called Scholle bags, after the company that commercialized them. They are not reusable — used for one trip only. Only minor investments in filling and unloading equipment are required. Filled Scholle bags can be stored and transported in simple plywood cases which can be reused up to 40 times. Transportation is done in box cars, and hence is about 40% cheaper per gallon of ketchup than transport by tanker. This is, however, more than compensated for by the cost of the bags. No decision on the number of bags needed has to be made. The number is proportional to the volume of tomato paste shipped.
3. A combination of options 1 and 2, with option 1 used for covering the steady transport needs all year round and option 2 used for meeting the excess demand for tomato paste at the conversion plants during the peak periods.

Note that options 1 and 2 are, in fact, simply limiting cases of option 3. In other words, option 3 includes the other two options. Hence, the analysis only needs to consider option 3, since it allows the optimal solution to be either a true combination or options 1 or 2 as limiting cases.

Input data

Rather than look at this problem as a whole, we will demonstrate the approach used by considering the transportation of paste from factory X to conversion plant Y. (Since the report in *Interfaces* does not contain any real data, all cost and demand figures are guesstimates coming from the inexhaustible store of numbers in our brains.)

The spreadsheet in Figure 12-4 summarizes the marginal analysis computations. It has three parts. The top portion lists cost components and other data. The middle part shows the incremental analysis. The months are ranked in descending order of demand. September has the largest demand level of 3700 tons and is ranked 1 (listed in the last monthly column of the sheet); January is lowest with 600 tons and is ranked 12 (first monthly column). The third part breaks down the total cost by mode of transport.

Since the useful life of the tankers is 12 years, an obvious way of analysing this problem is to determine the net present value of all costs incurred over that 12-year planning horizon for all possible numbers of tankers. The best solution is the one that minimizes the *NPV*. We shall, however, take a more insightful approach — marginal analysis.

DATA:	Rail:			Scholle bags:			COST EVALUATIONS:	
		Investment	$80,000 /tanker		Capacity of bag	1.1355 tonnes	Discount rate	0.15
		Useful tanker life	12 years		Cost of bag	$59 /bag	Equivalent annuity/tanker	$14,758
		Tanker capacity	18 tonnes		Plywood case cost	$73 /case	Tanker hauling cost/tonne	$54.00
		Tanker round trip	30 /year		Useful life of case	40 r'trips		
		Hauling cost	$972 /car		Rail hauling cost	$43 /case		
		Total annual volume	24000 tonnes		Return cost	$2 /case	Bag cost/tonne	$93.20

INCREMENTAL ANALYSIS BY DEMAND LEVELS (months ranked by increasing volume)

Months	Jan	Feb	June	July	Dec	May	Nov	March	Aug	Apr	Oct	Sep
Demand level	600	1100	1200	1300	1400	1800	2100	2300	2400	2900	3200	3700
Months at that level	12	11	10	9	8	7	6	5	4	3	2	1
Level increase	600	500	100	100	100	400	300	200	100	500	300	500
Additional volume	7200	5500	1000	900	800	2800	1800	1000	400	1500	600	500
Total volume	7200	12700	13700	14600	15400	18200	20000	21000	21400	22900	23500	24000
No. of tankers needed	13.33	24.44	26.67	28.89	31.11	40.00	46.67	51.11	53.33	64.44	71.11	82.22
No. of tankers used	13	24	26	28	31	40	46	51	53	64	71	82
Additional tankers	13	11	2	2	3	9	6	5	2	11	7	11
Volume by tankers	7020	12480	13400	14240	15360	18200	19820	20975	21340	22840	23490	23990
Volume by Scholle	16980	11520	10600	9760	8640	5800	4180	3025	2660	1160	510	10
Add. volume by tanker	7020	5460	920	840	1120	2840	1620	1155	365	1500	650	500
Marginal tanker cost/t	$81.33	$83.73	$86.08	$89.14	$93.53	$100.77	$108.66	$117.89	$134.87	$162.23	$212.93	$378.68
Marginal bag cost/t	$93.20	$93.20	$93.20	$93.20	$93.20	$93.20	$93.20	$93.20	$93.20	$93.20	$93.20	$93.20

TOTAL COST ANALYSIS (dollars)

by tankers	$0	$570,934	$1,028,112	$1,107,308	$1,182,184	$1,286,938	$1,573,120	$1,749,148	$1,885,308	$1,934,534	$2,177,872	$2,316,278	$2,505,616
by bags	$2,236,800	$1,582,536	$1,073,664	$987,920	$909,632	$805,248	$540,560	$389,576	$281,930	$247,912	$108,112	$47,532	$932
Total cost	$2,236,800	$2,153,470	$2,101,776	$2,095,228	$2,091,816	$2,092,186	$2,113,680	$2,138,724	$2,167,238	$2,182,446	$2,285,984	$2,363,810	$2,506,548

Figure 12-4 Spreadsheet evaluation of Heinz logistics problem

Usage of tankers by demand levels

The total annual volume to be transported is 24,000 tons. A tanker carries 18 tons per trip. For an average of 30 round trips per year, or 2.5/month, one tanker can carry an average of 45 tons per month. If the demand were constant throughout the year at 2000 tons per month, then a total of 2000/45 or about 45 tankers could do the job.

However, to meet the September demand requires 3700/45 = 82.22 or, rounded down, 82 tankers, with 10 tons (= 0.22 × 45 tons) carried by Scholle bags. The next-highest demand month, October with 3200 tons, only requires 71.11 tankers, rounded to 71, with the balance of 10 tons (= 2 months × 5 tons/month) by Scholle bags. If Heinz acquires 82 tankers, 11 are used for only one month of the year and remain idle for the rest of the year. The third-highest demand month, April with 2900 tons, requires 64 tankers. So, another 7 railcars are used only during two months of each year. (Calculate how many will be idle for nine months of the year.) Only 13 tankers are fully used every month of the year. This is depicted graphically in Figure 12-5.

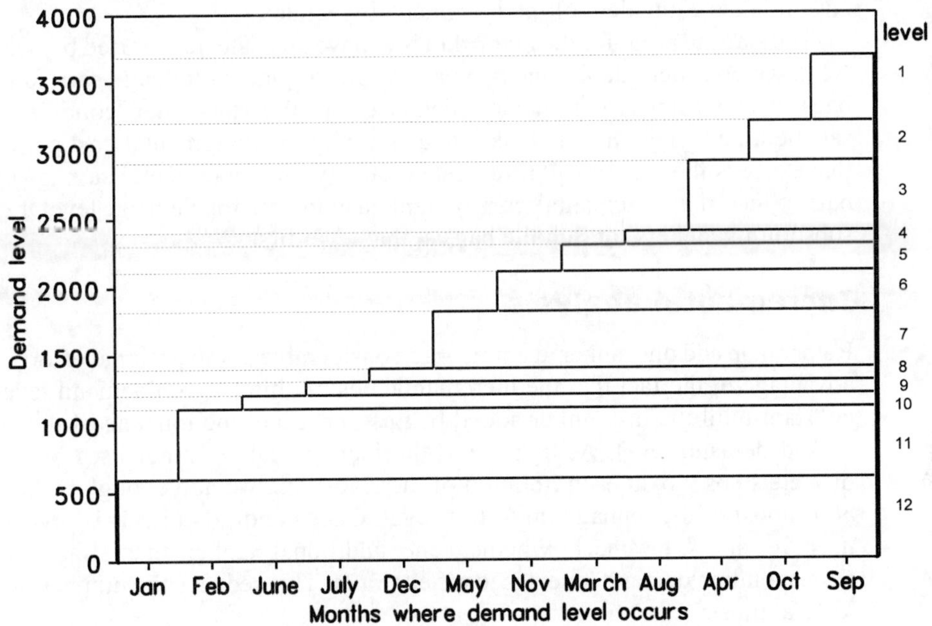

Figure 12-5 Demand pattern for paste by levels

The height of each horizontal band represents a monthly demand level that persist for $n = 12, 11, 10, \ldots, 1$ months during the year. The bottom band measures the lowest demand level 12 of 600, with all other months experiencing a higher demand. If tankers are used for transporting that volume, they are used all year round. Each next higher band requires additional tanker numbers, which are in use during n months and remain idle during $12–n$ months. So n represents also the number of months each set of railcars is used productively if the volume up to that level is transported by rail tankers.

Incremental reasoning — a motivation

If a tanker is in use most of the time, its initial investment can be spread over many tons. The investment cost per ton carried is low. As more tankers are added, they are used for fewer and fewer months of the year. As a result, the associated initial investment is spread over fewer tons and the incremental investment cost per ton carried increases as the demand increases from level 12 to level 1. In contrast, the incremental cost of transporting paste in Scholle bags remains unchanged, regardless of the volume transported in any month, since there is little or no initial investment needed, and all the remaining costs — bags, case, and freight — are constant per ton transported. Therefore, as the amount transported by tanker increases, one incremental cost goes up, while the other, the Scholle bag cost, remains constant.

We now cast this into the framework of incremental analysis, so that we can use the algorithm of Section 12.4 and apply condition (12-5) to find the optimal level of activity — the number of tankers to be bought. The trick is to interpret the incremental cost of transport by Scholle bag as savings — each ton switched to tanker saves that cost. It is the equivalent of the incremental revenue.

The starting point for the algorithm is to have all paste transported by Scholle bags. Next, we consider adding one tanker at a time, replacing tonnage carried by Scholle bags in increasing order of incremental costs. We stop when condition (12-5) is satisfied, i.e., when the last tanker added implies an incremental cost per ton carried that exceeds the 'incremental revenue', namely, the incremental savings by Scholle bags. Since the incremental cost by tanker is lowest for demand level 12, we start substituting tankers for Scholle bags at that level first.

Incremental analysis

Rather than add one tanker at a time — a considerable computational effort — we take advantage of the fact that the incremental cost within a given demand level remains constant until the last tanker added begins to eat into the tonnage of the next lower ranked demand level. At that point, the incremental cost increases by one or two discrete steps. So, at each iteration of the algorithm, we add enough tankers to carry all or most of the tonnage up to this level. Once condition (12-5) is invoked, all we need to do is to check whether one additional tanker that straddles the two corresponding demand levels is justified or not. This reduces the number of iterations to 12 at most.

Activity

- Why is the incremental tanker cost constant within each demand level (except maybe for the first few and the last few tons) and then increases by one or two steps as we eat into the next lower level? (Try out some numbers.)
- Why is the number of iterations needed 12 at most?

Intermediate results of these iterations are shown in the central part of Figure 12-4, under the heading 'Incremental analysis by demand levels'. We will demonstrate some of the calculations. First, we need to determine the annual cost implied by the initial investment of $80,000 for a tanker. This is the major cost incurred by Heinz for the use of the tankers over a 12-year productive life. We want to apportion this cost in equal amounts to each year, such that the *NPV*s of these costs add up to $80,000. This is the same concept we used in Sections 10.6 and 10.7 for comparing policies with different productive lives, namely, the concept of an equivalent annuity. For a discount rate of 15%, the equivalent annuity amounts to $14,758. The other cost incurred for transport by tanker is the tanker hauling cost of $972 per round trip, carrying 18 tons. It is constant at $54 per ton ($972/18). These are the numbers listed under 'cost evaluations' in the top right-hand corner of the spreadsheet in Figure 12-4.

The incremental cost per ton for transport by Scholle bag is based on the sum of the bag cost ($59), the transport cost for full bags in cases ($43), the return freight for the boxes ($2), and a portion of the initial cost for the plywood case. Since that case can be used for about 40 round trips, this is equal to 1/40 of $73. Adding these costs and dividing them by the weight carried per bag (1.1355 tons) results in a constant incremental cost for transport by Scholle bag of $93.20 per ton.

(Note: Forty round trips at about 2.5 trips per month cover 1⅓ years if the case is used all year round. But it could take several years if the case is only used for a few months. A more accurate treatment would express the case cost also in the form of an annuity, as a function of the number of years the case is in use. However, the added accuracy hardly justifies the complexity of these calculations.)

The incremental tanker cost for demand level 12 is then computed as follows. Demand level 12 amounts to 600 tons for each of 12 months, or a total of 7200 tons. This would require 600/45 = 13.33 or 14 tankers. Since the 14th tanker is only used to one third of its capacity, we arbitrarily decide to add only the 13 full-time used tankers. Hence, only 7020 tons (13 tankers times 18 tons times 2.5 × 12 trips per year) are carried. The balance of 180 tons for level 12 still goes by Scholle bags, together with the remaining 16,800 tons of the other 11 demand levels. These numbers are recorded in column 'Jan' in the spreadsheet.

The investment cost for 13 tankers is 13 times the equivalent annuity of $14,758, or $191,854. To express this on a per ton basis, we divide by 7020 — the amount carried by these 13 cars. The resulting investment cost per ton carried for demand level 12 is $27.33. Adding the constant hauling cost of $54 per ton gives a incremental tanker cost of $81.33 per ton. So, switching (most of) demand level 12 from Scholle bags to tanker increases tanker costs by $81.33 per ton, but saves $93.20 per ton in transport cost by Scholle bags. Hence, this switch is advantageous.

We now consider switching demand level 11 to tankers (plus the balance of 180 tons from level 12). The calculations now become a bit more complicated. Recall that, to cover level 12 completely, we need 13.33 tankers. To this, we now add the number needed to carry the additional 500 tons for each month of level 11 (all except January, as shown in Figure 12-4 in the row 'Level increase'). Since each tanker can carry 45 tons per month, this requires 500/45 = 11.11 tankers. The total number of tankers needed to cover both demand level 12 and 11 is 24.44 (i.e., 13.33 + 11.11). Again, the 25th car would only be used to 44% capacity, and we again arbitrarily decide not to use it. Therefore, the second iteration only adds 11 new tankers serving both levels. The additional tonnage carried is then: the 180 tons remaining from level 12, which uses 180/(45 × 12) = ⅓ of the capacity of one tanker; leaving 10⅔ of their capacity for level 11. This carries another $10\frac{2}{3} \times 45 \times 11 = 5280$. The additional volume carried by these 11 tankers is therefore 5460 tons, and the total for the 24 tankers amounts to 7020 + 5460 = 12480, as shown in column 'Feb'.

Eleven tankers incur an additional investment cost of $162,338. Expressed on a per ton basis, this is $29.73 (= 162,338/5,460). We add this to the tanker hauling cost of $54 and get an incremental cost of $83.73. This is still lower than the incremental savings from Scholle bags, so we continue.

We halt this incremental process when the incremental tanker cost for the last iteration rises above the incremental savings from Scholle bags. This happens for demand level 8. Hence, it pays to add at least 28 tankers to carry the tonnage of demand levels 12, 11, 10, and all except 360 tons ($^8/_9 \times 45$ tons $\times$ 9 months) of level 9. This amounts to a total tonnage carried by tanker of 14,240.

To carry the last 360 tons of level 9 would require $^8/_9$ of an additional tanker. So we have to check if it is advantageous to add a 29th tanker. It would also carry a fraction of the tonnage for demand level 8, in fact $^1/_9$ of 45 tons over 8 months, or 40 tons. The total tonnage carried by the 29th tanker is 400. Verify that the incremental cost per ton for this additional tanker is (14,758/400) + 54 or $90.90. Since this is still below the incremental savings from Scholle bags, tanker 29 is added. There is no need to repeat this for a further tanker, since the incremental cost for carrying the balance of demand level 8 is $93.53. We have found the optimal solution in five iterations of variable increments plus an additional iteration for one railcar.

Further discussion of solution

Although there is no need to continue these calculations beyond demand level 8, it is insightful to see how incremental tanker costs increase as more demand levels are switched to tankers. Since incremental tanker costs remain constant within each demand level, its graph is a step function, as shown in Figure 12-6. The steps become increasingly larger past demand level 4 (53 tankers).

Figure 12-4 also shows the total average annual cost as a function of the number of tankers used. It is an average because it includes not only the variable costs, but also the annual equivalent investment cost. Verify it! It also confirms that the minimum total cost is achieved around 28 tankers, as shown in Figure 12-7.

The total cost curve is quite flat over the range of 24 to 40 tankers. Given that the demand data used are future predictions whose reliability is not guaranteed, management has quite some leeway. A choice somewhere in that range will not affect total costs significantly. Any likelihood that demand may increase more than predicted will favour more, rather than fewer, tankers. Management may thus choose to be conservative and go for a higher number, such as 31 or even 40 covering level 8 or even level 7 demand, rather than a lower number.

Before making a final decision, management would also want to know something about how robust the solution is with respect to certain important assumptions. One of those is the discount rate. However, the average of 30 round trips per year assumed in all calculations may be more critical. (Exercises 8 and 9 of this chapter will ask you to investigate such aspects.)

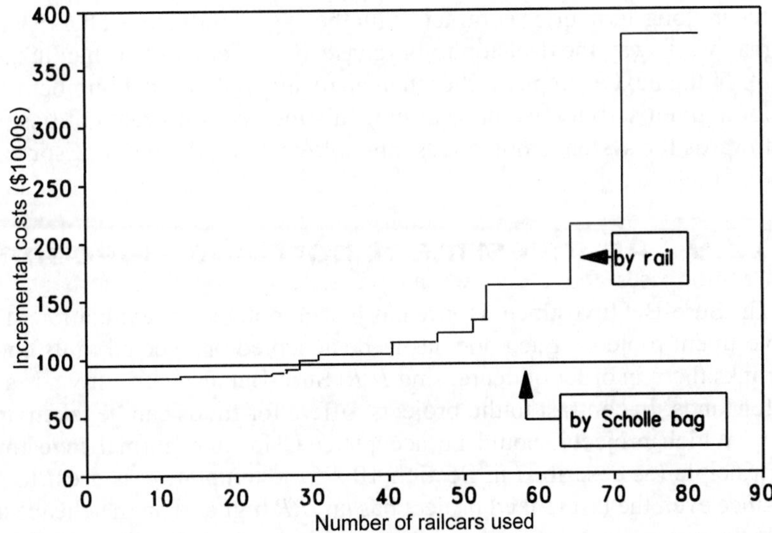

Figure 12-6 Incremental costs for tankers and Scholle bags

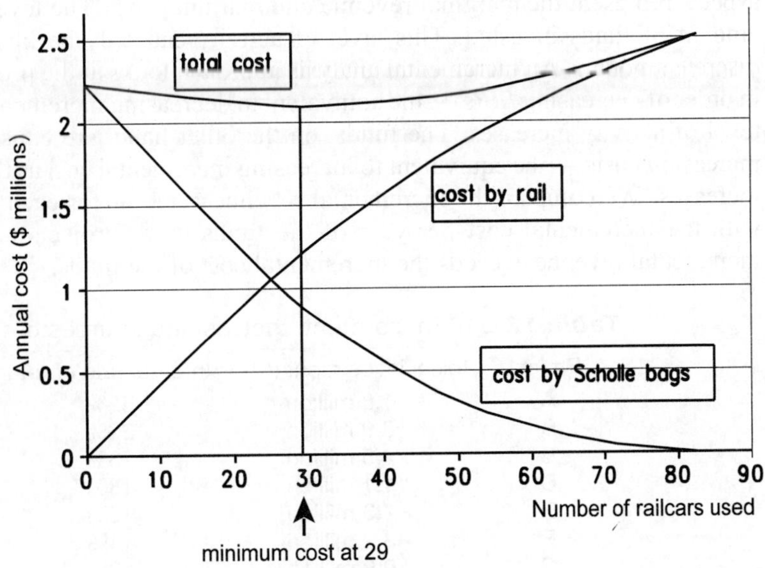

Figure 12-7 Total annual average costs for Heinz

Again, the incremental analysis approach provides insights that cannot be readily inferred from a total cost approach. For example, the difference in incremental costs between the two modes is only $7.50 for demand level 7 (May) per ton in favour of Scholle bags. A price increase for bags of less than 13% makes tankers the more attractive option also for May (and, by implication, for December). Unless Heinz can secure long-term price contracts with the bag manufacturer, the risk of a price increase may well sway the decision to purchase 40 tankers, rather than just 29.

In the next example, rather than analysing the optimal number of identical entities for a given activity, we have a set of distinct and different entities, each contributing towards the system's objectives, and all requiring the input of some shared resource.

12.9 An investment portfolio selection

The Sure-Bet Investment House has just completed the evaluation of nine potential investment projects. Each one has to be accepted or rejected in its entirety. Table 12-3 ranks them in order of decreasing *IRR*. Sure-Bet also currently has several firm offers for funds. In contrast to the projects, offers for funds can be taken up partially.

Which projects should be accepted? Using the normal investment accept/reject principle (as described in Section 10.2), the temptation is great to say 'all of them', since even the last ranked project has an *IRR* higher than the cheapest source of funds. If this were done, the annual return would be £5.477 million. Subtracting the annual cost of £3.55 million — the interest on the £30 million of funds used — gives an annual profit of £1.927 million. This naive approach, however, leads to the wrong decision.

The correct method is to apply incremental analysis. The trick is to identify which aspects represent the marginal revenue and marginal cost. The level of activity is the amount of funds invested. This level of activity can only be increased in unequal discrete amounts. An incremental analysis approach looks at the projects one at a time in order of decreasing *IRR*s — the equivalent to decreasing incremental revenues as the level of activity increases. The funds, on the other hand, are considered in order of increasing costs — the equivalent to increasing incremental cost as the level of activity increases. We compare the incremental revenue per year for each additional project with the incremental cost per year of the funds used. Projects are accepted if the incremental revenue exceeds the incremental cost of the funds.

Table 12-3 Investment choices and sources of funds

Project	Initial investment (£)	Internal rate of return
A	1.8 million	32%
B	6.9 million	26%
C	2.5 million	23%
D	1.1 million	18%
E	7.3 million	15%
F	3.2 million	14%
G	0.9 million	13%
H	2.2 million	12%
I	4.1 million	10%
Source	**Funds offered (£)**	**Cost/year**
1	up to 10 million	9.5%
2	up to 4 million	12.0%
3	up to 8 million	12.5%
4	up to 10 million	14.0%

Table 12-4 summarizes the steps of the analysis. We start with project A. Its incremental annual revenue is 32% on £1.8 million or £576,000. Funded from the cheapest source of funds, the incremental annual cost is 9.5% of £1.8 million or £171,000. Project A is accepted. This reduces the amount of funds available at a cost of 9.5% to £8.2 million.

Table 12-4 Incremental analysis for an investment portfolio (£ millions)

Project	Funds needed	Incremental revenue	Incremental cost	Accept/ reject	Unused sources of funds			
					9.5%	12.0%	12.5%	14.0%
A	1.8	0.576	0.1710	accept	8.2	4.0	8.0	10.0
B	6.9	1.794	0.6555	accept	1.3	4.0	8.0	10.0
C	2.5	0.575	0.2675	accept	0	2.8	8.0	10.0
D	1.1	0.198	0.1320	accept	0	1.7	8.0	10.0
E	7.3	1.095	0.9040	accept	0	0	2.4	10.0
F	3.2	0.448	0.4120	accept	0	0	0	9.2
G	0.9	0.117	0.1260	reject	0	0	0	8.3

The second-ranked project B has an incremental annual revenue of 26% on £6.9 million, or £1.794 million. It can be funded entirely from the cheapest source at an annual cost of £0.6555 million. This leaves £8.2 – £6.9 or £1.3 of the 9.5% funds. The third-ranked project C has an incremental annual return of £0.575 million; £1.3 million can be financed at 9.5%, and the balance of £1.2 million at 12%. This results in an incremental annual cost of £0.2675. Hence, C is accepted. The 9.5% funds are now exhausted, and £2.8 million of the 12% funds remain. This process continues until the next ranked project fails to recover all annual interest costs. This occurs for project G.

The optimal solution is to accept projects A to F for a total annual revenue of £4.686 million, using £22.8 million of funds. All the 9.5%, the 12%, and the 12.5% funds, and £0.8 million of the 14% funds are invested, leaving £9.2 million unused. The total annual cost of the funds used is £2.542 million, resulting in an annual total profit of £2.144 million, or £217,000 more than the naive approach.

In view of the order in which both the projects and the sources of funds were considered, there is no need to continue the analysis, once a project has been rejected. Any project further down in the rank order will stack up even more unfavourably.

12.10 Chapter highlights

- The marginal cost is the rate of increase in total costs at a given level of activity. Typically, as the level of activity increases, total costs initially exhibit increasing returns to scale, then constant returns to scale, and finally decreasing returns to scale. Marginal costs decrease during the first phase, remain constant during the second phase, and increase during the third phase.
- The latter phase is a manifestation of the universal principle of economics that all activities are ultimately subject to decreasing marginal returns.
- The average cost is lowest for a level of activity just prior to where the (increasing) marginal cost becomes larger than the average cost.

- Marginal revenue (or marginal benefit) is the rate of change in total revenue (or benefits) at a given level of activity. As the level of activity increases, marginal revenues will also ultimately decrease.
- Marginal and incremental analysis are useful tools for solving many relatively simple MS/OR problems. 'Simple' means that they only have one decision variable or activity and either a cost and a benefit or two cost aspects that vary in opposite directions as the level of activity increases. However, the ideas underlying marginal analysis also form the basis for a number of sophisticated mathematical OR tools.
- The principle of marginal analysis is to increase the activity level as long as the marginal revenue is larger than the marginal cost. The optimal level of activity occurs when they are equal.
- This principle easily extends to incremental analysis. The optimal level of a discrete activity occurs just prior to the point where the incremental gain in benefits for going to the next level of activity becomes smaller than the incremental increase in costs.
- Break-even analysis is a commonly used business tool. In its simplest form, it assumes constant unit variable costs and constant unit revenues or benefits. It determines the output or activity level for which total revenues (or benefits) become equal to or just larger than total costs (including fixed costs directly associated with the activity). At the break-even point, profits are zero (or have just become positive).

Exercises

1. What is the practical difference between marginal and incremental analysis, and why is the latter more useful for decision making?
2. An electrical goods manufacturer makes industrial transformers which it sells for £840 each. The material used in the manufacture consists of £120 for metal and plastic castings and wire costing £70 per km. The particular type of transformer produced on that machine requires 8 km of wire and 2 hours of labour per unit. The fixed annual cost of operating the machinery and overheads directly associated with the operation amount to £80,000. The machine operator is paid £800 per 40-hour week.
   (a) Assuming that the operator does other tasks when not operating the machine, determine the break-even point in terms of the number of transformers to produce per year.
   (b) If the machine operator remains idle when not operating the machine, what is the break-even point then?
3. A travel agent is contemplating opening another office in a different part of town. There is little or no overlap in potential clients expected. The cost of setting up a new agency is as follows: refurbishing the office £24,000; computer equipment and software licences £17,500; initial training of staff £3,600; initial promotion £6,900. The annual operating cost of the office consists of: office rental £10,400; staff salaries, including fringe benefits £58,000; various fixed office costs, such as telephone rentals, power, heating, and so on, £4,200; subscription to travel data sources, and so on, £6,000. Commission on travel ticket and accommodation sales, and so on, averages 10% of gross sales. Other variable sales costs amount to about 3% of gross sales.

(a) Determine the break-even point for annual gross sales needed for the agency to remain viable.

(b) The first office opened by the firm was able to operate at a sales level of 80% of the break-even point for the first year, 30% above the break-even point for the second year, 50% above the break-even point in the third year, and has maintained that level on average since then. If the same trend holds for the second office, how many years will it take to recover the initial investment?

4. An electric power company operates a number of hydro-electric and thermal power generating stations. Although the variable cost of using hydro power is essentially zero, power planners impute values for the water stored in hydro reservoirs based on the most expensive thermal power it can replace at some later time of the year. The table below lists the power increments available at the various stations and the associated real or imputed generating cost per megawatt hour (MWh) of power produced, valid for a given week:

Station	A			B		C	D			
Power increments	1	2	3	1	2	1	1	2	3	4
Output in MWh	50	50	50	40	40	20	30	30	30	30
Cost €1000/MWh	80	80	85	110	112	300	65	65	70	75

The company has firm contracts for supply of electricity of 170 MWh for that week. It can also offer additional power to other power companies at various prices: up to 40 MWh at €120,000/MWh, up to 50 MWh at €90,000/MWh, and up to 80 MWh at €82,000/MWh. What is the company's best power generating schedule for that week? Use marginal reasoning. It may help setting up a table similar to Table 12-1.

5. A firm produces ceramic tiles on a continuous basis. The daily output is 2 tons. They are stored temporarily at the plant and shipped periodically to its distribution warehouse in a box car that can carry up to 28 tons. The hauling cost, regardless of the amount shipped is £1,195. Each ton has a value of £12,000. The storage cost at the plant is 30% on the average stock investment. Compute the optimal number of days each shipment should cover using marginal analysis, as demonstrated in Section 12.5.

6. Earth Care, Inc., sells beauty products through house calls by its 'certified personal advisers'. A recent experiment selected three demographically similar areas of about 200,000 inhabitants, which could be considered typical for greater metropolitan Manchester. To each, a different number of 'advisers' was assigned for a two-month period. These numbers were changed for each of two consecutive two-month periods, in such a way that the number of 'advisers' assigned covered all numbers from 2 to 10. The following pattern between the number of 'advisers' assigned, the total annual sales volume, and the total travel costs reimbursed to the 'advisers' (all in €1000) was observed:

'Advisers'	2	3	4	5	6	7	8	9	10
Sales	500	750	1000	1240	1470	1690	1890	2050	2170
Travel costs	4	6	8	10	12	14.5	17	21	26

The reason for the ultimate decrease in additional sales is partially because less affluent urban areas have to be included. Travel costs increase more than proportionately for similar reasons.

Each 'adviser' gets a basic monthly salary of €1,000 and commission of 5% on sales. Earth Care makes 9% gross profit on sales, after sales commissions, but before travelling costs. Assuming the entire metropolitan area can be divided into corresponding homogeneous sub-areas, what is the optimal number of 'advisers' to assign to each?

7. A soft-drink bottling firm faces a seasonal demand (millions of bottles) as follows:

Period	Jan/Feb	Mar/Apr	May/June	July/Aug	Sep/Oct	Nov/Dec
Bottles sold	10	15	20	28	22	15

The firm can meet as much or as little of the demand as it wishes. The limited shelf life of bottled soft drinks means that no goods can be carried forward to a later period. The firm is currently modernizing its bottling plant by acquiring new bottling machines. Each bottling machine has a two-monthly capacity of 5 million bottles. The predicted total annual cost for each machine is $75,000. This includes all relevant fixed operating costs, as well as the recovery of the initial outlay less the salvage value at the end of its productive life, all expressed in terms of an equivalent annuity, as discussed in Section 10.3. The net contribution to profits is equal to $10,000 for each 1 million bottles sold. Use incremental analysis to determine the optimal number of machines to purchase.

8. Create a spreadsheet to reproduce the results in Figure 12-4.
9. Use the spreadsheet developed in Exercise 8 for the following sensitivity analysis, each done separately from the base case:
   (a) a change in the annual number of round trips from the current 30 to 25;
   (b) an increase in the cost of Scholle bags by 10%;
   (c) an increase in the carrying capacity of tankers from 18 to 20 tons;
   (d) an increase in the discount rate to 20%.
10. For the Heinz logistics problem, assume now that there is a second conversion plant Z with the following monthly demands:

Month	Jan	Feb	Mar	Apr	May	June	July	Aug	Sep	Oct	Nov	Dec
Demand	400	700	1500	1600	2500	3000	2200	2500	3200	2800	600	300

The number of round trips from factory X to factory Z is 40 and the tanker hauling cost for a return trip is $794. The freight cost for Scholle bags is $38/ton. The cost of returning the case remains at $2/case. Build a spreadsheet similar to the one in Figure 12-4 and find the optimal number of tankers to purchase. Hint: rather than express the demand levels in terms of incremental tons shipped, it is easier to express them in terms of incremental tankers needed. Determine for each destination the number of tankers needed in each month, add them for the two destinations, and then only rank the months in order of increasing numbers of tankers. Keep fractions here, only go to integers for the subsequent analysis.

11. A firm has the following indivisible investment opportunities, with the investment listed in £1000, and the internal rate of return (*IRR*) in % per year:

Project	A	B	C	D	E	F	G	H	I	J
Investment	20	40	60	30	50	10	20	50	40	30
IRR	28	27	25	22	21	21	18	15	12	10

Each of the following sources of funds can be taken up in its entirety or only partially:

Funds source	1	2	3	4
Limit in £1000	150	120	90	80
Cost/year %	12	16	20	24

Determine which investment projects should be entered into.

Further reading

Kerke, S. et al. (1990) 'A logistics analysis at Heinz,' *Interfaces*, September–October: 1–13

Samuelson, W.F. and Marks, S.G. (2012) *Managerial Economics*, 7th edn, International Student edn, New York: Wiley. Chapter 2 discusses marginal analysis. See also parts of chapter 6.

13

Constrained decision making

Learning objectives

- Find the optimal solution for a decision problem with a single decision variable in the presence of a resource constraint.
- Be able to determine the shadow price of a constraint and explain its interpretation.
- Apply the greedy algorithm for a resource allocation problem involving several decision choices.
- Use the Savage-Lorie benefit ratio to find its recommended fund allocation to a set of discrete investments.

Introduction

The decision problems studied so far did not involve quantitative restrictions on the decision variables or on the combination of alternative courses of action. For example, in the Lubricating Oil Division problem in Chapter 6 there was no restriction on the size of stock replenishments for the various products. Their optimal values were determined without consideration of any resource constraints. Although the mixing and filling capacity, and the warehouse space, were limited, and had to be shared by all products, we assumed that the capacities of these resources were ample and would not restrict the decision choices. This simplified the analysis considerably. It made it possible to look at each product individually, ignoring the fact that they shared the same resources. Similarly, when we evaluated investment projects, we assumed that there was no restriction on the amount of funds available.

In this and Chapter 14 we study the effect of constraints on the decision choices or on system behaviour. These constraints can be in the form of limited resources, such as funds, machine capacities, and so on. They could also be in the form of other conditions, such as minimum output requirements, minimum quality standards, or fixed relationships between activities. Some of the constraints may be physical or technical, such as maximum machine capacity — **hard constraints**. Others may be the result of management or policy decisions — **soft constraints**. An example of this is a budget allocation, e.g., the size of the advertising budget, which could be renegotiated or changed.

To keep things simple, this chapter only considers the case of a single resource constraint. In Chapter 14, we will study how to deal with several constraints when all mathematical relationships are linear.

We start out by considering a single activity the level of activity of which is restricted by a limited resource. We then study the effect of relaxing the constraint by increasing the amount of the resource marginally, i.e., we perform sensitivity analysis on the resource (see Section 6.17). This will lead us to the concept of the **shadow price** of a resource — an important theoretical and practical concept of constrained optimization.

Next, we show how the ideas of marginal analysis can be extended to the allocation of a limited resource to several competing uses. The last section looks at the allocation of a scarce resource when its use occurs in discrete and possibly unequal increments.

13.1 Resource constraint on a single activity

This section explores basic concepts of constrained optimization, demonstrating it with the simple EOQ model discussed in Chapter 6.

The optimal unconstrained solution

One of the LOD products has to be stored under refrigeration. Whenever the stock is depleted, a replenishment of size Q is initiated. The situation thus corresponds to the basic EOQ model. The annual cost is given by the sum of the annual stock holding cost and the annual replenishment set-up cost, expression (6-1A), reproduced here:

$$T(Q) = 0.5Qvr + sD/Q \qquad (13\text{-}1)$$

where D is the predicted number of cans sold over the coming year, s is the production set-up cost, v is the value of the product per can, and r is the annual investment holding cost per dollar invested. This function is well-behaved. It has a nice U-shape, i.e., it is convex. (See Figure 6-6, p. 151.) It has its minimum value at

$$Q^* = \sqrt{2Ds/vr} \qquad (13\text{-}2)$$

Table 13-1 lists the input parameters for this product in the top portion. Verify that expression (13-2) gives an order quantity of 1857.7 cans. Since cans are packed in boxes of 12, a practical order quantity is 1860 cans or 155 boxes. By expression (13-1), the relevant annual cost amounts to $3,274.

The boxes are stored on shelves in a cool store, eight boxes or 96 cans per pallet. A pallet area measures exactly 1 m^2; 1860 cans require $19^3/_8$ pallets. Since any partially used pallet uses the same storage space as a full pallet, each replenishment occupies 20 pallet spaces or 20 m^2. If there is no restriction on the amount of refrigerated space, then the (approximate) optimal replenishment policy for this product is to make a run of 1860 cans whenever the inventory is depleted. This occurs, on average, about 31 times per year, or about every 8 working days (assuming 250 working days/year). By definition, no other policy can have a lower annual cost.

Unfortunately, the current cool store space is only 8 m^2. This is equal to 64 boxes or 768 cans. In other words, there is a constraint imposed on Q, which is violated by the unconstrained optimal policy. Therefore, it is **infeasible**. To be a **feasible solution** the stock replenishment has to be decreased to at most 768 cans, with an annual cost of $4,637, an increase of $1,363 over the unconstrained solution.

Any deviation from the unconstrained optimal policy, by definition, results in a higher relevant annual cost. For what feasible value is this cost increase the smallest?

Incremental cost increases as storage space is reduced

Fractional pallet areas cannot be used as storage space, since a pallet requires a shelf measuring 1m^2. It only makes sense to consider reductions in the size of the replenishment equivalent to one pallet area, or 96 cans. We have, therefore, recourse to an incremental type analysis, except that this time we study the effect of decreases in an activity, rather than increases. This is demonstrated in the lower portion of Table 13-1 (ignore the last column, labelled 'shadow price' for the time being). Starting from the unconstrained optimal solution, we reduce the warehouse required by 1m^2. Since only $^3/_8$th of the 20th pallet is used, Q only has to be reduced by 3 × 12, or 36 cans. The resulting increase in costs is small — in fact, only $1. Further reductions in area imply a reduction in Q by 96 cans and increase costs by progressively larger amounts. They are listed in the column labelled 'Cost increase'.

Table 13-1 Stock replenishment with limited warehouse space

DATA		
Annual demand in cans	57,600	(*D*)
Value per can	$7.05	(*v*)
Production set-up cost/set-up	$52.80	(*s*)
Investment holding cost/$/year	$0.25	(*r*)
Warehouse space: cans/m^2	96	
Warehouse space available: m^2	8	
Unconstrained optimal solution:		
Economic order quantity Q in cans	1,858	
Total warehouse space needed in m^2	20	
Annual cost	$3,274	

Constrained optimal solution:

Available space	Order quantity		Annual cost	Cost increase	Shadow price
21	1860	(*EOQ*)	3,274		
20	1860	(*EOQ*)	3,274	0	0.00
19	1824		3,275	1	3.16
18	1728		3,283	8	13.18
17	1632		3,302	19	25.02
16	1536		3,334	32	39.15
15	1440		3,381	47	56.20
14	1344		3,447	66	77.03
13	1248		3,537	90	102.86
12	1152		3,655	118	135.40
11	1056		3,811	156	177.22
10	960		4,014	203	232.20
9	864		4,281	267	306.51
8	**768**		**4,637**	356	410.40
7	672		5,118	481	561.93
6	576		5,788	670	795.40
5	480		6,759	971	1,182.60
4	384		8,258	1,499	1,895.40

The constraint limits stock replenishments to values that require no more than 8 m^2 of storage space. The only values for the decision variable which satisfy this constraint are those involving a stock replenishment of 768 cans or less. From the 'Annual cost' in Table 13-1, we see that the cheapest feasible solution is the one that uses the entire space available (shown bold). The optimal constrained replenishment quantity is therefore $Q = 768$ cans at an annual relevant cost of \$4,637. Any lower value for Q results in higher costs, while any larger Q is not a feasible solution.

Generalizing the results

We can now generalize this result for the case of a single resource constraint. If the unconstrained optimal solution violates the constraint, i.e., is not feasible, then the optimal constrained solution is to choose a value for the decision variable that just satisfies the constraint, i.e., uses up all of the resource available. We then say that **the constraint is binding**. On the other hand, if the unconstrained optimal solution does not violate the constraint, i.e., requires less of the resource than is available, we say that **the constraint has slack**. The amount of slack is the difference between the amount available and the amount used. Slack is the amount of unused resource.

Finding the optimal solution subject to one constraint

This suggests the following optimization system O (see Figure 6-9, p. 162) for finding the optimal solution if the values of the decision variables are subject to a single constraint:

Step 1: Ignore the constraint and find the optimal (unconstrained) solution.

Step 2: Verify whether the constraint is satisfied by this solution. If 'yes', this solution is the optimal solution. If 'no', go to step 3.

Step 3: The optimal constrained solution is the one where the decision variables satisfy the constraint as a strict equality.

If there is only one decision variable, step 3 reduces to solving the constraint for the decision variable. If there are two or more decision variables, step 3 is somewhat more challenging, as we shall see in Section 13.5.

Activity

- For the data in Table 13-1, what is the optimal production run for a cool store capacity of 24 pallets? Why? Why is it not optimal to fill the cool store?
- Study the column labelled 'Cost increase' in Table 13-1. Note that successive reductions in the space available cause the cost to increase by progressively larger amounts. Try to explain why this is so.

13.2 Sensitivity analysis on a constraint

How does the optimal value of the objective function respond to changes in a constraint? We shall use incremental analysis to study this.

With only 8 m^2 of cool store space available, the optimal constrained replenishment is 768 cans. How much is it worth to acquire additional space? Such questions are regularly asked by a decision maker faced with limited resources. The worth of additional storage space is given by the decrease in the total annual cost. Increasing the available storage space from 8 to 9 m^2 results in a decrease in the annual cost of $356, as shown in Table 13-1 for the entry in column 'Cost increase' and row 'Available space 8'. If the annual cost of an additional square metre is less than $356, then it would be to the LOD's advantage to acquire at least one more square metre of space.

Often, a resource can only be acquired or used in a limited range of sizes or quantities. For instance, machine capacity may only be increased by adding further machines. In the LOD case, it is possible to rent refrigerated containers that increase the storage capacity by 6 m^2 at an annual rental cost of $600 per container. Should the LOD rent one? With the container, the total storage space increases from 8 to 14 m^2. For 14 m^2, the optimal constrained order quantity is 1344 cans with a total annual cost of $3,447 — a decrease of $1,190. Subtracting the container rental, the LOD will still be better off by $590. If technically acceptable, this option should be considered.

Should the firm consider renting two refrigerated containers, increasing the total storage space to 20 m^2? The storage space is no longer limiting, and the unconstrained solution becomes optimal, reducing the annual cost by another $173. This saving is less than the annual rental $600 for second container. The total combined cost increases. The answer to the question is thus 'No'.

13.3 Shadow price of a constraint

How does the optimal value of the objective function respond to relaxing a constraint? The answer to this question leads us to a fundamental concept in constrained optimization, namely, the shadow price of a constraint.

- **The shadow price of a constraint is the rate of change of the objective function at its optimal solution.**
- **A shadow price refers to a particular level of the constraint.**
- **As the level of the constraint changes, so may its shadow price.**

Note the similarity of this definition with the concept of the marginal costs and revenues, discussed in Section 12.4. Both refer to the rate of change of some 'output' for a marginal change in some input — a resource in this case. They differ, however, in one respect. The shadow price always refers to the rate of change at the optimal solution, while the marginal costs and revenues can be assessed for any arbitrary solution that may or may not be optimal.

Procedure for finding the shadow price

The shadow price at a given level of the constraint can be approximated by a similar approach as used in Section 12.1 for finding marginal costs and revenues. We relax the constraint by a very small amount and compute the resulting change in the optimal value of the objective function. Extrapolating that result to a unit change in the constraint provides an approximate value of the shadow price at that constraint level.

For the LOD, an increase of warehouse space from 8 m^2 to $8^1/_{96}$ m^2 reduces total costs by \$4.27. Hence, the shadow price at the constraint level 8 m^2 is approximately \$410 (= \$4.27/($^1/_{96}$)) per m^2. For a further increase of $^1/_{96}$ m^2 the shadow price reduces to about \$408. Relaxing the constraint causes the shadow price to fall.

Figure 13-1 shows how the shadow price behaves as the storage space increases. Initially, it drops quite steeply. As the constraint approaches 20 m^2, the curve becomes flatter. At 20 m^2, the unconstrained optimal solution can be implemented. Any further increase in storage space available will not decrease the minimum cost any further.

The shadow price drops to zero once the resource is no longer binding on the optimal solution.

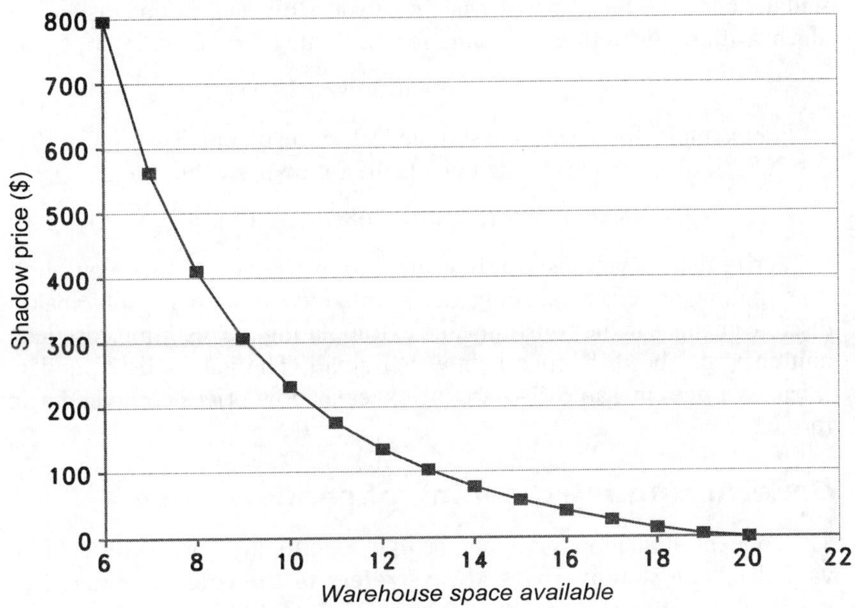

Figure 13-1 The shadow price of storage space

Analytic method for finding the shadow price

For a constraint that is a continuous variable, there is a more elegant way for finding the shadow price. The idea is deceptively simple! The trick is to add to the objective function a penalty for the use of the resource. In the LOD example, it is annual charge π per square metre of storage space used. Since 96 cans can be stored on one square metre, this additional charge for a replenishment of size Q amounts to $\pi Q/96$. Cost expression (13-1) becomes

$$T(Q) = 0.5Qvr + \pi Q/96 + sD/Q \tag{13-3}$$

or

$$= 0.5Q(vr + \pi/48) + sD/Q$$

The optimal replenishment Q^* is now

$$Q^* = \sqrt{2Ds/(vr+(1/48)\pi)} \quad (13\text{-}4)$$

Note the similarity with EOQ formula (13-2). There is an additional term of $(1/48)\pi$ in the denominator. If π is set equal to zero, expression (13-4) gives the same answer as the EOQ formula. This must be so, since a zero charge implies that storage space is abundant and additional space has no value. However, for any positive value of π, Q^* will be smaller than the EOQ.

Expression (13-4) can now be used for determining the value of this unknown charge π implied by the constraint. If the storage space is restricted, the constrained optimal order quantity is set to a value q which exactly uses up all storage space. We now simply assign π a value such that expression (13-4) yields a Q^* equal to q. We can find the correct value for π by trial and error. However, in this instance, some simple algebra allows us to find a formula for the value of π we are looking for:

$$\pi = 48([2Ds/q^2] - vr) \quad (13\text{-}5)$$

For example, for the current storage restriction of 8 m^2, we see from Table 13-1 that $q = 768$. Expression (13-5) then yields the following value for π:

$$\pi = 48([2(57600)(52.80)/(768^2)] - (7.05)(0.25)) = \$410.40$$

Verify that, if you insert this value into expression (13-4), you obtain $Q^* = 768$. This shadow price is an exact value — unlike the one obtained by making small, but discrete changes in the constraint and extrapolating the resulting cost decrease to a full unit change. The difference is however small. The values listed under the heading 'Shadow price' in Table 13-1 are the exact shadow prices computed using the above formula.

Generalizing the meaning of shadow price

The concept of shadow price can be extended to any type of restriction on decision variables. **The shadow price always refers to the rate of change in the optimal value of the objective function for relaxing or tightening the constraint by one unit.** Relaxing a resource constraint means providing additional amounts of the resource. The optimal constrained solution gets closer to the unconstrained optimal solution. Hence, the value of the objective function should improve, i.e., decrease if we minimize costs or increase if we maximize profits. Tightening a constraint has the reverse effect, i.e., increasing costs or decreasing profits, respectively.

Relaxing a constraint may take many different forms besides increasing the amount of a scarce resource. Here are a few examples to illustrate this.

Example 13-1: Value of irrigation water

A water reservoir is used mainly for irrigation, with any excess water generating power. The irrigation contracts may require a minimum release of 60 m^3 of water per minute. Relaxing this constraint means lowers the minimum release and makes more water available for power generation. The value of the additional power generated per m^3 corresponds to the shadow price of the minimum release constraint.

Example 13-2: Cost of air pollution emission

A constraint may be in the form of a maximum amount of output of a by-product for a given activity, for instance, the emission of air pollutants from a factory. Relaxing this constraint means allowing higher emissions, hence reducing the cost of air pollution abatement for the factory. It represents the shadow price of the current emission standards. (However, this neglects the increased social cost of air pollution — a cost not included in the cost function of a private enterprise).

Example 13-3: Tensile strength standard

The constraint may refer to minimum quality standards, such as the minimum tensile strength for a cable. Relaxing this constraint means making it easier to satisfy this quality standard. It hopefully results in a decrease in manufacturing costs, which represents the shadow price of the current standard. Obviously, decreasing this standard may result in a higher incidence of the cable breaking under stress, resulting in damage, injury, or worse — again, a cost not included in the firm's cost function.

13.4 Interpretation and uses of shadow price

Value of additional resources

The above discussion suggests the following interpretation for the shadow price:

The shadow price is the maximum amount the user of the resource should be willing to pay for additional (but possibly small) increments of the resource.

So, if the cost of the resource is less than the shadow price at the current constraint level, this is a signal for acquiring additional amounts of that resource. On the other hand, if the cost of the resource is more than the shadow price, this may be an indication that the firm either uses too much of the resource, or uses it inefficiently.

Although the shadow price gives a signal whether to acquire more of the resource or dispose of some of the resource, there still remains the question of 'How much?' The answer to that is made more difficult by the fact that the shadow price is a marginal concept and may be highly sensitive to even small changes in the constraint level.

As a first cut, we can study the curve of the shadow price as a function of the constraint level. For example, assume that the current cost of refrigerated storage space is about \$100 per m^2. Figure 13-1 shows that for storage space of 13 m^2 or less the shadow price is more than \$100. If storage space can be purchased at that unit price in any arbitrary amount (within reason), the optimal decision for the LOD is to increase the refrigerated storage space to 13 m^2. Hence, we see that knowing the shadow price at the current constraint level of 8 m^2 is not sufficient. In fact, we generally need to know more of the shadow price curve for answering the question of 'How much?'.

If the resource can only be acquired in a limited number of sizes or amounts, 'How much?' is not a question of marginal analysis, but one of incremental analysis. Section

13.2 demonstrated this approach for the storage problem. There, additional storage could be obtained in lots of 6 m^2 at a cost of \$600. This is also \$100 per m^2. We concluded that the optimal solution was to increase the storage space to 14 m^2. This is 1 m^2 more than the optimal solution derived from marginal analysis. The reason why the two answers differ is that marginal analysis assumes the resource is infinitesimally divisible, i.e., can be acquired in arbitrary amounts, while incremental analysis is based on the discrete realities of the real world.

Correct interpretation of shadow price

A clear grasp of the distinction between marginal and incremental analysis is the basis for a proper interpretation of the shadow price at a given constraint level. Only then will the use of shadow prices lead to the correct decisions.

There is a second source of potential confusion in the interpretation of shadow prices. If the objective function already includes a charge for the resource — say, the going purchase price — the shadow price also reflects this cost. It then only represents the highest additional premium that should be paid for the resource at the current constraint level. For example, suppose the scarce resource is hours of labour during regular work time. The regular-time labour cost is already included as a cost component in the objective function. Then the shadow price represents the maximum overtime premium the firm can afford to pay without being worse off. (Note that the question of 'How much?' still needs to be answered!)

A shadow price may not necessarily be expressed in monetary terms. In fact, it is always expressed in terms of the units used in the objective function. For example, if the latter deals with maximizing the amount of electric power produced, then the shadow price of the water in the reservoir, which limits the amount of power that can be produced, will also be in terms of units of electric power.

In conclusion, shadow prices provide indicators of whether or not it may be advantageous to change the current constraint level, and whether the change should be a relaxation or a tightening of the constraint. However, without further analysis, they do not tell us the best size of any change. To answer that question, we need to use incremental analysis.

Shadow prices are one of the more difficult concepts of hard MS/OR. They are an integral part of sensitivity analysis. They are also an important theoretical concept in MS/OR.

You may need to study this and the previous section again. We will demonstrate the usefulness of shadow prices in both this chapter and Chapter 14.

Activity

- Section 6-17 defines sensitivity analysis as the response of the optimal solution to changes in inputs (cost, demand, and so on). Compare sensitivity analysis with the concept of shadow price. What are the similarities?
- The shadow price of a resource used in a given activity falls to zero once it is abundantly available. But you will rightly claim that the value of that resource surely cannot be zero, that if the firm has no use for it, it could be sold. Discuss this apparent contradiction. (Hint: the shadow price only reflects what is in the model.)

13.5 Several activities sharing a limited resource

When several activities compete for the use of the same scarce resource, the optimal level of each activity cannot be determined individually for each activity. They are now linked together through the resource use. There will be trade-offs. Allocating more to one activity in order to capture high benefits will leave less for the other activities, reducing the benefits there. The optimal combination of activity levels needs to be determined jointly.

The Heinz logistics problem revisited

At this point, it is a good idea for you to review the Heinz USA logistics case of Section 12.8, in particular Figure 12-4. Using the idea of marginal costs and marginal savings, we found the optimal number of rail tankers by stepwise increasing their number until their marginal cost became larger than the marginal savings from the reduction in Scholle bag usage. This approach was possible because we only looked at the transport of tomato paste from a single factory to a single processing plant.

Heinz operates several factories and processing plants. Although the exact demand patterns at the various plants differ, their peaks and troughs tend to occur in the same months. Tankers may therefore not be switched between routes, since they are busy or idle in the same months. Each combination of factory and plant can thus be optimized individually. Let us now throw a spanner into the works. The tanker manufacturer can only supply a total of 60. To simplify things, we consider only four different combinations of factories and processing plants, each being a separate activity. How should we go about finding the optimal allocation of tankers to each factory-plant pair?

As is often the case, the basic idea is very simple — it just needed somebody to think of it. We will demonstrate it with this little story. After having seen the film classic 'Babette's Feast' with a group of friends, you invited them for a special treat. You planned to surprise them with 'caille au sarcophage' — the main course Babette offered to her guests. A crude translation is 'quail in a coffin'. But do not be deceived — it is delicious! Unfortunately, you forgot to order the quails. In a panic, you go to the local farmers' market. A quick check shows that several stalls still have a few suitable birds left and that the prices vary substantially. But no single stall can supply all the quails you need. Being a frugal gourmet — a rather interesting contradiction — you quickly note down prices and the number of quails at each stall. You use a solution-building heuristic for your purchasing strategy. You start by buying as many quails as are available at the stall with the lowest price, then proceed to the stall with the next lowest price, and so on, until you have bought the required number of quails. In other words, true to your character, you use a **greedy algorithm** — another version of incremental analysis. It will guarantee that you spend the least amount of money.

A greedy algorithm for resource allocation

This same type of greedy algorithm can be applied to the allocation of rail tankers. All we need is a schedule of the differences between the marginal Scholle bag cost and the marginal tanker cost per ton for each level of demand for each factory. We will call this difference 'the marginal advantage of rail over bags' (MARBs). We allocate the rail tankers sequentially in order of decreasing value of MARBs until all 60 tankers have been allocated to the four factories.

Table 13-2 lists the MARBs for each factory-processing plant pair. Factory 1 is the one we analysed in Figure 12-4 (p. 340). For example, the MARBs for demand level 12 is the difference between $93.20 for Scholle bags and $81.33 per ton transported by tanker for demand level 1. Only positive MARBs are shown, since we would never use tankers when the MARBs become negative (<0).

Table 13-2 Marginal advantage of rail over bags in decreasing value

Demand level	Factory 1 Tankers	Factory 1 MARBs	Factory 2 Tankers	Factory 2 MARBs	Factory 3 Tankers	Factory 3 MARBs	Factory 4 Tankers	Factory 4 MARBs
12	13 of 13	11.87 (4)	10 of 10	11.96 (2)	9 of 9	13.12 (1)	12	9.41
11	8 of 11	9.47 (8)	8 of 8	10.98 (5)	7 of 7	11.93 (3)	9	9.03
10	2	7.12	4 of 4	10.02 (6)	1 of 1	9.63 (7)	3	8.34
9	2	4.06	1	7.03	2	7.45	2	5.74
8	3	< 0.00	2	2.61	4	2.92	4	0.49
7			5	< 0.00	6	< 0.00	8	< 0.00
Allocation		21		22		17		0

The numbers in parentheses show how MARBs are ranked in decreasing value. This is also the sequence of successive allocations for a greedy algorithm. Factory 3 has the highest MARB of $13.12 per ton, valid for the first 9 tankers used. So, the first 9 tankers are allocated to factory 3. There are 51 tankers left. Factory 2 has the next highest MARB with $11.96, and is allocated 10. This leaves 41. The third allocation is again to factory 3, and so on. (How about testing your understanding by doing the remaining allocations?) After the seventh allocation (to factory 3), there are only 8 tankers left. These are allocated to factory 1. They only cover a portion of the 11 tankers which have the MARB of $9.47. The bottom row summarizes the number of tankers allocated to each factory.

The shadow price at the current constraint level of 60 tankers is given by the MARB to which the next available tanker should be allocated for an optimal solution. It is the highest MARB not yet allocated a tanker. This is the MARB of $9.47 for factory 1, valid for up to 11 tankers. So the 61st tanker would go to factory 1, increasing that allocation for the 11th demand level from 8 to 9.

Since the MARB is the difference between the rail cost and the Scholle bag cost per ton transported, this shadow price must be interpreted as a premium. It is the highest premium per ton carried by rail that Heinz should be willing to pay. So, if an additional tanker is allocated to factory 1, it can carry a further 45 tons in each of 11 months. Hence, the premium for this 61st tanker is 45 × 11 × $9.47 = $4,688. As long as any additional tanker has an equivalent annuity cost of less than the original equivalent annuity plus this premium, or $14,758 + 4,688 = 19,446, it should be obtained.

In the inventory control example the shadow price changed continuously. Here, for a limit of 60 tankers, this premium remains fixed for up to three additional tankers beyond those already allocated. Can you figure out why?

The answer to this question can be found in Figure 12-6 (p. 344). It shows how the marginal rail cost increases step-wise with each progressive higher demand level, but remains constant for additional tankers within each demand level. As a consequence, the shadow price for additional tankers also remains constant within a demand level, and increases when stepping to a higher demand level.

There is a close similarity between the greedy algorithm and the algorithm for marginal analysis. As a result, both require that the objective function is well-behaved. This means that the marginal costs have to be non-decreasing, i.e., they either stay the same or increase for additional allocations, and the marginal savings have to be non-increasing, i.e., they either stay the same or decrease for additional allocations. As a result, the marginal advantage will ultimately decrease as the amount allocated increases progressively further. If costs or benefits do not satisfy this property, then the greedy algorithm fails to find the optimal solution. It may also fail if the allocation has to be done in irregularly discrete chunks. The next section will demonstrate this aspect.

Activity

Think up a simple numeric example with two competing uses, where benefit functions are not well-behaved, and then show that the greedy algorithm fails.

13.6 Discrete and irregular sized resources

A firm is considering its investments for the coming year. Several operating departments have put forward investment proposals. Each proposal has been subjected to the usual financial accept/reject test in terms of the firm's desired rate of return on new investments (see Section 10.2). The first three rows in Table 13-3 list the candidate projects, their individual initial investment or cash outlay, and their *NPV*, i.e., the sum of the present values of all cash outflows (including the initial investment) and cash inflows associated with each project, all expressed in units of £1000.

The firm has an investment budget of £600,000. The firm's objective is to maximize the *NPV* of the portfolio selected. Which portfolio of projects should it undertake to achieve that objective?

A naive application of the greedy algorithm would choose the projects in terms of decreasing *NPV*s. The second set of rows in Table 13-3 shows that the projects have already been ranked in this order. Hence, A, B, and C are the first three projects chosen. They use up £490,000 of the £600,000 available. The fourth ranked project D has an initial investment of £133,000 and exceeds the balance of funds left. Hence, it is skipped. The initial investment of the fifth ranked project E can be accommodated, leaving a balance of unallocated funds of £28,000. Projects F, G, and H also have to be skipped. The final project selected is J, leaving an unused balance of £3,000. The sum of the *NPV*s of selected projects is £222,000.

This selection method has serious flaws. Consider the extreme case where there is another candidate L with an initial investment of £600,000 and an associated *NPV* of £120,000. Since it has the largest *NPV,* it is chosen first, exhausting the entire budget. This leads to a substantially inferior return than if project L had been ignored.

Table 13-3 Selection of investment portfolio

Project	A	B	C	D	E	F	G	H	J	K
Initial investment	107	201	182	133	82	141	30	37	25	12
NPV	84	50	45	39	35	26	24	9	8	2
Ranking by decreasing *NPV*:										
NPV rank	1	2	3	4	5	6	7	8	9	10
Cumul. investm.	107	308	490	-	572	-	-	-	597	-
Cumul. *NPV*	84	134	179	-	214	-	-	-	222	-
Ranking by decreasing ratio [*PV* of cash inflows/Initial investment]:										
PV cash inflow	191	251	227	172	117	167	54	46	33	14
Ratio	0.785	0.249	0.247	0.293	0.427	0.184	0.800	0.243	0.320	0.167
Ratio rank	2	6	7	5	3	9	1	8	4	10
Cumul. investm.	137	578	-	377	219	-	30	-	244	590
Cumul. *NPV*	108	240	-	190	143	-	24	-	151	242
Optimal solution:										
Cumul. investm.	107	-	289	422	82	-	534	571	596	-
Cumul. *NPV*	84	-	129	168	203	-	227	236	244	-

In the 1950s, two economists, J. Lorie and L. J. Savage, suggested that the projects be ranked in terms of the benefit/cost ratio [PV of all cash flows exclusive of the initial investment] over [the initial investment]. A more sophisticated version of the greedy algorithm would select projects in decreasing order of this ratio. This method is demonstrated in the third part of Table 13-3. Verify that this method selects the first six projects G, A, E, J, D, B in that order. Project C is ranked seventh. Its initial investment exceeds the unallocated balance of £22,000. Hence, it is skipped. So are projects F, G, and H. Only project K still fits into the budget. The *NPV*s of the projects chosen add up to £242,000, considerably better than the first method.

However, even the Lorie–Savage criterion cannot guarantee finding the optimal solution. The reason for this is that funds are allocated in discrete and uneven chunks. The Lorie–Savage criterion may leave a fairly large balance of funds unused. A different choice may use more of the funds and achieve a higher *NPV* total. For our example, the optimal solution is shown in bottom rows. It does not select the projects in terms of their decreasing benefit/cost ratio. More sophisticated solution algorithms are needed to find the optimal solution if the solution space is not well-behaved, as is the case here. However, for very large problems with many relatively small projects, the Lorie-Savage criterion often finds the optimal solution, or one very close to it.

13.7 Chapter highlights

- If the optimal unconstrained solution for a one-decision-variable problem violates the constraint, the optimal constrained solution is to set a value for the decision variable that satisfies the constraint exactly.
- The shadow price of a constraint represents the rate of change in the optimal value of the objective function (expressed in terms of a unit change in the constraint). If

the objective function is a nonlinear, but well-behaved function of the decision variable, then the shadow price may change continuously, becoming progressively smaller as the constraint is relaxed. It is zero when the constraint becomes slack.

- When several activities compete in equal unit increments for the same resource and the incremental improvement in the objective function is decreasing (or at least non-increasing) for any unit activity increase, then a greedy algorithm that allocates each additional unit of the resource in order of decreasing incremental improvements finds the optimal resource allocation.
- If the objective function is not well-behaved, or resource allocations are in different amounts for each activity, then a greedy algorithm fails to find the optimal resource allocation. More sophisticated methods are needed.

Exercises

1. For the cost and demand data in Table 13-1, use a spreadsheet to analyse a restriction on the average investment in inventories. Reduce the investment limit initially to the nearest multiple of \$100 and then by decrements of \$100 to a minimum of \$5,000. Plot the incremental cost change as a function of the average investment, i.e., the x-axis increases from \$5,000 to the unconstrained optimal average investment.
2. For the data in Table 13-1, find the shadow price for a warehouse constraint of 12 m^2:
   (a) using first the numeric approximation in the second subsection of Section 13.3;
   (b) using expression (13-5).
3. Using the numeric approximation described the second subsection of Section 13.3
   (a) find a reasonably accurate shadow price for the situation in exercise 1 for an average investment limit of \$5,500;
   (b) give the exact interpretation of this shadow price;
   (c) show that the cost difference between the constrained optimal solution for an investment limit of \$5,500 and the unconstrained optimal solution is substantially less than the product of the shadow price for a \$5,500 average investment constraint, and the difference in Q between the unconstrained and constrained optimal solutions.
4. For the problem in Exercise 1, develop an analytic expression similar to expression (13-5) for determining the shadow price on the average inventory investment and use it to evaluate the shadow price for a \$5,500 limit.
5. Determine the shadow price for the data given in exercise 6 of Chapter 12 (p. 349) if the number of 'advisers' is limited to 6.
6. Consider Exercise 5 in Chapter 12. Assume that a railcar can only carry 18 tons. Find the optimal constrained solution and its cost. Determine the shadow price of this constraint.
7. The original data in the Heinz case in Chapter 12 had a limit of 30 round trips per year and a tanker capacity of 18 tons. Using a spreadsheet, apply the approximation procedure demonstrated in the second subsection of Section 13.3 to determine the shadow price:
   (a) for 30 round trips;
   (b) for tankers of 18-ton capacity.
8. A chain of supermarkets has just received the last shipment of strawberries of the season, packed in cases containing 24 punnets each. From past observations, the fresh fruit marketing manager is able to develop the following table of total sales revenues (in €) for allocating n cases to each of the 6 stores in the chain:

	Store	1	2	3	4	5	6
Allocation:	1 case	36	36	32	30	30	29
	2 cases	70	68	64	60	58	57
	3 cases	95	96	96	90	84	84
	4 cases	112	116	128	118	105	104
	5 cases	122	125	152	138	126	118
	6 cases	122	125	172	153	135	125
	7 cases	122	125	181	160	135	125
	8 cases	122	125	181	160	135	125

The difference in revenues is due to location and customer propensity to buy strawberries. Each case has a cost of €20. Use a greedy algorithm for the following situation:

(a) If there is no restriction on the number of cases that can be obtained, how many cases should be purchased to maximize profits? How many are allocated to each store? What is the total gross profit (difference between revenue and cost)?

(b) If the number of cases that can be procured is 16, how should they be allocated to the stores? What is the total revenue? What is the shadow price of case 17?

9. The table below shows the choices of an electric power generating company for generating incremental amounts of power for a given day, where the numbers in the table represent the actual cost of thermal generation or the imputed value of the water used for hydro generation for incremental units of one MWh in £1000:

Source of power	Station 1	Station 2	Station 3	Station 4
Type of station	hydro	hydro	thermal	thermal
1st MWh	56	75	80	110
2nd MWh	72	75	80	110
3rd MWh	84	82	80	110
4th MWh	95	90	96	120
5th MWh	110	110	96	120

(a) If the amount of power required is 9 MWh, what is the optimal output for each station, assuming that there are no fixed start-up costs for thermal power stations? What is the total cost? Use a greedy algorithm.

(b) Assume now that there is a start-up cost of £20,000 for each thermal station. This means that the first MWh of power produced costs £20,000 more than listed in the table above, but the cost of further increments is the same as above. Discuss why a greedy algorithm will fail to find the optimal solution.

10. Consider the investment opportunities in exercise 11 of Chapter 12. Assume now that only £270,000 of funds are available (i.e., only the first two sources of funds). Using the ratio method of Section 13.6, find the resulting choice of projects to be approved.

Further reading

Lorie, J. and Savage, L.J. (1955) 'Three problems in capital budgeting', *Journal of Business*, October: 229–39.

Daellenbach, H.G,, George, J.A. and McNickle, D.C. (1983) *Introduction to OR Techniques*, 2nd edn, Boston: Allyn & Bacon. Section 19-7 has a detailed discussion with an example about constraint optimization for differentiable functions and the meaning of shadow prices.

14

Multiple constraints: linear models

Learning objectives

- Be able to formulate the objective function and constraints of a linear program.
- Be able to find the optimal solution using linear programming software, such as the Excel Solver.
- Be able to interpret the answer and sensitivity reports of Excel Solver.
- Be able to use the Excel Solver sensitivity report to determine the effect on the optimal value of the objective function for (a) changes in the right-hand-side parameters of constraints, and (b) forcing a variable that has a zero value in the optimal solution to become positive.
- Be able to use the Excel Solver sensitivity report to determine the minimum change required in the objective function coefficient of a decision variable that has a zero value for it to become a candidate to a assume positive value.
- Be able to formulate a transportation or assignment problem and find its optimal solution using Excel Solver.
- To be able to formulate simple integer linear programming problems and solve them using Excel Solver.

Introduction

We saw in Chapter 13 that a constraint on the decision choices may force a solution that is less advantageous than the unconstrained optimal solution. Multiple constraints will have an even greater effect. This chapter studies a special case of constrained optimization where the relationships between the decision variables are all linear. Although the assumption of linearity may look highly restrictive, there are numerous applications in engineering, business, industry, agriculture, and the public sector where linearity of all relationships between the variables holds, or is at least a very good approximation over the normal range of operations.

As an example, consider the construction of a highway through hilly countryside. Soil and rocks have to be shifted from places where the road cuts through hills to where fill is required to raise the road level, or to be discarded at other suitable sites. The construction firm wants to do this as cheaply as possible. For any two sites, one where excess material is to be removed, referred to as a source of material, and one where material is to be deposited or may be dumped, referred to as a sink of material, the cost of shifting this material is approximately proportional to the amount that is transported. The schedule for shifting material consists of a detailed list of how much is transported from each source to each sink — the decision variables of the problem. The constraints imposed are, on the one hand, the amounts of excess material required to be removed from each source and, on the other hand, the amounts of fill material required at each sink or the capacity of sinks serving as dumps for unwanted material. Clearly, the constraints are linear. They simply consist of a sum of material shifted. For instance, if site A has a capacity for receiving 120,000 m^3 of dumped material, then the sum of the amounts transported from all sources to sink A cannot exceed this limit.

This chapter starts out with a short general discussion on optimization in the presence of multiple constraints. We then demonstrate an application of one of the most important tools of MS/OR, namely, **linear programming**, to a small product mix problem. We formulate the problem as a mathematical model with the help of an influence diagram, and show that it satisfies the assumptions of linearity of linear programming. The appendix to this chapter discusses the graphical representation of a simplified version of the problem and illustrates some of the properties of linear programming models.

We next show how spreadsheet **solvers** or **optimizers** find the optimal solution and discuss the output reports, particularly sensitivity analysis and its limitations. The ease with which sensitivity analysis can be performed in linear programming is one of the strengths of this tool.

To demonstrate the power of this tool, we look at a real-life application dealing with developing a harvest processing plan for a pineapple canning factory. The final sections extend linear programming to related mathematical structures, such as the **transportation problem,** and to **integer programming**, where some or all variables may only assume integer values.

14.1 Constrained optimization

Section 13.1 suggests the following procedure for finding the best solution if there is a single constraint on the decision choices: (1) we first determine the optimal solution ignoring the constraint; (2) if this solution satisfies the constraint, we have found the optimal solution to the problem; (3) if the constraint is violated, then we know that the best solution will satisfy the constraint as an equality, e.g., use up all of the available resource. Often, a greedy algorithm will find the best constrained optimal solution.

New aspects with multiple constraints

Faced with many constraints, perhaps in the thousands, more powerful optimization systems are needed. Since the second half of the twentieth century, sophisticated algorithms have been developed. Some are of a fairly general nature, making few assumptions about the mathematical structure of the problem. The majority, however, deal with classes of problems and take advantage of their special mathematical structure. If all relationships are linear and the variables are continuous, the simplex algorithm — the solution technique of **linear programming** — can be applied. The detailed discussion of such optimizing algorithms are the topic of advanced university courses in MS/OR and are beyond the scope of this text. Our interest here is much more modest. We simply wish to get a better understanding of the nature of the difficulties of constrained optimization, gain some insights into the general form of the solutions, in order to enable you to formulate linear models for practical problems, and correctly interpret the information contained in the optimal solution.

In a multiple constraint decision problem, some of the constraints may be binding on the optimal solution, while others will not be. If the constraints are all in the form of scarce resources, a binding constraint implies that all of the resource is used up — in other words, the total amount of the resource consumed is equal to the amount available. A constraint that is not binding means that some of the resource remains unused — in other words, the constraint has slack.

From Section 13.1, we also know that the optimal constrained solution can never be better than the optimal unconstrained solution. In fact, unless all constraints have slack, the best constrained solution will be worse.

If we knew which constraints are binding on the decision variables at the optimal solution, we could simply discard all non-binding constraints. These will, by definition, have no effect on the optimal constrained values of the decision variables. With fewer constraints to be considered, finding the optimal constrained solution would be computationally simpler. At the optimal constrained solution, all the binding constraints would be in the form of equations. The computational problem would then boil down to solving a system of equations. Unfortunately, there is no simple way of identifying which constraints are binding and which constraints have slack.

An algorithmic analogy — South Sea island treasure hunt

So, how do many of these algorithmic methods go about finding the optimal constrained solution to a problem? The easiest way to explain the general principle is to take a geographical analogy. Consider this enchanting South Sea island. Your treasure map tells you that the treasure is hidden under a round rock at the highest point on the island. You arrive on the island in the middle of a pitch black night. You cannot wait until daylight before starting the ascent to the highest point since One-eyed Jack is in hot pursuit. You also know that the island has a very rugged coastline, with high cliffs at various places. In fact, the highest point on the island could well be at some cliff top.

You need an approach — an algorithm — that will guide you to the highest point. Recall from Section 6.19 that an algorithm is an iterative method that starts with an initial or incoming solution. It applies a set of rules to find a new improved solution. This then becomes the next incoming solution to which the rules are again applied for a new iteration. The process stops when no further improvement can be found.

You reason as follows: You land at a suitable spot where the ground rises slowly from the shore. This is your initial solution. Since you could land there, it must be a feasible solution. You now want to move away from this spot to a higher point. Each step up means that you get closer to the summit of the island. The height you reach after each step is your measure of success — your objective function. But you also consider only steps that do not lead you over a cliff. The cliffs are constraints on your movements. They limit the direction you can travel or, if a constraint is still some distance away, how far you may travel in its direction. So your rules are: Find a direction away from your current location that is feasible (i.e., does not go over a cliff) and at the same time goes uphill (i.e, improves your objective function) and take a step. Once you reach a point where you cannot take a step in a feasible uphill direction, you stop, having reached a top.

Appendix 14.1 provides additional insight into one particular algorithm for linear programming models, the simplex method.

Local and global optima

The question now is 'Is this the highest point on the island?' If the island has only a single peak and the ground rises from the shore steadily towards it from every feasible direction, even along the cliff edges, then you can be sure that you have reached the highest point. Mathematically speaking, we say that the surface of the island is **well-behaved**. In this case, this greedy algorithm will find the optimal solution.

On the other hand, if the island has many high points with peaks of various heights and possibly also some plateaux and valleys part-way up, we say that the surface of the island is not well-behaved. Then there is no guarantee that this algorithm will lead you to the highest point on the island. You could easily end up at a plateau part-way up, or at one of the minor peaks, i.e. a local peak rather than the highest or global peak. Had you started at some different initial point, you might have reached a different local peak or even the global peak. But in the dark you can never tell!

Back to the discussion of constrained optimization! If the mathematical form is well-behaved, an algorithm which at each iteration improves the value of the objective function, while remaining feasible, will ultimately find the optimal solution. If a problem does not have a well-behaved mathematical form, then no such guarantee can be given. You might have found a **local optimum** or the **global optimum**. The vexing question is that you will never know which one.

For some types of problem we can ascertain that the mathematical form is well-behaved. Hence, the solution algorithm is guaranteed to find the global optimal constrained solution. Linear programming — our focus — is one of these.

Activity

- Compare the above process of ascent with the greedy algorithm in Section 13-5.
- What happens if you combine this process and the greedy algorithm?
- If a problem has several optima, how could you try to find the global one?

14.2 A product mix example

A situation summary

Consider the following simplified example: An office furniture company produces ergonomic computer workstations on rollers. Each consists of a tubular frame with adjustable shelves for the keyboard, monitor, computer, printer, and other accessories. Three models are made: Basic, Standard, and Luxury. They are sold through the firm's own retail outlets. Manufacture of these workstations consists of five operations: cutting the tubular frame pieces, welding the frames, spray painting the frames, making the shelves, and final assembly of frames, shelves, and rollers. Table 14-1 lists the labour input required for the various operations, the production capacity for each operation, the costs of the parts and supplies used, and the wholesale price of the units.

Table 14-1 Computer workstation production problem

Product	Cutting tube	Welding frame	Making shelve	Assembly of unit	Material cost	Wholesale price
Basic	16 min.	25 min.	36 min.	22.5 min.	£43	£143
Standard	12 min.	22.5 min.	50 min.	25 min.	£60	£180
Luxury	20 min.	36 min.	80 min.	40 min.	£86	£246
Capacity/day	8 hours	15 hours	23 hours	15 hours		

The labour capacities imply that one worker cuts tubes, while two each weld and assemble, and three make shelves. Welding, shelf-making, and assembly all require a daily set-up time, hence the lost hour of production. The spray painting and curing facility has a capacity for 32 frames per day, regardless of which type. These five capacities are technical or physical output restrictions imposed by the current production process and the facilities used. They can only be increased by adding more workers, arranging for overtime, or a change in equipment. They are **hard** constraints of the production process.

Marketing considerations dictate that the number of Standard units should be at least equal to one third of the number of Basic units. In contrast to the five hard constraints, this requirement is a deliberate management policy. It can be changed by a simple management decision. It is thus a **soft** constraint on the choice of product mix.

Management would like to know the product mix which uses its current production capacities most effectively, while also meeting the marketing restriction. We shall interpret 'most effectively' as that use of resources which maximizes profit. Profit is the difference between the revenue generated by the output and all costs incurred. We shall arbitrarily set the basic planning period at one day.

Certain costs are fixed, regardless of the product mix, such as the various types of overhead. In the short run, even labour costs are fixed, since each worker is paid for the entire eight hours of each working day, even if he or she may be idle for a fraction of the time. In this example, the only cost items that vary as a function of the product mix are the material costs. Therefore, an appropriate measure of performance is given by the difference between revenues and material costs. We shall call this difference the gross profit (not the usual definition for this term).

An influence diagram

The influence diagram in Figure 14-1 depicts the chain of consequences associated with the control inputs, given here by the product mix choice (rectangle labelled 1). A product mix choice consists of specifying the exact number of each type of workstation to produce per day. The output of prime interest to us is the gross profit (shown as the oval labelled 24). However, there are other outputs we must observe; namely, whether the various operations capacities and the marketing restriction are violated or not. These are the other six ovals (labelled 5, 9, 12, 16, 20, and 22).

The uncontrollable inputs (shown as clouds) are the unit labour time for each operation and each model, the daily production capacity for each operation, the Basic/Standard output mix restriction, and the unit material costs and unit revenues.

Just to remind you of the principles underlying influence diagrams (Section 5.6), we briefly review the relationships ending in output 5 ('Status of cutting time constraint'). Each model takes a given number of 'Minutes of cutting time per unit produced' (cloud 2). Given a choice of 'Number of each type of workstation produced per day' (rectangle 1), this results in the state variable 'Total cutting time used/day' (circle 3). This total is compared with the 'Cutting capacity per day' (cloud 4). If it is less than or equal to the capacity, then the 'Status of cutting time constraint' (oval 5) is 'OK', i.e. the decision choice is feasible with regard to this constraint, otherwise the status is 'violated', i.e. the decision choice is infeasible with respect to this constraint.

A decision choice has to be 'OK' for all six constraints to be a feasible solution. Obviously, we wish to find a feasible solution that maximizes the 'Gross profit'. The influence diagram does not reflect this! Remember that the influence diagram does not deal directly with optimization. It only traces the consequences of a given control input choice. In terms of Figure 6-9 (p. 162), it only represents system S — the narrow system of interest. Our next task is to use system M to translate system S into a mathematical model — in this case, a linear programming model — to which we can then apply system O, the optimization system, to find the optimal solution.

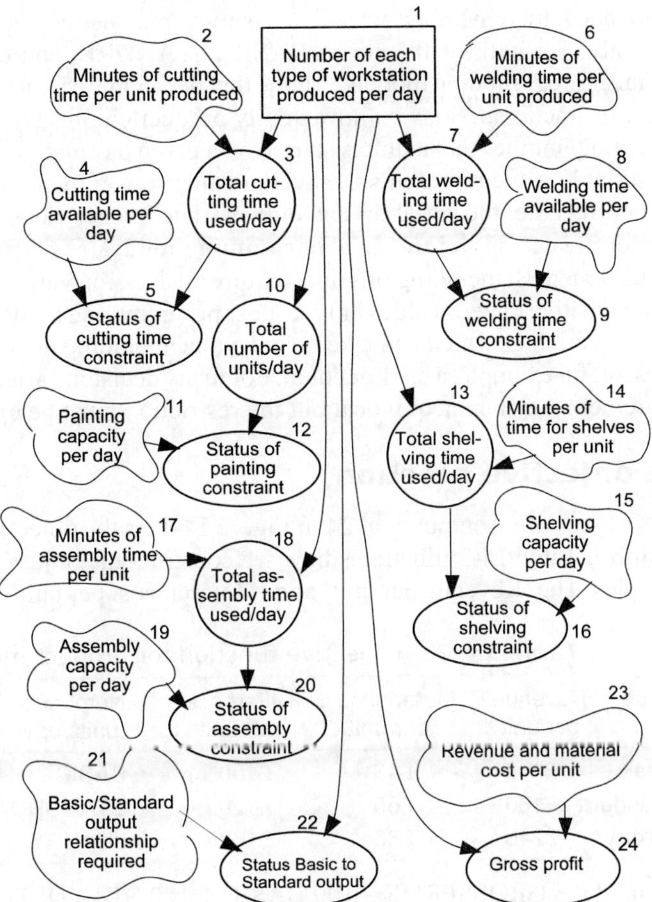

Figure 14-1 Influence diagram for product mix problem

14.3 A linear programming model

A linear programming model consists of an objective function and a set of constraints, all linear with respect to the decision variables. This means that the mathematical expressions used only involve sums of variables, where each variable may be multiplied by a coefficient. No expression contains products of two or more variables or powers of variables. The constraints may be in the form of inequalities, less than or equal to (≤), greater than or equal to (≥), or equalities (=).

Decision variables

A decision choice consists of the number of units produced per day for each product. Rather than denote the variables by letter symbols, such as x_1, x_2, and x_3, it is more helpful to use **mnemonic names** which suggest what the variables stand for. This is even more important if a problem involves hundreds or thousands of variables. You would need to remember what each subscripted letter symbol represented — a nightmare! We will use the names BASIC, STANDRD, and LUXURY.

Linear programming models assume that decision variables may take on any value, integer or fractional. So, we allow a daily production of, say, 5.4 Basic workstations. This simply implies that a unit is started on a given day and then finished the next day. The variable value represents the average output over many days. If this assumption is not correct, i.e. the variables can only assume integer values, then the problem has to be formulated as an **integer programming model**, as discussed in Section 14.10.

Many models, including this one, require all decision variables to be **non-negative**, take on positive or zero values only. Linear programming models, in general, allow for decision variables which can take on any value including negative values. This might represent, for example, a bank account. For many decision variables, the non-negativity requirement may be unequivocal but the restriction must be explicitly enforced.

The objective function

The 'Gross profit' (output oval 24 in Figure 14-1) is the objective function we wish to maximize. Table 14-2 illustrates how we construct the objective function from basic principles. The 'Revenue per unit' and 'Material cost per unit' come from Table 14-1.

Table 14-2 Objective function for product mix problem

Type	Revenue per unit	Material cost per unit	Difference per unit	Number of units/day	Gross profit per day
Basic	£143	£43	£100	BASIC	100 BASIC
Standard	£180	£60	£120	STANDRD	120 STANDRD
Luxury	£246	£86	£160	LUXURY	160 LUXURY

Total/day: GROSSPROF = 100 BASIC + 120 STANDRD + 160 LUXURY

The influence diagram shows that 'Gross profit' is a function of the decision variables (rectangle 1) and the 'Revenue and material costs per unit' (cloud 23). The last line in Table 14-2 is the expression for the objective function, representing the 'Gross profit'. For any combination of values of the decision variables, it has the value GROSSPROF. To indicate that it is to be maximized, we show it as

$$\text{Max GROSSPROF} = 100\ \text{BASIC} + 120\ \text{STANDRD} + 160\ \text{LUXURY} \qquad (14\text{-}1)$$

The coefficients multiplying the decision variables are called the **objective function coefficients**. Note that the expression is the sum of products, each involving a decision variable and a coefficient. It is linear as required by the linear programming model.

Constraints

In addition to the non-negativity conditions, there are five hard and one soft constraints that restrict the combination of values the decision variables may assume. Each could be formulated by a pattern analogous to Table 14-2 above.

Cutting time constraint: There are 8 hours, or 480 minutes, of 'Cutting time available' (cloud 4) to cut the tubular pieces that make up the frame. The 'Total time used per day' (circle 3) to produce any combination of workstations is the product of 'Minutes of cutting time per unit' (cloud 2) and 'Number of workstations produced per day' (rectangle 1), summed over all three types:

16 BASIC + 12 STANDRD + 20 LUXURY minutes

The coefficients of the decision variables come from Table 14-1. The time used cannot exceed 480 minutes. The cutting constraint thus becomes:

(CUTTING) 16 BASIC + 12 STANDRD + 20 LUXURY ≤ 480 (14-2)

This constraint says that the sum on the left-hand side (LHS) has to be less than or equal to the number on the right-hand side (RHS). The coefficients multiplying the decision variables are called the **left-hand side** or **LHS coefficients**, while the constant on the RHS is referred to as the **right-hand side** or **RHS parameter**. This constraint is linear.

Welding time constraint: There are 15 hours, or 900 minutes, of welding time available per day. Hence:

(WELDING) 25 BASIC + 22.5 STANDRD + 36 LUXURY ≤ 900 (14-3)

Painting capacity constraint: Only 32 frames can be processed per day; so

(PAINTING) BASIC + STANDRD + LUXURY ≤ 32 (14-4)

Note that an LHS coefficient of 1 is usually not shown explicitly.

Shelving time constraint:

(SHELVING) 36 BASIC + 50 STANDRD + 80 LUXURY ≤ 1380 (14-5)

Assembly time constraint:

(ASSEMBLY) 22.5 BASIC + 25 STANDRD + 40 LUXURY ≤ 900 (14-6)

Basic/Standard output mix: The daily output of Standard units has to be at least equal to one third of the number of Basic units produced. This gives the following greater-than-or-equal constraint:

STANDRD ≥ ⅓ BASIC

By convention, all decision variables are listed on the LHS, while the RHS only shows a constant, which may be zero. So, we subtract ⅓ BASIC from both sides. Adding or subtracting the same term on both sides or multiplying or dividing both sides by the same constant does not affect which values of the variables are admissible. This yields the following constraint:

(BAS/STD MIX) – ⅓ BASIC + STANDRD ≥ 0 (14-7)

To be a **feasible solution** to the product mix problem, the three decision variables have to be non-negative and satisfy all six constraints (14-2) to (14-7). The **optimal**

solution to the problem is the feasible solution that maximizes the objective function of expression (14-1).

This completes the formulation. Appendix 14.1 gives a graphical interpretation of a two-decision-variable version of this problem.

A linear programming model is often referred to as a **linear program** or an **LP**. In comparison to real-life applications, the above LP is very small. Real-life product mix situations may easily have hundreds and, more often, thousands of variables and constraints. Activity scheduling problems, such as the scheduling of aircraft and aircrews, or a representation of all operations of an oil company or forestry processing company — all classical applications of linear programming — may even have hundreds of thousands or millions of variables and constraints.

Neither decision variables nor constraints need to be in the same measurement units. Some variables may be in number of units, others in kilograms, still others in tonnes, and so on. Similarly, some constraints may be in minutes per day, e.g., constraint (14-2), while others may use a different measure, such as constraint (14-4) which is in units per day. However, each constraint must be dimensionally consistent, e.g., if the RHS is specified in minutes per day, each product of a LHS coefficient and decision variable must also be in minutes per day. Verify that this is the case for constraint (14-2).

14.4 Solution by spreadsheet

One optimization system O used for finding the optimal solution to an LP is known as the **simplex method**. It was developed in 1947 by the American mathematician George Dantzig. Its discussion goes beyond the scope of this text, however, Appendix 14.1 illustrates some of its principles using a graphical representation of an LP. Sophisticated LP computer software can find the optimal solution to problems of several thousand variables and constraints in seconds, and larger problems in minutes.

Excel includes an add-in 'Solver', which is effective for optimizing small problems. In general, for LPs with more than 100 variables and/or constraints, you should use specialized commercial **mathematical optimization software**, such as AMPL, AIMMS, CPLEX, GAMS, Gurobi, Premium Solver or Xpress, to name a few.

Linear programming spreadsheet model

Any LP optimizing software, whether in a spreadsheet or as a standalone package, needs to have a complete 'working' formulation of the model before it can be optimized. For Excel Solver, the input data for an LP model is best submitted in a structured tabular form, similar to the layout in Figure 14-2. The table has a column for each variable (here B, C, and D), one to indicate the direction of the constraints, i.e, ≤, =, or ≥ (column F), and one for the RHS parameters (column G). It has a row for the objective function (row 5) and one for each constraint (rows 7 to 12).

The row for the objective function holds the objective function coefficient for each variable. Each LHS coefficient is inserted in the cell intersected by its corresponding constraint and variable. It is important to use sufficient decimal places, otherwise the accuracy of the results may suffer. Zero entries may be left blank.

	A	B	C	D	E	F	G	H
1	**Decision Variables**							
2	Product	Basic	Standard	Luxury				
3								
4	**Objective function**							
5	Gross profit	£100	£120	£160		Max		
6	**Constraints**					type	RHS	Units
7	Cutting	16	12	20		≤	480	minutes
8	Welding	25	22.5	36		≤	900	minutes
9	Painting	1	1	1		≤	32	workstations
10	Shelving	36	50	80		≤	1380	minutes
11	Assembly	22.5	25	40		≤	900	minutes
12	Bas/Std Mix	-0.3333	1			≥	0	workstations

Figure 14-2 LP in detached coefficient form for product mix problem

Such a table is referred to as the **LP in detached coefficient form**. Its tabular structure implies the form of the mathematical expressions of objective function and the constraints. In particular, multiplying the coefficients of each row with its corresponding (column) variable and summing across all variables generates the objective function and the LHS of each constraint, respectively. Hence, the table contains all information needed for expressing the mathematical relationships of the LP.

Note that row 3 and column E are shown shaded. Excel Solver needs two ranges of cells dedicated to hold the varying (or 'working') parts of the LP. We use row 3, referred to here as 'the decision variables row,' to display the current values of the decision variables for a given solution. We usually set them all zero to begin with. Column E, referred to as 'the totals column' calculates the corresponding value of the objective function and the achievement level towards the constraints. Changing the values of the decision variables will change the totals in column E.

Figure 14-3 is the screen printout for an arbitrarily chosen initial solution of 6 Basic, 8 Standard and 9 Luxury workstations (cells B3, C3, and D3). This solution produces a gross profit of £3000 (cell E5) and lists the achievement towards the constraints (cells E7 to E12). All constraints are satisfied, but all resources are underutilized; so this solution is far from optimal.

When calculating the optimal solution, Excel Solver will **only** change the values in the decision variable cells. The values in the totals column will reflect this change. All the other data cells of the LP in detached coefficient form will remain unchanged.

Since in Excel all data, decision variables and the entries in the totals column are represented as cells showing values, it is helpful to use cell styles and formats that highlight their different roles in the model. In Figure 14-3, we use light shading for data cells and dark shading for decision variable cells, while the totals column numbers are shaded grey.

The entries in the totals column are obtained by the function

SUMPRODUCT(range 1, range 2)

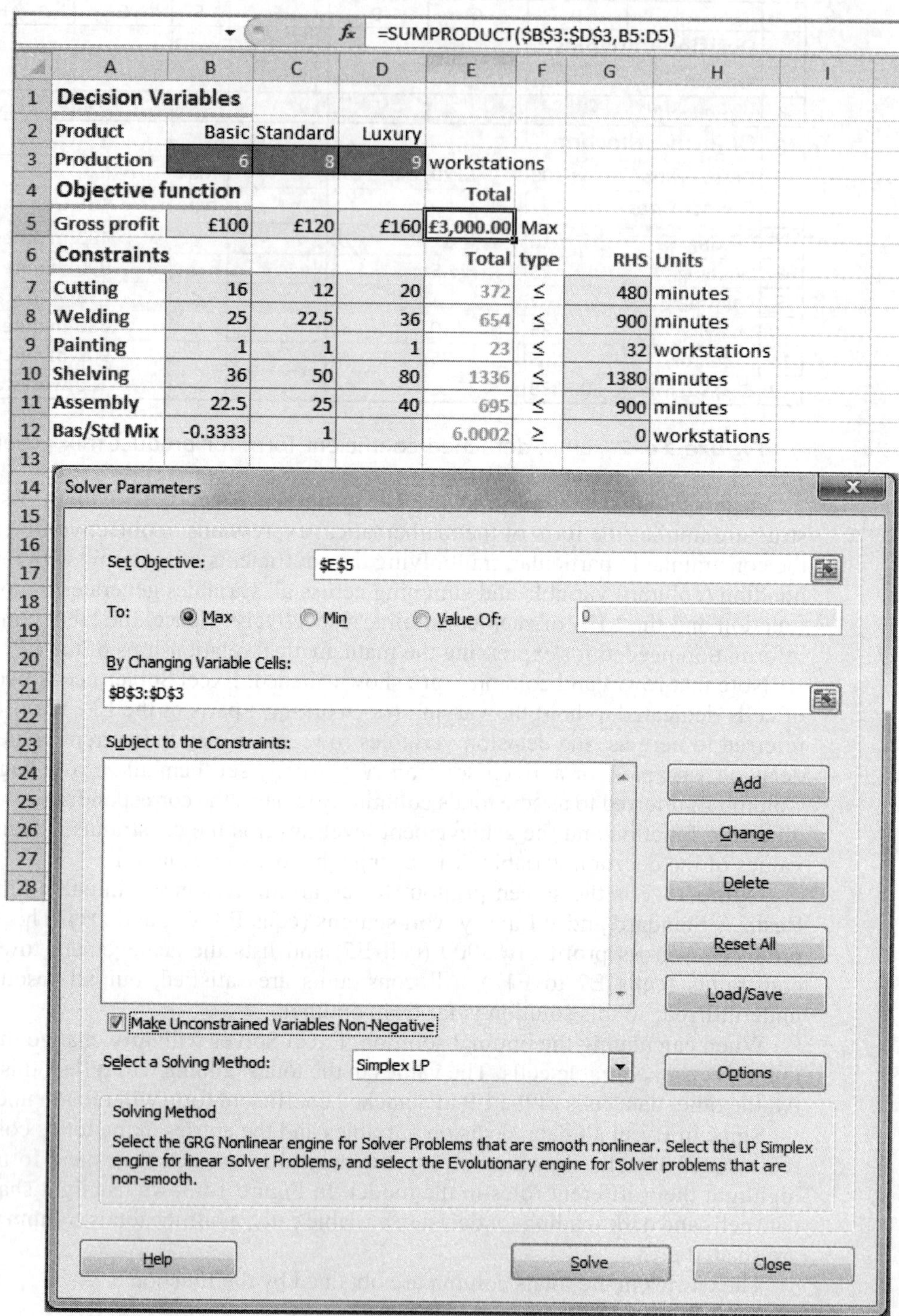

=SUMPRODUCT($B$3:$D$3,B5:D5)

	A	B	C	D	E	F	G	H
1	**Decision Variables**							
2	**Product**	Basic	Standard	Luxury				
3	**Production**	6	8	9	workstations			
4	**Objective function**				Total			
5	**Gross profit**	£100	£120	£160	£3,000.00	Max		
6	**Constraints**				Total	type	RHS	Units
7	**Cutting**	16	12	20	372	≤	480	minutes
8	**Welding**	25	22.5	36	654	≤	900	minutes
9	**Painting**	1	1	1	23	≤	32	workstations
10	**Shelving**	36	50	80	1336	≤	1380	minutes
11	**Assembly**	22.5	25	40	695	≤	900	minutes
12	**Bas/Std Mix**	-0.3333	1		6.0002	≥	0	workstations

Figure 14-3 Excel Solver dialog window for product mix problem

where 'range 1' refers to the decision variable cells, and 'range 2' refers to the objective function or LHS coefficients, respectively. The formula bar in Figure 14-3 shows this formula for the objective function, cell E5. The value of £3000 in this cell was calculated by Excel as $6 \times 100 + 8 \times 120 + 9 \times 160$. Corresponding formulas are used in cells F7 to F12, which give the resource use for constraints (14-2) to (14-6) and the excess of Standard output over its minimum of $^1/_3$ of Basic output.

Input to Excel Solver

Once we have a 'working' LP formulation in the spreadsheet, we are ready to invoke the Excel Solver from the 'Data' ribbon by clicking on 'Solver'. (If Solver is not on your Data ribbon, look up 'turn on Excel Solver' on the Internet for instructions.) The dialog box 'Solver Parameters' appears, as shown in the bottom portion of the screen reproduction in Figure 14-3. (For pre-2010 versions of Solver, the layout is slightly different.) This is where we tell Solver where to find the LP model in the spreadsheet.

The box labelled 'Set Objective' (or 'Set Target Cell') indicates which cell computes the value of the objective function — in our example, cell E5. To enter the cell reference, we move the cursor to cell E5 in the spreadsheet and click on it. This is less prone to error than typing it in. On the next line, we click the button for 'Max' or 'Min', depending on whether we want to maximize or minimize the objective function.

Next, we click the entry box labelled 'By Changing Variable Cells' (or 'By Changing Cells') and select the cell range from B3 to D3 in the decision variable row.

Finally, we enter the constraints. These can be entered in groups of the same type, i.e. ≤, ≥, or =. To add a constraint or constraint group, we click 'Add…', which opens the new three-part dialog box, shown in Figure 14-4.

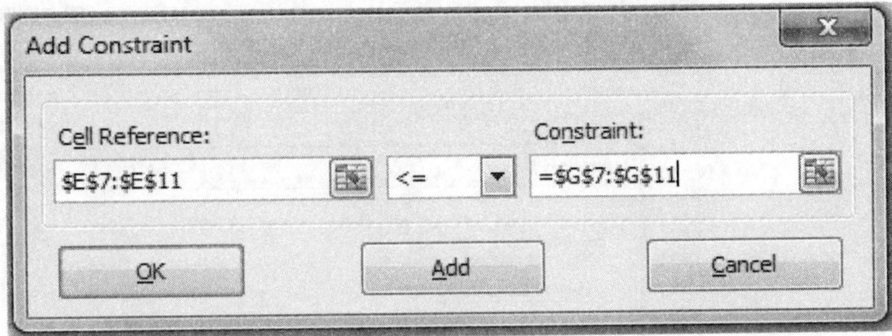

Figure 14-4 Dialog box for entering constraints in Excel Solver

Every constraint set is entered by first highlighting the range corresponding to LHS calculations for the 'Cell Reference' box; next, selecting the appropriate sign in the middle box (Excel uses the forms '< =', '=', and '> ='); and then clicking the 'Constraint' box and highlighting the corresponding range of the RHS.

Our first set of ≤ constraints correspond to rows 7 to 11. We highlight range E7:E11, select '< =', and then highlight range G7:G11. Clicking 'OK' enters that information into the dialog box in Figure 14-3. We repeat the same procedure for the single ≥ constraint (row 12). Notice that the constraint signs (in column F) are not used — they are for our own (visual) reference only. It is important to ensure that the visual reference matches the constraint type provided to Excel Solver.

Next, we tell Solver that (a) the model is a linear program by changing the 'Solving Method' to 'LP Simplex', and (b) all of the variables are required to be non-negative by selecting 'Make Unconstrained Variables Non-Negative'. (For older versions of Solver, these are set under 'Options…', by selecting 'Assume Linear Model' and 'Assume Non-Negative'.) Non-negativity restrictions can also be added explicitly as a set of constraints. We are now ready to optimize the model by clicking 'Solve'.

14.5 Output of Excel Solver — optimal solution

At the end of the computations, Solver tells us if it found a feasible solution and offers us reports on the results, as shown in the window of Figure 14-5. Any highlighted reports are saved as new worksheets when 'OK' is clicked. In Figure 14-5, row 3 now contains the optimal values of the three decision variables and column E shows the optimal value of the objective function and the LHS constraint totals.

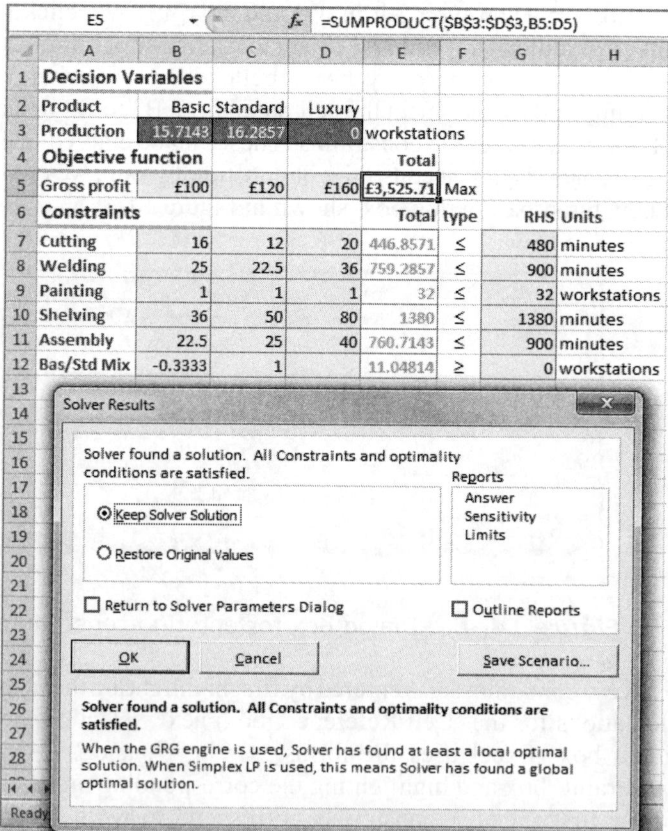

E5 =SUMPRODUCT($B$3:$D$3,B5:D5)

	A	B	C	D	E	F	G	H
1	Decision Variables							
2	Product	Basic	Standard	Luxury				
3	Production	15.7143	16.2857	0	workstations			
4	Objective function				Total			
5	Gross profit	£100	£120	£160	£3,525.71	Max		
6	Constraints				Total	type	RHS	Units
7	Cutting	16	12	20	446.8571	≤	480	minutes
8	Welding	25	22.5	36	759.2857	≤	900	minutes
9	Painting	1	1	1	32	≤	32	workstations
10	Shelving	36	50	80	1380	≤	1380	minutes
11	Assembly	22.5	25	40	760.7143	≤	900	minutes
12	Bas/Std Mix	-0.3333	1		11.04814	≥	0	workstations

Figure 14-5 Excel Solver result window

The Answer and Sensitivity Reports are shown in Figure 14-6. The top of the Answer Report, labelled 'Objective Cell' or 'Target Cell' lists the optimal value of the objective function. Solver combines the closest labels to the left and above the cell when naming the objective function, decision variables, and constraints. Hence, the objective cell is named 'Gross profit Total', and lists a maximal value of £3,525.71.

Answer Report

Objective Cell (Max)

Cell	Name	Original Value	Final Value
$E$5	Gross profit Total	£3,000.00	£3,525.71

Variable Cells

Cell	Name	Original Value	Final Value	Integer
$B$3	Production Basic	6	15.71428571	Contin
$C$3	Production Standard	8	16.28571429	Contin
$D$3	Production Luxury	9	0	Contin

Constraints

Cell	Name	Cell Value	Formula	Status	Slack
$E$7	Cutting Total	446.8571429	$E$7<=$G$7	Not Binding	33.14285714
$E$8	Welding Total	759.2857143	$E$8<=$G$8	Not Binding	140.7142857
$E$9	Painting Total	32	$E$9<=$G$9	Binding	0
$E$10	Shelving Total	1380	$E$10<=$G$10	Binding	0
$E$11	Assembly Total	760.7142857	$E$11<=$G$11	Not Binding	139.2857143
$E$12	Bas/Std Mix Total	11.04814286	$E$12>=$G$12	Not Binding	11.04814286

Sensitivity Report

Variable Cells

Cell	Name	Final Value	Reduced Cost	Objective Coefficient	Allowable Increase	Allowable Decrease
$B$3	Production Basic	15.71428571	0	100	1.333333333	13.6
$C$3	Production Standard	16.28571429	0	120	18.88888889	0.909090909
$D$3	Production Luxury	0	-2.857142857	160	2.857142857	1E+30

Constraints

Cell	Name	Final Value	Shadow Price	Constraint R.H. Side	Allowable Increase	Allowable Decrease
$E$7	Cutting Total	446.8571429	0	480	1E+30	33.14285714
$E$8	Welding Total	759.2857143	0	900	1E+30	140.7142857
$E$9	Painting Total	32	48.57142857	32	1.260869565	4.4
$E$10	Shelving Total	1380	1.428571429	1380	220	116
$E$11	Assembly Total	760.7142857	0	900	1E+30	139.2857143
$E$12	Bas/Std Mix Total	11.04814286	0	0	11.04814286	1E+30

Figure 14-6 Excel linear programming reports

The second part, labelled 'Variable Cells' or 'Adjustable Cells', shows the optimal values of the decision variables, labelled using the pattern mentioned above. The best product mix only produces 15.7143 Basic units and 16.2857 Standard units per day. Surprisingly, it is optimal not to produce any Luxury units at all in spite of their high gross profit contribution. This may not be desirable, and management may want to look into this aspect. We shall briefly do this in Section 14.6.

Recall that these numbers represent the average daily output over many days. So, on some days 15 Basic units will be finished, while on others 16. This implies that periodically an unfinished unit is carried forward to the following day. If this is not possible or desirable, then some of the binding constraints may have to be marginally violated. In practice, this is usually of little concern for a problem of this sort. Not only are the LHS coefficients for the various operation times estimates of observed averages, but the actual times vary from unit to unit. The workers may on some days do a few minutes overtime, while quitting a few minutes early on others, or they simply vary their work speed a little. Only if the constraints were of a hard physical nature would we have to adhere to them strictly. In modelling, it is always important to use common sense, particularly if human aspects are involved.

If no partially completed units can be carried forward to a following day, then the decision variables have to be restricted to integer values. The problem then has to be solved by an integer programming algorithm. This is the topic of Section 14.10.

The third part lists the constraints, the constraint achievement levels (as also shown in Column E in Figure 14-5), the status of the constraints — 'Binding' or 'Not Binding'— and the differences between the RHS and the actual level of the LHS level achieved, i.e., the amounts of **slack**. For the product mix problem, only two of the constraints turn out to be binding, namely the ones for the painting capacity and shelving time capacity. The other three operations and the marketing mix constraint all have various amounts of slack, e.g., there are about 33 minutes of cutting time unused per day.

The Sensitivity Report shows the result of sensitivity analysis on some of the inputs. The top part deals with the so-called 'reduced costs' associated with objective function coefficients.

At the optimal solution:

- **the 'reduced cost' is always zero for a decision variable that assumes a positive value;**
- **for variables whose optimal value is zero, the reduced cost represents the change in the value of the objective function for forcing that decision variable to assume a unit value.**

BASIC and STANDRD assume positive values: hence, their reduced costs are zero. LUXURY has a zero value. Its reduced cost is non-zero, i.e., –2.85714. By setting LUXURY = 1, the objective function would change by –2.85714 — a decrease of £2.86. This profit reduction can be explained as follows: At the optimal solution, it is not advantageous to let LUXURY assume a positive value. If the solution is forced away from the optimum, its objective function value must decrease by definition. (This would obviously mean that the values of some or all other decision variables would have to change accordingly for the solution to remain feasible, and that a unit change can be accommodated by the constraint set.)

The reduced costs are negative or zero if the objective function is maximized, signalling a possible decrease in the objective function. It is positive or zero if the objective function is minimized, signalling a possible increase.

What is the implication if the reduced cost is zero when the optimal value of the decision variable is zero? By the above logic, letting the variable become positive would cause no change in the objective function. In other words, the solution listed is not the only one that achieves that optimal objective function value.

If a decision variable is zero at the optimal solution and its reduced cost is non-zero, this implies that there are alternative optimal solutions with the same value of the objective function, but this variable at a positive value, with others adjusted accordingly to meet all constraints.

Activity

Explain why for variables, which are zero in the optimal solution, all 'Reduced Cost' values are positive (or zero) if the objective function is minimized.

The reduced cost can also be given an alternative interpretation. If the original objective function coefficient is changed by subtracting a value greater than the reduced cost, then the optimal solution will change to include this decision variable. For a reduction of less than the reduced cost, the optimal solution is not changed. If the objective coefficient is reduced by exactly the reduced cost, there will be alternative optimal solutions: one with the corresponding variable at zero and another with this variable taking on a positive value.

For example, if the objective function value of LUXURY increases by £2.86 to £162.86 (i.e., we subtract –2.86), then it would become attractive to produce some Luxury units, reducing the number of Basic and/or Standard units accordingly. An increase of only £2.85 would have no effect.

For all decision variables, the Sensitivity Report also shows by how much the value of its objective function coefficient can increase or decrease without affecting the optimal value of the decision variables. For example, the current optimal values of the three decision variables remain the same as long as the gross profit per unit of Basic is between 100 – 13.60 = 86.4 and 100 + 1.33 = 101.33. Obviously, a change in this objective function coefficient will result in a change in the value of the objective function. (The notation 'xE+p' means 'x times 10^p', i.e., '1E+30' is 1 multiplied by 10^{30}, a very large number that Solver uses to stand for infinity.)

The second part of the Sensitivity Report lists, for each constraint, its **shadow price** (see Section 13.4 for the correct interpretation of this term). For example, adding one minute of overtime for the shelving operation will increase the optimal value of the objective function by £1.4286 or about £85.70 per hour.

In contrast to the analysis of Chapter 13, which involved a nonlinear objective function, the shadow price of an LP constraint does not change gradually as the RHS of the constraint is changed. Rather, it remains constant over a given interval and then changes abruptly to a different value. This is the significance of the two columns 'Allowable Increase' and 'Allowable Decrease'. For the SHELVING constraint, the optimal value of the objective function increases by £1.43 for each additional minute up to a capacity of 1380 + 220 = 1600 minutes/day, or decreases by that amount for a decrease of up to 116 minutes. So, we see that if each of the three workers in the shelving operation does 30 minutes of overtime per day (adding 90 minutes in total), profits would go up by 90 times £1.4286 = £128.57. Since this must surely be more than the cost of 1½ hours of overtime, the firm should be advised to investigate having some workers go on overtime. (Figure 14-13 in Appendix 14.1 demonstrates how the shadow price for a problem with only two decision variables can be determined graphically.)

Note again that the shadow price for a constraint that has slack is zero.

Activity

Using what you learned in Chapter 13 about shadow prices, explain why the shadow price for the SHELVING constraint will decrease (in discrete steps) as more shelving time becomes available, but will increase (in discrete steps) as the time available becomes smaller.

Number of binding constraints and number of positive optimal values of decision variables

Only two of the three decision variables in the product mix problem assume a positive value in the optimal solution. Similarly, only two of the six constraints are binding. This is no coincidence.

Regardless of the number of variables in a linear program, the number that can assume a positive value at the optimal solution is never larger than the number of constraints that are binding, but may be fewer.

Even if the choice of workstation types had been in the hundreds, at most six would ever have been chosen in the optimal production mix if all six constraints were binding. If some constraints had been slack, the solution would have used even fewer types.

This relationship between the number of positive variables in the optimal solution and the number of binding constraints holds in general. It is a property associated with the mathematical structure of LP problems. For the non-mathematician — and most decision makers in business, industry, and government fall into this category — this property is a rather counterintuitive result. Most would expect that the larger the number of choices that can all be pursued jointly, the larger the number that is actually used. Not so! The number of constraints dictates the variety of choice that is optimal.

Unsuccessful termination of Solver

Solver may terminate without finding a solution. If no combination of decision variable values exists that satisfies all constraints simultaneously, the Solver Results window will have the message 'Solver could not find a feasible solution'.

The other unsuccessful termination is an **unbounded solution**. The Solver Result window will show the message 'The Set Cell values do not converge'. This means that the constraint set is such that some decision variables may be increased in value without upper bound and never be restricted by a constraint. Hence, the objective function value can go to plus infinity.

Although hypothetical problems can easily be devised that are infeasible or result in an unbounded solution, few economic or technical real-life problems are of this nature. Rather, getting this result is almost always an indication of errors in the computer input, or that something went wrong in the formulation of the problem. If you get either message you should painstakingly check the values of all LHS and objective function coefficients and all RHS parameters. A wrong sign — positive when it should be negative or vice versa — is an easy error to make. You may have left some LHS coefficients at zero by mistake. It is easy to enter a coefficient in the wrong column or row of the LP in detached coefficient form. Check in the 'Solver Parameter' window (Figure 14-3) whether the direction of each constraint (≤ or ≥) has been correctly entered. A >= entry instead of <= could let one or more variables go to infinity. If the input into your LP software is in equation form, carefully check the spelling of all variable names. One incorrect letter, and you have created a nonexistent variable which may allow another legitimate variable to become infinitely large.

If this does not remove the problem, carefully verify that all constraints have been correctly formulated. For instance, check that each constraint is dimensionally consistent. You may have to review your work more than once. Even better, have another person check it. If you are still unsuccessful, you may have to go back even further and have another look at your system definition. You may have overlooked other critical aspects — other decision choices or restrictions on them. Many optimization packages, including the latest version of Excel Solver, provide reports or tools to help track down such errors. Discussion of these reports is beyond the scope of this text.

14.6 Forcing a variable at zero to be positive

The reduced cost for LUXURY is only –2.85714. This means that forcing the production of some Luxury units might cause only a small decrease in the daily gross profit, while giving the firm a more balanced product line. Management may consider that not offering any Luxury workstations may be detrimental to its market image. They ask that the effect of forcing a minimum output of two Luxury units per day be studied. We add an additional constraint:

$$\text{LUXURY} \geq 2 \tag{14-8}$$

The complete problem and its optimal solution are shown in Figure 14-7.

	A	B	C	D	E	F	G	H
1	**Decision Variables**							
2	Product	Basic	Standard	Luxury				
3	Production	20	10	2	workstations			
4	**Objective function**				Total			
5	Gross profit	£100	£120	£160	£3,520.00	Max		
6	**Constraints**				Total	type	RHS	Units
7	Cutting	16	12	20	480	≤	480	minutes
8	Welding	25	22.5	36	797	≤	900	minutes
9	Painting	1	1	1	32	≤	32	workstations
10	Shelving	36	50	80	1380	≤	1380	minutes
11	Assembly	22.5	25	40	780	≤	900	minutes
12	Bas/Std Mix	-0.3333	1		3.334	≥	0	workstations
13	Min Luxury			1	2	≥	2	workstations

Figure 14-7 Expanded product mix problem with minimum Luxury output

The CUTTING constraint now also becomes binding. The additional trade-off needed for BASIC and STANDRD to accommodate this means that the GROSSPROF (cell E5) decreases by £5.71, i.e. by 2 × £2.85714. Management should be pleased that adding a requirement of a minimum Luxury production has such a negligible effect on daily gross profits. However, the rather large shift from Standard to Basic production may be not be so desirable.

Limitations of sensitivity analysis

If management had required a minimum of four Luxury workstations, Solver would have returned an optimal GROSSPROF of £3,453.04. This is a decrease of £72.67, significantly larger than four times the reduced cost of £2.85714 of the original formulation. A deeper analysis reveals that the reduced cost is valid only for an increase in Luxury of up to 2 workstations. Beyond 2, the reduced cost increases substantially. This points to one of the limitations of the Sensitivity Report. It gives no information on the permissible increase in the decision variable for which the reduced costs are valid.

An even bigger shortcoming of the Sensitivity Report is the assumption that only one objective function coefficient or one RHS parameter is changed, with all other inputs remaining at their original values. In many situations, a change in costs or in production rates, and so on, may affect more than one of these values. For instance, in the product mix problem, an increase in raw material costs will affect every single objective function coefficient. Similarly, management may feel obliged to offer overtime to all workers and not just those making the shelves. This too means that several RHS parameters will change simultaneously. Furthermore, the change may affect one or several LHS coefficients. Sensitivity analysis with respect to them is very complex. In such cases, the analyst has no choice but to re-optimize the problem for each new configuration.

The Sensitivity Report's main value is to highlight further aspects for analysis.

14.7 Pineapple Delight processing planning

A situation summary

Pineapple Delight, Inc., of Queensland, Australia, operates its own pineapple plantation. In most years, it processes its entire harvest in its cannery. Occasionally, some fruit is sold at the going market price to other processors. The current price for pineapple fruit sold on the market is $440 per tonne (= 1000 kg).

This coming season's crop is estimated at 24,000 tonnes. For processing, fresh fruit has to be skinned. This produces an average waste of 39.4%. The outer part of the skinned pineapple and its core, amounting to another 26.6%, can only be used for juice extraction. Juice is used in a finished pineapple product or sold at cost to beverage manufacturers. The balance of the flesh has traditionally been used for the firm's 'premium' pineapple rings. Offcuts in the form of crushed pineapple are used in fruit salad, and so on. With the market for canned pineapple rings becoming more competitive, Pineapple Delight has started to differentiate its products by marketing some output in novel shapes, such as spears and chunky pieces, or mixed with passion fruit.

Rings use 81% of the pineapple flesh, while 85% of the flesh can be cut into chunks. Flesh used for spears produces 60% spears and 28% chunks. In each case, the balance of the flesh is offcuts. Chunks are canned as chunky pieces or as passion fruit/pineapple chunks. Offcuts are used in fruit salad, fruit salad catering packs, and crush catering packs. The normal retail can has a net weight of 1 lb., or 454 grams, while catering packs have a net weight of 4.54 kg. The actual fruit content of each can is about 70% of the net weight.

Table 14-3 lists the pineapple products sold by Pineapple Delight, the amount of skinned flesh, the price ex-factory, and the sum of variable cutting, canning, and ingredient costs (mainly sugar) for each product. It also lists the upper limit for potential sales of each finished product. Naturally, these are only forecasts. They could be affected by advertising. For simplicity, we will ignore this aspect.

Table 14-3 Pineapple Delight product information

Product	Flesh	Revenue	Cost*	Contribution	Upper limit
Rings delight	0.31 kg	$0.74	$0.12	$0.62	9 million cans
Spears delight	0.27 kg	$0.82	$0.13	$0.69	6
Passion fruit/pineapple	0.31 kg	$0.88	$0.19	$0.69	4
Chunky pieces delight	0.34 kg	$0.68	$0.10	$0.58	8
Fruit salad delight	0.16 kg	$0.92	$0.51	$0.41	7
Fruit salad catering packs	1.6 kg	$6.20	$4.05	$2.15	3
Crush catering packs	3.4 kg	$5.10	$0.88	$4.22	unlimited

*exclusive of pineapple fruit cost

Management would like to develop a plan for the coming season. Its objective is to maximize profits. This means determining how much of its crop should be processed in its own cannery, how much sold to other processors, and how to allocate the usable flesh from the pineapple processed in its own cannery to the various products it sells.

A material flow diagram

You will agree that the firm's operations are difficult to grasp from this account. The systemic relationships are more effectively captured by a material flow diagram. Figure 14-8 shows the material flow associated with selling and processing pineapples.

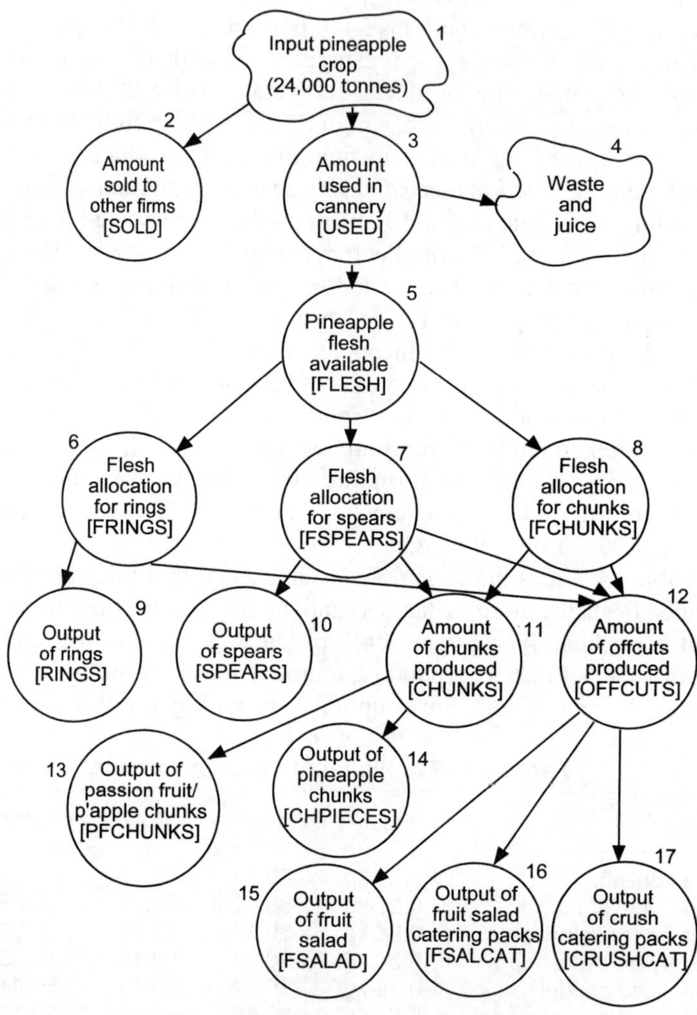

Figure 14-8 Material flow for pineapple processing

Cloud 1 denotes the input of 24,000 tonnes of fresh pineapples. It is either processed in the firm's own cannery (circle 3) or is sold to other processors (circle 2). Some 34% of the pineapples processed in its own cannery become usable flesh (circle 5), while the rest is either waste or is used for juice (cloud 4). Most of the juice is used in the firm's finished products and the balance sold at cost to beverage manufacturers.

Hence, there is no need to keep track of the use of juice since it does not affect profits. Pineapple flesh is then allocated to the production of the three main products: rings, spears, and chunks (circles 6, 7, 8). Each of these allocations is processed into its intended main product (circles 9, 10, 11), with part of it becoming offcuts (circle 12). Chunks are also a by-product of spears production. Finally, chunks and offcuts are allocated to the remaining five finished products (circles 13 to 17).

In this material flow diagram, each circle represents a variable whose optimal value we wish to find. In the next section, we shall see an example where it is more effective to let the arrows represent the variables.

Notice that some circles, i.e., 3, 5, 6, 7, 8, 11, and 12, refer to intermediate products, used as input into finished products, i.e. 9, 10, and 13 to 17. We will refer to all the variables (all circles) as 'decision variables'. This may not be strictly true, since some of them are simply consequences of another variable, i.e., we do not have the freedom to choose their values independently of each other. For example, the amount of pineapple flesh we get for any quantity of pineapples used in the cannery is 34%. Choosing the quantity of pineapples used immediately fixes the amount of pineapple flesh available. Constraints will be used to ensure such relationships.

Variable names and units

The variable names used for formulating the mathematical relationships are the mnemonic labels shown in brackets in the material flow diagram in Figure 14-8. In the formulation all variables are measured in terms of units of 1000. This is referred to as **scaling**. It is done for two reasons. First, it avoids writing all the extra zeros. More importantly, the accuracy of the computations performed by the LP computer packages increases if all LHS coefficients and RHS parameters are scaled such that they are close to 1, rather than some being extremely small, while others are very large. So, all intermediate products, including SOLD, are measured in 1000 kg, while all finished products are measured in 1000 cans of various weights. All variables are non-negative.

Objective function

The objective is to maximize profits, i.e., the difference between revenues and costs. However, fixed costs can be ignored. They will not affect the optimal operating plans. Revenues consist of the net receipts from selling fresh fruit and canned products, as listed in Table 14-3. The variable costs include the cost of preparing the fruit, cutting and canning it, as well as the cost of any ingredients used in the canning operation.

Should the cost of the pineapple fruit also be included? What is, in fact, the cost of the fruit? We could interpret it as the cost of harvesting it. If the entire harvest is used, either internally or sold, then this cost is a constant. Hence, it can be ignored. However, if less than the entire potential harvest is used, either sold or processed, with some fruit left in the fields, then the harvesting cost becomes a function of the pineapple used and must be included. In our case, all fruit is either processed or sold, so we will exclude the harvesting cost.

Economically, we should value any fruit not used at the opportunity cost of the best alternative use. This is selling the fruit to other processors, which is included as an explicit option in the linear programming model.

With the relevant variable costs directly allocated to the various finished products, the total contribution towards profit is simply given by the product of the amount of each finished product produced (and presumably sold) and its unit contribution, as listed in Table 14-3. To this we also add the receipts from fresh pineapples sold. The objective function therefore reads as follows:

MAXIMIZE 0.44 SOLD + 0.62 RINGS + 0.69 SPEARS
+ 0.69 PFCHUNKS + 0.58 CHPIECES + 0.41 FSALAD
+ 2.15 FSALCAT + 4.22 CRUSHCAT

Since all variables are in units of 1000, the objective function is also in \$1000.

Processing constraints

The material flow diagram helps us in determining the constraints. We associate one constraint with the set of flows (or arrows) coming out of each cloud or circle and one constraint with each set of flows (or arrows) ending at a circle.

Starting at the top of the diagram, we see two arrows coming from cloud 1, allocating the input of 24,000 tonnes of fresh fruit. One goes to SOLD, the other to USED in the firm's own cannery. Obviously, some of the crop could also be left over unused. We get the following inequality constraint:

$$\text{SOLD} + \text{USED} \leq 24{,}000$$

Stepping down the diagram, the next element is the circle for the amount of pineapple flesh, denoted by FLESH, resulting from the decision USED. From the description of the operation, only 34% of fresh pineapple fruit is suitable for further processing into canned products:

$$\text{FLESH} = 0.34\ \text{USED}$$

or expressed in the usual linear programming form:

$$\text{FLESH} - 0.34\ \text{USED} = 0$$

This is an accounting type **material balance** or **input–output constraint**.

The next constraint allocates the usable flesh for cutting into finished shapes, i.e., rings, spears, and chunks, represented by the arrows leaving the circle for FLESH:

$$\text{FRINGS} + \text{FSPEARS} + \text{FCHUNKS} = \text{FLESH}$$

or $$\text{FRINGS} + \text{FSPEARS} + \text{FCHUNKS} - \text{FLESH} = 0$$

The next layer in the diagram has four circles. The set of arrows leading into each generates a constraint. The first deals with the output of rings. Each unit of 1000 cans contains 0.31 tonnes of flesh. But only 81% of the flesh allocated for ring production is rings, the balance is offcuts. We get the following relationship for rings:

$$0.31\ \text{RINGS} = 0.81\ \text{FRINGS}$$

or $$0.31\ \text{RINGS} - 0.81\ \text{FRINGS} = 0$$

and we get a similar constraint for the output of spears:

$$0.27 \text{ SPEARS} - 0.6 \text{ FSPEARS} = 0$$

Chunks are produced as a by-product from spears as well as from the flesh allocated specifically to chunk production, each flow associated with one of the two arrows leading into the circle for CHUNKS:

$$0.28 \text{ FSPEARS} + 0.85 \text{ FCHUNKS} = \text{CHUNKS}$$

or

$$0.28 \text{ FSPEARS} + 0.85 \text{ FCHUNKS} - \text{CHUNKS} = 0$$

Verify that the amount of offcuts produced yields the following constraint:

$$0.19 \text{ FRINGS} + 0.12 \text{ FSPEARS} + 0.15 \text{ FCHUNKS} - \text{OFFCUTS} = 0$$

Finally, we have to allocate chunks and offcuts to their canned products:

$$0.31 \text{ PFCHUNKS} + 0.34 \text{ CHPIECES} - \text{CHUNKS} = 0$$

$$0.16 \text{ FSALAD} + 1.6 \text{ FSALCAT} + 3.4 \text{ CRUSHCAT} - \text{OFFCUTS} = 0$$

Note that, except for the first constraint on the total volume of fresh fruit available, all these constraints are equalities. They represent the flow of materials into or out of a node. For example, the total amount of material leaving circle 5 is equal to the sum sent along the arcs to circles 6, 7, and 8. Similarly, what is received by a given node, e.g., at circle 11, must be equal to the sum coming along the arcs from circles 7 and 8.

Marketing constraints

The output of each finished product, with the exception of crush in catering packs, should not exceed its upper limit listed in Table 14-4. This results in the following **upper bound constraints**:

$$\text{RINGS} \le 9000 \qquad \text{SPEARS} \le 6000$$

$$\text{PFCHUNKS} \le 4000 \qquad \text{CHPIECES} \le 8000$$

$$\text{FSALAD} \le 7000 \qquad \text{FSALCAT} \le 3000$$

Optimal solution

This linear program was solved using the Excel Solver. Figure 14-9 shows the Excel spreadsheet. The layout used almost exactly matches the layout from the product mix case, with one column per variable and one row for each constraint and the objective function. The lightly shaded cells hold parameter values and the calculations in the totals column are all sumproduct formulas. The dark shaded cells hold the decision variables, currently showing the optimal solution.

For this formulation the upper bound constraints are treated differently. The row immediately under the decision variables row holds the upper bounds for those variables with bounds. These constraints are added to Excel Solver with the other constraints. In the Add Constraint dialog box, the decision variable cell is the Cell Reference and the upper bound value is the Constraint (RHS parameter).

Decision Variables																			
Product	Sold	Used	Flesh	FRings	FSpears	FChunks	Rings	Spears	Chunks	Offcuts	PFChunks	ChPieces	FSalad	FSalCat	CrushCat				
Production	0	24000	8160	3444.44	2700	2015.56	9000	6000	2469.22	1280.78	4000	3615.36	7000	100.486	0				
Upper limit							9000	6000			4000	8000	7000	3000					
Units	tonnes	tonnes	tonnes	tonnes	tonnes	tonnes	1000 cans	1000 cans	tonnes	tonnes	1000 cans	1000 cans	1000 cans	1000 cans	1000 cans				
Objective function																Total			
Profit contribution	$0.44						$0.62	$0.69			$0.69	$0.58	$0.41	$2.15	$4.22	$17,663	Max		
Constraints																Total	type	RHS	Units
Total fresh fruit	1	1														24000	≤	24,000	tonnes
Useful flesh		-0.34	1													0	=	0	tonnes
Flesh allocation			-1	1	1	1										0	=	0	tonnes
Rings weight balance				-0.81			0.31									0	=	0	tonnes
Spears weight balance					-0.6			0.27								0	=	0	tonnes
Chuncks weight balance					0.28	0.85			-1							0	=	0	tonnes
Offcut weight balance				0.19	0.12	0.15				-1						0	=	0	tonnes
Chunck allocation									-1		0.31	0.34				0	=	0	tonnes
Offcut allocation										-1			0.16	1.6	3.4	0	=	0	tonnes

Figure 14-9 Excel Solver linear programming model for Pineapple Delight

The maximal value of the objective function is 17,662.95. Since the objective function is in units of \$1000, the total contribution is \$17,662,950. Information on all variables and all inequality constraints at the optimum is listed in Table 14-4. The shadow prices for the equality constraints are not shown since their interpretation is rather complex and beyond the scope of this text. When interpreting these numbers, remember that they are in units of 1000 kg or cans. Similarly, the reduced costs and the shadow prices are in thousands of dollars per 1000 kg or per 1000 cans, which equates to dollars per kg or dollars per can, respectively.

Table 14-4 Optimal solution to Pineapple Delight

Product	Variable	Optimal value	Reduced cost
Pineapples sold	SOLD	0	–0.1215
Pineapples processed	USED	24,000	0
Usable flesh	FLESH	8,160	0
Flesh allocated to rings	FRINGS	3,444.4	0
Flesh allocated to spears	FSPEARS	2,700	0
Flesh allocated to chunks	FCHUNKS	2,015.6	0
Chunks produced	CHUNKS	1,280.8	0
Rings	RINGS	*9,000	0.0856
Spears	SPEARS	*6,000	0.2343
Passion fruit chunks	PFCHUNKS	*4,000	0.1612
Chunky pieces	CHPIECES	3,615.4	0
Fruit salad	FSALAD	*7,000	0.195
Fruit salad catering packs	FSALCAT	100.5	0
Crush catering packs	CRUSHCAT	0	–0.3487
Constraint	**Status**	**Slack**	**Shadow price**
Total fresh fruit	binding	0	0.5615
Upper limits:			
on rings	binding	0	0.0856
on spears	binding	0	0.2343
on passion fruit chunks	binding	0	0.1612
on chunky pieces	slack	4,384.6	0
on fruit salad	binding	0	0.195
on fruit salad cat. packs	slack	2,899.5	0

*variable at its upper limit

What-if analysis

No catering packs of crush are produced. The output of fruit salad catering packs is only 100,500 cans. It is conceivable that this is too small for effective marketing of this product. The firm may wish to increase its marketing effort for retail cans of fruit salad to absorb the crush allocated to catering packs. It would imply raising the upper limit on fruit salad by about 1000 units of 1000 cans, i.e., one million cans — one seventh of the current output. The shadow price for the upper limit on fruit salad is 0.195, or \$195 per 1000 cans. It turns out that this shadow price is valid for any conceivable increase in the upper limit (not shown!). Hence if the upper limit on fruit salad can be lifted to at least 8 million cans through further advertising at a cost of less than \$195,000 (= \$195 times 1000), such a switch would be advantageous.

Note another interesting fact. The reduced cost for FSALAD is equal to the shadow price of its upper bound constraint. This is true in general.

All fresh fruit is processed. None is sold. The reduced cost coefficient for SOLD indicates that the total profit contribution would decrease by 0.1215 (= \$121.50/tonne) for every unit increase (= 1 tonne) of SOLD. It may be useful to ask 'What increase in price for fresh fruit would be required before selling some or all fresh fruit becomes attractive?' The reduced cost for SOLD again provides us with the answer. Its negative is the minimum price increase needed for the variable SOLD to assume a positive value without reducing the objective function. The market price for fresh fruit would need to increase by \$121.50/tonne to at least \$561.50 (= \$440 + \$121.50).

This is also the increase in contribution realized by increasing the amount of pineapple crop by 1 tonne, as indicated by the shadow price of the total fresh fruit constraint. If the firm could acquire fresh fruit on the open market for less than \$561.50 it could increase its profits by the difference for each additional tonne processed, up to a maximum of 5,158.4 tonnes (not shown!).

14.8 The transportation problem

An application of high practical importance deals with transportation problems. Goods are available in limited quantities at several sources and required in given quantities at various destinations. There is a cost of transporting the goods between sources and destinations. The problem consists of satisfying the requirements at all destinations so as to minimize the sum of all transportation costs. The shifting of soil and rocks in the highway construction problem referred to in the introduction to this chapter is an example of a transportation problem.

A production/transportation problem situation

Remember the Heinz tomato paste logistics case in Section 12.8? The problem consisted in finding the optimal number of railcars for transporting tomato paste from factory X to conversion plant Y. Obviously, Heinz processes tomatoes at more than one factory and has several conversion plants scattered all over the USA. Consider the following example: there are tomato processing plants in Stockton and Riverside, California, and Tuscaloosa, Alabama, and there are five conversion plants: Los Angeles, Dallas, Chicago, Atlanta, and Newark.

Table 14-5 summarizes the unit transportation cost from each tomato processing plant to each conversion station, the unit processing costs at each processing plant, the production capacity at each processing plant, and the tomato paste requirements at each conversion plant during a given 4-week period. For example, the transportation cost from Stockton to Chicago is \$54 per tonne, Stockton's production cost is \$524 per tonne, and it has a production capacity of 4,600 tonnes for the given 4-week period, while Chicago has a requirement of 1,600 tonnes for the corresponding 4-week period.

The firm would like to determine the production schedule which has the lowest total production and transportation cost.

Table 14-5 Input data for a transportation problem

Sources	Production cost	Capacity tonnes	Transportation cost to destinations				
			LA	Dallas	Chicago	Atlanta	Newark
Stockton	$524	4,600	$25	$48	$54	$67	$75
Riverside	$541	2,900	$11	$44	$57	$61	$81
Tuscaloosa	$612	1,700	$57	$33	$32	$10	$36
Amount required in tonnes			2,100	1,700	1,600	1,300	2,200

As in the previous example, a material flow diagram makes the transportation problem much more transparent. The network in Figure 14-10 depicts the flow of goods from the three source nodes to the five destination nodes.

Each arc from a source node to a destination node depicts a shipping option. For instance, the arrow from Stockton to Chicago is the option of shipping goods from Stockton to Chicago. The amount shipped along that arc is denoted by the mnemonic variable STCH, shown next to the arc. (We used the first two letters of each name.)

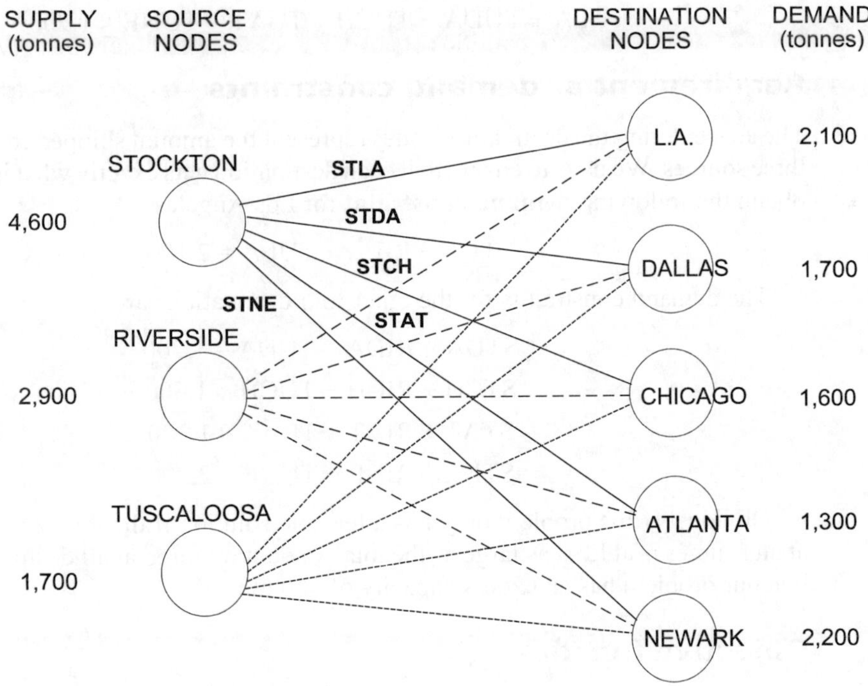

Figure 14-10 Goods flow diagram for transportation problem

In contrast to Figure 14-8, the flow of material from sources to destinations is represented by the arcs, rather than by the circles. If all options are available, the number of arcs leaving each source is equal to the number of destinations, denoted by n, while the number of arcs entering each destination is equal to the number of sources, denoted by m. The total number of variables is therefore equal to m times n, or $3 \times 5 = 15$ for our example.

The network flow diagram again helps us in determining all constraints. As in the previous example, we associate a constraint with each set of arcs leaving a source node (the nodes issuing material) and one with each set of arcs entering a destination node (the nodes receiving material).

Availability or supply constraints

Consider the five arcs leaving the Stockton node. Each represents the amount shipped from Stockton to one of the five destinations. The total amount shipped from Stockton cannot exceed Stockton's capacity of 4,600 tonnes for the four-week period in question. We obtain the following constraint, called a **supply constraint**:

$$\text{STLA} + \text{STDA} + \text{STCH} + \text{STAT} + \text{STNE} \leq 4{,}600$$

Each of the other two sources has a similar supply constraint:

$$\text{RILA} + \text{RIDA} + \text{RICH} + \text{RIAT} + \text{RINE} \leq 2{,}900$$

$$\text{TULA} + \text{TUDA} + \text{TUCH} + \text{TUAT} + \text{TUNE} \leq 1{,}700$$

Requirement or demand constraints

The arcs entering the destination nodes represent the amount shipped from each of the three sources. We have to ensure that each destination gets exactly what it requires. We obtain the following **demand constraint** for Los Angeles:

$$\text{STLA} + \text{RILA} + \text{TULA} = 2{,}100$$

The demand constraints for the other four destinations are:

$$\text{STDA} + \text{RIDA} + \text{TUDA} = 1{,}700$$

$$\text{STCH} + \text{RICH} + \text{TUCH} = 1{,}600$$

$$\text{STAT} + \text{RIAT} + \text{TUAT} = 1{,}300$$

$$\text{STNE} + \text{RINE} + \text{TUNE} = 2{,}200$$

Obviously, this problem only has a feasible solution if the total amount available at all sources is at least as large as the total amount required at all destinations. Verify that our problem has an excess capacity of 300 tonnes.

Objective function

The objective is to minimize total costs. In transportation problems, the relevant cost usually includes only the transportation costs. However, in our example the variable production costs at the three processing plants differ. Furthermore, there is excess processing capacity of 300 tonnes. Hence, some plants will operate below full capacity. The total production cost will depend on which plants are left with excess capacity. As a consequence the production costs become a relevant item. For example, from Table 14-5 it follows that the relevant cost of allocating one tonne of goods from Stockton to Chicago is equal to the variable production costs at Stockton of $524 plus the transportation cost from Stockton to Chicago of $54, or a total of $578.

The total cost is equal to the product of the unit allocation cost, computed from Table 14-5, and the amount shipped, summed over all allocation options:

$$\begin{aligned} z = {} & 549\text{ STLA} + 572\text{ STDA} + 578\text{ STCH} + 591\text{ STAT} + 601\text{ STNE} \\ & + 552\text{ RILA} + 585\text{ RIDA} + 598\text{ RICH} + 602\text{ RIAT} + 622\text{ RINE} \\ & + 669\text{ TULA} + 645\text{ TUDA} + 644\text{ TUCH} + 622\text{ TUAT} + 648\text{ TUNE} \end{aligned}$$

Activity

If the total supply is smaller than the total demand, the nature of the problem changes to one of allocating the goods so as to maximize net profits.

- How does this change the supply and demand constraints? (Hint: one or more of the destinations will not have their demand met completely.)
- What revenue and costs would enter into the objective function coefficients?
- Can variable production costs be ignored if total supply equals total demand?

Optimal solution

The problem has $m + n$ or $3 + 5 = 8$ constraints, plus the 15 non-negativity constraints on the decision variables. It was optimized using Microsoft Excel Solver. The spreadsheet model showing the optimal solution is illustrated in Figure 14-11. The layout of this spreadsheet linear programming model matches the layout of the previous models. Note the structure of the LHS coefficients for the constraints.

Table 14-6 lists the optimal production/transportation schedule. Tuscaloosa ends up with an excess capacity of 300 tonnes. The minimum cost is $5,202,300.

Table 14-6 Optimal production/transportation schedule

Destinations / Sources	LA	Dallas	Chicago	Atlanta	Newark	Total shipped
Stockton	0	900	1,600	0	2,100	4,600
Riverside	2,100	800	0	0	0	2,900
Tuscaloosa	0	0	0	1,300	100	1,400
Total received	2,100	1,700	1,600	1,300	2,200	

The optimal solution has some interesting features. As expected, the expensive Tuscaloosa plant does not work at full capacity. Far more unexpected, though, is that the optimal transportation schedule does not necessarily select the cheapest options. For example, Stockton ships nothing to Los Angeles — its cheapest option — but supplies

Decision Variables																			
Product	ST_LA	ST_DA	ST_CH	ST_AT	ST_NE	RI_LA	RI_DA	RI_CH	RI_AT	RI_NE	TU_LA	TU_DA	TU_CH	TU_AT	TU_NE				
Production	400	1700	900	1300	0	0	0	700	0	2200	1700	0	0	0	0	tonnes			
Objective function																Total			
Profit contribution	$549	$572	$578	$591	$601	$552	$585	$598	$602	$622	$669	$645	$644	$622	$648	$5,404,800	Max		
Constraints																Total	type	RHS	Units
Stockton capacity	1	1	1	1	1											4300	≤	4,600	tonnes
Riverside capacity						1	1	1	1	1						2900	≤	2,900	tonnes
Tuscaloosa capacity											1	1	1	1	1	1700	≤	1,700	tonnes
L.A. demand	1					1					1					2100	=	2,100	tonnes
Dallas demand		1					1					1				1700	=	1,700	tonnes
Chicago demand			1					1					1			1600	=	1,600	tonnes
Atlanta demand				1					1					1		1300	=	1,300	tonnes
Newark demand					1					1					1	2200	=	2,200	tonnes

Figure 14-11 Transportation problem spreadsheet LP model

almost the entire Newark requirement — its most expensive option. How can this rather counterintuitive result be optimal?

The answer lies in the unit cost differences between the shipping options. If Stockton supplied Los Angeles while Riverside shipped to Newark, there would be a $3 unit cost saving for Stockton shipments, but an additional $21 cost for Riverside shipments.

The third interesting feature is that all decision variables are integer, although we did not specify this as a condition. It turns out that this is a general characteristic.

At an optimal solution to a transportation problem, all variables assume integer values, provided that all availabilities at sources and all requirements at destinations are also integer.

Alternative spreadsheet formulation

Transportation problems have a special constraint structure which allows for a more streamlined spreadsheet formulation. We arrange the decision variables in an array, with the rows relating to the sources and the columns relating to the destinations. The cell at the intersection of a source row and destination column measures the amount shipped from that source to that destination, i.e., it is the value of the corresponding decision variable. The availability constraints are then formed by summing the rows, while the requirement constraints are given by summing the columns.

The top portion of Figure 14-12 displays this alternative input structure for the Heinz problem. We now have a totals column for the sources, but also a totals row for the destinations. For example, the formula for cell G3 is '=SUM(B3:F3)' and the formula in cell B6 is '=SUM(B3:B5)'. Below that first array is a second one which contains the objective function coefficients. The value of the objective function in cell G15 is computed as 'SUMPRODUCT(B3:F5,B12:F14)'.

	A	B	C	D	E	F	G	H	I	J
1	**Decision Variables and Constraints**									
2		L.A.	Dallas	Chicago	Atlanta	Newark	total	type	capacity	
3	Stockton	400	1700	900	1300	0	4300	≤	4,600	tonnes
4	Riverside	0	0	700	0	2200	2900	≤	2,900	tonnes
5	Tuscaloosa	1700	0	0	0	0	1700	≤	1,700	tonnes
6	total	2100	1700	1600	1300	2200				
7	type	=	=	=	=	=				
8	demand	2,100	1,700	1,600	1,300	2,200				
9		tonnes	tonnes	tonnes	tonnes	tonnes				
10	**Objective function**									
11		L.A.	Dallas	Chicago	Atlanta	Newark				
12	Stockton	$549	$572	$578	$591	$601				
13	Riverside	$552	$585	$598	$602	$622				
14	Tuscaloosa	$669	$645	$644	$622	$648				
15						Total profit	$5,404,800			

Figure 14-12 Alternative transportation problem spreadsheet model

Figure 14-12 displays the optimal solution, which obviously is identical to the one in Figure 14-11. These represent two different ways to submit the objective function and the constraints to Excel Solver. (Note, however, that the way sensitivity results are presented in Excel Solver will be differ between the two formulations.)

Other problem situations disguised as transportation problems

The Heinz problem above involves transporting goods **over space**, i.e., from several locations to several other locations. However, goods can also be 'transported', figuratively speaking, **over time** from a given period to a later period. For example, a firm has a production capacity that fluctuates in a known pattern over time, while it also has to meet a demand that varies in a different pattern over time. As a consequence, production in, say, March is stored in inventory until it is used in June. Obviously, there is a cost associated with storing goods. Furthermore, the firm may have the option of adding more production capacity by going to overtime, again at a cost. The firm would like to find a production and storage schedule, including the use of overtime, so as to minimize the total relevant cost. Total costs include the cost of storing goods for later use and the cost of regular and overtime production. (Any option that implies meeting demand in a given period by production in a later period is ruled out by simply penalizing it with a prohibitive cost.) This is often referred to as the **regular time/overtime production scheduling problem**.

The Crystal Springs problem in Section 12-2 is of a similar nature, except that it also included fixed costs for adding and discontinuing shifts. This aspect can only be handled by a more complex integer programming formulation.

A related situation is the **assignment problem**.* A number of jobs need to be done and there are a number of people to do them. Due to differences in training and experience, the people differ in their aptitude or suitability to do the various jobs. The problem is to find the best match of people and jobs. This can also be viewed as a sort of transportation problem. The persons become the sources, the jobs the destinations. Each source has an availability of 1. Each destination has a requirement of 1. The objective is to maximize the sum of the 'suitability indices' of the person-to-job assignments. With all RHS parameters equal to 1 and the optimal solution being integer, each job is assigned to one person only. There are no split or partial assignments.

*The assignment problem was used by George B. Dantzig, the inventor of the first efficient solution algorithm for LPs, to 'prove' that monogamy is the optimal social structure. When asked at a press conference in the late 1940s to explain in lay terms what the linear programming 'model' was, he used the following allegory: Assume that 100 men and 100 women get shipwrecked on a deserted island with no hope of any rescue in their lifetime. They decide to pair off men and women. But they wish to find the optimal set of pairings that maximizes happiness for their isolated society. This is an assignment problem. Since its optimal solution will have no split assignments, say several men partially assigned to one women, but only all or nothing assignments, this proves that monogamy is the optimal solution, i.e., the optimal social structure. As in real life, not all matches will be ideal, but viewed overall no other assignment will have a greater total happiness. After that explanation, one of the reporters present exclaimed: 'Man, you must have been playing with the wrong model!'

14.9 Combining data preparation and LP model in one Excel spreadsheet

So far, we have used the LP in detached coefficient form as the input into Excel Solver (except for the alternative structure of the transportation problem in Figure 14-12). This required that all objective function coefficients and all LHS coefficients are readily available in final form or, if not, have already been computed from original raw data in a separate spreadsheet before entering them into the LP spreadsheet.

Why not combine both operations into a single spreadsheet? The original raw numeric data are entered into a 'data' subsection. They are then used to compute all coefficients and the constraint right-hand sides in the subsection reserved for the LP in detached coefficient form.

The main advantage of this approach is that any changes occurring in the raw data, such as changes in employee pay rates and fringe benefit contributions, costs in raw material and supplies, or changes in the ingredient specifications, are instantly reflected in all entries in the LP in detached coefficient form. There is no need to change any coefficients or constraint right-hand sides individually. Changing them individually, it is easy to overlook some, which would invalidate the solution obtained.

B18 f_x =B5-B4

	A	B	C	D	E	F	G	H
1	ORIGINAL DATA							
2	One hour	60	minutes					
3	Product	Basic	Standard	Luxury				
4	Material cost	43	60	86	per workstation			
5	Wholesale price	143	180	246	per workstation			
6	Process	Cutting	Welding	Shelving	Assembly			
7	Basic	16	25	36	22.5	minutes		
8	Standard	12	22.5	50	25	minutes		
9	Luxury	20	36	80	40			
10	Capacity/day	8	15	23	15	hours		
11	Painting capacity/day	32	workstations					
12	Marketing requirements							
13	Standard at least	0.3333	Number of Basic workstations					
14	LP MODEL							
15	Product	Basic	Standard	Luxury				
16	Output/day	6	8	9	workstations			
17	Objective function				Total			
18	Gross profit	£100	£120	£160	£3,000.00	Max		
19	Constraints				Total	type	RHS	Units
20	Cutting	16	12	20	372	≤	480	minutes
21	Welding	25	22.5	36	654	≤	900	minutes
22	Painting	1	1	1	23	≤	32	workstations
23	Shelving	36	50	80	1336	≤	1380	minutes
24	Assembly	22.5	25	40	695	≤	900	minutes
25	Bas/Std Mix	-0.3333	1		6.0002	≥	0	workstations

Figure 14-13 A linear programming model with computed coefficients

Such an approach is part of good modelling practice.

When applying sensitivity analysis, it is also important to realize that the implied changes apply to the objective coefficients and RHS parameter values and not directly to the original data. The effect of a change to a single original data value which affects multiple LP coefficients or parameter values cannot be determined directly from the Sensitivity Report. The only option is to make the changes, re-optimize the LP, and observe the changes in the optimal solution produced.

Figure 14-13 displays the combined raw data input and LP formulation for the product mix problem of Section 14.2. The original data from Table 14-1 (p. 371), together with any other relevant numeric data, is entered in the top subsection of the spreadsheet. These entries are then used to prepare the LP in detached coefficient form shown in the bottom subsection. The formula window displays the calculation used to find the entry for cell B17.

Case study 14-1: The Nordic Forest Corporation of Norway

The operations manager of the Nordic Forest Corporation (NFC) is planning next month's production. NFC is currently logging two forests, F1 and F2. The logs harvested are used either in NFC's sawmill or in its pulp mill. Some of the logs can also be exported to England. The table below lists the average output of each forest per day, the maximum percentage of logs suitable for processing by the sawmill or for export (export logs need to be straight, otherwise they take too much space in the ship's hold), and the cost of harvesting and of transporting the logs from each forest to the plants or to the export port. Logs not suitable for the sawmill or for export can only be used for pulp. Export logs fetch 2,000 Norwegian Kroners (K) per cubic metre.

Logs processed by the sawmill are converted into construction and dressed timber in the proportions below. Offcuts and scraps are transferred to the pulp mill for use there. The logs from forest F2 offer two possible conversion patterns into construction and dressed timber that have different processing rates. The manager has the following data:

Forest	F1	F2	
Upper limit to log output in cubic metres	128	192	
Maximum percentage of logs harvested suitable for sawmill and export	41%	55%	
Cost of harvesting logs	K124	K132	/cubic metre
Transport cost from forest to sawmill	K42	K66	/cubic metre
pulp mill	K32	K45	/cubic metre
port	K62	K56	/cubic metre
Transport cost from sawmill to pulp mill	K24 /cubic metre		

Log conversion at sawmill for logs from forest	F1	F2	
		Pattern 1	Pattern 2
Construction timber	60%	40%	50%
Dressed timber	30%	48%	41%
Scrap and offcuts	10%	12%	9%
Processing time in hours/cubic metre:			
into construction timber	0.10	0.12	0.11
Into dressed timber	0.25	0.22	0.24
Selling price/cubic metre: Construction timber	K1,500	K1,500	K1,500
Dressed timber	K2,900	K3,100	K3,000

The sawmill operates for two shifts per day. Each shift has an average capacity of 6 hours; the remaining 2 hours for the shift are taken for stoppages and maintenance. The hourly operating cost of the sawmill is K2,500. Scraps and offcuts are a by-product of the sawmill process not using any capacity.

NFC wants to meet the demand for construction timber of at least 32 cubic metres per day, while the output of dressed timber should not exceed 40 cubic metres per day.

Logs, scraps, and offcuts are converted into chips at the pulp mill. The chips are then processed into pulp, used for newsprint production. Each cubic metre of wood yields 0.5 tonnes of pulp which has a value of K3,400/tonne and incurs a processing cost of K400/tonne. The pulp mill can process up to 160 cubic metres per day. NFC has to meet firm contracts for pulp of 60 tonnes per day.

The operations manager would like to know the best daily operating schedule, in terms of allocation of logs to the various finished products, and the output of finished products, so as to maximize gross profits.

(Note that most integrated forest products processing companies use MS/OR methods to help them determine suitable operating plans. Obviously, their problems are much more complex, involving hundreds of log types of different qualities, which have different conversion rates into final products. They also model their operations in much greater detail, with intermediate products going from machine to machine.)

(a) Develop a diagram depicting the material flow for this situation, similar to the one shown in Figure 14-8. However, you may find it easier to have the flows associated with the arcs, and let the nodes represent either sources, processes, or uses. This will be helpful for part (b) below.

(b) Formulate this problem as an LP. Note that in this example, it may be easier to associate decision variables with the arcs, rather than the circles.

(c) Solve the problem using an LP computer package, e.g., Excel Solver.

(d) Optional: show the numerical values of your solution on the flow diagram in (a) by attaching to each arc the value of the corresponding decision variable.

(e) Management is considering the possibility of shifting all or part of the maintenance work on the sawmill to overtime. What increase in profit can be achieved for an additional hour of capacity? It is also possible to add an additional logging gang to forest F1 at a daily cost of K4,800. The additional gang would be able to log up to 32 cubic metres of logs per day. Should NFC consider this option? Why or why not? The marketing manager would like to launch a campaign to increase sales of dressed timber, since it seems to provide such a high contribution towards profits. Should he be encouraged to do this? What would be the consequences of it and why?

14.10 Integer programming models

In many practical situations, some decision variables are restricted to assume only integer values. For example, the number of Airbus 380-800 operated by an airline has to be an integer. It cannot be 4.67. Often, the choice is restricted further to either 0 or 1, i.e., select something, such as an option (1), or do not (0). This is captured by **binary variables**, which assume the values 0 or 1.

If all decision variables are restricted to non-negative integer values, the formulation is referred to as an integer linear program or IP. If only a subset of variables need to be integers, while the rest may assume any non-negative value, we talk about a mixed integer program or MIP. In real life, the latter are the more common.

The formulation of IPs and MIPs follows largely the same pattern as for LPs, except that the solution software must also be told which variables are restricted to integers and which ones have to be binary variables.

Consider again the investment portfolio problem in Section 13.6. Table 13-3 (p,

364) contains all the data. The firm has an investment budget of £600,000 and a list of candidate projects (denoted by A to K), each with an initial investment and projected *NPV*. For purposes of demonstration, we alter the problem slightly. Projects D and H represent marketing events that can be repeated in up to four different urban centres, each requiring the same initial investment and providing the same *NPV*. The objective is to find a combination of investments from this list that maximizes the sum of *NPV*s.

We shall name the decision variables by their letter. All are restricted to integers. Variables D and H cannot exceed 4, while the remainder are binary variables, 0 or 1. This results in ten simple constraints, each of the form

$$X \le U_X, \quad X = A, B, C, \ldots, K, \text{ and } U_X = \text{upper limit of variable X.}$$

The objective function is

$$\text{MAX } 84A + 50B + 45C + 39D + 35E + 26F + 24G + 9H + 8J + 2K$$

In addition to the upper bounds, there is one additional constraint — the total amount invested cannot exceed the budget of £600,000:

$$\begin{aligned}\text{(BUDGET)} \quad & 107A + 201B + 182C + 133D + 82E \\ & + 141F + 30G + 37H + 25J + 12K \le 600 \text{ (thousand)}\end{aligned}$$

Figure 14-14 displays the input format for solution by Excel Solver.

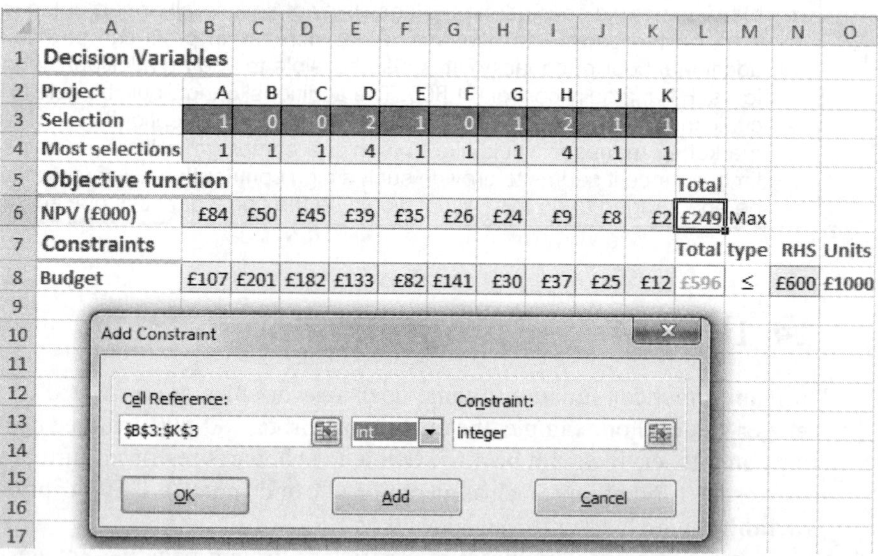

Figure 14-14 An integer programming model

Row 2 gives the names of the ten variables. Row 3 contains their current values (which normally are all set to zero to start with). Row 4 lists the upper limits of the variables, implying the set of constraints $X \le U_X$. For binary variables, rather than enter upper bound constraints of 1, we could have listed them individually or as a range in the 'Cell Reference' of the 'Add constraint' window and select constraint type 'bin'. The objective function coefficients are listed in row 5, with the value of the objective function computed in cell L6. Finally, the LHS coefficients of the budget constraint are listed in row 8. All monetary figures are in units of £1000.

To force the decision variables to take on integer values, another set of constraints has to be added, as depicted in the 'Add constraint' window in Figure 14-14. In the 'Cell Reference', we list the variables that are restricted to integers, either individually or as a range as done here, and select constraint type 'int'.

Figure 14-14 displays the optimal solution of projects chosen in row 3. Cell L6 shows the maximal value of the total *NPV* as £249. Not the entire budget is used up.

IP models allow complex conditions and restrictions to be modelled. Integer variables can be used to turn sets of constraints on and off when certain conditions occur, to select exactly one of a set of options, and to model mathematical logic conditions. Discussion of such complexities is beyond the scope of this text.

Integer programming models are not 'well-behaved'. They take longer to optimize than equivalently sized LPs. Some can take many hours to find an optimal solution. For highly complex situations, rather than attempt optimization with IP software, we may have to be satisfied finding a good solution by heuristic methods (see Section 6.19).

Unlike linear programming software, IP software provides little or no sensitivity analysis. The only recourse is to change the inputs and re-optimize.

14.11 Chapter highlights

- If all relationships — constraints and the objective function — are linear and all variables continuous, then a constrained optimization problem can be formulated as an LP and solved by LP computer software using the Simplex algorithm.
- The sensitivity report of Excel Solver provides useful information for decision making. At the optimal solution, the following properties hold:
  - → The number of decision variables that can assume positive values is at most equal to the number of binding constraints.
  - → The shadow price of a binding constraint is (normally) non-zero; it is the change in the optimal value of the objective function for a unit change in the RHS of the corresponding constraint.
  - → Slack constraints have zero shadow prices.
  - → The reduced cost coefficient of a variable that is zero is negative for maximizing and positive for minimizing the objective function. It represents the change in the objective function if that variable is forced to assume a value of 1. If its negative is added to the original objective function coefficient, this variable becomes eligible to assume a positive value at the optimal solution.
- The transportation problem deals with finding the optimal schedule for:
  - → transporting goods over space from sources with limited availabilities to destinations with minimum requirements;

→ allocating production capacity in given periods to meet demand in the same or later periods, i.e., 'transporting goods over time'.

- The assignment problems assigns 'people' to 'jobs' to best use their skills.
- Transportation and assignment problems are special types of LP that result in integer solutions.
- If some or all decision variables are restricted to integer values, it is an integer programming problem, solved by an algorithm built to cater for that aspect. Excel Solver is capable of solving relatively small integer programming problems.

Exercises

1. The manager of a camping trailer factory is offered a contract with the leading local distributor for producing two types of trailer, A and B, to the specifications supplied by the distributor. Trailer A offers a net profit per unit of $600, while B's unit profit is $900. A and B would share the same assembly and painting facilities. Type A requires 2 person-weeks of assembly time per unit, B requires $3^1/_3$ person-weeks per unit. There are 20 person weeks of assembly time available per month (= 5 people for 4 weeks each). The painting facilities can handle a maximum of 8 trailers per month. The distributor would leave it to the manufacturer to determine the product mix, provided that at least two trailers of type A would be available, and the number of type A is at least $^1/_3$ of the number of type B produced. This is to guarantee an acceptable product mix.
   (a) Draw an influence diagram for this problem.
   (b) Use it to formulate an LP with the objective of maximizing total monthly profits.
   (c) Enter the problem in a spreadsheet as an LP in detached coefficient form and prepare it for input into Solver or similar software.
   (d) Use it to find the optimal solution and verify that all constraints are met. What is the optimal number of each trailer to produce? What is the monthly profit?
   (e) How much should the manager be willing to pay for more assembly time per person-week? How much for increasing the throughput of the painting facility by one unit?
2. Management in the product mix problem of Section 14.2 is dismayed that no unit of the Luxury workstation is recommended in the optimal solution. They therefore add a soft constraint, requiring a minimum output of at least 3 Luxury units per day.
   (a) Add an appropriate constraint for this requirement and re-optimize the problem by computer. How has the solution changed in terms of binding constraints?
   (b) What is the daily cost to the firm of this new requirement?
   (c) Interpret the shadow price of this constraint. Why is it correct that it is negative?
3. A cabinet maker would like to use the current excess capacity in the factory to produce a combination of three different types of bathroom cabinet. The table below lists labour requirements for the various operations per unit and other input data:

Product	Cutting time	Glueing time	Sanding time	Finishing time	Profit/unit
Modern	24 min.	60 min.	20 min.	160 min.	$60.00
Provincial	36 min.	90 min.	60 min.	120 min.	$60.00
Colonial	48 min.	60 min.	60 min.	180 min.	$56.00
Capacity	8 hours	15 hours	8 hours	32 hours	per week

(a) Formulate this problem as an LP, maximizing weekly profits for the additional activity.
(b) Optimize the model. What is the optimal solution?
(c) The cabinet maker considers introducing overtime for some of the operations. Which ones are possible candidates and what is the maximum overtime premium the cabinet maker should consider paying?
(d) The optimal solution does not produce any colonial cabinets. The cabinet maker has been approached by a bathroom dealer to supply at least 1 colonial cabinet per week. Using the information from the sensitivity analysis report, by how much would the cabinet maker's weekly profit decrease if 1 colonial cabinet is produced per week? How much larger would the increase in the unit profit for a colonial cabinet have to be before it would become attractive to produce colonial cabinets?

4. An insurance company has £100 million of funds available for investments. It has a choice of three types of investment of unequal risk: blue-chip shares that offer an annual return of 6% with a risk rating of 1; government bonds at 4% with a risk rating of 0; and somewhat more risky industrial real estate that offers a return of 10% with a risk rating of 2.5. The choice is restricted by risk considerations, as well as legal constraints. Legal requirements are that at least 30% of the investment has to be in government bonds. The amount invested in real estate should not exceed 1.5 times the amount invested in blue-chip shares. The average risk rating should be no more than 1.2 (it is computed as the weighted average of the risk rating). The objective is to maximize the annual weighted return.
(a) Formulate this problem as an LP.
(b) Optimize the model by computer.
(c) How would you reformulate this problem so that you could give management an answer how to plan their investments to meet these conditions regardless of the amount of funds that becomes available?

5. During the construction of a reservoir dam, large quantities of aggregate for concrete mixing have to be prepared at some or all the four possible sites with sufficient quantities of deposits and then transported to the concrete mixing plant near the dam:

Deposit site	Available m^3	Cost/m^3
River-dredge material site A	8,000	£3.20
River-dredge material site B	16,000	£4.50
Island aggregate site C	8,000	£2.80
River bar aggregate site D	6,000	£4.00

The costs cover preparation and transportation to the concrete mixing plant. Three different aggregate blends are required at the quantities and additional costs shown:

Blend	Specifications	Cost/m^3	Requirement
1	$(A + B) \leq 50\%$, $C \geq 10\%$, D no limit	£4.80	6,000 m^3
2	$(A + B) \leq 60\%$, $C \geq 10\%$, $(C + D) \leq (A + B)$	£4.20	15,000 m^3
3	$A \geq 20\%$, $(C + D) \geq 0.5(A + B)$	£5.40	8,000 m^3

Formulate this problem as an LP minimizing total costs. Find the optimal solution.

6. The Western Paper Company (WPC) operates a cardboard plant in Seattle. The plant has been operating at only 75% capacity, producing 2700 tons per month at a total cost of $77.33 per ton. Included in the total cost per ton is the cost of wastepaper, one of the major raw materials used. For each 100 tons of product, 80 tons of wastepaper are required. Up to 1440 tons of wastepaper per month can be purchased locally at $18.75 per ton. Additional wastepaper may be purchased through brokers at $27.50 per ton delivered to the plant. Of the present total monthly costs at the plant, $59,400 is estimated to be fixed costs not dependent on the output level of the plant. The remainder of the cost varies in proportion to

the output level. WPC has a second plant in Oregon. That plant is operated currently at 60% capacity, producing 3600 tons per month at a total cost per ton of $85.00. Local wastepaper at the Oregon plant costs $20 per ton and is limited to 4000 tons per month. Again, additional wastepaper can be purchased through brokers at the same conditions as for the Seattle plant. Of the present operating cost at the Oregon plant, $108,000 is fixed cost.

(a) Determine the variable cost per ton of producing cardboard at each factory.

(b) The firm wants to determine the optimal output at each plant to produce the current combined output of 6300 tons per year. The objective is to minimize total combined production costs. Formulate this as an LP.

(c) Find the optimal solution.

(d) Using the information on sensitivity analysis provided by the LP computer printout, answer the following questions:

- What is the additional cost of increasing the total output to 6400 tons per year?
- What are the shadow prices for locally available wastepaper at each plant?
- Because of a slump in demand, WPC is approached with an offer of a substantial discount on wastepaper. What is the maximum price WPC would be willing to pay for wastepaper bought from a broker at each of the two plants?

7. BULL DIESEL produces two specialized lightweight diesel trucks. Production is done in four departments: the metal cutting and press department, producing body panels, engine assembly, Model A final assembly, and Model B final assembly. The monthly production capacities are as follows: The metal cutting and press department can either produce body parts for 1200 Model A or 857.14 Model B (fractional number represent averages of several months), or any corresponding combination of the two. The engine assembly department has a capacity to assemble either 800 Model A engines or 1200 Model B engines or any corresponding combination of the two. The two final assembly departments have capacities of 800 Model A and 600 Model B units. Note that each model can only be assembled on its own dedicated assembly line.

BULL can currently sell as many trucks as they can produce. However, dealers insist on a balance between the two models. In particular, they want to receive no more than twice as many of Model A as of Model B. This has not been a problem in the last few years. BULL tended to produce considerably more Model B trucks than Model A, since according to the accountants standard cost imputations Model B is much more profitable than Model A, as can be seen from the table below:

Standard costs of production for:		Model A	Model B
Materials and purchased parts		€7,400	€5,900
Direct labour:	Metal cutting and press	€1,200	€900
	Engine assembly	€900	€1,300
	Final assembly	€2,400	€1,800
	Total labour	€4,500	€4,000
Overhead:	Shared factory overhead	€1,512	€1,584
	Final assembly overhead	€4,008	€1,696
	Subtotal	€5,520	€3,280
	General overhead 25% of above	€1,380	€820
	Total overhead	€6,900	€4,100
Total cost		€18,800	€14,000
Net selling price		€20,000	€18,450

Overheads for the two shared manufacturing departments (metal cutting and press, and the engine assembly), expected to total €1,404,000 per month, are allocated to the two models in terms of the direct labour costs for these two departments, based on the preliminary plan of producing 300 Model A and 600 Model B trucks each month. Monthly overheads for the two final assembly departments are forecast at €1,202,400 for the Model A assembly department and €1,017,600 for the Model B department. The predicted monthly general overhead of €906,000 is allocated to the two models as 25% of manufacturing overheads. Note that the manufacturing overhead included 20% fringe benefits (vacation pay, pension fund contributions, insurance, and so on) on direct labour costs. The figures shown for direct labour above are exclusive of fringe benefits.

At the regular monthly planning session, the chief executive voiced his concern about the company's profit performance. The marketing manager immediately pointed out that it was impossible to raise the price of Model A trucks to yield a profit comparable to the Model B truck. He suggested that serious consideration should be given to dropping this model from the product line. He asked the production manager by how much the output of Model B could be increased by such a move. The production manager took out his calculator and, after 20 seconds, responded: 'About 200 more, but only if the Model A assembly line is converted to the production of Model B trucks! That would cost roughly €500,000!' The marketing manager nodded and expressed the opinion that most dealers would welcome an increased output of Model B, particularly if they were made aware of the firm's current plans to develop two new models for introduction in about 18 months time. The company's vice-president of finance objected to this suggestion. She pointed out that the seemingly bad profit margin on Model A was caused by trying to absorb the entire fixed overhead of the Model A assembly department with only a small number of units produced. She suggested that the firm should explore the possibility of producing more Model A trucks. The production manager interjected that this would only be possible by reducing the output of Model B trucks, although he thought that it would be possible to buy in engines to the required specifications from another engine manufacturer. This would obviously be considerably more expensive. At this point in the discussions, the chief executive decided that additional information was needed before a decision could be reached. He asked the production manager to inquire about the cost of buying in engines and report to him as quickly as possible. He asked the marketing manager to investigate the response of some of the important dealerships about the possibility of dropping Model A, as well as whether the market could absorb up to 800 Model B trucks, as well as possibly more Model A trucks, without forcing a price reduction in either model. Five days later the production manager reported that engines to the required specifications could be purchased for €5,980 for Model A engines and for €6,910 for Model B engines. Purchasing engines from outside would also reduce material costs by €1,600 for each truck. Obviously, no engine assembly costs would be incurred. Assume that you are the chief executive's analytic assistant. He asks you to analyse this situation. In particular, he wants recommendations about the following points:

(a) Should Model A be dropped from the production line and the output of Model B increased to 800 by converting the assembly line for Model A to Model B assembly?

(b) Should output of Model B trucks even be increased beyond 800 by purchasing engines from outside suppliers? If purchase of engines from outside suppliers is not on the cards at the current prices quoted, he would like to know the maximum price the firm would be willing to pay.

(c) Is the suggestion of the vice-president of finance to increase production of Model A units by reducing the output of Model B trucks or buying in engines a better solution than either of the two above? Again, he also wants to know the maximum price the firm should be willing to pay for engines purchased from outside.

Note that all questions can be answered by using a single model that allows all possible options and letting the model determine the optimal solution. Identification of relevant costs is an integral part of this exercise. (This exercise has been liberally adapted from an example in W.L. Berry et al. (1980) *Management Decision Sciences*, Irwin,, pp. 88–91.)

8. One of the earliest applications of linear programming is the diet or feed-mix problem. A feedlot farmer has bought a herd of 200 young steers for fattening up. He feeds his animals on a carefully chosen combination of feeds, such that they get just the right combination of nutrients in the form of starch, protein, and fibre. The table below lists the currently available feeds, the percentage by weight of the three nutrients, and their cost per 100 kg:

Feed	Starch	Protein	Fibre	Cost (€)
Potatoes	18.8	0.82	0.89	8.00
Swedes	7.4	0.68	1.12	5.50
Lucerne	6.9	3.1	6.15	8.80
Meadow hay	33	3.8	25.5	10.40
Dried grass	52.4	9.5	19.6	15.60
Barley	71.1	6.4	5.3	17.80
Wheat	71.8	9.4	2.2	18.90
Soya beans	68.9	17.8	4.1	27.50

The government farm consultant advises him that if he wants his steers to grow at a rate of 0.5 kg per day, each animal needs a daily nutrient intake of at least 4 kg of starch, 0.5 kg of protein, and 0.5 kg of fibre. The farmer would like to know which combination of feeds to choose so as to meet these requirements at least cost.

(a) Formulate this problem as an LP.

(b) Find the optimal solution by computer. What quantities of each feed does he have to prepare and mix each day to feed the herd? What is the total cost?

(c) How much cheaper would meadow hay have to become before it would become an alternative feed choice to use?

9. Continental Meats, a Dutch sausage factory in Tilburg, produces two types of sausage: beef frankfurters and luncheon meat. The firm uses meat off-cuts from other company divisions as major inputs into sausage production, namely, pork trimmings, pork heads, beef trimmings, and mutton. The recipes for beef frankfurters and luncheon meats allow some flexibility in the inputs, as long as certain other specifications, such as fat and water content, are met. The production manager of Continental Meats is confident that these two products can be produced from a wide range of inputs, while still maintaining product quality in terms of flavour, colour, and texture. The specifications for beef frankfurters require that: (1) the total fat content cannot exceed 31% of the finished product; (2) the total moisture must not exceed four times the protein content; (3) the amount of pork must be between 20% and 40% of the finished product; (4) the content of mutton cannot exceed 30%; and (5) the content of beef trimmings has to exceed 45%. For luncheon meat, the recipe states that it can contain any combination of mutton, beef trimmings, and pork, provided that: (1) the content of pork is at least 15%; (2) fat content cannot exceed 40%; (3) moisture content has to be at most 47%; (4) the protein content has to be at least 12%; and (5) mutton cannot be more than 35% of the total input into luncheon meat.

Although the different batches of the various inputs used vary slightly in terms of their fat, protein, and moisture composition, the production manager is confident that production plans can be based on past averages. These are as follows:

Input	Content of:	Fat	Protein	Moisture
Pork trimmings		61.7%	6.5%	28.9%
Pork heads		70.2%	4.5%	23.8%
Beef trimmings		12.2%	19.1%	66.0%
Mutton		15.3%	18.7%	64.3%

The current selling price per kilogram is €8.60 for beef frankfurters and €5.90 for luncheon meat. Although about 80% of the total inputs used come from other company divisions, with the balance purchased from external suppliers, the production manager considers that the value of the inputs received from other company divisions should be equal to the cost from external suppliers. The latest schedule specifies the following price schedule: pork trimmings €4.80; pork heads €2.85; beef trimmings €5.90; and mutton €2.80. However, the total amount of pork heads available from other company divisions, as well as other external sources is limited to about 2000 kg per week.

Marketing has supplied the following information about average weekly sales requirements: beef frankfurters between 4000 and 8000 kg; luncheon meat between 4000 and 6000 kg. The firm's daily production capacity is 2000 kg. The factory works 5 days per week. The wage cost for the production workers amounts to €4,236 per week. This includes variable overheads (fringe benefits) of 18%. Other production costs, such as other ingredients used (salt, pepper, spices, and so on), casings for the sausages, and electricity, amount to €0.27 per kg of output. The production manager's salary, including fringe benefits, is €2,800 per month. The sausage production department employs an office clerk who is paid €586 per week, including fringe benefits. The sausage department is assessed a charge for facility rental and general overhead contribution, totalling €8,800 per week.

(a) The production manager would like to have a detailed weekly production schedule, specifying exact quantities of each sausage type produced, together with an exact schedule of input requirements. Obviously, that schedule should maximize profits. Formulate this problem as an LP and find the optimal solution. Note that identification of the relevant cost factors is an integral part of this exercise.

(b) He would also like to know whether to schedule overtime. Up to up to 20% per week can be scheduled, at a wage premium of 50%. Overtime increases the maximum daily output proportionately. How much overtime should he schedule? Why?

(c) From across the Belgian border that there are up to 500 kg of pork heads available on a weekly basis. Pork heads sell for the same price as in Tilburg. However, there would be an additional cost of €0.70/kg incurred for the packing and transport under refrigeration from Belgium to Tilburg. Should he buy these pork heads? Why?

(d) The product quality supervisor approaches the production manager with the request that some pork trimmings should be used in place of pork heads in the production of beef frankfurters. This would improve the texture of the final product. Since the recent appearance of frankfurters imported from Germany, such an improvement might be important for Continental to maintain its share of the market. What effect would this have on the weekly profits?

10. A car rental firm projects the following distribution of its budget model for the coming Monday, listed as 'available', in contrast to its planned distribution, listed as 'planned':

Location	A	B	C	D	E	F
Available	18	6	22	11	7	4
Planned	12	9	15	18	6	6

Note that the planned distribution requires fewer cars than are available. Cars can be transferred between locations in either direction at the following cost/car in £:

To		A	B	C	D	E	F
From	A	0	48	92	65	74	126
	B		0	115	58	35	88
	C			0	50	78	105
	D				0	44	65
	E						38

(a) Draw a flow diagram similar to Figure 14-10.

(b) Use the diagram to formulate the corresponding LP.

(c) What is the least-cost redistribution schedule? Which location ends up with more cars than planned?

11. A firm faces a seasonal demand for its products. The firm has the policy to maintain a stable workforce, although the work force can be scheduled to work overtime up to 25% of its regular time capacity. Goods produced in any given month are available for sale in the same month. Any goods produced in a given month can be stored in inventory for sale in a later month at a cost of £4 per unit per month stored, assessed on the ending stock of each month. The regular time capacity of the plant is 6000 units per month. Each unit produced during regular time has a cost of £250, while a unit produced on overtime has a cost of £260. The firm faces the following demands over the coming 6 months:

Month	1	2	3	4	5	6
Demand	3000	4500	6500	9000	7000	6500

Demand cannot be back ordered.

(a) Draw a flow diagram similar to Figure 14-10.

(b) Use it to formulate the corresponding LP.

(c) Find the optimal regular time/overtime production schedule.

12. Reformulate the problem in exercise 3, restricting the number of each cabinet to be produced per week to be integers. Find the optimal solution. By how much are the maximal weekly profits reduced by this requirement?

13. Due to new emission standards, a firm has to upgrade its water treatment in its three factories (F1, F2, F3), which discharge waste water into the same river. The table below summarizes the options available: (ppm = parts per million)

Highest degree of treatment	Oxygen demand ppm			Installation costs (£100,000)		
	F1	F2	F3	F1	F2	F3
none	1.2	0.8	1.4	0	0	0
primary	0.6	0.6	0.9	8	4	10
secondary	0.3	0.4	0.5	14	8	15
tertiary	0.1	0.1	0.1	17	14	22

The combined oxygen demand over all three factories cannot exceed 1.6 ppm. What degree of treatment should be chosen for each factory if the firm wants to minimize the total installation cost? Formulate this problem as an integer program and optimize it using a spreadsheet IP solver. (Formulation hint: let the degree of treatment at each factory be a binary variable, one and only one of which must be chosen for each factory.)

Further reading

General MS/OR texts contain a chapter with LP formulations and often a separate one covering solution algorithms, as well as various extensions, such as duality, special algorithms for both the transportation and the assignment problems, and more elegant ways to deal with upper bounds on the variables. They also have chapters on IP algorithms and non-linear programming.

Appendix 14.1

Graphical solution to a linear program

Some insight into the form of the solution, the results of sensitivity analysis, and the general nature of the solution algorithm can be gained by studying the graphical representation of an LP and finding the optimal solution graphically. However, this restricts us to problems that have only two decision variables.

Recapitulation of revised product mix problem

Since the product mix problem does not recommend the production of Luxury workstations, the problem reduces to two decision variables, BASIC and STANDRD. Dropping the LUXURY variable from all expressions, we get the following LP:

Objective function:

Maximize GROSSPROF = 100 BASIC + 120 STANDRD (14-1A)

subject to

Cutting constraint:	16 BASIC + 12 STANDRD $\leq$ 480	(14-2A)
Welding constraint:	25 BASIC + 22.5 STANDRD $\leq$ 900	(14-3A)
Painting constraint:	BASIC + STANDRD $\leq$ 32	(14-4A)
Shelving constraint:	36 BASIC + 50 STANDRD $\leq$ 1380	(14-5A)
Assembly constraint:	22.5 BASIC + 25 STANDRD $\leq$ 900	(14-6A)
Basic/Standard mix:	$-^1/_3$ BASIC + STANDRD $\geq$ 0	(14-7A)
Non-negativity:	BASIC $\geq$ 0, STANDRD $\geq$ 0	

Graphical representation of LP

Each expression involves only two variables. Hence, it can be graphed in two dimensions, with values of BASIC along the Y-axis and the values of STANDRD along the X-axis. Each point in the positive quadrant and along the two axes represents a combination of non-negative values for the two decision variables. For any given value of GROSSPROF, equation (14-1A) is a straight line. Any straight line is defined by two points. We simply define two points and then draw the straight line that goes through both. Say GROSSPROF = 3600. Two convenient points can easily be found by setting each variable in turn to zero and solving for the other one. For BASIC = 0, STANDRD must be 3600/120 = 30, and for STANDRD = 0, BASIC becomes 3600/100 = 36. So the two points are (30, 0), falling on the X-axis, and (0, 36), falling on Y-axis, as shown in Figure 14-15. Drawing a straight line through these points gives all combinations of BASIC and STANDRD that yield a GROSSPROF of £3,600. It is called an **isoquant** or **equal profit line**. Two additional lines for a GROSSPROF of £2,400 and £1,200 are also shown. They are parallel to the first. As GROSSPROF increases, the corresponding lines move parallel up and to the right.

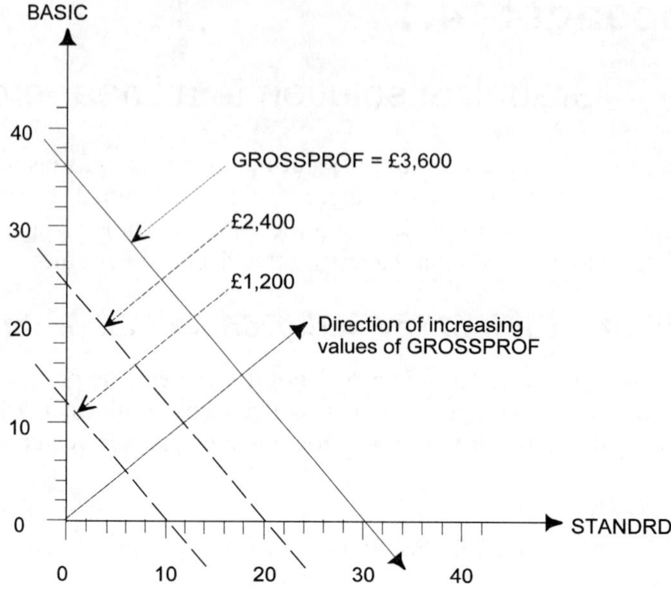

Figure 14-15 The graph of the objective function

Each of the constraints restricts the values of the decision variable to a given region. To identify that region, we draw the straight line corresponding to the constraint satisfied as an equality. Figure 14-16 shows the region of permissible variable values for the cutting constraint as the area below and to the left of the constraint line.

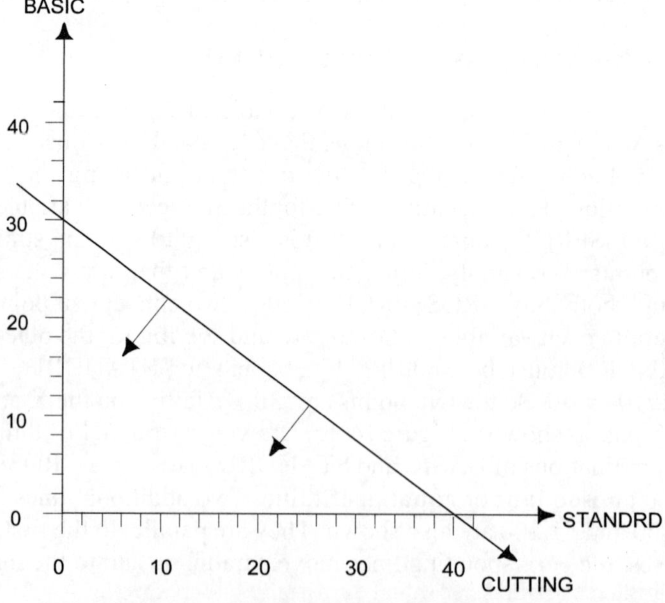

Figure 14-16 The graph of the cutting constraint

Figure 14-17 shows the lines for all six constraints on the same graph. Only those combinations of values for BASIC and STANDRD that satisfy all constraints including the non-negativity conditions simultaneously are admissible. The set of all those admissible points is called the **feasible region**. It is the shaded area.

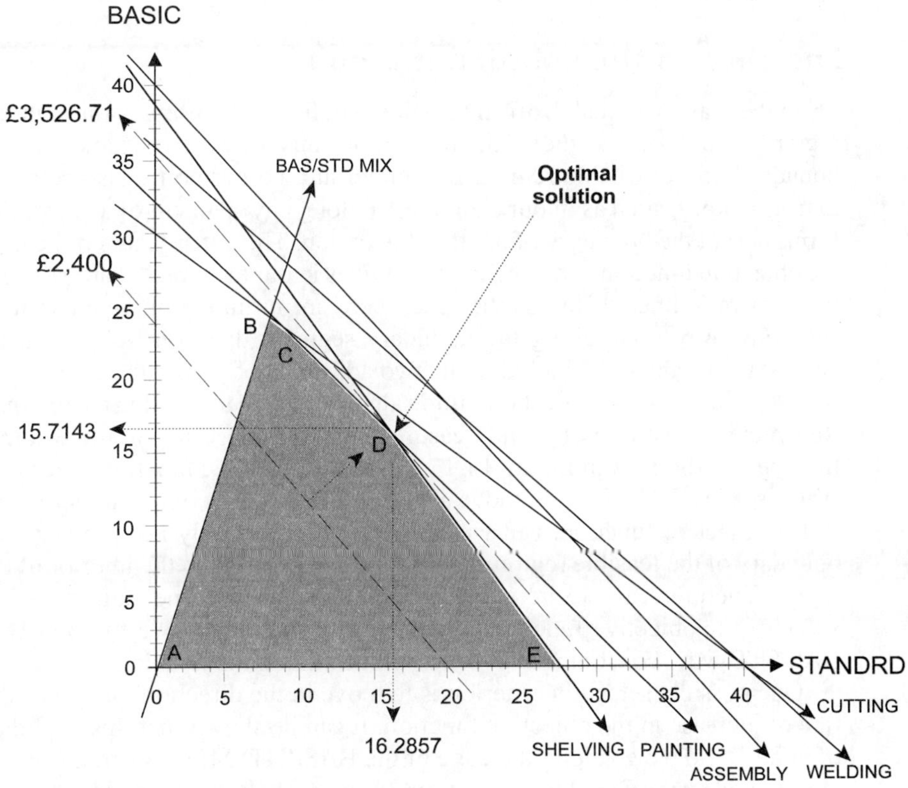

Figure 14-17 The feasible region and the optimal solution

The feasible region is bounded by four of the six constraint lines — CUTTING, SHELVING, PAINTING, and BAS/STD MIX, as well as the non-negativity condition on BASIC, while the constraint lines for WELDING and ASSEMBLY lie outside the feasible region. Neither restricts the two decision variables. They are **redundant**. We could delete them from the formulation. However, to get the correct ranges for the shadow prices it is essential that they remain.

To define the feasible region, we only needed the constraints. The objective function does not enter into consideration. It only becomes relevant when we want to find where in the feasible region the optimal solution is located. For this. we see what happens when we push the equal-profit lines to higher and higher values.

For a value of £2,400, the equal-profit line has a whole segment inside the feasible region with a multitude of other feasible solutions that lie on higher equal-profit lines. The highest permissible equal-profit line which still has at least one point in common with the feasible region is at the intersection of the PAINTING and SHELVING constraints. It has a value of £3,525.71. All equal-profit lines for larger values are completely outside the feasible region. So £3,525.71 is the maximal value of the objective function. It corresponds to values for BASIC of 15.7143 and STANDRD of 16.2857.

The optimal solution implies that painting and shelving time are completely used up — they are binding — while all other constraints have various amounts of slack.

Insights on the solution method

From the way the equal profit lines slide parallel to themselves through the feasible region, it follows that the optimal solution must always lie somewhere along the boundary of the feasible region. It is either at a corner point, also referred to as an **extreme point**, such as in our example, or along any segment of a constraint line that forms part of the boundary of the feasible region. The latter occurs if the isoquants for the objective function — the equal-profit lines in our example — are parallel to one of the constraint lines. If this is the case, there are infinitely many alternative optimal solutions. Any point along the boundary segment that coincides with the optimal isoquant is a candidate, including its two adjacent corner points.

These insights motivate the solution algorithm used for finding the optimal solution. Remember the South Sea island treasure hunt! Hence, we start at some corner, such as the origin — point A in Figure 14-17. At A, the objective function is zero, i.e., we are still at sea level. We want to move away from it in a direction that increases the value of the objective function. But we also know that we only need to search along the boundary of the feasible region. There is no point to search the interior of the feasible region. Therefore, at each iteration, we look for adjacent corner points that improve the value of the objective function. From A, we can either move to point B (along the BAS/STD MIX constraint line) or to point E (along the X-axis).

One possible selection criterion is to move in the direction that gives the steepest rate of increase in the objective function. It can be shown that this is in the direction of point B. So we go along the edge of the BAS/STD MIX constraint. At point B we are stopped by the CUTTING constraint. We now have completed the first iteration of the search algorithm, ending at an improved solution.

We start a new iteration, searching again for a feasible direction of improvement. Of the two directions along an edge, one leads back to where we just came from. Going along it would decrease the value of the objective function, hence, is no good. The other improves the value of the objective function. It follows along the edge of the CUTTING constraint to point C, where it intersects the PAINTING constraint — only a short hop. The third iteration finds again only one direction of improvement, namely along the PAINTING constraint to point D, where it intersects the SHELVING constraint. The fourth iteration shows that no direction of improvement can be found anymore. We have reached the optimal solution.

This is, in very broad terms, what the simplex algorithm does. The mathematical version if this algorithm was invented in 1947 by the American mathematical scientist George Dantzig. Ironically, the Russian mathematician Leonid Kantorovich discovered in 1939 a similar algorithm for solving LPs, but his work remained hidden in the USSR and never reached the West.

Sensitivity analysis

In Figure 14-18, we briefly look at changes in the RHS parameters of resource-type constraints and changes in the objective function coefficients. We have deleted the two slack constraints ASSEMBLY and WELDING to unclutter the diagram.

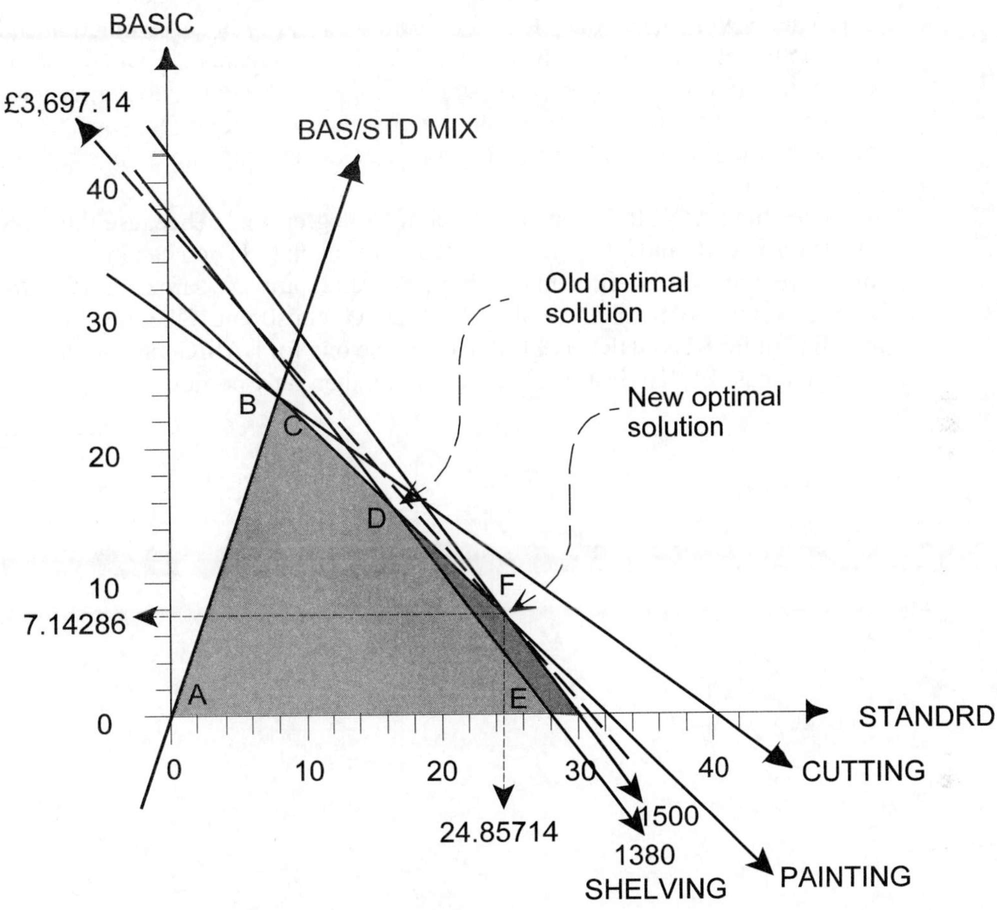

Figure 14-18 Increasing RHS parameter of SHELVING

Consider first adding more shelving time. This shifts the SHELVING constraint line up and to the right, as shown in Figure 14-18 for an increase of two hours. The RHS of the constraint goes to 1500 minutes. It now intersects the PAINTING constraint line at point F, and not at point D. The feasible region is enlarged by the dark grey area (enclosed by points E, D, F, and 32). The isoquant for the objective function can now be pushed up to point F (the dashed line in the graph). Its value increases by £170.43 to £3,697.14, or by £170.43/120 = £1.42857 per additional minute. This shadow price value is confirmed by the shadow price in the Solver Sensitivity Report in its 'Constraints' list.

Since there is now no decision variable at zero in the optimal solution, we cannot show how to find the reduced cost coefficients. Instead, we will show what happens as the objective function coefficient of BASIC is increased from its current value of £100. The reasoning for finding the reduced cost coefficient is similar.

The slope of the isoquants for GROSSPROF determines at which corner point of the feasible region the optimal solution occurs. A change in either objective function coefficients will change that slope. For example, as the objective function coefficient for BASIC increases (while the one for STANDRD remains the same), the slope will tilt counter-clockwise. When it is parallel to the PAINTING constraint line, point C becomes an alternative optimal solution, together with point D, as well as any point along the line from D to C. In other words, there is an infinite number of alternative optimal solutions.

Since the PAINTING constraint is at a 45-degree angle (because the LHS coefficients for BASIC and STANDRD are the same, namely 1) you can infer that when the objective function coefficients of both variables are the same, the GROSSPROF isoquant will be parallel to the PAINTING constraint. The objective function coefficient for STANDRD is £120. Hence, the one for BASIC must increase to £120, or an increase of £20. If it increases by more, then only point C remains optimal.

15
Uncertainty

'Everybody complains about their memory, but no-one complains about their judgement.' La Rochefoucauld (1613–80)

Learning objectives

- Be able to identify possible causes of uncertainty.
- Be able to determine whether a probability is of the objective type or subjective type.
- Be able to identify the major components used in forecasting and prediction.
- Be able to determine if a subjective probability assessment could be affected by a simplifying heuristic, by biases or illusions, identified by behavioural research.
- Be able to interpret the meaning of an objective probability statement.
- Appreciate that a subjective probability statement expresses the degree of confidence in the corresponding outcome.
- To be able to use probability distributions to represent uncertainty.

Introduction

The approaches to decision making within systems discussed so far implicitly assumed that if we take a given action, we can predict the resulting effect on the system with (absolute) certainty. In many problems, our knowledge of the situation actually may be good enough to satisfy this assumption, at least in a practical sense, if not in theory. Situations of this sort are called **deterministic**.

For example, XL Bakers has a firm contract with the Big-G chain of supermarkets for delivery of 2000 loaves of sliced white sandwich bread each day of the week. It enjoys a deterministic demand for that portion of its sales. Accordingly, it can make firm decisions regarding the number of loaves to be baked to meet that demand.

More often, however, the exact outcome that results in a given situation or from a given event may not be known in advance — in other words, may be **uncertain**. Take again XL Bakers. It has a firm contract to supply each of the 13 stores of the rival Bargain Barn chain daily with sufficient bread to satisfy customer demand, with the obligation to take back any bread that is not sold within 24 hours after delivery. On some days, all bread delivered to a given store is sold within the 24-hour period. In fact, had XL stocked more, all or a portion of the additional amount stocked might have been sold too. On other days it may have to take dozens of unsold (stale) loaves back from the same store. XL may be able to predict how many loaves are sold on average by each store, but not how many will be sold on any specific day. So, it faces an uncertain demand picture for that part of its daily operation.

And then there are situations which are unique, in the sense that they will not repeat themselves in similar way, or even if they do, we may have no recorded experience about them or no way to make comparisons. We may be able to list some or most of the possible outcomes, but how could we assess the likelihood of each?

Situations where we cannot predict which particular outcome will occur are referred to as **uncertain**, **risky**, **stochastic**, **or probabilistic**. The approaches used for decision making under certainty may not be appropriate any longer. Even the form or structure of the decision itself may need to be different. Rather than using decisions in the form of open-loop controls, it may be more appropriate to resort to decision rules involving closed-loop or feedback controls. Such decision rules are referred to as **strategies**.

This chapter first explores how uncertainty is expressed in everyday language, what causes uncertainty, the types of uncertainty we may face, and how to predict the occurrence of uncertain future events.

We then study the meaning of objective and subjective probabilities, and explore the biases, fallacies, and difficulties associated with assessing subjective probabilities.

Random variables and how to approximate their behaviour by theoretical probability distributions are the next topic, while the last two sections address the problems of how to reduce uncertainty, and the decision criteria relevant in the face of uncertainty.

The chapter aims to enhance your understanding of the diverse meanings of uncertainty on a conceptual level. We hope this will lead to a more informed grasp of decision making under uncertainty. It does not deal with the computational rules of probabilities and statistical data analysis. One chapter cannot do that. We assume that you are familiar with the basics of these areas.

15.1 Linguistic ambiguity about uncertainty

Uncertainty is an everyday occurrence. Just consider the large number of words in the English language related to this concept: chance, probability, likelihood, possibility, risk, hazard, fortune, random, stochastic, odds, to expect, believe, feel, or guess that something will or might happen, to name just a few. In fact, this proliferation of words may be an indication of the ambiguity, even of a certain degree of confusion, associated with the notion of uncertainty.

What is the meaning of phrases such as 'There is a possibility that ...' or 'It is very unlikely that ...'? Table 15-1 shows the responses from a group of over 500 students in a first-year university course to everyday language phrases indicating uncertainty to various degrees, with 0 denoting absolute impossibility and 100 absolute certainty. For comparison, a group of 40 older students (average age 33) in an executive-type MBA course was also asked the same questions. Their responses are shown in parentheses. The wide range of responses for both groups indicates highly divergent interpretations, even for statements suggesting a very high or a very low likelihood. No wonder that such statements lead to confusing and contradictory interpretations.

Table 15-1 Interpretation of statements about uncertainty

Phrase	Assigned probability in %		
	10th percentile	Median	90th percentile
It is highly likely that ...	75 (50)	90 (80)	95 (90)
There is a much better than even chance that ...	55 (50)	70 (65)	75 (75)
It is improbable that ...	5 (10)	20 (20)	40 (40)
There is a fair chance that ...	40 (35)	50 (50)	65 (70)
It is very unlikely that ...	5 (5)	10 (20)	25 (40)
It is quite possible that ...	30 (50)	60 (60)	80 (75)
It is almost impossible that ...	1 (3)	5 (5)	10 (30)
It was sunny today; it is likely to stay fine tomorrow.	40 (50)	50 (57)	75 (75)
The likelihood of a strong earthquake in the Los Angeles area next year is quite high.	10 (20)	60 (60)	80 (80)
The probability of a serious nuclear power plant accident anywhere is quite small.	2 (5)	10 (18)	40 (50)

Such ambiguity is not only exhibited by the 'person in the street'. 'Experts' and professional people, such as economic advisers or national security advisers to governments, or judges in courts of law, are equally prone to it., as the next two examples demonstrate.

Example 15-1: Bay of Pigs invasion

Peter Wyden (*Bay of Pigs*, New York: Simon and Schuster, 1979, pp. 89–90) reports on an instance where such divergent interpretation might have led to a serious international incident. In early 1961, President Kennedy ordered the Joint Chiefs of Staff to study the CIA's plan for an invasion of Cuba by expatriate Cubans. The general in charge of the evaluation concluded that its chances of overall success were 'fair'. Interviewed on this affair several years later he revealed that he intended this to mean a 30% chance. He recalled: 'We thought other people would think that a "fair chance" would mean "not too good".' When the report was sent to the White House, it stated 'This plan has a fair chance of ultimate success.' It is highly possible that this misinterpretation of the word 'fair' led President Kennedy to authorize this mission, which ended in disaster for the invaders and humiliation for the USA.

Example 15-2: National security analysts

C.W. Kelly and C.R. Peterson (*Probability estimates and probabilistic procedures in current-intelligence analysis*, Gathersburg, MD: IBM, 1971, pp. 4-1, 4-2) report on a test involving a group of national security analysts. They were asked to assign a numeric probability for the statement 'The cease-fire is holding, but it could be broken within the next week.' The author, a colleague of the group interviewed, intended the sentence to mean that there was a 30% chance of the cease-fire being broken. However, most of the other analysts thought that it meant a probability of 50% or higher.

Surveys of judges and jurors indicate that the commonly used court-room statement 'beyond a reasonable doubt' is variably interpreted as anywhere from 50% to 100% chance of guilt. This is rather alarming for both the innocent accused, as well as the victim of a guilty accused.

The ambiguity of language and the widely differing interpretations given to statements about uncertainty suggest that numeric statements about the probability of an event would lead to clearer understanding and, consequently, to better decision making. Although this will be so in many cases, even probability statements may not be unambiguous, as we shall see in Section 15.7, neither will they necessarily lead to more rational decision making.

Activity

Cover the numerical answers shown in Table 15-1 and then fill in your own. Once finished, critically (in the sense of careful judgement and judicious evaluation) compare yours with those in the table. Explain the differences.

15.2 Causes of uncertainty

Uncertainty about the exact nature of some phenomenon, some process, or the precise state of a system at a given point is due to one or combination of the following four reasons:

1. The most common reason is that the process or event in question is not known or understood in sufficient detail. Many physical phenomena, such as the weather or the time, strength, and duration of the next earthquake at a given location, are all processes that we do not fully understand yet, or for which it would be prohibitively expensive or even physically impossible to gather all relevant information. Clearly, if the processes that cause earthquakes could be understood to their last details, there would be nothing inherently random about the next earthquake in San

Francisco, California, or in Christchurch, New Zealand — two cities on highly active earthquake faults.

2. The second reason is that statements about a phenomenon or process are based on incomplete information. For instance, a statement about the percentage of all television viewers tuned in to a given station at a given time is, for cost reasons, usually based on a sample of some 500 to 1000 viewers, rather than the entire population of all viewers at that time. It is an estimate and, hence, it will only be exactly correct by coincidence. In other words, it is only an estimate, subject to sampling error. The uncertainty is again due to ignorance, except that this time it is ignorance by design. This type of uncertainty can be eliminated by surveying the entire population (provided no measurement errors occur) — a costly exercise.
3. A third important reason, particularly for economic phenomena, but also for competitive sports and games, is the inability to predict what moves other actors in the real world, such as competitors, customers, employees, or the government, will make, which could affect the outcome. Such moves may be made completely independently of our own decisions, or may be in response or in anticipation of our decisions. Take again the example of bread delivery. If — and this includes many sub-'ifs' — it were possible to ascertain by 6 pm each day exactly how many loaves of bread each of the supermarkets' potential regular and casual customers will buy over the 24-hour time span starting the next day at noon, then the bakery would know how many loaves of bread to bake and to supply. Clearly, such detailed information is not known, neither can it be reliably collected. Hence, the demand for bread remains uncertain.

   In some team sports, such as football, it is often impossible to predict what kind of strategy the opposing team will attempt to use. In other sports, such as cricket or tennis, past observations of the players' favourite strokes or placement of the ball will give a good indication of the play. But a smart opponent will be aware of that and vary his or her strategy deliberately.
4. The final and increasingly less important reason for uncertainty is measurement error about a phenomenon due to mistakes made by the observer or improper gauging or functioning of measuring instruments, both unknown to the observer. These measurement errors may lead to the erroneous conclusion that any variability observed is inherent in the phenomenon measured, rather than a result of the measuring process.

15.3 Types and degrees of uncertainty

Most of the uncertainties relevant to systems or faced by individuals or firms deal either with the numerical value (quantity, size, and so on), or the qualitative attribute (on, off; for against, and so on) associated with the phenomenon of interest, or with its timing. A firm being uncertain as to the size of the demand for one of its products during a given time period in the future, or at what price raw materials will have to be purchased next month on the commodity market, are examples of uncertainty about the numerical value of phenomena. The time between consecutive arrivals of patients at an accident and emergency facility is an example of uncertainty about timing, as well as the number of arrivals, since an ambulance attending an accident may bring in several people at the same time. Finally, the batsman in a cricket test does not know what kind of ball the bowler will deliver him next—its qualitative attribute is unknown prior to the delivery.

The degree of uncertainty may vary from knowing almost nothing about the process or phenomenon to knowing almost everything. For instance, a firm preparing a cash flow budget (a plan of the timing and amounts of cash receipts and cash disbursements over a given time interval) may know exactly the timing and amounts of cash needed for disbursements over the first two weeks, have fairly accurate data on disbursements for the next four weeks, with less and less reliable information the further in the future these disbursements will occur. For the far distant future, only rough guesstimates may be available, since these events are influenced by many other unknown events, such as the level of production, for example, which in turn depend on the level of sales far in the future.

When we are dealing with events involving competitors, any predictions about their responses may be even more precarious. We may not even have a complete list of all possible alternative courses of action available to them and their consequences for us. Similarly, for the introduction of a novelty product or service, a firm may have little to go on for predicting how successful it will be. Furthermore, knowledge about new technology, even just a few years from now, may be hazy or even completely absent — a case of complete uncertainty.

In the decision literature, we usually talk about **decision making under risk** if it is possible to list all outcomes and make numerical statements about the likelihood of each. If neither condition is met, then we talk about **decision making under complete uncertainty**. (However, 'decision making under uncertainty' is often loosely used for denoting both types!) As we shall see in later chapters, the approaches used for dealing with these two cases are radically different.

Activity

- For each of the four causes/reasons listed in Section 15.2, find two new examples that differ in their nature and explain why they match the cause/reason.
- Find two new examples of uncertain size, uncertain timing, and both.
- Find two new examples that fit the case of risk and the case of complete uncertainty.

15.4 Prediction and forecasting

Much of the uncertainty faced by decision makers deals with future events. How can we foresee the future? For thousands of years, the search for an answer has given rise to all sorts of professions: shamans, seers and soothsayers, travelling fortune-tellers, and high priests of all sorts, who often exploited their position of power and control over those who believed in their abilities. Economists and treasury officials are the modern version of these gurus (and they are also highly paid and all too often no more successful in their predictions!).

Persistence prediction

At least a partial answer to 'How do we foresee the future?' is 'By studying the past!' Even in the turbulent and often chaotic world we live in, there are some threads of continuity and stability. A phenomenon may not change its character, its form, or its range of possible outcomes. If its range changes, such a change itself may be stable. Such phenomena are called **stationary**. So, the first step toward prediction is the identification of characteristics that have persisted and have exhibited some degree of stability over time — hence the label 'persistence prediction'. It is by far the simplest approach!

Persistence prediction is good for phenomena that remain in their current position, or exhibit relatively small variations in an unpredictable pattern around a stable base. It could be likened to the erratic movements of a drunk who, after struggling to his feet, is equally likely simply to fall right over again or teeter in any direction — a **random walk**. Short-term daily fluctuations in share prices or foreign exchange rates, when these markets are in a stable phase, follow a random walk in response to unpredictable entry of buyers and sellers.

In weather forecasting, persistence prediction is sometimes almost as good as the forecast developed with highly sophisticated monitoring equipment, complicated air-mass theories, and running computer programs on very fast computers for hours. In fact, in many areas with relatively stable weather patterns, comparisons show that the weather office is correct only about 10% more often than the simple prediction that tomorrow's weather will be the same as today's. This is not because the methods used by the weather office are so bad. Rather, it is because persistence prediction is so good.

So, predictions about the number of newspapers sold each day at a location subject to a highly regular and stable pedestrian traffic pattern, such as at a corner on Piccadilly Circus, or for that matter in most suburban shopping malls, can safely be based on the average number sold in the most recent past. The sales pattern is stationary. The prediction error — the difference between the forecast and the actual realization — will on most days be fairly small, particularly if such factors, as the day of the week and so on, are also taken into account in the prediction.

Trend prediction

A slightly more sophisticated scheme for forecasting the future is trajectory or trend prediction. This method assumes that, although there is change, the change itself is stable. If bread sales by XL Bakers in Glasgow have shown a fairly regular increase of 4% in each of the past few years, presumably due to the increase in the region's population, it will be reasonable to assume that this trend will continue, at least for another few years, unless a serious downturn in economic activity hits the area. In other words, the trend remains stationary.

Trend prediction is without doubt the most successful and most used forecasting approach. Tests have shown that it tends to give more reliable forecasts than much more sophisticated methods based on econometric models. It usually provides good short-run forecasts, but may lead to absurd long-range predictions, particularly if the trend is assumed to be exponential.

Many phenomena initially exhibit an exponential-type growth, i.e., growth in successive time periods is ever-increasing. Such growth was observed in the 1960s and 1970s for the consumption of electricity, motor fuels, and vinyl music records; then in the 1990s with music CDs and cell phones and, more recently, with other electronic novelty items. But it is clear that such processes will ultimately change their pattern fundamentally. Electricity consumption is a case in point. Its growth pattern in the 1980s and 1990s did not follow the exponential trends of the 1960s and 1970s. The trend predictions for the 1980s based on the data of the 1960s and 1970s overestimated consumption systematically. The essays in Baumgartner and Midttun (1987), document the reasons that led to this systematic failure in a number of countries.

Cyclic prediction

Cyclic predictions are based on the principle that history repeats itself. Cyclic predictions for seasonal phenomena are highly successful. They may be superimposed over a trend prediction and, hence, give considerably better short-run forecasts. This is the case for demand forecasts for many products and services subject to seasonal consumption, such as beer, ice cream, electricity use, or tourism. But cyclic predictions are equally fickle when they try to forecast long-range phenomena, such as business cycles. Just look at the notoriously bad business forecasts made by economic research institutes or banks — fortunately as quickly forgotten by most people as they are issued by the forecasters — or the futile attempts to forecast stock exchange price cycles that, in today's world of large-scale speculation, may take a dive if the US president coughs.

Example 15-3: General Hardware

General Hardware is a New Zealand company that makes door furniture sold in the domestic market and exported to Australia. They have 100 product lines. Sales are seasonal. They want to forecast sales on a monthly basis, typically over a horizon of up to three months, for production planning, materials planning and cash-flow forecasting. Having read about influence diagrams in Section 5.6, the production manager sketches out a model that says:

> Sales = some function of: recent sales; the exchange rate between Australia and New Zealand; the amount spent on advertising; competitors' actions; building activity; Australian building activity, and probably some other variables as well.

Many of these variables will be difficult, expensive, or even illegal (approaching his competitors, for example) to collect. Estimating the parameters and functions for 100 product lines requires considerable expertise, and the use of software that could charitably be described as 'unfriendly'. And worse still, to produce forecasts of sales requires forecast values of all of these variables! If we can forecast exchange rates accurately, then why bother making door handles?

Luckily the production manager has also read Section 5.3 on essential properties of good models, especially points 3, 4, and 5, and realizes that, given the cost of the possible inputs listed above, and the output requirements, much simpler models are essential. For items with low unit cost, short forecast horizons and relatively stable demand patterns, methods based on trend and seasonality alone can work very well.

The factors originally identified by the production manager will not be ignored, but will be considered when the final forecasts are produced. Now that the modelling system has been restricted to consideration of trend and seasonality only, automated software is available that selects the best forecasting method by looking at how well it worked on past data, updates the models every month and forecasts our 100 series in a few seconds. Figure 15-1 shows output from one of these packages, Forecast Pro.

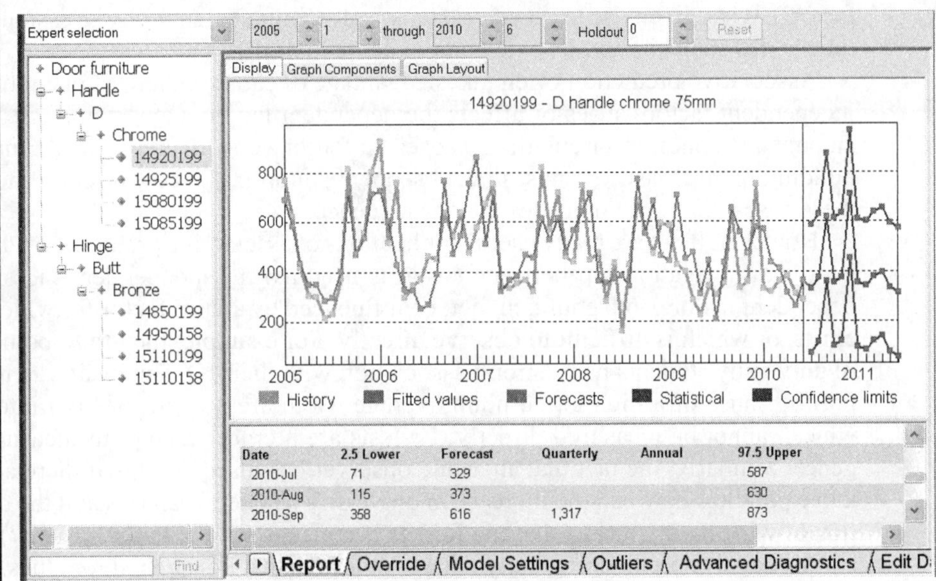

Figure 15-1 Part of the Forecast Pro output

As well as forecasts for each product line, it produces forecasts for product groups such as hinges (the left-hand pane in Figure 15-1). Forecasts can also be produced in units of dollars and of raw materials, satisfying the needs of the three clients of the forecasting process. Systematic **judgemental adjustments** (see Section 15.5) are allowed by use of the 'Override' button. Some versions of Forecast Pro even automate the desirable steps described in Section 15.5, recording the adjustments with written justifications in a permanent database, and highlighting series for which the forecasts were poor so that these can be considered at subsequent planning meetings.

Many of the users of programs such as Forecast Pro have limited knowledge of how the formulas in it work. Essentially, they are all smoothing methods that pick up patterns of trend and seasonality in the past values of the series, and extrapolate them to produce forecasts (see chapters 4 and 7 of Makridakis et al. (1998)). Instead, they sensibly concentrate on the essential human aspects of the forecasting system, getting the input data right, reviewing the results of the forecasts and any previous judgemental adjustments each month, and leave the program to do the maths. The program even sets up a framework for such a successful forecasting system.

Activity

- Compare the process by which the forecasting model evolved with the structure diagram for hard OR described in Figure 6-9 (p. 162). Identify systems M, S, and O in this example.
- For the situation described above, compare the original model that the production manager considered, with the Forecast Pro method finally used. Rate each method on the six properties of a good model discussed in Section 5.4.

Associative prediction

This method uses past data from one type of process (usually referred to as the 'independent factor') to predict another type of process (referred to as the 'dependent factor'). It has given rise to powerful statistical techniques, such as regression analysis, time series analysis, and its extension to econometrics.

Associative prediction often takes advantage of cause and effect phenomena. The independent factor causes or affects the dependent factor, such as an increase in the amount of money in circulation 'causes' inflation, or a decrease in the number of building permits issued 'causes' a subsequent slump in the construction industry. In these cases, the cause precedes the consequence.

However, there are many useful applications of associative predictions where there is no causal relationship between (what is used as) the independent factor and the dependent factor. Both could, in fact, be influenced by a third factor for which no data exists, or which is difficult to observe directly. For example, the grade-point average of university students has a strong association with their IQ. But clearly, a high IQ is not the cause of a high grade-point average. Both are a result of high intelligence, which cannot be measured directly. IQ tests are a crude attempt to measure intelligence. Similarly, the fact that an astute observer has discovered that there are remarkable parallels between the increase in university teachers' salaries and the consumption of wine hardly means that the former is the cause of the latter (or is it?).

Associative prediction greatly enlarges the area that is searched for clues. Much of regression analysis deals with discerning which independent clues are helpful — in other words, statistically significant — for predicting a dependent process or event of interest. Trend prediction is a special form of associative prediction, time being the independent factor or variable.

But without doubt, the method that uses all data available in the most effective way is hindsight prediction — the prediction of an event after it has already been observed and measured. Historians, TV commentators, economists, and politicians use this method to great effect. How often do you say 'I told you so'?

Is the past valid for predicting the future?

With the exception of hindsight prediction, all approaches mentioned so far use past data to predict future events. The crucial systemic assumption underlying these approaches is that the past is a good basis for predicting the future. However, structural or behavioural changes in the phenomenon observed render this assumption invalid. Structural changes could be due to changes in legislation, new technology, or economic relationships governing the phenomenon in question. Behavioural changes could be the result of psychological, moral, or life-style changes in the population concerned. A case in point is the surge of internet commerce, partially replacing the personal in-store shopping tradition.

However, there are many instances where there are no known past data that can be used for predicting future events. The occurrence and far-reaching consequences of technological innovations, such as the invention of electronic computers, microchips, or laser technology clearly could not be predicted even by experts in the fields, except the very few actually involved in their development. Hence, predictions based on past data without any knowledge of imminent technological breakthroughs were badly off. But even for less spectacular events, such as next year's fashion trends or the Christmas sales volume for a given toy, predictions are difficult to make and are often unreliable. This is why fashion and toy stores only stock these goods just prior to the season and only in quantities that they are fairly confident to clear by the end of the season. However, the large number of end-of-season sales, with price reductions to a fraction of the original selling price for fashion items and toys, is a clear indication of the difficulty of demand predictions in these areas (although nowadays many sales items are specially procured, and never sold at the undiscounted price, simply to attract customers during a sale in the expectation that they will also purchase other items).

Predictions should not be restricted to single estimates. The only way to assess the reliability of predictions is to obtain also some measure of the degree of variability inherent in the phenomenon predicted. If the predictions are part of an ongoing repetitive process, then it will be possible to compute some measure of the prediction error, such as an estimate of the standard deviation of the differences between corresponding pairs of predicted and observed values.

15.5 Predictions by expert judgement

In the second half of the twentieth century, several other prediction methods were developed and are used regularly by big business, market research consultants, and governments. Firms test new products on consumer panels to get some indication as to their likely appeal. Larger firms and governments use various techniques involving experts in the field of interest — in an attempt to pool the combined and considered judgement of a group of experts.

Delphi method

The best known of these is the Delphi method. It was used in the late 1970s by an MS/OR group that was evaluating the economic desirability of expanding the only oil refinery operated in New Zealand. A group of economic and energy experts from all over the world was asked to partake in a survey about the likely level of oil prices over a 30-year span. All participants were given a questionnaire. Their responses were collated and expressed in statistical form. The results of the first questionnaire were then fed back to the experts in summarized form (averages, median responses, range of responses, and so on). They were asked if, in the light of the first-round results, they wanted to change their original responses, and how. Their new answers were again processed in the same manner. The Delphi method usually repeats this procedure through two or three iterations, with the responses of the last iteration being used as the final predictions. Note that throughout the procedure complete anonymity of all responses received is strictly preserved. This ensures that no participant is influenced by the disclosure of the responses of persons recognized as leaders in the field.

The Delphi method has had many successful applications. It is not a cheap method and, unless the experts are all locally present, it takes considerable time to reach a conclusion. Each iteration can easily take weeks. It is therefore only suitable for relatively important projects. Before embarking on such an exercise, the analyst should perform considerable sensitivity analysis to determine how crucial it is to get a reliable estimate. In the oil price exercise, the price for a barrel of the type of crude oil processed at the refinery in early 1978 was around US$35. The final results of the Delphi exercise predicted a price by the end of the 1980s in the range of US$60 to US$95. The analysis for the expansion option chosen established that it would remain economically viable as long as the price remained above about US$29. The actual price in 1989 was well below US$20, reaching lows of US$15 at times. So, we see that even judgements by experts may be far off the mark.

Subjective or judgement predictions

What can be done for one-off cases, where no past history or comparable situations are available? In such instances, a person intimately familiar with the situation, usually the decision maker, is asked to make a subjective prediction. He or she may base it on general relevant experience, or on assessments obtained by other people, and sometimes on pure 'gut feelings'. Such a prediction could, for instance, take the form of: 'I estimate that the most likely outcome is X, with a 50:50 chance that the outcome will not deviate from X by more than 10%.' The latter part of the statement provides an indication of the confidence that the respondent puts into the prediction. It can be used as a measure of the perceived degree of uncertainty in the prediction.

Unfortunately, many decision makers are very reluctant to make subjective predictions that involves a statement of odds. They are not used to thinking or reasoning in these terms and may be wary of being held accountable at some future time if their prediction turns out to be wrong. They may also be unfamiliar with, or have forgotten, the most basic statistical concepts. Either case will require skilful and sympathetic questioning on the part of the analyst. Furthermore, such judgemental assessments are prone to various biases, as discussed in Section 15.7.

You may rightfully ask, why bother getting such predictions which smack of spurious accuracy, and then use them as input into some fancy decision model? Remember the principle of GIGO (garbage in, garbage out)! Why not ask the decision maker directly to choose the action he or she considers best? The answer is that the latter course solves nothing and may hide everything. The very process of obtaining subjective predictions will force the decision maker to a more thorough and logical assessment of the situation. Hidden elements may become explicit. This in itself is of considerable value. The use of the model will allow the situation to be explored fully through sensitivity analysis on the very bones of contention — the subjective predictions. It will allow the decision maker to assess the robustness of the solution(s). It may also lead to the re-evaluation of boundary judgements made on the narrow and wider system of interest, and even reveal hidden boundary judgements that may need to be questioned. Finally, the reason for going through the modelling process is not to relieve the decision maker of the responsibility of making the final decision, but to provide a consistent and rational framework and insights for reaching the best decision.

Judgemental adjustments to forecasts derived by other methods

Quantitative forecasting methods, by necessity, are based on past data. As we have seen, there may sometimes be reasons for believing that such past data are not entirely representative of the future, due to events which are not reflected in the data yet or which are only appearing on the horizon. The seemingly obvious action is to use judgemental inputs to 'correct' the quantitative forecasts obtained on past data. In many instances this is a highly appropriate course of action. However, empirical research has shown that such adjustments are prone to bias and that certain rules should be followed (Goodwin, 2005; Makridakis, 1988). Some of the biases showing up in such adjustments are wishful thinking (more on this in Section 15.7) and the illusion of control, i.e., that making the forecast will, in fact, help reduce the variability of the phenomenon in question, such as sales.

There is general agreement among experts that judgemental adjustments should be restricted to take into account extra information or insider knowledge, but definitely not to reflect 'gut feelings'. Any adjustment made should be fully justified in writing (say, as a footnote). Experience shows that this often reduces the incidence of unjustified adjustments. Furthermore, the person(s) should be made aware of the common types of biases prevalent, as discussed in detail in Section 15.7. Finally, the persons making judgemental forecasts or judgemental adjustments to forecasts should receive timely and personalized feedback on their performance, with emphasis on 'timely'. Again, research has shown that such feedback helps improve forecasting and tends to reduce biases. However, it is important that such feedback is not used for fixing blame, but for learning. If it is used for blaming, the forecaster will try to protect him- or herself by making highly conservative predictions.

Activity

Find two new examples each for which the methods below are most suitable:

- persistence prediction
- trend prediction
- cyclic prediction
- associative prediction
- subjective or judgement prediction
- Delphi method

15.6 Probability measures and interpretation

Uncertainty means that one of a number of possible outcomes will occur and that it is not possible to state, with certainty, which one of these outcomes will eventuate. The number of possible outcomes may be small (e.g., the number of cases of a rare notifiable disease in a given year, or the number of breakdowns of a machine over a short time period); it may be large (e.g., the number of CDs sold of the latest release by a famous band). In some instances, the potential or theoretical range of outcomes may be infinitely large (e.g., the time until the next earthquake in Paris, not located in an earthquake-prone region). The possible range of outcomes may not even be knowable — the case of complete uncertainty.

If we know the range of possible outcomes, the best thing is to make a numeric statement about the likelihood of each outcome if they are discrete (e.g., the number of arrivals at a service facility over a given period), or if the outcomes are real numbers (e.g., the time between consecutive arrivals) that the outcome falls into a given interval.

How should we interpret statements of probability? Say, I flip a fair coin. It spins and then lands either heads or tails. We all agree that the probability it will show heads is ½. How should we interpret this? Take a more complex problem, such as the case of firm A having submitted a tender for a major construction job. A number of other firms have done the same. The manager of firm A estimates the probability that her firm will be awarded the contract to be 0.6. What is the meaning of such a statement?

There are at least four major schools of thought on this subject. Although the literature gives the impression that there are great differences between these schools, the differences are largely of a philosophical nature. (Facetious tongues warn us that in this quest we should be particularly aware of academitis — a disease characterized by hairsplitting and, eventually, by 'rigour' mortis.) All schools agree on the numerical values for all simple problems (particularly hypothetical ones), the rules of manipulating probabilities, and the broad principles of using them for decision making. So, how do they differ? We shall now examine two of them.

Objective probabilities

For many simple situations, such as games of chance, or any process that may repeat itself in more or less the same form time and again, the numerical value of the probability of a given outcome or event E, denoted by $P(E)$, can be interpreted as the long-run relative frequency with which this outcome occurs. However, for any given repetition of the process, the event E may or may not occur. We cannot state categorically for which repetition event E will occur or will not occur.

In terms of prediction, we would be fairly safe in predicting that E will occur if the probability $P(E)$ is close to 1, say 0.9. In fact, in this situation we should always predict that event E will occur. In the long-run, only in about 10% of all predictions would we be wrong. It would be completely illogical to use a pattern of predicting the occurrence of E in 90% of the cases and *Not E* in the other 10%. Our betting average would decrease from 90% to 82% correct.

Probability assessments that are either based on physical properties of the phenomenon, such as rolling dice, or based on a vast pool of past experience, such as the number of newspapers sold by a vendor at a given location on a given day of the week, or the probability that a male aged 25 in normal health will survive another t years, where t assumes values 0, 1, 2, 3, and so on, as used by life insurance companies for setting their insurance premiums, can all be given this long-run frequency interpretation. Such probabilities are referred to as **objective probabilities**. Powerful statistical data analysis can be applied to such phenomena.

Subjective probabilities

Difficulties of interpretation arise if we are dealing with one-off situations — situations that are sufficiently unique and different from any previous experience. The majority of strategic decisions in business and government, such as the introduction of a new product, the effect of a given government intervention, or even a core melt-down at a nuclear power station, deal with unique situations. What is the meaning now of 'the probability that outcome X occurs is 60%'? The outcome X could be that sales of a revolutionary gadget exceed the break-even point. The repeatability argument cannot be applied — the product launch will not repeat itself ever under the same or similar circumstances. In fact, it may even be debatable whether assessing a probability measure makes logical sense.

It is in such cases where the subjective probability school comes to our rescue. It tells us that the numerical value, referred to as the **subjective probability** of an event, simply measures the confidence or degree of belief of a reasonable person, who is sufficiently informed about the situation, that the event in question will happen. Hence, two individuals, faced with the same situation, may assign different subjective probabilities to a given event. Their probability assessments are their personal, subjective perception and, hence, are valid — each for the individual who made it. Neither may that perception necessarily remain the same over even short time intervals of a day or a week.

It also seems obvious that, if an event is repeatable and sufficient data on past outcomes have been collected, a reasonable individual's subjective probability assessment should coincide with the observed frequencies, unless other known new factors call for an adjustment.

The use and validity of subjective probabilities sits rather uncomfortably with many people. Interestingly, we use them daily with such statements as 'it's highly probable' (about 0.9?), 'rather unlikely' (0.1?), 'impossible (0.01?), '50-50'. Punters at the races use intuition or hunches to assess the odds of a horse winning — subjective probabilities that are never explicitly stated, but still clearly enter into their choices. When you cross an intersection on your bike just in front of the oncoming car, you assess it as highly unlikely (about 0.02?) that you will not make it.

So, rather than use such assessments implicitly, it makes good sense to render them explicit. Not only could this lead to a re-assessment of what is the best decision, but it also allows us to carry out sensitivity analysis on these assessments. This helps in determining over what range of values for the subjective probability the decision remains unaffected. It will also lead to more consistent decision making.

Events whose occurrence is judged as highly unlikely are often ignored by decision makers. This is an implicit boundary judgement and its reasonableness should be justified. For example, the likelihood of a disaster may be so small that no protective measures are taken. The implicit boundary judgement is that the cost (monetary, social, or in human life) is zero. Unfortunately, such highly improbable events do occur time and again — the melt down of a nuclear power plant (Fukushima, 2011), the blowout of a deep sea oil well (Gulf of Mexico, 2010), ecological disaster caused by the grounding of a cargo ship (NZ North Island, 2011; English Channel, 2008).

Whether we are dealing with subjective probabilities, the event in question will either occur or will not occur. Since it is a one-off situation, it would be nonsense to interpret its probability as 'it occurs x% of the time'. The probability measure only reflects our strength of belief in the event occurring.

A probability statement is an *a priori* concept. It is made before the uncertainty has been resolved — before we know which one of the various possible outcomes has occurred. Once 'the die has been cast', one and only one of these outcomes has occurred, and it could well be one which, a priori, had a low probability. Once that outcome is known, no probability is associated with it any longer.

Activity

- Find two new examples of a different nature where objective and where subjective probability measures are appropriate.
- Assume now that the probability of event *E* is exactly 0.51 and you are repeatedly asked to predict the outcome. What sequence of prediction would you make, and why?

15.7 Behavioural research on subjective probabilities

Research into how individuals assess uncertainty and make judgements under uncertainty shows up a number of rather disturbing behavioural patterns. Miller (1967) states that people face severe limits on their capacity to process information. This is particularly the case in understanding and processing complex multi-faceted relationships. Most people can only cope with about five to nine different uni-dimensional pieces of information at the same time, hence 'the magical number seven, plus or minus two'. Miller noted that once this threshold has been exceeded, people tend to reformulate information into bigger and less detailed chunks. This leads to stereotyping and other gross simplifications. These findings follow naturally from Herbert Simon's concept of **bounded rationality** (see p. 9).

Simplifying heuristics for decision making under uncertainty

A. Tversky and Nobel Prize Laureate for Economics, D. Kahneman (1974, see also 1981, 1986, and 2011) wrote a fascinating paper on how human judgement tends to fail when faced with uncertainty — a 'must read' for any adult who strives for a position of responsibility. (See also the collection of papers in Wright and Ayton, 1994.) They found that research into how our minds cope with uncertainty indicates that we tend to rely on a limited number of heuristic principles, rules, or patterns, known as **representativeness**, **availability**, and **adjustment and anchoring**, which we use to reduce the complex task of assessing probabilities and transforming predictions into simpler judgemental operations. This process happens most of the time without our awareness. Although these heuristics are often useful, they may also lead to serious errors in assessment, systematic bias, and unjustified illusions of validity.

Research subsequent to the Tversky and Kahneman paper shows that the biases introduced by the use of these heuristic are reduced or attenuated when individuals have extensive experience and task familiarity, and are motivated, e.g., by professional ethics, rewards or sanctions (Wright and Ayton, 1994, pp. 116–25). In his popularized book, *Thinking, Fast and Slow*, Kahneman (2011) recommends that we resist our automatic intuitive response to judge events and information (the fast way) which may rise unbidden in our mind, and instead apply systematic and logical reasoning and deliberations (the slow way).

Representativeness

The likelihood or probability of an event is based on how closely it resembles a class of events for which it is seen as representative. For example, asked about the likely profession of a person described as 'very shy and withdrawn, invariably helpful, but with little interest in people or in the world of reality, a meek and tidy soul with a great need for order, structure, and a passion for detail', people tend to have recourse to **stereotyping**. Since that description is very representative of the mental image most people have about librarians, the likelihood that they will assign a person fitting this description to the class of librarians rather than the class of farmers is much larger. The fact that the proportion of farmers in the population is several times larger than the proportion of librarians does not enter into the assessment. The relative size of the corresponding statistical populations 'librarians' and 'farmers' are ignored. This is referred to as **base-rate neglect**.

Research also shows that the representativeness heuristic tends to **disregard the size of the sample** on which a probability judgement is based. A given outcome A in, say, two thirds of all observations is assumed (at least by people with little training in statistical analysis) as equally indicative of the true proportion of A regardless of whether it is based on 6 or 60 observations, when in fact the larger sample tends to provide more reliable estimates. The result is that too much confidence is placed in the findings based on small samples. The extreme case is making a judgement based on a single observation, even if that observation consists of several aspects, such as happens in job applicant assessment tests. Unless the various aspects observed are largely independent of each other — in statistical terms, have little or no correlation — the conclusion reached may be unreliable.

Another aspect of representativeness that is misunderstood or ignored is the tendency of **regression to the mean.** Stochastic phenomena where the outcomes vary randomly around stable values — stationary processes — exhibit the general tendency that extreme outcomes are more likely to be followed by an outcome closer to the mean or mode than by other extreme values in the same direction. For example, even a bright student will observe that her or his performance in a test following an especially outstanding outcome tends to be less brilliant. Similarly, extremely low or extremely high sales in a given period tend to be followed by sales that are closer to the stable mean or the stable trend. Ignoring this tendency and basing predictions on the latest observation leads to over- or underestimation.

Availability

In many situations, people tend to assign a higher likelihood to the occurrence of an event where instances can easily be retrieved from past experience than to those that are difficult to recall. Events that have left a strong impression, such as accidents one was involved in, or unpleasant episodes with the boss or a fellow employee, come more readily to one's mind and, hence, may be seen as being more numerous than they are. In contrast, events more difficult to retrieve, such as things that happened a long time ago or to other people, tend to be judged as occurring less frequently.

Similarly, having just experienced several such events in the recent past may contribute to overestimating their frequency. For example, having just gone through two floods in the space of three years, most people would scoff at the statement that both were 'one-in-a-hundred-years' events.

However, the bias of availability even works for things that you might not have experienced personally, but for which possible contexts under which they might occur can easily be imagined. For example, the likelihood of being caught in a terror attack is overestimated by most people, since it is easy to imagine potential scenarios.

Adjustment and anchoring

In most situations, people estimate something by starting from an initial value, usually based on past experience with comparable situations. Experiments have shown that, if people were fed with different starting points, any adjustment made to the starting point to account for the same additional information tended to be insufficient. The initial starting point acts like a ship's anchor that allows only a limited shift of position for the vessel in response to water currents or wind.

This has important consequences on how the quest for probability assessments or forecasts is framed, particularly for subjective probabilities. The frame may become such an anchor that leads to severe bias. It is therefore essential that considerable thought is given to framing the search for unbiased estimates of future events (Tversky and Kahneman, 1986). Unfortunately, for people familiar with a given situation, the frame is already provided by what they know.

It is crucial that whoever is involved in developing estimates for future events is fully aware of the danger of anchoring. It may be useful to repeat such an exercise with a different frame and then reconcile any differences in results.

Overconfidence and wishful thinking

Other research indicates that people tend to be overconfident in their ability to assess probabilities — not justified by their actual performance. They tend to overestimate the probability of rare events and underestimate the probability of highly likely events.

People are prone to the **gambler's fallacy** — expecting that an outcome that has failed to occur for a while is likely to occur in the near future, disregarding the fact that each outcome may be independent of what happened before.

We may also overestimate probabilities of events that we would like to happen or desire, and underestimate those that we would rather did not happen. Experiments with MBA students and executives clearly reveal the existence of this type of wishful thinking. In one experiment, the subjects were presented with a sales history on a new product of firm A as shown in part (a) of Figure 15-2. Sales increased dramatically after the product's launch, but then very recently have shown a small decline. The subjects were put into two groups. Group 1 were told to put themselves into the position of the marketing manager of firm A, while group 2 were told that they were the marketing manager of a major competitor. Each group was then asked to predict firm A's future sales pattern for that product. Most subjects in group 1 predicted that sales would recover promptly and continue their dramatic increase. In contrast, the subjects in group 2 predicted that the sales downturn would persist. This is depicted by the broken lines in part (b) of Figure 15-2.

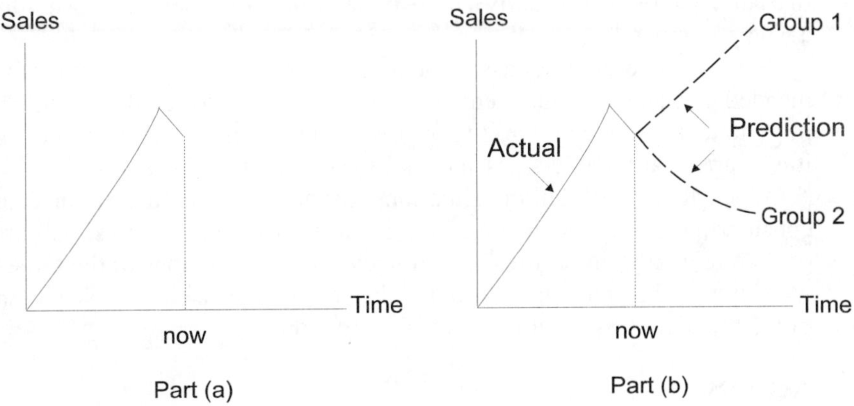

Figure 15-2 Sales predictions by wishful thinking

Each group reflects a high degree of wishful thinking because: (a) outcomes happen later in time and may not be easily attributable to the causal action; (b) variability in the environment degrades the reliability of feedback, especially for outcomes of low probability; (c) there is often no information about what the outcome would have been if another action had been taken; (d) most decisions for which such assessments are made are unique and therefore provide little opportunity for learning (Tversky and Kahneman, 1986, p. 274); and (e) information for learning is often suppressed by subordinates or colleagues of decision makers out of fear that revealing it may backfire on them, i.e., may be used for assigning blame rather than for learning.

Kahneman (2011) believes that biases had a hand in the 2008 and 2011 financial crises, producing what he describes as 'a collective blindness to risk and uncertainty'.

Lessons to be learned

What lessons can we learn from this research? First, the individual making subjective probability assessments or predictions must be aware of the potential short-comings of the heuristics of representativeness, availability, and the anchoring effect, as well as the tendency towards wishful thinking. It is best not to rush into an initial guess and then try to rationalize its validity. Instead, a good starting point is to decompose a complex problem situation and develop a complete list of all the factors that may affect it, how it is affected by each one, and weighing them carefully and deliberately against each other. It is also helpful to restate the same situation in a different framework, e.g., expressing a positive statement as the exact equivalent negative statement, and observe whether this leads to a different assessment and, why.

Rather than settle for a single number, it is more effective to select as the initial anchor or benchmark a fairly wide interval and then attempt to narrow it down in the light of the various influencing factors listed earlier. It is also useful to hold off on a definite assessment and first pool the judgement of other people who are sufficiently familiar with the situation. This is likely to lead to a more balanced and more representative answer, and reduce the anchoring effect. A final assessment in the form of a narrow interval is usually a more honest and more useful piece of information than a single number.

Finally, once the final assessment has been made, it is important that the recommended decision is subjected to extensive sensitivity analysis with respect to all important subjective probability or prediction inputs. This will reveal how important it is to arrive at reliable assessments for each input of this nature.

When faced with unique situations, the tendency is to take an 'inside' view by considering mainly the distinguishing features of the problem situation and ignoring or even rejecting similarities or analogies to other situations of the same general type, when it would be more insightful to take an 'outside' view, i.e., see them as instances of the broader class of situations and learn from them.

Activity

From your own personal experience, give examples of how you may have used each of the heuristics or biases: representativeness (stereotyping, disregard of sample size, estimates based on a single observation, misconception of regression), availability (ease of retrieving instances, lack or ease of imagining contexts), insufficient adjustment by anchoring, overconfidence, wishful thinking, the gambler's fallacy. Identify clearly which aspect(s) of your judgement was/were affected. The same example may often have elements of several factors.

15.8 Random variables, probability distributions

Random variables

Assume now that a situation has several alternative outcomes and that with each outcome we can associate a real number. An example will help. Sales for XL Bakers' fruit loaves at supermarket K vary from day to day. Occasionally, none are sold. The largest number ever sold, recorded in recent history, is 12. On most days, sales range somewhere between 4 and 8. Past history thus indicates that daily sales may assume any outcome between 0 and 12. Hence, we can associate with each possible outcome (= daily sales) one of the integers from 0 to 12. These numbers represent the values that the **random variable** 'daily sales' may assume.

Frequency and probability distributions

The historical frequencies with which each sales amount has been observed could be used as an approximate model for the probabilities with which each of these sales amounts will occur in the future. These probabilities are now seen to be a function of the integers from 0 to 12. We call this function a **probability frequency function** of the random variable 'daily sales'. It is also sometimes loosely referred to as a probability distribution, although in probability theory this term has more a precise meaning. The above case is an example of a discrete probability distribution. But remember, on any given day only one of these outcomes will actually be realized. (By analogy, these concepts can also be applied to one-off situations. The frequency interpretation is then replaced by 'the strength of belief' or 'the degree of confidence' in each possible value of the outcome.)

A probability distribution conveys considerably more information than does a single-valued prediction. Not only does it show the range of possible outcomes, but also their relative frequency for recurrent events, or the subjective strength of belief in each outcome for one-off situations. It should lead to better and more informed decision making than that associated with single-value predictions. However, it is also more costly to determine and usually leads to more complicated and expensive models.

Approximations by theoretical distributions

Since the determination of the exact probability distribution is difficult, we often resort to approximations. Sometimes, the process itself will suggest a distribution. Events that occur singly and are relatively rare, such as the breakdown of machines, traffic on a quiet road, or the arrival of customers at a service facility, are quite often approximated surprisingly well by a **Poisson process**. Here, the distribution of times between events has a **negative exponential distribution** or, equivalently, the number of events in any time period has a **Poisson distribution**.

If the outcome is affected by, or is the sum of, a large number of independent factors, with no factor having a predominant influence, the **normal distribution** provides an excellent approximation. Demand for bread — mentioned earlier — would be a good example. Daily sales are the result of many individuals independently making a decision to buy one or a few loaves, with no individual buying a very large number and thus having an undue influence over sales, whenever this occurs. It is completely defined by two parameters: the expected value and the standard deviation of the random variable.

The normal distribution is a continuous distribution, i.e., the random variable may assume any real value from minus infinity to plus infinity. In practice, the outcomes tend to be clustered more or less tightly around the expected value. For example, there is a 95% probability that any particular realization of a normal random variable lies within two standard deviations of the expected value. The distribution's position and shape is completely defined by these two parameters.

In the bread demand example, daily sales (number of loaves) are integer variables. However, if sales are sufficiently large, usually 20 or more, then using a continuous random variable may be a suitable approximation for many decision situations.

What if the situation does not suggest a theoretical distribution? We may be able to collect a sample of data — say, times between events — from the existing (or a similar) system and find a suitable candidate from one of the many theoretical distributions available, keeping in mind that the distribution must be suited to our modelling purposes. One family of distributions, for example, are the **Erlang-*k***

distributions. These are the distributions that result from adding k negative exponential random variables together. These distributions have little natural application. However, their probability functions have a number of useful shapes. Figure 15-3 plots the probability functions for $k = 1$ (negative exponential), 2, 4, 8. All the probability functions are for random variables with the same mean of 2.

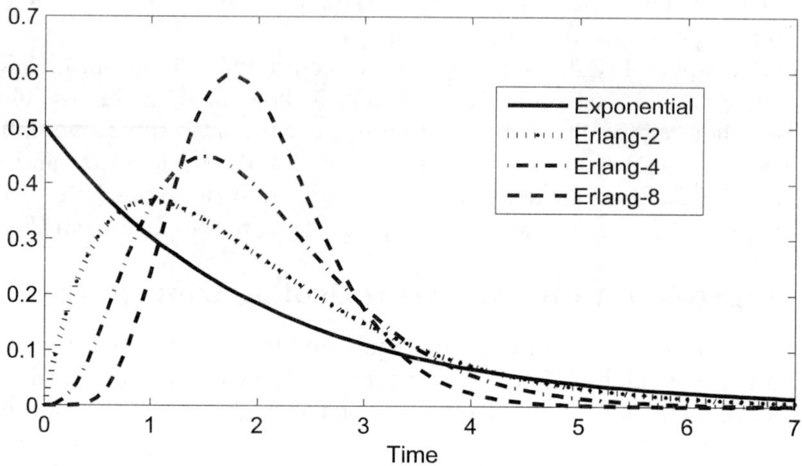

Figure 15-3 Erlang-1, -2, -4, and -8 probability distributions

For the negative exponential distribution, most of the times are short, hence its distribution decays away steadily. For $k = 2, 4, 8$... however, the distribution moves to a more and more 'normal' shape, just as the previous characterization of the normal distribution suggests it should. Their shapes suggest they would be good for modelling situations where most of the values are clustered close to the mean, there are no negative or zero values, and there are very occasional large values — say, times for cars paying at a car park, where most pay quickly, but the odd person has lost his or her ticket.

Figure 15-4 shows data collected on vehicles for the time taken to pay for parking as they leave the Lichfield Street car park in Christchurch. The data were used to test other configurations for the toll system — two toll booths served by one queue, or a special queue for vehicles with electronic tags, for example. The left-hand graph shows that the times between arrivals at the toll booth appear quite close to a negative exponential distribution (note that testing of the suitability of particular theoretical distributions is usually carried out on the cumulative distribution function). So, they may well be modelled by a Poisson process, as we might expect.

We have no intuition about the time taken to pay except that it must be non-negative, and probably less variable than a negative exponential distribution would imply. Some investigation of the basic parameters and a number of attempts, however, show that the times can be well approximated by an Erlang-4 distribution, as shown in the right-hand graph. From a modelling point of view, the acceptable fits of these two distributions is good news. If we decide to fit waiting line models such as those discussed in Chapter 16, assuming Poisson arrivals and Erlang service time distributions leads to calculable formulas for waiting times. If we opt for discrete event simulation (see Chapter 17), these distributions are particularly easy to use to generate additional observations for simulation. Thus, they meet the requirement of being suited to our modelling purposes, possibly over other distributions which might fit the observed data better.

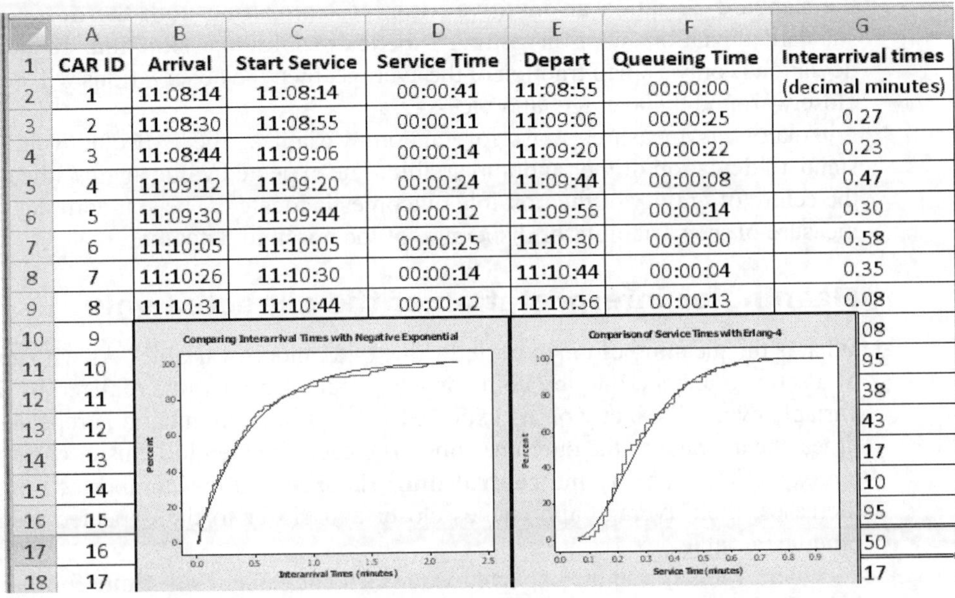

	A	B	C	D	E	F	G
1	CAR ID	Arrival	Start Service	Service Time	Depart	Queueing Time	Interarrival times
2	1	11:08:14	11:08:14	00:00:41	11:08:55	00:00:00	(decimal minutes)
3	2	11:08:30	11:08:55	00:00:11	11:09:06	00:00:25	0.27
4	3	11:08:44	11:09:06	00:00:14	11:09:20	00:00:22	0.23
5	4	11:09:12	11:09:20	00:00:24	11:09:44	00:00:08	0.47
6	5	11:09:30	11:09:44	00:00:12	11:09:56	00:00:14	0.30
7	6	11:10:05	11:10:05	00:00:25	11:10:30	00:00:00	0.58
8	7	11:10:26	11:10:30	00:00:14	11:10:44	00:00:04	0.35
9	8	11:10:31	11:10:44	00:00:12	11:10:56	00:00:13	0.08
10	9						08
11	10						95
12	11						38
13	12						43
14	13						17
15	14						10
16	15						95
17	16						50
18	17						17

Figure 15-4 Lichfield Street data and fitted distributions

Activity

- Collect a minimum of 40 times at which vehicles pass you in one direction on a quiet road. Make sure you are not downstream of something that would cause the vehicles to bunch up, such as traffic lights or stop signs. Use the Excel spreadsheet on the website, Event_time_Recorder.xlsm to record times, but a watch and clipboard will also work.
- Draw a histogram of the times between vehicles. For a Poisson process, it should have a decaying-away shape, but this can be very dependent on the class intervals selected.
- Draw a cumulative distribution function of the times between vehicles and compare it with that for a negative exponential distribution with the same mean. Some packages, such as Minitab, can do this automatically. It was used to draw the two graphs in Figure 15-3, but it can be done adequately as superimposed scatterplots using Excel. There is more detail on how to do this in Section 16.3. Usually, the cumulative distribution provides more convincing evidence that the process is close to Poisson.
- Is it acceptable to model traffic by a Poisson process for such a small-scale study?

15.9 Expected value and standard deviation

For any set of actual observations about a phenomenon, we can compute the average or mean value, which gives us an indication of their centre of gravity. We can also find the standard deviation, which provides us with a measure of how widely the observations are dispersed around the average. Although most of us have difficulties giving the standard deviation an intuitive meaning, comparing both the average and the standard deviation helps in getting a better feel for the situation. If the standard deviation is only a small fraction of the average, then the observations will be bunched closely around the average, and vice-versa.

Analogous measures exist for random variables: the expected value and the standard deviation of the random variable. The expected value again indicates where the centre of gravity of the possible outcomes is located. The standard deviation is a measure of the variability or dispersion of the possible outcomes.

Meaning or interpretation of the expected value

What is the meaning of the expected value of a random variable? As with an average of a set of numbers, only by coincidence will the actual value realized by a random variable ever fall exactly on its expected value. If a phenomenon is repeated several times, the average of the outcomes observed each time tend to cluster closely around the expected value. By the **central limit theorem**, as the number of observations increases, their average approaches closer and closer to the expected value of the random variable.

Often, we may use the expected value as a convenient substitute for the long-run behaviour of a random variable and base our decisions on this number. However, it is only an approximation — a modelling simplification. It never implies that the random variable will, in fact, assume its expected value. For a discrete distribution, the expected value may involve fractions, i.e., not equal one of the possible outcomes, while for a continuous distribution it will be a pure coincidence if the realized value of a random variable falls exactly on its expected value.

For subjective probability distributions, particularly for one-off situations, we do not even have the comfort of a long-run interpretation. No averaging can occur. The expected value has no meaning beyond its mathematical definition. Nevertheless, it can be shown that a decision based on the alternative which produces the highest expected value of the measure of performance is the best decision. But, do not fall into the trap of assuming that the outcome, when it occurs, will be equal to the expected value. This point cannot be stressed strongly enough!

15.10 Approaches to deal with and to reduce uncertainty

Most decision makers would rather make decisions under certainty than under uncertainty. The higher the uncertainty, the higher their discomfort and anxiety. Hence, it is not surprising that substantial efforts are made to reduce or avoid uncertainty. This is an important topic for theories in organizational behaviour and strategy. There are four basic approaches: we attempt to reduce uncertainty as such; we attempt to alleviate its effects; we postpone any firm commitments as long as possible, in the hope of dissolving some of the uncertainty as time passes; or we opt for greater flexibility for future responses by creating future options.

Collecting more information

The obvious approach to reducing uncertainty is to gather more information and, hence, improve our predictions, be it in terms of a single-valued guesstimate or a probability distribution. For instance, a firm has experienced a steady growth for one of its main product lines over the last 18 months. If this trend continues, sales will increase by another 40% over the next year. The existing production facilities are now taxed to the limit. Substantial investments in new plant and equipment are needed to expand capacity. There is, however, considerable uncertainty about the long-run potential for this product line. Will the growth trend be sustained and, if so, for how much longer? Faced with such a situation, most firms would undertake a comprehensive market research study to obtain a better picture of the market potential for the product line. In other words, they would gather more information to reduce the uncertainty faced.

Gathering more information is costly and time consuming. This is only justified, if the new information gained reduces uncertainty and leads to making better decisions. There is a whole branch of statistical decision theory dealing with these aspects: **Bayesian decision analysis**. The underlying mathematics are, unfortunately, beyond an introductory survey. The basic idea is simple and intuitively appealing. Starting with some prior, albeit imperfect, information, we decide to acquire additional information. This could be in the form of purchasing advice from experts, a Delphi study, consulting a consumer panel, a small market survey, a limited market test, or a small-scale experiment or trial run. The additional information or sample data obtained is then used to adjust the prior information.

Unfortunately, the conditions for applying this analysis are often not satisfied. Time pressure may not permit acquiring additional information. The cost of a trial run may be too expensive. Market testing may alert the competition and give them time to react. Delphi studies take too long.

Sensitivity analysis

The second approach is to ascertain how crucial it is to get accurate information about uncertain events. Sensitivity analysis comes to the rescue. We systematically evaluate over what range of values for any uncertain parameters the best decision remains the same as for the guesstimates used for deriving it. If that range is small, then this signals that acquiring more accurate information may be beneficial. If the range is wide and we feel fairly confident that the true value of the uncertain parameters lies well within that range, nothing will be gained by spending time and money to get better information.

Keeping options open

The third approach is to select a decision strategy that closes the fewest doors for future action. In other words, any action which commits us firmly to a given direction and eliminates a large number of other possible future actions is either avoided or postponed until more and better information becomes available. Naturally, most decisions will narrow down future choices. It is a problem of finding a good balance between maximizing the benefit of the course of action to be chosen and keeping our options open — a version of the perennial problem in decision making, of balancing benefits against costs. Robustness analysis, a problem structuring method briefly discussed in Section 7.8 (p. 211), addresses such issues.

Creating future options

Rather than simply keeping options open, it may be strategically advisable to take actions that create new future options. For instance, a firm located in a growth area where suitable land is becoming scarce may decide to purchase a site now in anticipation of possible future expansion of its production facilities, although no decision or even exploratory planning has been made at the time of the purchase. It simply creates a new option for the future. If no expansion is made within five to ten years, the land may be sold again — one hopes at a good profit.

Similarly, firms investing heavily in research clearly do this in anticipation of opening up new future options, i.e., new products or processes.

Scenario analysis

Organizations invariably have to plan for events in the far future and often face a highly turbulent environment in terms of potential technological change, potential moves by competitors or adversaries, or high uncertainty as to the future economic climate. Rather than consider only one possible future that tries to accommodate the variability and uncertainty involved in all factors, it may be more effective and insightful to consider several possible futures or scenarios.

Although an organization faces an infinite number of possible futures, the number of different scenarios explored is rarely more than three or four. Each scenario makes certain assumptions about crucial factors that drive what may happen in the future; in other words, each makes different boundary judgements, usually with regard to the wider system. It is important that these boundary judgements are clearly identified and justified as reasonable. Scenarios should not include decision choices and the possible response of the wider system to such choices. That should be part of the subsequent analysis once the scenarios have been developed.

The practice is to start with two scenarios, one somewhat optimistic about various aspects of the future, the other somewhat on the pessimistic side. One or two other scenarios in between complete the set, one of which may be the continuation of the status quo. For commercial ventures, the choice of scenarios should be such that each has a reasonable chance of eventuating approximately. On the other hand, for disaster planning, it may be essential to evaluate extreme scenarios that have a very small probability of occurring, but may have devastating consequences if they do.

For each of these scenarios, a preferred decision strategy that balances competing goals (see Chapter 19) is developed. Such a strategy should include contingency actions that allow recovery if another scenario occurs. Whenever possible, a strategy should consists of several stages, some to be implemented right away, others for future implementation and contingent on later events. Each decision strategy is assessed in terms of its robustness and risks with respect to the other scenarios, if this makes sense.

This process will enhance the understanding of the problem situation and thereby provide valuable insights for informed, rational decision making. It may even suggest actions that may increase the likelihood that the preferred scenario eventuates.

Any two or more of these five approaches may be used jointly for reducing the degree of uncertainty.

15.11 Decision criteria under uncertainty

When the outcome of each alternative course of action is known with certainty, the evaluation of which action is best boils down to identifying the one with the highest net benefit if the objective is maximizing benefits, or the lowest cost if the objective is minimizing costs. When the outcomes are uncertain, what criterion should be used for choosing the best decision? Chapters 16 to 18 will explore such questions with a number of examples. The discussion below is only intended as a cursory overview.

Expected value criterion

The most obvious approach is to adapt the criterion of maximizing benefits or minimizing costs for deterministic situations. Under uncertainty, each action leads to one of a number of possible outcomes. Which particular outcome will be realized is only known in terms of its probability. So, we substitute expected benefits or expected cost for benefits or costs in the above criterion. The best action is the one with the highest expected benefit or the lowest expected cost. Economic theory, in fact, shows that under fairly general conditions, this criterion achieves the best possible long-run results.

For repetitive risky situations, this statement has the usual long-run frequency interpretation. Applied to one-off situations, the meaning implied is that, using this criterion consistently will, in the long run, produce superior results to any other criterion. However, for any particular one-off situation, the outcome could still spell disaster!

Threshold approaches

In situations with extremely serious possible outcomes, such as large losses or bankruptcy, the decision maker may not be willing to make a decision based on the expected value criterion. Instead, he or she may select an outcome that has a lower expected benefit, but provides better protection against the risks involved. One such criterion chooses the best decision on the basis of reducing the probability of disastrous outcomes below a maximum acceptable level. In particular, the decision maker may eliminate any actions from further consideration if they imply that a probability of not achieving a certain minimum benefit, or of exceeding a certain maximum cost is larger than a given threshold value. For instance, when comparing several mutually exclusive risky investment opportunities, the decision maker may eliminate any which have a probability of 5% of leading to a loss of more than a certain amount. The actions passing the threshold are then evaluated using a secondary criterion, such as maximizing expected benefits or minimizing expected costs.

Unfortunately, for many real-life complex and sequential decision situations, determining the probability distribution of the final outcomes may be difficult. Risk analysis — a topic briefly discussed in Chapter 18 — is one attempt to overcome some of these difficulties.

Worst outcome approach

If there is a high degree of uncertainty about the outcomes and, furthermore, some may also involve serious adverse consequences, the decision maker may select the decision which offers the best protection against the worst outcomes. The probabilities are completely ignored. This criterion may be appropriate if some of the possible outcomes involve disasters, such as loss of life, serious injury, or irreversible damage to the environment, or if the outcomes are partially controlled by a vicious adversary who is out to get you.

In a business context, a firm may resort to this criterion in order to avoid any possibilities of going bankrupt. Discussion of this and similar criteria is the subject of **decision analysis** (Chapter 18) and **game theory** (a topic not covered in this text).

15.12 Chapter highlights

- Few things in the real world are known with absolute certainty. Deterministic models are often convenient simplifying approximations. Uncertainty results in new types of system behaviour.
- Expressions in everyday language about uncertainty are prone to ambiguity. This may lead to misunderstandings about their intended meaning.
- Uncertainty has three major causes: insufficient understanding of the phenomenon, information based on samples from the unknown population, and measurement errors.
- The degree of uncertainty may range from almost complete ignorance about the phenomenon to well-understood principles about it or to reliable and extensive observations of past occurrences.
- Much of decision making depends on having good information about future events. Methods for predicting the future fall into five groups: persistence prediction, trend prediction, cyclic prediction, associative prediction, and prediction based on expert judgement. The predictions are usually based on past behaviour. Hence, all methods assume, to a lesser or greater extent, that the past is a good predictor of the future.

- Objective probabilities can be interpreted as the frequency of various (usually repetitive) events occurring in the long run. Subjective probabilities express a person's strength of believe in the occurrence of various (usually unique) events.
- Behavioural research shows that we tend to use simplifying heuristics when making judgements about uncertain events. These are prone to biases and systematic errors, such as stereotyping, disregard of sample size, disregard for regression to the mean, deriving estimates based on the ease of retrieving instances of the event, anchoring to an initial frame or guess, the gambler's fallacy, wishful thinking, and illusion of validity. These arise unbidden in our mind, and lead to quick and simplified judgement and decision making, rather than the use of (slower) systematic and deliberate reasoning.
- Certain theoretical probability distributions, such as the Poisson and the normal, tend to approximate many phenomena in real life. For other situations, there are many theoretical probability distributions that can be used as an adequate means to capture the uncertainty of the process for modelling purposes.
- Much of decision making is concerned with dealing with or reducing uncertainty or the effects of uncertainty, such as collecting more information, performing sensitivity analysis with respect to uncertain aspects, exploring more than one possible future via scenario analysis, and selecting decisions that keep open or create new future options.
- Decision criteria for selecting the best option need to reflect the degree of uncertainty. For recurrent decisions, maximizing or minimizing the expected value of the outcomes is most appropriate. Theoretical arguments show that even for unique or one-off situations this remains the appropriate criterion, but the interpretation of the expected value changes. However, in decisions that can lead to extreme, adverse outcomes, e.g., large monetary losses, environmental disasters, or serious injuries and loss of life, other types of decision criteria that offer additional protection may be more appropriate.

Exercises

1. One of the major causes of uncertainty listed in Section 15.2 is ignorance about or a lack of complete understanding of a given phenomenon. It is then conceivable that ultimately uncertainty will disappear if advances in science allow us to understand all phenomena perfectly. Critically discuss this view.
2. A recent court case found a local council negligent for allowing the complainant to build a house on a 50-year flood plain. Although the council had informed the complainant of the danger, the court awarded him considerable damages, based on the fact that, within the first ten years after completion, the house was inundated in three of these years. The judge's verdict stated that the council's assessment of the flood risk clearly was in error, given that in three out of ten years flooding had occurred. Assume that the council's assessment of the house being on a 50-year flood plain was correct. Discuss the validity or otherwise of the judge's reason for siding with the complainant.

3. An analyst asked an economist whether he should collect additional data to have a more reliable basis for finding the best policy for a decision problem under uncertainty. The economist's answer was: 'You should collect additional information until the marginal cost of obtaining it is less than the marginal gain of improved decision making.' (This follows the principles developed in Chapter 12.) Why is this a rather naive recommendation? (Hint: consider the possible difficulties of doing this.)
4. 'The probability that I will have a car accident on my way home from work is one in 700.' Give an objective and a subjective interpretation of this statement.
5. Imagine you are in charge of an organization (business, school, sports club, government agency). Give an example for each of the following heuristics you may end up using for various uncertain events you may face:
   (a) stereotyping;
   (b) disregarding sample size;
   (c) making a judgement based on a single observation;
   (d) disregard for the regression to the mean;
   (e) the ease of recalling instances (based on past events);
   (f) the difficulty of recalling instances;
   (g) the ease of imagining situations where the event might occur;
   (h) the difficulty of imagining situations where the event might occur;
   (i) insufficient adjustment because of anchoring;
   (j) overconfidence;
   (k) wishful thinking, the gambler's fallacy.
6. Consider the heuristics discussed in Section 15.7. For each description listed below, identify which of these heuristics was or is likely to be used, and the potential error or bias it could introduce. Some situation may fit more than one heuristic.
   (a) Discussing politics, Mike says to Sue: 'You can't trust a politician — they are all liars!'
   (b) When Mike went swimming in the ocean, his partner asked him to be careful of rips. 'Oh, I'm more worried about sharks.'
   (c) Five of John's friends recently won sizeable sums in scratch lotto. John's aunt asks him whether the chances of winning in scratch lotto are good. He responds: 'Oh yes, just look how my friends are doing!'
   (d) Andrew goes to the supermarket. In the car park, raised on a slanted platform, is a beautiful cabriolet sports car — the latest model, offered as the first prize for a nationwide raffle organized on behalf of the Red Cross. He falls in love with the racy car. He has the firm feeling that if he buys a book of tickets for £10, he will win it.
   (e) Margaret got five A+s and three As in her first year at university. The head of department of her major subject is overheard making the following remark to one of his colleagues: 'I bet Margaret will do even better next year!'
7. For each of the situations described below, indicate one or more possible approaches to deal with or reduce uncertainty, and why each is a reasonable approach:
   (a) A firm has detailed data available of its sales, based on delivery documents for each sales transaction. However, for various reasons (suppliers' strikes and shipment delays, machine breakdowns, and so on), a substantial number of orders from customers could not be met. Because of these lost sales, the size of the true demand is therefore unknown.

(b) A firm faces the dilemma of whether or not it should invest in an expensive expansion of its product research facility. There is hearsay evidence that the competition is considering similar action. Recent rapid advances in technology relevant for both research and production has created added uncertainty as to whether this trend continues, in which case premature expansion may lock the firm in at a level of technology that may soon be partially obsolete. On the other hand, experience also indicates that advances in technology tend to go through cycles of high activity and stagnation.

(c) A new prosthesis for artificial hips has come on the market. The manufacturer claims that it will increase the length of time before it fails, reducing the need for replacement. However, the manufacturer has only limited data which, although promising, is not sufficient to back up the claim fully. The health department (who pays for the cost of such operations, including the prostheses) wants to make a decision now as to whether it should switch to the new prosthesis, which is considerably more expensive than the one currently used, or stick with the current one for the foreseeable future.

Further reading

Armstrong, J.S. (1985) *Long-Range Forecasting: From Crystal Ball to Computer*, New York: Wiley. Extensive coverage of forecasting methods. Armstrong is a provocative writer.

Baumgartner, T. and Midttun, A. (eds) (1987) *The Politics of Energy Forecasting: A Comparative Study of Energy Forecasting in Western Europe and North America*, Oxford: Clarendon Press. A fascinating collection of essays on energy forecasting in the 1970s and 1980s. Sets out reasons for the huge over-predictions of energy demand persistently produced by various official and quasi-official bodies in seven countries. These include excessively complex and poorly understood models, highly subjective probabilities, and advocacy and bias among forecasters.

Bross, Irwin D.J. (1953) *Design for Decision*, New York: Macmillan. The date of publication makes this a classic. It is a classic! Humorous, insightful discussion of many issues associated with uncertainty. Our discussion in Chapter 15 has been strongly influenced by this book. The relevant chapters are 1 to 5.

Goodwin, P. (2005) 'How to integrate management judgment with statistical forecasts', *Foresight* 1(1): 8–12. *Foresight* publishes practical applied articles of forecasting. This issue contains a special section on judgemental adjustment.

Goodwin, P. and Wright, G. (2009) *Decision Analysis for Management Judgement*, 4th edn, Chichester: Wiley. Chapters 5 and 6 discuss uncertainty and probability, chapter 10 heuristics and biases in probability assessments, and chapter 11 methods of eliciting probabilities.

Hogarth, R.M. and Makridakis, S. (1981) 'Forecasting and planning: an evaluation', *Management Sciences*, February: 115–38. This seminal paper first reviews some of the psychology of human judgement, followed by a review of reported applications of formal forecasting methods. It finds that the latter are as prone to similar problems as the former. It then concludes with some suggestions for overcoming some of these difficulties.

Kahneman, Daniel (2011) *Thinking, Fast and Slow*, New York: Farrar, Straus & Giroux. His most recent book on the faults, biases, and pitfalls of intuitive, but real-life decision making, versus the normative rational-choice model of economic theory that fails to recognize how the majority of real people behave. Popularized and updated versions of his papers.

Makridakis, S. (1988) 'Metaforecasting: Ways of improving forecast accuracy and usefulness', *International Journal of Forecasting*, 1988, 4: 467–91.

Makridakis, S., Wheelwright, S. and Hyndman, R. (1998) *Forecasting: Methods and Applications*, 3rd edn, New York: Wiley. A comprehensive coverage of quantitative and some qualitative forecasting methods. Also includes sections on biases and judgemental revision.

Miller, G. (1967) *The Psychology of Communications: Seven Essays*, New York: Basic Books.

Tversky, A. and Kahneman, D. (1986) 'Rational choice and the framing of decisions', *Journal of Business*, 4(part 2): S251–8. The more academic version on the same theme as their 1981 paper.

Tversky, A. and Kahneman, D. (1981) 'The framing of decisions and the psychology of choice,' *Science*, January, 453–8. A popular follow-on article to 'Judgement under uncertainty', which shows that preferences and, hence, decision choices are highly dependent on how the problem in question is presented or framed.

Tversky, A. and Kahneman, D. (1974) 'Judgment under uncertainty: heuristics and biases', *Science*, 185, September: 1124–31. The classic article discussed in Section 15.7.

Wright, G. (2001) *Strategic Decision Making: A Best Practice Blueprint*, New York: Wiley. Popular, easy reading on fallacies and pitfalls when dealing with uncertainties.

Wright, G. and Ayton, P. (eds) (1994) *Subjective Probability*, Chichester: Wiley. A collection of academic papers extending the Tversky and Kahneman research.

Wright, G. and Goodwin, P. (eds) (1998) *Forecasting with Judgment*, Chichester: Wiley. An authoritative series of articles on how judgement affects and biases predictions, and ways to overcome some of the difficulties.

Forecast Pro comes from Business Forecast Systems Inc.: www.forecastpro.com.

Minitab comes from Minitab Inc.: www.minitab.com.

16

Waiting lines: stochastic systems

Learning objectives

- To identify the components of a waiting line model.
- To be able to identify the causes of congestion in waiting line models.
- To use arrival–departure diagrams for modeling the time-dependent causes of congestion.
- To recognize how emergent properties may occur in stochastic systems.
- To apply simple queueing models to a practical situation.

Introduction

As we saw in Chapter 15, uncertainty about the behaviour of a system can range from knowing almost nothing, to having fairly reliable information in the form of 'objective' probabilities about the various events that may occur in the system. This chapter studies system behaviour that is often the realization of sequences of random events. We will use theoretical probability distributions to model each sequence. We shall see that under these conditions a system may exhibit new and interesting types of behaviour that is not present in deterministic systems — examples of 'emergent properties' (see p. 43).

While in a deterministic system each alternative course of action leads to a corresponding known outcome, in a stochastic system each alternative course of action leads to one of a number of possible outcomes. We cannot specify which particular outcome will result from a given decision, but only with what probability each of the possible outcomes will occur. Hence, the 'best' decision is the one that produces the most 'favourable' probability distribution for the outcomes. For most hard OR problem solving, the most favourable probability distribution is the one with the highest expected benefit or the lowest expected cost.

This chapter deals mainly with the long-run system behaviour of stochastic systems. This implies that the operation of the system continues (at least in theory) for a long time interval and that all inputs are stationary, i.e., the probability distributions governing all random events, as well as any other aspects, such as costs factors, remain unchanged.

We shall explore these ideas by studying a particular type of system, namely, waiting lines. They are ideal for showing some of the emergent properties of stochastic systems, and how the long-run behaviour of such systems is affected by controllable and uncontrollable aspects. The first two sections of this chapter describe the structure of waiting line situations and demonstrate that stochastic systems may exhibit emergent properties that comparable deterministic systems do not have. The mathematics of waiting lines has been studied extensively since 1917. Section 16.3 summarizes some of the most basic results. The remaining sections of the chapter study a real-life application in detail — the New Zealand Forest Products weighbridge problem.

16.1 Waiting lines

We are all familiar with waiting lines or queues. We wait at a bus stop for the next bus, we wait for lifts, and we wait at checkout counters in supermarkets, the student cafeteria, or the library until it is our turn to be served. We wait at the doctors', or for an operation in a hospital. Queues are also a common concern in commercial and industrial situations. For example, ships in a harbour have to wait for unloading cranes to become available. Every hour of waiting costs thousands of pounds in ship operating costs. On the other hand, additional cranes cost a great deal. Port authorities do not want to have them idle. How many cranes should the port authorities operate so as to keep the waiting costs of arriving ships reasonably low, while at the same time keeping the cranes busy much of the time?

The first queueing models were developed by the Danish engineer A.K. Erlang in 1917. They dealt with telephone exchanges. Computer/communications networks such as telephone networks, LAN's and the Internet, remain one of the most common areas of application of queueing models. The very first example in Chapter 1 — the services call centre — is an application of this kind. We want to know how many operators we need if we want, say, 99% of all incoming calls answered within ten seconds. A growth area for queueing theory recently has been in the modelling of the provision of health care, as countries everywhere struggle to cope with increasing demand, more expensive procedures, and the needs of ageing populations. The most famous telephone formula, the Erlang-B formula, originally derived to estimate the number of lines required in a telephone exchange, is now used in hospital staffing programs to estimate the daily number of resourced beds that must be provided, given the uncertain demand. Production management, new product development, road traffic engineering, and the emerging discipline of services engineering all make use of queueing models.

Basic structure

Figure 16-1 depicts the general structure of waiting line situations, while Table 16-1 lists a few typical examples. The three major components of a system involving queueing-type behaviour are:

- one or several sources of customers or **arrivals**;
- one or several **queues**, each with its corresponding **queue discipline**;
- one or several **service facilities**.

Arrivals of different types may all request service from the same service facility. For example, some arrivals at an accident and emergency clinic may suffer from a life-threatening condition that requires immediate attention, while others have had some minor accident, the treatment of which can be delayed within reason. Each group can be viewed as a separate source of arrivals. Similarly, aircraft requesting permission to land may be large commercial airliners or small private planes. In each case, one source may get priority of service over the other source. Furthermore, each source of arrivals may have different characteristics in terms of the kind of service requested or the length of time needed to complete it.

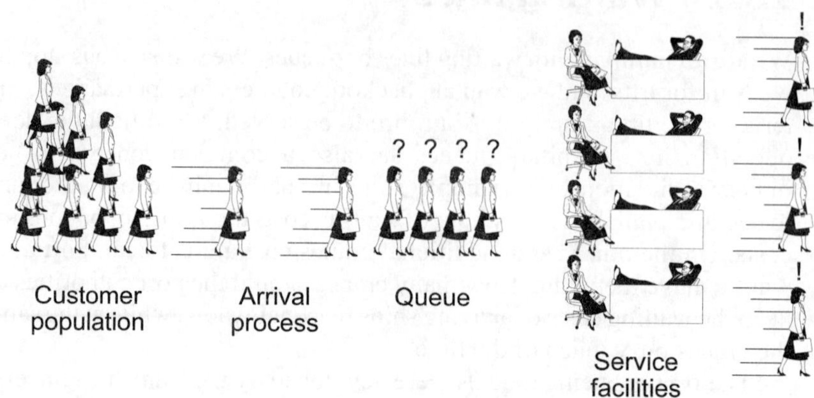

Figure 16-1 General structure of waiting lines

The priority with which the server attends to the entities waiting is called the 'queue discipline'. In most queues, arrivals are attended to by the server on a first-come/first-served sequence. There are, however, instances where the service priority follows a different rule. For example, some blood banks issue blood for transfusions on a last-in/first-out basis. The reason for this is that the oxygen-carrying capacity of the blood deteriorates with age. Hence using the freshest available blood is most effective from a medical point of view. In other instances, some arrivals meeting specified criteria are given priority over other arrivals. For example, customers may choose one or several charging rates for the service — the higher the charging rate, the higher the service priority. Or jobs arriving are classified by length of service required — the shorter the job, the higher the priority. This has the effect of minimizing the queue length.

There may be one queue, several queues, or no queue at all. For example, most banks and post offices nowadays have all customers join a single queue. The person at the front of the queue is first in line for the first teller to become free. On the other hand, in supermarkets each checkout counter has its own queue, while the usual single-line telephone connection without a call-waiting option has no queueing facilities. If the line is already in use, any other caller gets a busy signal. Their call is not accepted as an arrival. Each caller has to redial to try for a successful connection.

The length of a queue may be limited. For example, a psychotherapist may limit the number of clients waiting for a weekly time slot to become available to three at the most. Any potential clients arriving when the waiting list is full are referred to other therapists. Finally, potential arrivals may balk and depart immediately if they observe that the queue is too long. Some customers already in the queue may also become impatient and depart without service ('renege') if they expect that the additional waiting time will be too long. Arrivals finding the queue full, or balking and reneging customers are lost to the system. This may result in potential profits foregone.

As the examples in Table 16-1 indicate, the entities in the queues do not have to be at the same physical location, but may be awaiting service in separate locations, such as photocopiers owned or rented by different firms or organizations requiring repairs or service.

Table 16-1 Examples of waiting line situations

Source of arrivals	Nature of service	Service facility
customers in stores	sales transactions	store attendant
telephone calls	enquiry	call centre
jobs on the Internet	switching	switch
aircraft	landing and take-off	runway
ships in harbour	berthing	dock
ships berthed at dock	loading and unloading	cranes or/and gangs
cars	sea crossing	ferry
machines	repairs, change-over, etc.	technician/operator
mechanics on shop floor	tools or parts	attendants at counter
computing jobs	processing on machine	computer
computing jobs	hard disk file handling	file server
emergency/accident victims	medical attention	nurses/surgeons
welfare applicants	processing of application	case worker
stock withdrawals	stock replenishment	supply facility

Service facilities may be arranged **in parallel**. The checkout counters at a supermarket or tellers in a bank operate in parallel. Each service facility performs exactly the same type of service. Customers in the queue require service from only one such facility and may be serviced by any one of them. In contrast, an arrival may require service from several facilities in sequence. For example, a job in a machine shop may have to be cut on a lathe, then drilled on a drill, and finally finished on a polishing machine. There may be a queue in front of each of these machines.

This brief survey shows that the variety of possible waiting line configurations seems almost unlimited. In this chapter, we shall study only rather simple situations.

Activity

Show how each of the following situations can be viewed as a waiting line problem. Identify the source of arrivals and the nature of the service, and determine whether the server(s) act in parallel or in sequence:

- a fire station with a single crew to respond to fire calls;
- lifeguards on a public beach;
- a hotel reception operation where guests check in at a desk, are shown to their rooms by a uniformed clerk, and brought their luggage by a porter.

16.2 What causes queues to form?

On the edge of the desert, east of Perth, Australia, is a small store with a single fuel pump. It displays a tall sign warning motorists that this is the last petrol station for the next 300 kilometres. As a result, no car ever drives past without filling up. On average, about four cars stop at the service station every hour. Jake, the owner of the store, having seen many cars stop at his station, is never rushed, regardless of how many cars are waiting for fuel. If Jake takes a liking to a customer, he easily forgets himself and chats away for minutes on end. On average, he takes about 10 minutes to serve each car. Let's study what happens to this simple system under various assumptions about the rate at which customers are served.

Constant arrival and service times

Assume that cars arrive evenly spaced over time, i.e., the **interarrival time**, *a*, is constant. With four arrivals per hour, the interarrival time is exactly 15 minutes. We start observing the service station at 8 am. No cars are there, so the pump is idle. The first car arrives at 8:04. For some reason, Jake decides that today he will spend exactly the same length of time, $s = 10$ minutes, serving each car. So, he starts serving the first car immediately upon its arrival and finishes 10 minutes later at 8:14. The car departs. Jake goes back to his cup of coffee, kept warm on the stove. The next car arrives at 8:19, exactly 15 minutes after the first car. It gets immediate service, and leaves at 8:29. The third car arrives at 8:34, and Jake completes serving it at 8:44. This regular pattern continues all day long. No car ever has to wait. There is never a queue.

Because there is exactly one interarrival time and one service time for each customer, the service facility is busy a fraction of time equal to the ratio of the service time to the arrival time, or $s/a = 10/15 = 2/3$, and it is idle a fraction of time equal to (1 – [fraction busy]) or $1 - 2/3 = 1/3$.

Next day, Jake decides to tell each customer in dramatic detail the story about how this snake had climbed up his pump, and he mistook its tail for the nozzle of the hose. Hence, customers have to suffer an agonizing 24-minute wait before Jake finally sends them on their way. We again start observing the station at 8:00 with the first car arriving at an idle pump at 8:04. Jake completes the service at 8:28. In the meantime, the second car has arrived at the station at 8:19. It has to wait till 8:28 for the service to the first car to be completed before it gets its turn. The service is completed at 8:52. By then, the third and fourth cars have arrived at 8:34 and 8:49, respectively. Service for the third car begins at 8:52 and ends at 9:16, well after the fifth car has joined the queue of waiting cars . In fact, the number of cars in the queue will slowly but surely increase throughout the day as long as Jake keeps on telling his snake story. No more coffee breaks for Jake!

We conclude that, if the service time is longer than the interarrival time, or, equivalently, if the number of cars served per hour — the service rate — is lower than the number of cars arriving per hour — the arrival rate — the queue length will become progressively longer.

Random arrival and service times

What happens when either or both the interarrival times and the service times fluctuate randomly? We mimicked this for an eight-hour period for the case where the average rate of service is greater than the average rate of arrivals or, equivalently, where the average service time is smaller than the average interarrival time. Figure 16-2 shows how the queue length behaves for three values of the average service time, *s*, but the same average interarrival time of $a = 15$ minutes. We also assume that the interarrival and service times are both negative exponentially distributed.

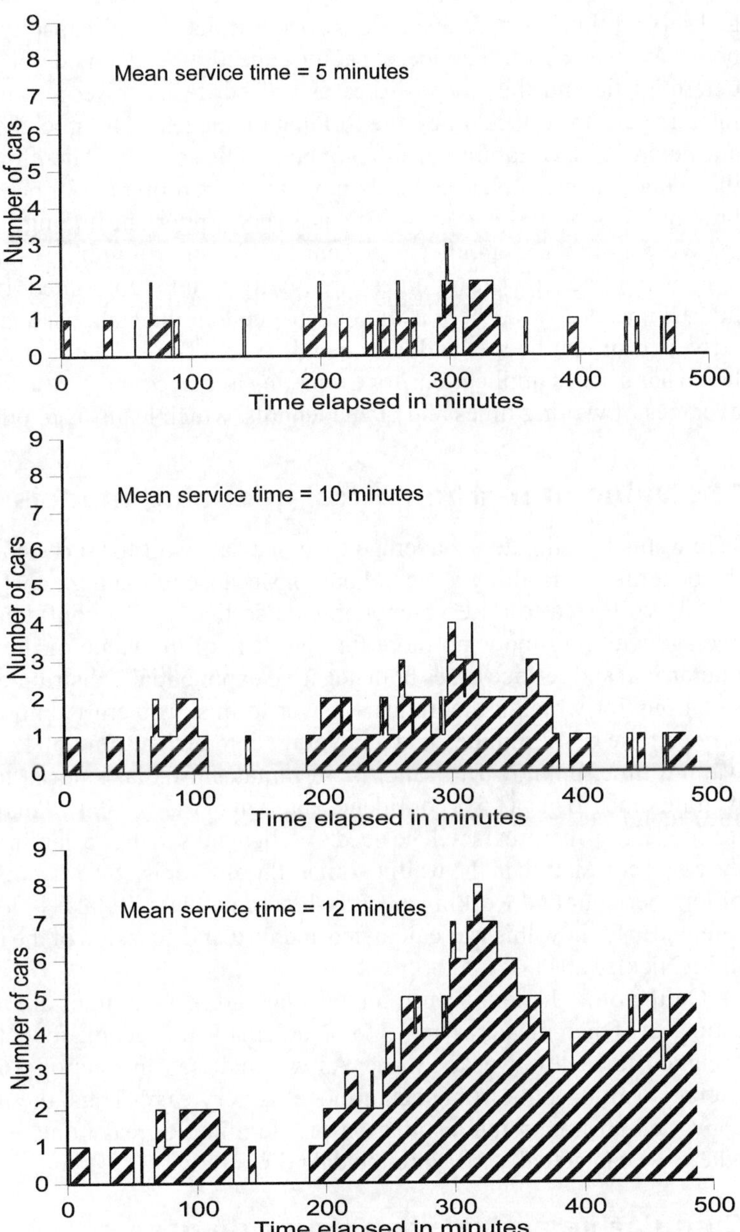

Figure 16-2 Queue behaviour for three different average service times and the same mean arrival rate of four cars per hour

Observe that for $s = 5$ minutes, queues occur rarely and are usually of no more than one or two cars. However, as s increases, and in particular gets closer to a, the frequency of queues increases and the length of the queues also tends to increase.

This happens even though, on average, the service capacity is sufficient to satisfy the service demand. Compare this with the deterministic case with constant interarrival and service times, where queues only occur if the service capacity is insufficient, but never as long as the service capacity exceeds the demand for service. Since the deterministic and the stochastic cases only differ with respect to the variability in interarrival and service times, the forming of queues in the stochastic case can only be attributed to the variability in either or both of these times. Therefore, we can conclude that, under uncertainty, systems exhibit emergent properties or behaviours that are not present in a world of certainty. This is a very important finding.

We can also see another emergent behaviour in Figure 16-2: successive queue lengths (and hence waiting times) are highly serially correlated. If you arrive to find 20 cars ahead of you, there is a good chance that the cars just ahead and behind you arrived to similar queues and, hence, will experience similar delays. This serial correlation has serious implications for estimating averages and confidence intervals for the averages of waiting times and queue lengths, which leads us to our next observation.

The value of mathematical queueing models

Jake wants to estimate the average time that cars wait for service in order to estimate the benefits of installing a second pump. Because of the high cost of this, he decides that he will need to observe enough cars so that a 95% confidence interval for the average waiting time is no more than +/− 5% of the value of the average. With the interarrival and service times both negative exponentially distributed, this is one of the situations for which a theoretical answer to this problem is known. For an average service time of 12 minutes and an average interarrival time of 15 minutes, the mean waiting time, unknown to Jake, is 48 minutes. So, Jake needs to measure enough waiting times to get a 95% confidence interval of (45.6, 50.4). This does not sound too difficult. How many cars will he need? Well, thanks to the variability and, in particular, the serial correlation in the waiting times, the answer is 189,776 cars! At an arrival rate of four per hour and working an eight-hour day, that will take 16 years! You can find references for how this was calculated and further discussion of the implications of this in McNickle (2011).

On the other hand, because interarrival and service times are independent, using estimates of their means as inputs to a mathematical queueing model will give the same accuracy for a few weeks' work. As we shall see in Section 16.3, estimating the average waiting time from such a model is very easy. Thus, the use of a model has converted an impossible estimation problem into an easy one, even for a situation where we can actually measure the data directly!

Cumulative arrival–departure diagrams

While Figure 16-2 shows us what the queue length is at any time, it is not easy to read off how long a particular customer had to wait. A cumulative arrival and departure diagram helps with this. For each customer, we plot the arrival time, the service starting and departure times, using customer number as the vertical axis. Obviously, if a customer arrives when the server is idle, the arrival and service starting times are identical. Table 16-2 lists these times for the first six cars used in the third plot in Figure 16-2.

Table 16-2 Times for the first seven cars

Car number	Arrival time	Service starts	Time of leaving
1	1.94	1.94	16.71
2	32.41	32.41	50.73
3	56.47	56.47	57.54
4	66.58	66.58	75.06
5	68.28	75.06	117.15
6	86.53	117.15	127.77
7	139.72	139.72	145.14

The cumulative arrival–departure diagram is plotted in Figure 16-3. From it we can see that cars 5 and 6 wait 6.78 and 30.62 minutes, respectively (the horizontal lengths of the shaded areas.) If we consider these shaded areas vertically, the diagram also tells us that there was one car waiting in the queue from 68.28 to 75.06 minutes, and one from 86.53 to 117.15 minutes.

Two other useful facts that can be read from arrival–departure diagrams are that the slope of the arrival graph gives the arrival rate, and that during those times when the server is busy the service rate is given (approximately) by the slope of the departure times (or start of service times) graph.

A virtue of cumulative arrival–departure diagrams is that they can be used in situations where the arrival rate of customers is temporarily greater than the service rate. Consider this situation. A self-service cafeteria has a rush of customers at lunch-time which is causing very long queues. The rush starts at about 11:30 am and continues until 12:30 pm However, even with all the cashiers operating, the queues do not disappear until about 1 pm. Over a number of days, we have recorded the arrival times and then plotted the average cumulative arrival time curve in Figure 16-4. (Since it is an average we, have joined up the values to give the relatively smooth curve in Figure 16-4, rather than a step graph such as that in Figure 16-3.)

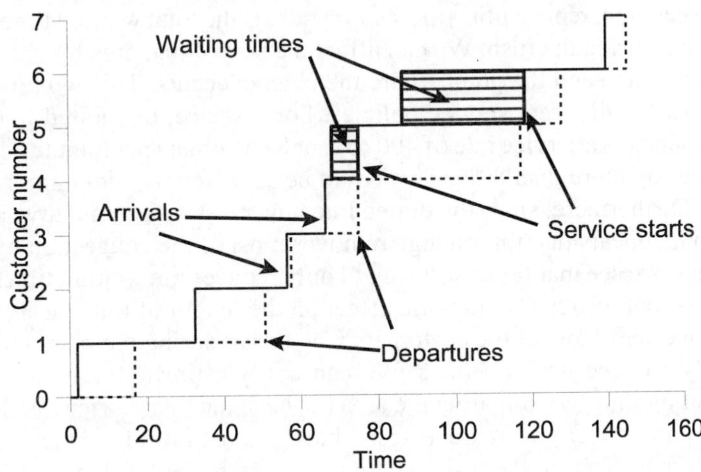

Figure 16-3 A cumulative arrival–departure diagram

We have also found that with the usual number of cashiers working during the rush, they can serve 500 customers in 90 minutes. The middle portion of the dashed line gives the slope corresponding to this service rate. Given that the service times are very short, it is a good approximation to the service start times (as well as customer departure times), from the time when the system usually becomes very busy until it meets the cumulative arrival curve again. When the system is not congested and waiting times are short, the dashed line follows the customer arrival curve closely.

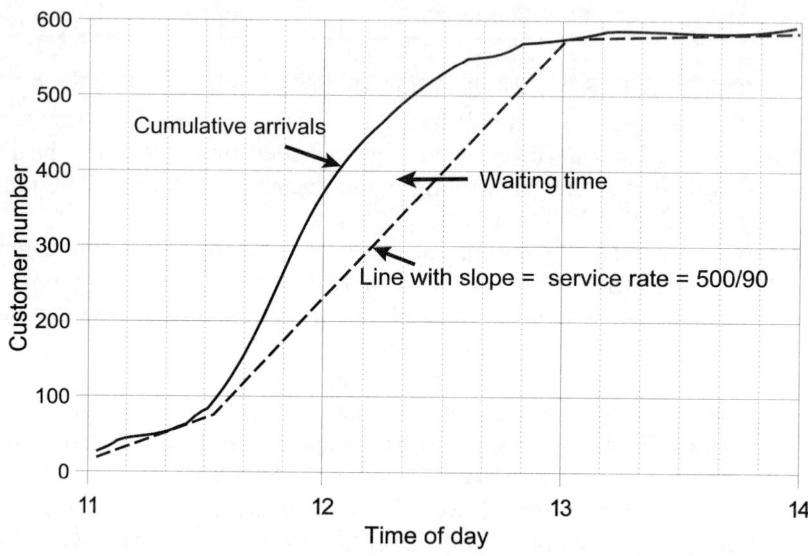

Figure 16-4 The cafeteria average cumulative arrival–departure diagram

The area between the customer arrival curve — the continuous line — and the dashed line, representing the service rate, is the total waiting time of all customers who arrive during the rush. We can affect the size of that area by changing the slope of the dashed line and the point where the change occurs. This will allow us to estimate the effects of different service policies. For instance, the dotted line in Figure 16-5 corresponds to a service rate of 400/50, or 8 customers per minute. It reduces total waiting times by more than 80%. This could be achieved by adding more cashiers at 11:30.

Furthermore, since the dotted line now meets the cumulative arrival curve at 12:20 pm it appears that this change removes most of the congestion by about that time too. Thus, we see that faster service not only reduces the waiting times of individual customers, but also has a dramatic effect on the length of time during which the system is congested. Most of the customers who arrive during the rush will now have considerably reduced waiting times. We can easily estimate the reduction in total customer waiting time by estimating the area between the two service rate lines. Another insight we can gain from Figure 16-5 is that we must introduce the faster service rate at or before the start of the rush to gain maximum benefit. Slide the 'Service rate = 400/50' line horizontally to the right to see the effect of delaying the start of faster service.

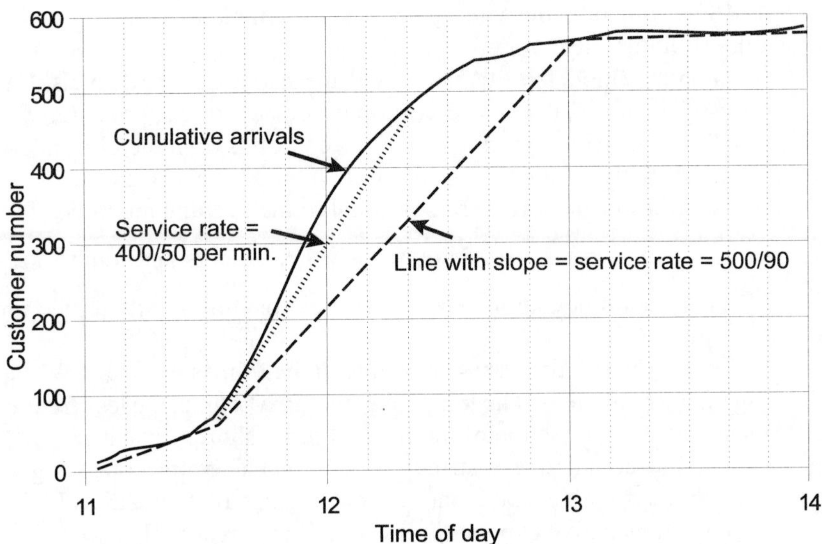

Figure 16-5 The effect of a faster service rate

Activity

For the situations listed below, would you expect the queues to be long most of the time, or short, or to vary highly in length depending on the time of day. Why?

- A lifeguard service at a beach (refer to activity on p. 455).
- A hotel reception operation (refer to activity on p. 455).
- A single-screen cinema ticketing desk.
- A multi-screen cinema ticketing desk.

16.3 Formulas for basic queueing models

Mathematical queueing models

Mathematical models of waiting line systems are the subject of **queueing theory**. *Queueing* is supposed to be one of the words in the English language with the most vowels in a row! Aside from this interesting fact, one of the nice aspects of queueing models is that some of them turn out to have surprisingly simple formulas for such system characteristics as the mean number of customers in the queue, denoted by L_q, and the mean time that a customer spends in the system, W. If we can determine that one of these theoretical models fits the situation studied reasonably well, then we can use these formulas for studying the performance of the system. As we saw in Section 16.2, this may well be faster and less costly than estimating performance measures by directly observing the operation of the system!

Since we are most interested in the implications of these formulas, we will not give proofs of them. Proofs can be found in, for example, Gross (2008) for M/G/1 (p. 220),

M/M/C (p. 66), or in the waiting line chapters of most of the general MS/OR texts listed in the Bibliography.

The simple models we consider will all assume that the arrivals come from a Poisson process. Therefore, the interarrival times are negative exponentially distributed with a cumulative distribution function $1 - e^{-\lambda t}$. It is completely specified by a single parameter, the arrival rate per unit time, λ. As we have seen for Jake's service station, the reciprocal of the arrival rate is equal to the average interarrival time, i.e.,

$$15 \text{ minutes} = 0.25 \text{ hours} = 1/(4 \text{ customers per hour}), \text{ or } a = 1/\lambda$$

The standard deviation of a negative exponentially distributed random variable is also equal to *a*.

For this distribution, very short interarrival times occur more frequently than very long interarrival times. The longer the interarrival time, the less frequently it will occur. When we plot the fraction of interarrival times shorter than a certain time against time (the sample cumulative distribution), we get a graph consisting of a sequence of irregular steps with a slope that becomes less and less positive. This can be used as a check that a negative exponential assumption is reasonable.

Figure 16-6 plots these steps for a (small) sample of 40 interarrival times. Note how there are many more short intervals in the sample than long ones, and hence the typical concave shape to the distribution function. The dashed line corresponds to the distribution function for a negative exponential random variable with a mean of 15 minutes. It appears from the obvious similarity between the two graphs that a negative exponential assumption for the interarrival times at Jake's service station is reasonable.

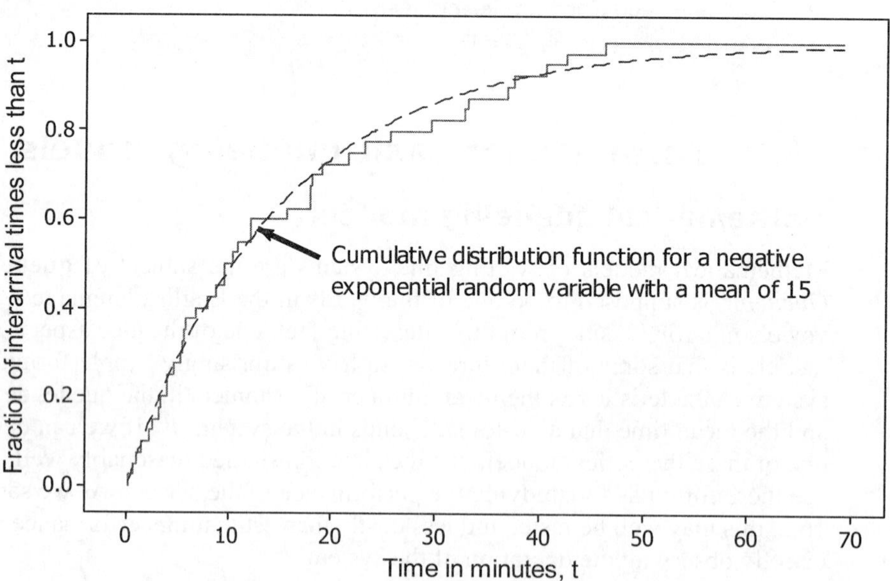

Figure 16-6 Cumulative sample and negative exponential distributions

Checking that the assumptions of the mathematical model — in our case, the form of the interarrival time distribution, the queue discipline, and the service-time distribution — are reasonable approximations to the characteristics of the actual queue are important steps in validating the mathematical model. In fact, because of the highly variable and correlated behaviour patterns we noted above, this may be the only practical way in which we can validate the model against the actual system. Figure 15-3 in Chapter 15 shows how Minitab, and some other statistical packages, can check distributions from observations on the actual queue, using an estimate of the mean interarrival time calculated from the same sample. If you have not already done so, you should carry out the activity in Section 15.8, on fitting a Poisson process to road traffic.

It turns out that for a surprisingly large number of waiting line situations, a Poisson process is a very good approximation for the arrivals. This is particularly the case if arrivals are generated independently of each other, such as individual customers or clients requesting a service, or individual machines breaking down.

The most basic queueing models assume that the service times also follow a negative exponential distribution with rate μ, (or a mean service time of $s = 1/\mu$). Although this may be an adequate first approximation for some cases, service times are usually less variable, as in the car park service times analysed in Section 15.8. Fortunately, the formulas for several important system characteristics of a basic class of models remain valid even if we allow the service time distribution to be of a more general form.

Formulas for the M/G/1 queue

A very useful class of queueing models is described by the shorthand notation of M/G/1, where 'M', short for '**Markovian**', refers to the fact that interarrival times come from a negative exponential distribution with rate λ, the service times come from any positive probability distribution with mean s and variance σ_s^2 (i.e., a **G(eneral)** service time distribution whose exact form does not need to be specified), and the '1' indicates that there is a single server.

The formulas listed below assume that the system has been running for a long time. This means that the system is in **steady state**, i.e., the state of the system no longer depends on the **initial state** of the system, such as how many customers were present at the start. (Check the precise meaning of steady state in Chapter 3, page 47.) The system's characteristics calculated from these formulas are then valid representations of the long-run behaviour. Note that we are not saying that the waiting time and queue lengths are no longer changing over time, simply that their distributions have stopped changing.

The mean number of customers in the queue will be given by:

$$L_q = \frac{\lambda^2\sigma_s^2 + (\lambda s)^2}{2(1 - \lambda s)} \tag{16-1}$$

where λs, which must be less than 1, is called the **traffic intensity**.

Just as in the case of Jake's store, the traffic intensity can be interpreted as the fraction of time that the server is busy. For this class of model, it is also the probability that an arriving customer will have to wait.

As was true for the deterministic case in Section 16.2, the traffic intensity has to be smaller than 1, or else the queue will continue to grow indefinitely. Hence we have the condition on Expression (16-1) that λs must be less than 1. Rewriting this condition as $\lambda < 1/s = \mu$, we can see that it is just the condition of requiring that the arrival rate be less than the service rate or, equivalently, that the average service time must be less than the average interarrival time.

Expression (16-1) illustrates rather nicely a couple of points that, in fact, hold for more models than just the M/G/1 class:

1. The mean queue length L_q (and the other operating characteristics, as we shall see) increase hyperbolically (i.e., in the shape of $1/(1-x)$) as the traffic intensity approaches 1. L_q is plotted in Figure 16-7 for an M/M/1 queue, where the service time distribution is also negative exponential.

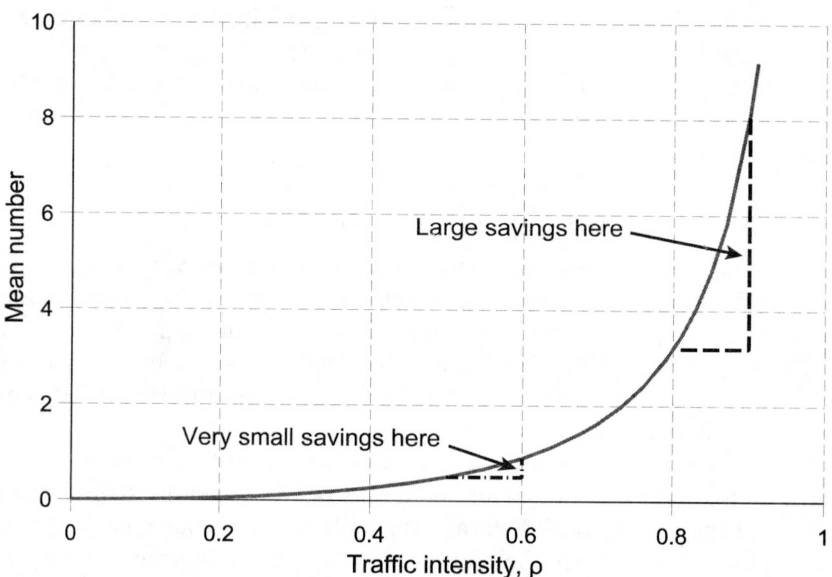

Figure 16-7 L_q for an M/M/1 queue

From Figure 16-7, we note that reducing the traffic intensity (by providing faster service or by reducing the arrival rate) will gain us a great deal if the traffic intensity is high (say, greater than 0.7), but that we make much smaller gains if the traffic intensity is already low. Changes in the traffic intensity that move us down from 0.9, above the 'knee' of the curve — roughly at 0.7 — to 0.8 are much more profitable than similar changes entirely below the knee from 0.6 to 0.5.

2. The average queue length (and hence the average delay, as we will show below) depends not only on how busy the server is, but also on how variable the service process is. Thus, we can decrease the average delay also by reducing the variability

of the service time. Fast food operations, for example, make explicit use of this by limiting the range (and hence variability in preparation time) of the items they sell. The same is also approximately true for arrival processes — the more variable the interarrival times, the longer the average waiting time.

L, the mean number of customers in the system, can be found from:

$$L = L_q + \lambda s \qquad (16\text{-}2)$$

This follows from noting that the mean number of customers in the system must be the sum of the mean number in the queue and the mean number in service, and that the latter is equal to the traffic intensity. The mean time that a customer spends in the queue, W_q, and the mean time that a customer spends in the system, W, are given by what are known as **Little's formulas**. They hold for a large number of queueing models.

Little's formulas

$$L = \lambda W \qquad (16\text{-}3)$$

$$L_q = \lambda W_q \qquad (16\text{-}4)$$

An elementary proof of (16-3) is given in the example below. Little's formulas also hold for observed data. That is, if you measure the mean queue length, the mean waiting time, and the arrival rate over a particular time period, they will be related by 16-3 (and 16-4) provided the observations finish with the queue empty.

Finally, the mean time a customer spends in the system is the sum of the mean time spent waiting in the queue and the mean service time:

$$W = W_q + s \qquad (16\text{-}5)$$

Activity

Referring to Figure 16-7, explain why successive 10% increases in the arrival rate tend to push the average queue length up by progressively larger amounts if the service rate remains the same.

Example 16-1: A one-crane container port

A small container port has only one dock with a single container crane. Hence, only one ship can be unloaded and loaded at any one time. Other container ships arriving while the dock is occupied will have to wait their turn until the dock becomes free. Suppose that a container ship arrives at the port, on average, every five days, i.e., $a = 5$. This implies that the arrival rate is $\lambda = {}^{1}/_{5}$ ships per day. It takes $s = 4$ days to unload and load a ship. The standard deviation of the service time is $s = 2$ days. To use the above formulas, we check first that the traffic intensity is indeed less than 1, i.e., $\lambda s = {}^{1}/_{5} \times 4 = 0.8 < 1$. Since it is, an estimate of the mean number of ships in the queue is given by expression (16-1):

$$L_q = (0.2^2 \times 2^2 + 0.8^2)/(2 \times (1 - 0.8)) = 2.0$$

and $\quad L = L_q + \lambda s = 2 + 0.2 \times 4 = 2.8$

The average time in days that a ship spends waiting in the queue for the dock to become free is obtained by rearranging expression (16-4) as

$W_q = L_q/\lambda = 2.0 / 0.2 = 10$ days,

while expression (16-5) gives the average time a ship is in the system, i.e., waiting or being unloaded and loaded, as $W = W_q + s = 10 + 4 = 14$ days.

Suppose that it costs $8,000 per day to operate a ship while in port. Hence, each ship calling into port incurs a total cost of $8,000 multiplied by the mean time a ship spends in the system, W, or $8,000 × 14 = $112,000. Another measure of interest is the average daily cost of the ships in port. This is given by $8,000 times the mean number of ships in port, L, or $8,000 × 2.8 = $22,400. Both these costs seem to be rather high. The port operator may, therefore, wish to increase the unloading and loading capacity, either by installing a second crane on the dock or by replacing the current crane with another one of a higher capacity. You should verify that, if the mean time to service a ship is reduced from 4 days to 2 days with a standard deviation of 1 day, the new system's characteristics are $L = 0.5667$ and $W = 2.8333$. Both measures are reduced substantially because we have reduced the traffic intensity from 0.8 to 0.4 (point 1 on p. 464), and the standard deviation of the service time from 2 to 1 (point 2 on p. 464). The average cost in port per ship falls to only $8,000 × 2.8333 = $22,667, while the average daily cost of ships in port falls to $8,000 × 0.5667 = $4,533. A doubling of the service rate has resulted in an almost fivefold decrease in these costs.

We can use this example to demonstrate a proof of Little's formulas (expressions (16-3) and (16-4)). Consider (16-3). We have just established above that the average daily cost of ships waiting or being serviced in port is $8,000 × L. On the other hand, your friend works it out this way. Each ship spends an average of W days in port. On any given day, we expect on average λ ships to arrive, each of which is going to spend W days in port. Hence, the additional cost, considering only that day's average number of arrivals, is $8,000 × W × λ. But this must also be the daily cost of all ships in port. Well, both arguments are right. Equating the answers, they produce expression (16-3). Note that this proof does not rely on properties of negative exponential distributions, or the number of servers, or even the way in which the service facility works. Little's formulas thus hold for very general queueing situations.

Multiple server queues

What about a system where the customers form a single queue and go to the first available server out of a number, C, of servers? Such systems are often used at banks, post offices, and other service counters. We now only get simple formulas if we assume that the service time distribution is also negative exponential with rate parameter μ, i.e., an M/M/C queue. Then, provided $\lambda/C\mu < 1$, the probability that there are no customers present in the system is:

$$P_0 = \frac{1}{\left[\sum_{n=0}^{C-1} \frac{(\lambda/\mu)^n}{n!} + \frac{(\lambda/\mu)^C}{C!(1-\lambda/C\mu)}\right]} \tag{16-6}$$

and

$$L_q = \frac{(\lambda/\mu)^{C+1}}{C\ C!(1-(\lambda/C\mu))^2} P_0 \tag{16-7}$$

The condition $\lambda/C\mu < 1$ ensures that the maximum service rate, when all the servers are busy, is greater than the arrival rate, as otherwise the queue will grow without limit. The characteristics for the number of customers in the system, L, the time in the system, W, and the waiting time, W_q, can again be found from (16-7) by using $L = L_q + \lambda/\mu$,

$L_q = \lambda W_q$, and $W = W_q + 1/\mu$. Note that the formulas here also hold for C = 1, although as Exercise 9 asks you to show, they are much simpler.

The formulas for the operating characteristics in this section are easily evaluated with a spreadsheet. In the website for this book there is a simple Excel spreadsheet named Queueing_formulas_for_Chapter_16.xlsx, which covers M/G/1 (16-1), M/M/C (16-6, 16-7) M/M/C/N (finite capacity with only a total of N customers ever allowed in the system), and the Erlang-B formula (M/M/C/C). Gross et al. (2008) give a much more extensive set of Excel queueing programs on the website for their book.

Example 16-2: Queueing for toilets

In 1995, New Zealand Works Consultancy was contracted to revise the Building Standards for the number of toilets that needed to be provided in public buildings. Data was collected from 13 types of building, including office buildings, schools, theatres, swimming pools and shopping plazas. Most of the data was collected electronically, with the times of arrival measured by the time a person cut a pair of infra-red beams.

Occupancy times were measured either by magnetic switches on cubicle doors or infra-red beams. One can be seen to the right of the urinal in the picture. The data was fed into a recorder in the box on the floor. Suppose that the criterion to be used is that 'the average waiting time in the queue is to be no more that one minute'. In a building where the arrival rate is 60 customers per hour, and for a toilet type where the mean occupancy time is two minutes, how many toilets will we need? The assumption that the times between arrivals come from a negative exponential distribution is quite reasonable for the reasons discussed in Section 16.3. This was checked by drawing graphs of the interarrival times such as Figure 16-6. We will also assume that the occupancy time distribution is negative exponential.

We start out by expressing all of our input information in the same time units. Using hours, we have $\lambda = 60$, $\mu = 30$. Next, we check for the minimum starting value for C to ensure that we have a feasible solution, i.e., that $\lambda/C\mu < 1$. Trying $C = 2$, we find that $\lambda/2\mu = 60/(2 \times 30) = 1$. Hence, it is clear that at least three toilets will be needed. Is this sufficient, or do we need more toilets to meet the criterion that $W_q \leq 1/60$ hours?

For $C = 3$, we find

$$P_0 = \frac{1}{\left[\sum_{n=0}^{2} \frac{(60/30)^n}{n!} + \frac{(60/30)^3}{3!(1-60/(3(30)))}\right]} = 0.11111$$

$$L_q = \frac{(60/30)^4}{3(3!)(1-60/(3(30)))^2}(0.11111) = 0.88889$$

Now $W_q = L_q/\lambda = 0.014815$ hours or 53.3 seconds, so the criterion is just met. Three toilets will be enough to meet the Building Standards.

The benefits of pooling

We can also use the multiple server formulas to quantify the effects of alternative system configurations without actually observing the system. The alternative in which we are interested is **pooling**, i.e., combining separate servers into a central facility, as depicted in Figure 16-8.

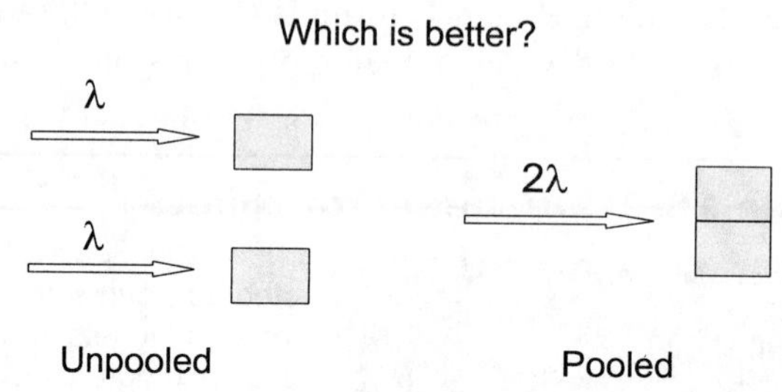

Figure 16-8 Two alternative configurations

Is it better to have arrivals join one of two separate queues, each feeding its own server, or have arrivals join a single queue that feeds both servers? In the 1980s, banks and post offices moved to the single-queue system. The reason for this is that it avoids the situation where any tellers are idle while other tellers have customers waiting. It appears likely that there would be some benefit in this change, but how large will it be? In Table 16-3, expressions (16-7) and (16-4) have been used for comparing the waiting times for the two systems.

We see that, for these models, pooling similar service facilities can reduce waiting times by a factor of about four for low traffic intensities and by a factor of at least two when the servers are busier. In fact, pooling together N service facilities can be shown to reduce average waiting times by at least a factor of N.

Provided other concerns, such as travel times or the quality of customer service, are taken into account, pooling similar service facilities will always reduce waiting times, often by a considerable amount. (The comparisons in Table 16-3 are valid for any equivalent ratio of λ/μ, even if the service rate $\mu \neq 1$.)

Table 16-3 W_q for equivalent unpooled and pooled systems

W_q (service rate = 1)		
λ	Unpooled	Pooled
0.3	0.428	0.099
0.5	1	0.333
0.8	4	1.780
0.9	9	4.260

This effect can be partially described in terms of feedback loops, such as those described in Section 3.11. In the pooled system, as we move from only one customer in the system to two or more customers present, the service rate will definitely increase when the second server is called into action. Hence, the waiting times are partially controlled by a self-regulating negative feedback loop. In the unpooled system, the effect will only occur if the customers arrive at the appropriate server, hence there may be no feedback.

Activity

- In queueing for toilets, cubicle occupancy times were actually much less variable than a negative exponential distribution would imply (curiously, urinal occupancy times were remarkably close to negative exponential.) How would this show up in a graph such as Figure 16-6? Would this necessarily invalidate results obtained using a negative exponential assumption? (Recall that we want to guarantee that 'the average waiting time in the queue is to be no more that one minute'.)
- We just saw that pooling is better than servers with individual queues. Why is it not necessary to have all servers located at the same place in order to take advantage of the benefits of pooling? If the server has to travel to the physical location of the user, what other considerations may become important in allocating 'idle' servers to users? What may this imply in terms of the home base for servers? (Think of desirable properties for locating fire stations.)
- Retrieve Queueing_formulas_for_Chapter_16.xlsx and use it to verify the results in the toilets study (Example 16-2, p. 467) and in Table 16-3.

16.4 NZ Forest Products weighbridge problem

This case history comes from one of the authors' involvement with a New Zealand company. However, any wood processing plant in any part of the world receiving truck loads of tree logs from forests may face a similar situation.

Description of the system

During the 1980s, some 2,500,000 m^3 of cut logs per year were transported from the forest to a pulp mill operated by New Zealand Forest Products (NZFP). The cartage was done by trucks owned by private contractors. Every truck had to enter the NZFP complex over a single-lane weighbridge, as shown here. The weight of wood carried formed the basis of the payments to the contractors. The weighing records were also used for monitoring the volume of fellings in the forest.

When the complex was busy, more than 400 truckloads passed over the bridge per day. A truck had to come to a complete halt on the weighbridge while it was weighed and documents were checked. If a truck arrived to find the weighbridge empty, it drove straight on to it. If the weighbridge was already occupied, the next truck in line stopped some distance from it and, for safety reasons, was only allowed to proceed on to the weighbridge when the preceding truck was completely clear. Therefore, a truck forced to wait lost additional time by having to drive on to the weighbridge as a separate movement. The resulting move-up time had the effect of slowing down the rate of progress of trucks. As a result, waiting times in 1989 sometimes exceeded 20 minutes per truck, especially, it seemed, if they attempted to bring in more than about 420 loads per day. This worried management: had the weighbridge reached its saturation point?

Various options were considered to deal with this problem. One was to build a second weighbridge in parallel with the existing bridge. Trucks would form a single queue and move to the first available weighbridge. It is important to note that the weighbridge forms a relatively small component in a very expensive complex, which has to be kept supplied with logs at all costs.

Data collection and system parameter estimation

To analyse this situation we needed data on the movement of trucks. For two days, we observed the weighbridge, starting at 5.30 am until the last load was allowed across at 5 pm. The arrival time, the time of entering the weighbridge, and the time of leaving it were recorded for each load in an hour–minute–second format. Table 16-4 reproduces a small sample of the data collected.

Table 16-4 A sample of weighbridge observations

Load number	Arrival time	Time of entry	Time of leaving
...	...	...	...
100	8 22 53	8 22 53	8 24 52
101	8 23 42	8 25 18	8 27 22
102	8 24 45	8 27 56	8 28 36
103	8 26 13	8 28 53	8 29 45
104	8 29 11	8 29 59	8 31 44
105	8 31 09	8 32 08	8 34 34
106	8 36 16	8 36 16	8 37 23
...	...	...	...

For load 100, the truck was able to drive straight on to the bridge. This follows from the ‘arrival time’ being equal to the ‘time of entry’. Its weighing time was 1 minute 59 seconds — the difference between ‘time of leaving’ and ‘time of entry’. Load 101 arrived 49 seconds after load 100, while that load was still being weighed. Hence, it had to wait for 1 minute 10 seconds for the weighbridge to become available — the difference between ‘time of leaving’ for load 100 and the ‘arrival time’ for load 101. It then took the truck 26 seconds to move on to the weighbridge — ‘time of entry’ for load 101 less the ‘time of leaving’ for load 100. Its weighing time was 2 minutes 4 seconds.

Table 16-5 Weighbridge parameters

Variable	Mean (minutes)	Standard deviation
Interarrival time	1.6782	1.7459
Move-up time	0.3323	0.2735
Weighing time	1.2070	0.7309

Working in this way, we can compile a list of interarrival times, move-up times, and weighing times. The averages and variances of these, as shown in Table 16-5, are estimates of the parameters for the corresponding probability distributions.

Generalizing the M/G/1 formulas to the weighbridge problem

Note that the mean and standard deviation of the truck interarrival times are in the same ball park. If truck arrivals are independent of each other, then a standard deviation equal to or very close to the mean is a good indication that the interarrival times are negative exponential — in this case with rate $\lambda = 1/1.6782 = 0.5959$. Statistical tests based on graphs such as those in Figure 15-4 confirmed that a negative exponential distribution gives an acceptable approximation. This discovery certainly increases our confidence in the use of an M/G/1 queueing model for the current operation of a single weighbridge. However, there are a couple of places where the system deviates seriously from the assumptions of the M/G/1 model.

1. The weighbridge starts from empty each morning. Hence, the first few trucks tend to experience very small delays. On the other hand, the W_q obtained from the M/G/1 model assumes the system is in steady state. The true average waiting time per truck over the day will therefore be slightly lower than the theoretical W_q based on the steady state.
2. Trucks arriving when the weighbridge is occupied take some time to move on to it. In some sense, the move-up time can be viewed as part of the service time. However, incurring this additional time depends on whether the bridge is 'free' or not. 'Not free' means that a truck occupies the weighbridge, or that a truck is moving up. Therefore, we cannot assume that the service times are all drawn from the same probability distribution, independent of the state of the queue, which is an essential assumption of the M/G/1 model.

We can analyse the effect that this will cause by considering the weighbridge as a feedback loop (see Section 3.11). Figure 16-9 shows the feedback loop associated with the weighbridge.

The longer the queue at the weighbridge, the higher the probability that a truck will have to come to a complete halt and then move on to the weighbridge (arc 1 in Figure 16-9). The higher this probability, the longer the total time that a truck occupies the weighbridge (arc 2), and the longer the total time that a truck occupies the weighbridge, the bigger the queue at the weighbridge will be (arc 3). Thus, a positive change in any of these elements causes a positive effect on the next element in the loop, as indicated by the 'plus' signs on each arc of the loop. Since all of the effects are of the same sign, the entire loop is clearly a positive feedback loop. As a queue starts to build up, the process generating the waiting times moves into a more unstable state, producing longer waiting times, which is only terminated when the weighbridge becomes idle.

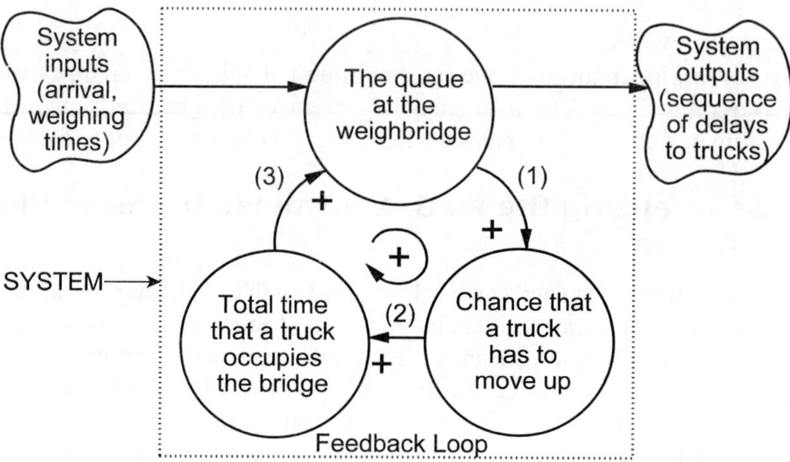

Figure 16-9 The weighbridge described as a feedback loop

Can we relate the actual characteristics of the weighbridge to those of the M/G/1 model? Recall that traffic intensity is the fraction of customers who wait:

$$\text{fraction of customers who wait} = \text{traffic intensity} = \lambda s$$

In the weighbridge case, the average service time s could be viewed as the average service delay a truck incurs for stopping at the weighbridge. This consists of the average weighing time plus the average move-up time for the fraction of trucks that have to wait. We use the interpretation of the traffic intensity as the probability that a customer will have to wait, giving:

$$s = \text{average weighing time} + \text{traffic intensity} \times \text{average move-up time} \quad (16\text{-}8)$$

Putting these two expressions together and inserting the known values for $\lambda = 1/1.6782 = 0.5959$, the average weighing time $= 1.2070$, and the average move-up time $= 0.3323$, we get:

$$\text{Traffic intensity} = 0.5959 \times 1.2070 + \text{traffic intensity} \times 0.3323$$

Rearranging this equation and solving it for the traffic intensity gives a value of 0.8968. As we have just seen, this is also the proportion of trucks that has to wait and incur a move-up time.

Now we consider the second way in which the actual weighbridge deviates from the M/G/1 model. Although an average of 89.68% of all trucks incur a move-up time, whether or not any particular truck is affected depends on the status of the weighbridge at the time of the arrival of that truck. As we have seen, this effect can be modelled as a positive feedback loop, which provides part of the explanation of the high waiting times. What if we simply ignored this and randomly assigned move-up times to trucks in this proportion? Then all the service delays of all trucks can be treated as if they were drawn from the same probability distribution, and the M/G/1 model is more appropriate. This modification is equivalent to removing arc 1 of the positive feedback loop, breaking the entire loop. So this suggests that the theoretical M/G/1 formula should underestimate the delay. Note that a systems view has told us this quite valuable piece of information without any further mathematical analysis of the model. We hope that this underestimate and the overestimate produced by the start-up effect will partially cancel each other out.

Using the modified M/G/1 model

Now we work out the values of the parameters for the M/G/1 formulas. Inserting the estimates of Table 16-5 into expression (16-8), we compute the average service time, s, as

$$s = 1.2070 + 0.8968 \times 0.3323 = 1.505$$

For the variance of the service times, we use the property that the variance of a weighted mixture of two random variables is given by

$$p\sigma_1^2 + (1 - p)\sigma_2^2 + p(1 - p)(m_1 - m_2)^2$$

Here, p and $1 - p$ are the weights (in our case the traffic intensity and its complement), and m_1, m_2, σ_1^2, and σ_2^2 are the means and variances of the two random variables. So

$$\sigma_s^2 = 0.897 \times (0.7309^2 + 0.2735^2) + (1 - 0.897) \times 0.7309^2 + 0.897 \times (1 - 0.897) \times 0.3323^2 = 0.61$$

We now have all input parameters needed for evaluating expressions (16-1) and (16-4). We obtain $L_q = 4.94$, and $W_q = 8.27$ minutes. The latter agrees quite well with the actually observed value of $W_q = 8.94$ minutes over the two days when data was collected.

Because we have a theoretical model which fits the observed system quite well, we can use it to show what the effect of varying some of the system parameters would be on the system performance. A spreadsheet calculated values of W_q as a function of the arrival rate of loads. These are plotted in Figure 16-10. Note again how the average waiting time increases hyperbolically as the traffic intensity tends to 1. The situation actually recorded in the two-day survey period corresponds to about 411 loads per day.

It is clear that the weighbridge is dangerously close to its maximum practical capacity. An increase of only 5% in wood requirements and truck loads (the dotted lines in Figure 16-10) will lead to impossibly long waiting times. In particular attempting to haul more than 420 loads, will, on average, lead to delays greater than 10 minutes. So, the effect management had noted was not just bad luck, but could be expected to be the normal state of affairs.

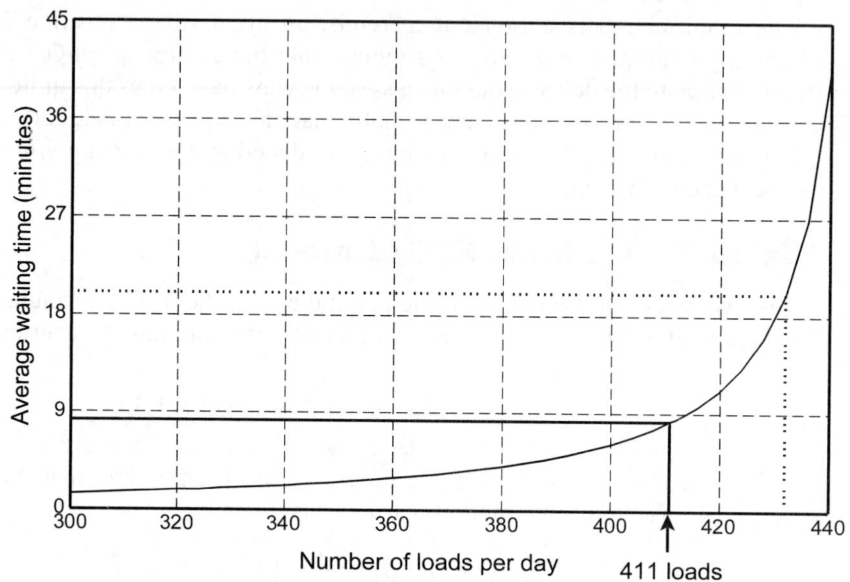

Figure 16-10 The effect of arrival rate on waiting times

16.5 The two-weighbridge option

To analyse the proposed extra weighbridge, we will need a theoretical model of a two-server queue. Unfortunately, the M/G/2 queue is one of the queueing models which does not have simple formulas for its operating characteristics.

Assuming that the service time distribution is also negative exponential implies that the standard deviation of service times is equal to the mean service time. In the weighbridge case, the standard deviation of service times is considerably smaller. From expression (16-1), we see that, for the single-server case, the larger the standard deviation of service times, the larger the mean queue length and mean waiting time. For multiple-server queues, it is also a reasonably safe rule of thumb that the more variable the service process is (i.e., the larger the standard deviation of service times), the greater the average delay. So, using the M/M/2 model will result in overestimating the mean waiting time. The M/M/2 model therefore provides a conservative upper bound on the average delay, and the savings estimated from the M/M/2 model will be smaller than those based on the true variability in service times. Underestimating savings is a much safer decision-making strategy than overestimating them.

What should we do about the move-up time problem? Intuitively, we should expect that now almost no trucks will have to wait. So, our initial approach is to simply ignore the move-up time. If the results confirm that few trucks will wait, then this approximation is suitable. If the fraction of trucks waiting is still significant, then we would have to build a more accurate and more complex model.

Using the same arrival rate of $\lambda = 0.5989$ trucks per minute, a service rate of $\mu = 1/1.2070 = 0.8285$, and $C = 2$ servers, the formulas for the M/M/C model give an estimate for W_q of 0.18 minutes. A good estimate of the minimum reduction in waiting time that will occur if a second weighbridge is built is $8.27 - 0.18 = 8.09$ minutes per load. For 400 loads per day, this amounts to 400×8.09 minutes, or almost 54 hours of truck time per day. This is the equivalent of the workload of about six trucks. Hence, the current workload of hauling logs from the forests to the mill could be accomplished by six fewer trucks.

Remember that the contractors are paid by the amount of wood hauled. Eliminating most of the time wasted waiting at the weighbridge means that each truck can carry more loads per day. Therefore, NZFP has a good case to negotiate a reduction in the haulage cost per load and still guarantee that each contractor's daily net earnings are at least as high as under the old system. At a running cost of \$80 per truck-hour, the reduction in hauling costs for the mill is slightly over \$1 million (54 hours × 250 days × \$80) annually. The additional wage bill for staffing the second weighbridge is less than \$100,000 per year. The cost of building a second weighbridge is around \$400,000. The cost of the second weighbridge can be recovered in the first six months of use. This sounds like a good proposition!

Activity

- Why do we want to underestimate the savings due to the second weighbridge rather than overestimate them? Go through the sequence of models we have used and decide if we have achieved this objective.
- If we assume that the arrival process of trucks at the weighbridge is a Poisson process, estimate the maximum arrival rate of trucks that is possible (i.e., for which steady state exists). Verify your answer from Figure 16-10.
- Use Queueing_formulas_for Chapter_16.xlsx to verify the estimated waiting times produced by the single weighbridge (M/G/1) and two-weighbridge (M/M/2) models.

16.6 Some conclusions

It is interesting to see how the models we have used for this problem stack up against the properties of a good model listed in Section 5.3. Certainly, they are simple, adaptive, and easy to manipulate. The formulas can easily be evaluated with a spreadsheet or even a calculator. Do they include all significant aspects of the problem?

The assumption that the trucks arrive as a Poisson process is critical for the use of simple mathematical models, yet the way the wood transport system operates raises serious questions about the validity of that assumption. In the actual system, the trucks each make about 8 round trips per day. Hence, it appears that a second weighbridge will change the arrival pattern since the round-trip time will be reduced. But note that the weighbridge is a very small part of a very expensive mill complex, which must be fed with the required amount of wood at all costs. Therefore, no matter how the weighbridge operation is altered, the flow of trucks across it will remain dictated by the needs of the mill. Knowing the part that the weighbridge plays in the entire system, we can safely conclude that more extensive modelling of the arrival process would be very unlikely to change the recommendation for installing a second weighbridge.

With such great savings, was the second weighbridge built in 1989? The answer is 'no'. As often happens with projects of this sort, by the time the recommendations are submitted to the decision makers, or shortly thereafter, other events may have changed the economic picture. In this case, it was a worldwide slump in the demand for newsprint. As a result, the level of operations of the mill was curtailed, reducing the number of daily loads required by the mill. As a consequence, the immediate pressure was off. There was to be no further increase in wood demand until the market had recovered. The additional bridge was finally built in 1993.

However, the wood yard manager was immediately able to put Figure 16-10 to good use. First, as we have seen, it showed that hauling 420 or more loads could not be done under the current method of operation. The second use of Figure 16-10 was in presenting a new proposal for a more effective operation of the wood yard. As it shows, if the number of loads entering the yard during the time from 5:30 am to 5 pm could be reduced to 350, the mean waiting time at the weighbridge would decrease to less than 3 minutes. This is one of those profitable changes that brings us down to below the 'knee' of the curve, as described in Section 16-3. One possible alternative would have been to extend the opening hours of the weighbridge by two hours or so to get the remaining 50 to 60 loads processed during this time. However, that would have required the entire workforce of the wood yard to be present, which would have been rather expensive.

A break-down of the types of wood coming in indicated that about 50 loads per day were thinnings. These were processed at a separate part of the yard employing only two people. The obvious solution was to restrict the loads coming in after hours to thinnings alone. Hence, the congestion at the weighbridge could be reduced dramatically at a minimum of additional labour cost. Figure 16-10 was very valuable for judging the merit of this proposal.

Case study 16-1: Do-it-yourself queueing

For most real-life MS/OR applications, obtaining details about the problem situations requires access to confidential information. Fortunately, for queueing theory, examples of queues are all around us. This activity deals with fitting a theoretical queueing model to a real-life queueing situation:

- Observe an actual queue. Collect enough data to fit a theoretical queueing model to your situation.
- Analyse the data following the steps described in the text. Estimate the interarrival time and service time distributions from your data. Fit what you feel to be the most appropriate theoretical model (or models) of those we have studied.

- Measure the mean waiting time and the mean queue length by direct calculation from the data set, and compare them with the theoretical values from your model.

Full details on how to complete this activity are given in McNickle (2011), available online at http://ite.pubs.informs.org/. It also describes how to compare the observed and theoretical waiting time- and state-distributions. This requires fitting an M/Erlang-k/1 model to the system using MATLAB, but will usually give more satisfying results than just comparing means.

16.7 Chapter highlights

- When we deal with stochastic phenomena, each alternative course of action leads to one of a number of possible outcomes. Prior to taking a particular action, all we may know is the probability distribution over the outcomes associated with that action. A decision is thus equivalent to choosing a particular probability distribution or measure of those outcomes.
- For stochastic systems, we are often primarily interested in their long-run behaviour. Hence, the decision criterion used for evaluating a course of action is often the expected value of the performance measure of interest.
- The simplest structure of waiting lines consists of customers arriving at a service facility, waiting in a queue until it is their turn for service, and then being served on a first-come/first-served basis. Queues form because both the interarrival and the service times are random variables.
- Simple queueing models assume that interarrival times have a negative exponential distribution and that service times are either also exponential (one or more servers) or can be characterized by their expected value and their standard deviation (one server only). This leads to simple formulas for the average queue length, average waiting time, and average time in the system.
- The variability and serial correlation of waiting times and queue lengths lead to the curious conclusion that we may be better to estimate means of these from a model, than to measure them directly.
- Pooling of two or more service facilities results in lower waiting times than operating each facility with its own queue.
- By making judicious simplifications to the actual processes occurring in a waiting line system, it may often be possible to estimate upper or lower bounds to crucial operating characteristics, such as the mean waiting time or the mean queue length, which suffice to make safe recommendations for improving the system.

Exercises

1. A firm operates a 20-tonne crane truck on a job contracting basis. Going through the firm's records over the most recent 100 days shows that 140 requests for jobs were received. They took, on average, 4 hours (half a working day) to execute, including the truck's travel time to the site and back to the yard.
   (a) Define the basic structure for this waiting line system, i.e., what constitutes an arrival, the service facility, and a service.
   (b) If you were to use an M/M/1 model, what assumptions must you make about the arrival and service processes? Indicate why they are reasonable, or why not.
   (c) Assume now that the M/M/1 model fits. Find the average number of jobs waiting for the truck, and their average waiting time. What fraction of time is the truck idle? Busy?
   (d) If you were to use an M/G/1 model, what assumptions must you make about the arrival and service processes? Are they more likely to be satisfied than those for an M/M/1 model. Why?
   (e) Assume now that the M/G/1 model fits, with a service time standard deviation of 2 hours or ¼ day. Find the average number of jobs waiting for the truck and their average waiting time. What fraction of time is the truck idle? Busy?
2. A thermal power station operates its own coal mine. The mine is only a short distance from a barge loading port, also owned and operated by the firm. The port consists of one berth with an automatic loading facility which takes 6 hours to load a barge, with a standard deviation of 1.5 hours. Given the distance between the port and the power station, as well as the variable ocean conditions, barges travelling back and forth between the power station and the port arrive at the port in an almost random pattern, with an average time between arrivals of 10 hours. (The port operates 24 hours/day.)
   (a) Find the fraction of time the port is idle. Compute the average time a barge is in the system, i.e., either waiting or being loaded in port, and the average total time in the system for all barges arriving at the port per day.
   (b) There is a fixed cost of \$1,200 to operate the port for one day. It costs \$1,500 to operate a barge for one day. Find the total cost for the port facility, consisting of the port's own operating cost and the cost of the time barges spend in the system.
   (c) The firm is considering upgrading the port's loading facility. The two options available are to decrease the average loading time to 4 hours at a daily operating cost of \$1,500 or to 3 hours at a daily operating cost of \$1,800, both with a one-hour standard deviation. Is any one of these options better than the current set-up?
   (d) What additional assumption is implicit in your answer to (c)?
3. Consider once more Exercise 2. Assume now that the time to load a barge is deterministic, i.e., the standard deviation of loading times is zero. Reassess the daily average cost of each of the three choices of facilities.
4. Compute the average waiting time of an arrival for a single-server waiting line system with a service rate of 1 and the following set of arrival rates: 0.1, 0.2, 0.3, 0.4, 0.5, 0.6, 0.7, 0.8, 0.9, 0.95, 0.99. Show the average waiting times graphically as a function of the arrival rate. (This is a simple 10-minute exercise on a spreadsheet!)
5. Consider Exercise 2 again. The power station plans to double its size, which will also result in a doubling of the number of barges that will transport coal from the mine to the power station. Management wishes to evaluate three possible options for upgrading the port facilities. Option 1 calls for the building of a second port at a new site that offers easier access and better shelter. This would mean that the firm would operate two separate ports,

each handling half of the volume. So, barges would arrive at each port, on average, every 10 hours and each barge would take, on average, 6 hours to load. The new port would have a daily operating cost of $1,000, while the cost of the existing port would remain unchanged. Option 2 calls for the building of a second identical loading facility at the existing port. Barges would arrive, on average, every 5 hours and then be loaded by the first berth becoming available. However, due to some economies of scale, the two facilities together would have a total daily cost of only $2,000. Option 3 calls for the replacement of the current facility by a completely new facility which can load a barge in 3 hours. Its daily cost would be $2,000. Barges would still arrive at that facility, on average, every 5 hours. So, all three options have the same total capacity of being able to load 8 barges per day. Assume that the service times for all three options follow a negative exponential distribution.

(a) For each option, determine the average time the port facilities would be idle and the total average time in the system of all ships arriving for loading per day. Note that for Option 2 you will have to use expressions (16-7) and (16-8). What additional approximation will you have to make?

(b) Cost out each option. Which one is the cheapest? Will the answer for Option 2 overestimate or underestimate the true cost?

6. (This problem uses a similar model to the weighbridge project with move-up time.) Customers arrive according to a negative exponential distribution at a single-server queue with unlimited waiting space. The mean time between arrivals is two minutes. 30% of the customers require a service of exactly one minute and the remaining 70% require a service of exactly two minutes. The customers are randomly mixed in the arrival stream, i.e., the chance that the next customer will require a service of one minute is always 0.3.

   (a) Calculate the steady state probability that an arriving customer does not have to wait.

   (b) Calculate the mean number of customers in the queue and the mean time that a customer spends in the system.

7. In Section 16-3, Little's formulas were stated as relations between the system's characteristics for mathematical queueing models that applied only after the system had been running for a long time. Use two copies of an arrival–departure diagram to show that, provided the server is idle at the end of the period, Little's formulas are also exactly true over any finite period. In other words, provided L_q, W_q and λ are measured over the same period, then $L_q = \lambda W_q$.

8. (a) From Figure 16-4 estimate what the total waiting time of all the customers who arrive during the rush time at the cafeteria will be. Assume the service rate is 500/90 customers per minute. What is the average wait of any customer over the rush time?

   (b) If the service rate is increased to 8 customers per minute, how much customer waiting time will this save? Although increasing the service rate obviously provides better service, it will also cost more staff time. From Figure 16-4, estimate approximately the maximum service rate that it would be sensible to consider?

   (c) Management has agreed with your suggestion that they provide more service capacity, so that the maximum service rate is 8 customers per minute. However, they are only prepared to provide this capacity from midday (12:00) until the congestion clears. Modify Figure 16-5 to demonstrate the effect of this change and estimate how this will affect the average waiting time.

9. The queueing formulas must be consistent when applied to the same model. In particular, M/M/1 is a special case of both M/G/1 and M/M/C. Show that for an M/M/1 queue, where μ is the service rate, expression (16-1) (p. 463) can be rewritten as

$$L_q = \frac{(\lambda/\mu)^2}{(1 - \lambda/\mu)}$$

(a) Verify that expressions (16-6) (p. 466) simplifies to $P_0 = 1 - \lambda/\mu$, and that the probability that there are no customers in the system and hence (for Poisson arrivals) the probability that an arriving customer does not wait is exactly as derived for an M/G/1 queue, i.e., $P_0 = 1 - \lambda s$. Finally, show that (16-7) (p. 466) gives the same answer as above for L_q when $C = 1$.

(b) Use a spreadsheet to draw a graph of L_q versus the traffic intensity, which should be the same as Figure 16-6.

Further reading

Bunday, B.D. (1986) *Basic Queueing Theory*, London: Edward Arnold. Easier coverage of the simpler theoretical models than Gross et al. (2008).

Gross, D., Shortle, J.F., Thompson, J.M and Harris, C.M. (2008) *Fundamentals of Queueing Theory*, 4th edn, New York: John Wiley. There has been a vast amount of work on theoretical models for queueing systems. This is the best general reference on them. More extensive spreadsheets for calculating queueing formulas are available from the Wiley ftp site.

Hall, R.W. (1991) *Queueing Methods for Services and Manufacturing*, Englewood Cliffs, NJ: Prentice Hall. Unique graphical methods for control and modelling of queues, such as the arrival–departure diagram.

Hall, R.W. (ed.) (2006) *Patient Flow: Reducing Delay in Healthcare*, New York: Springer. A collection of papers, many using queueing theory, to reduce delays in healthcare systems.

Kleinrock, L. (1975) *Queueing Systems, Volumes I and II*, New York: Wiley-Interscience. Another very comprehensive general reference on the theory of queueing models. Many interesting applications of waiting lines are concerned with computer/communications systems. Volume II concentrates on them.

McNickle, D.C. (2011) 'Fitting a theoretical model to a real queue', *INFORMS Transactions on Education*, 11(3):111–22. Available at http://ite.pubs.informs.org/. DOI:ited. 1110.0064.

McNickle, D.C. (1998) 'Queueing for toilets', *O. R. Insight,* 11: 2–5. The analysis of toilet standards was done using the method described in Section 16-3, except that the criterion used was that 90% of customers should wait less than one minute.

McNickle, D.C. (1991) 'Estimating the average delay of the first N customers in an M/Erlang/1 queue', *Asia–Pacific Journal of Operational Research*, 8: 44–54. The final theory that was actually used for the weighbridge problem.

McNickle, D.C. and Woollons, R.C. (1990) 'Analysis and simulation of a logging weighbridge installation', *New Zealand Journal of Forestry Science*, 20: 111–19. Analysis of the weighbridge problem.

Reinertsen, D.G. (2009) *The principles of product development flow: second generation lean product development*, Redondo Beach, CA: Celeritas Publishing. Queueing theory and arrival-departure diagrams used to illustrate efficient product development practices.

17 Simulation and systems dynamics

Learning objectives

- Differentiate between the various kinds of simulation used in MS/OR.
- Identify events, activities, temporary and permanent entities of a discrete-event simulation. Know how at least one style of discrete-event simulation works, and describe the advantages and drawbacks of this style.
- Describe how one random number generator works, how a range of random variates can be produced, and identify the advantages and disadvantages of random number generators in simulation problems.
- Be able to run a simulation experiment.
- Identify the important characteristics of situations for which Monte Carlo and Continuous Systems Simulation are appropriate.

Introduction

In Chapter 16, we studied system behaviour under uncertainty with the aid of mathematical models of queueing theory. If the situation can be captured adequately by such a model, this clearly is the preferred approach. However, there are many situations where either no suitable theoretical model exists, or the problem is so complex that a theoretical model cannot represent the interrelationships properly. In such cases, the analyst often resorts to simulation.

In MS/OR, simulation is used to explore the dynamic behaviour or operation of complex commercial, industrial, or technical systems. We do this by building a descriptive mathematical model of system behaviour over time. This model needs to include all aspects of the system that have been identified as essential to trace how the state of the system changes. It is then used to record in exact chronological order of **simulated time** (i.e., assumed or imitated time) each and every change in the state of the system that would have occurred had the actual system been operated in **real time** over the same time interval. At the end of the time interval, various simulated measures for analysing the performance of the system are computed from the system state changes. (You may have to read this paragraph again to get its full meaning!)

Would it not be more accurate to observe the real operation directly? This may be true. However, it may be neither economically affordable, nor technically feasible. As we saw in Chapter 16, it may take years of actual observations to accumulate reliable performance measures for a given mode of operation, let alone alternative modes. Any answers derived may be of little or no relevance by then. Implementing alternative modes of operation may be disruptive or impossible. Finally, the system may still be on the drawing board. The simulation may be done precisely to finalize which option should be implemented.

On the other hand, a simulation can often be completed in a few days, weeks, or months, depending on the complexity of the system in question. Therefore, a simulation may turn out to be a far more effective approach.

The first part of this chapter is mainly devoted to **discrete event simulation**. Changes in the state of the system are triggered by events, such as the arrival of a customer, the start or end of an activity, and so on. Discrete event simulation is particularly suitable for the study of the dynamic behaviour of complex waiting line situations which are beyond representation by theoretical queueing models.

Discrete event simulation may also be used to verify whether a theoretical model used for a situation that does not satisfy all assumptions of the theoretical model is a sufficiently good approximation. For example, in the weighbridge problem we incorporated the move-up time as a random component of the service time and argued that this will tend to underestimate the true waiting times slightly. Any reduction in waiting time for the two-weighbridge option would therefore be on the conservative side. A simulation that models the move-up time properly could be used to verify whether our argument is correct.

The first section of this chapter sets the stage by illustrating the simulation process with the weighbridge problem of Chapter 16. Nowhere in MS/OR modelling is the systems view as evident as in simulation. The next section uses systems concepts to explain the basic structure of event simulation. We then discuss how to plan and run simulations. This is followed by a discussion on simulation software.

Discrete event simulation is by far the most common type of simulation. However, there are other forms of simulation, such as fixed-time incrementation, and **Monte Carlo simulation**.

The last part of the chapter deals with the simulation of continuous systems, in particular with **system dynamics**. We introduce the concepts with a simple accident and emergency situation, followed by a real-life application to interactions between the UK health care and social services.

The last section discusses some of the pitfalls of simulation.

There are at least one hundred discrete event simulation packages at prices ranging from free to many thousands of dollars. We assume you have access to a preferred package. So, rather than go through the details of one package, we concentrate on the basics of how discrete event simulation works, and how to run effective simulation experiments. However, we do describe briefly a favourite package, especially when cost and benefits are considered: Simul8.

Luckily, Monte Carlo packages in MS/OR all have a very similar look and feel, as do system dynamics packages. We consider two representative examples, ModelRisk and *ithink.*

17.1 The weighbridge problem revisited

We will use the NZFP weighbridge case to demonstrate the process of discrete event simulation. You should re-read the description of the problem in Section 16-4. We will start with the original situation of one weighbridge. With simulation there is now no need to approximate the move-up process or to use steady-state assumptions. We can easily model what actually happens.

Detailed record of processing trucks at the weighbridge

The initial eight columns shown in Table 17-1 show how the first 20 trucks arriving at the weighbridge on a given day were processed. All times are expressed in seconds of time since the weighbridge starts.

The first truck is just driving up to the weighbridge when it opens. Its arrival time is recorded as 2 seconds (column 1). Since the weighbridge is unoccupied, there is no move-up time (columns 2 and 3 are blank). Weighing starts immediately at time 2 (column 4). The weighing time is 38 seconds (column 5), hence weighing ends at time 40 (column 6), and truck 1 leaves the weighbridge, i.e., leaves the system.

Truck 2 arrives at time 23. It finds the weighbridge occupied; hence it has to wait until truck 1 leaves the weighbridge at time 40. At time 40, truck 2 starts moving up to the weighbridge (column 2). This takes 61 seconds (column 3). As a result, weighing starts at time 40 + 61 or 101 (column 4). Weighing takes 59 seconds and truck 2 vacates the weighbridge at time 160. In the meantime, truck 3 arrives at time 87, finds the weighbridge occupied, and waits until time 160, when it starts moving on to the weighbridge, and so on.

Column 7 records the total time each truck spends in the system, i.e., the difference between its departure time from the weighbridge and its arrival time. Column 8 shows the unproductive time that each truck spends waiting in the queue and moving up to the weighbridge. The time truck 1 spends in the system is simply equal to its weighing time, namely 38 seconds. Its unproductive time is zero. Truck 2 spends 78 seconds of unproductive time — the table entry in column 4 minus the table entry in column 1. Its total time in the system is 137 seconds.

These detailed records allow us to determine some overall measures of performance. For example, the average of column 7 tells us that each truck spends, on average, 192.8 seconds in the system. Of this, 118.25 seconds, on average, is lost either waiting in the queue or moving up to the weighbridge (average of column 8). The weighbridge was busy 71.2% of the time. This percentage is calculated by dividing the sum of the weighing times of all 20 trucks by the weighing ends time for truck 20.

Generating random events

So far, we assumed that columns 1 to 8 of Table 17-1 are an actual reconstruction of how the first 20 trucks arriving after 5.30 am on a given day were processed over the weighbridge. For this, we would have needed an exact record of arrival times, move-up times, and weighing times for each truck.

Table 17.1 Simulation of truck processing over weighbridge

Column	1	2	3	4	5	6	7	8	9	10	11	12
Truck number	Arrival time	Move-up starts	Move-up time	Weighing starts	Weighing time	Weighing ends	Time in system	Waiting time	Inter-arrival time	Random number	Random number	Random number
1	2			2	38	40	38	0	2	0.0166	0.0474	0.1064
2	23	40	61	101	59	160	137	78	21	0.1916	0.9531	0.3418
3	87	160	60	220	78	298	211	133	64	0.4706	0.9510	0.5582
4	238	298	10	308	30	338	100	70	151	0.7756	0.4001	0.0113
5	506			506	54	560	54	0	268	0.9297	0.6985	0.2832
6	568			568	98	666	98	0	62	0.4603	0.8185	0.7864
7	584	666	28	694	48	742	158	110	16	0.1468	0.7524	0.2143
8	707	742	15	757	90	847	140	50	123	0.7059	0.5264	0.6932
9	717	847	22	869	82	951	234	152	10	0.0963	0.6721	0.6023
10	731	951	38	989	85	1074	343	258	14	0.1276	0.8513	0.6435
11	828	1074	16	1090	92	1182	354	262	97	0.6181	0.5496	0.7197
12	832	1182	13	1195	107	1302	470	363	4	0.0434	0.4808	0.8895
13	1308			1308	89	1397	89	0	476	0.9911	0.8391	0.6838
14	1387	1397	5	1402	53	1455	68	15	79	0.5412	0.2189	0.2785
15	1432	1455	42	1497	58	1555	123	65	45	0.3571	0.8806	0.3362
16	1435	1555	19	1574	77	1651	216	139	3	0.0259	0.6200	0.5482
17	1442	1651	60	1711	115	1826	384	269	7	0.0627	0.9505	0.9785
18	1623	1826	9	1835	91	1926	303	212	181	0.8337	0.3561	0.7126
19	1867	1926	11	1937	74	2011	144	70	244	0.9114	0.4248	0.5106
20	1901	2011	9	2020	73	2093	192	119	34	0.2894	0.3669	0.5002
Average			26.13		74.55		192.80	118.25	95.05			

What if we have not collected such detailed records, but only have summary statistics on the arrival and processing pattern, as shown in Table 16-5? Can we construct a table, similar to columns 1 to 8 of Table 17-1, that represents a good imitation of what might happen at the weighbridge on a typical day? All we need is a method for generating for each truck an artificial but typical triplet of times consisting of an interarrival time, a move-up time (which may be zero), and a service time. These times should be consistent with what we know about their corresponding probability distributions. This is what simulation is all about! It is simply an imitation of the real process, using artificially created times for the various activities and events that typically occur in the real thing.

To generate these activity and event times, we start by generating **random numbers**. These are fixed-length sets of digits from 0 to 9, which we hope appear to be uniformly distributed and independent of each other. In spite of their name, 'random numbers' are always produced from a **deterministic** formula. What we want is a formula that produces a sequence that *appears as though* the numbers in it are independent, and are uniformly distributed over their range.

Many random number generators are variations of a Multiplicative Congruential Generator. We specify a very large prime number m, and a multiplier a. For example, in one package $m = 2^{31} - 1$, $a = 742{,}938{,}285$. Then, from the previous random number Z_{i-1} we calculate the integer: $Z_i = (aZ_{i-1})(\text{mod } m)$, i.e., Z_i is the remainder after dividing aZ_{i-1} by m. Finally, we turn Z_i into a random variate uniformly distributed between zero and 1 by dividing Z_i by m. The Excel function for this process is RAND.

Activity

From this chapter's website, retrieve the spreadsheet random_number_demo.xlsx. This is a (deliberately badly) executed implementation of the generator described above. Answer the questions on the second page of the spreadsheet. You should be able to show that:

- if you run the same simulation starting at the same settings you get *exactly* the same answers;
- the generator will start to repeat after a (hopefully long) time;
- you can jump out to any number in the sequence in one mathematical operation.

Our next task is to turn uniformly distributed random variates into random variates from any desired distribution. Consider the weighing times. According to Table 16-5, the weighing time has a mean of 1.21 minutes or 72.6 seconds and a standard deviation (s.d.) of 0.73 or 43.8 seconds. Assume that the weighing time is normally distributed. Recall also that any value of a normal random variable can be expressed as its mean plus or minus a multiple of its standard deviation. We use the z-values from the normal distribution tables for this purpose. They measure how many standard deviations the value of the normal variable is away from its mean, either in a positive or a negative direction. The first uniform random variate listed in column 12, u = 0.1064, can therefore be transformed into a normal random variate v as follows:

$$v = \text{mean} + z_{u-0.5}(\text{s.d.}) \qquad (17\text{-}1)$$

$$= 72.6 + z_{(0.1064-0.5)}(43.8) = 72.6 + (-1.25)(43.8) = 17.85$$

where $z_{u-0.5}$ corresponds to the normal distribution table entry $u - 0.5$. If $u - 0.5$ is negative, then you look up the z-value for the absolute value of $u - 0.5$ and make the z-value negative. This is the case in the above example. Since $0.1064-0.5 = -0.3936 < 0$, we look up the z-value closest to 0.3936, which is 1.25. Hence, $z_{(-0.3936)} = -1.25$. Excel has a function called NORMINV which performs this transformation for you.

For some distributions, the transformation can be done algebraically. For example, a random variate that is uniformly distributed over the range going from $a = 28.8$ to $b = 116.4$ seconds can be produced as follows, using again the first uniform random variate listed in column 12, $u = 0.1064$:

$$v = a + u(b-a) \qquad (17\text{-}2)$$

$$= 28.8 + 0.1064 \times (116.4-28.8) = 38.12 \text{ seconds}$$

Sometimes, we may have an empirical frequency distribution, compiled from observations of an actual process. In such instances, it may be best to use this distribution for generating random variates directly, rather than some theoretical approximation to it. Assume that we have the following frequency distribution:

Observed value	0	1	2	3	4
Frequency	0.23	0.39	0.19	0.13	0.06
Cumulative frequency	0.23	0.62	0.81	0.94	1.00

Say the uniform random variate to be transformed is $u = 0.7692$. We find the first cumulative frequency which is just larger than 0.7692. This is 0.81 in the above list. Its corresponding observed value is 2. This is the random variate associated with u. Had u been equal to 0.8100, then according to the above rule 0.94 would have been the cumulative frequency just larger than 0.8100, with an associated random variate of 3.

Figure 17-1 shows this transformation graphically. It plots the graph of the cumulative frequency distribution for the above example. Note that the vertical axis goes from 0 to 1, while the horizontal axis lists the values that the random variate can take. We first locate the point on the vertical axis corresponding to the uniform random variate (0.7692), then go across until we meet the graph. Next, we drop a vertical line down to the horizontal axis. This will identify the corresponding value of the random variate. Because the vertical steps in the graph are in proportion to the frequencies of each value, the process will generate random variates with the correct frequencies. Since we go from the vertical axis to the horizontal axis, the method is known as the **inverse transform method**. It is the basis of most methods for generating random variates from empirical distributions, as well as from discrete probability distributions.

In this example, the random variate had only four possible values, but clearly the same look-across and then look-down process would apply to distributions with more values, and even, at the limit, to continuous distributions. Luckily, for some random variables, notably negative exponential, the formula for the mathematical inverse of the distribution function is known, and can be used to bypass the graphical process.

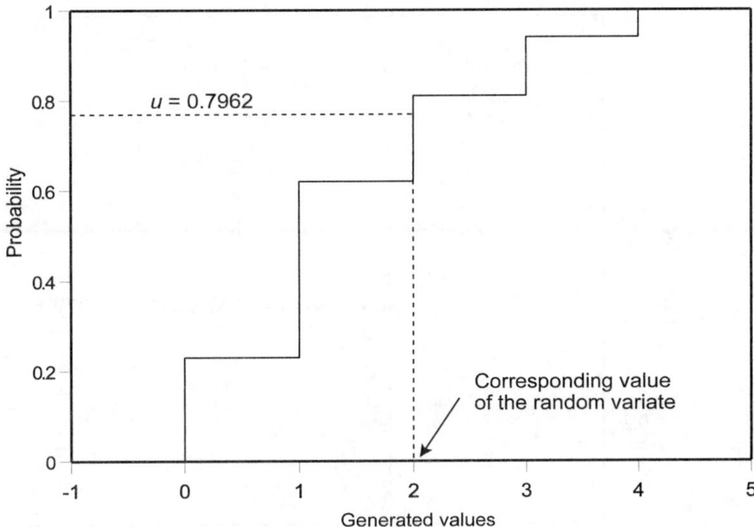

Figure 17-1 The inverse transform of the cumulative distribution function

Suppose that we want to a produce random variate v from a negative exponential distribution with a mean of a. Let u be the uniform random variate we have generated. Then, from Figure 17-2 it must be true that

$$u = 1 - e^{-v/a}$$

Rearranging and taking the natural logarithm (ln) of both sides of this gives:

$$v = -a(\ln(1 - u)) \qquad (17\text{-}3)$$

This simple logarithmic operation transforms a uniform random variate into a random variate from a negative exponential distribution.

Figure 17-2 illustrates this process for generating the interarrival times of trucks at the weighbridge. According to Table 16-5, the mean interarrival time of trucks at the weighbridge is $a = 1.68$ minutes, or 100.8 seconds. Applying expression (17-3) to the same uniform random variate (0.7692) produces an interarrival time of 147.79 seconds, as shown in Figure 17-2. You should check your understanding by verifying that the first uniform random variate in column 10 of Table 17-1 (0.0166) transforms into an interarrival time of 1.69 seconds.

There are a number of other exponential-type variates that can be generated by extensions to the log transform method, for example, Weibull (used in reliability) and Erlang-k. In fact, you will find that most simulation packages offer much the same set of random variates, included because they are the ones that are easy to generate.

Activity

We have already made use of the inverse transform method without defining it. Draw the cumulative distribution function for a uniform random variable from $a = 28.8$ to $b = 116.4$ seconds. (Hint: it's a straight line.) Show that the transformation method in equation 17-2 s using the inverse transform method to generate uniform random variates.

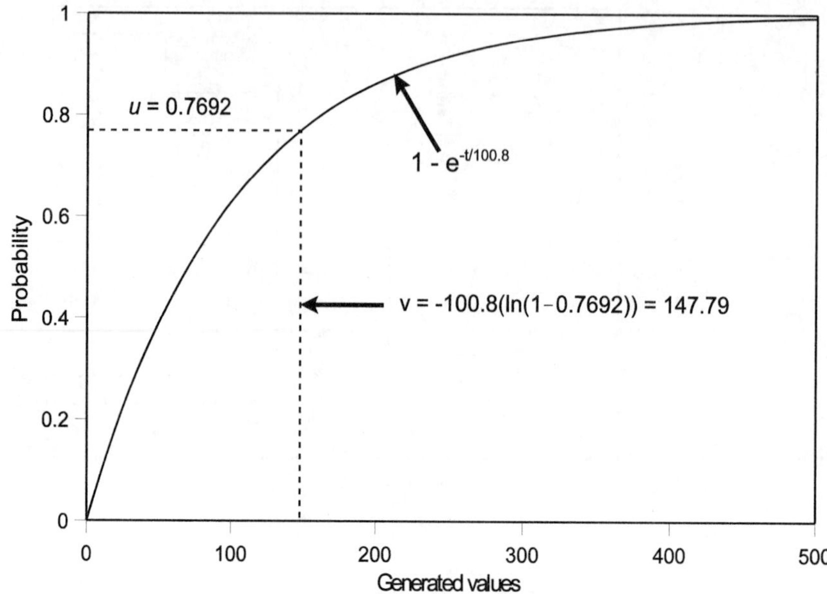

Figure 17-2 The inverse transform for a negative exponential distribution

Simulating the weighbridge operation

For each truck, we have to generate an interarrival time, a move-up time if the truck has to wait, and a weighing time. Table 16-5 shows that the standard deviations of the truck interarrival times and move-up times are very close to their corresponding averages. If this is the case and each occurrence is independent of all other events, then the negative exponential distribution is often a good approximation. The interarrival time is thus assumed to have a negative exponential distribution with a mean of 1.68 minutes, or 100.8 seconds, while the move-up time has a negative exponential distribution with a mean of 0.33 minutes, or 19.8 seconds.

The weighing time, on the other hand, seems to follow a different, but unknown, distribution. A tempting choice would be to use a normal distribution with a mean of 1.21 minutes or 72.6 seconds and a standard deviation of 0.73 minutes or 43.8 seconds. However, given the relatively large standard deviation in comparison to the mean, very small uniform random variates could easily result in negative weighing times, which is impossible. We have to choose a different approximating distribution.

In a real application, the preferred approach would be to compile an empirical frequency distribution, based on a sample of, say, 100 observed weighing times. This could then be used find a suitable theoretical distribution (Erlang-3 worked well), or to generate directly corresponding random variates, using the method in Figure 17-1. Since we ultimately wish to use a spreadsheet for simulating the weighbridge problem, such an approach is computationally rather demanding. Hence, we will use a rather rough approximation, based on a uniform distribution. Its range (a, b) is chosen to correspond to a = mean – s.d. = 72.6 – 43.8 = 28.8 and b = mean + s.d. = 72.6 + 43.8 = 116.4 seconds, i.e., one standard deviation on either side of the mean. This distribution will underestimate the standard deviation of the weighing times by about 40%, and from what we know of waiting-line models (Section 16-3), we conjecture that this should result in the simulation underestimating the average waiting times. From a modelling point of view, this is preferable. We do not want to represent the current situation as worse than it is in reality, and thereby produce a bias in favour of a change.

Consider again Table 17-1. The simulation starts at simulated time '0'. We now generate the first arrival. For this, we need an interarrival time. We use the uniform random variates in column 10 to generate interarrival times. The first entry is 0.0166. We already used that entry in expression (17-3) to generate a random variate from a negative exponential distribution. We obtained a value of 1.69 seconds, which we rounded to the nearest integer. So, the first interarrival time is 2 seconds. This is the entry in column 9. Hence, truck 1 arrives 2 seconds after the start of the simulation (entry in column 1). Since the weighbridge is empty, no move-up time has to be generated. The next random variate needed is the one for the weighing time of truck 1. We use the uniform random variates in column 12 for that. The first entry is 0.1064, which we used above in expression (17-2) to demonstrate how to generate a uniformly distributed random variate in the range of 28.8 to 116.4. We obtained 38.12 seconds, which we round to 38 (entry in column 5).

We now create the arrival of truck 2. Using the second entry in column 10, 0.1916, expression (17-3) gives an interarrival time of $100.8 \times (-\ln(1-0.1916)) = 21.44$ seconds, rounded to 21 (column 9). Truck 2 arrives at simulated time $2 + 21 = 23$ seconds (column 1). It has to wait, and we generate a move-up time from a negative exponential distribution with mean 19.8 seconds. Using second entry in column 11, 0.9531, produces a move-up time of $19.8 \times (-\ln(1 - 0.9531)) = 60.58$ seconds, rounded to 61 (column 3). Note that if a truck does not have a move-up time, we simply skip the uniform random variate reserved for this calculation in column 11. This was the case for the first truck. The second entry in column 12, 0.3398, gives a weighing time of $28.8 + 0.3398 \times (116.4 - 28.8) = 58.57$ or 59 seconds (column 5).

This process continues until the simulation is stopped. To test your understanding, verify the generation of random variates in the simulation for another few arrivals. In this example, the simulation was stopped after 20 arrivals. A more common **stopping rule** is to run the simulation until the simulated time reaches a specified time, such as a whole working day for the weighbridge problem. Table 17-1 covers only the first 40 minutes of simulating a full working day at the weighbridge.

It is worth noting these points about this simulation, which apply to all discrete-event simulations:

- **Trucks do not really 'move' in the simulation. Movement is modelled by having them change state.**
- **Time is simply a variable. The value of time required to get to the next event is calculated and added to the simulated time.**
- **What makes the simulation a satisfactory model of the real situation is a set of rules (here implicitly defined by the rows of the spreadsheet) to determine what event happens next.**

Activity

- Why do trucks 5 and 6 each have no entry in the move-up time column?
- Verify the times in columns 2, 4, 6, 7, 8 of Table 17-1 for trucks 3 to 6.
- What if there were two weighbridges in parallel, where a truck goes to the first available one? Would this spreadsheet approach extend easily to this case? What implicit ordering of events are we relying on for the spreadsheet to work?
- How would you convert uniform random variates into random variates from a uniform distribution with a range from −2 to +3?
- Verify that you can get (17-3) by rearranging and taking natural logarithms

17.2 Structure of simulation models

The simple spreadsheet approach to simulating the weighbridge problem worked because there was an inherent ordering of the events in the single queue model. A truck could not move on to the weighbridge until the previous arrival had left. For more complex situations, we need a more general method of describing how the components of a system interact. In this section, we will classify the components of a simulation system, and describe one method — entity life cycles — for capturing the complex interactions of these components.

In the terminology of discrete event simulation, the components of the system are called **entities**. The simulation traces the behaviour of entities through the system. There may be several types or **classes of entities**, such as people, machines, goods, or pieces of information, interacting with each other. For example, consider the simulation of a job shop, where various jobs arrive for processing on one or a sequence of machines. The sequence may be different from job to job. The jobs form one class of entities. Each group of interchangeable machines forms another class of entities.

Some types of entities may be **permanent**, such as the machines in the job shop. They remain part of the system throughout the entire simulation run. Others are **temporary** entities, such as the jobs. They are created at the time they arrive and are then cancelled or destroyed at the time they have finished all processing.

Entities engage in **activities**. For example, a job and a machine engage jointly in an activity, separate, and then may join another entity for a new activity, or become idle (for machines) or leave the system (for jobs).

The exact sequence of processing a given job in the job shop example is called an **attribute** of the job. This is an example of a permanent attribute. The machine on which a job is processed at any given point in simulated time is another attribute of the job — a temporary attribute in this case, since it changes once the processing at that machine ceases. Machines also have permanent attributes, such as the speed of processing, and temporary attributes, such as whether a machine is idle or busy.

At any given point in simulated time, the system has a given configuration, defined by the current activities of the entities and the value(s) of their temporary attributes. This is the **state** of the simulated system. A change in the state of the system is referred to as an **event**. For instance, in the job shop system the arrival of a new job, the start and the end of processing a job on a machine, are all separate events.

Some events may be imposed on the system from outside, i.e., they may be specified as an input to the system by the analyst. A typical example is the event that causes the simulation to stop, such as the value of the simulated time signalling the end of the simulation run. Other events are generated by the simulation itself, either by the completion of an activity or by another event. For example, in the job shop the event 'machine X starts processing job K' may be the consequence of the event 'machine X finishes job L', with job K waiting for processing at machine X (a temporary attribute of job K), or the event 'job K arrives at machine X', with machine X being idle at that time (a temporary attribute of machine X).

The weighbridge simulation structure

The weighbridge itself is a permanent entity. The weighing time distribution is its permanent attribute, while 'idle', 'waiting for a truck to move up', and being 'busy' are its temporary attributes. The trucks are temporary entities. Their permanent attribute is their arrival pattern, as indicated by the interarrival time distribution. 'Waiting in the queue', 'moving-up', or 'being weighed' are their temporary attributes.

Trucks engage in three activities. They 'arrive', 'move up', and are 'being weighed'. The weighbridge engages in one activity only: 'weighing'. However, it is standing by while a truck 'moves up'. During that time, the weighbridge is blocked — a sort of pseudo-activity it goes through if a truck has been 'waiting' while the bridge finished a 'weighing'. A truck engages in the activities 'arriving' by itself, while for 'moving-up' and 'weighing' it also requires the presence of another entity, the weighbridge. So, a truck and the weighbridge engage jointly in the activities 'moving up' and 'weighing'. The events are 'the arrival of a truck', 'the start of moving up', 'the end of moving up', 'the start of weighing', and 'the end of weighing'. So, most events are associated with the start or end of an activity.

Some activities and events can only occur if the state of the system satisfies a given condition. For example, the activity 'moving up' can only start when two conditions are satisfied: a truck must be waiting and the event 'weighing' has been completed. On the other hand, once the truck has completed 'moving up', it and the weighbridge unconditionally engage in the joint activity 'weighing'. We will use this linkage between activities to capture the interaction between the components of the system.

Entity life cycles

Each type of entity goes through a sequence of activities and changes of temporary state attributes. For example, a truck first 'arrives' and then 'waits in the queue' if the weighbridge is 'busy' or 'waiting for a truck to complete moving up'. Sooner or later the truck 'moves up', followed immediately by 'being weighed', and finally leaves the system. Alternatively, if a truck arrives while the weighbridge is in the 'idle' state, it goes through 'wait in the queue' without stopping and immediately engages in 'being weighed', and then leaves. We see that each truck goes through a **life cycle** of activities, and inactive times or queues. This can be depicted graphically. Figure 17-3 shows the two paths for the truck life cycle. Activities are depicted as rectangles and queues as circles. The source and the sink of temporary entities are depicted as clouds.

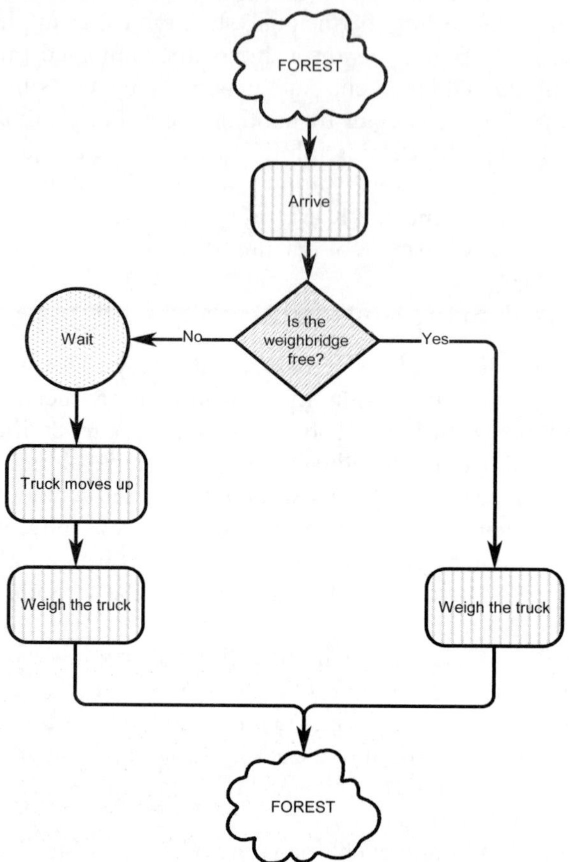

Figure 17-3 Life cycle diagram for truck entities

This entity cycle diagram has a special feature. The truck can take alternative paths, depending on whether or not the weighbridge is 'free' at the time of its arrival. A diamond is used to depict this switching mechanism.

The entity weighbridge also has a life cycle, as shown in Figure 17-4. Since it is a permanent entity, it repeats that life cycle for each truck it processes. As for trucks, the path involves a switch, depending on whether or not the queue of trucks is empty. If the weighbridge is 'idle', which can only happen if no trucks are 'waiting in the queue', then it remains 'idle' until a truck 'arrives'. At that point, the weighbridge engages in 'weighing' (right-hand side of diagram) and then returns to the switch. If in the meantime a new truck has 'arrived' and is 'waiting in the queue', then the switch sends the weighbridge onto the left-hand path where it first 'waits for truck to complete move-up', after which it 'weighs' the truck, and returns again to the switch for a new cycle.

Note that we show 'idle' as a queue. If there is only one weighbridge, it may not seem so obvious that being 'idle' has the nature of a queue. In state 'idle', the weighbridge is waiting for a truck to arrive. If there are several weighbridges that could be in the state 'idle', it becomes immediately clear that this is a queue structurally no different from the queue 'wait' for trucks.

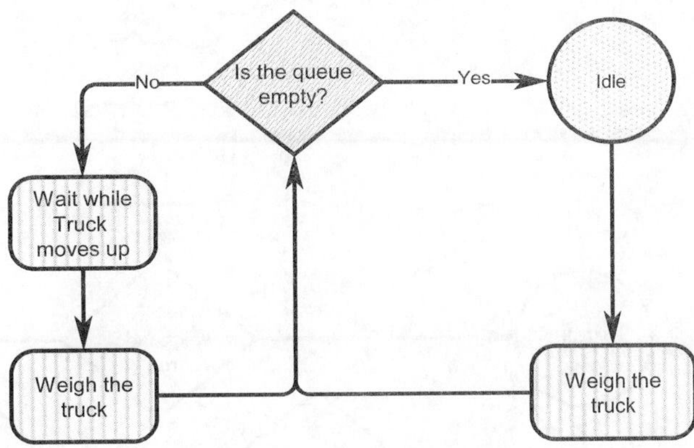

Figure 17-4 Life cycle of weighbridge

To show the interactions between the two types of entities, we combine the two life cycles, such that they coincide for activities engaged in jointly by a truck and the weighbridge. This is shown in Figure 17-5. Since 'moving up' and 'waiting for truck to complete move-up' must always occur together, nothing is lost by referring to both as 'truck moves up'. The two cycles merge there and separate again after 'weighing'. For the alternative path, a truck and the weighbridge only join for 'weighing'.

Note that if trucks do not need to go through a 'move-up', but can enter the weighbridge directly once it becomes free, there is no need for a switch mechanism for either the truck or the weighbridge. In this case, each has a single, unique path for its activity cycle. After 'arriving', a truck 'waits' until the weighbridge becomes 'idle' and then immediately joins with the latter for 'weighing' before departing. The weighbridge also remains in the queue 'idle' until a new truck arrives, at which point it joins the truck for'weighing' and returns to 'idle'. If another truck is already waiting, it simply zooms through'idle' and immediately starts another 'weighing'. As an exercise, draw the combined activity cycle diagram for this simpler situation.

The model used for the weighbridge creates the truck entities coming from the forest and then destroys them after weighing. In reality, the trucks are involved in round trips, picking up logs in various forests, bringing them to the mill over the weighbridge, unloading them in the wood yard, and returning to the forest, starting another round trip. Given that the weighbridge operation occupies only a small part of each round trip, we use this as justification for separating it out from the round trip. However, any time lost waiting at the weighbridge will reduce the number of round trips a truck can undertake per day. As long as the congestion at the weighbridge remains minor, the reduction in round trips will be negligible. If the waiting times become excessive, say longer than 15 minutes, the effect may become significant.

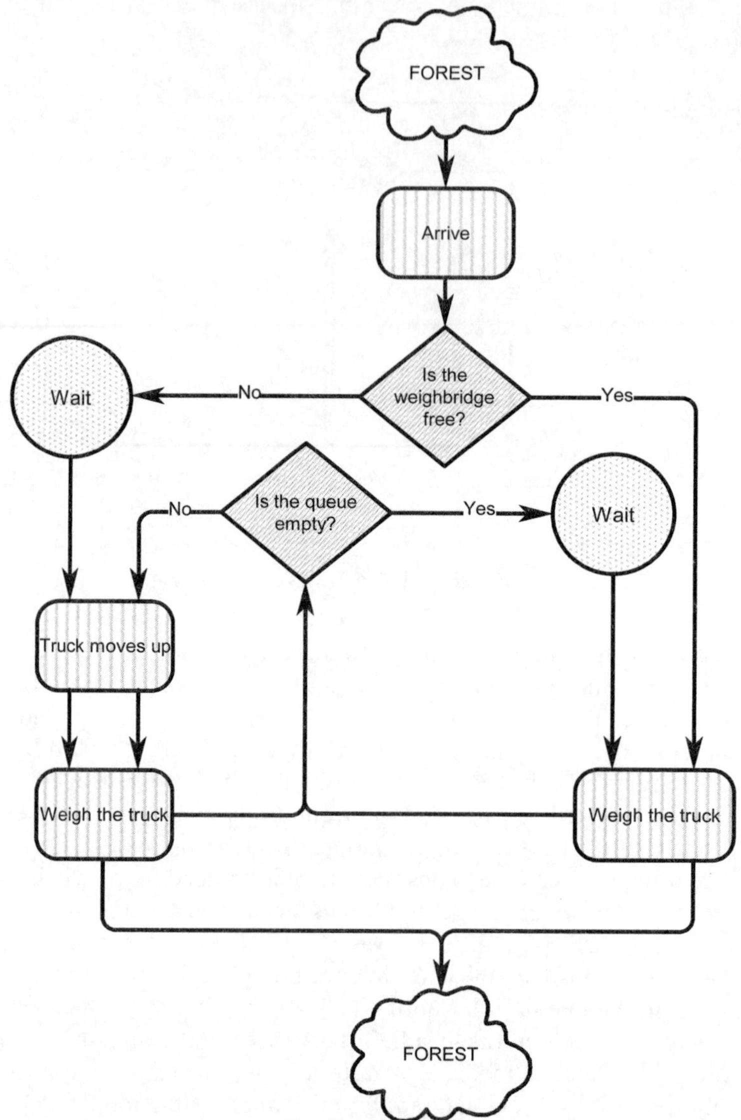

Figure 17-5 The combined truck and weighbridge cycles

A better approximation might be to model the round trips explicitly. The life cycle diagram for trucks is then also a closed loop, and the trucks become permanent entities, executing several new activities and queues, such as 'trip to forest and back', 'travel from weighbridge to wood yard', 'waiting for unloading', and 'unloading of logs'. Additional permanent entities, such as log unloaders, may have to be introduced. (Such a simulation would be very difficult, or even impossible, to set up for a spreadsheet. The use of specialized simulation software would be essential.)

As with influence diagrams, entity life cycle diagrams have several uses. They are a powerful display device for facilitating communication between problem owners and analysts or between analysts. They clearly show the interactions between entities and therefore facilitate better understanding of the complexities of the system. Because they capture these interactions, they can serve as a first step for writing a simulation program. In fact, the class of simulation packages known as activity cycle diagram (ACD) packages explicitly view discrete event simulations in the form of entity life cycles. Some require the input to be organized and submitted in this form.

Activity

Get together a group of friends and play the following game (matchboxes can be substituted for friends):

- Divide into two groups of similar size and form two lines.
- Draw a circle on the ground between the two groups.
- The two people at the head of each line must each randomly decide to move into the circle. They hold hands for another randomly selected length of time and then each rejoin the back of their respective lines. Repeat this step a number of times.

You have been simulating a queue with a number of servers using the activity-cycle method. Does it matter which group represented the customers and which were the servers? This illustrates one problem with ACD packages: they work best for very simple entity behaviours, where all the entities in a class behave in exactly the same way.

17.3 How is a simulation planned and run?

Performing a simulation for a sufficiently large number of events or a sufficiently long period of time is called a 'simulation run'. For all realistic practical applications, this has to be controlled by the computer. How should we plan such simulation runs in order to get useful and reliable results? This is a rather difficult question, so do not expect a comprehensive and definitive answer, if one even exists! We will simply be able to point out some of the more basic and obvious rules to follow and pitfalls to avoid. More details can be found in the books by Law (2007) and Robinson (2004).

Measures of performance

The analyst has to be very clear what kind of measures are needed to judge and compare the performance of alternative systems, such as one weighbridge versus two weighbridges. The simulation program has to be capable of collecting the information for compiling these measures. For instance, in the weighbridge problem we are interested in measures such as the average time a truck spends in the system, as well as how that time breaks down into waiting, moving-up, and being weighed. In a spreadsheet simulation, these measures can be computed from the details recorded. Other simulation packages may require setting up to capture this information. Management may also wish to know what percentage of trucks has to wait longer than, say, 3 minutes. Hence, the data collected may have to be organized in the form of a frequency distribution, rather than the simple cumulative totals needed for averages.

The performance of the real system usually varies over time. In the weighbridge operation, there will be days when everything moves smoothly over the weighbridge, with few long delays. On other days, the congestion may be very bad, with many trucks delayed up to 20 minutes. So, the average waiting time per truck varies from day to day. A good simulation of the weighbridge operation should, therefore, exhibit a comparable pattern of daily performance measures. Table 17-2 lists the results of 64 simulation runs, each for one day's operation covering about 400 truck arrivals. These results were obtained using the spreadsheet format of Table 17-1. With the help of a simple Excel macro, all 64 runs were made in succession, taking only a few seconds.

The average time trucks are waiting in the queue and moving up varies widely from a minimum of 172 seconds for day 21 to a maximum of 1084 seconds for day 40. In fact, each run is one observation on a random experiment. The times listed in Table 17-2 are 64 observations of the random variable 'average daily waiting time per truck'.

Table 17-2 Sum of waiting and move-up times for 64 days

Day	Time	Day	Time	Day	Time	Day	Time
1	426	17	173	33	405	49	560
2	915	18	278	34	582	50	835
3	327	19	641	35	302	51	317
4	954	20	199	36	400	52	329
5	782	21	172	37	426	53	350
6	330	22	394	38	325	54	241
7	289	23	331	39	607	55	308
8	475	24	386	40	1084	56	459
9	256	25	333	41	677	57	558
10	242	26	279	42	603	58	325
11	330	27	615	43	243	59	347
12	432	28	392	44	627	60	183
13	589	29	277	45	342	61	186
14	316	30	655	46	705	62	524
15	729	31	449	47	875	63	372
16	601	32	258	48	517	64	545
		Average	452.9		Standard deviation		207.8

Variability of simulation results

In contrast to most MS/OR models, the inputs into a simulation model are often sequences of random variates (such as the sequence of truck arrival times), rather than the single parameter estimates we might need for a theoretical queueing model. For example, although we based the generation of interarrival times on an average of 100.8 seconds, the observed average for the first 20 interarrival times shown in Table 17-1 is, in fact, 95.05 seconds. Hence, the output measures of system performance collected from the simulation model will also reflect this variability. Figure 17-6 attempts to capture the problem (and one possible solution) for the weighbridge.

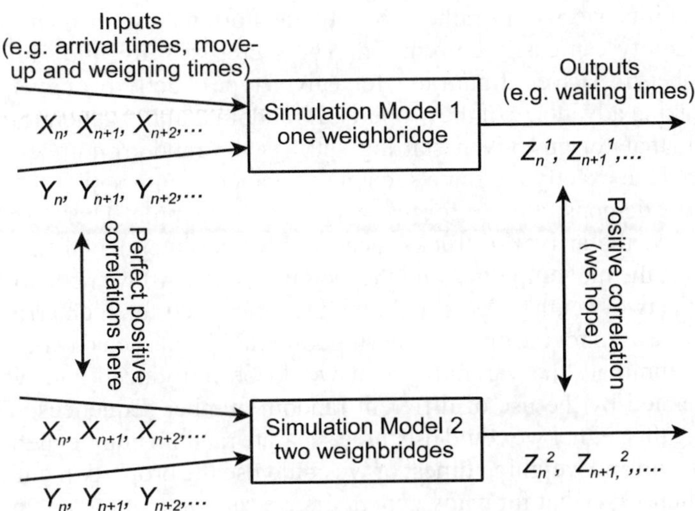

Figure 17-6 Variability of simulation results

We want the variable inputs in order to have a valid model. However, as a result of this, we can expect to observe variable output measures, such as the waiting times in a queue. As we have seen in the example above, the variations observed may be surprisingly large. To get a sufficiently reliable picture of the long-run performance of the system simulated, we have to make a sufficiently large number of simulation runs. This will not only give better estimates of the average values for all performance measures, but will also allow us to estimate their variability. We can then calculate confidence intervals for the performance measures of interest. Narrow confidence intervals give more certainty about the conclusions. It is essential that the presentation of simulation results always includes some measures of the variability of the results as an indication of their reliability.

For our example, the overall average for the 64 days is 7 minutes and 32.9 seconds. This is fairly close to the values predicted by the theoretical model in Chapter 16. The standard deviation of average waiting times is 207.8 seconds. Because the daily results are independent, we can thus specify an approximate 95% confidence interval on the average total waiting time of 400.9 to 504.9 seconds (i.e., $452.9 \pm 1.96 \times 207.8/\sqrt{64}$). Note that this is a rather wide interval. Unfortunately, the number of runs needed to get confidence intervals that bracket the overall average by just a few per cent can easily be in the hundreds or thousands.

Much of the more sophisticated simulation methodology is, in fact, concerned with reducing some of the variability in the simulation output measures. Let us briefly touch on one of those — the use of common random numbers.

Simulations are usually done to explore how crucial performance measures are affected by different operating options or configurations, such as one or two weighbridges. If each option is simulated with a new set of random numbers, then the simulation results are affected by two sources of variability. The first is the variability inherent in the operation itself. That variability we want to measure. The second is the variability introduced by using different random number sequences. That second variability we would rather do without. Fortunately, in many instances, this second variability can easily be reduced. The secret is to use the same sequence of random numbers in each configuration, for a given type of activity or event. This can be achieved by taking advantage of the property of random number generators mentioned in Section 17.1, that for any given starting settings the random number generator will always reproduce exactly the same sequence of random numbers.

We demonstrate this for the weighbridge example. There are three types of random activity: the arrival of trucks measured by the interarrival time between consecutive trucks, the move-up time, and the weighing time. All we need to do is to make sure that for the two-weighbridge simulation the times used for each arriving truck are identical to those used for the one-weighbridge simulation on each day of the simulation run. This will eliminate the variability that would be introduced had we used different times generated by the use of different random number sequences. There are two ways of doing this: either we could use three separate random number generators for interarrival, move-up and weighing times; or we could use the property mentioned in the Activity in Section 17-1, that for many generators we can jump out to any number in the sequence in one operation. We could thus use, for example, the first million numbers for interarrival times, the second million for move-up times, and the third million for weighing times.

Intuitively, what we are doing is just what you would do if you were running an agricultural experiment to determine the difference between the yields from two brands of carrot seed: you would ensure that as many as possible of the inputs (water, sunlight, fertilizer) to the two plots were the same, in order to reduce the variance of the difference of the outputs. In Figure 17-6 we show two models, Model 1 and Model 2, producing outputs Z_n^1, Z_{n+1}^1, ... and Z_n^2, Z_{n+1}^2, ... respectively. By ensuring that as many as possible of the inputs X_n, X_{n+1}... and Y_n, Y_{n+1},... are the same for the two models, we hope that Z^1 and Z^2 will be positively correlated. If this is true then the variance of their differences will be less than the sum of their variances. When the objectives of the model are taken into account, what initially appeared in Section 17.1 to be serious defects of random number generators, non-randomness and predictability, are often exploited to produce more accurate model results.

Simulation output analysis

This is a complex topic, so we start with a simple example. Figure 17-7 shows how the cumulative average waiting time in a simple queueing model behaved in an simulation run of 1,000 arrivals. The model is an M/M/1 queue (see Section 16-3) with a mean time between arrivals of 15 minutes and a mean service time of 10 minutes. Because the first simulated customer arrives to an empty queue, the average waiting time also starts from zero. Although initially it rapidly increases towards the steady state value of 20 minutes (calculated from formulas (16-1) and (16-4), pp. 463, 465), it is clearly affected by the initial empty state of the system. This effect is referred to as the **transient effect**. We may obtain more accurate results if we discard the observations collected during this transient period, because this means that data collection is now starting in a more representative state. For example, if we wish to model a busy café from 12 to 1 pm, it makes sense to start the simulation at 11 am, and then start measuring the characteristics of interest at 12, so they will only be collected over the period of interest. On the other hand, the weighbridge naturally starts from empty at 5.30 am, so there is no transient period and discarding initial observations is not appropriate.

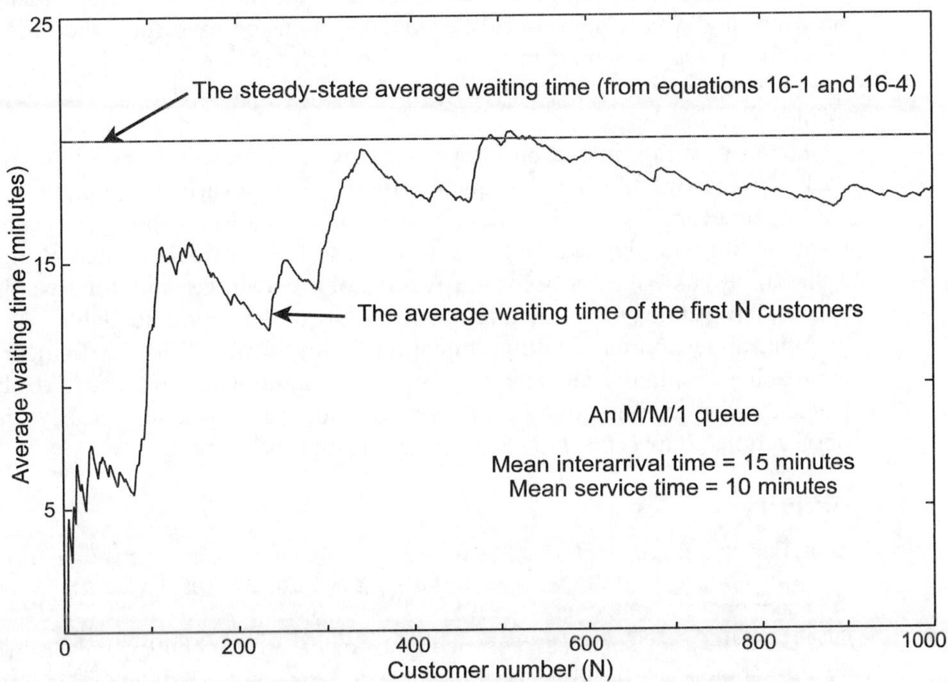

Figure 17-7 Behaviour of waiting time with run length

The second effect we can note from Figure 17-7 is that the convergence of the estimated average waiting time towards its steady state value is very slow. In Section 16.2, we discussed how in waiting line models the positive serial correlation of waiting times accounts for the very slow convergence of system characteristics towards their steady state values. In simulations we are also often observing highly correlated random variables, such as the simulated waiting times of successive trucks at the weighbridge. If the simulated waiting time of the 300th truck is abnormally long, then there is a good chance that the simulated waiting time of the 301st truck will also be abnormally large. So, we can expect the same very slow convergence of system characteristics towards their steady state values. Because of this serial correlation, calculating a confidence interval over successive observations using the conventional formulas in Excel or most statistical packages will not give the right answers, as they assume they are dealing with independent (uncorrelated) observations. For one class of simulations, however, there is a way around this problem.

In the weighbridge, the system starts at 5.30 am every working day with an empty queue. No trucks arrive after 5.00 pm, although any truck waiting at that time will still be processed. There are many real-life applications with this daily or periodic pattern, with each period terminating with an empty system, i.e., with no temporary entities present. This class of simulations is called 'terminating'.

In the job shop example, the operation is also interrupted at the end of each working day. However, the system starts each new day in exactly the state it was stopped the previous day. Any temporary entities in the system simply resume their life cycle at the point the system was interrupted at the end of the previous day. Hence, the operation does not go through a regular daily cycle, but continues indefinitely. It would be classed as 'non-terminating'.

For terminating simulations, if we take the average result over each period (e.g., over each day) then we now have a sequence of independent variables (e.g., the daily average waiting time) and the usual confidence interval calculation is appropriate. This is exactly what we did with the data from Table 17-2, so the confidence interval there, $452.9 \pm 1.96\times207.8/\sqrt{64}$, is actually for the average of the average daily total waiting time per truck! While clumsy, the calculation is at least statistically defendable.

What about non-terminating simulations? This is a much more difficult problem. One approach is to split the data into very large chunks (say 10,000) successive observations, calculate the average over each chunk, and treat these as 'nearly' independent observations. Law (2007) gives more details on this method.

Activity

- Describe in general terms how you might modify the spreadsheet simulations of the weighbridge in order to reduce the variability of the results due to using different sequences of random numbers.
- Does the transient effect present a problem for the weighbridge simulation?
- From your own experience, identify an example that would be best modelled by a terminating simulation, and an example for which a non-terminating simulation would be appropriate.
- Does the problem of serial correlation apply to the results of separate days of the weighbridge simulation? Note that each day starts from empty.
- Can a terminating simulation sometimes need a transient period? (Hint: read p. 499.)

17.4 Discrete event simulation software

Most simulations are performed by specialized software, such as GPSS/H, Simul8, or ARENA. For all but the simplest types of simulation, using one of these packages is recommended. Although spreadsheets can do rudimentary simulations, they do lack many of the facilities needed and, furthermore, only handle simple systems where each temporary entity can be processed through all operations with reference only to the event times of the entity that just preceded it. This is the case for the single weighbridge problem. For the two-weighbridge problem, the two bridges may not necessarily process two trucks that arrived consecutively, but trucks that were separated by other truck arrivals. Writing spreadsheet macros to deal with this complexity would be tricky, increasing the computational time many-fold.

Simulation packages have facilities to generate random variates from many distributions, often with individually controlled random number generators. They automatically keep track of the state of the system and properly execute all events at their scheduled times. They automatically collect performance measures on all queues and allow the programmer to specify other statistics to be collected, including frequency distributions for various passage times, such as waiting times. Programming time is therefore reduced to a fraction of what it would take to use one of the general-purpose computer languages, such as Visual Basic or C.

To give you an indication how simple such a program may be, Figure 17-8 lists the core of the GPSS/H statements used to simulate the weighbridge problem. The entire program consists of only 37 lines. GPSS/H uses a slightly different problem representation method to that of entity cycles, called the **process-interaction** approach. The GPSS/H statements describe the process through which temporary entities pass. Specialized statements describe the way these entities interact with the permanent entities in the model. For example, SEIZE and RELEASE statement pairs have the property that only one temporary entity may be in the section of instructions bordered by them at a time. Thus, when a truck reaches SEIZE Bridge, then no other temporary entity can enter that statement until the truck has reached the RELEASE Bridge statement, thus modelling the way in which each truck has exclusive use of the weighbridge. Within the SEIZE Bridge and RELEASE Bridge pair are two ADVANCE statements which delay the truck for a negative-exponentially distributed move-up (if needed) and an Erlang-3 distributed weighing time. Each truck has been given an attribute called PH(Empty), reflecting the state of the weighbridge (busy or idle) when the truck arrived. The TEST statement checks this to see the if weighbridge was idle when the truck arrived and, if so, jumps the temporary entity over the first ADVANCE so that it is delayed for a weighing time only.

```
     SIMULATE
     GENERATE RVEXPO(3,1.6782)
     BLET PH(Empty)=F(Bridge)
     QUEUE    Wait
     SEIZE    Bridge
     DEPART   Wait
     TEST G PH(Empty),0,Idle
     ADVANCE   RVEXPO(4,.3323)
Idle ADVANCE   RVERL(5,3,1.207)
     RELEASE   Bridge
     TERMINATE
     GENERATE 690
     TERMINATE 1
     START 1
     END
```

Figure 17-8 Instructions for simulating the weighbridge in GPSS/H

Windows and personal computers have contributed to the rise of visual interactive modelling system (VIMS) simulation packages such as ARENA, WITNESS and Simul8. The simulation model is drawn on the screen, using predefined icons. The package then creates a hidden language-based simulation, which finally, as part of its job, makes the temporary entities move on the screen.

In these packages, the model is created by dragging and dropping pre-defined icons for various permanent entities onto the screen. For example, dragging and dropping the four icons in Figure 17-9 is enough to set up a Simul8 model of a simple queue like those discussed in Section 16.3. (The '8' in Simul8 was inspired by the minimum number of key strokes or mouse clicks needed to set up simple models!)

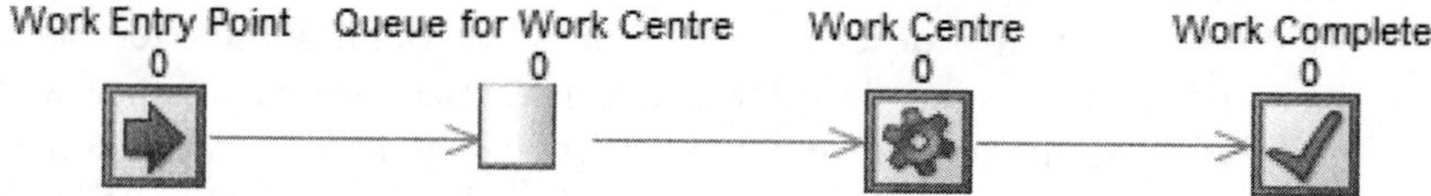

Figure 17-9 A simple queue modelled in Simul8

Temporary entities are created in the Work Entry Point. They wait for service in the Queue for Work Centre and then engage in the activity Being Served at the Work Centre. Finally, they are destroyed and some statistics are gathered at Work Complete. Double clicking on an icon allows the attributes of temporary and permanent entities in it to be set or changed. A considerable advantage of these visual interaction packages is that an apparently realistic model can be created very quickly, even in front of the client. They are also much easier and more rewarding to learn initially. A disadvantage is that it may be difficult, or even impossible, to model particular kinds of complex entity behaviour if these are not provided by the predefined icons. Because the usual attributes of Simul8 temporary entities are less flexible than those of GPSS/H , for example, it is difficult to expand the model to capture the move-up behaviour of trucks at the weighbridge without resorting to some programming.

An alternative modelling strategy here could be to exploit the simplicity and speed of Simul8 to run a range of models which could be expected to over- and underestimate the results like the queueing models discussed in Section 16.4.

Figure 17-10 shows a screen of part of a model of a hospital accident and emergency department in Simul8. We changed the icons to more appropriate pictures and sketched an outline of the facility on the screen to enhance the appeal of the model to the client. Although the initial program was sketched out in less than a day, the model in Figure 17-10 again required more programming to model the complex behaviour of different classes of patient, and the different patterns of patient arrival over times of day and days of the week.

Fixed-time incrementation

Event simulation is particularly suitable for queueing and sequencing situations of all sorts. Simulated time is always updated to the time when the next most imminent event is scheduled to occur.

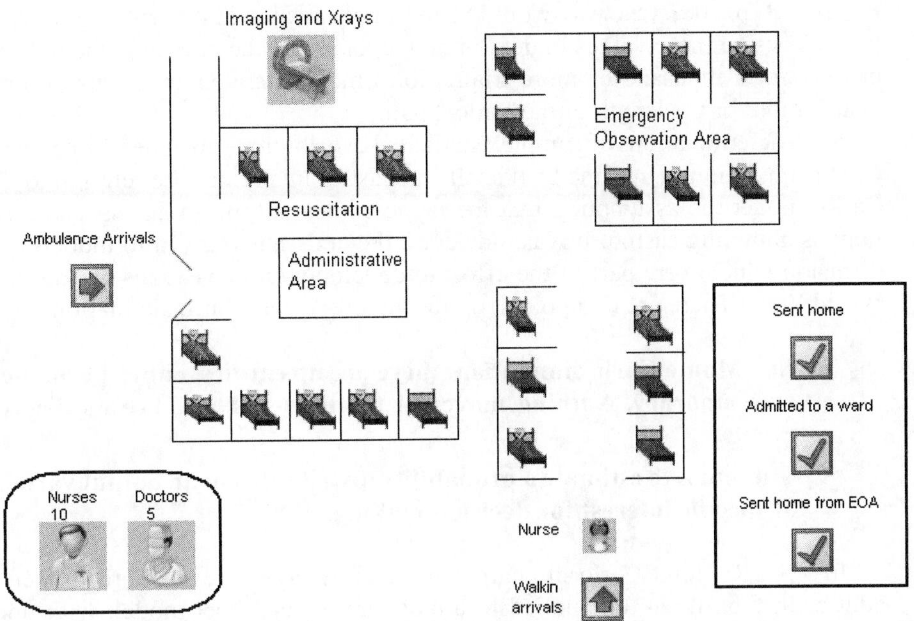

Figure 17-10 An accident and emergency department in Simul8

For other situations, it is more appropriate or adequate to update simulated time in equal discrete time intervals, such as a day or a month. Recall the production scheduling problem for the Crystal Springs Mineral Water Company in Chapter 11. There, we traced out exactly what would happen month by month for a given shift level and production schedule. In fact, we simulated the response of the system to various policies, trying to identify the best policy. We did not refer to it as a simulation, but it was a deterministic simulation with monthly time intervals.

This type of time updating is called **fixed-time incrementation**. It is a suitable modelling approach if some events occur regularly in each period and it is not important to record exactly at which precise point in time within a period events occur, as this has little effect on the performance measures. It is usually convenient to assume that all events occur either at the beginning or the end of a period. For example, a simulation of a production/inventory control situation, such as the one described in Chapter 6, would assume that any replenishments arrive in stock at the beginning of a day, while all stock withdrawals to meet customer orders occur at the end of each day. All costs would be assessed as of the end of each day.

17.5 Monte Carlo simulation and risk analysis

Sometimes, the problem we are interested in refers directly to random sampling of probability distributions. For example, how would you determine the probability distribution for the length of the **critical path** of a project, such as that described in Figure 5-8 (p. 108). One way would be to sample a value of the length of time that each task takes, use these values to determine the length of the critical path, and repeat this process for a thousand or more trials. The times generated are a sample probability distribution for the length of the critical path.

Such determinations of complex statistical distributions go under the name of **Monte Carlo** simulations. (In some books, all stochastic simulations are referred to as 'Monte Carlo', under the assumption that the name comes only from an association with the famous gambling casino. It was, however, the code name given to models of neutron diffusion which were part of the effort to develop atomic weapons during the Second World War.) There are two points to grasp about Monte Carlo simulation:

- **In a Monte Carlo simulation, there are no entities, either permanent or temporary. Nothing moves in the model. There are no discrete events.**
- **The aim is to estimate a probability distribution of an output variable of specific interest for decision making.**

In MS/OR, Monte Carlo simulation is almost always done on a spreadsheet, using an add-in. In fact, it can be applied to almost any spreadsheet model, with uncertainty represented by probability distributions on input cells, giving us measures of uncertainty on the output cells as described above. Popular add-ins include @RISK, Crystal Ball, and ModelRisk, which we will use.

We illustrate these points on a very simple model. In Chapters 15, 16, and Section 17.1, we described **Erlang-k distributions**, which are the distributions of sums of k negative exponential random variables, and a handy modelling family. Suppose we wanted to estimate what the probability distribution was for an Erlang-4 distribution with a mean of 2? The theoretical answer to this problem is easy. But let's do it by simulation. All we need to do is add together four negative exponential random variates, each with a mean of 0.5, and do this 1,000 or more times.

Figure 17-11 shows this being done using ModelRisk. When the add-in is run, a menu to set up and run the simulation appears at the top of the Excel screen. A number of special functions (such as VoseExpon(.5), which will generate the required exponential random variates) are now available, and are copied into cells B2:E2. The sum of these cells is collected in F2. The histogram and cumulative plot of the values in F2 are shown in Figure 17-11. Compare the histogram with the Erlang-4 probability density function in Figure 15-4, and the cumulative plot with the shape of the right-hand graph in Figure 15-3. The simulation gives convincing evidence that those theoretical graphs are correct.

A more realistic and very common use of Monte Carlo methods is to provide estimates of the likely outcomes of multi-stage decision processes where variables, such as cash flows, are subject to uncertainty. This is known as **risk analysis** and will be studied further in Sections 18.6 and 18.7. Thus, another way of characterizing Monte Carlo simulation is as a sophisticated form of sensitivity analysis on spreadsheets.

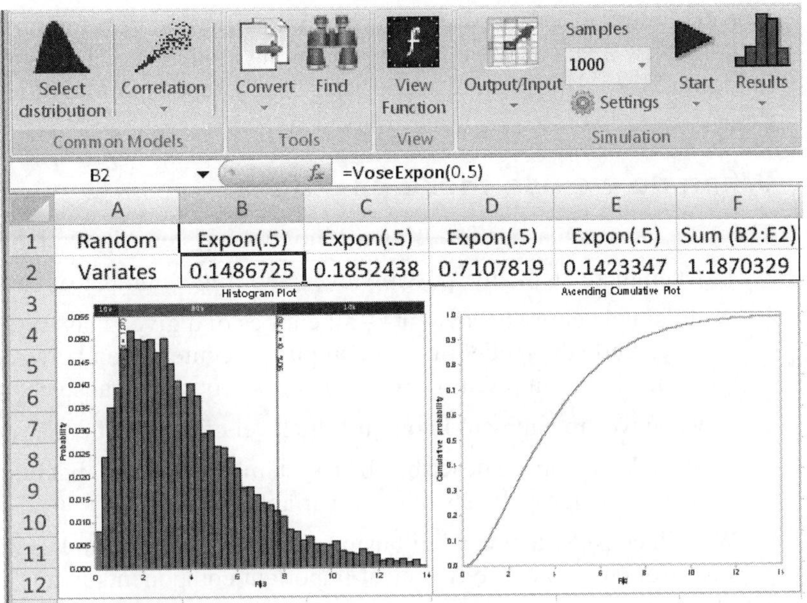

Figure 17-11 Simulating an Erlang-4 distribution using ModelRisk

Activity

ModelRisk Standard comes from Vose Risk Consulting (see www.vosesoftware.com).

- Use it to verify that Erlang-1(negative exponential), -2, -4, -8 probability density functions, all with the same mean, have the shapes described in Figure 15-3.
- Under ModelRisk Help, read the item called 'Your first model'. Carry out the steps in it to build a Monte Carlo model for the cost of building a house. This can also be found in the Example models as Building_a_house.xls.
- To get an understanding of the range of problems for which Monte Carlo simulation is used, you should run any other problem that can use 'any' version of the software — e.g., Wine problem (an infection model), or Basel II — estimating the risk of loss due to defaults in a bank's loan portfolio.

17.6 System dynamics — continuous system simulation

Sometimes, we do not need to know what happens to each individual entity in a simulation, but are happy enough to know simply the **level** and **rate-of-change** of a particular type of entity. Examples of such systems include large biological populations, money in an economy, chemical processes, staff recruitment systems for large organizations, such as the military or police, and ecological systems.

There are several simulation packages specifically for such problems, including Vensim, *ithink*, and DYNAMO. Usually, this kind of system modelling in terms of feedback loops (see Section 3.11, pp. 47–9) is associated with **system dynamics**. Causal-loop diagrams, as described in Section 5.5, are used for developing suitable models. In fact, the New Zealand Wine Industry planning model, depicted as a causal loop model in Figure 5-3 (p. 100), served as the basis of a system dynamics model, evaluated using *ithink.*

When do we use these packages?

There are various reasons for using a continuous system simulation model:

- when there are many, possibly even an infinite number of entities;
- for simple entity behaviour — all entities of a given class must behave the same way; while the model may be complex, the interaction between entities can only be modelled simply. It is often feedback loops that cause complex behaviour;
- when we are happy to know just the level of a type of entity over time;
- when levels can be described by a system of equations that relate the levels to the rate of change or levels of other variables over time.

We will consider a model built using the *ithink* package, and use the notation of this package from now on. The two most important components in any continuous system simulation package are:

Levels: In *ithink* these are referred to as **stocks** and denoted by rectangles.

Flows: These represent activities which lead to changes in the magnitude of stocks, and in *ithink* have an icon which looks like a pipe with a valve on it. The valve ('flow regulator') contains an algebraic or graphical expression which determines the volume that flows through the pipe.

17.7 *ithink* model of health and social services

We consider a simple model of part of a health care system. Elderly, infirm, or mentally ill patients often receive much of their care either in their own homes or in facilities other than hospitals. This is known as 'community care', and has become very popular as a means of both (ideally) providing appropriate care, and (often) reducing the total costs of care.

In our simple model, patients are assigned from the community to a waiting list. They are treated or assessed in hospital and then discharged into community care. Thus, we have three stocks: *Waiting List*, *Hospital*, and *Community Care*. Four flows (*Assignment rate*, *Admission rate*, *Discharge rate*, and *Leaving rate*) control the flow of patients through the model. The dynamic environment of the system, which provides inputs or receives outputs (infinite sources and sinks), is represented by clouds.

Since hospital capacity is limited, we have used the two other remaining *ithink* building blocks to build a feedback loop to control the hospital admission rate. These building blocks are **converters** (circles), which typically take information in and transform or store it for use by another variable in the model, and **connectors** (arrows or wires). Connectors carry information, not flows and, in this case, the information is:

'how full the hospital is'. Thus *Fraction full* is calculated at each time step as the ratio of *Hospital* to *Hospital capacity*. The *Admission rate* is then modified, either by a formula, or here by a graph, which shows how the *Admission rate* is to reduce as *Fraction full* increases towards one.

The system dynamics diagram for this model can be drawn interactively on the *ithink* screen window by the simple drag-and-drop facility provided. It is reproduced in Figure 17-12. Furthermore, *ithink* automatically creates most of the equations associated with the diagram, as listed in Figure 17-13.

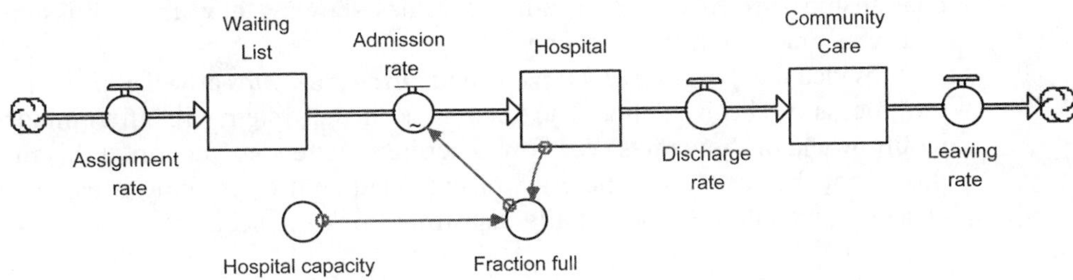

Figure 17-12 A system dynamics diagram

```
Community_Care(t) =
Community_Care(t–dt) + (Discharge_rate – Leaving_rate) * dt
INIT Community_Care = 30
INFLOWS:
Discharge_rate = 19
OUTFLOWS:
Leaving_rate = 20

Hospital(t) =
Hospital(t–dt) + (Admission_rate – Discharge_rate) * dt
INIT Hospital = 40
INFLOWS:
Admission_rate = GRAPH(Fraction_full)
(0.00, 20.0), (0.333, 20.0), (0.667, 20.0), (1.00, 0.00)
OUTFLOWS:
Discharge_rate = 19

Waiting_List(t) =
Waiting_List(t–dt) + (Assignment_rate – Admission_rate) * dt
INIT Waiting_List = 10
INFLOWS:
Assignment_rate = 20
OUTFLOWS:
Admission_rate = GRAPH(Fraction_full)
(0.00, 20.0), (0.333, 20.0), (0.667, 20.0), (1.00, 0.00)
Fraction_full = Hospital/Hospital_capacity
Hospital_capacity = 100
```

Figure 17-13 Automatically generated model equations in *ithink*

The first lines in each section show the equations that the package has created. It solves these numerically to give the levels of the three stocks for each time step dt. For example, adding the net change in the level of patients in *Community Care* over the time step dt, (Discharge_rate – Leaving_rate)*dt, to the level at the previous time step, Community_Care(t–dt), gives the level at time t, Community_Care(t). The remainder of the program specifies initial values for the stocks (for example, INIT Hospital = 40) and specifies the inflows and outflows for each stock. These are mostly set equal to constant values specified by the analyst except that Admission_rate is determined by a graphical relationship specified by four pairs of values showing how the admission rate is to reduce as Fraction_full approaches 1.

Provided the *Assignment*, *Leaving*, and *Discharge rates* are all approximately equal, the process will be in balance. The three stocks in the system will buffer minor variations in inflow and outflow rates. We now describe an extended version of this model where this is not the case, and where a well-intended control system on part of the model created unintended and potentially disastrous consequences.

17.8 UK health care and social services — a process design

(This section is based on a case study first published in the '*ithink* Business Applications Guide for versions 4-7'. It is used with the permission of High Performance Systems, www.hps-inc.com, and the authors, Professor Eric Wolstenholme, OLM Consulting, UK and Richard Stevenson, Cognitus Ltd, UK.)

In the United Kingdom, the National Health Service (NHS) provides all citizens with free medical care from cradle to grave, regardless of their circumstances. Reorganizations of the NHS have created an 'internal market' for the purchase and provision of health services in the hope of providing better and more efficient services.

Another government department — Social Services (SS) — is responsible for people with special needs. In this context, SS provides community care for elderly, disabled, or mentally ill people, who often require medical treatment or assessment by the NHS in hospitals before and/or during their period under SS care.

The interface between the NHS and SS subsystems is therefore crucial to considerations of patient welfare and efficient public spending. Patients flow back and forth across the boundary between these two organizations. The processes which drive these flows are of particular interest, as the NHS reforms have placed new responsibilities on managers on both sides of the boundary. At this point, you should look at the system dynamics diagram in Figure 17-14, which shows Wolstenholme and Stevens' generic model of such a community care system. The three subsystems — the community, the NHS and SS — are defined by rectangles. Representing them in this way allows each subsystem to be built up independently, and hidden when all the detail is not needed. Before 1993, the discharge rate from hospitals was solely under the control of the NHS. From 1993 onwards, local SS managers became responsible for managing all community care under cash limited budgets. The discharge rate from hospitals thus moved at least partly under control of local SS managers. If cash resources were limited, they could slow down the rate of acceptance of patients into community care and, hence, reduce

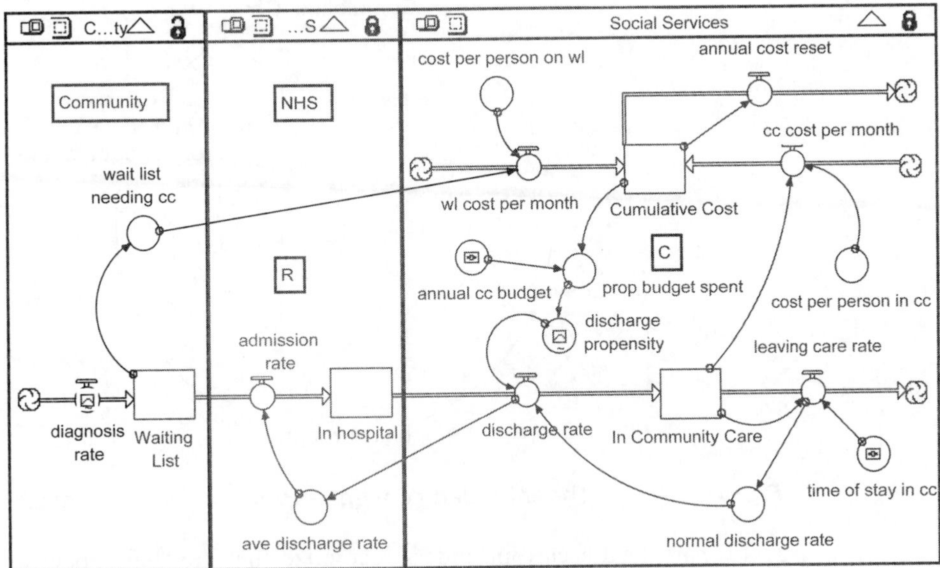

Figure 17-14 Expanded *ithink* model of the interactions between community, NHS, and Social Services

the discharge rate from hospitals. We model this change from the simple model in Figure 17-12 by shifting the *discharge rate* regulator into the SS subsystem, where it is now controlled by the *leaving care rate*. This, in turn, is found by dividing the number *in Community Care* by the *time of stay in c(ommunity) c(are)*.

The intention is that this would assist local SS managers to keep to their budgets, albeit possibly by adopting short-term and localized actions. In Figure 17-14, the feedback loop which models this intended behaviour is labelled 'C'. As the annual budget is used up, managers will be less willing to accept new patients from the NHS hospitals into Community Care (*discharge propensity*), which will reduce the *discharge rate* and, hence, the number of patients *in Community Care*. The anticipated result is that the *c(ommunity) c(are) cost per month* will reduce, and therefore the *Cumulative Cost* will rise at a lower rate, allowing managers to meet annual budget targets. Thus, we have a negative feedback loop. In *ithink*, negative feedback loops are called **C**ompensating loops, hence the letter C for compensating on it.

For clarity, this feedback loop is reproduced in Figure 17-15. *ithink* drew this loop diagram directly from the system map — a very useful attribute of the package. Separating out the causal loops from the clutter of the entire systems map makes it easier to explain to stakeholders key aspects of the system which the model captures.

However, if SS managers can now restrict the discharge rate from hospitals, one or more of three things must happen:

1. The number of patients in hospital will rise. But hospital capacity is limited.
2. Waiting lists will increase, as the admission rate must be reduced to ease congestion in the hospitals. This is the most likely outcome.

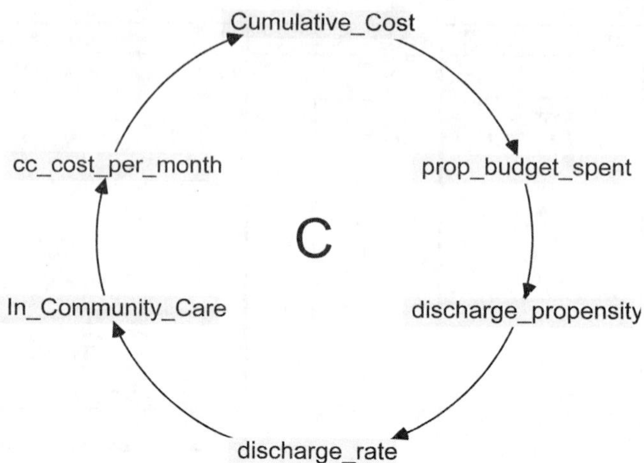

Figure 17-15 The intended consequences of controlling discharge rates

3. Primary health care providers recognize that hospital capacity is limited and assign fewer patients to the waiting list. Thus patients are deprived of appropriate care.

In practice, we could expect all three of these things to occur simultaneously but, in particular, the waiting list, and the time which a patient spends on the waiting list, will rise. Many of these patients will need home care by nurses and social workers while they are on the waiting list. The increased cost of this will have to come from the very same SS budget which the original action was intended to control! In Figure 17-14, this is captured by connectors, which go from the *Waiting List* through a convertor which calculates the number on the waiting list needing community care, and then feeds this, i.e., *w(aiting)l(ist) cost per month* into the *Cumulative Cost* in the Social Services sector of the model. The resulting loop is labelled 'R', for **R**einforcing.

The causal loop associated with this aspect of the model is seen more clearly in Figure 17-16. As the *Waiting List* increases, so will the number of patients on the *wait list needing cc*. The cost of this is captured as the *wl cost per month* and fed into the *Cumulative Cost*. As the budget is used up (*prop budget spent*), SS managers will be less inclined to accept patients from hospital into community care (*discharge propensity*). The *discharge rate* and, hence, the *admission rate* for hospitals reduce, causing still further growth in the *Waiting List*. It can thus be seen to be a positive feedback loop or, in *ithink* notation, a **R**einforcing loop. This loop is particularly worrying, as SS has no control mechanism for controlling community care expenditure in the community.

Positive feedback loops are discussed in Sections 3.11 and 5.5. In the absence of any control mechanism, they lead to instability and the levels in them can explode. Thus, the model suggests that there is a possibility that an action which was intended to impose control within part of the system, the SSs, may have an opposite and unintended serious consequence on another part of the system, the community.

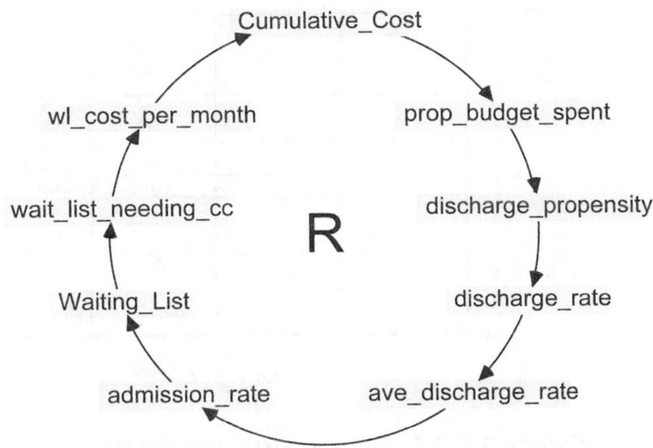

Figure 17-16 The unintended consequences

Activity

An important aspect of causal loop diagrams is to determine whether the loop is reinforcing or compensating. Two methods are:

- Assume a small increase in any variable and trace this round the loop. If, when you return to that variable the feedback effect increases the variable the loop is reinforcing, otherwise it is compensating. A fast way (see Section 5.5) is to count the number of negative links. If this is even, the loop is reinforcing; if odd, it is compensating (we need to have a net change in sign to turn an increasing change into a decrease).
- Verify, by both of these methods, that the intended and the unintended consequences in Figures 17-15 and 17-16 are compensating and reinforcing loops.

We ran the program over the time horizon of five years. *ithink* solved the system of differential equations using a numerical technique. The usual outputs from continuous system simulation packages are graphs showing the magnitudes of the stocks or levels over time. With the input variables originally specified by the authors for this problem, the system remains nicely in balance. Figure 17-17 shows that the annual expenditure on community care is comfortably less than the budget of £600,000 every year.

As you can see, the annual expenditure on community care is always less than £500,000. So, why not reduce the budget to this amount? The same amount of money that was previously adequate for community care would still be available, and the £100,000 released could be used to employ another SS manager (with car and expense allowance). In Figure 17-14, there is a tiny 'slider' on *annual cc budget* indicating that this change can easily be done from what *ithink* calls the **control panel** without altering the program. We make this change, and the surprising results can be seen in Figure 17-18.

For the first two years, the expenditure remains exactly as expected, under £500,000. But from then on, annual expenditure starts to rise, until by year 5 it is exceeding the budget by 60%. The reason for the budget blowout is easy to see if we look at the patient levels in the three subsystems, as shown Figure 17-19.

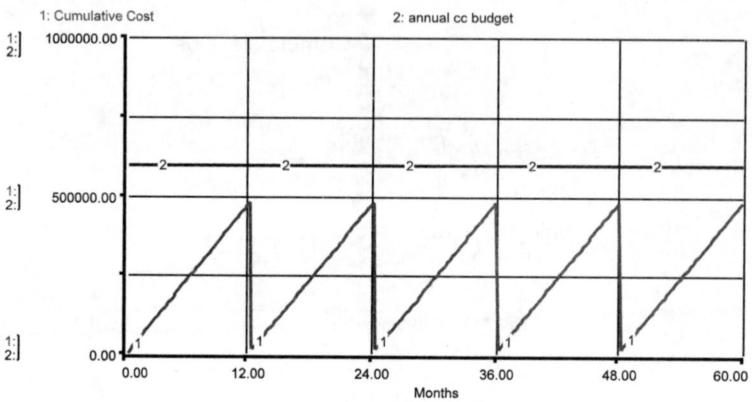

Figure 17-17 Annual costs and budget for community care

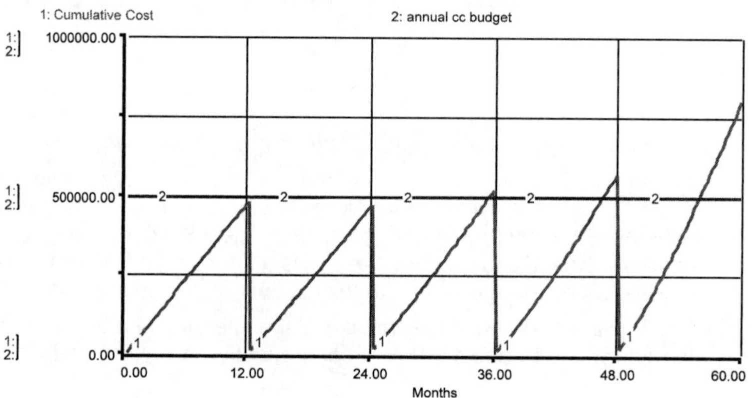

Figure 17-18 Community care budget reduced to £500,000

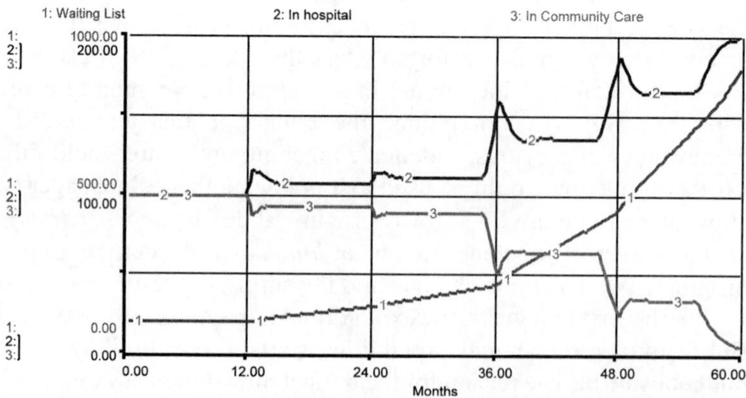

Figure 17-19 Patient levels in the three subsystems

In order to reduce the number of patients in community care and balance their budgets, SS managers reduce the discharge rate from hospital towards the end of every year. Thus, the patient numbers in hospital also rises sharply until, by the end of year 3, the NHS hospitals are almost continuously full. In the meantime, the number of patients on the waiting list rises at an increasing rate, from almost no one to nearly 1000. Since some of these will require home care while on the waiting list, this further eats into the community care budget, which now can support fewer and fewer patients officially in community care.

Some comments on continuous system simulation

More so than other kinds of simulations, system dynamics modelling requires careful thought about the formulation of the model and system boundaries. Many parameters must be estimated, often with little information. If the quantitative results of the model are to be taken seriously, extensive sensitivity analysis on input parameters is often needed, especially in the case of models with several feedback loops, to ensure that the results are not just artefacts of either the limitations of the model or specific parameter settings. In the SS above, it would be equally unwise to assume that exactly the unstable behaviour depicted in Figure 17-19 would occur if the budget were cut, as it would be to assume that a budget of £600,000 always led to a system under smooth control.

Often, a better way of using continuous simulation models is as a basis for discussion with all of the stakeholders, rather than assuming that the model can be fitted to the point where it exactly predicts system behaviour.

As Wolstenholme and Stevenson say:

> 'The simple maps and models discussed here are only a starting point for investigation of overall system behaviour, which is certainly much more complex than this. Other strategies are available to SS (reducing the quality of care, or well care/preventative medicine.) These strategies can be implemented into the model and their effects assessed ... Management of these complex issues requires effective cross-boundary discussion between *all* of the players involved. The model provides a conceptual framework and a common language on which to base those discussions.'

Case study 17-1: NetSim Models

Go to www.iseesystems.com/community/downloads/NetsimModels.aspx#4, where a number of system dynamics models can be run directly on the Web. When run under NetSim, they do not require access to *ithink*. While you cannot change the model, you can see it and experiment with input parameters. Study the following two models:

- From the Education and Research section, load the model **H1N1 Flu Outbreak**. It provides a good example of a reinforcing loop. It deals with a highly infectious disease, where the sufferers remain infectious for a long time. Explore the model and use it to determine if vaccination, or forcing infected people to stay at home (or a combination of both policies) is most effective.
- From the Business and Public Policy section, load the model **Tobacco Use Prevention Lab**. Use the model to confirm the three Insights (accessed from the Simulate 'Simulation Control Panel' page).

17.9 Conclusions on simulation as a tool

Simulation is one of the most spectacular MS/OR modelling techniques. Yet, curiously, perhaps because of its obvious value and applicability, it also tends to be associated with more failed projects than any other technique. All too often, the results of effort spent on simulation are disappointing. All there is to show for months of work is a 'nearly running' model, which may never produce useful results. Most of the reasons for failure relate to excessive concentration on the modelling phase of an MS/OR project — systems M and O in terms of Figure 6-9 (p. 162) — with too little thought and effort spent on problem formulation — system S — and implementation (see Chapter 8). So, what aspects tend to go wrong in simulation modelling?

Selecting simulation because you don't know what else to do

Simulation is sometimes described as a last-resort technique, to be used when attempts to fit some kind of analytical model have failed. While this may sometimes be true, in practice it is not a particularly good way of thinking about the place of simulation in the range of MS/OR tools. As we have seen, the use of simulation models in no way reduces the data requirements or the need for a thorough understanding of the system that is being modelled. Starting to build a simulation model before the system has been fully understood may lead to excessively detailed modelling of unimportant parts of the system while crucial parts are overlooked. In addition, the analyst is faced with acquiring simulation software which is often very expensive, learning how to use it, and writing the simulation program.

A better way of thinking about simulation is that it is a technique that may require large inputs: data collection, study and understanding of the system being modelled, knowledge of the simulation software, and knowledge of the special statistical problems that occur in the analysis of simulation output. On the other hand, a simulation model:

- may produce detailed output on performance measures for various parts of the operations;
- may be a flexible model that can include aspects of the system for which no easy analytical model is available;
- has the ability easily test the effect of varying system parameters; and
- in the case of a visual package, may be seen by unsophisticated management as more convincing than a model based on formulas.

Poor initial planning

Often, a modeller simply drifts into simulation. The project is dumped on a junior team member who starts building the model so that at least something will appear to be getting done. No initial scoping assessments are made and a small model, using whatever language or package happens to be lying around, eventually grows into a monster. The time taken to complete the model is usually grossly underestimated. Practically all large computer-based developments are late. Two major reasons for this are:

- **Premature coding:** the irresistible urge to begin writing the simulation before the system and the problem are properly defined.
- **Optimistic scheduling:** underestimating the time required for known tasks, such as problem scoping and data collection, and neglecting to allocate time for the inevitable, unanticipated problems.

Failure to define achievable goals or objectives

The goal of a simulation project should never be 'to model the ...'. As with all MS/OR projects, modelling itself is not a goal; it is a means of achieving a goal. An essential ingredient for successful simulation is a clearly articulated and agreed set of realizable objectives. These depend on answers to questions, such as 'What do we need to learn about the system under study?' or 'What decisions will be based on the simulation results?'.

The objectives cannot be correctly defined without the participation of the problem owner, and they must, of course, be realizable. As we saw in Chapter 4, setting these objectives is an important early step in any MS/OR project.

Wrong simulation software

It is possible to write simple simulations in general-purpose languages, such as Visual Basic. However, for most models it is much easier and safer to use a simulation package. These provide features such as complex control of the flow of events, reliable random variate generation, and visual output. However, no matter which package is chosen, there comes a time when it will simply not do what you want it to do. When simulation software was first designed years ago, fundamental and unalterable decisions were made about how temporary and permanent entities work, the level of detail they offer, and the complexity of behaviour they can handle. Many of these could not be changed as the software subsequently evolved. So, make sure the software can handle the degree of complexity you will need.

Incomplete mix of essential skills

A successful simulation project calls for a combination of at least four areas of knowledge and experience:

- **Project leadership:** the ability to motivate, lead, and manage the simulation team.
- **Modelling:** the ability to design a conceptual model that imitates the system under study at the required level of detail.
- **Writing the simulation:** the ability to transform the model into a logical, modifiable, working simulation.
- **Knowledge of the modelled system:** sufficient understanding of the system to guide the modelling and to judge the validity of the simulation results.

Teams typically concentrate on programming, to the exclusion of other aspects. In addition, people knowledgeable about the system, together with those who will use the results of the simulation study, often do not track the development in sufficient detail to assure that the end product satisfies their needs.

Inadequate level of user participation

All too often, model developers simply go off by themselves for six months and then proudly drop the 'completed', never-to-be-used model on the project clients. Inevitably, there will be some defect in the model, or the results will exhibit odd and counterintuitive behaviour. Either event immediately destroys confidence in the model.

The model-building team must work with the intended users of the results in order for both to have the confidence and understanding necessary to make and encourage effective use of the completed work. There should be regularly scheduled briefings, progress reports, and technical discussions with the users. The users are also the only ones who can inform the team about realistic considerations, such as politics, bureaucracy, unions, and budget limitations. These can affect the success of the project as much as the quality of the technical work. (See also Sections 8.1 and 8.2, pp. 224–9.)

Inappropriate level of detail

A model is a simplified representation of a system, and it should incorporate only those features of the system thought to be important for the users' purpose.

In modelling a complex system, difficult questions must be addressed — often for the first time. There is a tendency to spend a great deal of effort modelling in unnecessary detail those portions of the system that are well understood, while glossing over poorly defined portions that may be more important. The goals of the project determine the appropriate level of detail, which must be consistent with the availability of data and other resources.

Using an unverified or invalid model

Verification ('internal validation') involves comparing the programmed computer model with the system model. Does the program correctly implement the system model as designed? Validation ('external validation') involves comparing the system model with the real world (Section 6.4, pp. 126–8, discusses validation). Does the model adequately represent the real world? One effective verification–validation technique is a walk-through, with the modeller explaining what has been done to someone who is familiar with the system under study. This technique frequently turns up design errors that can be corrected at an early stage.

Poor presentation of results

The results from simulation studies are often presented in a way that the user finds incomprehensible. A model that gives unexpected or illogical results may do so because certain parameters turn out to be far more or less significant than expected, or because unanticipated interactions between system elements, such as feedback loops, greatly affect system performance. Insight into hidden problems of this sort is often the major gain from a simulation. However, unexpected or unusual simulation results that cannot be explained are usually caused by errors, invalid assumptions, or lack of understanding of the real system. Someone familiar with the system under study must examine the simulation results to determine whether they are reasonable, and the simulation results must be presented in a way that the user can easily relate to the system under study.

17.10 Comparison of the weighbridge queueing and simulation models

In Chapter 16, we analysed the weighbridge problem by using queueing formulas. It is instructive to compare the advantages and disadvantages of the two approaches. Some of the advantages of using simulation are:

1. The move-up time can be easily and realistically modelled by a line in the GPSS/H simulation instructions (the third line in Figure 17-8, p. 501), which assigns an arriving truck an attribute which takes the value '1' if the bridge is in use when it arrives. The value of this attribute is tested when the truck arrives at the head of the queue (line 7). If it is '1', the truck is delayed for a move-up time, otherwise the truck jumps to the 9th line, which delays it for a weighing time only.
2. The simulation can be started with an empty queue and is stopped at the end of a (simulated) day. There is no need to use steady state formulas.
3. It is easy to model the two-weighbridge situation because the computer package specifically provides for multiple servers in parallel.
4. It was easier to convince management that we had 'solved' the problem because a visual version of the program made little trucks move across the computer screen.

While the simulation model is easy to program and works well, its distinct disadvantage is the variability of the outputs that it produces and, hence, the large number of simulation runs needed to produce sufficiently narrow confidence intervals for the results. Because the queue is so sensitive to slight variations in its inputs, the simulated daily mean waiting time varied from 3 to 25 minutes. A total of 10,000 days was required to reduce the standard deviation of the mean daily waiting time down to 0.05 minutes.

For management, the most valuable part of the original study using the theoretical queueing model was the sensitivity analysis for the number of loads that could be carried per day, shown in Figure 16-10 (p. 474). Producing such a plot by simulation could easily take days of computer time.

We can also consider the two approaches in terms of the properties of good models listed in Section 5.3. Both approaches could be classed as **appropriate for the situation** and **relevant**. They produce the required economic information for management to make the decision about the second weighbridge at very small cost. We would probably conclude that, while the simulation model is superior on the **completeness**, **simplicity**, and possibly the **credibility** criteria for a good model, it is distinctly inferior to the queueing formulas for **ease of manipulation**, being **easy to communicate with**, and **adaptivity**.

Some of the guidelines for modelling listed in Sections 5.3 and 5.4 can also be related to the weighbridge problem. In particular, the ability to adequately model the arrival process of trucks at the weighbridge by assuming that the interarrival times were sampled from a negative exponential distribution is vital for the use of simple queueing models and also results in a much simpler simulation program. We are also applying **Ockham's Razor**, i.e., we exclude aspects that do not contribute to the predictive power of the model. For example, we exclude the fact that the trucks actually make round trips. We justified this simplification in Section 16.6 (p. 475).

Where the simulation model proved vital was in validating the queueing formulas that were used. These were slightly more complex than those shown in Chapter 16. (The analysis there was, in fact, our first attempt to produce a quick approximate answer to the problem. This was later refined into a more elegant method which gave very similar answers. Thus, we were also following the advice given under 'An iterative process of enrichments' in Section 5.4, p. 96.) By determining that the simulation and formula results are in close agreement for a few selected input values, we can reasonably assume that the formulas will be correct for intermediate values, hence saving a substantial amount of computer time and data analysis. Management appeared to be happy with this validation and found the results of the analytical models acceptably accurate.

17.11 Chapter highlights

- Simulation is the management scientist's tool of experimentation for exploring the effect of different combinations of control inputs on aspects of dynamic system behaviour.
- Stochastic events or phenomena are imitated by generating random variates. Using the inverse transformation method, random variates from many theoretical probability or empirical frequency distributions can be obtained.
- Event simulations imply a system structure consisting of permanent and temporary entities that have permanent or temporary attributes and engage individually or jointly in activities. The state of the system is given by the values of all attributes at a given point in simulated time. System behaviour is summarized by collecting statistics of these attributes.
- An entity life cycle diagram captures the sequence of activities for a class of entities.
- When comparing different combinations of control inputs, the results of simulation runs are affected by two types of variability: the variability associated with the stochastic behaviour of the system proper, which is the one we wish to measure, and the variability introduced by the use of different sequences of random numbers. The latter we can often eliminate by using the same sequence of random variates for each configuration of control inputs.
- The reliability of performance estimates can be improved by having long simulation runs, by a large number of simulation runs and, where appropriate, by reducing the transient effect through the choice of initial conditions, or a warm-up period.

- Computer simulation software contains features, such as random variate generators, updating of simulated time and entity attributes, and collection of statistics, that simplify simulation modelling.
- Event simulations update simulated time in variable increments by finding the next most imminent event. Fixed-time incrementation updates time in regular fixed periods. It is suitable for only for situations where it is not crucial when exactly in the period each event occurs.
- Monte Carlo simulation is a method for sensitivity analysis on spreadsheets. There are no temporary or permanent entities.
- In continuous system simulation, system behaviour is modelled by the levels (stocks) and the rate of change of levels over time, rather than by individual events.
- Simulations hide many pitfalls for the beginner. Simulation should not be used in preference to suitable analytic or numeric methods which can usually produce valid and useful results more quickly and more cheaply. For no other MS/OR technique is the proper choice of the system boundaries, the system components and their interactions, and the appropriate level of modelling detail as important as for simulation. Great care must be taken in scoping and planning simulations, in seeking crucial user participation, in using the most appropriate software, in adequate verification and validation of the model, and in documenting the model.

Exercises

1. Develop a spreadsheet similar to Table 17-1 to simulate the behaviour of the weighbridge, and simulate the arrival and processing of 80 trucks. Determine statistics for the amount of idle time of the weighbridge and the total waiting time for the first 80 trucks.
2. The table below is a partial simulation of ships arriving at a port for unloading and loading. The average interarrival time between ships is 48 hours. Interarrival times follow a negative exponential distribution. It takes, on average, 12 hours to unload a ship. The unloading time also has a negative exponential distribution. The loading time is uniformly distributed between 8 and 32 hours. There is only one berth in the port. Thus, only one ship can be unloaded or loaded at a time. Loading commences immediately after unloading has been completed. At the start of the simulation, no ship is in the port. This system is to be simulated for 12 ship arrivals, using the table format below. Note that the first 2 ships have already been processed to indicate the pattern.
   (a) Define the structure of this system, i.e., the permanent and temporary entities, the activities, and associated events. What would you use to define the state of the system?
   (b) Draw a combined life cycle diagram for the entities.
   (c) Simulate the behaviour of this system by hand for 12 arrivals. Round all times to the nearest hour. The following set of uniformly distributed uniform random variates should be used:
   (.0196) (.0674) (.1064) (.1584) (.6801) (.9531) .4418 .1916 .7706 .6510 .5582 .0112
   .9296 .6985 .2832 .4603 .8185 .7864 .1268 .7524 .2143 .7059 .5264 .6932 .0963
   .6721 .8095 .4541 .6392 .1983 .8791 .5023 .1276 .8512 .6435 .6181 .5496 .7197

   The random numbers already used for the first 2 ships are shown bracketed and resulted in the times listed below. Continue generating times starting with .4418.

Ship no.	Interarrival time	Arrival time	Unload time	Start unload	End unload	Loading time	Start of loading	End of loading
1	1	1	1	1	2	11	2	13
2	8	9	14	13	27	31	27	58
3								

(d) What is the waiting time for ship number 3? What is the total time the berth is idle, exclusive of the initial period at the start of the simulation?

3. A firm uses the following policy to control its inventory: whenever the stock on hand has been reduced through sales to 8 units, a replenishment of size 24 is placed. This replenishment arrives at the firm's premises in the morning of the third day after the order has been placed and becomes immediately available to meet customer demand. If the demand on a given day is larger than the stock on hand, then the amount short is lost, i.e., the customer goes elsewhere. The daily demand pattern is as follows:

Demand	0	1	2	3	4	5	6	7
Frequency	0.25	0.20	0.15	0.12	0.10	0.08	0.06	0.04

Simulate the behaviour of this system by hand for an interval of 30 days. Use a table format that has one row for each day and appropriate columns for the amount of stock on hand at the beginning of each day, the demand generated using the set of random numbers listed in exercise 2 above, the stock level at the end of the day, the amount of goods on order (stock replenishment orders are placed at the end of the day after sales have been processed), and the amount of lost sales. To generate the random demands, use the scheme described in Section 17.1 — in particular, the method demonstrated in Figure 17-1 (p. 487).

4. A product is assembled on a two-station assembly line. Station A assembles the first part (Part A) of the product, while Station B finishes the assembly of the product (Part B). Station A takes any time between 40 and 50 seconds to assemble one unit of Part A. The time is uniformly distributed. Station B takes on average 46 seconds to finish the assembly of one unit of Part B, with a standard deviation of 9 seconds. The distribution of the Part B assembly time is approximately normal. Station A starts assembling a new Part A immediately after having completed the previous unit. Any completed units are put on a counter within reach of the operator at Station B. Station B also starts a new assembly (Part B) after having completed the previous assembly, provided there are any Part A units ready (waiting) on the counter for completion at Station B. If no Part A units are available, then the operator at Station B is temporarily idle until the next Part A has been completed at Station A. Assume that the work day begins at 8:00 am and Station A starts the first Part A assembly. Station B starts work as soon as the first Part A has been placed on the counter.

   (a) Define the structure of this system, i.e., temporary and permanent entities and their attributes, the activities, and the various events. How would you define the state of the system?

   (b) Draw a combined life cycle diagram for the entities.

   (c) Set up a computer spreadsheet and simulate this system for 60 assemblies. It should show when each event occurs. Use a new row for each new assembly started. Round all times to the nearest second. Use the following approach for generating approximate normal random variates with a mean of 0 and a standard deviation of 1: generate 12 uniformly distributed uniform random variates and compute their average. (This needs to be repeated for each normal random variate.) You want to collect statistics for the length of time taken to complete the assembly of 60 complete items, as well as the fraction of time each of the two stations are idle during that time. Do not include the time at Station

B at the beginning of the work day when Station B is waiting for the first partially completed assembly to be released by Station A as idle time.

(d) (*Advanced*) Write a spreadsheet macro that allows you to repeat this simulation for 20 different runs, each one using a different set of random numbers. Compute the average of the statistics and a measure of the variation of the 20 runs.

5. An inner city service station has one pump and only space for two cars in total, i.e., the one being served and, at most, one waiting. Any potential customer seeing both spaces taken (i.e., two cars in the service station) will not enter and simply drives by to go to some other service station. These potential customers are thus lost to the system. Potential customers arrive at the service station at a rate of 10 per hour, or on average every 6 minutes. Given that each potential customer independently makes the decision to fill up or not, a negative exponential arrival distribution is a good assumption. The service takes, on average, 5 minutes. It is uniformly distributed over the range from 1 to 9 minutes. Service is on a first-come/first-served basis. The service station owner would like to determine the effect of the limited space available to serve customers — in particular, the average number of customers lost due to lack of space. On average, each customer buys about 25 litres of petrol on which the service station earns £3.75. The owner would also like to know a number of other performance measures that could be of interest or useful. Think carefully about which performance measures you want to observe.

   (a) Define the structure of the system, i.e., the temporary and permanent entities, the activities and the events. What would you use to describe the state of the system?

   (b) Draw a combined life cycle diagram for the entities.

   (c) Develop a computer spreadsheet and simulate this system for a total of 40 potential arrivals. Round all times to the nearest minute. It should enable you to collect/observe all performance measures of interest. List the formulas used for every cell in the row of your spreadsheet for the second arrival.

   (d) (*Advanced*) Write a spreadsheet macro that allows you to repeat this simulation for 10 different runs, each one using a different set of random numbers. Compute the average of the statistics and a measure of their variation for the 10 runs.

6. (*Advanced*) Consider a somewhat simplified computerized system for telephone horse race betting. The system has two lines. When a punter calls, the call is answered by a free line and the punter connected to the computer touch-tone betting system to enter the bet(s). If both lines are occupied, the call is lost. When a punter has completed entering the bet(s), the line becomes free again. During the hour just prior to a given race, calls arrive at a rate of 1 per minute. It is reasonable to assume that interarrival times have a negative exponential distribution. Assume that a punter takes anywhere from 20 to 120 seconds to enter the bet(s), i.e., the time is uniformly distributed.

   (a) Draw a combined life cycle diagram for all entities involved.

   (b) Develop a computer spreadsheet and simulate the arrival of 60 calls. Round all times to the nearest second. Collect statistics on the total amount of idle time of the two lines together, and the number of calls lost.

Further reading

Banks, J., Carson, J.S. and Sy, J.N. (1995) *Getting Started with GPSS/H*, 2nd edn, Wolverine Software Corporation, 4115 Annandale Road, Annandale, VA 22003-3910. The introductory manual for the GPSS/H package mentioned in Section 7.3. It includes a functioning version of the software, available at http://wolverinesoftware.com/.

Law, A.M. (2007) *Simulation Modeling and Analysis*, 4th edn, Boston: McGraw-Hill. A very good reference for details of data analysis, modelling strategy, and output analysis in simulation, authored by a leading practitioner.

Maani, K.E. and Cavana R.Y. (2007) *Systems Thinking, System Dynamics: Managing Change and Complexity*, Auckland: Pearson, An introduction to system dynamics with computer models, including the New Zealand Wine Industry planning model.

Pidd, M. (1998) *Computer Simulation in Management Science*, 4th edn, Chichester: Wiley. A readable, general introduction to simulation either using packages or general-purpose (Pascal, Basic) programs. Also includes a section on system dynamics modelling.

Robinson, S. (2004) *The Practice of Model Development and Use*, Chichester: Wiley. A very good study of both software and the often-neglected modelling aspects of simulation, concentrating on discrete-event simulation.

Sterman, J. (2000) *Systems Thinking and Modeling for a Complex World*, Boston: McGraw-Hill. System dynamics texts often concentrate on ecological or social systems. This book covers business and policy applications, along with excellent general sections on modelling and analysing complex systems.

Simul8 comes from Simul8 Corporation: www.Simul8.com.

ModelRisk comes from Vose Risk Consulting: www.vosesoftware.com.

ithink comes from isee Systems Inc.: www.iseesystems.com.

The INFORMS Simulation Society has links to various simulation resources on its website: http://www.informs.org/Community/Simulation-Society/.

A survey of simulation software can be found at http://www.orms-today.org/surveys/Simulation/Simulation.html.

18

Decision and risk analysis

Learning objectives

- Be able to structure a sequential decision problem involving conditional actions that depend on uncertain outcomes as a decision tree, and attach probabilities and numeric pay-offs to each branch.
- Be able to evaluate a decision tree with monetary pay-offs by backward induction and determine the best decision strategy.
- Be able to prepare a pay-off table for a two-stage sequential decision problem and determine the expected value of perfect information.
- Be able to determine the minimax strategy for a decision problem summarized as a pay-off table.
- Be able to assess whether a utility function exhibits a risk averse, risk neutral, or risk seeking form.
- Be able to use the five-point assessment procedure to derive an approximate graphical shape of a utility function.
- Be able to set up a spreadsheet form that captures a multi-stage sequential decision problem involving unconditional and conditional random events with known probabilities or probability distributions, use spreadsheet-based risk analysis software to generate frequency tables and risk profiles of the outcomes, and perform sensitivity analysis on critical inputs.

Introduction

Chapters 16 and 17 explore dynamic systems behaviours where uncertainty can be captured by theoretical or empirical distributions. System behaviour is affected by random events occurring individually at random points in time. We study the system's long-run behaviour. Its effectiveness can be judged on the basis of its average performance over a long period, or a large number of trials or experiments.

In contrast, this chapter studies situations where the uncertainty about future outcomes is confined to a single event or a relatively small sequence of events. The problems analysed are often unique situations, where the decision maker has only one chance to get it right, such as the introduction of a new product or embarking on a new, but risky venture. Uncertainty is often expressed in the form of subjective probabilities about future events. What the future holds in store is called the **state of the future** or the **state of nature**. The benefits and costs associated with the decision choices may be different for each possible state of the future. Furthermore, being one-off, each situation is 'played' only once. There is no long-run behaviour to be observed.

What are effective and insightful ways for modelling such situations? What criteria are suitable for finding the 'best' alternative course of action? This chapter attempts to give partial answers to these questions. They are part of the vast topic of **decision analysis** and of **risk analysis**. Our purpose for studying aspects of decision analysis is not to give you a thorough working knowledge of these tools but, rather, to let you gain further insights into systems modelling and decision making under uncertainty.

Although the focus of this chapter will be on unique and independent decision situations, there are some recurrent decision problems, which have the same basic structure. A fast food stall or cafeteria daily faces the problem of how much of each of various dishes to prepare in anticipation of the coming day's sales. Similarly, 6 to 12 months prior to the start of the new clothing season a fashion manufacturer has to decide what assortment, in terms of sizes and materials, to produce. Usually only a single run is made, so it is important to get it right the first time.

We first set the stage with a simple, but by no means trivial decision situation that captures the basic aspects of decision and risk analysis. The problem is borrowed from the fascinating book *Quick Analysis for Busy Decision Makers* by Behn and Vaupel (1982, Chapter 2). Sections 18.2 and 18.3 study a business situation, which involves risky monetary outcomes, and demonstrates the general approach of finding the 'best' solution and the kind of insights that can be gained from the analysis. We then explore approaches for dealing with situations where the monetary value of a risky outcome is not a true reflection of the intrinsic worth of an outcome, which leads us to discuss the use, meaning, and practical application of utility functions.

The mathematics of decision analysis becomes intractable when the interdependencies between random outcomes over time become more intricate and some outcomes may be governed by continuous probability distributions. Furthermore, the decision maker may not be willing to make a decision on the basis of expected outcomes alone, as is the case with decision analysis, but may want to know something about the risk profile of a venture. The last two sections of the chapter look into risk analysis — a tool specifically designed to do just that.

18.1 Setting up a decision problem

Ollerton Watt, a busy executive, must make one of the most important decisions of his life. It has nothing to do with his job. Olly suffers from angina pectoris — chest pains often caused by narrowing of the coronary arteries. This deprives the heart muscle of blood when the heart needs to pump harder in response to physical exertion, excitement, or stress. Medication prescribed to Olly relieved some of the symptoms, but was not successful in clearing the problem. Olly has just had a complete cardiac examination. His doctor now sets out the options available to him. He can continue with his medication, taking it easy, and suffer the occasional painful and frightening angina attack, or he can elect to have bypass surgery. This will almost surely be successful in relieving the problem completely. There is only a small chance that the pain is not totally eliminated. However, the doctor also informs him that, in view of his age and previous medical history, there is one chance in ten that he could die on the operating table — more than twice the average death rate for this type of surgery! The doctor also explains to him that there is currently little medical evidence suggesting that surgery increases the patient's life expectancy. Olly could live as long with angina pectoris as with surgery, provided he took it easy. Should he decide to have surgery or not?

Olly's problem is far from unique. There are millions of people all over the world facing similar decision problems. Not all of them involve life-and-death decisions. Many may simply involve other risky outcomes, such as whether or not to accept the job offer in a new city, or getting into a stable relationship with a partner, or getting into a venture with possibly large monetary gains and losses.

Structuring the decision problem

A **decision tree** lays out sequential problems of this sort in a schematic form by decomposing it into simple single stage components. It clearly highlights the chronological structure of the problem and its sequential, conditional logic. Figure 18-1 is a graphical representation of Olly's decision problem.

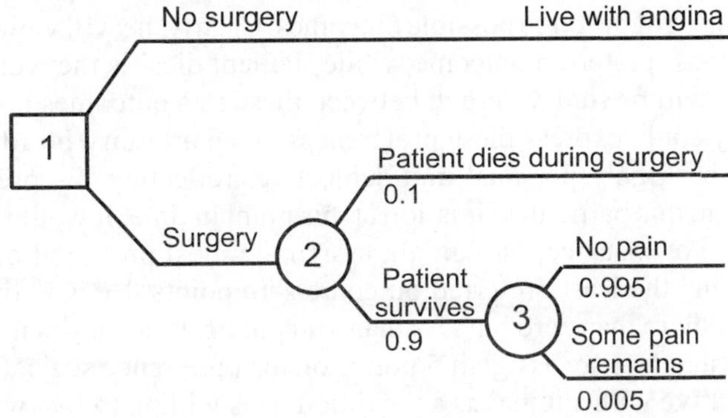

Figure 18-1 Decision tree for angina pectoris problem

This decision tree is read from left to right. It begins with a **decision node** — whether or not to undergo surgery — depicted as a square (labelled 1). The two branches leaving the square denote Olly's two decision choices 'Surgery' and 'No surgery'. The top branch 'No surgery' leads to the outcome 'Live with angina'. The bottom branch leads to a **chance node**, denoted by a circle (labelled 2). Each branch leaving the circle denotes one of the possible outcomes. In our example, there are two: 'Patient dies during surgery' and 'Patient survives'. The bottom branch 'Patient survives' leads to another chance node (labelled 3), also with two branches: 'No pain' and 'Some pain remains'. The 'Surgery' decision thus leads to one of three possible outcomes.

The branches leaving a chance node represent uncertain outcomes. We associate a probability (subjective or objective) with each outcome. These are shown below each branch. Since one of the outcomes must occur, the probabilities attached to the outcome branches originating at a given chance node add up to 1. For example, according to the surgeon, there is a 10% chance that Olly dies during surgery. Hence, there must be a 90% chance that he survives. So, we attach a probability of 0.1 to the top branch and a probability of 0.9 to the bottom branch. Similarly, Olly is told that if he survives the odds are 1 in 200 that 'Some pain remains'. Hence the odds for 'No pain' are 199 in 200. The probabilities attached to these two outcome branches are 0.995 and 0.005.

Evaluating the decision choices

We will initially ignore the small likelihood that, although Olly survives the surgery, some pain will remain. Surviving surgery is now assumed to mean 'surgery is successful'. With this small approximation, Olly faces a choice between a certain outcome of 'Live with angina' if he decides on 'No surgery', and an uncertain outcome if he decides on 'Surgery'. That uncertain outcome — either 'Surgery is successful' or 'Patient dies during surgery' — is equivalent to participating in the following gamble with Nature. An urn contains 90 white and 10 black balls. If Olly decides on 'Surgery', Nature draws one ball at random from the urn. A white ball means 'Surgery is successful', while a black ball means 'Patient dies during surgery'.

Whether or not Olly should choose 'No surgery' or 'Surgery' will depend on his assessment of the three possible outcomes. Clearly, he will view 'Surgery is successful' as the most preferred outcome, while 'Patient dies' is the worst outcome. 'Live with angina' will be somewhere in between these two outcomes in his preference ranking.

Olly could express these preferences on an arbitrary **point scale**. This point scale would be highly personal and subjective, reflecting his preference structure with respect to this particular situation at this point in time. It would be different for another person. For instance, Olly might assign the most preferred outcome 100 preference points and the least preferred outcome zero points. He would then assign 'Live with angina' more than zero but less than 100 points. If he judges it as only a little bit better than dying, he may assign it 5 points on his preference scale. On the other hand, if he views 'Live with angina' as a condition he is willing to live with, he may assign it 80 points.

A low preference point value for 'Live with angina' will push Olly towards 'Surgery' and accepting the gamble this option entails. A high point value will tip the scale towards the 'No surgery' option. For example, he might prefer 'Live with angina' to the gamble if he positions 'Live with angina' at 25 points, but prefer the gamble if it is only 10. As the point value decreases from 25 towards 10 his preference switches from 'Live with angina' to the gamble. Somewhere along his preference scale there is a **switch point** where he will be indifferent between the two options.

In the above discussion, we assumed that the probability of dying was given and known. An alternative way of looking at this problem is as follows. Assume that the proportions of white and black balls are not fixed yet. It is a fair guess that if the proportion of white balls is low, say only 50%, Olly, like most people, would opt for 'No surgery'. This choice may remain the same if the proportion of white balls increases to 70%. On the other hand, a very high proportion of, say, 95% would lead him to choose 'Surgery'. His choice would not change any more if the proportion were even increased to 99%. So, we see that as the proportion of white balls increases, there comes a critical level where Olly switches from the riskless 'No surgery' option to the risky 'Surgery' option. In our example, this critical level turns out to be higher than 70%, but less than 95%.

This critical level V is called the **switch probability** or **indifference probability**. If the proportion of white balls is just equal to V, then Olly would be indifferent between the two options. Neither is preferred over the other — he could let the decision be made by the toss of a coin. The two options are equivalent to each other. One could be substituted for the other. However, if the proportion of white balls is less than V, Olly prefers the riskless 'No surgery' option; if it is more than V he prefers the risky 'Surgery' option.

Viewed in this way, Olly's decision rule would be: choose 'No surgery' if the proportion of white balls is less than the indifference probability, choose 'Surgery' if it is more than the indifference probability, and flip a fair coin, with 'heads' meaning 'No surgery' and 'tails' meaning 'Surgery', if it is equal to the indifference probability. Finding this indifference probability is no simple matter. We will postpone this task to a later section.

The discussion in this section captures most of the conceptual features of decision analysis. It has given us some important insights. First, decision makers are able to rank final outcomes, even of a non-monetary nature, in order of their preference, from the least preferred outcome to the most preferred outcome. If the outcomes can be expressed in monetary terms, their values may well reflect the ranking order. In other instances, particularly highly risky situations, such as large financial gains or losses that could mean bankruptcy, or situations involving emotional, aesthetic, ethical, or environmental concerns, the decision maker may be willing to express the preferences along an arbitrary point scale. It is then possible to compare a riskless option with a risky option in terms of this scale.

Second, faced with three outcomes, A, B, and C, where A is preferred to B, and B is preferred to C, we can compare an (assumed) riskless option B to a risky option involving outcomes A and C in either of two ways:

1. We find the switch point at which the decision maker is indifferent between the riskless and the risky option. If the valuation of B is higher than the switch point, the riskless option B is preferred to the risky option, and vice versa.
2. Alternatively, we find the indifference probability for A at which the decision maker is indifferent between the riskless option B and the risky option involving A or C. If the best assessment for the probability for A is higher than the indifference probability, then the risky option is preferred to the riskless option and vice-versa, since $P(C) = 1 - P(A)$.

At the switch point or the indifference probability, the riskless option is equivalent to the risky option. The importance of this discovery is that it allows us to substitute a riskless option for a risky option. This property will be very useful when we compare risky options, as we shall in Section 18.5.

Activity

- Consider the original problem of Figure 18-1. The risky option 'Patient survives surgery' leads to either 'No pain' or 'Some pain remains'. How would you rank those? What point score would you assign to each?
- By substituting the certain outcome 'Surgery successful' for the risky option 'Patient survives surgery', we ignored the possibility that some pain remains. In our discussion on assigning point scores to outcomes in Section 18.1, how could this aspect have been taken into account? Would it affect the value of the switch probability between 'Patient dies' and 'Surgery successful and how?

18.2 A decision problem with monetary outcomes

Barry Low, the founder and major shareholder of FIRST US SOFTWARE (FUSS) has just been informed by his lawyer, Debbie Deft, that the Ying-Yang Computer Software House (YY) has informed her through their lawyer that YY plans to sue FUSS for copyright infringements by FUSS's EASY-OPT What-If Solver Release 2.1. YY claims damages of \$500,000 for loss of sales plus triple punitive penalties of \$1,500,000. Debbie Deft also tells Barry Low that YY's lawyer has hinted that YY would be willing to settle out of court by granting FUSS retroactively a flat-fee licence for using the software in contention for \$2,000,000. This would allow FUSS to continue selling Release 2.1. Barry Low estimates that the future revenue potential for Release 2.1 amounts to roughly \$3,000,000. If FUSS chose to defend the law suit and lost, these sales would also be lost. Debbie Deft estimates that the cost of defending the law suit will amount to \$600,000. If FUSS wins, YY will have to pay FUSS about \$500,000 of this. Similarly, if FUSS loses, it will have to pay YY an equal amount of costs.

Development of EASY-OPT Release 3.0 has just been started. With its completely new format, it will definitely not run any danger of infringing copyrights. Its development can be accelerated. This will allow Release 3.0 to be introduced four to eight months earlier than currently planned, provided its development starts within a month. The difficulty is that, without some preliminary analysis, no prediction can be made by how much. Such a preliminary analysis has a cost tag of $100,000. Accelerating the development will also increase the cost by $200,000 for a four-months-early release and $400,000 for an eight-months-early release. However, FUSS would recoup about $300,000 of the potential loss on abandoning Release 2.1 for every month of early introduction. Upon questioning Debbie Deft, Barry thinks that YY would be willing to accept an out-of-court settlement for $600,000 in compensation for past copyright infringements, if FUSS stopped marketing the Release 2.1 immediately. He also thinks that YY would be willing to accept a licence fee of $1,250,000 if Release 3.0 is introduced eight months earlier and $1,600,000 if it is introduced four months earlier.

Debbie stresses that Barry has at most five or six weeks available to make up his mind whether or not to accept an out of court settlement. Once YY has initiated the court case, there is little chance that they will still be interested in a deal.

There are two major uncertainties in this situation. What are FUSS's chances of successfully defending a court case? And, how much earlier can Release 3.0 be marketed if FUSS decides to accelerate its development? Debbie's subjective assessment is that FUSS has about a 70% chance of winning the case. Prior to a preliminary analysis, the EASY-OPT development project leader estimates that there is a 60% chance of accelerating completion of Release 3.0 by eight months and a 40% chance of accelerating it only by four months.

Setting up a decision tree

What is the sequence of decisions and uncertain events? Within five weeks, Barry has to make up his mind whether to abandon marketing Release 2.1 immediately, or accept a licence agreement with YY, or defend the case in court. Which of these decisions is 'best' may depend on whether or not Barry decides to accelerate the development of Release 3.0. Indeed, acceleration or no acceleration must be Barry's first decision. This is the decision node labelled 1 in the decision tree in Figure 18-2. While 'Do not accelerate' has no immediate cost, 'Accelerate' incurs an immediate cost of $100,000. This is shown as –$0.1 (in millions).

'Do not accelerate' leads to decision node 2. Since it is quite obvious that abandoning Release 2.1 without acceleration is a very unattractive option in comparison to taking out a 'Licence', there is little point in showing it as one of the decision alternatives. Hence, the two alternatives left are taking out a 'Licence' or going to 'Court'. The first one results in a licence fee of $2 million (shown as –$2.0), but will also generate revenues of $3 million. The second one incurs a cost of $0.6 million and leads to chance node four with branches 'Win' and 'Lose', with probabilities of 0.7 and 0.3, respectively. A 'Win' results in revenues of $3 million plus a refund of $0.5 in court costs, while 'Lose' means penalties and court costs paid to YY totalling $2.5 million. (Recall that costs are shown as negative numbers!)

'Accelerate' leads to chance node 3 with two branches: Release 3.0 is ready '4 months' earlier at an additional cost of $0.2 million with a probability of 0.4, and Release 3.0 is ready '8 months' earlier at an additional cost of $0.4 million with a probability of 0.6.

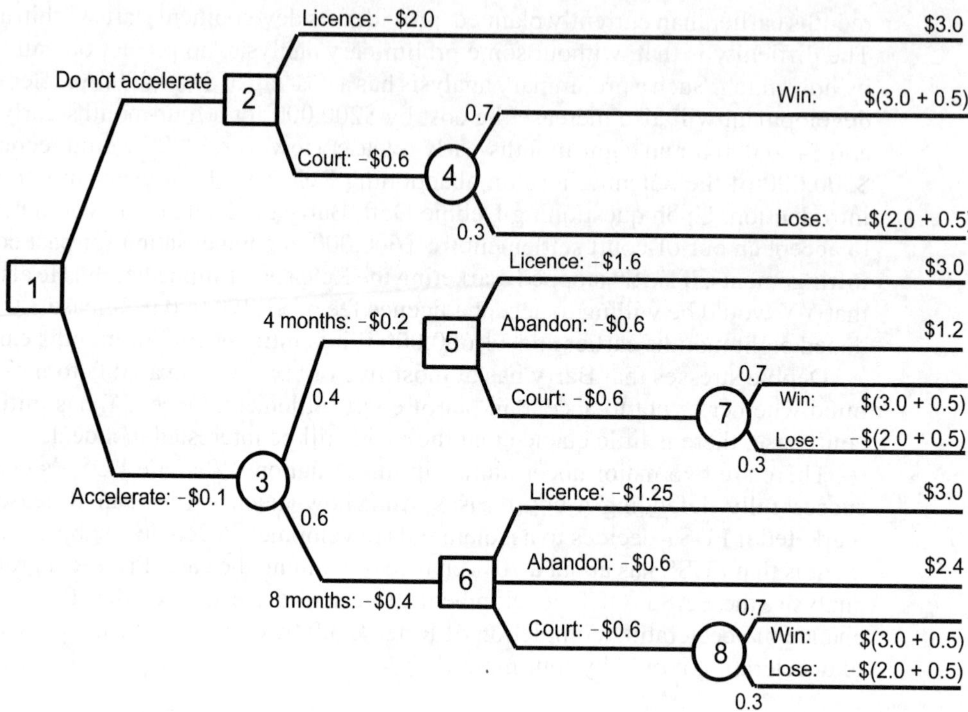

Figure 18-2 Decision tree for Barry Low's copyright infringement problem

Each of those branches leads to a new decision node, labelled 5 and 6, respectively. Both have the same three choices: take out a 'Licence', 'Abandon' Release 2.1 immediately, and go to 'Court'. Taking out a 'Licence' from node 5 has a cost of $1.6 million and will generate revenues from sales of $3.0 million. 'Abandon' causes costs of $0.6 million. With Release 3.0 ready '4 months' earlier, lost sales of $1.2 million can be recovered. Going to 'Court' has exactly the same structure as for the branch leaving decision node 2.

Activity

Verify the net cash flows and probabilities from chance node 3 on.

Evaluating the decision tree by backward induction

What is Barry's 'best' choice of decisions? Before we can answer this question, we need a criterion for 'best'. One criterion listed in Section 15.11 (p. 445) is to identify the decision or alternative course of action that **maximizes the expected monetary return**. For Barry, this is the expected value of net cash flow. But 'Wait!' you may interject. 'Does it make sense to base a decision for a unique non-repetitive situation on the concept of expected values?'

It can be shown that, under certain assumptions, choosing the action, which maximizes the expected value of the outcomes is a rationally consistent criterion. What the expected value criterion implies is that the decision maker is willing to 'play the average' even for one-off situations — the argument being that averaging over a string of unique decision situations is not necessarily different from averaging over recurrent decisions. However, this reasoning does not sit well with everybody. Section 18.4 considers other criteria for selecting the 'best' action.

For an expected value criterion, the first step in evaluating the decision tree is to find the cumulative net cash flow associated with each end point of the tree. This is the **pay-off** associated with the chain of actions and events leading to this end point. It is equal to the sum of the monetary outcomes attached to all branches on the path from the origin — node 1 — to each end point. For example, the top path in Figure 18-2 goes from node 1 through the branch 'Do not accelerate' to node 2 and continues to the branch labelled 'Licence'. The dollar amounts associated with these two branches are \$0 and (–\$2.0 + \$3.0) million, adding up to \$1.0 million.

Figure 18-3 reproduces the tree of Figure 18-2. Instead of showing the detailed cash amounts associated with each branch, it only lists the cumulative pay-off for each end point of the tree. So, the top end point shows \$1.0 million. The second end point consists of the path from node 1 to node 2 to node 4 and branch 'win', with cash amounts totalling \$2.9. Check the pay-offs associated with the remaining end points in Figure 18-3. For evaluating the tree, we only need these pay-offs.

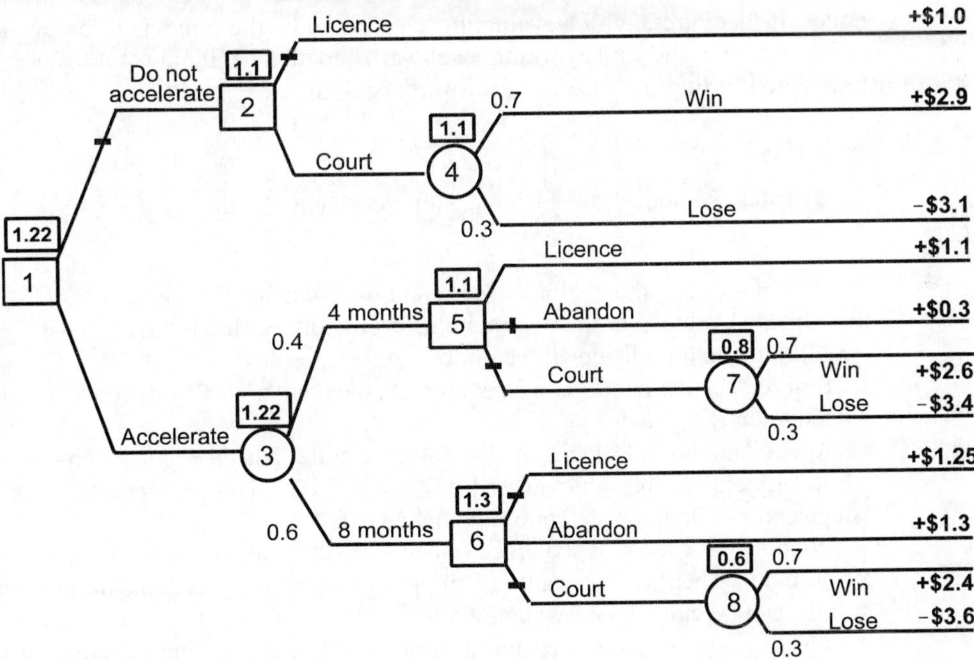

Figure 18-3 Evaluating the decision tree by backward induction

Using the expected value criterion, we find the best action by evaluating the nodes in the decision tree from right to left. Evaluating a chance node means computing the expected value of the outcomes associated with all branches originating at that chance node. Take node 8. It has two branches. The top branch has a pay-off of +\$2.4 with probability 0.7 and the bottom branch has a pay-off of –\$3.6 with probability 0.3. The expected value is equal to the sum of the products of the pay-offs and the corresponding probabilities. For node 8, this is (+\$2.4) × 0.7 + (–\$3.6) × 0.3) = \$0.6 million. We insert this result above chance node 8 (shown in the small rectangular box).

Evaluating a decision node means finding , which of the decision branches originating at that node has the highest monetary value. Consider decision node 6 in Figure 18-3. It has three decision branches. 'Licence' has a pay-off of \$1.25 million. 'Abandon' has a pay-off of \$1.3 million. We just computed the expected pay-off for 'Court' at node 8 as \$0.6. 'Abandon' has the highest value of \$1.3 million. This is the amount inserted in the rectangle above node 6. Hence, at decision node 6, the best action to take is to 'Abandon' Release 2.1 immediately and wait for Release 3.0 to become available. To signal that this is the best decision, the other two actions are blocked off (shown by the two cross-bars).

Note that we used the expected pay-off we computed for node 8 as an input into finding the expected pay-off for the 'Court' branch at node 6. In fact, if we had not already evaluated node 8, we would not have been able to determine the expected pay-off for 'Court' and, hence, evaluate node 6. Since we need the results of all successor nodes, if there are any, for evaluating a given node, the tree has to be evaluated by starting at the end and working backwards to the beginning — hence the term **backward induction** (also called 'rolling back the tree').

Activity

Verify that, for node 5, the best decision is 'Licence', with a value of \$1.1 million.

With nodes 5 and 6 evaluated, we can now evaluate chance node 3. This is again the expected value over the two branches from node 3, that is \$1.1 × 0.4 + \$1.3 × 0.6 = \$1.22, the amount listed above node 3.

Before decision node 1 can be evaluated, decision node 2 and, hence, chance node 4 need to be evaluated.

At decision node 1, decision 'Do not accelerate' has an expected pay-off of \$1.1, while 'Accelerate' has an expected pay-off of \$1.22. Hence, the best decision is to 'Accelerate'. 'Do not accelerate' is blocked off.

We now have the best sequence of decisions. It is to 'Accelerate' development of Release 3.0. Then, if the results of the preliminary analysis indicate that only four months can be gained, Barry should take out a 'Licence'. On the other hand, if eight months can be gained, then he should 'Abandon' Release 2.1 immediately. One of two possible final outcomes will occur: \$1.1 million with probability 0.4 or \$1.3 million with probability 0.6. The average of these two outcomes, weighted by their probabilities is \$1.22 million.

Only the first decision is firm. The second decision, taken either at node 5 or 6, is conditional on what happens at chance node 3. So, under uncertainty the best alternative course of action is not a single decision, but a sequence of conditional decisions. This is referred to as a **strategy**. We also do not know what the final outcome will be. All we have is a list of possible final outcomes. Their corresponding probabilities can be inferred from the path of branches that leads to each final outcome, as the product of the probabilities of each chance branch. In contrast, in deterministic situations the best course of action can be specified as a firm single decision or a firm sequence of decisions. We know exactly what will happen and what the final outcome will be.

Sensitivity analysis

Remember that much of the input to Barry's problem was based on educated guesses. Would YY really settle out of court for the amounts used on the decision tree under the various options of abandoning Release 2.1 right away? And what about the probability of winning the case, or of introducing Release 3.0 several months earlier than originally scheduled? Let us analyse what happens as the probability of winning, p, becomes larger than 0.7.

Verify that when the probability of winning increases to 0.72, 'Do not accelerate' also has an expected pay-off (at chance node 4) of $0.72 \times 2.9 + 0.28 \times (-3.1) = \$1.22$ million. (Note that an increase in p does not change the best choices at decision nodes 5 and 6.) So, as this probability increases beyond 0.72, the preferred sequence of decisions is 'Do not accelerate' at decision node 1, followed by go to 'Court' at decision node 2. These decisions are unconditional. However, the final outcome is still either \$2.9 million with probability $p > 0.72$, or –\$3.1 million with probability $1 - p < 1 - 0.72$. The best current strategy is, therefore, quite precariously poised on the probability of winning. A small increase in it will tilt the balance towards a different alternative course of action. If Barry is even a bit of a gambler, he may well decide to go to court regardless.

Activity

Assuming all data remain the same, except for the probabilities of accelerating the development by four or by eight months, will a change in these probabilities affect the optimal strategy? Why, or why not? (Hint: compare expected outcomes of 'Do not accelerate' with those of '4 months' and '8 months'.)

18.3 The expected value of perfect information

Debbie Deft suggests that Barry Low consult with a famous business tycoon, whose phenomenal success record, it is said, implies a perfect nose for predicting the future. As expected, this person does not come cheap. How much should Barry be willing to spend at the most for acquiring a 'perfect' prediction on which state of the future will become true? If Barry had such perfect knowledge, he could plan exactly what he has to do to get the best result for that future state. However, prior to receiving such **per-**

fect information Barry can only make contingency plans about which strategy is best for each possible future state. Then, knowing the probability for each future state, he can compute an expected pay-off associated with his contingency plans. Comparing the expected value of his contingency plans, based on receiving perfect information, with the expected value of the best strategy without it, he can then see how much better off he will be with perfect information.

The states of the future are given by the various combinations of the two types of events, i.e., the outcomes of the court case and the acceleration of Release 3.0. The four possible combinations of events are listed under the heading 'Joint state of nature' in Table 18-1. The probability of each of the combinations occurring is given by the product of the corresponding probabilities of each type of event. For example, based on the currently available (subjective) information about the future, the probability of the joint outcome 'Court case win' and '4 months gained by acceleration' is the equal to the probability of winning (0.7) times the probability of accelerating Release 3.0 by 4 months (0.4) which equals 0.28. Verify the remaining three joint probabilities, listed in the bottom row of Table 18-1. Note that the joint probabilities for the four combinations of outcomes must add up to 1, since one of them will occur.

The combinations of 'Do not accelerate' or 'Accelerate', and 'Get licence', or 'Abandon', or 'Go to court' yield six possible strategies. ('Do not accelerate' and 'Abandon' are listed here for completeness, but were left out of Figure 18-2.) The entries at the intersections of strategy rows and state of nature columns are the pay-offs (in $1 millions) — hence the name **pay-off table**. For some strategies, such as 'A: Do not accelerate and get licence', the monetary outcome does not depend on the state of nature. Hence, it is the same for all states. This also occurs for strategy B. For C, the outcome only depends on 'win' or 'lose', but not whether the firm accelerates or not. The probabilities for the combinations win/4 months and win/8 months acceleration add up to 0.7, as they should, and so on.

Table 18-1 Pay-off table for combined actions and joint states of nature

EVENT	JOINT STATE OF NATURE			
Months gained by acceleration	4	4	8	8
Court case outcome	Win	Lose	Win	Lose
STRATEGY				
A: Not accelerate and get licence	$1.0	$1.0	$1.0	$1.0
B: Not accelerate and abandon	–$0.6	–$0.6	–$0.6	–$0.6
C: Not accelerate and go to court	$2.9	–$3.1	$2.9	–$3.1
D: Accelerate and get licence	$1.1	$1.1	$1.25	$1.25
E: Accelerate and abandon	$0.3	$0.3	$1.3	$1.3
F: Accelerate and go to court	$2.6	–$3.4	$2.4	–$3.6
Best strategy for state of nature	C	D	C	E
Pay-off	$2.9	$1.1	$2.9	$1.3
Probability of state of nature	0.28	0.12	0.42	0.18

For each state of nature, the best strategy can now easily be identified. It is given by the strategy with the most favourable monetary outcome of its column of pay-offs, shown shaded. For example, for '4 months gained and court case win', the strategy with the highest pay-off is 'C: Do not accelerate and go to court'. Its pay-off is \$2.9. Check out the other three states.

So, prior to receiving this perfect information, the expected value of the pay-offs for the best strategies is given by the sum of the products of these pay-offs with their corresponding probabilities, or

$$\$2.9 \times 0.28 + \$1.1 \times 0.12 + \$2.9 \times 0.42 + \$1.3 \times 0.18 = \$2.396 \text{ million}$$

But remember that the actual pay-off will be one of the four pay-offs, not their weighted average.

Without getting any information about the true state of the future, all Barry can 'expect' for using his optimal strategy is a weighted average pay-off of \$1.22 million. Getting perfect information, the expected pay-off goes up to \$2.396 — a gain of \$1.176 million. This increase in the expected pay-off is called the **expected value of perfect information.** It represents the upper limit that Barry should be willing to pay to get perfect information. Naturally, the perfect predictor does not exist, and imperfect information is worth considerably less.

So, we get a new, albeit not unexpected, insight into decision making under uncertainty. It may pay to acquire better information about the true state of the future. Furthermore, we can put an upper limit on how much the decision maker should be willing to spend for better information.

The decision maker may be able to obtain better information through various means, such as market research and test markets (i.e., trying out the product on a small, reasonably self-contained market), additional scientific research to gain a better understanding of the underlying principles and causes, or by having recourse to expert advice, e.g., through a Delphi study (see Section 15.5).

18.4 Capturing the intrinsic worth of outcomes

In many situations, the intrinsic worth of an outcome can be adequately measured by its monetary outcome. This is particularly so for routine type decisions, where the monetary outcome falls well within the decision maker's normal range of experience. However, for strategic or unique decisions the monetary outcomes are usually outside this range. Furthermore, the outcomes may involve a high degree of uncertainty. In such instances, few decision makers are willing to 'play the averages'. Other factors, such as the decision maker's financial ability to absorb large losses, or the personal likes and dislikes of engaging in risky situations, may well influence how such uncertain outcomes are viewed.

You can easily check this out by imagining the following situation. It is the 20th of the month and you have £80 left for food and other necessities to carry you through the end of the month, when you get your next sustenance payment. You have no other means to get money. A 'friend' takes you to a party where you are invited to participate in a game. Upon payment of £60 you can flip a coin. If it falls heads, you win £360, tails, you get nothing. If you take the offer, you end up with either £380 or £20 in your pocket. The expected value of your financial situation is 0.5 × £380 + 0.5 × £20 or £200. Given that right now you have just barely enough to get through the remainder of the month, would you be willing to participate in this game? You might have to live on watery porridge for 10 days! If you are like most people, you would decline. The great majority of people in such a dire financial position would rather have £80 in their pocket for certain, than a 50:50 chance of £20 or £380. 'But then hope springs eternal!'

Similarly, most of us carry insurance on our cars and other property. Some of us buy lottery tickets or gamble at the races. Clearly, these decisions are not based on a simple criterion of maximizing the expected monetary outcome. How else could insurance companies or lottery and gambling operators cover their operating costs, their payouts on claims or wins, and at the same time also make handsome profits? Should we infer from this that decisions to buy insurance or to gamble are not made on a rational basis? Far from it! It simply means that factors other than simply monetary outcomes affect how decision makers view outcomes that involve a great degree of uncertainty and other possible thrills or anxieties.

Furthermore, for many decision situations the outcomes often cannot be measured in monetary terms alone without introducing rather questionable value judgements. This is clearly so for Olly's problem. What is the monetary equivalent for 'Living with angina' or 'Dying in surgery'? Similarly, for many decisions in the public sector the outcomes of various courses of action could be the preservation or the destruction of scenic beauty, wilderness areas, or other important sites of public interest, changes to public safety, public health, or equity, and so on. Assigning monetary values to such things is fraught with controversy.

Take the notorious proposals to build a third international airport for London in the late 1970s. The preferred option offered by the planners would have destroyed a Norman church built in the eleventh century. The analysts valued the church at its fire insurance value (to be ridiculed in the public hearings held)! In such cases, a simple criterion of maximizing expected monetary values will not do. Some of the approaches discussed in this and the next section may help. In other instances, decision criteria that explicitly consider multiple conflicting objectives may have to be invoked. Dealing with multiple conflicting objectives is the topic of the next chapter.

To measure the intrinsic worth or desirability of highly risky outcomes outside our normal range of experience, we have to go beyond monetary values. This section discusses two approaches, which are not based on 'playing the averages'. The next section gives a short introduction to **utility theory** — an approach that expresses the intrinsic worth of outcomes along a numeric scale that expresses the decision maker's worldview, her or his personal value judgement and attitude towards risk.

The minimax criterion

Consider again Barry Low's problem, but with an additional twist. Losing the court case would mean that Barry's firm goes bankrupt. Barry is not so much of a gambler to run that risk. Therefore, any action which runs this risk is excluded. In fact, Barry is even more of a risk averter. He really wants to play it safe. He wants to choose a decision strategy that guarantees him at least the best of the worst outcomes possible over all alternatives, no matter what happens. In this example, this means finding the strategy with the maximum lowest pay-off. This decision rule is known as the **minimax criterion** (derived from **mini**mizing the **max**imum loss; when dealing with benefits, it is also referred to as the **maxmin criterion**, derived from **max**imizing the **min**imum benefit).

Finding the minimax strategy could be done on the decision tree. However, since we have already summarized the information of the decision tree in the form of a pay-off table, it is simpler to work directly with this table. Table 18-2 reproduces those parts of Table 18-1 we need for this evaluation. We find for each strategy its worst outcome or pay-off (shown shaded) and enter it in the last column of the table. For example, for strategy 'C: Do not accelerate and go to court', the worst pay-off is –$3.1, obtained for two of the states of nature.

Table 18-2 Pay-off table for combined actions and joint states of nature

EVENT	JOINT STATE OF NATURE				Worst pay-off for action
Months gained by acceleration	4	4	8	8	
Court case outcome	Win	Lose	Win	Lose	
STRATEGY					
A: Do not accelerate and get licence	$1.0	$1.0	$1.0	$1.0	$1.0
B: Do not accelerate and abandon	–$0.6	–$0.6	–$0.6	–$0.6	–$0.6
C: Do not accelerate and go to court	$2.9	–$3.1	$2.9	–$3.1	–$3.1
D: Accelerate and get licence	$1.1	$1.1	$1.25	$1.25	$1.1
E: Accelerate and abandon	$0.3	$0.3	$1.3	$1.3	$0.3
F: Accelerate and go to court	$2.6	–$3.4	$2.4	–$3.6	–$3.6

The best of the worst outcomes or, in our case, the maximum of the minimum pay-offs, is $1.1 million, obtained for strategy 'D: Accelerate and get licence' — the cell with the heavy lines. It is the **minimax strategy**. Interestingly, it is the same as the one, which maximizes the expected pay-off. But this is by coincidence, rather than by rule.

Note that at no point did the probabilities of the various outcomes at chance nodes enter into the decision process. Even if the chance of losing the court case is, say, only one in a 1000, or 1 in a million for that matter, the minimax criterion will choose the same strategy. This seems to be rather unreasonable. In business, conservative decision makers of that sort end up accepting only riskless ventures. But most riskless ventures are also low-return. They miss most good opportunities. Their businesses stagnate and ultimately will be squeezed out by competitors who are willing to assume some reasonable risks.

On the other hand, if the decisions involve ethical, safety, or environmental aspects, such as life-and-death outcomes, or the possible destruction of unique ecological or scenic areas, a minimax approach may be more appropriate as a decision criterion than maximizing the expected pay-off.

A risk threshold approach

In this approach, any decision choices that carry a probability of certain specified adverse outcomes larger than some critical level are eliminated. The 'best' alternative course of action is then chosen from the remaining ones, based on some other criterion, such as maximizing the expected net cash flow.

Referring back to Figure 18-3 (p. 531), assume that Barry is not willing to run a risk of more than 1 in 5 of going bankrupt. Any strategy that has a probability of bankruptcy of more than 0.2 is eliminated. 'Do not accelerate' followed by 'Court' has a probability of 0.3 of bankruptcy. It is ruled out. This leaves only 'Licence' to follow 'Do not accelerate', at a net cash flow of \$1.0 million. 'Accelerate' can lead to bankruptcy for both chance outcomes at node 3 if 'Court' is the follow-on choice. However, using an expected value criterion, 'Court' is not a contender. The 'best' follow-on choices for 'Accelerate' have a zero chance of bankruptcy. Based on that reasoning, the expected net cash flow for 'Accelerate' is \$1.22 million (as for the original situation). This turns out also to be the best strategy under the constraint of a probability of bankruptcy of, at most, 0.2. It turns out to be a robust strategy.

Sensitivity analysis on this subjectively fixed limit for going bankrupt gives additional insight into how critical it is in terms of its effect on the expected outcome of the best decision strategy. If the expected value is highly sensitive to the constraint, this may lead the decision maker to review and possibly change it.

Rather than impose a constraint on the probability of a certain type of outcome, the constraint could be imposed on the maximum possible loss.

The risk threshold approach has considerable appeal. It formalizes the intuitive decision behaviour used by many decision makers, and produces more consistent and insightful decision making, particularly when coupled with systematic sensitivity analysis. Its major difficulty is that it may become quite intractable for complex decision situations with a large number of possible combinations of decision choices and random events.

The literature on decision analysis discusses several other criteria. Most are mainly of academic interest, with little or no practical use for real-life situations.

Activity

Consider the controversial development of a cancer treatment based on gene technology. Proponents claim that the chances of inadvertently creating dangerous genes are minuscule, while opponents argue that, if anything goes wrong, it could threaten life on earth as we know it. Discuss these stands in terms of various decision criteria.

Case study 18-1: Airport Château Hotel strategy

Michel d'Hôtelier, the Quebec-born manager of Vancouver's Airport Château, is in a serious quandary about his best business strategy for the coming year in the light of the potential slump of the British Columbia tourist industry. Airport Château, a boutique hotel, has 26 rooms, which offer a theoretical total of 9,490 room nights per year. In practice because of guest number fluctuations, it is unrealistic to expect that an occupancy of more than 9000 room nights can ever be achieved.

In the past four years, 5000 room nights were booked by Green Tours (GT), one of the hotel's prime customers, at a room fee per night of $300 and another 3500 by casual customers, the latter at a room rate of $420.

According to the latest industry forecasts, there is a 40% chance that tourist numbers will be down by 20% for the coming year. This will, however, only affect casual guests, since contracts with tour operators are set for a fixed number of room nights per year. However, in view of these forecasts, the CEO of Green Tours hinted at the recent tourist industry convention in Montreal that their agency might have to cancel the bookings for next year. Michel thinks that the CEO's message may have been a ploy to get reduced room rates. He guesses that there is still a 70% chance Green Tours will renew the current 5000-room-night contract if he reduces the room fee from $300 to $250 per night, but only a 40% chance if he does not.

Michel could also look for alternative tour operator business. Initial indications are that there is a 75% chance he should be able to negotiate a contract with a Japanese tour operator (JT) at a fee of $240 per room for either 3000 or 4000 room nights, with probabilities of 80% and 20%, respectively. This alternative will, however, incur a $60,000 promotion cost, regardless of whether the negotiations are successful or not.

By far the most reliable arrangement is in 'air-crew contracts', where an airline books a fixed number of rooms every night at a contractual sum for the entire year, regardless of whether the rooms are used or not. He has already been approached by Bamboo Airlines (B), which serves the lucrative tourist trade to South East Asia, with a contract proposal for eight rooms each night for a one-year period at a fixed contract sum of $500,000. This averages to about $171 per room per night, considerably less than the price paid by other guests, although it is guaranteed income.

The hotel capacity of 9000 room nights only allows for either the Green Tours or the Japanese tour contract, but not both. However, either of them can be combined with the airline contract, although this could reduce the number of casual guests that can be accommodated, which may not necessarily be a good outcome, given the much higher room rate obtained from them.

If no tour operator contract eventuates, the hotel's variable operating costs would decrease from $960,000 to $720,000 per year, mainly because of lower staff numbers and other incidental costs.

Can you help Michel d'Hôtelier to analyse his problem and recommend his best strategy for the coming year?

18.5 Utility analysis

In 1944, Von Neumann and Morgenstern, a mathematician and an economist, proposed an index designed to quantify the personal subjective worth of a risky outcome to a given decision maker, valid for a particular decision situation at a particular time. They called it **utility** — a rather unfortunate choice, given the earlier discredited usage made of this term in economic theory. For this reason, some authors prefer to label this approach **preference theory**, rather than utility theory.

A **utility function** expresses a decision maker's valuation of risky outcomes on a numerical scale. We already used this concept for capturing Olly's preference structure. The scale used is arbitrary; it could cover a range from 0 to 1, 0 to 100, or −1000 to +1000. The lower limit reflects the worth of the least desirable outcome, the higher limit the most desirable outcome, with all other outcomes in between.

Basic forms of utility functions

Figure 18-4 shows three different utility functions. The horizontal axis measures the monetary outcomes. The vertical scale shows the intrinsic worth of that outcome on the arbitrary scale from 0 to 1. The straight line in the middle represents the utility function for a person who is **risk neutral**. Such a person does not need to have recourse to a utility function — the 'best' decision will be the same as for maximizing expected monetary outcomes. Most of us are risk neutral when we deal with outcomes , which are clearly within our everyday range of experience. This may be a few dollars for an individual, but could be in the millions for large business corporations.

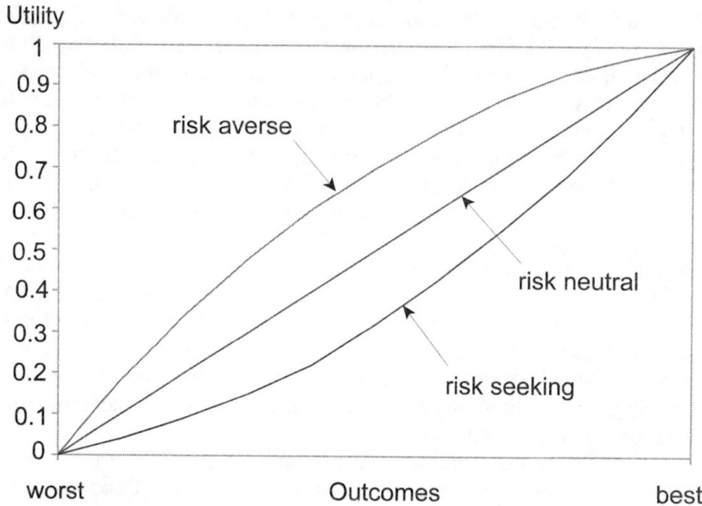

Figure 18-4 The three basic shapes of utility functions

The concave curve above the straight line is the general shape of the utility function for a decision maker who is **risk averse**. Consecutive equal increments in the monetary outcome result in smaller and smaller increments in utility. Most people exhibit some degree of risk aversion, particularly for large monetary gains or losses in their private and professional lives.

The convex curve below the straight line depicts the utility function for a person who is a **risk taker**. Doubling the monetary outcome increases the utility more than proportionately. Few people exhibit such a pattern for outcomes of important business and private decision choices. The exception is the pathological gambler. However, all of us occasionally are risk takers when we are looking for thrills or fun, such as gambling at the races, playing cards with high stakes or engaging in a dangerous sport.

So, we see that the same person may make some decisions from a risk-neutral position, others from a risk-averse position, and a few from a risk-seeking position. Each position is perfectly rational within its proper context and consistent with the person's worldview.

A five-point assessment procedure

Recall the insights we gained from Olly's problem situation. We concluded that, given a risky option with outcomes A or C, we can construct an equivalent riskless option with outcome B, where A is preferred to B , which is preferred to C, such that the decision maker is indifferent between choosing the risky or the riskless option. The equivalent riskless option can be constructed by either adjusting the value of B or by adjusting the probabilities of the risky option. Indifference between the two options implies that their intrinsic worth is the same. These surprisingly simple ideas form the basis for finding the utility function for a given decision situation.

We now demonstrate the procedure with Barry's problem. We start by assigning the worst outcome an intrinsic value or a utility of zero, and the best outcome a utility of 1. The choice of these values is arbitrary. It will not affect the relative ranking of the various decision strategies open to Barry. In Barry's case, the worst outcome is –\$3.6 million (i.e., a loss of \$3.6 million) and the best outcome a gain of \$2.9 million.

We now offer Barry a choice of two options: (1) a 50-50 gamble involving the best and the worst outcomes, and (2) a riskless option involving a net cash flow somewhere in between the worst and the best outcomes. The technical term for the gamble is **reference lottery**. We could start out with a cash flow exactly half-way, i.e., –\$0.35 million. (Keep in mind that negative outcomes represent losses!) Knowing that Barry is risk averse, we expect that he will prefer the sure pay-off of –\$0.35 million to the gamble. This is indeed the case. So, we know that his utility for –\$0.35 million is higher than the utility of the gamble. We now lower the monetary value of the riskless option. Say, we reduce it to –\$2.0 million. We again ask him to rank the original gamble and the sure outcome of –\$2.0 million. He now says that he prefers the gamble. This implies that his utility for –\$2.0 is lower than the utility of the gamble. Our next try is a value between –\$0.35 and –\$2.0 million. We continue presenting Barry with a choice of the original gamble and a sure outcome of X dollars, increasing the value of X if he prefers the gamble and decreasing it if he prefers X. After a few more trials, he finally settles on a value of –\$1.5 million, for which he is indifferent between the gamble and the riskless outcome. Indifference between the original gamble and the sure thing of –\$1.5 implies that these two options have the same intrinsic worth, or the same utility. But we know the utility of the gamble. It is equal to the expected utility of the outcome of the gamble. For a 50-50 gamble, this is $0.5 \times 1 + 0.5 \times 0$, where 1 is the arbitrary utility value assigned to the best outcome, and 0 the value assigned to the worst. So, the utilities of the gamble and of the riskless outcome of –\$1.5 million are both 0.5.

We now repeat this procedure a second and third time. But instead of choosing a 50-50 reference lottery involving the worst and best outcomes, we replace either the worst outcome or the best outcome with the value –\$1.5 million just found. So the second reference lottery is given by a 50-50 chance of –\$1.5 and \$2.9 million. Again, we can easily compute the expected utility of this reference lottery as $0.5 \times 1 + 0.5 \times 0.5$ or 0.75. After a number of trials, Barry agrees on an equivalent riskless option of \$0.4 million. Hence, an outcome of \$0.4 million must have a utility of 0.75, the same as the second reference lottery. For the third round, we set the reference lottery to a 50:50 chance of –\$3.6 and –\$1.5. Verify that the expected utility of this reference lottery is 0.25. After a few more trials, Barry settles on an equivalent riskless option of –$2.8 million. Hence, –$2.8 must have a utility of 0.25.

We now have determined the utility of five outcomes in the range from the worst to the best outcome for this particular decision situation under uncertainty. They are depicted in Figure 18-5 by the solid squares. Fitting a smooth curve through these five points yields a good approximation to Barry's utility function for this problem. As expected, Barry is clearly risk averse. His utility function is everywhere above the straight line representing a risk neutral utility function.

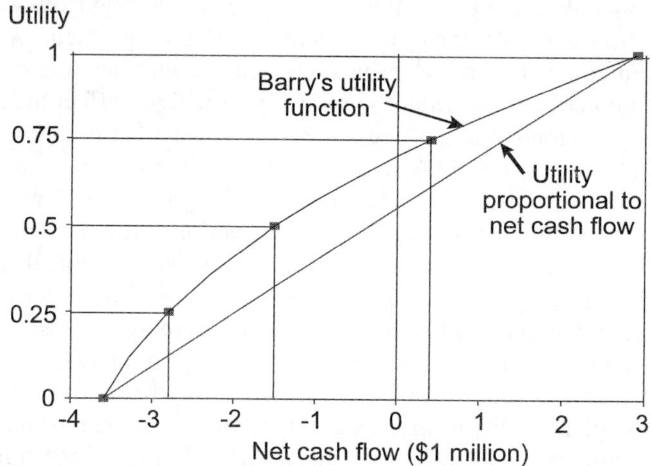

Figure 18-5 Barry Low's utility function

Activity

Put yourself into each of the following two situations and develop your corresponding utility function, using the five-point assessment procedure. Plot the results and draw an approximate curve through the points.

- You worked hard to accumulate savings of £3,000 that will allow you to complete the last year of your degree only needing to work weekends and assured to get good average grades. You get an invitation from a reputable stock broker to participate in a risky venture that, if it pays off, would yield £10,000 — no need to work and, hence, have a good chance of getting those important top grades. But if it goes wrong, you lose all your savings, opening up the possibility of failing some courses and needing a further miserable year to complete the degree.
- Having some £20 spare cash, you go to the races for an afternoon of fun. Your fancy is caught by a particular horse , which offers rather long odds of £26 for every pound placed on it. So, if you put your entire £20 on a win, you will make £500 net for a win, but lose £20 for a loss.

Finding the best decision using utility functions

If the full worth of an outcome can be measured on a monetary scale, the best decision strategy is based on an expected monetary value criterion. If the intrinsic worth of outcomes is measured by utilities, it can again be shown that the best strategy is the one that **maximizes expected utility**. We simply replace the net cash flows at all end points in the decision tree by the corresponding utility values, and then proceed to evaluate the tree by backward induction as before. I suggest that you insert into Figure 18-3 the utility values corresponding to all end-point net cash flows in Figure 18-5, and evaluate all nodes again. For Barry's utility function, the overall best strategy remains the same. (However, the best action at the blocked-off node 2 switches from 'Court' to 'Licence'.)

Some reflections on utility measures

It is important to stress that the utility measures obtained in this manner not only reflect a decision maker's valuation of outcomes, but also the attitude towards risk. Therefore, these utility functions are not valid for decisions that do not involve uncertainty. Furthermore, they are valid for the particular situation for which they were assessed at a particular point in time. Each new situation needs to be assessed anew. Furthermore, a decision maker's attitude towards risk may change over time. Even facing the same type of situation at some later time, the utility function may need to be reassessed.

The procedure can also be easily adapted to situations that do not involve monetary outcomes, such as is the case in Olly's problem. In fact, there have been serious efforts made since the early 1980s to introduce utility-type concepts into decision situations in the health and medical fields.

As we have seen, the method for assessing approximate utility functions is surprisingly simple. Increased accuracy for drawing the curve can easily be obtained by finding equivalent riskless options for additional utility values between the ones assessed in the five-point procedure. It may also be possible to fit algebraic functions to the points found.

So, given the simplicity of the procedure, why have utility functions largely remained an academic curiosity, and this in spite of the fact that this topic has been part of the curriculum of most college and university business courses since the early 1960s? There are a number of reasons. Although the procedure is simple, most decision makers find it difficult to think in terms of reference lotteries and equivalent riskless options. Hence, they are reluctant to be pinned down to definite answers. Their answers may not be consistent, requiring a delicate process of re-assessment. In fact, it needs a fairly skilful analyst to get results , which the decision maker feels truly reflect her or his preference structure for the problem situation in question. Up to now, few real-life applications outside academic institutions have been reported.

Research by McCord and de Neufville (1986, pp. 56–60) and Delquié (1993, pp. 1382–95) indicates that the utility functions derived may differ depending on the exact sequence and form of assessments made, the framing of the assessment, as well as other unexplained factors. Hence, this casts serious doubts on their validity and reliability.

However, even if the utility functions derived are never explicitly used in finding the 'best' decision strategy, the process of assessing such utility functions will enhance the decision maker's awareness of her or his preference structure, and thereby lead to better and more informed decision making.

18.6 Risk analysis — basic concepts

(Sections 18.6 and 18.7 require basic knowledge of simulation concepts, in particular, the generation and use of random variates in Section 17.1, and the concept of Monte Carlo simulation in Section 17.5. Similarly, they assume familiarity with the discounting of cash flows over time (Section 10.1), and the associated spreadsheet function in Section 10.5.)

For investment decisions, the exact amounts of future cash flows are usually not known with certainty, particularly on the revenue side. They are random variables. Conventional methods of investment evaluation approximate these random cash flows by their expected values or other conservative estimates. Similarly, the cost and revenue figures attached to some branches of decision trees may also be random variables, again substituted by expected values. Furthermore, decision trees suffer from the need to restrict any chance events to only a few discrete outcomes, or else the tree explodes in size and becomes unwieldy and difficult to use.

Backward induction, or rolling back the tree, eliminates all but a few end points that are possible pay-offs of the best strategy. For instance, in Barry Low's problem, the best strategy results in an outcome either of $1.1 million (accelerate/4 months/ licence) with probability 0.4, or $1.3 million (accelerate/8 months/ abandon) with probability 0.6. In reality, acceleration may result in a reduction of development time ranging anywhere from 3 to 10 months, each with a different development costs. Similarly, the cost of the preliminary analysis is hardly $100,000 exactly, but could be between a low of $50,000 to a high of $200,000; the guess as to the size of the licence fee that YY is willing to accept may be inaccurate. It is a random variable, and so are the costs of defending the law suit, or the revenues generated from sales under the various conditions. Most are continuous variables. They are not restricted to a few values. The decision tree reduced all this myriad of possible outcomes to just two numbers: 1.1 and 1.3 million.

Faced with risky situations, few decision makers will be satisfied with such scant information. They would want to see a better profile of the variability of outcomes associated with a given strategy. They would want to get answers to such questions as: What is the probability that the strategy threatens the survival of the firm? What is the probability that the monetary outcome is less than the break-even point? and so on.

To answer such questions about the risk of a venture, what is needed is a probability distribution over the possible range of outcomes. Except for the simplest situations, there is no analytical way to determine the probability distribution of the final outcome if some of the intermediate chance events are, in turn, conditional continuous random variables. Risk analysis is an attempt to find an empirical approximation based on the idea of Monte Carlo simulation.

Risk analysis repeatedly simulates the sequence of unconditional and conditional random outcomes that result from a given decision strategy and records their effect on various performance measures, such as the project's cumulative cash flow and its profitability. For investment ventures that span several years, the measures may well be expressed as net present values (*NPVs*). The results over all these simulations are then captured by frequency tables and histograms.

Repeating this process for various possible good strategies, and performing sensitivity analysis on some of the more 'uncertain' aspects, will provide the decision maker with the insight as to the risk profile of such ventures.

Commercial software, such as @RISK, Crystal Ball, or ModelRisk considerably simplifies performing risk analysis. ModelRisk is used in the next section for assessing the risk profile of an investment in a new ski-field.

18.7 Risk analysis for a ski-field development

Situation summary and narrow system of interest

Italia Neve is considering launching a new ski-field in a north-facing valley on Mount Etna, adjacent to a rival facility. Based on a comprehensive investigation for the development design, it has accumulated information about:

- construction costs for each of three years;
- operating costs for various patronage levels;
- effect of pricing structure on market share;
- number of skiable days in the region based on records over the past 20 years for the neighbouring ski-field;
- future levels for the region's skiing market over time.

All of these aspects involve considerable uncertainty. The values they will assume in any given year are random variables. Furthermore, they are affected to various degrees by three other factors. The first is the general economic conditions affecting the main customer catchment area, in this particular instance, a major metropolitan region within driving distance. An economic slump may reduce the patronage by up to half. The second is the fact that the area is on the slopes of a mountain , which over the last 100 years has shown regular volcanic activity. Just a few years prior, a major eruption necessitated the temporary closure of the neighbouring ski-field, thereby ruining the better part of the ski season for that year. A conservative estimate is that patronage will be reduced by 40% in any year an eruption occurs. Finally, the amount of natural snow fall, the average temperature, and the frequency of warm sirocco winds during the skiing season — all three captured by the catch-all term 'weather conditions' — can only partially be 'corrected' by artificial snow-making facilities and, hence, affect the number of skiable days and patronage for that year.

The firm would like to get a better feel for the economic viability of this project, in particular the financial risks, both in terms of profitability and the cash flow profiles over time. The latter could lead to liquidity problems even if the project has a satisfactory rate of return on investment. Risk analysis is the ideal tool for this. We will arbitrarily select a planning horizon of 10 years.

The first step is to get a clearer picture of the narrow system of interest S. Based on S we can then build a quantitative model, using the spreadsheet technology and ModelRisk as the mathematical modelling system M, which will allow us to explore the solution space. An influence diagram seems the ideal vehicle for defining S. This is done in Figure 18-6.

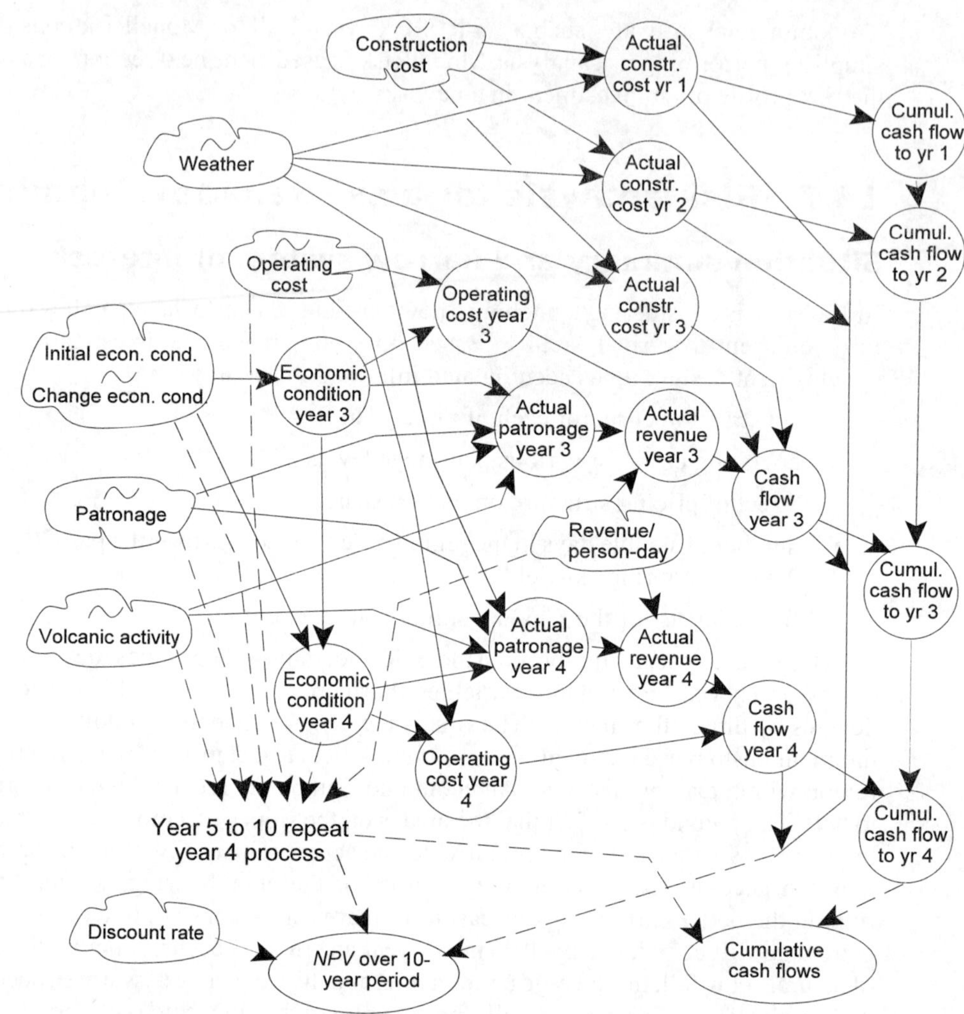

Figure 18-6 Influence diagram for ski-field project

Several inputs are random variables, depicted as input clouds with a tilde (~) above the name. The actual variate values generated are system variables, depicted by circles.

Construction occurs in the first three years. Its 'Actual cost' — generated from the assumed probability distribution for 'Construction cost' — is affected by the overall 'Weather' conditions — another random input. In year 3, the field begins partial operations. The 'Actual operating cost' is also affected by the general 'Economic conditions'. The latter may change from year to year. An economic slump means less patronage, hence fewer staff hired. 'Actual patronage' is affected by the 'Weather', by 'Volcanic activity', and by the general 'Economic conditions'. It affects 'Actual revenue'. The various cash flows of year 3 produce the 'Total cash flow' in year 3, which added to the 'Cumulative cash flow' to the end of year 2 results in the 'Cumulative cash flow' to the end of year 3. The year 3 pattern for the operating costs and patronage, as well as the revenue flows, is then repeated for year 4 and on to 10, as indicated by the broken arrows.

Spreadsheet implementation

To formulate a spreadsheet model, we need to specify probability distributions for each of the random aspects. The construction costs are assumed to follow a normal distribution with means and standard deviations entered as input into the top portion of the spreadsheet in Table 18-3 on page 548, cells C5 to E6. For example, costs in year 1 have a mean of €4.1 million and a standard deviation of €0.2 million.

Based on the advice received from meteorologists, the effects of the weather conditions in each year can be approximated by a triangular (or triangle) distribution, as in Figure 18-7. It generates a weather factor between 0.9 and 1.1, with the majority falling around 1, as indicated by its peak. Multiplying these factors by the patronage produces the desired effect. The distribution parameters are listed in cells J4 to L4.

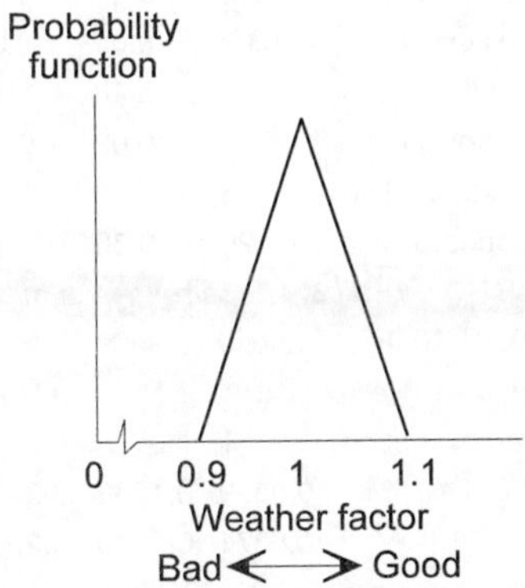

Figure 18-7 Triangular distribution

Engineering estimates indicate that bad weather will increase the construction cost by up to 11%, while good weather will decrease it by at most 9%. Again, we can get the desired effect, but this time by dividing the construction cost by the weather factor.

Our volcanologist adviser predicts that the chance of an eruption, serious enough to disrupt operations, in any year is about 5% (input cell L5). During a year of volcanic eruptions, patronage is assumed to be reduced to 60% of a normal year (input cell L6).

Economics consultants guess that a change in the general economic conditions occurs, on average, in three out of ten years. In each year there is, therefore, a 30% probability that the economic conditions change, either from 'Good' to 'Bad' or vice-versa (input cell L2), while there is a 70% chance of no change.

'Bad' economic conditions mean that operating costs are only 80% (input cell L3) of those under 'Good' conditions (input rows 12 and 13). To reflect the impact of the economic conditions on patronage, we use a different normal distribution for each case: input rows 8 and 9 for 'Good', 10 and 11 for 'Bad'. These are guesstimates, made by a committee of top staff and advisers.

Even for this cut-down problem, we needed to specify 30 probability distributions, as well as guesstimates for several other uncertain factors. There is no doubt that, for any real life risk analysis, assembling the needed information about all uncertain aspects, for many of which little hard data may be available, easily escalates into a massive data collection and data fitting exercise.

Table 18-3 Risk analysis for ski-field investment (single run)

	A	B	C	D	E	F	G	H	I	J	K	L
1	**SKI-FIELD DATA:** *(monetary outcomes in millions of euros)*						Discount rate					0.12
2	Current economic conditions			GOOD			P(economic conditions change)					0.30
3	Revenue per skier-day €			78.00			Cost reduction					0.80
4	Predicted construction		Year 1	Year 2	Year 3		Weather triangular dist.			0.9	1	1.10
5	Average cost €1 million		4.1	5.2	1.6		P(volcanic eruption)					0.05
6	Standard deviation		0.2	0.4	0.3		Reduced patronage in volcanic eruption					0.60
7	Year		1	2	3	4	5	6	7	8	9	10
8	Good patronage:	average			0.10	0.20	0.30	0.33	0.35	0.36	0.37	0.38
9	(million skier-days)	standard deviation			0.02	0.05	0.08	0.06	0.06	0.06	0.06	0.06
10	Bad patronage:	average			0.05	0.10	0.20	0.22	0.23	0.24	0.25	0.25
11	(million skier-days)	standard deviation			0.01	0.02	0.05	0.05	0.05	0.05	0.05	0.05
12	Nominal operating cost: average €1 mill.				8	12	16	17	17	17	17	17
13			standard		0.20	0.30	0.40	0.40	0.40	0.40	0.40	0.40
14	**SIMULATION OF STOCHASTIC EVENTS:** *(patronage in million skier-days)*											
15	Weather factor		1.0391	0.9794	1.0019	0.9909	0.9845	0.9799	0.9664	1.0440	1.0050	0.9643
16	Volcanic eruption		No	No	No	No	No	No	No	No	No	No
17	Patronage multiplier for volcanic eruptions				1	1	1	1	1	1	1	1
18	Unadjusted good patronage				0.0859	0.1938	0.3447	0.2498	0.3575	0.4292	0.5022	0.2735
19	Unadjusted bad patronage				0.0371	0.1116	0.2911	0.1962	0.3157	0.2649	0.3145	0.2875
20	Change in econ. cond.		No	No	No	No	Yes	Yes	No	Yes	Yes	Yes
21	Economic conditions		Good	Good	Good	Good	Bad	Good	Good	Bad	Good	Bad
22	Actual patronage				0.0861	0.1920	0.2865	0.2448	0.3455	0.2765	0.5047	0.2772
23	**CASH FLOWS:** *(€1 million))*											
24	Actual construction cost		3.850	5.097	2.194							
25	Actual operating cost				7.793	12.090	12.756	17.200	17.484	13.393	17.102	13.013
26	Actual revenue				6.712	14.975	22.350	19.092	26.95	21.568	39.365	21.620
27	Net cash flow		-3.850	-5.097	-3.275	2.885	9.594	1.892	9.466	8.175	22.263	8.607
28	Cumulative cash flow		-3.850	-8.947	-12.22	-9.337	0.257	2.150	11.615	19.79	42.053	50.660
29									***NPV* over planning horizon**			16.787

The last two parts of Table 18-3 show one simulated realization of the project over all ten years. It follows the sequence of events depicted in the influence diagram. Row 15 generates the weather factor, row 16 volcanic eruptions (yes or no), while row 17 shows the corresponding multiplier on patronage (1 for no, 0.6 for yes). Rows 18 and 19 are the normal random variates for unadjusted patronage for both good and bad economic conditions, based on the input rows 8 to 11. Although only one of the two entries will ever be used in any given year, calculating both at this point simplifies the formulas for actual patronage in row 22. Row 20 finds whether a change in economic conditions occurred or not. Its effect is reflected in row 21. The first change occurs in year 5. Hence, the economic conditions in years 1 to 4 carry forward the initial conditions 'Good' (input cell D2), and only changes to 'Bad' in year 5. The patronage (row 22) is calculated by multiplying the product of the weather factor (row 15) and the volcanic eruption multiplier (row 17) by the entry in row 18 if the corresponding cell in row 21 shows 'Good', or the entry in row 19 if it shows 'Bad'.

The bottom section calculates the resulting cash flows. The construction costs in cells C24 to E24 are the ratios of the normal random variates generated from the input data cells C5 to E6 and the weather factors in row 15. Operating costs are equal to the random variates generated from rows 12 and 13, reduced to 80% (input cell L3) if the economic conditions are 'Bad'. Finally, the revenues (row 26) are the product of the unit revenue per skier-day (cell D3) and the patronage in row 22. The net cash flow in each year (row 27) is equal to revenue less construction cost and operating cost. The row 28 entries are the cumulative sums of row 27, while the *NPV* (cell L29) is the sum of the discounted net cash flows, using the discount rate in cell L1.

Table 18-4 Result of 1000 simulations for ski-field project

Output name	*NPV* (millions €)	Cum. cash 5 years	Cum. cash 7 years	Cum. cash 10 years
Average	7.890	-7.076	5.284	30.067
Std Dev	7.6256	7.974	11.609	16.274
Std Err	0.241	0.252	0.367	0.5146
Max	31.120	23.73	40.116	77.258
Min	-14.440	-25.91	-28.145	-15.778
Percentiles				
5%	-4.436	-18.95	-12.454	3.868
10%	-1.647	-16.84	-9.687	9.212
15%	0.295	-14.870	-6.600	13.383
20%	1.272	-13.961	-4.409	15.981
25%	2.464	-12.786	-2.276	19.004
30%	3.494	-11.864	-0.967	21.125
35%	4.624	-10.836	0.491	23.300
40%	5.907	-9.856	1.711	25.557
45%	6.737	-8.660	2.931	27.914
50%	7.671	-7.800	4.569	29.836
55%	8.500	-6.786	6.028	31.221
60%	9.669	-5.563	7.534	33.675
65%	10.778	-4.734	9.620	36.279
70%	11.648	-3.304	10.87	38.386
75%	12.872	-1.783	12.655	41.085
80%	14.154	-0.158	14.740	43.709
85%	15.758	1.482	17.169	46.947
90%	17.884	3.913	21.070	51.952
95%	21.182	7.642	25.071	57.948
100%	31.120	23.733	40.116	77.258

This particular simulation results in a healthy €16.8 million *NPV* over the chosen 10-year period. It recovers the initial investment by the end of year 5. However, it would be foolhardy to make a decision as to the desirability of such a risky project on one single simulation run. Usually, several hundred or thousands of runs are made and the results combined to get useful and reliable results.

18.8 Results of risk analysis for ski-field

To get risk profiles for the project, we ran the simulation 1000 times. Risk analysis software automatically produces frequency tables and histograms. The top portion of the printout in Table 18-4 on page 549 shows that the average *NPV* is close to €8 million. What is, however, rather unexpected is that the standard deviation is almost equally large. The bottom portion reveals that there is almost a 15% probability that the *NPV* is negative — a sizeable risk. There is little chance of recovering the construction costs within the first five years and, even by the end of seven years, it is still more than 35% likely that not all funds have been recovered. What is also alarming is that the worst case scenario may end up with a net loss of more than €14 million.

A second run of 1000 simulations, using different random variates, yielded very similar overall results.

Since the average *NPV* of €7.8904 million is larger than the mode of 7.6708 (the 50% percentile), this means that distribution is slightly skewed to the left. Its right tail, extending to 31.12, is longer than its left tail, going to €–14.44 million.

Figure 18-8 shows the graph for the risk profile of the *NPV*, while Figure 18-9 maps the profiles for the cumulative cash flows after 5, 7 and 10 years.

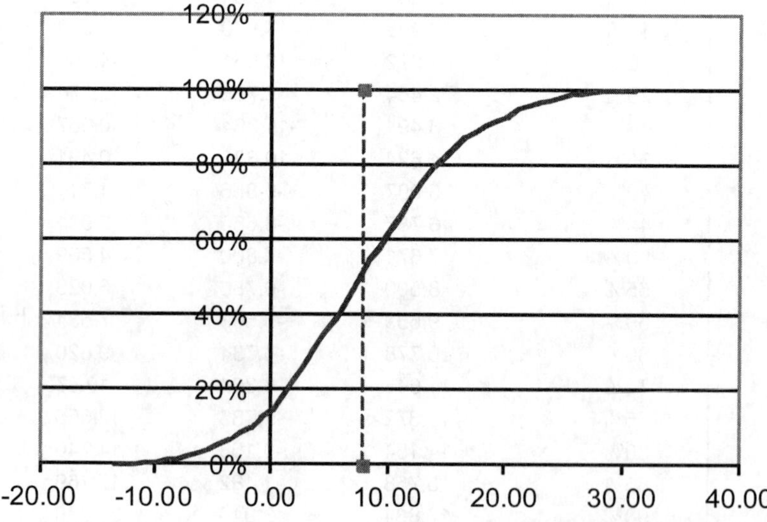

Figure 18-8 Risk profile of *NPV* (€1 million) over a ten-year horizon

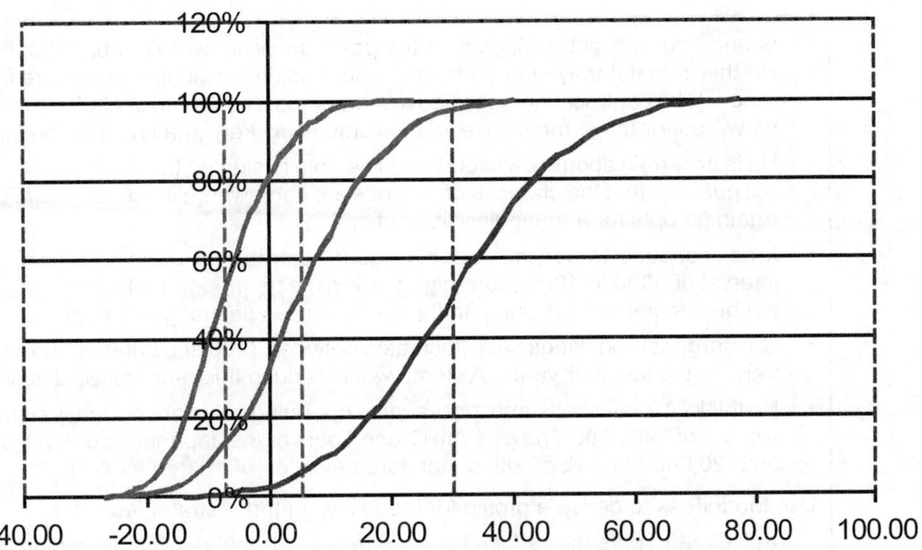

Figure 18-9 Cumulative cash flows (€1 million) Risk profile after 5, 7, 10 years

Properly used, risk analysis is a powerful tool for quantifying the risk involved in a venture. It provides valuable insights that cannot be gleaned from decision trees. However, it is important to realize that the actual outcome is a single point in the range of possible outcomes, e.g., €16.8 million as for the run in Table 18-3. Potentially, it could even fall outside the range produced by the risk analysis. Furthermore, the reliability of the results is only as good as the reliability of the inputs and, in particular, how well the various uncertainties have been captured by the probability distributions used. For this reason, it is important to do extensive sensitivity analysis. For our example, it is crucial to explore what happens to the risk profiles for:

(a) different levels of reduction in patronage because of volcanic eruptions;

(b) different unit revenues per skier-day; and

(c) wider ranges of the distribution for weather conditions (e.g., 0.8 to 1.2).

Sensitivity analysis is greatly facilitated by commercial software. Systematic exploration of the response to changes in the various inputs will reveal , which ones are critical and need to be assessed with extra care. This will allow the analyst to direct data collection into these areas. The size and the difficulties of the data collection effort needed to get reliable results is, without doubt, the Achilles' heel of risk analysis.

Case Study 18-2: Airport Château Hotel analysed by Monte Carlo simulation (see summary, Case study 18-1, p. 538)

Michel d'Hôtelier provides you with the following additional information:

- He thinks that if a slump occurs, the casual room bookings could reduce by between 5% and 35%. Shown various distribution shapes, he opts for a triangular distribution.

- Green Tour actual bookings over the past four years were 4720, 5280, 5600, 4400. He thinks that if they sign up again, room bookings will be somewhere in the same range. (The contract only specified a guaranteed a minimum of 4000 room-nights, and he will go for the same clause.) The slump is unlikely to affect their bookings.
- He is uncertain about how likely he will be able to sign up the Japanese tour operator, but guesses that the chances of success are somewhere in the range of 70% to 80%. Again he opts for a triangular distribution.
- If he manages to get the Japanese tour contract, he projects a 95% confidence interval of 3000 to 4000 room-nights. He expects though that the average bookings will be affected by the slump in the same way as casual guest nights.
- Casual guests bookings have fluctuated between 3200 and 3800 without showing any trend in the last four years. A slump would reduce this range accordingly.
- He thinks it is fair to assume that variable operating costs are normally distributed with a mean of $960,000 if he gets the Green Tours or the Japanese contract, and a mean of $720,000 otherwise, with a standard deviation of 12,000 for both.

Use ModelRisk to derive a profile for the following three strategies: Offer

(a) Green Tours the reduced room rate of $250, but decline the airline contract.

(b) Green Tours the original room rate of $300, but decline the airline contract.

(c) the Japanese tour operator the $240 room rate and accept the airline contract.

Tour operators and the airline get priority. Hence casual guest room bookings cannot exceed the room nights left over. (If a slump occurs, simply generate room bookings using the 'no slump' distribution and then reduce the result by the percentage above.)

Which is the more attractive strategy, both in terms of total revenue less operating costs and their risk profile?

18.9 Chapter highlights

- Decision trees capture the sequence and conditional dependence of multi-stage decision processes involving uncertain events. They are a useful aid for forcing the decision maker to clearly and comprehensively map out all possible sequences of decisions and contingent events that lead to all possible final outcomes.
- The best sequence of decision choices is usually in the form of a strategy of conditional actions that achieves the highest expected value of benefits or the lowest expected cost. It is determined by backward induction, blocking off decision branches that lead to inferior outcomes.
- Given that some of the input used may be highly subjective, it is important to perform extensive sensitivity analysis. This will identify , which inputs are critical. These should be assessed with extra care.
- For single or two-stage processes, it is possible to determine the value of perfect information. This provides an upper limit to the amount that may be spent on collecting better and more reliable input data.
- For decision problems that are subject to high degrees of uncertainty, or that involve outcomes with serious environmental, health, or security implications, or for which the monetary outcome may not reflect the true intrinsic value, decision

criteria other than maximizing or minimizing expected values may be more appropriate. The minimax criterion minimizes the worst possible outcome, regardless of the probability associated with the various outcomes. Threshold criteria eliminate actions that lead to extreme outcomes, or have unacceptably high probabilities for unfavourable outcomes.

- Utility functions are another approach to measure the intrinsic value of numeric outcomes, both monetary and other, particularly those that fall outside the everyday range of experience. Such utility functions are, however, specific for a given risky situation experienced by a given decision maker at a specific point in time. They are not valid for other decision problems of a different nature, or for other decision makers. They may change over time. Based on the concepts of indifference or switch points, it is possible to derive empirical approximations to the utility function for a given risky outcome using a five-point assessment procedure.
- Risk analysis is an approach for assessing the risk profile associated with a particular strategy used for multi-stage and/or multi-period ventures that involve uncertain outcomes, some of which may be conditional upon other outcomes. It allows random outcomes to be represented in the form of discrete or continuous probability distributions or empirical frequency functions. Each simulation represents one particular realization of the venture. Performing a large number of such simulations, it is possible to derive frequency distributions of the outcomes associated with that strategy. However, for one-off ventures only one outcome will be realized, which only by coincidence will be equal to the expected value.

Exercises

1. Sally Smart is planning how to survive her coming academic year. The way matters stand, she will lose her government assistance since her parents have just joined the class of 'nouveau riche', created by the government to raise the morale of the population. With another brother struggling to finish his engineering degree, chances are nil that her parents will be able to support her with more than a few carrot cakes. Her options are limited:
   - Drop out and join the ranks of the unemployed. Using her skills in present value calculations recently acquired in MSCI 101, she calculated that the *NPV* of her lifetime loss in earning power would amount to £25,000 if the finance minister's naive ECON 101 policies continue to depress the economy, while the loss would only be £5,000 if the prime minister finds the courage to sack her with most of her Treasury advisers, who always have 100% hindsight. Sally figures that the chance that the prime minister can find the necessary courage is only 25%.
   - Take out a loan, finish her degree and then pay it back over the next 10 to 20 years. The *NPV* cost of that action is £15,800 with the present finance minister remaining in office and £12,400 if she is replaced.
   - Enter into a marriage of convenience and then automatically retain her government assistance. With the cost of the parties her friends would insist she throw for both 'tying the knot' and 'cutting it again after graduation', as well as the potential 'intangible' costs associated with this action, she figures that the net cost to her would be £4,000

with the present finance minister remaining in office, but £16,000 without her (because of entering a fictitious marriage without there being a real need for it).

(a) Develop a decision tree, attaching costs and probabilities to the various branches. Using this tree, find the best action for Sally based on monetary considerations only.

(b) Using the method of Section 18.3, determine the value of perfect information.

2. After making her choice, Sally decides to sleep on it before taking any irrevocable action. On the second morning, it dawns on her that the Minister of Education might stumble on the marriage of convenience scheme. She deduces that there is a 40% chance that the government would introduce a questionnaire asking embarrassing personal questions about the civil state of the applicants for government assistance. She might then have incurred the expense of getting married (£4,000) only to find that she does not qualify for assistance anyway, given her marriage is one of convenience only. She would be worse off by £4,000, but obviously could still settle on one of the first two choices open to her.

   (a) Draw up a new decision tree for this problem and find the strategy that minimizes expected costs now.

   (b) Using the method in Section 18.3, determine the value of perfect information.

3. In the mid-1970s, a small car was blown off the access road to a ski-field in the Southern Alps of New Zealand, resulting in a fatality. The car's owner had ignored warnings not to use the road during gale force winds that had sprung up in the early afternoon. Several other cars had close shaves during other storms. The management of the ski-field was faced with the dilemma as to what action to take, if any, to prevent further accidents of that sort. Three alternatives were investigated:

   (1) Relocation of the road away from exposed areas at a cost of $2.5 million, completely eliminating any further danger.

   (2) Erection of protective wind barriers at a cost of $1.5 million, which would prevent any vehicle from being blown off the road, except under the most severe storm conditions. The chance of such a storm occurring over the next 10 years was estimated at 20%, but, since the road would be closed to traffic if such a storm was predicted, the chance that a car would actually be caught in such a storm was only 10%. If, however, an accident would happen, the ski-field company would be liable to punitive damages and possible loss of income due to adverse publicity to an amount of $4.2 million. Furthermore, the company would have little choice but to relocate the road then.

   (3) Do nothing, but close the ski-field whenever there is the slightest danger of any winds in excess of 20 knots. This would not involve an immediate costs, but would lose considerable revenues. These are estimated at $1 million. There still remained a residual 10% chance of a major accident because of the inability to predict the frequent sudden weather changes in the region. An accident would have the same financial consequences as those for option (2), i.e., punitive damages and the cost of relocating the road. Assume all amounts are already expressed in present values.

   (a) Develop a decision tree, attaching costs and probabilities to the various branches.

   (b) Determine the action with the lowest expected cost.

   (c) Using the method of Section 18.3, determine the value of perfect information.

4. The BlueSky Recording company is faced with whether or not to record and market an album for a promising, but as yet unknown continental rock band. The usual method to reach a decision is as follows: Two songs from the group's repertoire are recorded in the firm's Belgian studio. These are submitted for appraisal to a consumer panel. These two steps cost of €3,000. The panel rates the songs as 'potential hits' or 'questionable'. The talent scout and the music director of the firm agree that, from what music they have heard of the group and the perceived current preference patterns of the potential buyers, the

probability that the panel will rate the songs as 'potential hits' is 0.7. If the panel rates the songs as 'questionable', the firm normally decides not to go ahead with any further recordings of that band. If the panel rates the songs as 'potential hits', the firm will record a full album and prepare its release on the market. This has a fixed cost of €50,000. They will then decide whether to make an initial production run of 10,000 or 40,000. Two months after the release, the market response will be evaluated. It is either 'success' or 'failure'. "Success" means all disks will be sold at a gross unit profit of €7. 'Failure' means that the majority will have to be dumped at a heavy discount, at an average gross profit of €1.50 if 10,000 are made and €0.50 if 40,000 are made. Past experience shows that, out of 10 cases where the panel rated the songs as 'potential hits', 8 turned out to be a 'success'.

(a) Draw a decision tree for this situation, attaching costs, gross revenues, and probabilities to the various branches.

(b) Find the best action for the firm for this particular band.

(c) Determine the pay-off table and the value of perfect information.

5. A firm has just placed an order for a special-purpose machine. Since this is one of a kind, it is cheaper to include an order for some essential spare parts for the machine at the same time, rather than waiting until later when they are actually needed. Consider a particular part. If ordered with the machine, each part has a cost of £2,100. If ordered later on at the time of an actual breakdown, the cost of the part is £6,000. In addition, the loss in profit due the machine being down for several weeks amounts to another $4,000. Past experience with similar machines indicates that the probability of needing *n* spare parts over the machine's productive life is as follows:

Number of parts needed	0	1	2	3	4
Probability	0.1	0.3	0.3	0.2	0.1

Any parts remaining unused at the end of the machine's productive life only have a scrap value of £100. (Ignore the fact that various cash flows may occur over a span of several years.) The decision is the number of spare parts to be included in the original machine order. Develop a decision tree for this situation and find the best action.

6. A bookshop is considering how many copies of an exclusive connoisseur art calendar to buy. The purchase price is £240 per copy. They would be sold for £440 each. From past experience, the owner predicts the following probability distribution for the demand for this calendar:

Demand	4	5	6	7	8
Probability	0.4	0.3	0.15	0.1	0.5

Any calendars not sold are disposed of below cost for £50.

(a) Draw a decision tree depicting the decision choices and associated outcomes for this problem. Show the revenues and costs associated with each branch and the probabilities associated with all branches issuing from chance nodes.

(b) Use the decision tree to determine the optimal number to procure and find the associated expected profit.

(c) Interpret the meaning of the expected profit in terms of the possible outcomes.

7. For the decision tree developed in Exercise 3, find the corresponding pay-off table and determine the minimax strategy that minimizes the maximum cost.

8. Consider again the decision tree developed for the recording company in exercise 5 above. Find its corresponding pay-off table and determine the minimax strategy.

9. Assume that your mechanic just told you that there is a 50:50 chance that your beloved BMW's motor will seize within the next six months. If this happens, other major damage will occur to your motor. The total repair bill will amount to about €2,000. He advises you to have the motor overhauled now at a fraction of that cost. What is the maximum amount

that you personally would be willing to spend on an overhaul, such that you would just be indifferent between the 50:50 chance of the motor seizing and the overhaul? Using the other steps of the five-point assessment procedure, determine the approximate shape of your personal utility function for expenditure on your BMW.

10. Gérard Mousse, manager of Champignons Galore (see Appendix 9.1, p. 265), wants to determine the risk involved in mushroom exports to London from his French factory. He contemplates daily shipments. The truck freight forwarding company is willing to reserve a daily cargo space of 10 tonnes (= one truck) at a daily cost of €2,400. The current excess production capacity is 9.6 tonnes ± 25%. If actual excess production is less than 10 tonnes, only that excess will be shipped. If it is more than 10 tonnes, the amount shipped is 10 tonnes. Mushroom shipments are auctioned in London and fetch on average £1,800 ± 400 per tonne. The fluctuations in the currency exchange rate of £ into € is a random variable with an expected change of zero from week to week and a range of €0.03. The current rate is £1 = €1.515. Bob Moss would like to get an indication of the weekly revenue in €. Note the exchange rate is always rounded to three decimal places. Assume a uniform distribution for changes in the exchange rate, while the actual production and the London price both follow a normal distribution. (Take the ranges given as covering 90% probability.)
    (a) Map out the sequence of outcomes.
    (b) Use a spreadsheet to simulate 50 days of outcomes and use them to construct a histogram of net € revenues. Plot it. What percentage of days is the net € revenue below €24,000? (If you have access to risk analysis software, use it.)

Further reading

Evans J.R. and Olson, D.L. (1998) *Introduction to Simulation and Risk Analysis*, Englewood Cliffs, NJ: Prentice-Hall. Includes a student version of Crystal Ball, a risk analysis software.

Delquié, P. (1993) 'Inconsistent trade-offs between attributes: New evidence in preference assessment biases', *Management Science*, November: 1382–95.

Hertz, D.B. and Thomas, H. (1983) *Risk Analysis and its Applications*, New York: Wiley. Chapters 1 and 2 give an introduction to the basics of risk analysis.

Hertz, D.B. (1979) 'Risk analysis in capital investment', *Harvard Business Review*, 57(5). A popularized first introduction to risk analysis by its inventor.

McCord, M. and de Neufville, R. (1986) '"Lottery equivalents": Reduction of the certainty effect in utility assessment', *Management Science*, January: 56–60.

Savage S.L. (2003) *Decision Making with Insight (with Insight.xla 2.0)*, Florence, KY: Cengage Learning. Covers Monte Carlo simulation, decision trees, queuing simulations, optimization, Markov chains, and forecasting with Insight add-ins to Excel.

Vose, D. (2008) *Risk Analysis: A Quantitative Guide*, 3rd edn, Chichester: Wiley. More advanced, particularly useful for the discussion on probability distributions and Monte Carlo simulation.

Winston, W. (2008) *Financial Models Using Simulation and Optimization II*, Newfield, NY: Palisade Corp. A detailed, step-by-step guide for Excel and Palisade's Decision Tools software covering risk analysis using @RISK for financial modelling.

19

Decisions with multiple objectives

Learning objectives

- Appreciate the meaning of an 'optimal solution' for a decision situation with multiple objectives.
- Be able to determine whether an outcome involving two objectives is dominated and find the set of efficient outcomes or solutions.
- Be able to create a hierarchy diagram for multiple objectives with second- and third-level objectives.
- Be able to apply the aggregate value method for finding the most preferred solution for a decision problem with discrete choices and multiple objectives.
- Be able to represent the results of an aggregate value analysis graphically in the form of performance profiles and composition of performance scores.

Introduction

In most of the examples and case studies discussed in Chapters 9 to 14 and 16 to 18, we assumed that, for any given decision problem, the decision maker pursues a single objective. Often that objective was to minimize costs or maximize net benefits. You will rightly point out that, in real-life, most decision makers attempt to satisfy a variety of objectives and goals simultaneously. Some of these objectives or goals are fully or partially conflicting. Multiple conflicting objectives and goals are an integral part of each person's worldview — a word you have not heard for a while! It is not just politicians who promise to deliver the 'maximum benefits' to the 'largest number of people' at the 'least cost' — an impossibility.

Few business people are so single-minded as to look only for maximum returns on their investment. Most also wish to provide high quality products or services, maintain excellent customer service, keep a happy and cooperative work force, and achieve the largest market share possible. Similarly, most decisions dealing with environmental and social issues strive to meet multiple, and usually conflicting, goals. On a personal level, have you not allowed yourself to dream of that ideal job that offers daily challenges, involves a variety of interesting duties, has responsibility and prestige, offers excellent promotional opportunities, has a pleasing work environment, is high paying with lots of fringe benefits, and involves extended stays on the French Riviera? In each instance, the actual decision taken is usually a compromise. It does well on some objectives or goals, worse on others.

But even our daily life is a sequence of compromises between conflicting goals and objectives. This means that we must be experts in decision making with multiple objectives! And we do this without any support of a formal approach. So, why should we need such support in a managerial or planning context? In part, it is for the same reasons that led us to have recourse to formal decision models when we ignored all but one objective, namely as a means for overcoming, at least in part, the complexity of the situation. Remember our discussion in Section 15.7 (p. 434) on people's limited cognitive abilities for processing complex, multi-faceted relationships? This is not only a reality when faced with decision making under uncertainty, but becomes even more pronounced when faced with weighing several partially conflicting objectives.

There are other reasons. A formal approach allows a fuller exploration of the solution space, thereby providing deeper insight into the problem — one of the prime aims of MS/OR. The joint performance of the objectives in response to the various potential decision alternatives can be observed, compared, and weighed. This may reveal that certain objectives are much more sensitive, while the performance of others is hardly affected, no matter what action is taken. The decision maker is thus provided with a more effective basis for finding the most preferred compromise. It may lead to a partial or complete re-evaluation of the importance of the various objectives and ultimately to better, more defensible, and wiser decision making.

This chapter will only scratch the surface of this vast topic. To set the stage, we will summarize three real applications reported in the literature. We then review how 'traditional' MS/OR methods deal with multiple objectives. The following two sections give a brief overview of the difficulties and aims of multi-criteria decision making, commonly abbreviated as MCDM — not a roman numeral — and the approaches to MCDM suggested in the literature.

The discussion is largely restricted to the case where the choice has to be made from a set of discrete alternatives. This sidesteps the rather more complex situation of continuous decision variables, for which multiple objective mathematical programming techniques, similar to linear programming, have been invented.

We end the coverage by applying one of the simplest MCDM approaches to the selection of the 'best' venue for a conference of a software users' group.

19.1 Three real MCDM problem situations

Multiple land use planning

The Federal Land Policy and Management Act, passed by the 94th US Congress in 1976, gave the following mandate to the Bureau of Land Management (BLM) for the management of the over 400 million acres of federally owned land under its control: Land management is:

- to be on the basis of multiple use and sustained yield;
- to protect the quality of scientific, scenic, historical, ecological, environmental, air and atmospheric, water resource, and archaeological values;
- preserve and protect certain public lands in their natural condition;
- to provide food and habitat for fish, wildlife, and domestic animals;
- to provide for outdoor recreation and human occupancy and use.

Many of these objectives are in direct conflict with one another. For some areas, the BLM would be under fire from different pressure groups to have their vested interest prevail. These groups include farm lobbies who want more grazing land, mining companies who want prospecting rights, and conservation groups who want to keep some areas in their natural state. How should the BLM resolve these conflicts?

Assume a BLM district officer has to develop a multiple-use land programme for an area in his district which is mainly used for grazing, but for which a geological survey indicates the likely presence of oil or gas deposits of potentially economic significance. The area's recreational value is mainly for big game hunting and winter use by snow-mobiles. BLM's assessment procedure consists of compiling detailed inventories of the area's topography, soil, vegetation, other physical features, and its existing uses. This is followed by a detailed assessment of the area's unlimited potential for each possible use — grazing, recreation, mineral exploitation, habitat conservation for native flora and fauna — without regard to any other uses. Independently of this, a socioeconomic profile is compiled that provides relevant information on attitudes of current and prospective users of the area, on special interest groups, and on the economic importance of exploitable natural resources. Armed with these documents, the area manager attempts to develop a compromise solution that reflects both the best intrinsic uses of the area and relevant socioeconomic factors. This is a very difficult task of weighing conflicting objectives against each other.

A pilot study by K.F. Martinson at the University of Colorado in 1977, implemented on a trial basis by some BLM districts, demonstrated how a multiple-objective linear programming approach can be used for gaining insights into how the objectives respond to each other, leading to more effective and more defensible management plans. (Section 22-5 in Daellenbach et al. (1983) demonstrates this approach.)

The Mexico City Airport development

One of the classical examples deals with the Mexico City airport development, undertaken in 1971 for the Ministry of Public Works (MPW) of Mexico by two MIT professors, H.R. de Neufville and H. Raiffa, both pioneers in the field of decision analysis. As in many other large urban centres, the growth in the volume of air traffic, the difficulties of further expansion of the existing major airport, with its take-off and landing flight patterns largely over built-up areas, lent considerable urgency for providing an acceptable airport service development strategy over the next 30 years. The then existing Texcoco airport was sandwiched between the remains of Lake Texcoco to the east and the sprawling city expanse to the west. Upgrading Texcoco on the highly unstable former lake bed or by displacement of large populations would make construction and maintenance very expensive. The continued increase in air traffic that this would allow would further aggravate the current noise problem and increase the danger of serious air accidents, with potentially numerous casualties among the residents in the densely populated surrounding areas. The advantage of upgrading Texcoco was its close proximity to the city centre. The most attractive alternative sight was at Zumpango, an undeveloped rural area some 25 miles north of the city. It would not suffer any of Texcoco's problems, but would increase travel times to and from the city substantially.

Based on a consensus of the directors of MPW, a partial list of objectives included:

- minimizing total construction, maintenance, and operating costs;
- minimizing travel times to and from the airport;
- maximizing airport operating safety;
- minimizing the effect of air traffic noise pollution;
- minimizing social disruption and displacement of the population; and
- raising the air traffic service capacity for Mexico City.

There were many uncertainties associated with any decisions. For instance, what was the future growth in air traffic likely to be? Would the noise levels of future aircraft engines be considerably lower? What safety standards were the IATA and international pilot associations going to impose for future airport operations?

Faced with the multiple objectives and such uncertainties, how should the MPW go about developing a strategy that was 'best' in terms of social, economic, safety, and political considerations? After attempts to 'solve' this problem using traditional cost-benefit analysis (an adaptation of project evaluation of Chapter 10 for public projects), the two professors, together with the senior staff of the MPW, applied a form of decision analysis based on multi-attribute utility functions to come up with a set of recommendations.

This method develops individual utility functions for the performance on each objective. These are then combined into a single complex aggregate utility function which is used for comparing various development strategies. Daellenbach et al. (1983, Chapter 22) apply this approach to a search and rescue service.

As happens with the recommendations of many major projects — their findings to have a staged move to Zumpango — were never implemented. Forty years later, Texcoco is still Mexico City's major international airport and is still facing the same problems. (As a footnote, at about the same time, a similar planning exercise, based on a multi-million-pound cost–benefit analysis and public hearings, was undertaken for selecting the location of the third London airport. Its recommendations, to convert the small airport at Stansted into a fully-fledged international airport, were not implemented at that time either.)

Blood bank stock management

Recall the blood bank Case study 3-1 (p. 54). Blood is collected from donors, classified according to type, and stored for use in emergency and elective surgery. Some is used to produce by-products, such as plasma and platelets. A blood bank manager tries to avoid two types of undesirable events:

- running short of blood needed for emergencies and scheduled operations; and
- outdating of unused blood.

The first may have serious consequences, such as endangering life, or require expensive remedial action, such as calling up suitable emergency donors and/or postponing elective surgery. The second is a waste of a valuable product. If donors give blood without compensation, outdating of blood is morally undesirable. Avoiding both shortages and outdating of blood are the major objectives of fresh blood management. Cost considerations may only be a secondary consideration.

Relatively large stocks of each type of blood will help to keep shortages to low levels. On the other hand, outdating can be kept to a minimum by keeping low levels of blood stocks. The achievement levels of the two objectives thus vary inversely with each other. The solution must be a compromise. Naturally, most managers will view blood shortages as more serious than outdating of blood. They will therefore risk more outdating of blood in order to keep shortages to acceptably safe low levels.

In the 1970s and 1980s a great deal of research was devoted to this problem. The policies derived from the models developed led to a reduction in outdating of blood from well over 25% of all blood collected in the early 1970s to well below 5% by the late 1980s, without an increase in the rate of shortages.

19.2 Traditional hard MS/OR approach

The traditional approach for modelling multiple objectives is to single out the one viewed as the most important from an economic perspective — usually this is benefits or costs — and find the optimal solution with respect to it, while meeting minimal performance targets on all other objectives. In other words, arbitrary boundary choices are used as a substitute for all but one objective. Often, little or no justification is given for these choices.

For most issues involving safety, such as the operation of means of transport, seabed drilling for and extraction of oil, operations of underground mines or nuclear power station, an acceptable 'solution' is obtained by minimizing operating costs, subject to meeting minimum legal or regulatory safety standards. Usually, the economic, environmental, and social impacts on future generations are ignored.

The targets substituting for all but one objective become firm **surrogate constraints** on that objective. Therefore, they restrict — in fact, dictate — the best level of achievement that is possible for the most important objective. In other words, this approach first guarantees that the targets on the lesser objectives are satisfied, before it allows any look at the most important objective. So, by a rather ironic twist, the most important objective becomes subordinated to what are often seen as the less important objectives.

Mind you, when dealing with safety issues, this may be preferable. However, there are many situations where this inadvertent reversal of priorities is more questionable. In particular, such minimal performance targets may involve a considerable degree of arbitrariness; neither do the performance targets chosen have the inviolate nature of hard constraints. They are often the result of a policy decision and, hence, have the character of soft constraints. They reflect what is seen as a reasonable or a desirable level of achievement — both rather fuzzy and highly subjective notions. Furthermore, they may even result in a suboptimal solution when other feasible solutions exist that perform better on several objectives without being worse on any of the others — a highly undesirable outcome. It is, therefore, important that the MS/OR analyst performs extensive sensitivity analysis with respect to all these surrogate constraints. The decision maker should be presented not simply with the 'optimal' solution for the target levels chosen, but also with the insights gained from the sensitivity analysis exercise.

The traditional approach is a fairly arbitrary ad hoc procedure. It really shirks the fundamental issues in MCDM. The next two sections look at some of these.

Activity

- In the LOD problem in sections 6, 6.7 to 6.1 and 6.13 to 6.17, the objective used was cost minimization. There were other objectives, such as achieving a high inventory turnover rate, as specified by the vice-president of finance, providing top service to customers in terms of fast execution of their orders, smoothing the level of mixing and filling capacity usage over time. How were these handled?
- Consider the NuWave Shoes situation (Section 4.8, p. 74). List Elly's possible objectives. How did she deal with them?

19.3 Some basic issues in MCDM

A new meaning for 'optimal solution'

Finding the optimal solution with respect to a single objective has a precise meaning. It identifies that solution which either achieves the maximum 'benefit' or the minimum 'cost' — taking these two terms in their broadest sense — whichever is the aim of the optimization. What is the meaning of an optimal solution in the presence of several objectives?

Clearly, it cannot be a maximum or a minimum of something. For instance, only by coincidence will all objectives take on their maximum outcome simultaneously for the same decision choice. If this should happen, the objectives are not conflicting and the problem is trivial in this respect.

In general, one decision choice does better with respect to some objectives, while another fares better for others. By necessity, the decision chosen as the 'best' one is a compromise. It may achieve the optimum outcome for some objectives, but falls short to various degrees on others. So, rather than refer to the solution finally chosen as 'the optimal solution', it makes more sense to call it the **most preferred** solution.

Dominance

Some decision choices can be ruled out as potential candidates for the most preferred solution. If a decision choice A performs no better than decision choice C with respect to all objectives and worse for at least one, then A is **dominated** by C. It can be eliminated from further consideration. A rational decision maker will never consider A as a potential candidate for the most preferred solution (provided the objectives used capture everything that counts about the decision choices).

Figure 19-1 depicts dominance graphically for the case of two conflicting objectives. Each axis measures the achievement level on one objective. The higher the level, the more desirable it becomes. The joint achievement levels on both objectives for each decision choice represent a point in the positive quadrant.

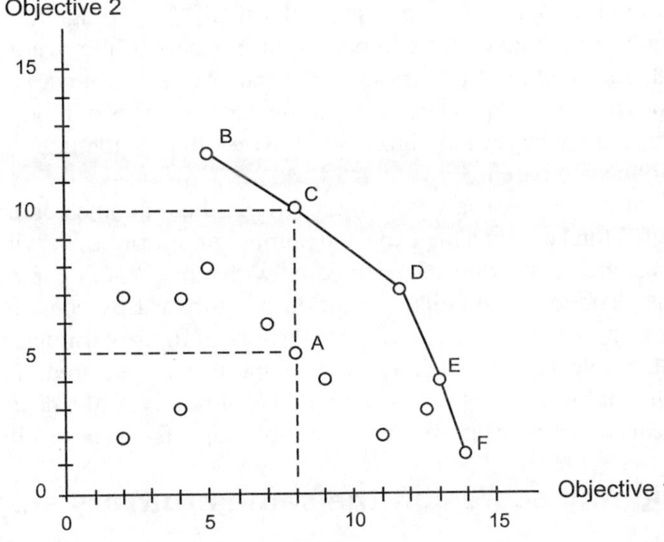

Figure 19-1 Dominance and efficient solutions

For example, alternative A achieves an outcome of 8 on objective 1 and 5 on objective 2, while alternative C achieves 8 on 1 and 10 on 2. Alternative A is no better than C for objective 1, but worse for objective 2. Hence, A is dominated by C. On the other hand, alternative B with outcomes of 4 on objective 1 and 12 on objective 2 does not dominate either A or C and is dominated by neither

The solid line in Figure 19-1 from B to F connects all those alternatives that are not dominated by any other alternative. They are referred to as **efficient solutions**. They should be the only candidates for the most preferred solution. (In economics, the concept of dominance is also referred to as **Pareto optimality**.)

Activity

> In the light of the discussion of dominance, what do you see is another potentially serious shortcoming of the traditional MS/OR approach of substituting targets or constraints for all but one objective.

Measuring outcomes for objectives

The performance of a decision choice is given by a set of outcomes, one for each objective. Some objectives may readily be measured in terms of a natural physical unit — pounds, dollars or euros, or pollutant emission levels in parts per million. For others, such as beauty, safety, or convenience, no natural measuring scales exist. Ultimately, the various decision choices must be compared with one another in some way. This comparison is either made in terms of a single overall numeric performance, which aggregates the individual numeric performance measures over all objectives, or on a holistic basis, which ranks alternatives from best to worst. In the latter case, the outcomes achieved for the objective need not be measured along a cardinal scale.

Sometimes, different objectives are commensurable. For example, the performance of a blood bank can be expressed in terms of the average number of pints of blood outdated over a given time interval and in terms of the average number of units of blood requested for transfusions which cannot be delivered, i.e., pints of blood short. Although the consequences of outdating and shortages of blood are vastly different — shortages may be seen as significantly worse than outdating — the two measures can readily be compared.

Contrast this to a safety problem, where the outcomes of any decision choice are expected total cost and the expected number of injuries of varying severity and deaths. How can monetary values be compared with numbers of people injured or numbers of deaths? The rather simplistic solution put forward by economists suggests that we express injuries or deaths in terms of the loss of future earnings. However, that ignores all intangible aspects, such as the pain and trauma suffered, the potential loss of life enjoyment, or the emotional personal loss of relatives of a dead person. Furthermore, how can we even measure such intangible aspects meaningfully?

Assigning scores on the same arbitrary scale

The commonly accepted way out of many of these difficulties is to express outcomes in terms of a **score** along an arbitrary scale from, say, 0 to 1 or 0 to 100, similar to the way to assess utilities in Chapter 18. The worst possible outcome is given a score of 0, while the best possible outcome is given a score of 1 or 100. All other outcomes are scored inside the interval selected.

This approach is used for all objectives. For outcomes with a natural scale, the scores are linear transformations. For example, if the range of monetary benefits runs from $10,000 to $260,000 over the various alternatives, the maximum outcome is assigned a score of 100, with all other scores proportionately less; $80,000 is then given a score of 28. For intangible objectives, the scores assigned are, by necessity, highly subjective to the person doing the scoring. The scores assigned are not valid for another person, neither may they remain the same over time, even for the same person.

The difference in the scores achieved by pairs of alternatives for a given objective reflects the differences in desirability. Suppose alternatives A, B, and C have scores of 10, 50, and 70. A switch from A to B is interpreted as twice as desirable as a switch from B to C, since the gain in the score is 40 for the first and only 20 for the second. The same conclusion is reached if the three scores are 20, 60, and 80. It is not affected by the initial choice of a score of 10 or 20 for A. It only depends on the difference between scores. However, the ratio of two scores no meaning. So, the ratio of scores for B and A of 50/10 = 5 does not mean that B is five times more desirable than A. That ratio is affected by the initial choice of the score for A. It reduces to three if A is scored at 20 and B at 60, while the difference between them remains at 40.

Scores from 0 to 100 may also be interpreted as the percentage achieved on a given objective by the alternative in comparison with the highest scoring alternative.

The decision maker's preference structure

How decision makers value various outcomes forms part of their **preference structure**. The latter reflects their worldview. It is therefore highly personal to each decision maker. Naturally, it also enters into the valuation of outcomes for single-objective decision making, as we have seen in the discussion on utility functions in Chapter 18. However, in MCDM a new dimension is added. It is now not simply a question of valuing outcomes of individual objectives, but also a question of the relative importance of each objective. In order to assess the relative worth of an alternative, we need a measure of both. Only then can the alternatives be ranked from best to worst.

Multiple decision makers

Situations with more than one decision maker create new difficulties. All decision makers bring their own personal preference into the evaluation. They may assign different scores to the same outcome and give each objective a different importance weight. As a result, each may end up with a different ranking of the alternatives. Furthermore, they may have a different personal stake in the problem, so that it is a legitimate question whether each should have the same degree of say in the matter. For example, one may be the major investor in the firm, while others may be employees at different levels in the hierarchy. Should their inputs all be given equal weight?

The group as a whole will have to agree on a common ranking. This calls for a partial reconciliation of the individual preferences and 'rights' of the participants. A discussion of suitable processes for resolving such conflicts goes beyond the scope of this text. Problem structuring methods, covered in Chapter 7, may help to resolve them.

19.4 Process of evaluating choices

The two predominant approaches for finding the most preferred of a set of discrete alternatives are **aggregate value function methods**, mainly used and developed in the USA and the UK, and **outranking methods**, originating in France and Belgium.

Aggregate value functions

These methods in their most basic form assume that:

- a favourable outcome for one objective can be traded off with a less favourable outcome on another objective; and
- the overall or aggregate score of an alternative is a function of the outcome scores and the weights for the relative importance of the individual objectives.

Usually, the weights are normalized such that their sum adds up to 1. Each weight is a number in the range from 0 to 1.

An example may help. For simplicity we use a linear aggregate value function. This means that the overall score is equal to the weighted sum of the individual scores, with the relative importance of each objective serving as the weights. Consider two objectives, X and Y. Objective Y is viewed as being three times more important than X. X is therefore assigned a raw weight of 1 and Y a raw weight of 3. The sum of the raw weights is 4. We normalize the raw weights by dividing each by the sum of the raw weights. Hence, objective X gets a normalized weight of $1/(1+3) = 0.25$ and Y one of $3/(1+3) = 0.75$. Their sum adds up to 1 as desired. Assume further that alternative A achieves outcome scores of 90 and 60 for objectives X and Y, while B has outcome scores of 75 and 65. The overall scores are then

$$\text{Alternative A: } 0.25 \times 90 + 0.75 \times 60 = 67.5$$
$$\text{Alternative B: } 0.25 \times 75 + 0.75 \times 65 = 67.5$$

They are the same. If a choice was made exclusively on the basis of the overall scores, the decision maker would be indifferent between the two alternatives. We can conclude that a loss of 15 score points on objective X from 90 to 75 is compensated by a gain of 5 points on objective Y from 60 to 65. In other words, score points of one objective can be traded off for score points on another objective, such that the aggregate score remains unchanged.

Outranking methods

In contrast, outranking methods assume that the decision maker is unwilling or unable to define trade-offs between objectives. It implies that no aggregate value function can be derived. Any ranking of the alternatives has to be done on the basis of pairwise comparisons of alternatives. This is done either on a holistic basis or based on the (possibly incommensurable) outcome scores and the relative importance of the objectives for each alternative. Each comparison has one of three outcomes: (1) one alternative is preferred to the other, (2) the two alternatives are indifferent to one another, or (3) the comparison is inconclusive. The end result of this process is a partial or complete ranking of the alternatives.

The various methods offer little theoretical justification for how these indices are computed. In contrast, the theoretical justification for the aggregate score of aggregate value function methods is based on utility theory. Any discussion goes well beyond the scope of this text. There is also little evidence of practical applications of outranking methods beyond those undertaken by academics.

19.5 Conference venue selection

We shall now study an application of the aggregate value function method to the selection of a conference venue where the final choice should be the best compromise over several desirable features.

The alternatives

Nancy Clare, the promotions manager of XL SOFTWARE, has to decide on the venue for next year's European XL Users' Group conference. Such meetings are always preceded by one or more workshops for new users of XL's products. Geneva has been chosen as the location for the conference. Nancy visited the four potential venues on the short list and made the following brief comments:

Venue A: A first class airport hotel; well-known for hosting international meetings, with experienced, helpful and flexible staff; good conference facilities; all-round good accommodation and reasonable catering; social meeting places limited to its several busy in-house restaurants and bars; direct access to airport and railway station; fairly expensive.

Venue B: A luxury city centre hotel; extensively used for international conferences of all sorts, with experienced, helpful, but overworked staff, well-equipped modern conference facilities, including computer networking, and luxury accommodation; good but rather expensive catering; a wide choice of in-house and nearby social meeting places; fast and easy access from the airport and the railway station; very expensive.

Venue C: The university conference venue; used mainly for scientific and cultural conferences; its staff somewhat bureaucratic and not known to be helpful; with a wide choice of good, but somewhat stark conference facilities, including computer labs; modest, barely adequate accommodation and catering; few attractive nearby social meeting places; a nice, park-like environment; reasonable access to transport means; cost-wise, by far the cheapest.

Venue D: A newly renovated chateau in a nearby village, overlooking Lake Geneva with the Alps as a backdrop; a recent newcomer on the scene of conference venues, with limited staff experience, reasonable facilities for small conferences, and excellent modern accommodation; famous for its catering; good social meeting places at the venue and in the several small restaurants in the village; access from the airport and the railway station would have to be organized by bus; still reasonably priced.

Nancy recently studied Prof. Belton's tutorial on MCDM (in Hendry and Eglese, 1990) which demonstrates various aspects of the use of MCDM on exactly the type of problem she is facing now. She wants to give the simple multi-attribute value function approach a trial.

Step 1: Selecting objectives

The first step is to come up with a list of objectives considered important for evaluating each alternative venue. In fact, this step has to be done before making up a list of possible venues. It tells the analyst(s) what aspects to look out for and what information to collect about each venue.

In consultation with the conference director and the pre-conference workshop leaders, Nancy develops the following list:

1. low overall cost of facilities;
2. easy transport access;
3. a wide range of top-quality conference rooms and other conference facilities;
4. high-quality accommodation;
5. outstanding catering for conference meals;
6. highly experienced and helpful staff available to organizers and participants;
7. a wide range and high quality of informal social meeting places and restaurants easily accessible to the participants; and
8. a congenial, pleasant overall environment.

These objectives fall into three groups: (a) those associated with the 'Location' of the venue, (b) those associated with the 'Facilities' offered by the venue, and (c) its 'Cost'. They become the **first-level objectives**, while the original list with the exception of 'Cost' is referred to as the **second-level objectives**. It is conceivable that even some of the latter might already be groupings of third level objectives. This **hierarchy of objectives** is depicted in Figure 19-2. Objectives that are not broken down further are called **end objectives**.

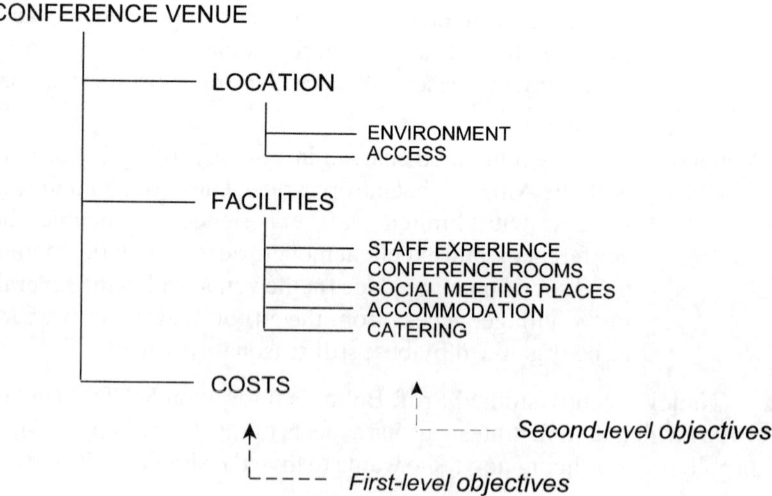

Figure 19-2 Hierarchy of objectives for evaluating a conference venue

Step 2: Setting importance weights

The next step is to assess weights of the relative importance of each objective. These are numbers between 0 and 1. They are usually chosen so that the weights of the first-level objectives add up to one, and similarly the weights of the second-level objectives associated with each first-level objective also add up to one (and so on for further level objectives). This is demonstrated in the two columns headed 'Level 1' and 'Level 2' of Table 19-1. Note that column 2 sums to 1, and similarly the weights for each grouping of second level objectives also sum to 1. Again, Nancy settles on these weights after two animated sessions with the conference director and workshop leaders. These may not be the final weights, but serve as a good starting point.

Table 19-1 Spreadsheet evaluation of conference venues

DATA	WEIGHTS		SCORES FOR VENUE			
OBJECTIVES	Level 1	Level 2	A	B	C	D
Location:	0.35					
Environment		0.50	0	25	40	100
Access		0.50	100	80	35	0
Facilities:	0.45					
Staff experience		0.10	100	80	40	0
Conference rooms		0.30	75	100	50	0
Social meeting places		0.15	25	100	0	75
Accommodation		0.20	80	100	0	90
Catering		0.25	60	70	0	100
Cost	0.20		5	0	100	60
EVALUATION	Location score		50	52.5	37.5	50
	Facilities score		67.25	90.5	19	54.25
	Cost score		5	0	100	60
	Overall score		48.76	59.1	41.68	53.92
	Rank		3	1	4	2

Setting weights that truly reflect the importance a decision maker attaches to the objectives is no easy task. The decision maker may well be prone to similar biases as in the assessment of subjective probabilities (see Section 15.7 for a discussion on potential biases). Naturally, being aware of these biases is the first step towards overcoming them. However, it is essential that the analyst provides the decision maker with meaningful information about the sensitivity of the overall scores and their ranking in response to changes in the weights.

Step 3: Assessing achievement scores

Assessing the scores achieved by each alternative for each end objective is the next task. Since Nancy is the only person who has inspected the facilities, this task falls exclusively upon her shoulders. After much agonizing and a few phone calls to Geneva, she comes up with the scores in the last four columns of Table 19-1.

For all end objectives with the exception of 'Cost', the higher the level of achievement of a given venue the more attractive it becomes. Hence, the highest achievement level is assigned a score of 100, while the lowest achievement level gets a score of 0, with all other scores in between. On the other hand, the higher the cost of a venue, the less attractive it becomes. The highest cost is therefore given a score of 0 and the lowest cost a score of 100.

These scores are relative. Adding other alternatives may require some to be re-assessed. Suppose we add a new venue E that does better for 'Accommodation' than venue B, which previously had the highest score of 100. Then venue E gets a score of 100, while all other venues, except the one with the score of 0, have their relative scores adjusted down. A similar re-adjustment occurs if an alternative is dropped. Although these readjustments may be a nuisance, relative scores based only on the alternatives included are generally easier to assess.

Another approach is to use scores for each end objective that are relative to arbitrary worst and best reference achievement levels. For example, the scores for 'Catering' could be with reference to the Paris Ritz and a typical university student cafeteria. Adding or deleting alternatives would then not require re-adjustments of any scores. Such **absolute scores** require considerably more effort to derive, since a suitable set of reference pairs has to be selected for each objective. This effort is, however, well justified if we are dealing with a recurrent decision problem. For example, if XL has several such conferences in different parts of the world every year, then developing such an absolute scale could well be worthwhile. It would also lead to a more consistent assessment over time between successive uses.

Step 4: Evaluating the alternatives

Armed with this information, we can now compute a weighted overall score for each alternative. The steps are similar to the roll-back procedure in a decision tree. We first determine a weighted score for each grouping of end objectives. These weighted scores become an input into the next higher level in the hierarchy of objectives, until we can determine the weighted score for the first-level objectives.

In our example, using the second-level objectives that make up 'Location' and 'Facilities', we find the weighted scores for these two first-level objectives. For example, for venue A the weighted score for 'Location' is equal to $0.5 \times 0 + 0.5 \times 100 = 50$ and for 'Facilities' $0.1 \times 100 + 0.3 \times 75 + 0.15 \times 25 + 0.20 \times 80 + 0.25 \times 60 = 67.25$. The first-level score for 'Cost' is simply its score of 5. The first-level scores are shown under 'Evaluation' at the bottom of Table 19-1.

With all first-level scores computed, the 'Overall score' can now be obtained. Again, for venue A it is found by summing the products of the first-level weights and the first-level scores, i.e., $0.35 \times 50 + 0.45 \times 67.25 + 0.2 \times 5 = 48.76$ (rounded).

As a first cut, the four alternatives are ranked from best to worst in the order of B - D - A - C. The city centre hotel scores highest, with the chateau coming in as a respectable second. However, this ranking should not be taken as the final answer. It should be used as a catalyst for discussion and for learning more about the problem. But more on this in the last section of this chapter!

Activity

Is it possible that an alternative, A, that is dominated by another alternative, B, can end up with an overall score that is better than B? Why, or why not?

Graphical representation

As usual, displaying the results in graphical form allows the decision maker to gain a better 'feel'. Figures 19-3 and 19-4 show two different charts for the first-level objectives. Similar charts can be constructed for the second-level objectives.

Figure 19-3 shows a profile of the performance of each alternative on the first-level objectives. The three objectives are spaced along the x-axis. Their scores are measured along the y-axis. Each line connects the scores on the three objectives for a given alternative. Such a chart shows whether a given alternative dominates another alternative. But even if no strict dominance occurs, it reveals whether such dominance is close. In our example, no venue dominates, although venue B comes close to topping A. It is just a bit better for 'Location', far outstrips it for 'Facilities', and is just marginally worse for 'Cost'. On this basis, Nancy Clare may well eliminate venue A as a serious contender.

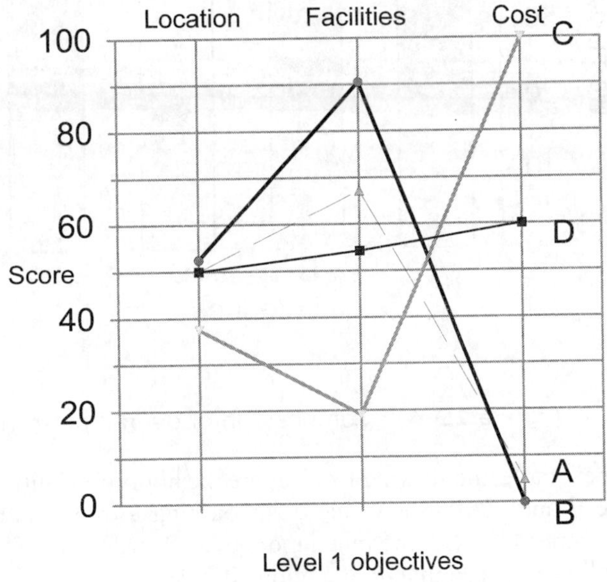

Figure 19-3 Performance profile of alternatives

However, that dominance of first-level objective does not imply dominance over all end objectives. First-level scores may be weighted averages over end objectives farther down the hierarchy. (Just compare the scores for 'Environment' and 'Access' of A and B. There is no dominance there, although the weighted score for 'Location' of B is better than for A.)

The graph also helps clarify the overall performance pattern of an alternative. Is it a good all-rounder or does it have significant weaknesses? A good all-rounder may be an attractive choice, even if it does not achieve the highest overall score. In our example, venue D comes close to being a good all-rounder — its 'Facilities' score being a minor weakness. The chart also clearly highlights that 'Cost' is the major weakness of venue B — our highest-scoring venue.

Figure 19-4 contrasts the overall score of the alternatives and how each breaks down into first-level objectives. Each first-level objective score has been scaled by its corresponding weight. This reveals the relative weighted contribution of each objective towards the overall scores. An alternative's weakness with respect to a particular objective, as revealed in the performance profile chart (like Figure 19-3), may be viewed as less damaging if the importance weight of the objective is relatively small in comparison to all other objectives.

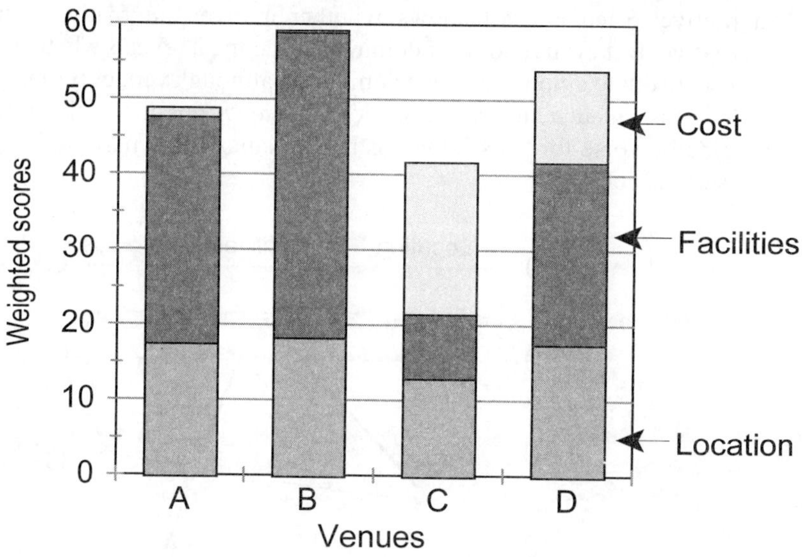

***Figure* 19-4** Composition of overall performance scores

In our example, the striking features are the high contributions made by 'Facilities' for venue B and 'Cost' for venue C, amounting to more than 50% of their overall scores. Contrast this with the much more even distribution of venue D. It now has an even more pronounced image of a good all-rounder.

19.6 Sensitivity analysis

Subjectivity of MCDM methods

As for decision analysis, personal subjective judgments play an important role. In fact, every step requires some subjective inputs. The choice of objectives, their grouping into a hierarchy, the choice of importance weights for the objectives, the assessment of the end objective scores for each alternative, all involve subjective judgments. Even the choice of the evaluation criterion is, in part, subjective. In the conference venue example, we used a criterion for maximizing the weighted overall score. An alternative criterion could have been to maximize the lowest weighted score on any first-level objective (analogous to the minimax criterion in decision analysis). Given this high degree of subjectivity, it is essential to perform extensive and thorough sensitivity analysis, at least for those aspects that involve numerical inputs, such as the importance weights and the end objective scores.

Sensitivity analysis with respect to importance weights

Table 19-2 shows the results of sensitivity analysis on the importance weights. The first set of three rows shows the response of the overall score distribution as the importance weight for 'Location' decreases from 0.45 to 0.25 in steps of 0.1, with the weights of the other two objectives increasing by 0.05 at each step. The second set of three rows decreases the weight for 'Facilities' from 0.55 to 0.35, the third set the weight for 'Cost' from 0.3 to 0.1, while adjusting the other two weights accordingly. The striking feature of this analysis is the fact that the overall score for venue D changes only marginally, in contrast to the scores for the other three venues. The performance for D is thus very robust, reinforcing its quality as a good all-rounder. However, note that B remains the highest scoring venue as long as 'Facilities' has a relatively high importance weight.

Table 19-2 Sensitivity analysis for conference venue selection

Weights			Venues			
Location	Facilities	Cost	A	B	C	D
0.45	0.40	0.15	50.2	59.8	39.5	53.2
0.35	0.45	0.20	48.8	59.1	41.7	53.9
0.25	0.50	0.25	47.4	58.4	43.9	54.6
0.30	0.55	0.15	52.7	65.5	36.7	53.8
0.35	0.45	0.20	48.8	59.1	41.7	53.9
0.40	0.35	0.25	44.8	52.7	46.7	54.0
0.30	0.40	0.30	43.4	52.0	48.9	54.7
0.35	0.45	0.20	48.8	59.1	41.7	53.9
0.40	0.50	0.10	54.1	66.3	34.5	53.1

Firming up the preference structure

When embarking on such an analysis, the decision maker(s) may often have somewhat vague ideas about the relative importance of the various objectives. In other words, the preference structure is not yet clearly defined. Helping the decision maker(s) to firm up the preference structure is frequently an essential and integral part of an MCDM analysis. Access to an appropriate spreadsheet template or a dedicated MCDM computer package will facilitate this task.

In our example, notice the relatively subdued response of the scores to major changes in the relative importance of 'Location', as revealed by the first three rows in

Table 19-2, in contrast to the much stronger response to major changes in each of the other two weights. 'Location' is a less discriminating objective than either 'Facilities' or 'Cost'. This could well lead Nancy to re-appraise the importance she initially attached to 'Location'. She might settle for the weight distribution in row 3 of Table 19-2. Although this does not change the relative ranking, it reduces the difference between venues B and D further, with the all-rounder D becoming even more attractive.

19.7 Chapter highlights

- In real life, decision makers often have multiple objectives or goals. The traditional MS/OR approach substitutes target constraints for all but the most important objective and then finds the best solution for this objective, subject to the targets.
- MCDM approaches find the best compromise solution that balances the achievement levels for all objectives to satisfy the decision maker's preference structure.
- The decision maker should never settle for a dominated solution, but select an efficient solution.
- The two major approaches in MCDM are aggregate value function methods and outranking methods. The first allow trade-offs between objectives; the second do not and derive a ranking of the alternatives by different criteria.
- The simplest aggregate value function approach assigns for each decision choice an achievement score for each objective. Each objective is given an importance weight. An overall score for an alternative is given by the weighted average over all objectives. The alternative with the highest overall score is the most preferred one according to the decision makers preferences.
- Sensitivity analysis with respect to the importance weights assigned to the various objectives provides valuable insight into how robust the overall score of an alternative is. It helps firming up the setting of these weights.

Exercises

1. Assume that you are two months away from graduating and you are already actively looking for a job. You have arranged three interviews with prospective employers. Think about possible things and aspects that you are looking for in a job and arrange them into a hierarchy of first- and second-level objectives. These have to be chosen such that appropriate measures for their performance levels can be determined, either using a natural or a point scale. Indicate how each would be measured. What are their importance weights? Such information will be essential in order to know what questions you will want to have answered from the firms about the job(s) for which they are recruiting.
2. Consider the blood bank problem (p. 561). Assume that there are three areas of concern: shortages, outdating, and costs (for collection of blood, storage, emergency call-up of donors, rescheduling of elective surgery, and so on). What numerical attributes would you use to measure each? Think about how you could get the data to assess their values.

3. The waters discharged in Deep Cove from the Manapouri Power Station in Fiordland National Park at the bottom of New Zealand's South Island (Example 1-3, p. 4) is so pure that it does not need chemicals to neutralize harmful bacteria or other contaminants. A firm applied for the rights to capture this water and transport it in large ocean-going tankers to the US West Coast and Middle Eastern countries. It would have entailed building a floating dock close to the tail race of the power station in order to allow water to be pumped into the tankers. The project would provide employment for about 30 people in an economically depressed area, and the New Zealand government would collect a substantial water royalty. The firm showed considerable environmental concern: no permanent staff residence inside the park, all staff flown in by helicopter; all rubbish removed; extensive safety measures to avoid oil spills, and so on.

   Not surprisingly, environmental groups opposed the project: non-tourist commercial activities are against the charter of national parks; removal of up to 60% of the tail race water would affect the sound's unique flora and fauna, which has evolved over millions of years; large tanker traffic would speed up the mixing of the surface fresh water layer with the salt water underneath, affecting flora and fauna even more; because of the severe weather conditions accidents resulting in oil spills with potentially disastrous consequences would be difficult to prevent; it would make poaching of rare birds and lizards easier and could introduce rats into the park; it would reduce wilderness enjoyment by tourists. Assume you have been asked by the government to assess this project. Define a first- and second-level hierarchy of suitable objectives. How would you measure each?

4. Consider Sally Smart's problem in Exercises 1 and 2 of Chapter 18. Indicate why a single objective approach dealing with monetary outcomes alone may not capture all essential aspects of the problem situation. Define a set of three to four suitable objectives, goals, or targets which any option chosen should either meet or achieve as well as possible. These have to be chosen such that appropriate measures for their performance levels can be determined, either using a natural or a point scale. Indicate how each would be measured.

5. Consider the following hierarchy of objectives, associated importance weights, and achievement scores for selecting a location for a factory:

	Weights		Locations			
Objective	Level 1	Level 2	A	B	C	D
Locality:	0.5					
Transport access		0.6	0	60	100	50
Tater availability		0.4	80	100	0	50
Cost:	0.5					
Construction		0.3	100	30	0	50
Operating		0.7	70	0	100	50

Using an aggregate value function approach, which location is the highest scoring? Is there a close second? Show your results in performance profile graphs.

6. The manager of a BLM district office (see p. 559) has been asked to come up with a management plan for a 16 square mile area in southern Colorado. The area consists of two mesas with adjoining gullies and deep canyons. The vegetation consists of low brush, junipers, and other bushes that thrive in the semi-arid low rainfall area, with a few stands of pines and other trees in sheltered parts. The few open places on the mesas are currently used for sheep grazing at a very low stocking rate. The current run holder would like to get permission for clearing brush and increasing the stocking rate. The mesas and canyons get the occasional visit from backpackers. One of the gullies between the two mesas contains an abandoned silver mine which was worked in the late nineteenth century. It has the potential for being developed into a tourist attraction, as have the interesting rock formations in the canyons. The area has considerable wildlife, particularly deer and various

big birds. The deer stalkers' association would like the area preserved for hunting, excluding all grazing by domestic animals which severely compete for the limited fodder available. No human habitation is currently in the area. Seven management options have been put forward by various interest groups. The district manager would like to select the option which best achieves the intrinsic values and characteristics of the area. He has captured these by four objectives: (A) preservation of scenic beauty, (B) recreational potential, (C) economic potential, (D) watershed protection, each being a first-level objective. (There are no second-level objectives.) All objectives are to be maximized. The table below lists the seven management options and their achievement scores for each objective:

Options Objectives:	A	B	C	D
Exclusive intensive grazing of mesas*	50	0	$50,000	30
Exclusive 4-wheel vehicle recreation*	30	80	–$40,000	0
Exclusive hunting*	90	60	$40,000	90
Canyons tourism, grazing of mesas	60	80	$100,000	50
Canyons tourism, 4-wheel use of mesas	40	100	$30,000	20
Continuation of current usage	70	40	$20,000	70
Exclusive wilderness area use	100	30	$0	100

*The options marked by an asterisk assume that most of the current other low intensity recreational use would continue.

(a) The district manager, after extensive consultation with various experts, comes up with the following set of importance weights: A: 0.2, B: 0.4, C: 0.15, D: 0.25. Which option would you recommend on the basis of an aggregate value function approach? Note that to apply this method you will need to convert the economic achievement levels into a suitable point scale. Show your results in a performance profile graph.

(b) Perform sensitivity analysis, increasing and decreasing the weight of each objective individually by 0.12 at the expense or benefit of the other three objectives. How does this affect your conclusion derived under (a)?

Further reading

Belton, V. and Stewart, T. (2002). *Multiple Criteria Decision Analysis: An Integrated Approach*, Dordrecht: Kluwer.

Belton, V. (1990) 'Multiple criteria decision analysis - Practically the only way to choose', in L.C. Hendry and R.W. Eglese, *Operational Research Tutorial Papers 1990*, Operational Research Society, Neville House, Waterloo St, Birmingham B2 5TX, England: 53–102. Elementary but instructive introduction to the basics of MCDM, similar to the coverage here, but more extensive. Shows an application of the VISA software.

Gal, T., Stewart, T.J. and Hanne, T. (eds) (1999) *Multicriteria Decision Making: Advances in MCDM Models, Algorithms, Theory and Applications*, Boston: Kluwer.

Keeney, R.L. and Raiffa, H. (1993) *Decisions with Multiple Objectives — Preferences and Value Tradeoffs*, 2nd edn, New York: Cambridge University Press. Classic text for multi-attribute utility analysis, with several case studies. Demanding both mathematically and conceptually.

Goodwin, P. and Wright, G. (2004) *Decision Analysis for Management Judgement*, 3rd edn, Chichester: Wiley.

20
Reflections on MS/OR

Introduction

It is now time to take stock of the vast and rugged landscape of MS/OR. In fact, since the 1960s it has grown to the point where most practitioners and academics of MS/OR only can claim to have expertise in a small niche of it, and no more than a superficial knowledge of the scenery beyond. As a result, there is often the danger that they try to fit any problem into one of their three or four favourite methods or techniques by making questionable boundary judgements. The risks are obvious. They end up with an elegant solution to the wrong problem.

Unfortunately, the vast majority of practitioners fall either into the camp of 'hard OR' or 'soft systems and soft OR', when it would enhance their professional effectiveness if they had a more balanced background and view.

Although this text has a partial bias towards hard OR, it is firmly based on the principles of systems thinking and thus shares this focus with soft OR. It also exposes hard OR practitioners to a brief overview of the underlying philosophy of soft OR and a few of the more widely applied problem structuring methods — not to allow them to apply any of these without further in-depth study, but as in incentive to step back when they approach a problem situation and evaluate whether a hard OR approach really is the most appropriate one.

The methodology for hard OR presented here unashamedly borrows aspects of soft approaches, particularly for the problem formulation phase, if they contribute to a more comprehensive picture of the problem and its wider context. This is in stark contrast to the narrow-focused treatment given in most MS/OR textbooks, which blind the reader with the beauty, the power, and intricate computational details of various quantitative techniques, as if their mastery guarantees good MS/OR, at the neglect of the most important aspect of successful problem solving, i.e., identifying the real problem within its full context.

20.1 Problem situations, not problems

Although the occasional MS/OR project starts out with a relatively well-structured, well-defined problem, most projects begin life as vague feelings of dissatisfaction or concern about the current or future state of affairs. Therefore, much of the time what analysts face is not a problem, but a problem situation of interconnected issues. Getting a proper grasp of the context in which these issues occur is a crucial and critical phase for any project.

The seeds of success or failure are quite often sown at this early stage. Homing in on a 'problem' without exploring its full context can be costly. The issue that has given rise to dissatisfaction may not be the 'real' problem, or can only be tackled once one or several other issues have been resolved. The 'problem' may be solved at the wrong level of resolution, or the form of the solution may not be appropriate for decision making. Even its true nature may be misunderstood, as the following telling story demonstrates.

For several years, the management of a high-rise office building in New York was inundated by complaints about the excessive time people had to wait for lifts in the main lobby. Successive MS/OR teams were asked to investigate the 'problem of excessive waiting times'. A number of 'solutions' were tried out, such as having some lifts operate exclusively for the lower floors, while others were express lifts to the higher levels. But each project team reached the conclusion that waiting times could only be reduced significantly by installing additional lifts — precluded by its horrendous cost. Each team basically took the problem as it was defined by management — a problem of excessive waiting times — except for the last team, where one team member suggested studying why people objected to waiting for lifts in the main lobby. They discovered that it was mainly boredom. So, if boredom could be overcome, then complaints about excessive waiting times would to a large extent disappear. The same team member suggested that they install mirrors along all the walls in the main lobby. This would surely alleviate boredom. Some people would take advantage of the mirrors to make last minute checks on how they looked and put on some finishing touches. Others could observe people standing around without being too obvious about it. This was the essence of his argument, although he put it rather more bluntly by stereotyping people by gender. This surprisingly cheap solution was implemented and complaints almost completely disappeared. Nowadays, instead of or in addition to mirrors, TV screens showing the latest stock exchange prices would do the same trick. The lesson of this story is that it clearly pays to look at the problem situation in very broad terms, rather than launch immediately into the 'issue' that may have been the trigger of the study.

20.2 The aim of MS/OR

The aim of MS/OR is not to come up with 'optimal' solutions, as more traditional textbooks profess, but to provide a basis for more insightful decision making. As we have seen, optimality is a rather misleading concept. Any solution recommended is only optimal with respect to the model chosen to capture the system. Both the system definition and the model imply boundary choices, some of which are arbitrary, affected by the resources available for the analysis (time, funds, computing power, and so on), the experience and background of the analyst and, last but not least, the particular worldview on which it is based. Widen any of these, and the 'optimal' solution may not be optimal any longer. What is optimal for a particular narrow system, may only be suboptimal for the wider system, and each system is always embedded in a wider system. So, the concept of optimality loses much of its gloss. All MS/OR can really strive for is to achieve some degree of improvement over the previous situation or an ad hoc decision process. This is why one of the founders of OR defined it as 'the art of giving bad answers to problems to which otherwise worse answers are given'.

If the focus shifts from optimality to improvements, the insights gained from sensitivity analysis about boundary choices becomes even more important.

Hard OR methodologies ≠ scientific method of natural sciences

Hard OR methodologies are not a version of the 'objective' scientific method of the natural sciences, consisting of formation of hypotheses, experimental design, data collection, and refutation or conditional confirmation of the hypotheses, performed under conditions that allow replication. While the scientific method aims at advancing scientific knowledge, MS/OR is aimed at problem solving within a real context with much of its complexity preserved. Most problem situations are unique, subject to change due to external factors. The analysis can rarely be replication under exactly the same conditions.

MS/OR practice cannot claim to be 'objective', but must recognize that many of its aspects are tainted with a fair degree of subjectivity. There is no distinct data collection phase. Different data are collected throughout most phases. All hard OR shares with the scientific method is that the methodology should be transparent, all assumptions and boundary choices should be spelled out and justified, data used should be conserved, and full documentation should be written up.

The admission that the hard variety of MS/OR cannot claim 'objectivity' or being a version of the scientific method will be seen as heretical by a large section of the academic MS/OR community, particularly in the USA, where the foundation stones of operations research are still seen at the time of writing as 'optimization' and 'mathematical modelling'. In the late 1970s, Russel Ackoff (1977), one of the US pioneers in MS/OR, coined the slogan 'Optimization + objectivity = opt out'.

20.3 Potential improvements from widening the boundaries of the system

Focusing on the narrow problem as it is presented by the decision maker, without exploring its context fully, may also make you miss the potential for really big savings that can be made at little or no cost. Here are three examples.

Example 20-1: Container loading problem

A firm experienced high container shipping costs for its products, a variety of electrical cables wound on wooden drums of various sizes. The problem was presented to the MS/OR team — OR students — as a container packing problem, i.e., which items of a shipment to load into each container and in what sequence, so as to minimize the number of containers needed and the extra cost of less-than-full container loads for any goods left over. A plethora of heuristic algorithms exists to deal with such problems. Rather than launch into the search of which algorithms suited this particular problem best and then write appropriate software, the students watched an experienced dispatcher direct the loading of several shipments. In one shipment for large-size drums, only two layers of drums could be inserted into the container. A third layer would have exceeded the container dimension by 4 cm. Hence, almost a third of the container capacity remained unused. Tough luck!

Similar observations were made for other shipments. While the firm has no control over the dimensions of the shipping containers, it has control over the dimensions of its drums. One of the students asked if the diameter of the wooden drums could not be reduced by 2 cm, which would allow 100% usage of the container capacity. A priori, there seemed to be no obstacle to this, even without reducing the length of cable, since most drums had enough unfilled space. Therefore, by enlarging the boundaries of the system, i.e., allowing drum sizes to become part of the problem, huge savings in shipping costs could be achieved, even without the use of a container packing algorithm. Further savings of applying such algorithms were, in fact, small in comparison.

Example 20-2: A cutting stock problem

Another team of students was presented with a trim problem for an appliance manufacturer. For certain sizes of the steel sheets, the unusable off-cuts amounted to 15% and 20% — an expensive waste of raw material. In general, optimization algorithms shave trim losses by only few per cent over those of an experienced scheduler. One of the students asked if it would be possible to procure different sheet sizes from the supplier. The procurement clerk's answer was a firm 'no'; these were the only standard sizes available. He also speculated that special sizes, more suitable for their needs, would be more expensive, since the supplier would have to make special set-ups for them.

The student did not give up that easily. He requested permission to approach the supplier. To his surprise, the latter said that since the appliance manufacturer was one of their important customers they would be willing to cut the steel sheets to any feasible length. A bit of further analysis showed that with different sheet lengths the trim losses could be reduced by 10% to 15% using the method currently used by the staff, without the use of any optimization techniques.

Example 20-3: The LOD problem revisited

In the LOD problem, the grease manufacturing supervisor claimed that the greases produced in huge pressure mixers required the mixer to be full. He had 30 years of experience. So, the problem was reduced to allocating grease manufacture to the three sizes of mixers available, leaving little or no room for lowering overall costs. Again, the analyst did not give up. He checked with the engineering section of the firm and, after some analysis, was told that grease quality would not be affected if the mixers were filled to at least 40% capacity. Suddenly, a highly restrictive constraint was substantially relaxed, opening up room for considerable savings in total inventory and production costs.

Each of these examples shows that often small changes to the boundary of the system — in particular, in what are taken as uncontrollable inputs — can give rise to improvements that may exceed those that 'optimization' of the originally defined problem could have produced. Without exploring the wider context in which the problem occurs, such improvements may be missed.

A vital lesson from these examples is the importance of asking 'Why?' and then following up the answer with another 'Why?', until a sufficiently comprehensive picture of all underlying factors has been obtained.

A systems thinking approach is no guarantee of effective problem solving. However, by its very nature of rendering explicit all boundary choices made in the analysis and their implications, it leads to more comprehensive, more balanced, less biased, and hence more insightful and more effective decision making.

Further reading

Ackoff, R.L. (1979) 'Resurrecting the Future of OR', *Journal of the Operational Research Society*, March: 189–99.

Ackoff, R.L. (1979) 'The future of OR is past', *Journal of the Operational Research Society*, February: 93–104.

Ackoff, R.L. (1977) 'Optimization + objectivity = opt out', *European Journal. of Operations Research*, 1: 1–7.

Feigin, G. (2008) 'Has academic OR lost its way?', *OR/MS Today*, February: 16–17.

Index

Bold numbers refer to principle definitions